# TORT

# TORT

## Sweet & Maxwell's Textbook Series

**Paula Giliker, M.A. (Oxon.), B.C.L., Ph.D. (Cantab.)**
*Barrister, Professor of Law, University of Bristol*

and

**Silas Beckwith, LL.B (Lond.)**
*Barrister, Senior Lecturer in Law, London Metropolitan University*

**SWEET & MAXWELL**

 THOMSON REUTERS

First edition      (2000)
Second edition   (2004)
Third edition     (2008)
Fourth edition   (2011)

Published in 2011 by Sweet & Maxwell,
100 Avenue Road, London NW3 3PF
Part of Thomson Reuters (Professional) UK Limited
(Registered in England & Wales, Company No 1679046.
Registered Office and address for service:
Aldgate House, 33 Aldgate High Street, London EC3N 1DL)

Typeset by LBJ Typesetting Ltd of Kingsclere
Printed in Great Britain by Ashford Colour Press, Gosport, Hants
For further information on our products and services,
visit www.sweetandmaxwell.co.uk

No natural forests were destroyed to make this product;
only farmed timber was used and re-planted.
A CIP catalogue record for this book is available from the British Library.

ISBN: 978-0-41404-608-5

# Preface

This book is designed for readers approaching tort law for the first time. We have sought to set out clearly and succinctly the rules applicable to each tort and illustrate how they work in practice by reference to case law. Whilst our discussion of case law can by no means replace reading the cases themselves, we have set out the salient points to serve as an *aide mémoire* and to enable the reader to consider the law in a factual context. Similarly, we have outlined the main statutory provisions in this area of law and have sought to help the reader understand the wording and impact of these provisions.

The book has a traditional structure. In the first chapter, we give an overview of tort liability and consider its aims and objectives, the interests it seeks to protect, and its role in modern society. In Chs 2–6, we examine the tort of negligence. Negligence is the most commonly used tort and forms an essential part of any tort law course. It is therefore considered in some detail and is divided into a number of issues which tend to be studied separately. Chapter 6 examines the law relating to causation. This is dealt with in the context of negligence, although it is relevant to all torts. The second half of the book deals with negligence-related liability, strict liability, and other torts. Chapter 7 explores tort liability arising in an employment relationship, whilst Ch.8 examines tort liability arising from occupation of premises. Chapter 9 considers two examples of strict liability statutes—the Consumer Protection Act 1987 and the Animals Act 1971—and their role within the law of tort. The book then deals with other torts, namely nuisance (and associated liability under the rule in *Rylands v Fletcher*), trespass, economic torts, defamation and privacy law. Our final two chapters deal with the important subjects of defences and remedies.

No understanding of the law would be complete without an appreciation of possible reforms. This new edition discusses significant new proposals to reform the law of defamation published by the government in March 2011, which put forward the most sweeping changes to the law of defamation in more than 150 years in an attempt to protect freedom of speech and bring an end to "libel tourism" from abroad. We also discuss the Government's responses to previous consultations proposing changes to the law relating to damages for personal injury or death, and illegality. This new edition equally highlights key recent decisions concerning public authority liability in negligence and under the Human Rights Act 1998 (*Van Colle v Chief Constable of the Hertfordshire Police*,[1] *Mitchell v Glasgow City Council*,[2] *Jain v Trent SHA*[3]), causation (*Sienkiewicz v Greif (UK) Ltd*[4]) and defamation (*Spiller v Joseph*[5]).

---

[1] [2008] UKHL 50; [2009] 1 A.C. 225.
[2] [2009] UKHL 11; [2009] 1 A.C. 874.
[3] [2009] UKHL 4; [2009] 1 A.C. 853.
[4] [2011] UKSC 10; [2011] 2 W.L.R. 523.
[5] [2010] UKSC 53; [2010] 3 W.L.R. 1791.

In writing this book, we have received considerable support from our colleagues, friends and family, to whom we express our thanks. We would particularly like to thank Susan Hawker and Keith Syrett for their help and encouragement. We would also like to thank all at Sweet and Maxwell, in particular Nicola Thurlow. In a book of this kind, inevitably work must be divided. Silas has therefore taken primary responsibility for chapters on negligence and economic torts, whilst Paula has done so in respect of chapters on negligence-related liability, strict liability statutes, nuisance, trespass, defamation, privacy, defences and remedies. The book remains, however, a joint effort. Needless to say, any errors therein are ours alone. We have attempted to state the law as it stood on March 31, 2011.

Two final points on terminology. The Civil Procedure Rules came into force on April 26, 1999. Their aim is to speed up and simplify civil litigation. Accordingly, in an effort to demystify the law, the term "plaintiff" was replaced in 1999 by the term "claimant". We therefore use the latter term when discussing principles of law and recent cases. The term "plaintiff", however, is used when discussing cases decided prior to the date of the change. More recently in October 2009, the Supreme Court replaced the Appellate Committee of the House of Lords as the highest court in the United Kingdom. For cases decided after this date, the term "Supreme Court" will be used; prior to that date the text will refer to "the House of Lords". Both signify the highest court in the United Kingdom.

Paula Giliker
Silas Beckwith
Bristol and London, April 2011.

# Table of Contents

# 4   Negligence: Psychiatric Illness

# TABLE OF CASES

# TABLE OF STATUTES

# TABLE OF STATUTORY INSTRUMENTS

# TABLE OF EUROPEAN AND INTERNATIONAL LEGISLTION

# Chapter 1

## THE NATURE OF TORTIOUS LIABILITY

Liability in tort can be imposed for a diverse range of conduct, extending from negligent behaviour to attacking a person's reputation or limiting a person's freedom of movement. This book aims to provide an understanding of the nature of tortious liability by explaining how and why a defendant can be liable in these and other situations. This chapter provides a starting point. Here, we shall examine what is meant by "tort", the aims and objectives of the current system of tort law, and the factors that seem to influence tortious liability. We shall also consider how tort law fits in with other forms of civil liability, namely contract and restitution. The second part of this chapter addresses some different questions: How well does tort law fulfil its role in English law? Are there any alternatives to tort law which could or should be adopted? By gaining a basic understanding of the scope and nature of tort, the reader will be better able to understand the law in following chapters.    **1–001**

### What is tort?

Tort takes many forms. It includes, for example, negligence, nuisance, libel, slander, trespass, assault and battery. It is therefore more accurate to speak of a "Law of Torts", rather than a "Law of Tort". To provide a definition which encompasses the whole of this area of law is impossible. Each tort has its own particular characteristics. Some torts, such as negligence, require proof of damage, whilst others, such as trespass and libel, are actionable without proof of damage. Whilst the tort of negligence obviously requires "negligent" behaviour, other torts, such as trespass, require intentional behaviour or at least recklessness. It is best, therefore, to confine ourselves to a statement that the law of tort is the law of *civil wrongs*[1] that is to say, it is concerned with behaviour which is legally classified as "wrong" or "tortious", so as to entitle the claimant to a remedy.    **1–002**

It must be conceded that this definition is somewhat circular, but it is the only one that will suffice. More precise definitions, such as that of the great tort lawyer Professor Winfield, have been widely criticised. Winfield defined tort as arising "from the breach of a duty primarily fixed by law; this duty is towards persons generally and its breach is redressible by an action for unliquidated damages".[2] This definition has been criticised because it ignores the fact that

---

[1] The word "tort" is in fact Norman-French for "harm" or "wrong". It dates from the times when Norman-French was used within the English judicial system.
[2] *The Province of the Law of Tort* (1931), p.32.

some tortious duties arise by consent,[3] some are owed only to specific individuals,[4] and a breach of duty does not automatically make the defendant liable.

Whilst it may not be possible to provide a precise definition of "tort", it is certainly possible to identify a number of principles that determine when liability in tort will arise. It is to these that we now turn.

## PRINCIPLES OF LIABILITY

**1–003**    Tort law determines who bears the loss which results from the defendant's actions. For example, driver A knocks down pedestrian B in the street. B suffers personal injury. Tort law will determine who bears the loss suffered by B. If A is not liable, B bears the loss. If A is liable, A (or rather his or her insurance company) will bear the loss. The aim of shifting loss does not tell us, however, what makes a court choose between A and B. A number of principles seem to underlie the decision whether or not to impose liability on A, and it is important to note that no one principle predominates. These principles may be broadly summarised as:

- compensation
- fault
- retributive justice (punishment)
- deterrence
- economic efficiency (market deterrence)
- loss distribution (spreading losses in a socially fair way)

We examine each principle below.

## (1) Compensation

**1–004**    Perhaps the most obvious objective of tort law is to award compensation for loss. In doing so, the courts are guided by the principle known as restitutio in integrum. Lord Blackburn, in *Livingstone v Rawyards Coal Co*,[5] explained the meaning of this principle when he said that compensation in tort should take the form of:

> "the sum of money which will put the party who has been injured, or who has suffered, in the same position as he would have been in if he had not sustained the wrong for which he is now getting his compensation or reparation."

The goal of compensation, of course, is subject to practical constraints. For example, where the claimant has lost an arm, the best tort law can do is to provide a sum of money which represents that loss. Tort law has also recognised that liability must be subject to certain rules

---

[3] e.g. if you invite someone into your home (see Occupiers' Liability, discussed in Ch.8).
[4] e.g. duties owed to employees (see Employers' Liability, discussed in Ch.7).
[5] (1880) 5 App. Cas. 25 at 39 per Lord Blackburn.

which limit the availability of compensation. Fears of indeterminate liability (the so-called "floodgates of litigation") and of disproportionate liability (or "crushing liability") have dictated that tort law must set limits to the types of loss it will compensate. Thus, for example, compensation for mental distress is rarely awarded, and a restrictive approach is adopted towards liability for "pure economic loss" and psychiatric illness. The idea of full compensation, therefore, translates into "compensation within reason".

Tort law has been supported in its compensatory goal by the growth of the insurance industry.[6] Statistically, most tort claims for personal injury arise from road traffic accidents or accidents in the workplace. In both cases it is compulsory for the defendant to insure against liability. The Road Traffic Act 1988 makes liability insurance compulsory for motorists[7] and its objectives are underpinned by the existence of the Motor Insurers' Bureau, which administers schemes to compensate victims of uninsured drivers and hit-and-run incidents.[8] Similarly, the Employers' Liability (Compulsory Insurance) Act 1969 provides that employers must be insured against accidents in the workplace. In these areas, then, legislation and the law of tort work in tandem. The legislation ensures that deserving claimants are guaranteed compensation (rather than being at the mercy of the defendant's resources), whilst the law of tort provides the mechanism through which they can obtain it.

Of course, compensating misfortune is not an objective peculiar to the law of tort. Tort operates in the context of a wider regime which includes statutory compensation schemes such as the Criminal Injuries Compensation Scheme and, ultimately, the cushion of social security payments. The law's efforts to reconcile the relationship between these different ways of providing compensation are examined in Ch.17. What should be noted here, however, is that the existence of tort law means that society applies the principle of full compensation selectively. In the absence of a universal system of compensation for all accident injuries, successful tort claimants are likely to receive substantial compensation, whilst victims of naturally occurring accidents (unless they are privately insured) receive no compensation, except possibly low-level social security payments.

## (2) Fault

Fault is the idea most commonly used to *justify* an award of compensation. Fault-based **1–005** liability embodies the idea of taking personal responsibility for one's own conduct and may serve as a deterrent. It also serves a retributive purpose—a claimant's anger at being the victim of a wrong is more likely to be placated if he or she receives compensation from the person who has been at fault, rather than from an alternative source. Both of these matters are considered in later sections.

Liability for fault has become particularly significant because of the growth of the tort of negligence. As we shall see in Ch.2, liability for negligence was opposed by most of the judges in the nineteenth century, because it ran contrary to the ideas of individualism and laissez-faire that dominated the political philosophy of the age. But this philosophy gradually

---

[6] See Davies (1989) 9 L.S. 67.
[7] See ss.143 and 145.
[8] See *Byrne v Motor Insurers' Bureau* [2008] EWCA Civ 574; [2009] Q.B. 66 (limitation provisions of the Untraced Drivers Agreement held incompatible with EC law). In the light of this decision, the government has asked the Motor Insurers' Bureau to reconsider claims that were formerly assumed to be time-barred.

changed, so that in 1932, Lord Atkin in *Donoghue v Stevenson*[9] was able to justify fault-based liability by saying that members of society ought to take reasonable care to avoid harming their "neighbours". The idea of fault nowadays pervades many areas of tort law, but it is not to be thought that all torts are fault-based. In libel, for example, a defendant who writes a defamatory article in a newspaper may be liable even if he or she has taken all due care in researching the article.

It should be noted that the context in which tort law operates in modern society means that, whilst the notion of "fault" is used to justify imposing liability, often, legal "fault" does not equate with moral blame. In relation to driving accidents, for example, the administrative advantages for the law in being able to settle claims easily have triumphed over moral considerations. Thus, as we shall see in Ch.5, a driver can be held legally at "fault" for a mistake that by the standards of society is morally excusable. Moreover, in many areas of tort law, the widespread practice of insuring against liability means that, in reality, it is an insurer rather than a morally guilty defendant who foots the bill for compensation. The fault principle is similarly undermined by the doctrine of vicarious liability.[10] Vicarious liability renders one person responsible for the torts committed by another. The most common example is that of employer and employee. If an employee commits a tort in the course of employment, the claimant is perfectly entitled to sue the employer for damages in tort. In these circumstances, then, the burden of the wrong done may be shouldered by the innocent employer, rather than by the employee who is to blame. Insurance and vicarious liability subordinate the fault principle to the overriding need to compensate victims of accidents. In the light of this, fault can be only *one* possible explanation of how the tort system works.[11]

## (3) Retributive justice

1–006    Vengeance or retribution is the most ancient justification for imposing liability on a defendant who has committed a wrong. It was to fulfil the objective of preventing "blood feuds" that the law developed an action for compensating harm, which eventually became the law of torts. In modern times, perhaps, this objective is less relevant. Even today, though, it should be recognised, for example, that a person is less likely to commit an act of "road rage" against a driver who has dented his or her bumper if a tort claim (settled by insurers) will pay for a new one.

Nowadays, the idea of retribution as an objective of tort sits very uneasily with the existence of the criminal law. It is the function of the criminal law to punish the wrongdoer and see that he gets his "just deserts". It is hard to justify importing the concept of punishment into civil proceedings for two reasons. First, in a civil trial, the punishment may be meted out in the absence of the evidential and procedural safeguards to which a defendant is entitled in criminal proceedings. Secondly, because tort law and criminal law operate concurrently, the defendant may receive "double punishment" for a single wrong. Nevertheless, in the modern law of tort there are certain circumstances where the courts may punish a defendant by an award of "punitive" damages. Such damages are justified on the basis of their deterrent effect. This is discussed below.

---

[9] [1932] A.C. 562 at 580. See also *Sedleigh-Denfield v O'Callaghan* [1940] A.C. 880 (expanding the tort of nuisance on the basis of fault).
[10] See Ch.7.
[11] For a more detailed critique of the fault principle, see Cane, *Atiyah's Accidents, Compensation and the Law* (7th edn, 2006), Ch.7.

## (4) Deterrence

In its basic form, the concept of tort liability acting as a deterrent is a simple one: if I cause   **1–007**
harm through my actions or inaction and have to pay compensation, I will try to behave differently next time. We can see the deterrence principle at work in various contexts. Publishers,
for example, aware of the high cost of compensation if they publish defamatory material,
often employ lawyers to screen publications so as to avoid liability. Equally, professionals
such as doctors and lawyers may be encouraged to take care in their work because they
fear the consequences of liability—not just in terms of financial cost, but in terms of the harm
litigation may cause to their professional reputations.

The objective of deterrence is supported by the courts' power to award "exemplary" or
"punitive" damages in tort.[12] These are damages which seek not to compensate the claimant,
but to punish a defendant for acting deliberately with a view to profiting from his or her tort,
or to punish the executive arm of government for acting in an arbitrary, oppressive or unconstitutional manner.[13] Their goal is to show that tort does not pay and thereby deter the defendant
from contemplating such conduct in future.[14] A good example is the American case of
*Grimshaw v Ford Motor Co*[15] concerning the Ford Pinto. Here, Ford was alleged to have
discovered a defect in the car which rendered it susceptible to explosion when struck from the
rear. Nevertheless, it continued to market the car on the basis that it would be cheaper to
pay compensation to victims of the defect than to redesign the car. Such cynical disregard
for human safety led a jury[16] to award exemplary damages of $125 million, reduced to
$3.5 million on appeal.

In the tort of negligence, however, deterrence theory has limited application. This is
because, in a case where A has injured B by simple *inadvertence* (which the law may call
"negligence"), it is difficult to see how making A liable can alter the behaviour of a person in
A's position. A is liable because he or she has failed to meet the standard of behaviour expected
of the "reasonable person". As we shall see in Ch.5, this is an *objective* standard—which
means that in applying it the court takes little account of the personal characteristics of the
defendant. What this means is that a defendant can be held liable even though he or she is
already taking all the care which he or she could possibly take in pursuing a particular activity.
The point is well illustrated by the decision of the Court of Appeal in *Nettleship v Weston*[17]
(discussed further in Ch.5). Here, a learner driver on her third lesson was held liable in negligence for driving below the standard of the "reasonable driver"—which was set at the standard
of an ordinary, competent, qualified driver. No concession was made to the fact that she was a
learner (or even that she was being sued by her instructor—arguably the very person whose
skill was supposed to prevent the accident!).

There are further objections to regarding deterrence as an important aim of tort law—a
deterrent can only work if the people whose actions or inaction cause damage are the same
people who have to pay for that damage. We have seen that the doctrine of vicarious liability
means that the employer pays for the damage, rather than the negligent employee. In such

---

[12] Discussed more fully in Ch.17.
[13] See *Rookes v Barnard (No.1)* [1964] A.C. 1129.
[14] [1964] A.C. 1129 at 1228 per Lord Devlin.
[15] 119 Cal. App. 3d 757 (1981).
[16] Juries are still used in tort cases in the US, but are rarely used in English courts, save for torts such as defamation,
fraud and false imprisonment: see Supreme Court Act 1981 s.69.
[17] [1971] 2 Q.B. 691.

circumstances, it cannot be said that the prospect of having to pay compensation has an effect on the amount of care taken by the employee in his or her work. Similarly, the existence of liability insurance removes the sting of arguments based on deterrence. When a motorist gets in a car, it is rather far-fetched to say that his or her mind is concentrated by the prospect of civil liability for careless driving, because that is a prospect against which he or she is insured. To the careless motorist, the cost of a car crash is likely to be no more than the loss of a "no-claims bonus", entailing a small increase in premiums (against which, nowadays, it is even possible to insure). In the context of employers' liability to their employees, whilst it is true that the threat of liability may provide an incentive for employers to adopt safer working practices, in a commercial world, these will only be adopted where they are cost effective. Moreover, because of the way the insurance industry works—spreading the cost of accidents amongst all policyholders—the full force of the incentive is seldom brought to bear on employers.

All of the problems with deterrence theory we have examined, then, are really part of the same problem: the objective of deterrence is accorded less importance in tort law than the objective of compensation. This is so for two reasons. First, by social consensus, vicarious liability and insurance make compensation available at the expense of deterrence. Secondly, there are limits to the extent to which deterrence arguments can be considered in the context of a tort trial. If a court seeks to deter a whole class of potential defendants from wrongful conduct by imposing liability on the particular defendant in the case (or by awarding punitive damages), then the result of the case may be unjust—the particular defendant is singled out to pay the price for wrongful conduct that may be the common practice of his or her peers, and (in the case of punitive damages) the particular claimant receives a windfall in addition to compensation.[18] Similarly, effective deterrence requires that potential defendants be given guidance about how to avoid liability. Whilst the courts occasionally provide such guidance, constraints of time and resources prevent them from going into details. Moreover, because the guidance is given in the context of a particular case, it may be difficult to interpret in terms of general application. In the light of these factors, such guidance is better provided by statute (for example, health and safety legislation) than by ad hoc decisions in tort.

## (5) Economic efficiency (market deterrence)

1–008      If, through the operation of law, a manufacturer of products (for example) is forced to bear the cost of harm caused by those products, and to pass that cost on to consumers, he or she will seek to maximise the safety of the products in order to obtain the best price in the marketplace. Logically, therefore, as a result of this process the safest products will become the cheapest, and market competition should operate to reduce the *total amount* of harm caused in society by all products on the market. This idea is known as the principle of "market deterrence".

Once we start to explore such arguments, we venture into the difficult realm of economic analysis of law. To use the language of economists, every product (or activity) has the potential to produce "externalities" ("extra costs" not reflected in the price) when either it causes harm, or necessitates precautions to prevent harm from arising. Economic analysis of law seeks to discover how these "externalities" are paid for. Economists argue that the framework

---

[18] But note that the Law Commission in its report No. 247 "Aggravated, Exemplary and Restitutionary Damages" (1997) recommended a more generous approach to punitive damages, which will be discussed in Ch.17.

of any legal system should be such as to ensure that externalities are paid for in a way that maximises "efficiency". In economic language, the most "efficient" way of doing things is the way that produces the least cost to society as a whole. What all this means for the law of tort is that the courts should seek to develop rules under which the risk of harm in any given situation is borne by the person who will expend the least amount of society's resources in taking precautions against it. This person is sometimes known as the "best cost-avoider".

We can see that this principle already operates in the law to some extent by considering a simple example. Suppose that a number of televisions are sold with wrongly wired mains plugs, presenting risks of fire and electric shock. It is likely that tort law will make the manufacturer of the televisions liable if these risks materialise. Whilst this result will accord with the principles of compensation and fault, it will also fulfil the objective of efficiency. This is because, whilst it will be relatively inexpensive for the manufacturer to change his or her production methods so that the wires are put in the plug the right way round, it would be relatively expensive (in terms of missed opportunities to create wealth) if all of the individuals affected by the problem had to rewire a plug themselves.

Whilst it is clear that tort law can be analysed in terms of economics, economic concepts are seldom referred to by English judges.[19] This might be explained by the fact that the "economics and law" debate is largely an American one,[20] and reflects the political trends of that country, namely right-of-centre market economics. It is sometimes also suggested that much of the academic commentary on the subject may be rather impenetrable to non-economist judges— yet it should be remembered that the current House of Lords comprises a large number of commercial judges who are undoubtedly familiar with economic concepts. Perhaps the true explanation for the lack of judicial enthusiasm in this area is that economic analysis of tort law cannot in many cases be reconciled with more pressing objectives of the tort system. Economic analysis takes as its starting point the assumption that in most, if not all cases, the potential human cost of the defendant's actions can be given a monetary value. Whilst, arguably, this is just a cold fact of life, it is one which society and the judiciary are understandably reluctant to face. Society may not be prepared to quantify in monetary terms the cost of a young child being hideously disfigured, so as to weigh it against the purely financial cost of preventing such an occurrence. Equally, whilst an economic perspective can be instructive in explaining decisions in negligence and nuisance[21] cases, it is less helpful in explaining torts like trespass and defamation, whose primary aim is to protect the integrity of the individual.

## (6) Loss distribution

As stated earlier, tort law shifts loss from the victim to the tortfeasor by imposing liability. In a broader context, however, it can be seen that tort law operates to shift losses so that they are borne by the whole (or large sections) of society. This function of tort law is known as "loss spreading" or simply "loss distribution". It is fulfilled mainly through vicarious liability—part of tort law itself—and through liability insurance—part of the context in which it operates.

**1–009**

---

[19] But see, e.g. the analysis of Lord Hoffmann in *Stovin v Wise* [1996] 1 A.C. 923 at 944 in the context of liability for omissions.

[20] Most of the relevant academic commentary is American. See, e.g. R. Posner, *Economic Analysis of Law* (7th edn, 2007).

[21] The role of economic deterrence in the tort of nuisance is discussed in the influential article of A. Ogus and G. Richardson [1977] C.L.J. 284.

Vicarious liability makes employers liable for accidents caused by their employees, but employers cover themselves by insurance and pass the cost of the premiums on to consumers in the prices of their goods and services. In this way, the cost of compensating accident victims is spread throughout the community, in much the same way that social security payments, funded by taxation, spread the cost of compensating social need. Similarly, because the legislature has imposed compulsory liability insurance for road traffic accidents, the cost of accidents will be met first by insurance companies, who will then pass on this cost in the form of premiums paid by their clients. The cost of accidents is thereby spread amongst the (insured) driving community.

Clearly, "loss distribution" can be criticised for a number of reasons. It can be criticised for ignoring the importance of fault and undermining the objective of deterrence. It can also be criticised as unjust: why should a careful driver or employer subsidise the cost of accidents caused by the tortious activities of others? It can only be justified by acceptance of its underlying rationale—that a certain amount of "distributive justice" is desirable in a civilised society.[22]

## Conclusions

**1–010**     Tort law is an amalgam of all six of the concepts considered above. Its mixed aims are the inevitable result of the common law system of justice where law is developed on a case-by-case basis. Although compensation is the most common reason for bringing a tort action, claimants may have a number of other reasons, including deterrence and retribution. In *Hill v Chief Constable of West Yorkshire*,[23] for example, the mother of the last victim of Peter Sutcliffe (a serial killer known as the "Yorkshire Ripper") sued the police for negligence, mainly in order to criticise their carelessness in failing to apprehend the murderer soon enough, and to make the point that police practices should be improved. In Lord Templeman's view, the action was misconceived. His Lordship pointed out that

> "an action for damages for alleged acts of negligence by individual police officers in 1980 could not determine whether and in what respects the West Yorkshire police force can be improved in 1988".

Lord Templeman's remarks emphasise that an adversarial system is ill-suited to a proper consideration of broad questions of social and economic policy. The focus of the courts' attention is whether compensation should be awarded to do justice in the particular cases before them. This does not prevent courts using their skill and experience to address broader concerns, but it is important to recognise that there are constraints on their ability to do so.

## THE INTERESTS PROTECTED BY TORT

**1–011**     Tort law aims to protect the individual from actual or threatened harm to certain specific interests. In this section, we examine the degree of protection afforded to each interest. Tort law does not protect *all* interests from harm, and certain interests, such as personal safety,

---

[22] The concept of "distributive justice" is referred to in a number of negligence cases, most notably *McFarlane v Tayside Health Board* [2000] 2 A.C. 59 (discussed in Ch.2 ) and *White v Chief Constable of South Yorkshire* [1999] 2 A.C. 455 (discussed in Ch.4).

[23] [1989] A.C. 53.

receive better protection than others. As tort law has developed, the nature of protection offered to each interest has reflected the importance of that interest to society at the relevant period in history. Thus, whilst in feudal times trespass to land was the most sophisticated and important tort, in the modern industrial age protection against personal injury has dominated the agenda.

## (1) Personal harm

The industrial revolution brought with it new threats to the safety of individuals with the intro- **1–012** duction of heavy machinery, motor vehicles and railways. Tort law responded by developing the tort of negligence. This supplemented the existing protection provided by trespass to the person, where the torts of assault, battery and false imprisonment serve to protect individuals from intentional interference with their personal freedom and bodily integrity.[24] Yet, whilst tort law has clearly offered protection against physical injury, the judiciary has been reluctant to offer protection against other forms of personal harm, such as psychiatric illness and distress. Considerable scepticism was expressed in the nineteenth century towards claims for "nervous shock", on the basis that they would leave "a wide field open for imaginary claims".[25] Although claims for psychiatric illness may now be brought, the law still adopts a restrictive regime of recovery, as will be seen in Ch.4. Claims for mental distress still cannot be brought in their own right,[26] although this is a developing area of the law. The problem of harassment has become more significant in recent times and developments in tort law have now been replaced by a statutory tort under the Protection from Harassment Act 1997. We shall see in Ch.2 that the Human Rights Act 1998 has had an effect on the scope of negligence liability so as to protect, for example, victims of child abuse in circumstances where the state has failed to offer them appropriate protection. In Ch.15, we consider the extent to which the law provides a remedy for invasion of privacy.

## (2) Harm to property

Protection against harm to property remains important, but no longer has the primacy accorded **1–013** to it during feudal times. "Property" here is used to signify both personal property and land (real property). Personal property is protected by the torts of trespass to goods and conversion (civil theft). Real property is protected by a number of torts, including trespass to land, nuisance, and the rule in *Rylands v Fletcher*, which are discussed in Chs 10 and 11. Property loss is also recoverable in other torts such as negligence.

## (3) Harm to reputation

Reputation is protected by the tort of defamation, which creates liability for untrue statements **1–014** which diminish the claimant's reputation in the eyes of right-thinking members of society. Defamation is examined in Chs 13 and 14 of this book. It should be noted that defamation protects the claimant's *reputation* and not his or her *feelings*, so that there will be no action

---

[24] See Ch.11.
[25] See *Victorian Railway Commissioners v Coultas* (1888) 13 App. Cas. 222 at 226.
[26] On claims for mental distress in tort generally, see Giliker (2000) 20 L.S. 19.

for defamation if the claimant is insulted in private or if the statement fails to diminish his
or her reputation. As will be discussed, protection of reputation must be weighed against
the public interest in free speech and a free press. In practice, this balance is far from easy
to achieve.

## (4) Harm to financial interests

**1–015**    Tort law gives limited protection to financial interests. Such interests are usually protected
outside tort law, for example by contract law or by legislation such as the Competition
Act 1998 and the Enterprise Act 2002. In this area, tort law is particularly conscious of
the potential number of claims and the threat of "liability in an indeterminate amount for an
indeterminate time to an indeterminate class".[27] Whereas the cost of compensating physical
injury tends to be limited, the potential for "crushing liability", resulting from a flood of
claims for financial loss, presents a problem for the law. Courts are therefore reluctant to
impose liability for *negligent* infliction of financial loss, save in the specific situations where
the defendant has voluntarily assumed responsibility for the claimant's interests, or where the
loss is consequential on physical damage.[28]

However, tort law does offer some protection where the defendant has *intentionally* interfered with the claimant's economic and trading interests. The tort of deceit (fraud) imposes
liability where the defendant has made a false statement[29] to the claimant in the knowledge
that it is false, or reckless as to its truth, with the intention that the claimant will act on it.[30] The
claimant may recover damages for economic loss suffered by acting on the statement.[31]
Likewise, the "economic torts", which we examine in Ch.12, impose liability in a limited
number of situations for intentional interference with business interests.

## (5) Harm to the due process of law

**1–016**    This will be dealt with briefly. Certain torts seek to protect the claimant against misuse of the
legal system. In this book, we refer specifically to one such tort: malicious prosecution.[32] In a
system where the criminal law permits individuals to instigate prosecutions, this tort affords
the claimant valuable protection against prosecutions which are brought maliciously without
reasonable and probable cause. In the leading case of *Martin v Watson*[33] the tort was used to
protect the plaintiff where the defendant had maliciously made a groundless accusation of
indecent exposure against the plaintiff, leading to his prosecution. Although it is a difficult tort
to prove, it demonstrates the willingness of the English legal system to intervene to prevent
abuse of the law.

---

[27] See Cardozo C.J. in *Ultramares Corp v Touche* 255 N.Y. Rep. 170 at 179 (1931); 174 N.E. Rep. 441 at 444 (1931).
[28] See Ch.3.
[29] Which must be of an existing fact: *Edgington v Fitzmaurice* (1885) 29 Ch. D. 459.
[30] See *Derry v Peek* (1889) 14 App. Cas. 337.
[31] The claimant can recover for all the losses directly flowing from the fraudulent misstatement: *Doyle v Olby
(Ironmongers) Ltd* [1969] 2 Q.B. 158. Deceit or fraud generally appears in the context of contract law and reference
should be made to works on contract law.
[32] See Ch.11.
[33] [1996] 1 A.C. 74.

## THE ROLE OF TORT IN THE LAW OF OBLIGATIONS

In this section, we compare the role of tort with two other aspects of civil law, namely the law **1–017** of contract and the law of restitution (or unjust enrichment). Together with tort, these heads of liability are sometimes referred to as the "Law of Obligations". In English law, the same defendant may be liable under more than one of these heads of liability. This is known as "concurrent liability". A claimant is not obliged to choose between bringing an action in contract, tort or restitution[34] and may plead all three. Nevertheless, the three causes of action perform different roles in English law, which are examined below.

### The distinction between tort and contract

The role of contract law is, put simply, the enforcement of promises.[35] Liability is therefore **1–018** centred around the contract itself: Has it been formed? What are its terms? Have they been breached? Contractual remedies seek to place the claimant in the position, so far as money can do it, that he or she would have been in had the contract been performed.[36] By contrast, tort is concerned with compensating the victim who has suffered injury as a result of conduct classified as a civil wrong by law. The aim here is not to enforce a bargain, but to compensate the victim for his or her out-of-pocket expenses, thereby placing the victim in the same position as he or she would have been in had the victim not sustained the wrong for which compensation is being awarded.[37]

Readers should be wary of attempts to distinguish contract and tort on the basis that contract consists of obligations imposed by consent and tort consists of obligations imposed by law. Contract law is subject to considerable legislative and judicial intervention and terms may be imposed by statute[38] or by the courts. Equally, the defendant in tort law may, in a sense, agree to undertake certain tortious responsibilities, for example by inviting a guest into his or her household[39] or by undertaking to advise the claimant on the merits of a particular business transaction.[40] Such a theory, therefore, is really too general to be of much use. In practice, the distinction between contract and tort is determined simply by asking the question: "Have the rules of contract law been complied with?" If the answer is "no", the obligation or wrong in question cannot be classified as contractual, but may be classified as tortious.

### The distinction between tort and restitution

Restitution is a growing area of civil liability, the proper scope of which remains unclear. The **1–019** law of restitution intervenes where the defendant has been unjustly enriched at the expense of

---

[34] See *Henderson v Merrett Syndicates Ltd (No.1)* [1995] 2 A.C. 145, overturning the doubts experienced following Lord Scarman's equivocal judgment in *Tai Hing Cotton Mill Ltd v Liu Chong Hing Bank Ltd* [1986] A.C. 80 at 107. This is not the case in all jurisdictions. The position is different, e.g. in France.

[35] Although it has been argued that its real role is in the protection of detrimental reliance: see, e.g. Atiyah (1978) 94 L.Q.R 193 and in P.S. Atiyah, *Essays on Contract* (1990, Clarendon Press).

[36] *Robinson v Harman* (1848) 1 Ex. 850 at 855 per Parke B.

[37] Lord Blackburn in *Livingstone v Rawyards Coal Co* (1880) 5 App. Cas. 25 at 39.

[38] e.g. under the Sale of Goods Act 1979.

[39] See Ch.8.

[40] See Ch.3.

the claimant. Rather than compensating the claimant, it seeks to restore to the claimant the amount by which the defendant has been wrongfully enriched. Whilst its goal is therefore distinct from that of tort, it is clear that restitutionary damages may be awarded as an alternative to tort in certain limited circumstances. These are discussed in Ch.16.[41]

## THE IMPACT OF EUROPEAN AND HUMAN RIGHTS LAW

1–020    In examining the English law of torts, it is important to recognise the impact of European law and policy. Sometimes this impact is direct. For example, in Ch.9, we examine liability for defective products, which is now largely dealt with under the Consumer Protection Act 1987. This was introduced to comply with Directive 85/374 on liability for defective products. In other cases, the impact is indirect—there is a body of case law which states that certain breaches of European Union law may be actionable in the national courts of Member States. Where a provision of European law (contained either in a treaty or in secondary legislation) has direct effect, giving claimants a remedy in national law,[42] actions by such claimants have been recognised as falling within the tort of breach of statutory duty.[43] This area—sometimes referred to as the law of "Eurotorts"—is likely to become increasingly significant.[44]

The European Convention on Human Rights, incorporated into English law by the Human Rights Act 1998, has also had some impact on the development of tort law[45] and has broadened the circumstances in which claimants are entitled to sue in the tort of negligence. Litigants are no longer required to pursue their case before the European Court of Human Rights in Strasbourg. They are able to raise breaches of the Convention in the English courts. Section 6 of the Act provides that public bodies, including courts[46] must not act in a way which is incompatible with a Convention right. This means that courts must take account of the rights established in the Convention and by the case law of the Strasbourg court.[47] Where legislation is concerned, s.3(1) of the Act provides:

> "So far as it is possible to do so, primary legislation and subordinate legislation must be read and given effect in a way which is compatible with the Convention rights".

However, the Act does not affect the validity of any incompatible primary legislation,[48] although a court may make a declaration of incompatibility.[49]

---

[41] For a more detailed discussion, see Jackman [1989] C.L.J. 302; Birks, "Civil wrongs: a new world", Butterworths Lectures 1990–1 (1992); Rotherham [2007] C.L.J. 172; and leading texts on the law of restitution.
[42] The concept of direct effect has been developed by the European Court of Justice from the case of *Van Gend en Loos v Nederlandse Administratie der Belastingen* [1963] C.M.L.R. 105.
[43] *Garden Cottage Foods Ltd v Milk Marketing Board* [1984] A.C. 130, HL: breach of art.86, Treaty of Rome (now art.102, TFEU).
[44] Consider, e.g. *Francovich v Italian Republic* [1993] 2 C.M.L.R. 66 and, more recently, *Brasserie du Pecheur v Germany; R. v Secretary of State for Transport, ex p. Factortame* (No. 4) [1996] 1 C.M.L.R. 889. See Downes (1997) 17 L.S. 286 and Craig (1997) 113 L.Q.R. 67.
[45] See, e.g. *Osman v United Kingdom* (1998) 5 B.H.R.C. 293 and *Z v United Kingdom* (2002) 34 E.H.R.R. 3, discussed in Ch.2.
[46] See *Aston Cantlow v Wallbank* [2004] 1 A.C. 546, HL, discussed by F. Meisel [2004] P.L. 2.
[47] See s.2.
[48] s.3(2). It also does not affect the validity, continuing operation or enforcement of any incompatible subordinate legislation if (disregarding any possibility of revocation) primary legislation prevents removal of the incompatibility.
[49] s.4(2).

The question for us to consider in this book, of course, is the impact of the Human Rights Act 1998 on the law of torts. We shall see in Ch.2 how art.6 (right to a fair trial) has affected the courts' practice of "striking out" cases where the claimant has no real prospect of success. We shall also see how art.3 (right not to be subject to inhuman or degrading treatment) has given child abuse victims an action against local authorities in respect of their child welfare functions. We also discuss the effect of the 1998 Act on other torts, for example nuisance (in Ch.10). In Ch.14 we specifically consider the effect art.10 (the right to freedom of expression) on the tort of defamation and in Ch.15 whether the 1998 Act has introduced a right to privacy into English law.

## TORT IN MODERN SOCIETY

Detailed study of tort law sometimes tends to obscure the fact that, especially in personal injury cases, there are often other means by which a claimant may be compensated for his or her loss. It is appropriate, therefore, to say something about tort law in its wider social context, to give the reader a clearer view of where it fits in modern society. In this section, we explore the role of tort in providing compensation and consider proposals for its reform, focusing particularly on the New Zealand experience of replacing tort with a no-fault system of accident compensation.    **1–021**

### Tort and other compensation systems

It is important to realise that in practice tort law plays a minor role in compensating accident victims. The Pearson Commission,[50] which undertook a survey of accident compensation in England and Wales in the 1970s, reported that only 6.5 per cent of accident victims received any form of tort damages.[51] This means that the bulk of compensation comes from sources outside the tort system. These include payments from employers, from insurance, from schemes such as the Criminal Injuries Compensation Scheme, and social security payments. Whilst the level of such payments is usually well below that of tort damages, which are unique in seeking to provide full compensation for the victim, in practice they provide financial assistance for the majority of accident victims. This assistance is supplemented by the provision of publicly funded health care under the National Health Service. As we shall see in Ch.17, there are sometimes problems involving "double-counting" where a claimant has received tort damages and also benefits from insurance, or perhaps a charitable donation. The courts (with the help of legislation) have evolved a number of complicated rules which govern the relationship between different sources of compensation.    **1–022**

The importance of these alternative sources of compensation varies. Social security payments are obviously significant, particularly for those on low incomes. However, the amounts are relatively small. As at March 2011, income support for a single person over 25 was set at £65.45 per week.[52] Insurance is also important, particularly in respect of property

---

[50] Royal Commission on Civil Liability and Compensation for Personal Injury (Cmnd 7054 1978).
[51] Royal Commission on Civil Liability and Compensation for Personal Injury (Cmnd 7054), Vol. 1, Table 5(i).
[52] See *www.jobcentreplus.gov.uk/JCP/Customers/WorkingAgeBenefits/*

damage, where tort actions are rarely brought.[53] Health insurance, critical or terminal illness cover, and unemployment insurance are also significant, as are payments from the accident victim's employer, such as occupational sick pay and pensions. The Criminal Injuries Compensation Scheme makes provision for victims of crimes of violence and those sustaining injuries in the course of apprehending an offender, although a tariff system is adopted and compensation in respect of a single injury is capped at £500,000.[54] Criminal courts also have the power to make compensation orders when sentencing in a criminal court,[55] but the amounts awarded tend to be nominal and the awards have limited impact if the convicted defendant does not have the means to pay.

## Why not tort?

**1–023**    Given that tort compensation tends to be paid at a higher level than the other forms of compensation, why is it that the majority of claimants do not bring an action in tort? One reason is that, in many circumstances, the rules of tort are well established. This means that whilst a tort *claim* may be made (perhaps on a very informal basis) and quickly settled, it is unnecessary to bring a tort *action*. The Pearson Commission found that 86 per cent of tort claims were disposed of without the issue of writ or summons, and that, of the total number of claims made (including those where no legal proceedings were commenced) only 1 per cent actually reached the courts. There are, however, a number of additional reasons why tort litigation is seldom used.

*Cost*

**1–024**    Litigation is extremely expensive. A claimant must be able to fund litigation and take the risk that if he or she loses, the court is likely to order the claimant to pay not only his or her own costs, but also those of the defendant. The burden of cost has to some extent been alleviated by the introduction of conditional fees. Under this system, a solicitor agrees to take on a client's case on the basis that no fee will be charged if the client loses,[56] but a larger fee will be charged if the client succeeds in his or her action which will normally be recoverable in whole or part from the losing party. This is not, however, a universal panacea: a solicitor is only likely to take on cases with reasonable prospects of success, and may be reluctant to take on complicated and time-consuming cases.

In 2008, the government set up an inquiry in response to concerns about the rising costs of civil justice. This led to a report, in 2010, by Jackson L.J.[57] In the forward, his Lordship states:

> "In some areas of civil litigation costs are disproportionate and impede access to justice. I therefore propose a coherent package of interlocking reforms, designed to control costs and promote access to justice."

Some of the key reforms proposed include the introduction of US-style contingency fees, under which the lawyer is paid a percentage of the winnings or nothing at all, and the abolition

---

[53] See Cane, *Atiyah's Accidents, Compensation and the Law*, (7th edn, 2006), p.495.
[54] See Criminal Injuries Compensation Act 1995. See generally Cane, *Atiyah's Accidents, Compensation and the Law* Ch.12.
[55] Powers of Criminal Courts (Sentencing) Act 2000.
[56] See Access to Justice Act 1999.
[57] *Review of Civil Litigation Costs Final Report* (HMSO, 2010)

of "referral fees"—fees paid by clients to organisations that "sell" damages claims to solicitors. It remains to be seen whether these reforms will have the desired effect.[58]

*Time*

Litigation moves very slowly (which of course adds to its cost). Despite the attempts of the  **1–025** Woolf reforms to speed up litigation[59] and despite time limits (set under the Limitation Act 1980) within which actions must be brought, it remains the fact that many cases take years to get to court, during which the claimant will generally have to wait to receive any compensation.

*Risk*

The adversarial system makes litigation a risky option. Indeed, the risk of litigation is often  **1–026** used by defendants to force the claimant to settle, rather than face the possibility of losing everything in a court of law.

*Difficulty*

Despite the intervention of Lord Woolf, going to law is often a complicated process. The  **1–027** workings of the law seem impenetrable to many lay people. Few would attempt a claim in tort without the assistance of qualified lawyers, and getting this assistance may be expensive, time-consuming and often alienating to an individual who simply wishes to be compensated for his or her injury.

*Absence of litigation consciousness*

Traditionally, there has been a lack of litigation awareness in this country. Accident victims  **1–028** have been far more likely to contact their insurers, or blame bad luck, than seek a possible defendant on whom to transfer their loss.[60] This, however, seems to have changed in recent years with the introduction of conditional fees. Few can have missed the aggressive advertising of numerous firms offering to take on personal injury claims. Such advertising has raised litigation awareness, but its effect must, of course, be balanced against the other problems with litigation which we have considered. Datamonitor, an organisation which tracks personal injury litigation, has found only a gradual increase in the number of personal injury claims in recent years, with claims rising by 8.3 per cent in 2006–07 and 10.9 per cent in 2008–09.[61]

Whilst the statistical reality is that there is no alarming growth of a "compensation culture" in the UK, the Government has felt the need to address a *perception* to the contrary—this perception was apparently held by some local authorities, who had acted defensively to protect themselves from the prospect of litigation, in one case, for example, by closing down a popular public beach to avoid any risk of drowning.[62] The Compensation Act 2006 therefore puts on a statutory footing what has always been the position at common law, namely that the courts, in deciding whether to impose liability in negligence, can take into account the question of whether such liability might be adverse to the public interest by preventing "desirable

---

[58] Comment: A Zuckerman, "The Jackson Final Report on Costs: plastering the cracks to shore up a dysfunctional system" [2010] C.J.Q. 263.

[59] See the final report of Lord Woolf, *Access to Justice* (1996).

[60] A survey conducted by researchers at the Centre for Socio-Legal Studies in Oxford in 1976 found that only 14 per cent of personal injury victims consulted a lawyer: Harris et al., *Compensation and Support for Illness and Injury* (1984).

[61] UK Personal Injury Litigation (*http://www.datamonitor.com* [Accessed April 11, 2011]).

[62] *Tomlinson v Congleton BC* [2004] 1 A.C. 46, discussed in Ch.8.

activities" from taking place.[63] The Act also provides that "an apology, an offer of treatment or other redress, shall not of itself amount to an admission of negligence"[64] and makes provision for the regulation of the claims management industry.[65]

## Proposals for reform

**1–029**　It is clear that tort law is far from perfect. A number of suggestions for reform have been made, which we consider below. These suggestions are not without problems and all require the legislature to take tough political decisions about the aims of any reformed compensation system. On current thinking, the possibilities for reform are threefold:

### (1) A mixed system

**1–030**　The Pearson Commission made a number of recommendations about reforming the system of compensation in England and Wales.[66] Its main proposal was that a mixed system of tort law and social security should be retained, but with greater emphasis on the role of social security payments.[67] Greater attention would also be paid to how tort and social security worked together. For certain accidents, such as road traffic accidents[68] (which represent a large proportion of total accident claims) special provision would be made. The Commission proposed a no-fault system for road traffic accidents funded by a 1p tariff per gallon of petrol.[69] This would spread the cost of such accidents, whilst placing the greatest burden on those who consume the most petrol. This was justified on the basis that drivers who use the most petrol–either by driving long distances or by driving vehicles with high petrol consumption– are those most likely to cause an accident.

　　The proposals were criticised for singling out road traffic accident victims and giving them preferential treatment over victims of other types of accident.[70] They can also be criticised, of course, for ignoring the functions of tort law in terms of deterrence and retribution (although the Commission felt that these ends could be adequately served if tort law were retained concurrently with a no-fault scheme). Delivered in 1978, immediately prior to the election of the new Thatcher Conservative Government, a plan of reform based on increasing state involvement in individual welfare stood little chance of success. In the event, of the Commission's 188 recommendations, only a handful have been implemented.[71] It is most unlikely that this situation will change.

### (2) No-fault liability

**1–031**　This is a more radical proposal. It is based on the proposition that if tort law primarily aims to compensate victims, it achieves this in an inefficient and often arbitrary way. Tort law is

---

[63]　See Compensation Act 2006 s.1.

[64]　Compensation Act 2006 s.2.

[65]　Compensation Act 2006 Part II. For further discussion, see Rebecca Herbert [2006] 4 J.P.I. Law 337.

[66]　See J. Fleming (1979) 42 M.L.R. 249.

[67]　Vol.1, para.275, on the basis that social security payments were quick, certain and inexpensive to administer and already covered the majority of accident victims.

[68]　Specific proposals were also suggested for airline and vaccination accidents, defective products and extraordinary risks.

[69]　Vol.1, Ch.18.

[70]　See, e.g. Ogus, Corfield and Harris (1978) 7 I.L.J. 143.

[71]　e.g. special treatment for vaccine-damaged children was implemented in the Vaccine Damage Payments Act 1979, which provides for a tax-free lump-sum payment of £120,000 where serious mental or physical damage has been caused by the administration of specified vaccines.

inefficient because of the sheer costs of administering the system. The Pearson Commission reported that the operating costs of the tort system amounted to a figure representing about 85 per cent of the money paid out in compensation. In other words, for every £100 paid out, it costs about £85 (in insurers' handling fees, lawyers' fees, etc.) just to make the payment. Clearly this can be seen as a waste of society's resources. The costs of running a no-fault scheme may be much lower.

Tort is arbitrary in the sense that only those victims who can point to a tortfeasor can recover full compensation. All other accident victims must fall back on other forms of compensation which are likely to be paid at a lower level. By contrast, no-fault liability seeks to compensate all accident victims on the basis of need.

Although the Pearson Commission felt that the adoption of a comprehensive no-fault scheme to the exclusion of tort was beyond their terms of reference,[72] a different view was taken by the Woodhouse Commission in New Zealand, which in 1967 recommended that such a scheme should be adopted in that country.[73] A comprehensive system of state-run compensation for all "accidents" causing personal injury and death was brought in by the New Zealand Labour Government in 1974 and tort actions for personal injury were abolished. The term "accident" has been extended to cover medical misadventure and intentional acts such as battery and rape. With its five aims of community responsibility, comprehensive entitlement, real compensation, complete rehabilitation and administrative efficiency, the system provides a dramatic contrast to our own system of tort law. The scheme is funded by citizens paying premiums into relevant funds. Accordingly, employers and the self-employed pay to cover work-related injuries, and drivers to cover road traffic accidents.[74] Accidents which occur outside of these contexts are funded by general taxation.

The New Zealand scheme has run for over 35 years, and the New Zealand experience is useful in evaluating our own system.[75] A number of conclusions can be drawn. First, a comprehensive system which seeks to replace tort law damages in every respect is inevitably expensive. The escalating cost of the New Zealand scheme led to the passing of legislation to curtail the scheme and reduce the level of benefits available to accident victims. Generally speaking, the scheme now compensates only lost earnings, although additional lump-sum payments for victims with permanent disability have been re-introduced, in response to criticism from claimants that the scheme was unfair by comparison to a tort action. Compensation for non-financial loss (such as pain and suffering), however, is not available. The scheme is administered by the Accident Compensation Corporation, whose tasks now include the promotion of accident-prevention measures (such as speed limits) and the promotion of rehabilitation of accident victims. Secondly, it is clear that the success of a no-fault scheme depends on the political mood of the country. This, of course, may change over time. In the early 1970s, many contemplated that the New Zealand scheme would expand, but in fact it has contracted. In the United Kingdom, the political mood is not in favour of the no-fault option, which requires a dominant philosophy of state intervention and responsibility.

In 2003, the Chief Medical Officer, Sir Liam Donaldson, rejected the option of a comprehensive no-fault compensation scheme for treatment under the NHS, when faced with an

[72] Vol.1, para.274, although it may be questioned whether this was an excuse to avoid discussion due to the obvious disagreement within the Commission as to the relationship between tort and no-fault liability.

[73] See Report of the Royal Commission of Inquiry on Compensation for Personal Injury in New Zealand (1967).

[74] By means of part of the motor vehicle licensing fee and a percentage of petrol sales.

[75] Information can be gathered from the website of the Accident Compensation Corporation which administers the scheme: *http://www.acc.co.nz* [Accessed April 11, 2011]. See, further, Oliphant (2007) 15 Med L Rev 357.

estimated cost of £4 billion a year.[76] Instead, a fault-based scheme has been provided for, under the NHS Redress Act 2006.[77] This scheme (which allows for claims only where there is "qualifying liability in tort") aims to supplement tort law by providing victims of medical negligence with up to £20,000 in compensation, together with an apology or remedial care, as appropriate. Patients are able to withdraw from the scheme if they decide they would rather take their claim to court. The idea behind the scheme is to settle claims in a non-adversarial way. This is in the interests of patient welfare, since it avoids the stress and delay associated with litigation. It is also in the interests of the medical profession—it is hoped that, free from the prospect of court action, medical professionals may be more willing to admit their mistakes and treat them as opportunities for learning. The scheme has not been without its critics, however, who fear that it will deprive claimants of their right to have claims decided by a judge (not least because claimants may be denied legal aid if they fail to use the scheme).[78]

*(3) Insurance*

**1–032**    This proposal is perhaps more consistent with current political views on free market economics. It is primarily advanced by Professor Atiyah, who explains it in his book *The Damages Lottery*.[79] Insurance, as we have seen, is an important adjunct to the law of tort, yet the influence of insurance on the law of tort is a matter of some dispute.[80] Whilst the orthodox position is that the courts should ignore the presence of insurance cover,[81] judges such as Lord Denning have used the presence of insurance cover to justify developments in the law aimed at achieving the principle of loss distribution.[82] Professor Atiyah's approach is more radical. Put simply, he argues that the tort system should be replaced by a system of first party insurance. By purchasing "first party" insurance, a person insures himself or herself against suffering *harm*. (It should be distinguished from "third party" insurance, where a person insures against *liability* for harm suffered by others.) The argument runs that, if everyone were covered by first party insurance, there would be no need for an inefficient system of tort law. Accident compensation and prevention could be dealt with through the more efficient medium of the market.

There are a number of objections to this suggestion,[83] the strongest of which is that not everyone in society has the means to pay for first party insurance. One must also have doubts about the morality and the wisdom of placing all accident compensation in the hands of insurers. At present, tort law provides the benchmark against which the appropriate levels of compensation for personal injuries are assessed. It is questionable whether justice would be seen to be done if this function were removed from the judiciary and placed in the hands of insurance companies.

---

[76] See *Making Amends* (NHS, 2003): *http//www.dh.gov.uk* [Accessed April 11, 2011].

[77] At the time of writing, consultation is still taking place before the scheme is brought into force by statutory instrument.

[78] See Peter Gooderham, "Special Treatment?" (2007) 157 N.L.J. 694.

[79] (Hart, 1997).

[80] See Stapleton (1995) 58 M.L.R. 820 and Morgan (2004) 67 M.L.R. 384.

[81] See Lord Bridge in *Hunt v Severs* [1994] 2 A.C. 350 at 363 who held that at common law the fact that the defendant is insured can have no relevance in assessing damages. See also Viscount Simonds in *Lister v Romford Ice and Cold Storage Co Ltd* [1957] A.C. 555 at 576–577.

[82] See, e.g. *Nettleship v Weston* [1971] 2 Q.B. 691 at 700.

[83] See the excellent review of Professor Atiyah's book by Conaghan and Mansell (1998) 25 J.L.S. 284.

## Tortious liability: conclusion

Tort law is a stimulating, if sometimes complicated and often frustrating subject to study. It **1–033** faces a number of challenges, some of which are of quite recent origin. The effects of the Human Rights Act 1998, a growing body of European law, and the Woolf reforms on civil litigation continue to shape the contours of tortious liability. Despite its failings, tort law continues to offer a humane and pragmatic response to the problems of twenty-first century life.

# Chapter 2

## NEGLIGENCE: THE DUTY OF CARE

### Introduction

The tort of negligence is the most frequently used of all the torts and is therefore perhaps the most important. It has flourished in the latter part of the twentieth century, rising to a dominant position because of the flexible nature of its rules, which have allowed the judges to expand the tort to protect many claimants who would otherwise have been left unprotected by the law. Unfortunately for the law student, however, this broadness of judicial approach can make the principles of the tort seem frustratingly vague.   **2–001**

This book explores negligence over five chapters, taking each ingredient of the tort in turn. This chapter introduces these ingredients and then, from a general perspective, discusses the first of them, namely the duty of care. The next two chapters explore some of the special difficulties the courts have encountered in deciding whether a duty of care should exist in relation to economic loss and psychiatric illness. The last two chapters on negligence deal with the remaining ingredients of the tort, namely breach of duty and causation.

This chapter begins with a basic definition. There then follows a short section describing the correct approach to be taken when studying negligence and a section giving a brief overview of the tort. These sections introduce certain important ideas which, once grasped, will help dispel some of the frustration often experienced by those who approach the subject for the first time.

### Definition of "Negligence"

The tort of negligence has been usefully defined as:   **2–002**

> ". . . a breach of a legal duty to take care which results in damage to the claimant."[1]

The tort is not usually concerned with harm inflicted *intentionally*. Rather, it is concerned with harm inflicted "accidentally" or through want of care. We shall see, however, that establishing negligence involves much more than simply showing that the defendant behaved "carelessly"—careless behaviour is only one ingredient of the tort.

---

[1] W.H. Rogers, *Winfield and Jolowicz on Tort*, 18th edn (2010), p.132.

To establish the tort of negligence, the claimant must prove three things:

(1) the defendant owes the claimant a duty of care;

(2) the defendant has acted in breach of that duty, and

(3) as a result, the claimant has suffered damage which is not too remote a consequence of the defendant's breach.

For the purpose of learning the law, it is convenient to consider each element of the tort in turn. Rarely in practice, however, will disputes ever involve all three elements. Moreover, the courts have a tendency to blur the distinctions between each of the separate elements of negligence. Quite often, therefore, a judgment may indicate that the defendant is not liable but may not make it clear which of the three separate requirements of the tort has not been fulfilled.[2] This difficulty stems from the fact that, as we shall see, the concept of "reasonable foreseeability" is used by the courts in establishing all three elements of the tort.

## STUDYING NEGLIGENCE

**2–003**     The tort of negligence covers such a wide range of factual situations that the search for a single "set of rules", applicable to all types of negligence case, will be fruitless. The correct approach, then, is to focus on the *type of interest* which the claimant is trying to use the tort to protect (physical safety, the safety of property, financial well-being, or psychological well-being), and then to think about the *policy reasons* why the courts have felt either able or unable to extend the scope of negligence to protect that interest in particular situations. The language of the judges, and the pattern of their decision-making, will only begin to make real sense when considered alongside the political and economic forces which motivate decisions in negligence cases.

When one looks at what negligence is trying to achieve within society—the redistribution of certain risks associated with day-to-day activities—it becomes clear why the judges have had such difficulty in formulating workable rules for the tort. The point to grasp is that negligence is essentially concerned with a conflict of values within society. The driver of a car, for example, wishes to go fast to reach his destination, but the pedestrian crossing the road wishes the driver were going more slowly so as to lessen the likelihood of being knocked down. In essence, therefore, in order to decide the question of negligence, the judge must make a *political and moral value-judgment* as to the relative merits of fast driving and road safety in society. Making this sort of judgment, however, is not a task with which judges feel very comfortable, because it is one for which the British Constitution does not equip them. As Lord Scarman put it in *McLoughlin v O'Brian*[3]:

---

[2] This is not necessarily to be regarded as a failing. See *Sam (aka Al-Sam) v Atkins* [2005] EWCA Civ 1452, [2006] R.T.R. 14 where the CA noted that although negligence is habitually analysed in compartments, it is a single composite concept. See also *Calvert v William Hill* [2008] EWCA Civ 1427; [2009] Ch.330, where the CA expressed a similar view (but note Morgan (2009) 68(2) C.L.J. 268, who suggests that this led to an over-complicated analysis).
[3] [1983] 1 A.C. 410 at 431.

"... the policy issue where to draw the line is not justiciable. The problem is one of social, economic and financial policy. The considerations relevant to a decision are not such as to be capable of being handled within the limits of the forensic process."

Clearly, his Lordship is referring to the fact that, in constitutional theory, the role of the judge is not to make law, but only to interpret it. Much of the interest in studying negligence, however, comes from exploring the way in which the judges have managed to make new law, usually without explicitly stating that they have done so. For constitutional reasons, the judges are not able to use the explicit language of politicians or economists in their judgments. This means that where the relevant political and economic reasoning is present in cases, it is often encoded in "judicial", rather than "political" language. A proper understanding of the tort of negligence, then, requires a good deal of "reading between the lines".

## AN OVERVIEW OF NEGLIGENCE

In 1932, Lord Atkin, in the landmark case of *Donoghue v Stevenson*,[4] formulated a general **2–004** principle (known as the "neighbour principle") by which the existence of a legal duty to take care could be determined, thus effectively inventing the modern tort of negligence. The problem with Lord Atkin's general principle, however, was that it contained too little by which, on the basis of logic, the limits of the tort could ever be confined.

As the tort of negligence developed, the courts sought to qualify Lord Atkin's general principle with a number of complex, inherently vague and sometimes rather arbitrary rules. These rules were necessary in order to keep the scope of negligence within acceptable bounds. In particular, the courts felt it important to avoid being overrun with a multiplicity of negligence claims (they were afraid to open the so-called "floodgates of litigation") because, as was noted in Ch.1, the tort system is very costly to administer. The courts were also afraid of allowing what is sometimes called "crushing liability". Crushing liability would occur if one particular defendant were made liable for a very large amount of loss, of which the defendant's actions were the logical cause, but for which it would be unfair or economically inefficient to make the defendant responsible in law.

In studying negligence, we shall see how, during the period from 1963 until the mid–1980s, the House of Lords was willing to apply Lord Atkin's "neighbour principle" fairly broadly, so that, from its beginnings in *Donoghue v Stevenson*, it came to be applied to factual situations which were far removed from the facts of that case. During this period, the tort of negligence grew from a tort protecting only property and physical well-being into one which, to a limited extent, now protects the financial and psychological well-being of claimants. We shall then see how, in recent years, faced with the problems of indeterminate and crushing liability, their Lordships have retraced their steps, diminishing the scope of the tort.

To some extent, it can be seen that the expansion of negligence, and its subsequent contraction, have mirrored certain changes in political thought that took place in the latter half of the twentieth century. This period saw a gradual change away from a philosophy of welfarism and state control towards a philosophy of individualism and contraction of state responsibility. The long rule of a Conservative Government, from 1979 to 1997, brought arguments about economic efficiency into tighter focus than ever before. It is likely that these arguments have

---

[4] [1932] A.C. 562.

influenced the courts, resulting in their reluctance to make people responsible for certain types of loss when, under a contract, the risk of that loss (and the reward for taking that risk) has been allocated to someone else. This point is further explored in Ch.3.

## THE DUTY OF CARE

### An overview

**2–005**   As the courts have struggled to determine the proper scope of negligence, they have used each of its three ingredients—duty, breach and causation—as a *control mechanism* to set limits to the tort. This multi-faceted approach can sometimes be rather confusing. What is clear, however, is that in recent times there has been a marked tendency to deal with the question of liability by reference to the scope of the duty of care. Logically, establishing the existence of a duty of care is the first hurdle a claimant must overcome. It therefore makes sense for a court to deal with this first, because it simplifies the decision-making process.

In many situations it will be obvious from established case law that the defendant owes the claimant a duty of care. The real problem for the courts has been to decide whether a duty of care should be owed in novel factual situations which are not covered by authority. Because of the political and economic considerations involved, the courts have found it difficult both to decide this question and to express their decisions in appropriate language. In order to limit the scope of the duty of care, they have repeatedly asserted the importance of the *relationship* between the defendant and the claimant. This approach, however, has not resulted in a universally applicable test for determining the existence of a duty of care in all cases. The qualifications on Lord Atkin's "neighbour principle" have become so numerous that the House of Lords has been forced to abandon the search for a single workable test. Thus, in *Caparo v Dickman*,[5] Lord Roskill concluded:

> "It has now to be accepted that there is no simple formula or touchstone to which recourse can be had in order to provide in every case a ready answer."

With this in mind, we can now examine more closely the historical development of the duty of care, and the modern approach to deciding whether it exists.

### The historical background

**2–006**   Negligence was not regarded as a tort in its own right until the late nineteenth century. The traditional system of writs, under which claims would not be recognised unless they had been made in the prescribed form, did not include a specific writ for negligence. Early case law, however, did suggest that in certain situations liability based on carelessness could arise. For example, it was established from early times that innkeepers and common carriers could be liable for the careless performance of a specific task. Later, in the seventeenth century, it became established that a surgeon or an attorney would be liable if his conduct was less than that expected of a reasonably skilled professional. Although, at the time, such cases were not

---

[5] [1990] 2 A.C. 605 at 628.

considered in terms of a separate tort of negligence, with hindsight they show us how the courts came gradually to accept that liability could arise where a defendant had merely been careless, as opposed to having committed an intentional act of wrongdoing.

In the nineteenth century, the technology of the industrial revolution brought with it great potential for personal injury. In addition, as urban areas became more densely populated, congestion on city streets led to an increase in the number of "running down" cases. These factors brought about a change in judicial attitudes. As Professor Winfield observes:

> "Early railway trains, in particular, were notable neither for speed nor for safety. They killed any object from a Minister of State to a wandering cow, and this naturally reacted on the law."[6]

The stage was set for the emergence of a new tort which could meet the needs of claimants in an increasingly dangerous age.

## The first step: identifying a general principle

Whilst, in the nineteenth century, the courts came to recognise that liability could be based on     **2–007** careless conduct, there was no general principle of law applicable to these situations. Instead, a body of case law emerged consisting of a collection of isolated instances where such liability had been imposed. The major obstacle to the development of a general principle seems to have been the Victorian belief that individuals should bear all responsibility for their own welfare and that they could not be expected to look out for the welfare of others unless they were being paid to do so. The concept of "collectivism"—the idea that every member of society can benefit if each member takes some responsibility for the well-being of others—whilst central to our modern way of thinking, was alien to Victorian political culture. Thus, whilst the courts were happy to make defendants liable where they had *assumed* responsibility for the care of another by entering into a contract with that other for reward, they were less happy about *imposing* on defendants a gratuitous duty to look after others.

This attitude was apparent in the decision in *Winterbottom v Wright*.[7] The plaintiff was a coach driver, employed by the Postmaster-General, who suffered serious injuries when he fell from a coach that had been defectively built by the defendants. It was held that the driver could not recover compensation from the builders of the coach because he was not a party to the contract with the Postmaster-General, under which the defendants had supplied the coach. The idea, of course, was that since it was the Postmaster-General, rather than the coach driver, who had paid the coach builders to assume responsibility for the safety of the coach, there was no reason why the coach driver should benefit when the coach proved dangerous.

In *Winterbottom v Wright*, then, it was decided that where a person had assumed responsibility under a contract for the quality of a thing supplied, and that thing turned out to be defective, he would be liable only to the person to whom he had supplied it under a contract. He could not also be liable for damage suffered by a third party who was not privy to the contract. This idea later became known as the "privity of contract fallacy". It persisted in the law until it was overturned by the decision in *Donoghue v Stevenson*[8] in 1932.

---

[6] Winfield (1926) 42 L.Q.R. 184 at 195.
[7] (1842) 10 M. & W. 109.
[8] [1932] A.C. 562.

The first real suggestion that there could be a general principle of law governing the existence of the duty of care came in 1883. Brett M.R., in *Heaven v Pender*,[9] observed that the following proposition appeared to cover all of the recognised cases of liability for careless conduct:

"... whenever one person is by circumstances placed in such a position with regard to another that everyone of ordinary sense who did think would at once recognise that if he did not use ordinary care and skill in his own conduct with regard to those circumstances he would cause danger of injury to the person or property of the other, a duty arises to use ordinary care and skill to avoid such danger."

The majority of the Court of Appeal, however, were unwilling to adopt such a broad principle of liability,[10] and in his later decision in *Le Lievre v Gould*,[11] Brett M.R. (now Lord Esher M.R.), declined to apply the principle to a case involving purely financial loss. In a sense, Brett M.R.'s formulation of a general principle came before its time. It was not until 1932 that a change in judicial attitudes, which mirrored the political and economic changes that had taken place in society, allowed for a unified approach to cases of careless conduct.

A further problem with Brett M.R.'s formulation of the principle was that, although it referred to the "position" of one person "with regard to another" as giving rise to a duty of care, it did not go very far in describing the nature of the relationship which had to exist between the claimant and the defendant. This meant that, on the face of it, Brett M.R.'s general principle would have given rise to liability in any case where a person should have foreseen that his conduct might cause harm to another. We shall see that Lord Atkin's reformulation of the principle in *Donoghue v Stevenson*[12] makes it much clearer that foreseeability of harm alone should not be sufficient to establish the existence of a duty of care.

*Lord Atkin's "neighbour principle"*

**2–008**      In 1932, the House of Lords decided the famous case of *Donoghue v Stevenson*.[13] The facts of the case have become legendary,[14] although it should be noted that, because the case was decided by the House of Lords on a point of law and was then settled before going to trial, these facts were never actually proved. It was alleged that Mrs Donoghue and her friend visited Minchella's Wellmeadow Café, in Paisley.[15] At the café, the friend bought for Mrs Donoghue a "ginger beer float", consisting of ginger beer, supplied in an opaque bottle, and ice-cream. Mrs Donoghue drank some of the mixture, and when her friend topped up the drink, out of the ginger beer bottle floated the decomposed remains of a snail. Mrs Donoghue claimed that the sight of the snail, together with the ginger beer she had already drunk, made her ill.

Now, Mrs Donoghue, of course, could not sue the retailer of the ginger beer for breach of contract because, not having bought the ginger beer herself, she was not in a contractual relationship with him. The contract had been made between the retailer and her friend. She therefore brought an action in tort against the manufacturer of the ginger beer. It was not worthwhile

---

[9] (1883) 11 Q.B.D. 503 at 509.
[10] (1883) 11 Q.B.D. 503 at 516 per Cotton and Bowen L.JJ.
[11] [1893] 1 Q.B. 491 at 497.
[12] [1932] A.C. 562.
[13] [1932] A.C. 562.
[14] For an entertaining review of the case, see Rodgers Q.C. [1988] C.L.P. 1.
[15] Paisley is in Scotland and the case was therefore brought in Scots law. The House of Lords accepted that no difference existed between English and Scots law in this instance.

suing the *retailer* in tort, because he was not at fault. The ginger beer had been supplied to him in an opaque bottle, so that he could not have looked inside the bottle to check that its contents were wholesome, and there was no possibility that the snail could have entered the bottle at any stage after it had been supplied by the manufacturer.

Mrs Donoghue's position, however, was very similar to that of the coach driver in *Winterbottom v Wright*. She had been the victim of a defective product that had been supplied to another person under a contract to which she was not a party. According to *Winterbottom v Wright*, it appeared that the manufacturer would only be liable under his contract with the retailer. Yet Mrs Donoghue succeeded in her claim. A majority of the House of Lords distinguished *Winterbottom v Wright*, holding that a manufacturer of products, which he sells in such a form as to show that he intends them to reach the ultimate consumer in the form in which they left him, with no reasonable possibility of intermediate examination before the products are consumed, would be liable to the consumer in tort if he failed to take reasonable care to ensure that the products were safe. Their Lordships rejected the so-called "privity of contract fallacy" of *Winterbottom*—privity of contract did not prevent a third party bringing an action in tort.

At first sight, it seemed that the decision in *Donoghue v Stevenson* had simply added yet another category to the separate instances of negligence recognised by the law. What has become significant about the case, however, is Lord Atkin's analysis of the law and his subsequent formulation of a general principle for determining the existence of a duty of care. This is what Lord Atkin said[16]:

> ". . . in English law there must be, and is, some general conception of relations giving rise to a duty of care, of which the particular cases found in the books are but instances. The liability for negligence . . . is no doubt based upon a general public sentiment of moral wrongdoing for which the offender must pay. But acts or omissions which any moral code would censure cannot in a practical world be treated so as to give a right to every person injured by them to demand relief. In this way rules of law arise which limit the range of complainants and the extent of their remedy. The rule that you are to love your neighbour becomes, in law, you must not injure your neighbour; and the lawyer's question who is my neighbour? receives a restricted reply. You must take reasonable care to avoid acts or omissions which you can reasonably foresee would be likely to injure your neighbour. Who then, in law is my neighbour? The answer seems to be—persons who are so closely and directly affected by my act that I ought reasonably to have them in contemplation as being so affected when I am directing my mind to the acts or omissions which are called in question."

Lord Atkin's general principle contained two elements. First, there was the element of "reasonable foreseeability". Thus, a duty of care would be owed where the defendant ought reasonably to foresee that his failure to take care may cause injury to another. (This, of course, is the same as what Brett M.R. had said in *Heaven v Pender*.) The second element was the test of "neighbourhood"—a duty of care would be owed only where the claimant was "closely and directly" affected by the defendant's conduct. Brett M.R.'s simple test of foreseeability of harm, therefore, became qualified by the additional need to show, as Lord Atkin put it, a degree of "proximity"[17] between the claimant and the defendant, not in the sense of physical proximity, but in the sense of "close and direct relations".

---

[16] [1932] A.C. 562 at 580.

[17] Interestingly, the term "proximity" was first used by Brett M.R. in *Thomas v Quartermaine* (1887) 18 Q.B.D. 685 at 688.

Lord Atkin's general test of foreseeability plus "proximity", then, gave the courts a basis on which the existence of a duty of care could be decided in all cases. It allowed them to view negligence as a tort in its own right, capable of being developed to meet any new factual situation which arose.

It is important, however, not to overestimate the significance of Lord Atkin's general principle. It has already been noted that, in modern times, it is recognised that this principle alone fails to provide a workable solution to the problem of imposing a duty of care. The principle suffers from a number of fundamental flaws. First, although Lord Atkin speaks of "acts or omissions", we shall see that the law treats liability for acts very differently from liability for omissions. Secondly, as the law has developed, it has become clear that, besides identifying the defendant's "neighbour", it is also necessary to identify the *type of loss* which the "neighbour" is likely to suffer (or, in other words, the *type of interest* which the claimant is seeking to use the law to protect) before any decision can be made about whether to impose a duty of care. Lord Atkin's words, spoken in the context of personal injury caused by a defective product, gave little indication of the degree of "proximity" which would be required in other factual situations. We shall see that, especially where other types of harm are in issue, the courts, for policy reasons, have had to say that a far greater degree of "proximity" is required in some situations than in others. In *Donoghue v Stevenson*, Lord Atkin observed:

> "There will no doubt arise cases where it will be difficult to determine whether the contemplated relationship is so close that the duty arises".[18]

Such prescience, it will be seen, was all too accurate.

## The second step: applying the general principle

**2–009**    Without Lord Atkin's "neighbour principle", the decision in *Donoghue v Stevenson* would simply have been another isolated example of negligence liability. (The case did indeed establish liability in English law for defective products, which is discussed in Ch.9.) It should be noted that Lord Atkin's principle did not form part of the ratio of the case, because the two other majority judges in the case refrained from adopting it. As might be expected, then, the first response of the courts was to treat the case as a narrow example of liability. The judges were particularly reluctant to apply the principle in situations where there was clear authority which excluded liability in negligence, such as where the claimant suffered financial loss because of a carelessly-made statement. And so things might have remained, but for a number of radical decisions in the 1960s and 1970s, in which the House of Lords was prepared to overturn previous authority to extend the scope of the duty of care.

*The decision in Hedley Byrne*

**2–010**    The first of these cases came in 1964. The decision in *Hedley Byrne v Heller and Partners*[19] established, contrary to previous authority, that there could be liability in English law in respect of financial loss caused by negligent misstatement. The case is examined more fully in Ch.3, but it will be convenient to state the facts here.

---

[18] [1932] A.C. 562 at 582.
[19] [1964] A.C. 465. For an insightful review of *Hedley Byrne v Heller* and its law-making effect, see Buxton (2009) 125 L.Q.R. 60.

Hedley Byrne, who were advertising agents, were about to enter into certain contracts on behalf of one of their clients—a company called Easipower—on terms which meant that, if Easipower failed to honour its obligations under the contracts, Hedley Byrne would become liable to pay Easipower's debts. Hedley Byrne therefore wished to find out whether Easipower was creditworthy, so, through their own bankers, they sought a reference from Easipower's bankers, Heller and Partners. Heller and Partners wrote saying that although the amounts in question were larger than they were accustomed to see, they considered Easipower to be good for the ordinary course of business. But they made it clear that they were providing this advice "without responsibility" on their part. In other words, they included a disclaimer of liability.

On the basis of the favourable credit reference, Hedley Byrne went ahead with the advertising contracts. It turned out, however, that Heller and Partners had carelessly failed to realise that, at the time they gave the reference, Easipower was in a very bad way financially. Easipower went into liquidation shortly after the contracts had been made, so that Hedley Byrne became liable to pay Easipower's debts. Hedley Byrne therefore brought an action against Heller and Partners for the negligently given advice.

Two major problems faced Hedley Byrne. First, their action concerned a statement which had been made carelessly, but previous authority had decided that there could only be liability where a statement had been made fraudulently.[20] Secondly, their action was for financial loss, rather than for personal injury or damage to property—the areas where the courts had so far been willing to impose negligence liability.

Nevertheless, the House of Lords was prepared to hold that, but for the disclaimer of liability, Heller and Partners would have been liable for their negligent statement. Whilst their Lordships were prepared to use Lord Atkin's "neighbour principle" as a starting point in establishing liability, they were not prepared to decide the case purely by analogy to the facts of *Donoghue v Stevenson*. Their Lordships made it clear that there were important differences between negligently made statements causing financial loss and negligently manufactured products causing personal injury. These differences meant that Lord Atkin's principle could not be applied without qualification in negligent misstatement cases. The reasoning in *Hedley Byrne v Heller and Partners* is considered more fully in Ch.3. For present purposes, however, it is sufficient to note that, in order to avoid the problems of indeterminate and "crushing" liability, their Lordships held that in negligent misstatement cases a high degree of "proximity", or closeness of relationship, would be required. It was held that for liability to arise, a "special relationship" had to be shown between the maker of the statement and the person who subsequently relied on it.

*The decision in Dorset Yacht*

The next landmark case was *Home Office v Dorset Yacht*.[21] This case was important because **2–011** it imposed a duty of care on the defendant to prevent damage being caused by the actions of others. Liability for the acts of third parties has proved to be a difficult area for the courts and is further discussed later in this chapter.

In *Home Office v Dorset Yacht*, the Home Office had established a Borstal (a prison training camp for young male offenders) on an island off the Dorset coast. One night, because of the carelessness of the guards, a number of the prisoners escaped and caused damage to some yachts moored in the harbour. The House of Lords was prepared to impose liability on the

---

[20] See *Derry v Peek* (1889) 14 App. Cas. 337 and *Candler v Crane Christmas & Co* [1951] K.B. 164 (discussed in Ch.3).
[21] [1970] A.C. 1004.

guards (for whom the Home Office was responsible in law), holding that there were "special relations" between the Home Office and Borstal boys, so that the Home Office could be liable for its failure to prevent the boys from causing damage. This, together with a high degree of foreseeability—escaping and causing the damage was the "very kind of thing" the boys were likely to do—made the Home Office liable.

Lord Reid made the following observation:

> "*Donoghue v Stevenson* may be regarded as a milestone, and the well-known passage in Lord Atkin's speech should, I think, be regarded as a statement of principle. It is not to be treated as if it were a statutory definition. It will require qualification in new circumstances. But I think the time has come when we can and should say that it ought to apply unless there is some justification or valid explanation for its exclusion."[22]

*Lord Wilberforce's "two stage test"*

**2–012**  This positive affirmation of Lord Atkin's principle was approved by the House of Lords in the next important case—the now discredited case of *Anns v Merton LBC*.[23] Here, a local authority had failed to notice that the foundations of a new block of maisonettes had not been dug to an adequate depth. The plaintiffs, who had taken long leases of the maisonettes, found that cracks appeared in the walls. They sued the local authority for the cost of rebuilding. (Nowadays, this case is regarded as one of economic loss. It was overruled in 1990 by the decision in *Murphy v Brentwood DC*,[24] discussed in Ch.3.)

In *Anns*,[25] Lord Wilberforce reformulated the test for determining the existence of a duty of care. According to his Lordship, the judges should ask themselves two questions, one after the other. This became known as Lord Wilberforce's "two stage test" and can be summarised as follows:

*Stage one*: is there, between the claimant and defendant, a sufficient relationship of "proximity or neighbourhood" such that the defendant can reasonably foresee that carelessness on his or her part would be likely to cause damage to the claimant? If the answer to this question is "yes", then a prima facie duty of care arises.

*Stage two*: are there any considerations which should nevertheless lead the court to deny a duty of care, or to limit its scope, in these particular circumstances?

This straightforward test had the appeal of simplicity, but unfortunately was flawed. Essentially, the problem was that it was unclear what Lord Wilberforce meant by the word "proximity" in stage one of the test. We have seen that Lord Atkin thought that "foreseeability" and "proximity" were two separate things. Foreseeability of harm alone would not give rise to a duty of care—there had also to be "close and direct relations" between the claimant and the defendant. Lord Wilberforce, on the other hand, now appeared to say that foreseeability *was* the test for proximity. This meant that, in applying the two stage test, if a judge felt that, although harm was foreseeable, liability should not be imposed because the relationship between the claimant and the defendant was not sufficiently close, the judge would have to find some way of expressing this idea by answering Lord Wilberforce's second question, i.e. by explicitly stating a policy reason for denying the existence of a duty of care.

---

[22] [1970] A.C. 1004 at 1027. Contrast the more reserved approach of Lord Diplock at 1060.
[23] [1978] A.C. 728.
[24] [1991] A.C. 398.
[25] [1978] A.C. 728 at 751.

Lord Wilberforce's approach proved difficult, and was eventually abandoned, because, on this interpretation, it did not truly reflect the way the courts decide the existence of the duty of care. The courts do not assume a duty of care and then consider, as a matter of policy, whether in the circumstances the type of damage in question should be compensated. Rather, the policy question of whether certain types of damage should be recoverable in certain circumstances goes to the central question of whether, in each case, a duty should exist in the first place. Reading between the lines, we might observe that the problem with Lord Wilberforce's formulation was that it made it difficult for judges to avoid explicit reference to *political* and *economic* considerations when answering the second question in the two stage test. Although there is no logical reason why liability cannot depend on a composite test of foreseeability plus politics and economics, the judges have not felt able to adopt such a direct approach.

Lord Wilberforce's two stage test, then, embodied a more generous approach to the duty of care issue—a *presumption* that a duty of care would exist unless clear policy objections could be found. This approach was adopted in *Junior Books Ltd v Veitchi & Co Ltd*[26] (discussed in Ch.3), where the majority of the House of Lords supported a claim brought by factory-owners against specialist sub-contractors who had negligently installed a floor in their factory. By so doing, their Lordships extended the tort of negligence so that, in special circumstances, it would provide a remedy not just for damage to property caused by the supply of a defective product, but for the cost of replacing the defective product itself. This was important because, previously, only contract law had provided a remedy for defects in the quality of products.

Following *Junior Books*, however, the courts began to express concern about the way in which the duty of care was expanding. Insufficient attention seemed to be given to the problems of indeterminate and crushing liability. Moreover, if tort were prepared to intervene and upset the delicate contractual allocation of risk between a main contractor and a sub-contractor, this would have implications for the prices charged by sub-contractors: if the law said that sub-contractors could be liable in tort for financial losses, even though they had expressly excluded this sort of liability in contract, they would need to take out insurance, and it was unclear whether, in terms of economic efficiency, these sub-contractors were always the best people to do so. Therefore, the courts have declined to follow the decision in *Junior Books*.

In *Donoghue v Stevenson*, Lord Atkin had recognised these problems when he said:

"... it is of particular importance to guard against the danger of stating propositions of law in wider terms than is necessary, lest essential factors be omitted in the wider survey."[27]

From the mid–1980s, then, the courts began to examine these "essential factors" more closely and to stress their importance in limiting the scope of the duty of care.

## The third step: refining the principle

In a series of decisions, from 1985 onwards, the House of Lords began to reject Lord Wilberforce's     **2–013**
broad approach to the duty of care. Lord Keith in *Governors of the Peabody Donation Fund v Sir Lindsay Parkinson & Co Ltd*[28] criticised the tendency to treat Lord Wilberforce's simple two

[26] [1983] 1 A.C. 520.
[27] [1932] A.C. 562 at 583.
[28] [1985] A.C. 210 at 240. See also Lord Bridge in *Curran v Northern Ireland Co-ownership Housing Association Ltd* [1987] A.C. 718.

stage test as a definitive formula, saying that the temptation to do so should be resisted. In *Leigh & Sillivan Ltd v Aliakmon Shipping Co Ltd (The Aliakmon)*,[29] Lord Brandon stated that Lord Wilberforce's two stage test should only be applied in novel factual situations where the courts had not previously ruled on the existence of a duty of care. Where a precedent existed (either directly or by analogy), the court should follow it, rather than apply the test. In *The Aliakmon*, this approach allowed the House of Lords to reject a claim by a buyer for damage caused by the negligent stowage of goods on board a ship. Whilst the claim may well have satisfied Lord Wilberforce's criteria, their Lordships preferred to follow previous authority which excluded such claims where the buyer had not yet acquired a proprietary interest in the goods.

In 1988, the Privy Council, deciding *Yuen Kun Yeu v Att-Gen of Hong Kong*,[30] was openly critical of the approach adopted in *Anns*. Lord Keith commented that the two stage test appeared to have been elevated to a degree of importance that it did not deserve and that it should not in all circumstances be regarded as a suitable guide to determining the existence of a duty of care. His Lordship highlighted the danger of misinterpreting stage one of the Wilberforce test as a simple test of foreseeability and stated that, henceforth, it should be presumed that by using the expression "proximity or neighbourhood" in stage one, Lord Wilberforce had intended to import into stage one of the test all of the ideas about "close and direct relations" that Lord Atkin had expressed in *Donoghue v Stevenson*. This meant that stage two would be reserved for considerations of "public policy", such as whether a common law duty of care would be inconsistent with the purpose of legislation, or would not be in the public interest.

In the light of their Lordships' growing reservations about Lord Wilberforce's approach, it was perhaps unsurprising that in 1990, a seven-member House of Lords took the unusual step of using the 1966 Practice Statement[31] to overturn its own decision in *Anns*. In *Murphy v Brentwood DC*,[32] their Lordships expressed their concerns about the potentially extensive liability permitted under the two stage test, and asserted that *Anns* should no longer be regarded as good law.[33] Instead, the courts should favour the approach suggested by Brennan J., an Australian judge, in *Sutherland Shire Council v Heyman*,[34] that is to say, novel categories of negligence should be developed incrementally and by analogy with established categories, rather than under a general principle which permits a massive extension of a prima facie duty of care, restrained only by indefinable policy considerations. This "incremental" approach is now the accepted means of finding a duty of care in English law.

## The modern approach

**2–014**    The leading case is now *Caparo v Dickman*.[35] This case concerned a claim for financial loss which resulted when an investor relied on published annual accounts and a company report that had been prepared carelessly by the company's auditor. The significance of *Caparo* in terms of claims for negligent misstatement will be discussed in Ch.3. For present purposes, we

---

[29] [1986] A.C. 785 at 815.
[30] [1988] A.C. 175. Applied in *Davis v Radcliffe* [1990] 1 W.L.R. 821 at 826.
[31] Practice Statement (HL: Judicial Precedent) [1966] 1 W.L.R. 1234.
[32] [1991] 1 A.C. 398.
[33] Contrast the position in Canada, where the Supreme Court retained the *Anns* test and declined to follow *Murphy*, although its recent reformulation of the *Anns* test in *Cooper v Hobart* (2002) 206 D.L.R. (4th) 193 has brought it closer to the position in English law.
[34] (1985) 60 A.L.R. 1 at 43; (1985) 157 C.L.R. 424 at 480.
[35] [1990] 2 A.C. 605.

need to note that the House of Lords gave guidance as to how to decide whether a duty of care should exist.

Their Lordships rejected as impractical the task of articulating a single general principle for the existence of a duty of care and concluded that, in future, to establish a duty of care, either:

(1) the claimant must point to a direct precedent, or to a closely analogous precedent, where a duty of care had been imposed, or

(2) in cases where no relevant precedent exists, the court should apply three criteria (which their Lordships identified) to determine whether there is a duty of care.

## The *Caparo* criteria

According to the dicta in *Caparo*, in novel factual situations all of the following three criteria       **2–015**
must be satisfied before a court should be willing to impose a duty of care:

(1) the damage must be foreseeable;

(2) there must be a sufficiently proximate relationship between the parties;

(3) it must be "fair, just and reasonable" for the court to impose a duty of care in the light of policy considerations with which the court is concerned.

The application of the three *Caparo* criteria is sometimes referred to as a "threefold test". It should be noted that, unlike the "two stage test" put forward by Lord Wilberforce in *Anns*, the *Caparo* criteria are designed to be considered all at once, not one after the other. This follows from the fact that the criteria cannot be precisely defined or evaluated in isolation from one another. As Lord Oliver noted in *Caparo* itself, the three criteria are, in most cases, "facets of the same thing".[36] On this basis, then, it might be said that the more foreseeable the harm suffered by the claimant, the closer the proximity of the parties, and vice versa. Equally, the closer the proximity, or the more foreseeable the damage, the more likely it is that the third criterion will be satisfied.

The House of Lords considered these issues in *Customs & Excise Commissioners v Barclays Bank*[37] (discussed in Ch.3) and concluded that, although the *Caparo* criteria provide (in the words of Lord Mance) "a convenient general framework"[38] for determining the existence of a duty of care, they can only give the courts limited help. It is therefore necessary for the courts to consider the detailed factual circumstances of each particular case, and especially the nature of the relationship between the parties. As Lord Walker put it, the courts, since *Caparo*, have shown an

> "increasingly clear recognition that the threefold test . . . does not provide an easy answer to all our problems, but only a set of fairly blunt tools."[39]

---

[36] [1990] 2 A.C. 605 at 633.
[37] [2006] UKHL 28; [2007] 1 A.C. 181.
[38] at para.93.
[39] at para.71.

It will be appreciated, then, that the *Caparo* criteria are somewhat vague.[40] On one view, though, it is this very vagueness which makes them so useful. We have seen that the problem with the approach in *Anns* was that it required the judges openly to refer to policy considerations in their judgments. Their reluctance to rule on policy meant that the expansion of the duty of care was inevitable. Under the modern approach, however, judges are no longer forced to confront policy issues so directly. Of course, they continue to make decisions based on policy, but they are now able to frame those decisions in appropriate judicial language by finding that there is insufficient proximity between the parties, or by declaring that the imposition of a duty would not be "fair, just and reasonable".

That said, it can be seen from the reasoning in more recent cases like *Customs & Excise Commissioners v Barclays Bank* that open and detailed consideration of policy factors is enjoying something of a renaissance as a mechanism for deciding novel and difficult cases, because the *Caparo* criteria alone fail to provide a very meaningful way of doing this. The problem with this approach, however, is that it can lead to uncertainty in the law—in the *Barclays Bank* case, for example, different weight placed on various different policy factors meant that a unanimous Court of Appeal decision ended up being overruled by a unanimous House of Lords. In these circumstances, it is very difficult for potential litigants to know whether their cases stand any chance of success.[41]

Although each of the *Caparo* criteria is a "facet of the same thing", it is nevertheless possible to say something about each criterion in turn:

*(1) Foreseeability*

**2–016**    It should be remembered that the relevant question is not what the defendant *actually did foresee*, but what a "reasonable person" in the circumstances of the defendant *ought to have foreseen*. The duty of care can only be owed in respect of preventing loss if the type of loss in question is "reasonably foreseeable". Implicit in this idea is that it must be reasonably foreseeable that the conduct of the defendant will affect the *particular claimant* in the case. This point is examined below:

*The foreseeable claimant*

**2–017**    In English law, it is said that negligence cannot exist "in the air". This is simply another way of saying that the particular claimant in the case must be, as Lord Atkin put it, someone who is "closely and directly affected" by the defendant's conduct. Thus, it is not sufficient to say that the defendant breached a duty of care owed to person A and the claimant (person B) was affected because he or she happened to be in the general area of the negligence.

This principle is illustrated by the House of Lords' decision in *Bourhill v Young*.[42] A heavily pregnant woman was descending from a tram when she heard a road traffic accident some 50 feet away from her, caused by the defendant's negligence. She arrived at the scene of the accident and saw blood on the road where a motorist had been killed (although his body had been removed) and subsequently suffered a miscarriage and psychiatric illness. Their Lordships were unsympathetic. Whilst the defendant would be liable for damage suffered by other

---

[40] The *Caparo* test has been rejected by the High Court of Australia in favour of a multi-faceted approach which addresses the policy issues arising in the case itself: see *Perre v Apand Pty Ltd* (1999) 198 C.L.R. 108, and *Sullivan v Moody* (2001) 207 C.L.R. 562.

[41] See Morgan (2006) 22 P.N. 206.

[42] [1943] A.C. 92.

road-users, the claimant was too far removed from the scene of the accident to be a reasonably foreseeable victim.

A more graphic illustration is the well-known United States case of *Palsgraf v Long Island Railroad*,[43] where the negligence of railway employees caused a passenger to drop a box of fireworks as he was boarding a moving train. The fireworks exploded and knocked over some heavy metal scales several feet away, which struck the plaintiff. The New York Court of Appeals rejected her claim for damages, holding that if any wrong had been committed, it had not been committed against *her*, because she was not a foreseeable victim of the railway company's negligence.

*Is an unborn child a "foreseeable claimant"?*

Obviously, the "no negligence in the air" principle serves to prevent indeterminate liability by restricting the range of claims that can result from a single negligent act. Its distinguishing feature is that it will not allow a claimant to base his or her claim on a wrong done to someone else. A difficult question of policy has arisen, however, in determining how far this principle should be applied in respect of children who are born disabled because of a wrong done to one of their parents before they are born.   **2–018**

For people born on or after July 22, 1976, the sort of claim that can be made is determined by the provisions of the Congenital Disabilities (Civil Liability) Act 1976.[44] In summary, this states that if a child is born disabled as a result of an injury to either parent which affects that parent's ability to have a normal child, or which affects the mother during pregnancy, or affects the mother or child during birth, the child may sue for his or her resulting disability.[45] It is not necessary to show that the parent has suffered personal injury of a type which would enable the parent to maintain an action in his or her own right.[46] However, any defences (and the principle of contributory negligence) which would apply if the parent were suing for injuries to himself or herself will be available to the defendant in fighting the child's claim.[47] It should be remembered that the Act not only covers injury to the foetus, it extends to cover situations where, before a child is conceived, a wrong is done to either of the parents which prevents them from conceiving a normal baby.

For policy reasons, the Act does not allow children to bring claims against their mothers, except in one particular situation, namely where the mother injures the child by negligently driving a motor vehicle when she knows (or ought to know) that she is pregnant.[48] The moral objections against children suing their mothers are overcome in this situation because the mother is, by law, obliged to be insured.[49] In such cases, the insurance company will meet or

---

[43] 248 N.Y. 339 (1928); 162 N.E. 99.

[44] As amended by the Human Fertilisation and Embryology Act 1990 and the Human Fertilisation and Embryology Act 2008. Note that in 1992, *Burton v Islington Health Authority* [1993] Q.B. 204 finally established that a duty of care could be owed at common law to an unborn child, even though a foetus has no independent legal personality. It was held that the wrong done to the parent would "crystallise" into a cause of action, maintainable at the suit of the child, once the child was born.

[45] Congenital Disabilities (Civil Liability) Act 1976 s.1. See also Consumer Protection Act 1987 s.6(3) (specific application of the 1976 Act to situations where the parent is affected by a defect in a product, e.g. a drug).

[46] Congenital Disabilities (Civil Liability) Act s.1(3).

[47] Congenital Disabilities (Civil Liability) Act ss.1(4), 1(6), and 1(7). Note, however, that contractual exclusions or limitations cannot be relied on where the case concerns the supply of a defective product: Consumer Protection Act 1987 s.6(3).

[48] Congenital Disabilities (Civil Liability) Act s.2.

[49] Road Traffic Act 1988 s.143.

defend the child's claim. It should be noted that the general immunity granted to mothers does not extend to fathers.[50]

Moral objections have prevented the courts from holding that an unborn child is a foreseeable claimant in so-called "wrongful life" cases. These are cases in which disabled claimants argue, in effect, that they should never have been born, and were only born because of the defendant's negligence. The defendant may, for example, have failed to recommend an abortion to the mother, in circumstances where it was likely that the claimant would be born disabled. In *McKay v Essex Area Health Authority*,[51] the court struck out such a claim as contrary to public policy. It was not prepared to state that in law a disabled life was to be regarded as less valuable than that of an able-bodied person. Equally, the court was reluctant to set a precedent under which an action might be maintained by a child against a mother who, knowing of the risk of the child's disability, refused to have an abortion.[52]

Although children themselves have not been allowed to sue for "wrongful life", the courts have in the past been prepared to allow *parents* to sue for the cost of bringing up "unintended children" where the negligence of the defendant has prevented them from choosing not to conceive, or choosing to terminate the pregnancy. In recent times, however, the House of Lords has declined, for public policy reasons, to allow such claims to succeed. The relevant cases are considered later in this chapter, in the context of the liability of the NHS.

*(2) Proximity*

2–019    It is impossible to define the concept of "proximity" in concrete terms. What can be said, however, is that it refers to the *closeness of the relationship* between the defendant and the claimant. The degree of closeness which the law will require before imposing a duty of care differs according to the *type of damage* for which the claimant is seeking redress. Therefore, as we shall see, in cases of economic loss and psychiatric illness, the courts require a very close relationship between the parties, whilst in cases of physical injury, the requirement of proximity is more easily satisfied.[53] Thus, if I negligently make a statement causing you financial loss, I must (generally speaking) know who you are and how you will rely on that statement before I can be made liable, but if I negligently drive my car, causing you personal injury, I will be liable to you without knowing who you are or that you, in particular, were relying on me to drive carefully.

The fact that the courts' insistence on "proximity" appears to be confined to certain types of situation, then, indicates that questions of *policy* are relevant to the question of whether or not, in a given situation, the required degree of proximity exists. As Lord Oliver put it, in *Alcock v Chief Constable of South Yorkshire*[54]:

> ". . . no doubt 'policy', if that is the right word, or perhaps more properly, the impracticability or unreasonableness of entertaining claims to the ultimate limits of the conse-

---

[50] Although the Pearson Commission thought that it should (see Cmnd 7034, Vol.1, para.1471).

[51] [1982] Q.B. 1166 at 1180. The court, obiter, also ruled out any claim under the 1976 Act. See also Symmons (1987) 50 M.L.R. 269.

[52] The difficulty of assessing the level of damages also concerned the court.

[53] See Lord Oliver in *Murphy v Brentwood DC* [1991] 1 A.C. 398 at 487; *Mobil Oil Hong Kong Ltd v Hong Kong United Dockyards Ltd (The Hua Lien)* [1991] 1 Lloyd's Rep. 309 at 368; *Perrett v Collins* [1998] 2 Lloyd's Rep. 255; *Pearson v Lightning* (1998) 95(20) L.S.G. 33. Note, however, that in *Sutradhar v Natural Environment Research Council* [2006] UKHL 33; [2006] 4 All E.R. 490 the HL stressed the necessity of showing proximity in claims for personal injury caused by negligent statements.

[54] [1992] 1 A.C. 310 at 410.

quences of human activity, necessarily plays a part in the court's perception of what is sufficiently proximate . . . in the end, it has to be accepted that the concept of 'proximity' is an artificial one which depends more upon the court's perception of what is the reasonable area for the imposition of liability than upon any logical process of analogical deduction."

In determining "what is the reasonable area for the imposition of liability", the courts will often have to ask themselves how the relationship between the parties (i.e. what actually happened in their dealings with one another) should define the *scope* of the defendant's duty of care. Thus, in some cases, although a certain duty is owed, the relationship (degree of proximity) between the parties may indicate that the defendant has not assumed responsibility for safeguarding the claimant against the actual loss suffered.

Consider, for example *Calvert v William Hill*.[55] The claimant was a compulsive gambler who made use of the defendant bookmakers' telephone betting service. Realising he had a problem, he sought to enter into a "self-exclusion" arrangement—a service offered by the defendants to problem gamblers, whereby they would accept the gambler's instructions to close the telephone account, and undertake to refuse telephone bets for six months. Through carelessness on their part, however, this arrangement was never implemented. The claimant was allowed to continue placing telephone bets, and lost £1.8m in various "betting frenzies".

It was accepted by the Court of Appeal that the dealings between the parties had created a duty of care, but the important question was the *scope* of the duty. The defendants had only assumed a responsibility to prevent the claimant from placing telephone bets with them, not to prevent him from gambling at all. The claimant was a pathological gambler, and the probability was that even if the "self-exclusion" arrangement had been implemented, other forms of gambling would have brought about his financial ruin. The defendants had not undertaken to save the claimant from financial ruin, and so could not be liable. The court cited with approval the observations of Lord Oliver in *Murphy v Brentwood District Council*:[56]

"The essential question which has to be asked in every case, given that damage which is the essential ingredient of the action has occurred, is whether the relationship between the plaintiff and the defendant is such . . . that it imposes upon the latter a duty to take care to avoid or prevent that loss which has in fact been sustained."

*(3) "Fair, just and reasonable"*

Because policy concerns are relevant to the degree of proximity required, it is often unclear what useful purpose is served by an additional consideration of whether the imposition of a duty of care is "fair, just and reasonable". In *Marc Rich & Co A.G. v Bishop Rock Marine Company (The Nicholas H)*,[57] Balcombe L.J. doubted whether the criterion added anything to the requirement of proximity. There may be exceptional cases, however (such as the old cases of advocates' immunity, discussed elsewhere in this chapter) where the courts wish to deny the existence of a duty of care, but where it will be a nonsense for them to speak in terms of an

**2–020**

---

[55] [2008] EWCA Civ 1427; [2009] Ch.330. Comment: Morgan (2009) 68(2) C.L.J. 268.
[56] [1991] 1 A.C. 398 at 486, cited by Sir Anthony May P. in *Calvert v William Hill* [2008] EWCA Civ 1427 at para.45.
[57] [1994] 1 W.L.R. 1071.

insufficiently close relationship between the parties. In such cases, the "fair, just and reasonable" criterion provides a "long stop", enabling the courts to determine liability on the basis of policy.

## Applying the *Caparo* criteria: factors relevant to the imposition of a duty of care

**2–021**    To understand how the *Caparo* criteria are applied in practice, it is useful to identify a number of factors which the courts take into account in deciding whether to impose a duty of care. We have already noted that the *type of harm* the claimant has suffered (physical, financial, or psychiatric) has a profound effect on whether a duty of care will be owed. This factor is further considered in Chs 3 and 4. In the following sections of this chapter, we examine two other relevant factors:

- whether the damage in question is caused by a positive act (misfeasance), or by an omission (non-feasance);

- the *type of defendant* who is being sued.

## MISFEASANCE AND NON-FEASANCE

**2–022**    It will be recalled that Lord Atkin, in *Donoghue v Stevenson*, spoke of a duty of care arising in respect of "acts or omissions", yet, as Lord Goff notes in *Smith v Littlewoods Organisation Ltd*[58]:

"... the common law does not impose liability for what are called pure omissions."

The law draws a distinction between a positive act which causes harm (misfeasance) and a mere failure to prevent harm from arising (non-feasance), there being no liability for the latter. The distinction between misfeasance and non-feasance is sometimes very difficult to draw and has given rise to problems. A motorist who causes an accident by failing to stop at a red light is guilty of an omission, but the law says that he or she is liable because this omission cannot be considered in isolation from the positive act of driving. The key question, therefore, is whether the "omission" in question can be seen as having been made *in the course of doing some positive act*. In a number of cases concerning the liability of local authorities, the courts have explored this question and have used the distinction between misfeasance and non-feasance to justify findings of no liability.

In *Curran v Northern Ireland Co-ownership Housing Association*,[59] Lord Bridge endorsed academic commentary which had pointed out that duties to *prevent* harm being caused (as opposed to duties to *refrain from causing* harm) would normally only arise where one person, under a contract, had promised to make another person better off, and that it may not be appropriate for such duties to be imposed in tort.[60] In *Curran*, their Lordships held that a local

[58]  [1987] A.C. 241 at 271.
[59]  [1987] A.C. 718.
[60]  Smith and Burns (1983) 46 M.L.R. 147.

authority was not liable for its failure to prevent financial loss caused by a defective part of a building. The plaintiffs had bought a house on which an extension had been built, by the former owners, with the help of a home improvement grant from the local authority. When the extension proved defective and had to be rebuilt, the plaintiffs sued the authority, arguing that it had been negligent in failing to supervise the building works. It was held that the purpose of the statutory powers under which the authority had acted was to ensure that public funds were well spent, rather than to protect individuals from the financial consequences of poor work-manship. It followed that if the local authority was not engaged in any positive supervisory activity for the benefit of the plaintiffs, the plaintiffs' case must fail, because it was an allega-tion of mere non-feasance, for which there could be no liability.

More recently, in *Sutradhar v Natural Environment Research Council*[61] (discussed later in this chapter) similar reasoning was employed by the House of Lords to deny the existence of a duty of care on the part of a scientific advisory body which reported on the quality of water in Bangladesh. The defendants' failure to test the water for arsenic was regarded as a case of mere non-feasance, because they had not assumed any positive obligation to do so.[62]

In *Stovin v Wise*,[63] which is discussed later in this chapter, Lord Hoffmann made the following important observations about liability for omissions:[64]

"There are sound reasons why omissions require different treatment from positive conduct. It is one thing for the law to say that a person who undertakes some activity shall take reasonable care not to cause damage to others. It is another thing for the law to require that a person who is doing nothing in particular shall take steps to prevent another from suffering harm . . . One can put the matter in political, moral or economic terms. In political terms it is less of an invasion of freedom for the law to require him to consider the safety of others in his actions than to impose upon him a duty to rescue or protect. A moral version of this point may be called the 'why pick on me?' argument. A duty to prevent harm to others or to render assistance to a person in danger or distress may apply to a large and indeterminate class of people who happen to be able to do something. Why should one be held liable rather than another? In economic terms, the efficient allocation of resources usually requires an activity should bear its own costs. If it benefits from being able to impose all or some of its costs on other people (what economists call 'exter-nalities') the market is distorted because the activity appears cheaper than it really is. So liability to pay compensation for loss caused by negligent conduct acts as a deterrent against increasing the cost of the activity to the community and reduces externalities. But there is no similar justification for requiring a person who is not doing anything to spend money on behalf of someone else."

It can be seen from the reasoning in these cases that whether a case is one of misfeasance or non-feasance depends essentially on the *nature of the relationship* between the claimant and the defendant. The issue therefore overlaps with the idea of "proximity". This is illustrated by the decision in *Yuen Kun Yeu v Att-Gen of Hong Kong*.[65] Here, the plaintiffs alleged that the

---

[61] [2006] UKHL 33; [2006] 4 All E.R. 490.
[62] See Lord Hoffmann, at para.27.
[63] [1996] A.C. 923.
[64] [1996] A.C. 923 at 943.
[65] [1988] A.C. 175.

Commissioner of Deposit-Taking Companies in Hong Kong had failed to prevent them from losing their investments, because he had negligently granted a licence to a fraudulent deposit-taking company, and had failed to stop that company from continuing to trade when he had reasonable grounds to suspect it was trading fraudulently. The Privy Council held that there could be no liability. The key finding was that there was insufficient proximity between the Commissioner and the investors, but the case might equally be regarded as one of non-feasance. The Commissioner's statutory powers did not require him to take steps actively to safeguard the financial well-being of investors. It followed that he could not be liable for his omission to act. Lord Keith noted that negligence liability is not based solely on foreseeability of harm. There is, for example, no liability "on the part of one who sees another about to walk over a cliff with his head in the air, and forbears to shout a warning".[66] His Lordship was here citing a classic example of non-feasance—in the absence of a "special relationship", there is no duty to go to the rescue of another. By analogy, the Commissioner owed no duty to save the investors from their fate, or, for that matter, to prevent a third party (the fraudulent company) from acting so as to cause them loss.

The rule against liability for non-feasance, then, gives rise to two important propositions:

- in English law, in contrast to civil law jurisdictions,[67] there is no general duty to rescue another;

- there is no *general* duty to prevent other people from causing damage.

These matters are considered below.

## Non-feasance: no duty to rescue

2–023    In *Smith v Littlewoods Organisation Ltd*,[68] Lord Goff stated that the refusal of English law to impose liability for mere omissions might one day need to be reconsidered, in the light of the "affirmative duties of good neighbourliness" imposed in other countries.[69] It seems, however, that that day is still some way off. In order for a duty to rescue to arise in English law, a prior relationship of care must exist between the defendant and the person who needs rescuing. Thus, whilst parents may be liable in negligence if they stand by and let their children drown in shallow water, the same cannot be said of a mere bystander at a swimming pool.[70] There is a related point that should be noted here: because there is no duty to rescue, it follows that in cases where a rescuer chooses to intervene, he or she cannot be liable in negligence unless it can be said that the intervention has made the claimant's position worse than if it had not taken place.[71]

---

[66] [1988] A.C. 175 at 192.
[67] See, e.g. art.233–6 of the French Penal Code, which punishes (with corresponding tortious liability) anyone who wilfully refrains from assisting a person in danger, when he or she could have done so without risk to himself or herself or to third parties.
[68] [1987] A.C. 241 at 271.
[69] Citing Fleming, *The Law of Torts* (6th edn, 1983) at 138.
[70] per Lord Nicholls in *Stovin v Wise* [1996] A.C. 923 at 931.
[71] *Horsley v MacLaren (The Ogopogo)* [1971] 2 Lloyd's Rep. 410, applied in *Capital & Counties v Hampshire CC* [1997] Q.B. 1004 and *Day v High Performance Sports Ltd* [2003] EWHC 197.

## Non-feasance: no general duty to prevent others from causing damage

In the same way that there is no duty to save others from natural perils, there is, generally **2–024** speaking, no duty to save them from perils arising from the actions of others. This was affirmed by Lord Goff in *Smith v Littlewoods Organisation Ltd*. The defendants had acquired a disused cinema, intending to develop the land where it stood. Shortly after they had taken possession of the cinema, vagrants occupied the building. On two occasions, small fires had been started using rubbish that had been left lying outside the cinema, but these fires had not been reported to the defendants or to the police. Then, one evening, the cinema was set on fire, damaging the plaintiffs' neighbouring property. The plaintiffs argued that the defendants ought to have prevented the vagrants from starting the fire. It was held that whilst the defendants were under a duty to prevent their property from becoming a source of danger to neighbouring property, on the facts, this duty did not extend to controlling the activities of the vagrants. Because the defendants had not known about the previous fires, it was not reasonably foreseeable that a fire would be started that would damage neighbouring property.

The decision in *Smith v Littlewoods* represented the culmination of a number of judicial attempts to identify the legal basis on which a defendant should be absolved from liability for the consequences of a wrong committed by a third party. Previously, there had been three Court of Appeal decisions on similar facts to *Smith v Littlewoods*, each of which had used a different element of the tort of negligence to deny liability. In *Lamb v Camden LBC*[72] it had been held that the third party's actions were too remote a consequence of the defendant's breach, whilst in *P.Perl (Exporters) Ltd v Camden LBC*[73] it had been held that, because the defendant could not be expected to control the third party, no duty of care was owed, and in *King v Liverpool CC*[74] it had been held that although a duty was owed, the defendants were not in breach of their duty because there was nothing they could reasonably have done to prevent the third parties from causing the damage.

Lord Goff's approach in *Smith v Littlewoods*, however, centred firmly on the absence of a duty of care as the appropriate legal mechanism for confining liability for wrongs committed by other people. Although this approach was not adopted by the other Law Lords in the case (who spoke in terms of breach of duty) it has met with subsequent approval by the House of Lords in the recent case of *Mitchell v Glasgow City Council*.[75] Here, the complaint was that the council had failed to protect the life[76] of one of its tenants when it took no steps to give a warning about the possible actions of a violent neighbour who was facing eviction.

Mitchell, a council tenant aged 72, had informed the council about the violent and abusive behaviour of his next-door neighbour, Drummond. The council summoned Drummond to a meeting, where he was told that he might be evicted if his behaviour did not improve. Shortly after the meeting, Drummond assaulted Mitchell with a stick or an iron bar, which led to Mitchell's death. His widow and daughter brought an action claiming that the council had

---

[72] [1981] Q.B. 625.

[73] [1984] Q.B. 342.

[74] [1986] 3 All E.R. 544.

[75] [2009] UKHL 11; [2009] 2 W.L.R. 481, applied in *X v Hounslow LBC* [2009] EWCA Civ 286 (no duty to re-house a couple with learning difficulties so as to prevent abuse by local youths). Comment: J O'Sullivan [2009] C.L.J. 270.

[76] The claim was brought in negligence and also under the Human Rights Act 1998, for breach of art.2. Both claims failed, the latter because it did not satisfy the "real and immediate risk" test for art.2 liability. This is discussed later in this chapter in the context of police liability.

owed a duty to warn Mitchell that the meeting was taking place, so that he could take steps to avoid the danger posed by Drummond.

The House of Lords rejected the claim. Whilst landlords owed some duties to their tenants, these did not extend to warning tenants of steps taken to evict other tenants. Nor could the council be liable for a wrong committed by a third party (Drummond) unless the case had some extraordinary "feature" going beyond mere foreseeability of harm (such as clear evidence that they had assumed responsibility for Mitchell's safety).

Their Lordships endorsed the approach taken by Lord Goff in *Smith v Littlewoods*. That approach takes as a starting point the proposition that, as a general rule, there is no duty of care owed to prevent third parties from causing damage, but acknowledges that there appear to be certain exceptions to this rule, in cases which have extraordinary features. Thus, there are four particular situations where liability for the acts of third parties can arise. These can be summarised as follows:

*(1) Special relationship between the defendant and the claimant*

2–025    The first situation is where the defendant has assumed responsibility to look after the claimant's property. Thus, in *Stansbie v Troman*,[77] the plaintiff employed a decorator who went out and left the premises unsecured. The decorator was held liable for losses caused by a thief who entered the premises and stole some of the plaintiff's property. The contractual relationship between the plaintiff and the decorator justified the imposition of liability—the decorator had agreed to look after the premises.

*(2) Special relationship between the defendant and the third party*

2–026    In *Home Office v Dorset Yacht* (discussed above), the defendants were liable because they had a relationship of control over the third parties who caused the damage.

*(3) Creating a source of danger "sparked off" by a third party*

2–027    The defendant may be liable for creating a dangerous situation which is subsequently "sparked off" by the foreseeable actions of third parties. This principle may apply, for example, to a defendant who keeps an unsecured shed full of fireworks that are subsequently ignited by mischievous children.[78] The principle was applied in *Haynes v Harwood*,[79] where the defendants left their horses unattended in the street and a boy threw a stone at them and caused them to bolt. The defendants were liable when the plaintiff was injured trying to save people from being injured by the horses.

*(4) Failing to take reasonable steps to abate a danger created by a third party*

2–028    Where the defendant knows, or reasonably ought to know, that third parties are creating a danger on his or her premises, the defendant is under a duty to take reasonable steps to abate that danger. Thus, in *Clark Fixing Ltd v Dudley Metropolitan Borough Council*,[80] where known trespassers on a vacant development site started a fire which burned down neighbouring property, the Court of Appeal, distinguishing *Smith v Littlewoods*, held the defendant council liable for failing to remove combustible material from the site, so as to prevent the

---

[77] [1948] 2 K.B. 48.
[78] per Lord Goff in *Smith v Littlewoods* [1987] A.C. 241 at 273.
[79] [1935] 1 K.B. 146.
[80] [2001] EWCA Civ 1898.

spread of fire. If, in *Smith v Littlewoods*, the previous fires had been reported to the defendants, they too may have been held liable on this principle.

## THE TYPE OF DEFENDANT

It goes without saying that before imposing liability on a particular defendant the court will look beyond the individual case to the broad consequences of establishing that a duty is owed by this type of defendant. If the defendant is a member of a particular profession or group, a precedent will be set fixing all members of that profession or group with the duty in question. Decisions on liability can have far-reaching implications about the allocation of financial resources by potential defendants. This is of particular concern where the defendant in question is providing a public service. For example, if Doctor X is held liable to Patient Y in undertaking a certain procedure, then in future, all doctors will be liable in similar circumstances. This may increase the insurance costs of the hospitals employing the doctors and may even lead to doctors becoming reluctant to undertake the procedure in question, or to their insisting that excessive safeguards be taken. The cost of the safeguards will increase the cost of the procedure and may reduce its availability in a financially constrained health service.

    The problem of increasing the scope of negligence liability affects a number of different professions and groups. In relation to each of these, the courts have adopted a slightly different approach. In relation to NHS medical services, for example, the usual mechanism for limiting negligence liability is not to restrict the scope of the duty of care. Rather, it is to hold that a doctor (or other medical professional) will not be in *breach* of the duty of care if his or her behaviour lives up to the standard of other responsible medical professionals.[81] In relation to some other public services, however, the courts are at times prepared to hold that, for policy reasons, no duty of care is owed. This discrepancy in approach between different types of defendant has attracted judicial comment,[82] but it remains the case that certain types of defendant may escape negligence liability because they owe no duty, whilst others are judged by the standard of their profession.

    For the sake of convenience, we deal with different types of defendant under four headings:

**2–029**

- local authorities
- other public servants
- regulators and advisory bodies
- lawyers

### (1) Local authorities

Actions against local authorities are common. Often, a claimant will seek to show that he or she is owed a duty of care by a local authority, even though its contribution to the damage has

**2–030**

---

[81] *Bolam v Friern Barnet Hospital Management Committee* [1957] 1 W.L.R. 582 (discussed in Ch.5).
[82] See *Capital and Counties Plc v Hampshire CC* [1997] Q.B. 1004 per Stuart-Smith L.J. at 1040.

been minor, because the authority has the funds to pay compensation. To succeed, however, a claimant must overcome a number of hurdles. In exploring these hurdles, it is helpful to appreciate that, in essence, the courts are here faced with the difficult task of determining the terms of the "social contract" under which taxpayers pay for the services the authorities provide. The fundamental question in most local authority cases is simply this: how far is it appropriate to provide a remedy in negligence where the state fails to confer a benefit on an individual?

*Policy arguments*

**2–031**     There are a number of policy objections to the imposition of a duty of care on local authorities.[83] A common objection is that the threat of liability may lead to the local authority adopting overly cautious practices at the public expense. Another objection is that allowing liability in tort will undermine or distort the framework of public protection provided by statute[84] or available in another area of the common law. In many cases, the claimant will have an alternative means of redress. He or she may be able to seek judicial review, for example, or take advantage of a remedy provided by the statute under which the local authority has acted. Moreover, it is argued that making a local authority pay compensation is contrary to the general public interest, because it forces the authority to divert scarce financial resources away from general public welfare, reallocating them to a small number of litigants.

In recent years, the courts have been keen to stress the distinction between contract and tort and have made it clear that there are political, moral and economic reasons why tort should not be used to impose a duty to *confer a benefit* on others, as opposed to a duty to refrain from causing harm. These reasons were cogently enunciated by Lord Hoffmann in *Stovin v Wise* (the relevant passage is set out earlier in this chapter). The question arises, however, whether it is appropriate to maintain this sharp distinction in the context of the welfare state, when to do so may create an unacceptable social divide between those who rely on the state for their welfare and those who look after themselves privately. In the context of the National Health Service (discussed later), the courts have clearly found such a divide unacceptable—therefore an NHS patient has substantially the same remedy in tort as a private patient would have for breach of contract.

Similarly, in the context of state education, the House of Lords has held in *Phelps v Hillingdon LBC*[85] that a local authority can owe a duty of care when providing educational services. This mirrors the legal position which would arise if the pupil (or his or her parents) had contracted privately for educational services. In relation to other state services, however, such as the provision of safe roads (*Stovin v Wise*), the courts have been unwilling to hold that a local authority owes a duty of care. Arguably, the courts have only been able to deny a duty of care in these cases because this does not create an obvious contrast with services provided in the private sector.

With this in mind, we can now examine some of the reasoning the courts have employed to determine liability. Before we do so, however, it will be helpful to consider the remarks of Lord Steyn, speaking in *Gorringe v Calderdale MBC*[86] about the difficult relationship between

---

[83] In line with the courts' general opposition to claims for pure economic loss, such claims against local authorities will normally be disallowed. (See *Murphy v Brentwood DC* [1991] 1 A.C. 398.) The policy reasons preventing economic loss claims are considered in Ch.3. Here, we concentrate on other issues, and examine the extent to which a local authority owes a duty of care in relation to physical and psychiatric harm.

[84] See *X v Bedfordshire CC* [1995] 2 A.C. 633 at 750; *Yuen Kun-Yeu v Att.-Gen. of Hong Kong* [1988] A.C. 175 at 198; *Harris v Evans* [1998] 3 All E.R. 522.

[85] [2001] 2 A.C. 619.

[86] [2004] 1 W.L.R. 1057 at para.2.

the tort of negligence and the performance of statutory functions by public bodies. His Lordship said:

> "This is a subject of great complexity and very much an evolving area of the law. No single decision is capable of providing a comprehensive analysis. It is a subject on which an intense focus on the particular facts and on the particular statutory background, seen in the context of the contours of our social welfare state, is necessary. On the one hand the courts must not contribute to the creation of a society bent on litigation, which is premised on the illusion that for every misfortune there is a remedy. On the other hand, there are cases where the courts must recognise on principled grounds the compelling demands of corrective justice . . . Sometimes cases may not obviously fall into one category or the other. Truly difficult cases arise."

In recent years, some of these "truly difficult cases" have arisen where claimants have argued that the exercise of (or failure to exercise) a statutory function has resulted in a violation of their human rights. These cases have forced the courts to re-evaluate their traditional approach to public authority negligence liability and address a difficult question: should the scope of the duty of care be widened to accommodate the demands of human rights law, or should a restrictive approach remain? As this issue has unfolded, some cases have suggested that negligence liability should expand to encompass human rights law. Later cases, however, have made it clear that negligence liability and liability under the Human Rights Act 1998 should be treated separately. It is therefore possible to find cases where a duty of care is denied (for policy reasons) but a human rights claim based on the same facts might succeed.

*Statutory functions and the intention of Parliament*

One important question in all of these cases is whether, on a proper construction of the statute, **2–032** Parliament intended that a failure to carry out the statutory function in question should give rise to claims for compensation from individuals affected by that failure. Where this *is* the case (and provided the statute imposes a *duty* rather than grants a mere *power* to act), there may be a claim for breach of statutory duty (a separate tort, considered in Ch.7), but the courts may disallow negligence liability, so as not to create an overlap with another cause of action. Where Parliament did *not* intend to create a right to compensation, there can be no claim under the tort of breach of statutory duty. In these circumstances the courts will not normally disturb the intention of Parliament by imposing liability in negligence. As Lord Hoffmann put it, in *Stovin v Wise*:

> "Whether a statutory duty gives rise to a private cause of action is a question of construction . . . if the policy of the Act is not to create a statutory liability to pay compensation, the same policy should ordinarily exclude the existence of a common law duty of care."[87]

*"Policy matters" and "operational matters"*

In many cases, the courts draw a distinction between activities involving matters of "policy" **2–033** and activities which can be regarded as "operational" (i.e. activities which *implement* policy).

---

[87] [1963] A.C. 923 at 952. The same view is expressed in *Gorringe v Calderdale MBC* [2004] 1 W.L.R. 1057 by Lord Hoffmann (at para.23) and Lord Scott (at para.71).

This distinction is a persistent feature of the reasoning in local authority cases, and was explored at some length in *Anns v Merton LBC*. On the basis of the policy/operational distinction, so the argument ran, it could be said that the way in which buildings were inspected was an "operational" activity, to which negligence liability might attach, whilst a decision to allocate financial resources which resulted in too few building inspectors being appointed would be immune from a negligence suit, because such policy decisions are not justiciable.

The problem with the policy/operational distinction, however, is that it is difficult logically to identify "operational" activities which do not involve any element of "policy". This is because, whenever a person exercises *discretion* in the performance of a task, some element of "policy" will be involved. Is this task to be done quickly or slowly? How much money will be spent in performing this task? Logically, these matters are just as much matters of "policy" as resolutions passed in committee meetings. As Lord Slynn noted in *Barrett v Enfield LBC*,[88] "even knocking a nail into a piece of wood involves the exercise of some choice or discretion".

The attempt in *Anns v Merton LBC*[89] to assert the relevance of a policy/operational distinction met with considerable criticism. In *Rowling v Takaro Properties*,[90] Lord Keith observed:

> ". . . this distinction does not provide a touchstone of liability, but rather is expressive of the need to exclude altogether those cases in which the decision under attack is of such a kind that a question whether it has been made negligently is unsuitable for judicial resolution, of which notable examples are discretionary decisions on the allocation of scarce resources or the distribution of risks."

Whilst the distinction is attractive, because it enables the court to wash its hands of political matters by declaring them not justiciable, the impossibility of drawing a logical distinction between, on the one hand, matters of "high policy", and, on the other hand, "operational" matters involving the exercise of discretion, makes the distinction problematic.

*When does a local authority "assume responsibility" for a claimant's welfare?*

2–034    As has been noted, the damage in suit will usually have resulted because a local authority has exercised (or failed to exercise) a statutory function. In deciding the question of liability, the court will examine the wording of the statute under which the local authority has acted and determine whether the function in question has been given for the benefit of individuals, or whether it serves only a general governmental purpose.[91] In the latter case, there may be no liability, because it cannot be said that the authority has assumed responsibility to the aggrieved individual. The approach of the courts may be illustrated by considering a number of cases involving road traffic accidents.

In *Stovin v Wise*[92] the plaintiff was involved in a road traffic accident at a dangerous junction. The question arose whether the local authority, which had resolved to carry out improvements to the junction, could be liable for its failure to do so. By a 3:2 majority, the House of

---

[88] [2001] 2 A.C. 550.
[89] [1978] A.C. 728 at 754.
[90] [1988] A.C. 473 at 501.
[91] See, e.g. *Governors of the Peabody Donation Fund v Sir Lindsay Parkinson & Co Ltd* [1985] A.C. 210, *Yuen Kun-Yeu v Att-Gen of Hong Kong* [1988] A.C. 175 and *Curran v Northern Ireland Co-ownership Housing Association Ltd* [1987] A.C. 718.
[92] [1996] A.C. 923.

Lords held that the local authority was not liable for its omission to act. The local authority had a statutory *power* to improve the junction, but not a *duty* to do so. Thus, its omission to improve the junction could not be seen as having occurred in the context of any positive obligation to protect the plaintiff from harm.[93]

In any event, and whether or not the statute in question confers on the local authority a *power* or a *duty*, the key issue appears to be whether, in the light of the statutory framework and other relevant policy concerns, the local authority can be said to have assumed reponsibility for preventing specific losses to individual claimants. An example of the courts' restrictive approach to this issue is to be found in *Gorringe v Calderdale MBC*.[94]

The claimant, Mrs Gorringe had been severely injured when she had driven her car head-on into a bus which was concealed from view on the other side of a steep hill. She argued that the council had caused the accident by failing to give her proper warning of the danger of driving fast over the hill when she could not see what was coming. In particular, she argued that the council should have painted "SLOW" on the road. Their Lordships were unsympathetic, and Mrs Gorringe lost her case. They pointed out that drivers were expected to look after themselves by driving at an appropriate speed, and that the law did not impose a duty to give warnings about obvious dangers.[95]

Moreover, Parliament, in giving local authorities statutory obligations in respect of signs and road markings, had not intended compensation to be payable to individuals injured by a breach of those obligations. Such a breach, therefore, could not give rise to a duty of care. Similar reasoning was employed by the Court of Appeal in *Sandhar v Department of Transport, Environment and the Regions*[96] to deny liability when a driver was injured after a failure to salt a road so as to prevent the formation of ice.

Despite the courts' reluctance to find a duty of care where local authorities have failed to exercise statutory functions, there remains the possibility of liability in truly exceptional circumstances. Consider, for example, *Kane v New Forest District Council*.[97] Here, the claimant was seriously injured when he emerged from a footpath on to a main road and was hit by an oncoming car. The council had required the construction of the footpath as a condition of planning permission for surrounding development. It had intended to see that the main road was widened, so that people emerging from the footpath could be seen by drivers, but at the time of the accident this had not been done. Since the footpath was a source of danger that had been *created* by the council's positive act (insisting that it be built), the court was able to distinguish *Stovin v Wise* (which concerned a mere failure to act). Their Lordships went on to hold that it was irrational for the council not to have used its powers to prohibit the opening of the footpath until it was safe to use. The circumstances were such as effectively to place the council under a duty to exercise such powers for the benefit of the claimant—the authority had created a danger by insisting on the presence of the footpath, and so had assumed an obligation to protect the claimant from harm.

---

[93] Compare *Rice v Secretary of State for Trade and Industry* [2007] EWCA Civ 289; [2007] P.I.Q.R. P23. (Duty of care imposed on managers of dock workers where the very purpose of the statute was to create a relationship entailing the necessary proximity.)

[94] [2004] 1 W.L.R. 1057. Comment: Howarth [2004] C.L.J. 546.

[95] Their Lordships cited *Tomlinson v Congleton BC* [2004] 1 A.C. 46 (discussed in Ch.8).

[96] [2004] EWCA Civ 1440; [2005] 1 W.L.R. 1632.

[97] [2002] 1 W.L.R. 312. It has been pointed out that this decision places a very onerous burden on planning authorities to monitor and enforce planning conditions where a source of danger may have been created. See Pether, [2003] J.P.I. Law 48.

The approach taken in the road-traffic cases is, of course, one of general application. Earlier in this chapter, we noted the decision of the House of Lords in *Mitchell v Glasgow City Council*[98] where it was decided that the council, in exercising its statutory functions in managing social housing, could not be said to owe a duty to protect its tenants from violent assaults by their neighbours.

The reasoning in *Mitchell* was applied by the Court of Appeal in *X v Hounslow LBC*.[99] The issue here was whether the local authority owed a duty to re-house a married couple, both of whom had learning difficulties, in time to prevent them being seriously abused by local youths. The council knew (through its social services department) that the couple had taken to allowing youths to make use of their flat, and were at risk of serious harm. Eventually, the youths subjected the couple to a number of degrading sexual and physical assaults.

In denying a remedy in negligence, the Court of Appeal held that the mere fact that the council was exercising its statutory functions in relation to the claimants, by actively trying to re-house them, was not sufficient to create a duty of care. In order for a duty of care to exist, there had to be an assumption of responsibility for the claimants' welfare arising *independently* of the mere exercise of statutory functions. Thus (as Lord Hoffmann had explained in *Gorringe*) an NHS doctor might provide care to patients pursuant to statutory duties in the National Health Service Act 1977, but it is not the exercise of this public law function which creates a duty of care towards the patient. Rather, the duty of care arises from an *independent* assumption of responsibility, namely the acceptance by the doctor of a professional relationship with the patient no different from that which would be accepted by a doctor in private practice.[100] On the facts of *X v Hounslow LBC*, there had been no comparable independent assumption of responsibilty, so no duty of care could arise.

We might usefully compare this with the factual situation in *Connor v Surrey CC*.[101] Here, the claimant was a headteacher who suffered psychiatric illness after she was subjected to criticism and inappropriate behaviour by school governors. She argued that her illness had been caused by the local authority's failure to intervene and replace the board of governors with an interim executive board. The Court of Appeal held that the local authority owed the claimant a duty of care. This did not arise because of its statutory functions in managing schools, but because the claimant was the authority's employee. In the circumstances, this duty of care had been breached by a failure to exercise a statutory discretion. The court made it clear, however, that negligence claims would only succeed in cases where fulfilling such an independent duty to the claimant could be achieved consistently with a defendant's proper performance of its statutory obligations.

*Human rights issues*

**2–035**   There are certain cases where, although the claimant is denied a remedy in negligence for poor performance of statutory functions, he or she might instead have a remedy for breach of human rights. Below, we consider the courts' developing attitudes to the question of whether or not human rights law should be accommodated within negligence by expanding the duty of care, or whether the two legal regimes should be kept separate. The picture is not altogether

---

[98] [2009] UKHL 11; [2009] 2 W.L.R. 481
[99] [2009] EWCA Civ 286.
[100] Per Lord Hoffmann in *Gorringe v Calderdale MBC* [2004] 1 W.L.R. 1057 at para.38, cited by Sir Anthony Clarke M.R. in *X v Hounslow LBC* [2009] EWCA Civ 286 at para.46.
[101] [2010] EWCA Civ 286.

clear because, although some case law on the issue has indicated a partial convergence of the two areas of law, the most recent decisions suggest that negligence will not generally be modified to accommodate human rights law.

*The "child abuse" cases: a partial accommodation of human rights law*

There have been a number of cases where claimants have sought damages for psychiatric   **2–036**
harm, alleging that this has been caused by the negligence of local authorities in the exercise
of their statutory functions in protecting child welfare. The earliest response of the courts was
to dismiss such claims, holding that, for policy reasons, the local authorities could owe no
duty of care. This approach can be illustrated by the reasoning of Lord Browne-Wilkinson in
*X v Bedfordshire CC*.[102] In *X*, the House of Lords considered five appeals. In the first group of
cases, it was alleged that a local authority had negligently failed to take children into care,
with the result that they suffered neglect and abuse at home and, conversely, that a local
authority had wrongly decided to take a child into care, causing psychiatric harm to the child
and its mother. The second group of cases concerned allegations that the local authority had
negligently failed to provide adequate education for children with special needs.

On the facts of these cases, Lord Browne-Wilkinson thought that it would not be fair, just
and reasonable to impose a duty of care. In the abuse cases, a duty of care would have been
inconsistent with the operation of the statutory system set up for the protection of children at
risk. This system involved a number of agencies besides the local authority, and to place
liability only on one agency would be manifestly unjust. Equally, to state that all parties owed
a duty of care would cause untold problems in ascertaining which party had been in breach or
had caused the damage. In the education cases, the claimants had access to a statutory appeals
procedure, and their Lordships felt that this, rather than litigation, was the most appropriate
way of dealing with the claimants' concerns.[103]

The problem with this complete denial of a duty of care, however, was that it was inconsistent with upholding the claimants' human rights. Some of the claimants in *X v Bedfordshire
CC* had been subjected to "inhuman or degrading treatment", contrary to art.3 of the European
Convention on Human Rights. When they were denied a duty of care by the UK courts, they
complained to the European Court of Human Rights (the Human Rights Act 1998 not being in
force at the time). This human rights litigation proceded under the name *Z v United Kingdom*.[104]

*The decision in Z v United Kingdom*

The claimants in *Z* were four siblings who had suffered terrible abuse at the hands of their   **2–037**
mother—they had, for example, been locked in filthy unlit bedrooms, which they had been
forced to use as toilets, and had been left so hungry that they had had to scavenge for food in
dustbins. The local authority had repeatedly decided not to appoint a social worker for the
children and had declined to place them on the Child Protection Register.

The ECHR was prepared to award the claimants compensation, to be paid by the UK
Government, on the basis that the UK had breached two of its obligations under the
Convention—it had allowed the claimants to be subjected to "inhuman and degrading

---

[102] [1995] 2 A.C. 633.
[103] Compare Lord Templeman's view in *Hill v Chief Constable of West Yorkshire* [1989] A.C. 53.
[104] (2002) 34 E.H.R.R. 3. It was this litigation which gave rise to the "Article 6.1 controversy" about the legitimacy of using the *Caparo* criteria to "strike out" claims disclosing no prospect of success. We discuss this controversy in a separate section at the end of this chapter.

treatment" (contrary to art.3) when it failed to act to ensure their welfare, and it had denied them a right to an effective remedy in respect of that treatment (contrary to art.13). The ECHR made it clear, however, that the "effective remedy" which must be provided for breach of Convention rights did not *necessarily* have to be a remedy in the tort of negligence—another form of remedy would suffice. This left open the possibility that, in future cases, where claimants could show a breach of the Human Rights Act 1998,[105] UK courts might decide to grant a remedy under the Act, but still hold that policy reasons prevented the existence of a duty of care in negligence.

Recent cases have evidenced some judicial disagreement about whether such a separation of negligence and human rights law is desirable. On the one hand, as Lord Brown has pointed out in *Van Colle v Chief Constable of Hertfordshire*[106] there is a good reason for maintaining the separation: negligence claims and human rights claims serve different purposes. The main purpose of negligence claims is to compensate losses, whilst the purpose of human rights claims is to uphold standards of behaviour and vindicate rights. On the other hand, as Lord Bingham observed in his dissenting speech in *D v East Berkshire NHS Trust*[107]:

> ". . . the question does arise whether the law of tort should evolve, analogically and incrementally, so as to fashion appropriate remedies to contemporary problems or whether it should remain essentially static, making only such changes as are forced upon it, leaving difficult and, in human terms, very important problems to be swept up by the Convention. I prefer evolution."

Inevitably, separating the two areas of law involves a certain incoherence: where a local authority (an organ of the state) is ordered to pay human rights damages because the state has failed to take care of its citizens, it seems rather artificial to suggest that such liability can arise without someone acting on behalf of the state being negligent. Avoiding this incoherence, however, would require a wholesale re-evaluation of public bodies' negligence liability. Recent case law suggests that this is not something the courts are prepared to entertain. Nevertheless, there has been a partial accommodation of human rights law within negligence, in the sense that the inflexible approach taken in *X* has been abandoned, so that in some circumstances human rights liability and negligence are now aligned. This is apparent from the decision of the House of Lords in *D v East Berkshire NHS Trust*.

*The decision in D v East Berkshire NHS Trust*

2–038    The claimants in *D* were a mixture of children and parents who alleged that they had suffered psychiatric harm because various health authorities (and in one case a local authority) had wrongly diagnosed that the children had been suffering from abuse at the hands of the parents. As a result, the claimants' family life had been disrupted in various ways—either the child had been removed from the parents, or the child had been placed on an "at risk" register with the

---

[105] The Act creates statutory rights that individuals can enforce directly against local authorities, without needing to invoke the tort of negligence. Under the Act, it is "unlawful for a public authority [e.g. a local authority] to act in a way which is incompatible with a Convention right": s.6(1). An "act" includes a "failure to act": s.6(6), and victims of a breach of a Convention right by a public authority are entitled to bring proceedings against that authority: s.7. The UK courts are empowered to grant such relief or remedy as they see fit, including damages: s.8. (Damages under the Act are discussed in Ch.17.)

[106] [2008] UKHL 50 at para.138. *Van Colle* is a police liability case, discussed later in this chapter.

[107] [2005] UKHL 23; [2005] 2 A.C. 373 at para.50.

parents under a cloud of suspicion, or limitations had been placed on the parents' contact with the child.

The House of Lords held that a duty of care was owed to *children* by public bodies when exercising their child welfare functions. This aspect of the decision entailed a finding that the broad policy-based reasoning that had prevented a duty of care in *X v Bedfordshire CC* was incompatible with the Human Rights Act 1998, and should no longer be applied.

In relation to the wrongly suspected *parents*, however, there were cogent reasons for denying a duty of care, namely that to allow such a duty would conflict with the duty owed to the child, and would constrain the public body's ability to discharge its statutory duties properly. The welfare of the child was paramount, and to impose on health professionals a duty towards parents would compromise their ability to investigate suspicions of child abuse effectively.[108]

In the light of this decision, with its departure from the reasoning in *X*, it seemed as if negligence liability and human rights liability might be set to converge. Later cases, however, have indicated that, although the slight widening of negligence liability represented by *D* remains good law, the decision does not represent an emerging trend in terms of the convergence of negligence liability and human rights. Indeed, there is now a tendency to view negligence and human rights liability as separate entities, each requiring separate consideration. This approach is exemplified by reasoning of the House of Lords in *Jain v Trent Strategic Health Authority*.

### *Jain v Trent Strategic Health Authority: negligence and human rights kept separate*

As Lord Scott succinctly explained in his leading opinion, *Jain* was a case in which the appellants, Mr and Mrs Jain, "had their nursing home business destroyed by executive action taken against them by a regulatory authority".[109] The home had been closed down following an application to magistrates made by the Health Authority that the registration needed to operate the nursing home should be cancelled. This application was made without notice and ex parte (that is, without allowing the Jains to be present in court). As a result, the residents, most of them elderly, were moved out. The Jains successfully appealed against the decision (which had been made in the absence of sufficient evidence, and on the basis of irrelevant and prejudicial information) but the four-month delay in hearing the appeal was sufficient to cause them financial ruin.

**2–039**

Their Lordships declined to impose liability in negligence. Despite sympathy for the Jains' plight, they were not prepared to hold that a local authority should owe a duty of care to nursing home owners when exercising its statutory power to regulate homes. The purpose of the power was to protect vulnerable residents. Therefore, as was the case with the parents' claims in *D v East Berkshire NHS Trust* (above) the potential for conflict—between a duty to protect the vulnerable and a duty to others affected by actions designed to do so—dictated that a duty of care would be inappropriate.[110]

---

[108] As to whether denying a remedy to the parents infringes their human rights, note the reasoning of Field J., approved by the CA in in *Lawrence v Pembrokeshire CC* [2007] EWCA Civ 446. His Lordship pointed out that (by art.8.2) art.8 (right to family life) must be applied to give effect to the public interest, which would include effective investigation of suspected child abuse. See also: *Merthyr Tydfil CBC v C* [2010] EWHC 62 (a local authority could owe a duty of care to a child and a parent where the parent was not suspected of abusing the child.)

[109] *Jain v Trent Strategic Health Authority* [2009] UKHL 4; [2009] 1 A.C. 853, at para. 1.

[110] In addition, clear authority establishes that where the instigation of proceedings has the potential to cause damage to a party to the proceedings, a remedy for that damage cannot be obtained by the imposition on the opposing party of a common law duty of care: see *Elguzouli-Daf v Commisioner of Police of the Metropolis* [1995] Q.B. 335.

What is interesting, for present purposes, however, is that their Lordships went on to consider whether the Jains might have had an alternative claim under the Human Rights Act 1998. The issue was academic, because the Act had not been in force when the order to close the home had been made. Nevertheless, Lord Scott justified considering the issue as having a bearing on whether the courts should, in light of the Act, now develop the common law so as to provide a remedy in cases such as this.[111]

Two particular human rights were in issue: the right to enjoy possessions (art.1 of the First Protocol to the Convention) and the right to a fair and public hearing (art.6.1). The legal right to run a nursing home qualified as a possession.[112] The right to enjoy possessions is a qualified right, and the state is entitled to impose limitations on it where other important interests are at stake. However, their Lordships found it difficult to see how even the need to consider the interests of vulnerable patients could justify the draconian approach of ruining the Jains' business by means of an application made ex parte and without notice. The House of Lords condemned the authority's use of this procedure as unsatisfactory in the circumstances. Additionally, Lord Scott found it very difficult to see how such a procedure could satisfy the art.6.1 requirement of a "fair and public hearing". His Lordship was clearly of the view that such arguments should be brought before the European Court of Human Rights in Strasbourg, once the Jains had exhausted their domestic remedies. It was made clear, however, that violations of human rights law did not necessarily mean that a duty of care should be imposed. Lord Scott endorsed the view that Lord Brown had expressed in *Van Colle v Chief Constable of Hertfordshire*, namely, that in view of the Human Rights Act 1998, "it is quite simply unnecessary now to develop the common law to provide a parallel cause of action".[113]

*The education cases*

**2–040**  In *Phelps v Hillingdon LBC*,[114] the House of Lords was prepared to hold that, in certain circumstances, a local authority could owe a duty of care in respect of the provision of educational services. In *Phelps*, the claimant had suffered from dyslexia as a child, causing her severe learning difficulties when she was at school. She had been referred to an educational psychologist when she was 11, but the psychologist failed to notice her dyslexia. She subsequently left school with no qualifications, and later sued the local authority for negligence in having failed to provide her with an appropriate education. The appeal in *Phelps* was consolidated with three other cases in which it was alleged that local authorities had been negligent in their provision of education for children with special needs. The House of Lords found in favour of all the claimants,[115] emphasising that *X v Bedfordshire* did not lay down any principle that there should be a blanket immunity in respect of local authority liability for the provision of educational services.

In the wake of *Phelps*, it seems that a general duty of care on the part of local authorities to look after the welfare of children in state schools is becoming firmly established. Thus, in *Kearn-Price v Kent CC*[116] a local authority was liable when the claimant, a boy of 14, was

---

[111] By contrast, Lord Roger (at para.41) declined to deal with the issue, on the basis that it had not been addressed by counsel.

[112] See *Van Marle v Netherlands* (1986) 8 EHRR 483.

[113] *Van Colle v Chief Constable of Hertfordshire Police* [2009] 1 A.C. 225 at para.136.

[114] [2001] 2 A.C. 619. *Phelps* was applied in *Carty v Croydon LBC* [2005] EWCA Civ 19; [2005] 1 W.L.R. 2312.

[115] Note that in only one of the appeals (*Phelps* itself) did this mean that the claimant won the case. In the other cases, the issue was simply whether they should be allowed to proceed to trial.

[116] [2003] P.I.Q.R. P11, CA.

struck in the eye by a leather football. The school had banned the use of such footballs, because of the potential danger to pupils, but had done little to enforce the ban. The claimant was injured in the playground shortly before the start of the school day. The Court of Appeal dismissed the local authority's argument that it could not be expected to supervise the welfare of pupils outside of school hours. In the particular circumstances, a duty of care was owed and had been breached. It is clear, however, that the scope of a local authority's "out of school" supervisory duty is limited. Thus, in *Bradford-Smart v West Sussex CC*,[117] Garland J. held that it would not be fair, just and reasonable to hold that the duty extended to protecting a child from bullying outside school.

## (2) Other public servants

In this section, we consider the duty of care in relation to the following types of defendant: **2–041**

- the police
- the fire brigade
- the coastguard
- the ambulance service
- the NHS
- the armed forces

### *The police*

To understand the courts' approach to police liability, it is necessary to distinguish two different **2–042** types of case. In the first type of case, the courts have little problem in holding that the police owe a duty of care. In the second type of case, however, the courts deny liability, applying what Lord Steyn has called a "core principle", namely that important policy reasons prevent the police owing a duty of care in respect of their general public functions of investigating and suppressing crime.[118] We consider each type of case below.

### *1. Cases where the police owe a duty of care*

Some of these cases are examples of so-called "operational negligence", where the police cause damage by negligent performance of their day-to-day activities, in much the same way that any other defendant might do. A good example would be where a pedestrian is hit by a negligently driven police car. These cases are treated in the same way as any other negligence claim. Thus, in *Rigby v Chief Constable of Northamptonshire*,[119] the plaintiff's gun shop had been under siege and the police had negligently fired a canister of C.S. gas into the shop without taking adequate precautions against the high risk of fire. When a fire occurred, the plaintiff was successful in his negligence claim.

---

[117] [2002] EWCA Civ 7; [2002] 1 F.C.R. 425. See also *Shaw v Redbridge LBC* [2005] EWHC 150.

[118] See *Brooks v Commissioner of Police* [2005] UKHL 24, per Lord Steyn at para.30.

[119] [1985] 1 W.L.R. 1242. See also *Knightley v Johns* [1982] 1 W.L.R. 349.

Also in this category are cases where the police assume a very specific responsibility to safe-guard particular individuals against harm. This might be because the individuals in question are police employees, suspects in custody, or police informants. In *Mullaney v Chief Constable of West Midlands*,[120] for example, the police authority was liable when a probationary constable suffered serious injury whilst attempting an arrest, in circumstances where fellow officers had failed to respond to his calls for assistance. In *Reeves v Metropolitan Police Commissioner*,[121] the police were liable for failing to safeguard the welfare of a suspect, a known suicide risk, who hanged himself in his cell, and in *Swinney v Chief Constable of Northumbria Police*,[122] a duty of care was owed to an informant who had received threats from a violent suspect after her contact details had been stolen from an unattended police car. The facts of the case suggested that the police had assumed responsibility for the informant's safety.[123]

### 2. Cases where policy reasons preclude the existence of a duty of care

In this type of case, the claimant suffers loss because the police have made an error in the course of fulfilling their general public functions of investigating and preventing crime. The courts have persistently refused to allow negligence liability in such circumstances, for reasons which we explore below. As we shall see, the position is complicated by the fact that, although no common law duty of care is owed, in many cases claimants will have a right to compensation under the Human Rights Act 1998 (or by applying to the ECHR in cases where the loss occurred before the Act came into force).

The "core principle" of no liability in these cases was established in *Hill v Chief Constable of West Yorkshire*.[124] The mother of the last victim killed by Peter Sutcliffe (a serial killer known as the "Yorkshire Ripper") sued the police authority for negligence, alleging that it had failed to use reasonable care in apprehending him. Sutcliffe had been interviewed by the police and subsequently released. It was argued that the police had carelessly failed to realise, at an earlier stage in their investigations, that Sutcliffe was the murderer. Had they done so, his last victim, Jacqueline Hill, would not have died.

The House of Lords refused to impose a duty of care. Lord Keith held that, since it could not be shown that there was any exceptional risk to Jacqueline Hill personally, there was insufficient proximity between her, as the potential victim of a crime, and the police.[125] His Lordship also objected to liability on policy grounds, identifying some important reasons why

---

[120] [2001] EWCA Civ 700. See also *Costello v Chief Constable of Northumbria Police* [1999] 1 All E.R. 550; *Waters v Commissioner of Police of the Metropolis* [2000] 1 W.L.R. 1607, HL. Compare *Leach v Chief Constable of Gloucestershire Constabulary* [1999] 1 All E.R. 215 where, by a majority, the Court of Appeal struck out a claim by the appropriate adult who had sat with Frederick West (a serial killer) in police interviews. The police had not assumed responsibility for her psychological well-being. Their only obligation was to provide counselling during or within a short time of the interviews.

[121] [2000] 1 A.C. 360; see also *Keenan v United Kingdom* (2001) 33 E.H.R.R. 38. Compare *Orange v Chief Constable of West Yorkshire* [2002] Q.B. 347 and *Vellino v Chief Constable of Greater Manchester* [2002] 1 W.L.R. 218.

[122] [1997] Q.B. 464. The court was conscious of the strong public policy argument in favour of allowing liability in such cases, so that informants would be encouraged to give information vital to the suppression of crime. At the full hearing, however, it was held that the police had not been in breach of their duty of care. See *Swinney v Chief Constable of Northumbria Police (No.2)* (1999) 11 Admin. L.R. 811.

[123] Per Lord Brown in *Van Colle v Chief Constable of Hertfordshire* [2008] UKHL 50; [2009] 1 A.C. 255 at para.120.

[124] [1989] A.C. 53. The application of the police "immunity" established in *Hill* was subsequently challenged before the ECHR in *Osman v United Kingdom* (1998) 29 EHRR 245 as being contrary to art.6.1 of the European Convention on Human Rights (right of access to a court). It was this litigation that gave rise to the "Article 6.1 controversy" discussed at the end of this chapter.

[125] *Hill v Chief Constable of West Yorkshire* [1989] A.C. 53 at 62.

the police should owe no duty of care in this type of case. The two reasons[126] which have proved most enduring in the light of later cases might be summarised as follows:

- The prospect of liability would lead to defensive practices—excessive record-keeping, for example, or a preoccupation with "closing the loop" by following up all lines of enquiry, however apparently unhelpful. These practices would be likely to impede the progress of investigations.[127]

- Defending this type of claim would involve much time, trouble and expense. It would involve police officers in (amongst other things) preparing documents and attending court as witnesses. This would cause the police to divert considerable time and resources from their most important function—the suppression of crime.

The reasoning in *Hill* has been applied broadly and consistently in subsequent cases, in a variety of different factual contexts.[128] There have been a number of recent cases in which the House of Lords has considered the *Hill* principle and has confirmed that it remains good law.

In *Brooks v Commissioner of Police*[129] the claimant, Duwayne Brooks, was a black youth who had been with his friend, Stephen Lawrence, on the night the latter had been murdered in a racist attack by white youths at a bus-stop in south-east London. A subsequent public inquiry found that the police had not dealt properly with Mr Brooks. In particular, the inquiry found that Mr Brooks had been:

"stereotyped as a young black man exhibiting unpleasant hostility and agitation, who could not be expected to help, and whose condition and status simply did not need further examination or understanding."[130]

Mr Brooks brought a negligence claim against the police, alleging that they had owed him a duty of care to take reasonable steps to assess whether he had been the victim of a crime, afford him appropriate support and assistance, and give reasonable weight to his account of how his friend had been murdered.

---

[126] Lord Keith also opined (at 63) that: (1) the police did not need the threat of liability as an incentive for maintaining high standards. (This is no longer accepted as a justification for the *Hill* principle—see the reasoning of the House of Lords in *Brooks v Commissioner of Police* [2005] UKHL 24, summarised by Lord Bingham in *Van Colle v Chief Constable of Hertfordshire* [2008] UKHL 50 at para 48.); and (2) it would be undesirable to conduct the "elaborate investigation of the facts" needed in many cases to determine whether discretionary and policy decisions were such as could be called into question by the courts.

[127] A further possible assumption here is that fear of liabilty might affect interrogation methods, including the length of time for which suspects are held and questioned, upsetting the delicate balance between civil liberties and law enforcement. This assumption has not been made explicitly by the courts, although it is perhaps hinted at: Lord Keith, in *Hill*, for example, refers to investigations being "carried on in a detrimentally defensive frame of mind" and says that conducting investigations "must necessarily involve a variety of decisions to be made on matters of policy and discretion". *Hill v Chief Constable of West Yorkshire* [1989] A.C. 53 at 63.

[128] See *Ancell v McDermott* [1993] 4 All E.R. 355, applied by analogy to the Crown Prosecution Service in *Elguzouli-Daf v Commissioner of Police of the Metropolis* [1995] Q.B. 335 (but compare *Welsh v Chief Constable of the Merseyside Police* [1993] 1 All E.R. 692). See also *Alexandrou v Oxford* [1993] 4 All E.R. 328, CA (police owed no duty to owners of business premises who had a burglar alarm connected to a police station) and *Cowan v Chief Constable of Avon & Somerset* [2002] H.L.R. 44 (police at the scene owed no duty to a tenant to prevent a landlord committing the criminal offence of wrongful eviction).

[129] [2005] UKHL 24; [2005] 1 W.L.R. 1495.

[130] See *Macpherson Report* Cm 4262-I, at para.5.12.

Lord Steyn, delivering the leading speech in a unanimous House of Lords, held that the "core principle" of *Hill* dictated that no such duty of care could be owed to Mr Brooks. Whilst it was desirable that the police should treat victims and witnesses properly and with respect, his Lordship thought that "to convert that ethical value into general legal duties of care . . . would be going too far." It would require the police to devote time and resources to ensuring that potential victims and witnesses were not caused offence, and this would "tend to inhibit a robust approach in assessing a person as a possible suspect, witness or victim".[131] Mr Brooks would therefore have to be content with pursuing a complaint under the police complaints procedure.

Subsequently, the House of Lords decided the conjoined appeals in *Van Colle v Chief Constable of Hertfordshire* and *Smith v Chief Constable of Sussex*.[132] An examination of these appeals is instructive not only because it confirms the application of the *Hill* principle, but because it throws light on the relationship between the tort of negligence and the Human Rights Act 1998. The cases were heard together because they concerned, as Lord Bingham put it, a common underlying problem: if the police are alerted to a threat that D may kill or inflict violence on V, and the police take no action to prevent that occurrence, and D does kill or inflict violence on V, may V or his relatives obtain civil redress against the police, and if so, how and in what circumstances?[133]

In the *Van Colle* case, Giles Van Colle was shot dead by Daniel Brougham shortly before he was due to give evidence for the prosecution at Brougham's trial on charges of theft. In the weeks preceding the trial Brougham had approached witnesses, including Van Colle, and attempted to dissuade them from giving evidence. Over the same period, incidents of fire damage to the witnesses' property had occurred and had been investigated, but they had not been attributed to Brougham. Some of the incidents had been reported to the police, including two telephone calls from Brougham to Van Colle, during one of which Brougham had said:

> "Drop the charges. We know where you live and where your parents live and where your business is. You'll be in trouble if you don't."

Despite all this, the police officer dealing with the matter had taken no action to protect Van Colle, and a police disciplinary tribunal subsequently found him guilty of failing to perform his duties properly.

The claimants, Van Colle's parents, brought an action under the Human Rights Act 1998, alleging a breach of art.2 (the right to life) by a public authority (the police). A concurrent claim in common law negligence was considered by the High Court, but rejected in the Court of Appeal, who were content to assume that the *Hill* principle would preclude the existence of a duty of care.[134] The Court of Appeal's finding of liability under the Human Rights Act 1998 was challenged in the House of Lords.

In dismissing the appeal, their Lordships applied *Osman v United Kingdom*,[135] in which the European Court of Human Rights had held that the duty of a state to protect the lives of its citizens under art.2 involved not only putting in place effective criminal law provisions, but,

---

[131] *Brooks v Commissioner of Police* [2005] UKHL 24, per Lord Steyn at para.30. See also *M v Commissioner of Police for the Metropolis* [2007] EWCA Civ 1361. (The police owe no duty of care to victims in deciding whether or not to prosecute an offence.)

[132] [2008] UKHL 50; [2009] 1 A.C. 225.

[133] *Van Colle v Chief Constable of Hertfordshire* [2008] UKHL 50 per Lord Bingham at para 1.

[134] *Van Colle v Chief Constable of Hertfordshire* [2007] 1 W.L.R. 1821, CA per Sir Anthony Clarke M.R. at para.95.

[135] (1998) 29 EHRR 245.

in appropriate cases, taking positive steps to protect individuals whose lives were at risk from criminal actions. According to *Osman*, however, the threshold of state liability was a high one. Liability could only arise where:

". . . the authorities knew or ought to have known *at the time* of the existence of a *real and immediate* risk to the life of an identified individual or individuals from the criminal acts of a third party and . . . failed to take measures within the scope of their powers which, judged reasonably, might have been expected to avoid that risk."[136]

Their Lordships held unanimously that, on the facts of *Van Colle*, this threshold had not been met. Brougham's criminal record was that of a petty offender not given to extreme violence, and the phone calls he had made were unpleasant, but did not contain explicit death threats. In these circumstances it would have been unrealistic for the police to conclude that there was a real and immediate risk to Van Colle's life.

The appeal in *Smith v Chief Constable of Sussex* concerned a claim for common law negligence. No human rights claim was brought.[137] The claimant, Smith, reported to the police that he had received persistent and threatening telephone, text and internet messages from his former partner, Gareth Jeffrey, following the break-up of their relationship. The messages were extremely abusive and contained explicit death threats, e.g.: "I am looking to kill you and no compromises." Smith also told the police about Jeffrey's previous history of violence, and provided them with Jeffrey's contact details, so that they could investigate the matter.

The police, however, declined to look at or record the messages, took no statement from Smith and completed no crime form. They did not visit or arrest Jeffrey, but informed Smith that the telephone calls would need to be traced, and that this would take four weeks to do. Shortly thereafter, Jeffrey attacked Smith with a claw-hammer in such a way that, had Smith been killed, it would have been a clear case of murder. Unsurprisingly, perhaps, Smith brought an action in negligence.

The House of Lords (Lord Bingham dissenting) refused to impose liability. The "core principle" of no liability established in *Hill* operated in the interests of the whole community, by ensuring that police resources were well-used. It should not, therefore, be abandoned, even in extreme cases such as this, where it might produce injustice for the individual claimant. As Lord Hope put it: "We must be careful not to allow ourselves to be persuaded by the shortcomings of the police in individual cases to undermine that principle."[138]

Their Lordships were not, of course, directly concerned with whether a human rights claim for breach of art.2 might have succeeded, had one been brought by Smith. Nevertheless, Lord Brown commented that:

". . . the apparent strength of this case might well have brought it within the *Osman* principle so as to make a Human Rights Act claim here irresistible".

His Lordship was clear, however, that this did not mean that it was desirable to enlarge the scope of the duty of care in negligence so as to accommodate human rights concerns. On the

---

[136] *Osman v United Kingdom* (1998) 29 EHRR 245 at para.116. Emphasis added.

[137] By the time of the appeal, Mr Smith had long run out of time for bringing a claim under the Human Rights Act 1998, which by s.7 (5) imposes a one year limitation period on claimants.

[138] *Van Colle v Chief Constable of Hertfordshire* and *Smith v Chief Constable of Sussex* [2008] UKHL 50 at para.75.

contrary, the very existence of the Act made it ". . . quite simply unnecessary now to develop the common law to provide a parallel cause of action."

Whilst acknowledging that the prospect of human rights claims somewhat weakens the value of the *Hill* principle insofar as it is based on safeguarding the police from the expense of defending litigation, his Lordship saw no great difficulty in allowing the principle to co-exist with the state's duty to protect human rights. As Lord Brown pointed out, negligence claims and human rights claims serve different purposes—the main purpose of negligence claims is to compensate losses, whilst the purpose of human rights claims is to uphold standards of behaviour and vindicate rights.[139]

Lord Bingham delivered a dissenting judgment in the *Smith* appeal. His Lordship pointed out that ". . . the public policy consideration which has first claim on the loyalty of the law is that wrongs should be remedied."[140] He therefore thought that Mr Smith should be entitled to look to the courts for recompense if the police had obviously failed to protect his safety. Lord Bingham proposed that a common law duty of care should be found in cases where the police were aware of apparently credible evidence that an identified individual was presenting a specific and imminent threat to life or safety. The adoption of this narrow "liability principle" would not, in his Lordship's view, distract the police from their primary function of suppressing crime and catching criminals—it would simply require reasonable performance of that function. This approach, however, was rejected by the majority, who thought that it would prove unworkable in practice. (When is evidence "credible"? When is a threat "imminent"?)[141]

The combined result of the *Van Colle* and *Smith* appeals, then, is as follows:

- the police continue to be protected from negligence claims arising from poor performance of their general public functions of investigating and preventing crime;

- in appropriate cases, art.2 human rights claims may be brought instead, but these will only succeed if the claimant can satisfy the stringent test for liability set out in *Osman v United Kingdom*.[142]

*The fire brigade*

**2-043**   In *Capital & Counties Plc v Hampshire CC*,[143] the idea that the fire brigade should be immune from liability on public policy grounds was examined by the Court of Appeal. The case was consolidated with three other appeals in which it was alleged that the fire brigade had been negligent in tackling fires. In the first two cases (*Capital & Counties* and *Digital Equipment*), the alleged negligence consisted of ordering that a sprinkler system, which had been operating at the location of the fire, be turned off. In the third case (*John Munroe*), it was alleged that,

[139] *Van Colle v Chief Constable of Hertfordshire* and *Smith v Chief Constable of Sussex* [2008] UKHL 50 at para.138. Lord Brown also points out that, in human rights cases, the courts appear to adopt a looser approach to causation—claimants need only establish some lost chance of (e.g.) being kept safe by the police. They do not need to prove that police action would probably have kept them safe.
[140] *Van Colle v Chief Constable of Hertfordshire* and *Smith v Chief Constable of Sussex* [2008] UKHL 50 at para.56.
[141] *Van Colle v Chief Constable of Hertfordshire* and *Smith v Chief Constable of Sussex* [2008] UKHL 50. See Lords Hope, Carwell and Brown at paras 77, 109 and 129.
[142] Further consideration is given to *Osman v United Kingdom* in "The Article 6.1 Controversy", a later section of this chapter.
[143] [1997] Q.B. 1004. Consolidated with *Digital Equipment Co Ltd v Hampshire CC, John Munroe (Acrylics) Ltd v London Fire and Civil Defence Authority* and *Church of Jesus Christ of Latter-Day Saints (Great Britain) v West Yorkshire Fire and Civil Defence Authority*.

after fighting a fire on adjacent premises, the fire brigade left the scene without ensuring that the fire was properly extinguished, with the result that it re-ignited, damaging the plaintiff's premises. In the fourth case (*Church of Jesus Christ of Latter-Day Saints*), it was alleged that the fire brigade had negligently failed to take proper steps to ensure that an adequate supply of water was available at the scene of the fire.

The plaintiffs faced two main problems. First, they faced policy objections that were similar to those advanced in *Hill*—for example that making the fire brigade liable for negligence in the course of its duties would lead to defensive practices, diverting resources away from the task of fighting fires. Secondly, they faced the reluctance of the courts to find that a sufficient degree of proximity exists where the case is one of "general reliance" by the public on services provided by a public body.

Stuart-Smith L.J., giving the judgment of the Court of Appeal, held that the fire brigade's attendance at the scene of a fire did not, of itself, give rise to the requisite degree of proximity. In the court's view, this followed from the fact that the fire brigade was under no duty to attend the fire in the first place. As Stuart-Smith L.J. put it:

". . . the fire brigade are not under a common law duty to answer the call for help, and are not under a duty to take care to do so. If, therefore, they fail to turn up, or fail to turn up in time, because they have carelessly misunderstood the message, get lost on the way or run into a tree, they are not liable."[144]

It would be strange, therefore, if, being under no duty to attend, the fire brigade could be liable where it had attended but had not made a claimant's position any worse. Accordingly, the plaintiffs in *John Munroe* and *Church of Jesus Christ of Latter Day Saints* could not succeed because, although the fire brigade had intervened, its actions had not caused any damage that would not have occurred had it failed to attend the fire. In the first two cases, however, the position was different. Here, it could be said that the incompetence of the fire brigade in ordering the sprinklers to be turned off had created a fresh source of danger, making the plaintiffs' position worse. So their claims succeeded.

So far as public policy immunity arguments were concerned, the court did not accept that the arguments which had been used in *Hill* were applicable, finding no close analogy between the activities of the fire brigade and the function of the police in investigating and suppressing crime. Neither did the court accept arguments based on the fear of indeterminate liability and the fact that property owners should bear the risk of fire because they are generally insured against it.

*The coastguard*

The familiar policy arguments for immunity have been applied to the coastguard, which has **2–044** been held not to owe a duty of care in respect of its watching, search and rescue functions. In *O.L.L. v Secretary of State for the Home Department*,[145] it was alleged that the coastguard, by misdirecting a rescue operation, had substantially increased the risk of injury to those in peril and that it should therefore be liable on the same basis that the fire brigade had been liable in *Capital & Counties*. It was held, somewhat questionably perhaps, that on the facts this had not been the case. The coastguard had not directly inflicted physical injury on those who were lost

---

[144] *Capital and Counties Plc v Hampshire CC* [1997] Q.B. 1004 at 1030. See also *Alexandrou v Oxford* [1993] 4 All E.R. 328.
[145] [1997] 3 All E.R. 897. See also *Skinner v Secretary of State for Transport, The Times*, January 3, 1995.

at sea, and May J. declined to draw an arbitrary distinction between situations where the coast-guard had misdirected itself (for which, in the light of *Capital & Counties*, it would not be liable) and situations where it had misdirected other organisations such as the Royal Navy. Clearly, though, his Lordship's decision reflected sympathy for a publicly funded service partly staffed by volunteers.[146]

*The ambulance service*

**2–045**     In *Kent v Griffiths*,[147] the Court of Appeal held that the policy arguments applicable to the police, and the "no liability unless the claimant's position is made worse than by failing to attend" argument, applicable to the fire brigade, had no general application to the ambulance service. The ambulance service was to be regarded as part of the health service rather than as a "rescue" service. The claimant suffered an asthma attack, and her doctor called an ambulance which took 40 minutes to arrive. Whilst waiting for the ambulance, she suffered a respiratory arrest, which would probably have been prevented if the ambulance had arrived within a reasonable time. Lord Woolf M.R., giving the judgment of the court, stated that the acceptance of the 999 call established a duty of care. Although cases might arise where policy considerations could exclude a duty of care—such as where the ambulance service had properly exercised its discretion to deal with a more pressing emergency before attending the claimant, or where it had made a choice about the allocation of resources—this was not such a case.

The decision in *Kent v Griffiths*, then, illustrates the idea that the courts are unwilling to deny a duty of care where this would create a divide between the standards to be expected from public and private sector service providers. Had Mrs Kent contracted privately for health care services including emergency ambulance provision, she would have been able to claim for breach of contract. It would be socially unacceptable if she were placed in a worse position because of her reliance on the National Health Service. In relation to firefighting and the suppression of crime, however, such arguments do not arise, because people do not commonly contract privately for those services.[148]

*The National Health Service*

**2–046**     The normal way for a claimant to proceed in a medical negligence case is to allege that a medical professional has been negligent and that an NHS provider (e.g. an NHS Trust or Health Board) is vicariously liable.[149] In most cases, the duty of care owed by such professionals is well established. The courts therefore confine the scope of negligence liability by reference to the concept of breach of duty. This is discussed in Ch.5. There is one group of cases, however, in which the courts have been willing to limit NHS negligence liability by using the scope of the duty of care as a control mechanism—the "unintended children" cases.

**2–047**     **The "unintended children" cases.** Until quite recently, the courts had been prepared to entertain claims against the NHS for the cost of bringing up children born as a result of

---

[146] *O.L.L. v Secretary of State for the Home Department* [1997] 3 All E.R. 897 at 907.
[147] [2000] 2 All E.R. 474. Compare *King v Sussex Ambulance NHS Trust* [2002] EWCA Civ 953, [2002] I.C.R. 1413.
[148] In this context, it is also worth considering whether *Alexandrou v Oxford* [1993] 4 All E.R. 328 (no liability where police failed properly to inspect premises after a burglar alarm had sounded) might have been decided differently had the defendants been a private security firm, or had the plaintiff been in a contractual relationship with the police. See the remarks of Glidewell L.J. in that case at 338, and compare *Bailey v HSS Alarms, The Times*, 20 June, 2000 (2000 WL 345011).
[149] Vicarious liability is discussed in Ch.7.

negligent advice or treatment having been given to the parents.[150] Then, in *McFarlane v Tayside Health Board*,[151] the House of Lords decided that, in the case of healthy, able-bodied children, the law would no longer entertain such claims. In rejecting a claim in respect of a healthy baby girl, who was conceived as a result of wrong advice that a vasectomy had been successful, Lord Millett said that "the law must take the birth of a normal, healthy baby to be a blessing, not a detriment".[152] Their Lordships declined to compensate the claimant for the cost of bringing up the child—damages were to be confined to compensating the pain and suffering endured as a result of the pregnancy. Various reasons were advanced by their Lordships for reaching this conclusion. In particular, their Lordships were unwilling to accept that the law might regard a baby as being "more trouble than it was worth"[153]—parenthood had its burdens but also its rewards, and since the rewards of parenthood were incalculable, they could not sensibly be weighed up against the burdens, so it was impossible to quantify what the parents had lost by having a child. Their Lordships were also conscious of the fact that awarding compensation to the parents of a healthy child, at the expense of a financially constrained NHS, might offend against ordinary people's views of how public money should be spent.

The decision in *McFarlane* did not resolve the question of whether compensation should be available for the costs of bringing up a *disabled* child. In *Parkinson v St James NHS Trust*[154] the claimant, who already had four children, underwent a sterilisation operation. The operation was carelessly performed and she subsequently became pregnant. She eventually gave birth to a child with significant disabilities. The Court of Appeal, mindful of *McFarlane*, could not award the claimant the normal costs associated with bringing up a child. Nevertheless, it felt able to award damages in respect of the *additional costs* associated with providing for a disabled child's special needs. This was so, even though the negligence of the doctors in performing the sterilisation operation had not been the cause of the child's disabilities.

Hale L.J. justified a departure from the approach taken in *McFarlane* by saying that, whatever ordinary people might think about the NHS having to pay the costs of bringing up a normal, able-bodied child, they would not regard it as unfair that where the NHS had undertaken to prevent the birth of further children, and had negligently failed to do so, it should meet the additional costs of bringing up a disabled child.[155] A departure from the *McFarlane* principle in such circumstances did not entail a suggestion that a disabled child was any less valued by its parents than an able-bodied one. It simply reflected the reality of the situation, which was that significant extra expenses were incurred by parents of disabled children in seeking to provide them with an upbringing comparable with that of an able-bodied child.[156]

In *Rees v Darlington Memorial Hospital NHS Trust*,[157] the House of Lords was faced with a new factual variation. Here, a healthy, able-bodied child was born to a blind mother, as a result

---

[150] See, for example, *Emeh v Kensington & Chelsea AHA* [1985] Q.B. 1012; *Thake v Maurice* [1986] Q.B. 644; *Benarr v Kettering Health Board* (1988) 138 N.L.J. 179; *Nunnerley v Warrington Health Authority* [2000] P.I.Q.R. Q69.

[151] [2000] 2 A.C. 59. Compare the approach of the High Court of Australia in *Cattanach v Melchior* [2003] HCA 38.

[152] [2000] 2 A.C. 59 at 113–114.

[153] [2000] 2 A.C. 59 at 82 (per Lord Steyn) and 114 (per Lord Millett).

[154] [2002] Q.B. 266. See also *Hardman v Amin* [2000] Lloyd's Rep. Med. 498; *Groom v Selby* [2001] EWCA Civ 1522; *Greenfield v Irwin* [2001] 1 W.L.R. 1279 (causing an unwanted child involves no breach of art.8 of the European Convention on Human Rights).

[155] *Parkinson v St James NHS Trust* [2002] Q.B. 266 at 295.

[156] [2002] Q.B. 266 at 293.

[157] [2004] 1 A.C. 309. Comment: P. Cane (2004) 120 L.Q.R. 189; A. Pedain [2004] C.L.J. 19; M. Mildred, J.P.I. Law 2004, 1, C19–21.

of a negligently performed sterilisation. The mother claimed the additional costs of bringing up the child that would be attributable to *her* disability. By a 4:3 majority, a seven-member House of Lords held that no exception to the principle in *McFarlane* was justified in such circumstances—the task of bringing up a normal, healthy baby could not be regarded as a loss that deserved compensation. In reaffirming this principle, however, their Lordships held that the law set out in *McFarlane* should be changed to a limited extent—there should be an award of a modest sum in all cases where negligence had caused an unintended pregnancy. The purpose of this award—which their Lordships called a "conventional award"—was to mark the courts' recognition of the fact that a legal wrong had been done, and to compensate the parents for having lost their right to limit the size of their family. The level of the award was fixed at £15,000.

In the light of *Rees* the status of the decision in *Parkinson* is uncertain. Three of their Lordships broadly endorsed the decision,[158] whilst three doubted its correctness.[159] The remaining Law Lord, Lord Millett, expressly stated that the question whether *Parkinson* was correct should be left open. Thus, the decision in *Rees* did not overrule *Parkinson*, so future claims for the additional costs of bringing up a disabled child remain a possibility.

*The armed forces*

**2–048**    The armed forces have never been treated as ordinary employers. Thus, in *Mulcahy v Ministry of Defence*,[160] the Court of Appeal held that, in battle conditions, common sense and sound policy dictated that the army could not owe a duty of care to its members. The plaintiff had been injured during the Gulf War, his injury being due to the negligence of his sergeant in causing a gun to fire whilst he was in front of it fetching water, rather than to active enemy involvement. The court accepted the argument that a duty of care would lead to defensive practices and undue caution, which would be wholly inappropriate to battle conditions. Whilst the immunity is likely to apply to all war-time activities, it is unlikely to apply to activities in peace-time. Thus, in *Jebson v Ministry of Defence*,[161] where the claimant was injured as a result of drunken horseplay in the back of an army truck, on the way back from an organised social event, the Court of Appeal held that the defendants were in breach of their duty to provide suitable transport and supervision for soldiers in high spirits.

## (3) Advisory bodies and regulators

**2–049**    In this section, we consider the liability of a number of advisory and regulatory bodies. Although in some cases these bodies receive government funding, they cannot be regarded as "public authorities" (like local authorities or NHS Trusts) because they do not act on behalf of the state. They are essentially "clubs" formed for the promotion or protection of certain

---

[158] Lords Steyn, Hope and Hutton.

[159] Lords Bingham and Nicholls were in favour of a conventional award in all cases, whilst Lord Scott thought that the additional costs of bringing up a disabled child might be recoverable where the reason for seeking the advice or treatment was precisely to avoid having a disabled child (e.g. where there was a likelihood of congenital abnormalities).

[160] [1996] 2 All E.R. 758. Compare *Multiple Claimants v Ministry of Defence* [2003] EWHC 1134. (*Mulcahy* applied, but it could not be said that all claims for personal injury sustained in combat were not justiciable.)

[161] [2000] 1 W.L.R. 2055. See also *Barrett v Ministry of Defence* [1995] 1 W.L.R. 1217 and *Bici v Ministry of Defence, The Times*, June 11, 2004 (peacekeeping and policing functions in Kosovo). Note that in respect of incidents occurring before 1987, Crown Proceedings Act 1947 s.10 confers immunity. In *Matthews v Ministry of Defence* [2003] 1 All E.R. 689, the House of Lords held that preserving this immunity does not involve violation of art.6.1 of the European Convention on Human Rights.

interests. In some cases, however, they perform a public service role that would otherwise have to be performed by a government organisation.

*Ship classification societies*

The same kind of arguments that were employed in *Hill* and elsewhere to deny liability have     **2–050**
been applied in relation to ship classification societies. Thus, in *Marc Rich & Co v Bishop Rock Marine Co Ltd (The Nicholas H)*,[162] a classification society issued a certificate which indicated the seaworthiness of a ship. The ship subsequently sank. The House of Lords asserted that despite the presence of physical loss resulting from the carelessly made report of the society's surveyor, and despite the fact that the loss was clearly foreseeable, no duty of care was owed to the owner of the cargo that was lost. The classification society was an independent and non-profit-making entity, created and operating for the sole purpose of promoting the safety of lives and ships at sea. In this way, it fulfilled a role akin to a public service which would otherwise have to be fulfilled by individual states. In this light, it would not be fair, just and reasonable to impose a duty of care.

There are suggestions, however, that the courts may be willing to overcome traditional policy objections where a classification society inflicts physical loss in a more direct way. Lord Steyn commented in *The Nicholas H*[163] that if the surveyor had caused an explosion by carelessly dropping a lighted cigarette into a hold known to contain combustible cargo, he would have been more willing to find that the society owed a duty of care. This approach was followed by the Court of Appeal in *Perrett v Collins*[164] where an inspector's role in certifying the airworthiness of light aircraft was critical, and, as a direct result of his negligence, the plaintiff suffered personal injury. The court saw no reason why the inspector should not owe the plaintiff a duty of care. Although the inspector worked for the Popular Flying Association, whose aim was to facilitate the construction and flying of light aircraft by amateurs, the imposition of a duty of care was not inconsistent with this aim.

The reasoning in *Perrett v Collins* was followed in *Wattleworth v Goodwood Road Racing Co Ltd*.[165] Here, a racing driver died when he crashed into the tyre-faced side of a race track. His widow sought to recover damages from the Royal Automobile Club, which had approved the track as safe. The court was prepared to hold that the RAC owed racing drivers a duty of care when approving the track. However, in the circumstances of the case, the RAC was not in breach of this duty, because the design of the track met a reasonable standard of safety.

*Scientific advisory bodies*

In *Sutradhar v Natural Environment Research Council*[166] the defendants were a UK govern-     **2–051**
ment-funded agency, established under Royal Charter, whose purpose was to undertake research, disseminate knowledge, and provide advice relating to the earth sciences and ecology. As part of a project to assist development in Bangladesh, they undertook a hydrological survey in that country which aimed to provide an understanding of how water might be used for irrigation and fish farming. They therefore conducted a number of tests on samples of groundwater

---

[162] [1996] 1 A.C. 211. See also *Reeman v Department of Transport* [1997] 2 Lloyd's Rep. 648 (Department of Transport surveyor causing economic loss).
[163] [1996] 1 A.C. 211 at 237.
[164] [1998] 2 Lloyd's Rep 255. See also *Grinstead v Lywood* 2002 WL 31397573.
[165] [2004] EWHC 140 (QB); [2004] P.I.Q.R. P25.
[166] [2006] UKHL 33; [2006] 4 All E.R. 490, Comment: D. Howarth [2005] C.L.J. 23.

to identify the presence of harmful chemicals. Unfortunately, they did not test the water for the presence of arsenic, having no reason to believe that arsenic was likely to be present.

The claimant was one of 700 Bangladeshi residents who had suffered from arsenical poisoning by drinking contaminated water from the sources which had been tested. He argued that the defendants were negligent in having issued a report which gave the impression that the water was safe to drink. In dismissing his claim, the House of Lords pointed to the lack of proximity between the claimant and the defendants, and noted that the purpose of the report had not been to protect the claimant from harm. The decisions in *Perrett v Collins* (above) and *Watson v British Boxing Board of Control* (below) were distinguished because, in those cases, the defendants had had complete control of the danger in question—in *Perrett*, for example, the inspector had had the power to ground the aircraft if he thought it was not safe to fly. Here, by contrast, the defendants had had no control whatsoever over whether and how water was supplied in Bangladesh.

*Sports regulators*

**2–052**    In *Watson v British Boxing Board of Control*,[167] the Court of Appeal was prepared to hold that the BBBC, a private organisation formed for the regulation of boxing, owed a duty of care to ensure an adequate standard of ringside medical treatment for an injured boxer. The case was novel because the claimant's allegation was that the defendant had been negligent in failing to formulate satisfactory rules for the conduct of the sport. The case arose as a consequence of the world super-middleweight title fight between Chris Eubank and Michael Watson. In the final round, the referee stopped the fight when it appeared that Watson was unable to defend himself. He had, in fact, suffered a brain haemorrhage. He was examined by a doctor at the ringside, and subsequently taken to hospital where he was given resuscitation treatment, but by this time he had already suffered permanent brain damage leading to disability. Watson claimed that immediate resuscitation treatment should have been available at the ringside, and that the BBBC was in breach of its duty of care by not providing for this in its rules.

Lord Phillips M.R., giving the judgment of the court, dismissed the BBBC's argument that Watson, knowing of the rules, had been the author of his own misfortune by consenting to box in accordance with them. His Lordship also regarded the fact that the BBBC was a non-profit-making organisation, without insurance, as irrelevant to its liability. Finding that there was a sufficient degree of proximity between Watson and the BBBC, his Lordship pointed out that Watson was one of only a limited class of individuals affected by the rules, so there could be no question of indeterminate liability.[168] Moreover, the BBBC had exclusive control over the provision of ringside medical assistance. Accordingly, it was fair just and reasonable for Watson to rely on the BBBC to look after his safety.

In *Vowles v Evans*,[169] the issue was not whether the rules of the game were adequate to protect the claimant, but whether they had been properly applied by the referee. The claimant was left confined to a wheelchair as a result of an injury he sustained during an amateur game of rugby. The injury had occurred when the referee had decided to allow the game to continue with "contestable scrummages" (in which the players are allowed to push against one another to gain possession of the ball) even though the substitution of an inexperienced player by one of the teams meant that this could not be done safely. The Court of Appeal saw no reason why

---

[167] [2001] 2 W.L.R. 1256. See George (2000) 65 M.L.R. 106.
[168] The High Court of Australia had found this a bar to liability in *Agar v Hyde* [2000] HCA 41, where the allegation was that inadequate rules governing rugby scrums had exposed the claimants to injury.
[169] [2003] 1 W.L.R. 1607.

the referee should not owe a duty of care. Even though the referee was acting in an amateur capacity, the second defendants (Welsh Rugby Union Ltd) who had appointed him could be expected to take out insurance against the negligence of their referees. The fact that serious injuries of this kind were comparatively rare meant that this would not create an unfair financial burden, or discourage amateurs from volunteering to act as referees.

## (4) The legal profession

Generally, judges[170] and arbitrators[171] cannot be sued in respect of their activities during a     **2–053**
case. Prior to the decision of the House of Lords in *Hall v Simons*,[172] barristers and solicitor advocates enjoyed a similar immunity—they could not be sued for negligently conducting a case in court, or for matters intimately connected with the conduct of the case in court.[173] In *Hall v Simons*, however, their Lordships abolished advocates' immunity, stating that the traditional arguments used to support it could no longer be sustained.

Although the immunity has been abolished, it remains difficult for a claimant who feels he or she has been the victim of incompetent advocacy to succeed in negligence against an advocate. For reasons we explore below, this is especially true in criminal cases where the claimant has been convicted. In all cases, of course, the claimant must show that the advocate is in breach of the duty of care, and that his or her negligence caused the loss suffered.[174] As we shall see in Chs 5 and 6, this can be difficult to establish.

*The old law*

Under the old law, the immunity enjoyed by barristers and solicitor advocates[175] applied only     **2–054**
in the context of litigation. Where non-litigious work was concerned, a duty of care was owed. The immunity granted to lawyers had somewhat different justifications from the restrictions on liability of the police and public bodies we have considered above, and its existence had been questioned by academics and practitioners alike.[176] Moreover, the distinction between "litigious" and "non-litigious" work proved very difficult to draw in practice and led to a lack of clarity in the law. In order to appreciate the modern law, it is convenient to set out below the arguments that were formerly used to support advocates' immunity[177] and to explore how each was addressed by their Lordships in *Hall v Simons*.

*Arguments for advocates' immunity*

**(1)  The advocate's duty to the court**. The integrity of our legal system relies on advo-     **2–055**
cates adhering to their overriding duty to the court whilst representing their clients'

---

[170] *Sirros v Moore* [1975] Q.B. 118; *FM (A Child) v Singer* [2004] EWHC 793.
[171] *Arenson v Arenson* [1977] A.C. 405. (Provided they are acting in an arbitral capacity. The immunity does not extend to mutual valuers.)
[172] [2002] 1 A.C. 615. Applied in *McFaddens (A Firm) v Platford* [2009] EWHC 126. Note that *Hall v Simons* has been held to apply retrospectively: *Awoyomi v Radford* [2007] EWHC 1671 (QB); [2008] Q.B. 793.
[173] *Saif Ali v Sydney Mitchell & Co (a Firm)* [1980] A.C. 198.
[174] See *Moy v Pettman Smith (A Firm)* [2005] UKHL 7; [2005] 1 W.L.R. 581, HL. Comment: C. McIvor (2005) 21 P.N. 131.
[175] See Courts and Legal Services Act 1990 s.62(1).
[176] See Hill (1986) 6 O.J.L.S. 183 and D. Pannick, *Advocates* (OUP, 1992).
[177] The leading case was *Rondel v Worsley* [1969] 1 A.C. 191, in which the relevant arguments were set out by Lord Reid.

interests. Thus, the advocate must not mislead the court, cast aspersions on the other party or its witnesses for which there is insufficient evidence, or withhold authorities or documents relevant to the case. In this context, then, it was argued that the immunity helped to ensure that advocates did not succumb, through fear of being sued, to pressure from their clients to breach their duties as officers of the court. Whilst the chief guarantee of integrity was the ethical code of the advocate's profession, it was argued that the existence of the immunity served to underpin this code, ensuring that advocates could carry out their duties "fearlessly" without "looking over their shoulders" for the reaction of their clients, who may feel that their interests are better served by breaking or bending the rules.

In *Hall v Simons*, their Lordships dismissed this "divided loyalty" argument.[178] Lord Steyn pointed out that it was difficult to see how the argument could justify the immunity of advocates when doctors, for example, enjoyed no such immunity, even though they too could be faced with questions of "divided loyalty", as where a patient with AIDS asks his doctor not to disclose this fact to his wife. Moreover, their Lordships noted that there was no evidence to suggest that in jurisdictions where advocates had no immunity (Canada, for example) their overriding duty to the court was compromised.

2–056    **(2) The "cab-rank" rule and "vexatious" clients**. Barristers (but not solicitor advocates) are obliged to act for any client who requests their services, provided that the client's claim is within their field of expertise and a proper fee is offered. This is known as the "cab-rank" rule. It was traditionally thought that the operation of this rule justified advocates' immunity because, if a barrister could not stop representing a client, even when that client threatened to sue the barrister for refusing to behave unethically, it was only fair that the barrister should be immune from suit. It was argued that were matters otherwise, barristers might be beset with unmeritorious negligence claims from "vexatious" clients whose cases they had no choice but to take.

This argument, too, was dismissed in *Hall v Simons*. Lord Hope said of the cab-rank rule that "its significance in daily practice is not great".[179] Lord Steyn went so far, perhaps, as to hint that the rule is more often honoured in its breach than its observance when he noted that "in real life" barristers' clerks were free, within limits, to raise the fees for unwanted briefs (i.e. so as to discourage clients from briefing the barrister of their choice).[180] Lord Hoffmann thought that although there could be a number of reasons why a barrister might not wish to take on a particular client, for example because the client was "tiresome or disgusting", the barrister's fear of an unwarranted and vexatious negligence action was seldom one of those reasons.[181]

In any event, their Lordships thought that the Civil Procedure Rules, which allow for "summary disposal" of claims where "the claimant has no real prospect of succeeding"[182] would ensure that barristers were not subject to a flood of unmeritorious claims following the abolition of advocates' immunity. It was also observed that recent reforms of the legal aid system, under which negligence claims are dealt with by way of conditional fee agreements, should prove a substantial obstacle to "vexatious" litigants—they will have to convince another lawyer to take on their case, and, according to Lord Hoffmann, a fellow lawyer "will be able to recognise a vexatious claim when he sees one".[183]

---

[178] A minority of judges believed, however, that it still had force in relation to criminal cases.
[179] [2002] 1 A.C. 615 at 714.
[180] [2002] 1 A.C. 615 at 678.
[181] [2002] 1 A.C. 615 at 696.
[182] Civil Procedure Rules 1998 r.24.2, applied in *Hussain v Cuddy Woods* [2001] Lloyd's Rep. P.N. 134.
[183] [2002] 1 A.C. 615 at 692.

**(3) The need to avoid a retrial.** To sue successfully for compensation resulting from an   **2–057**
advocate's negligence, the claimant must show that the advocate's negligence has caused him
or her to lose the case. To assess whether the unfavourable outcome of the trial was in fact the
consequence of the advocate's negligence (or whether the client would have lost in any event),
a court would effectively have to re-hear the case, evaluating the effect of the advocate's contribution to its outcome in the light of all the evidence. Clearly, permitting the courts to do this
does little to uphold the certainty of the judicial process and the finality of justice.

Although the avoidance of re-trials was often used as an argument to support advocates'
immunity, in fact, the "no re-trial" objective was already met in the law by different means.
The House of Lords' decision in *Hunter v Chief Constable of the West Midlands Police*[184]
confirmed that, at least in criminal cases, a collateral attack on the correctness of the final decision of a court would be struck out as an abuse of process where the claimant had had the
opportunity of appealing against that decision. *Hunter* was a case in which six convicted
I.R.A. terrorists (the "Birmingham Six") had alleged at their trial that the police had beaten
them to extract confessions. The trial judge had found that this had not been the case, and they
were convicted. They applied for leave to appeal (on other grounds) and this was refused.
Whilst in prison, they brought proceedings for assault against the police, alleging the same
beatings that had been alleged at the criminal trial. The House of Lords struck out their claim
as an abuse of process, because the men were attempting to relitigate issues which had already
been decided at their trial.

The rule in *Hunter* reflects considerations of public policy, namely the importance of finality
in administering justice, the affront to a coherent system of justice which would arise if there
subsisted two inconsistent decisions of the courts, and the virtual impossibility of fairly
re-trying, at a later date, issues of fact a court had decided on an earlier occasion.[185] Their
Lordships in *Hall v Simons* stressed the importance of maintaining the prohibition on collateral attacks on judicial decisions in criminal cases, but felt that this concern was relatively
unimportant in relation to civil cases.

**(4) Other grounds: the length of trials and the "witness analogy".** It was traditionally   **2–058**
argued that advocates' immunity ensured that trials were not unnecessarily prolonged by defensive conduct by the advocate, such as over-cautious questioning. Equally, it was asserted
that the immunity was consistent with the general immunity from civil liability that attaches
to all persons participating in court proceedings, such as the judge, court officials, witnesses
and parties.

Both of these arguments were addressed in *Hall v Simons*. In relation to the first, it was
noted by Lord Hoffmann that lengthy submissions by advocates were a problem even with the
immunity in place. His Lordship thought that the disapproval of the court, together with the
possibility of the judge making a wasted costs order against the advocate in question, would
be sufficient to contain the length of trials in the absence of advocates' immunity. In relation
to the second argument, their Lordships thought that advocates' immunity was an unwarranted
extension of the protection of free speech given to witnesses. The rationale for witness immunity was that, without it, witnesses might be less willing to assist the court. The same could
not be said for advocates.

---

[184] [1982] A.C. 529. Applied in *Hurnam v Bholah* [2010] UKPC 12. For an explanation of the *Hunter* principle, see
*R. v Belmarsh Magistrates' Court, ex p. Watts* [1999] 2 Cr. App. R. 188.
[185] *Smith v Linskills* [1996] 1 W.L.R. 763.

*The decision in Hall v Simons*

**2–059**     In *Hall v Simons* the House of Lords considered a number of appeals in which it was alleged that solicitors had been negligent in reaching settlements subsequently approved by the court. Since none of the appeals involved solicitors acting in the capacity of advocates, it was, as Lord Hope pointed out,[186] not strictly necessary to question the fundamental rule of advocates' immunity. Nevertheless, the seven-member House of Lords ruled unanimously that the immunity could no longer stand in civil cases, dismissing the traditional arguments, for the reasons we have examined above. By a majority, their Lordships also held that the immunity should be abolished in criminal cases, although a minority of three[187] thought that it should be preserved in such cases, because the conduct of criminal trials made advocates particularly vulnerable to unmeritorious complaints and the risk of "divided loyalties".

The majority thought that the rule against collateral attack, established in *Hunter*, would be sufficient to prevent the administration of justice being brought into disrepute by negligence claims against advocates. They noted that the rule in *Hunter* will operate differently in relation to criminal and civil cases. In relation to civil cases, it will seldom be possible to say that an action for negligence against a legal representative will bring the administration of justice into disrepute. This is because the correctness of the decision in a civil trial is a matter of concern only to the parties. Unlike a decision in a criminal court, it serves no wider purpose. Therefore, according to Lord Hoffmann, the rule in *Hunter* is unlikely to be used in a civil context, except in rare cases where allowing an action to proceed against an advocate would be unfair to a third party, for example, where a defence of justification[188] has been rejected in a defamation action.

In relation to criminal cases, a distinction was to be drawn between, on the one hand, cases where the accused has been convicted—either after a trial or a guilty plea—and, on the other hand, cases where the accused has had the conviction set aside after a successful appeal. Where the accused still stands convicted of the offence, any attempt to challenge the competence of his or her advocate will generally fall foul of *Hunter* and will be struck out as a collateral attack on the correctness of the conviction. The appropriate way for the accused to challenge a conviction is by an appeal rather than a negligence action against an advocate. On the other hand, if the accused has had his or her conviction set aside on appeal, there can be no such objection to a negligence action.

# THE ARTICLE 6.1 CONTROVERSY

**2–060**     We have already noted that, under the Human Rights Act 1998, which incorporates the European Convention on Human Rights into UK law, individuals who have their convention rights violated by a public authority can apply to a UK court for compensation. We have also noted that one of the recent concerns in the development of the tort of negligence has been whether, in the light of this, the scope of the duty of care should expand to accommodate human rights law.

In this section, we are concerned with a slightly different point, namely the extent to which art.6.1 of the Convention (the right of access to a court) has been regarded as inconsistent

---

[186]  *Hall v Simons* [2002] 1 A.C. 615 at 709.
[187]  Lords Hope, Hutton and Hobhouse.
[188]  See Ch.14.

with the UK courts' practice of striking out negligence claims. By this practice, the courts refuse to allow a full trial in cases where application of the *Caparo* criteria indicates that no duty of care should be owed. In *Osman v United Kingdom*, the ECHR held that this striking-out procedure denied the litigants proper access to a court, and so constituted a breach of art.6.1. Subsequently, however, in *Z v United Kingdom*, the ECHR retreated from this position.

Article 6.1 states:

> "In the determination of his civil rights and obligations . . . everyone is entitled to a fair and public hearing within a reasonable time by an independent and impartial tribunal established by law . . ."

The controversy surrounding the implications of art.6.1 began with the decision of the Court of Appeal in *Osman v Ferguson*.[189] Ahmet Osman was a school pupil. One of his teachers, who was psychologically disturbed, formed an obsessive attachment to Ahmet, giving him money, following him home, and even changing his own name by deed poll to "Ahmet Osman". When Ahmet's father asked for him to be moved to another school, the teacher began a campaign of violence against the Osman family, smashing the windows of their house and car. After each incident, the police questioned the teacher, but failed to arrest him. Eventually, the teacher went to the Osmans' house with a stolen gun, shot and injured Ahmet, and shot and killed Ahmet's father.

The Osmans sued the police in negligence, but the Court of Appeal struck out their claim. McCowan L.J. stated that, in the light of *Hill v Chief Constable of West Yorkshire*, their case was "doomed" to fail[190]—for policy reasons, the police enjoyed an immunity from negligence claims in respect of their investigation and suppression of crime. The Osmans then applied to the European Court of Human Rights, arguing, inter alia, that by striking out their claim, the Court of Appeal had denied them their human right to a fair and public hearing, as guaranteed by art.6.1.

In *Osman v United Kingdom*, the ECHR upheld this claim, stating that striking out the case on the basis of the police immunity rule established in *Hill* had constituted a disproportionate restriction of the Osmans' right of access to a court. In the ECHR's view, the Court of Appeal should have given proper consideration to countervailing arguments that liability was in the public interest, and balanced these against the arguments for immunity before reaching its decision. The court pointed out that the Osmans had satisfied the rigorous "proximity" test, that this was an allegation of grave negligence in failing to protect the life of a child, and that it was alleged that the police had assumed responsibility for the victims' safety. The Osmans were awarded compensation for their lost opportunity to have their case considered in a full trial.

Unsurprisingly, in the wake of *Osman v United Kingdom*, there followed a line of cases in which the courts were reluctant to strike out negligence claims, for fear that this behaviour would be seen by the ECHR as the application of a "blanket immunity" rule, falling foul of art.6.1. (Most of the relevant cases concerned the duties of local authorities in relation to children. See, for example, *Barrett v Enfield LBC* and *Phelps v Hillingdon LBC*,

---

[189] [1993] 4 All E.R. 344.
[190] [1993] 4 All E.R. 354.

considered above.[191]) In *Barrett v Enfield LBC*, however, Lord Browne-Wilkinson was critical of the ECHR's decision in *Osman*. The gist of his Lordship's opinion was that the ECHR's view (i.e. that the applicability of a policy-based exclusionary rule should be decided afresh in every case) represented a failure to understand the operation of precedent in UK law, and a failure to appreciate the legal mechanisms by which negligence cases are decided.

His Lordship pointed out that, although the word "immunity" is often used in an imprecise way, it is not wholly accurate to say that a finding that, on policy grounds, it is not "fair, just and reasonable" to hold a certain class of defendants liable, amounts to granting "immunity" to those defendants. Rather, it represents the proper application of the rules of negligence liability. His Lordship expressed the hope that the decision in *Osman* would be reconsidered by the ECHR (as indeed it subsequently was, in *Z v United Kingdom*) and expressed the view that, in the meantime, the courts had little choice but to be wary of striking out negligence claims, lest they fall foul of *Osman*.[192] The decision in *Osman* undoubtedly influenced the House of Lords' decision in *Hall v Simons* to abolish advocates immunity, and, for a time, it looked as if the ECHR's dim view of policy-based exemptions from negligence liability might effectively put a stop to any line of reasoning which would deny negligence liability on the basis of policy-based "immunities".

Then came the decision of the ECHR in *Z v United Kingdom*.[193] This case arose out of the *X v Bedfordshire* litigation, and has already been considered in that context. In *Z*, the ECHR stated, in effect, that it had changed its mind about what it had said in *Osman*. It was now persuaded that the UK courts' practice of striking out negligence claims, where the *Caparo* criteria indicated the claims could not succeed, did not amount to a breach of art.6.1. The court conceded that, in deciding *Osman*, it had misunderstood the effect of the *Caparo* criteria. The application of the *Caparo* criteria did not, in fact, operate to exclude claimants from the courts, or mean that certain types of defendant were above the law because they were exempt from legal proceedings. Rather, the *Caparo* criteria served to define what the law was. If, having applied those criteria, a court came to the conclusion that the law could not possibly assist the claimant, it was not a breach of art.6.1 for the court to save time and expense by declaring that proceedings should be discontinued.

The Article 6.1 controversy appears to have left a lasting mark on the contours of negligence liability. In cases like *Phelps v Hillingdon LBC* and *Hall v Simons*, we have seen a new-found reluctance to restrict the scope of the duty of care by granting policy-based exemptions to particular classes of defendant. That said, the courts have continued to apply policy-based exclusionary rules to claims against local authorities, and the decision in *Smith v Chief Constable of Sussex* has confirmed that, in relation to police investigations, the policy-based "immunity" in *Hill* remains, albeit now "reformulated" as an "absence of duty of care".

---

[191] See also *W v Essex CC* [1998] 2 A.C. 592, HL; *S v Gloucestershire CC* [2001] Fam 313, CA. Contrast *Palmer v Tees Health Authority* [2000] P.I.Q.R. P1, CA (*Osman* did not prevent striking out for lack of proximity).
[192] Compare the approach of Lord Woolf M.R. in *Kent v Griffiths* [2000] 2 All E.R. 474 at 484.
[193] (2002) 34 EHRR 3. See also *TP v United Kingdom* [2001] 2 F.C.R. 289 (where the ECHR rejected a claim of breach of Art. 6 for similar reasons to those given in *Z*) and *Roche v United Kingdom* (2006) 42 E.H.R.R. 30 (where the ECHR re-affirmed that art.6.1 created only procedural, not substantive, rights).

## Duty of care: conclusion

In recent cases, we have seen some judicial speculation that cases might be more fairly and **2–061** cogently decided if the courts were to use breach of duty (rather than the existence of the duty of care) as the primary control mechanism to limit the scope of negligence liability.[194] We have also seen frank judicial acceptance of the fact that the *Caparo* criteria, by themselves, are too vague to provide a principled and transparent basis for decision-making. A greater emphasis on the factual matrix of cases is required, as well as a more open recognition of policy factors. As Lord Hoffmann put it, in *Customs & Excise v Barclays Bank*[195]:

> "Questions of fairness and policy will enter into the decision and it may be more useful to try to identify these questions than simply to bandy terms like 'assumption of responsibility' and 'fair, just and reasonable'."

The (denial of a) duty of care remains one of the most important mechanisms available to the courts in determining the scope of the modern tort of negligence. We have seen that the question whether a duty should exist in a given situation is answered by reference to a number of considerations, in particular the ideas of ensuring that liability remains proportionate to the defendant's fault, yet consistent with the structure and general objectives of the law. In the chapters which follow, we shall explore the way the courts have incorporated these considerations into their decisions in cases of economic loss and psychiatric illness.

---

[194] See, e.g. *D v East Berkshire NHS Trust* [2005] 2 A.C. 373 (especially the dissenting opinion of Lord Bingham and the remarks of Lord Nicholls at paras 92 et seq.)
[195] [2006] UKHL 28, at para.36.

# Chapter 3

## NEGLIGENCE: ECONOMIC LOSS

---

### Introduction

We have seen that it is generally much more difficult to establish a duty of care in respect of "economic loss" than in respect of damage to property or personal injury. This chapter examines the reasons why this is so. We shall see that, broadly speaking, no duty of care is owed to avoid causing economic loss by careless activities, but that very different rules apply to careless statements, making it easier for a claimant to recover. The division between the two situations is largely a matter of historical accident in the way the law has developed, but it also has to do with the fact that, in the "activity" cases, the courts have been more heavily influenced by public policy arguments, in particular the need to limit the liability of local authorities.

**3–001**

### Definition of "economic loss"

"Economic loss" may be defined as *loss that is purely financial, in the sense that it does not result from damage to the claimant's property or injury to the claimant's person.*

    For the non-lawyer, many losses resulting from negligence might appear to deserve the title "economic"—if a claimant's car is "written off" by a negligent driver, for example, a lay person might call the loss "economic" because the claimant has lost a financial asset. Similarly, a claimant who is seriously injured and must give up work suffers a financial loss. In tort law, however, the term "economic loss" has a more precise meaning. It is used to describe losses which are "purely" financial, in the sense that the claimant has suffered "damage to the pocket" without suffering personal injury or property damage. This is the case, for example, where a person buys a product which is defective, although it does not cause personal injury or damage to property. The person is said to have suffered "economic loss" because the only loss in question is the cost of repairing or replacing the product.

**3–002**

### "Pure" and "consequential" economic loss

Tort lawyers generally use the term "economic loss" as shorthand for "pure economic loss" (of the type described above) but they sometimes need to draw a distinction between this type of loss and what they call "consequential" economic loss. The term "consequential economic

**3–003**

loss" simply means financial loss that is *consequent upon damage to property owned by the claimant*. (Lost profits, for example, resulting from damage to a profit-making machine.) Whilst this sort of loss is, of course, "damage to the pocket", the law has little difficulty in holding that it is recoverable, because it results directly from damage to the claimant's property. As a rule of thumb, then, we can say that "consequential economic loss" is recoverable, but "pure economic loss" (except where it results from negligent misstatement or negligent provision of services) is not.

## An illustration: *Spartan Steel*

**3–004**     The distinctions between "(pure) economic loss", "consequential economic loss" and "damage to property" are neatly illustrated by the decision in *Spartan Steel & Alloys Ltd v Martin & Co (Contractors) Ltd*.[1] The defendants, who were construction workers, negligently cut through a cable which supplied power to the plaintiffs' factory, causing a power cut which lasted for 14½ hours. Without electricity, the plaintiffs' furnace could not operate and they had to close their factory. The metal that was in the furnace at the time the power went off (the "melt") began to solidify, and to save damaging the furnace the plaintiffs had to throw it away. The plaintiffs brought an action for three types of loss:

- damage to the melt that was in the furnace at the time of the power cut (physical damage to property);

- loss of the profit which would have been made on the sale of that melt (consequential economic loss resulting from property damage);

- loss of profits on four further melts which would have been processed during the 14½ hours the factory was closed because of the power cut (pure economic loss).

A majority of the Court of Appeal held that the first two claims were recoverable, but the third claim was not. The defendants owed the plaintiffs a duty not to damage their property, and therefore had to pay for the damaged metal and the loss of profit resulting directly from that damage, but they did not owe a duty of care in respect of the further lost profits, because these did not result from the fact that the plaintiffs' property had been damaged.

   Lord Denning M.R. was unsure whether to approach the question from the point of view of duty of care or remoteness of damage. His Lordship observed:

> "At bottom I think the question of recovering economic loss is one of policy. Whenever the courts draw a line to mark out the bounds of duty, they do it as matter of policy so as to limit the responsibility of the defendant. Whenever the courts set bounds to the damages recoverable—saying that they are, or are not, too remote—they do it as matter of policy so as to limit the liability of the defendant."[2]

His Lordship then referred to the policy considerations which precluded liability for the further loss of profits. Observing that power cuts are a fact of life and that they can often cause

[1] [1973] Q.B. 27.
[2] [1973] Q.B. 27 at 36.

economic loss, his Lordship stated that people should bear that loss themselves, either by taking out insurance or by installing emergency generators, concluding: ". . . the risk of economic loss should be suffered by the whole community . . . rather than be placed on one pair of shoulders". His Lordship also noted that if claims for pure economic loss due to power cuts were allowed, it would be very easy to make inflated claims–plaintiffs could assert that they had intended to use their machinery for the duration of a power cut, but it would be impossible to prove whether, in fact, they really would have done so. If the courts simply took the plaintiffs' word for it, exaggerated damages awards would result.

## Policy considerations

The reasoning of the majority in *Spartan Steel*, then, reflects the two central policy considerations that have traditionally made pure economic loss non-recoverable in tort:                      **3–005**

### (1) Tort law should not undermine contract law

Those who contract for the installation and maintenance of emergency generators, for example, have a contractual remedy if they break down during a power cut causing economic loss. It would therefore be inconsistent to give a remedy in tort to others who have not so contracted.                      **3–006**

### (2) The desire to avoid "crushing liability"

Whilst a negligent act is likely to cause personal injury or property damage only to a limited number of people, the same act may cause an enormous number of people to suffer pure economic loss. The classic illustration of the point is that of a defendant who crashes his car, blocking a busy tunnel. This may cause a plumber on his way to work to be late and lose pay. In turn, the plumber's lateness may cause financial loss to others—a builder, for example, who is waiting for the plumber to complete his tasks before starting his own—and then to a property developer who misses a market opportunity by waiting for the completion of the building works. People's financial interests are so closely interrelated that causing economic loss to one person usually produces a "domino effect". The law's way of dealing with this phenomenon is to allow people, through the mechanism of contract law, to fix the extent of their economic liabilities to others—they will only be liable to others with whom they have contracted. This prevents one defendant from being liable for an indeterminate amount of loss.                      **3–007**

From a moral standpoint, it may be thought objectionable that a defendant who has caused foreseeable loss is allowed to escape liability. We have seen in Ch.2, however, that countervailing considerations sometimes dictate that a defendant should not be liable in tort without having accepted responsibility for the welfare of others. These considerations also have moral weight, in the sense that the law is regarded as just only if it recognises that people's willingness to look after the interests of others is limited. People are generally more willing to assume a duty to look after the physical safety and property of others than to look after the financial wellbeing of others. In denying recovery for economic loss, then, it may be argued that tort law simply reflects the feelings of society.

Whilst moral justification may be found, it is harder to find a justification in logic for the way in which the courts have sought to limit liability for economic loss. As can be seen from *Spartan Steel*, the courts have drawn a rather arbitrary line between economic loss resulting from damage to the claimant's *own* property (which they call "consequential") and economic loss resulting from damage to property in which the claimant only has a *contractual interest* (non-recoverable "pure" economic loss). In *Spartan Steel*, Edmund-Davies L.J., dissenting, objected to this arbitrary distinction. In his Lordship's view, the law would be clearer if it stated that all foreseeable economic loss was recoverable. His Lordship could not see why the recovery of economic loss should depend on the purely fortuitous circumstance of who happened to own the piece of property that was damaged.[3] The gist of his Lordship's argument, it is submitted, is this: suppose that the contractors had entered the factory, perhaps in pursuance of a statutory power, and had damaged a part of the power cable that *belonged to the plaintiffs*—all the economic loss would then have been recoverable, because it would have resulted from damage to the plaintiffs' own property. There is no logical basis on which to distinguish this type of situation from what happened in *Spartan Steel*. Despite its logical force, however, Edmund-Davies L.J.'s view has not found favour with the courts.

With the law's policy objectives in mind, it is now appropriate to examine the relevant case law in more detail. We shall begin with the "activity" cases and then consider the question of liability for economic loss caused by statements, and the extension of such liability to the negligent provision of services.

## ECONOMIC LOSS CAUSED BY NEGLIGENT ACTIVITIES

### The traditional approach

3–008    A convenient place to start is *Cattle v Stockton Waterworks*.[4] Here, the defendants, who had laid a pipe under land belonging to a certain Mr Knight, were under a statutory duty to keep the pipe in good repair. A road ran through Mr Knight's land which made it difficult for him to get easily from one side to the other, so he contracted with the plaintiff, Mr Cattle, to have a tunnel dug underneath the road. Mr Cattle agreed to do this for a fixed price, but after he had started work, he noticed that the land was becoming hard to excavate because it was water-logged. He realised that the defendants' pipe was leaking and contacted them about this, but they negligently failed to repair it. The result of this negligence was that Mr Cattle lost profit on his contract, so he sought to recover this from the defendants.

Blackburn J. held that Mr Cattle could not sue in his own name for damage that had been done to land belonging to Mr Knight. In other words, because Mr Cattle had no proprietary interest in the damaged land, he had no cause of action. In modern terms, we should say that Mr Cattle's loss was purely economic. Blackburn J. made reference to what we now call the "floodgates" argument, or the argument against "crushing liability". Considering his earlier (and more famous) decision in the case of *Rylands v Fletcher*,[5] where the defendant flooded the plaintiff's mine, his Lordship noted that if liability for damaged contractual interests were allowed in tort, then in *Rylands v Fletcher* it would have meant that not only could the owner of the flooded mine sue, but so could every workman who lost wages as a result of the flood. This would clearly be unacceptable because it would place the defendant under a financial liability disproportionate to his fault.

---

[3] [1973] Q.B. 27 at 41.
[4] (1875) L.R. 10 Q.B. 453.
[5] (1868) L.R. 3 H.L. 330 (discussed in Ch.10).

The *Stockton Waterworks* case, then, established that a claimant could not recover economic loss resulting from damage to property in which he or she had only a contractual interest. The point was tested again, however, in *Weller & Co v Foot and Mouth Disease Research Institute*.[6] (In 1963, the House of Lords, in *Hedley Byrne v Heller & Partners*, had radically extended the scope of the duty of care in respect of economic loss, as will be discussed below. It was in the wake of this expansion that the plaintiffs in *Weller* felt able to bring their case.) The plaintiffs were auctioneers of cattle. The defendants, by their carelessness, allowed an imported African virus to escape from their research institute and infect cows in the vicinity. This led the Minister of Agriculture to order the closure of all local cattle markets, with the result that the plaintiffs lost profit. It was held that, whilst the Institute might be liable to the owners of infected cows (i.e. for property that had been damaged by the virus), it could not be liable to the auctioneers because they did not have a proprietary interest in anything that had been physically damaged. It was true that they had such an interest in the premises in which cattle markets were held, but it could not really be said that these premises had been "damaged" by the virus. At best, it could be said that the plaintiffs had missed an opportunity to contract to sell the cows, but this missed opportunity was the same sort of loss that would be suffered by all other local traders—owners of shops and pubs, for example—while the cattle market was closed. Policy dictated that a line must be drawn somewhere, otherwise all of these traders would be able to claim compensation. This policy of avoiding wide and disproportionate liability was subsequently confirmed in *Spartan Steel*, which we have already examined.

## A brief period of expansion: *Anns* and *Junior Books*

At the beginning of this chapter, it was stated that where a person buys a product, and that product suffers from a defect in quality (although it does not damage anything or injure anyone), the cost of repairing or replacing the product is a classic example of economic loss. This type of loss (commonly called "defective product economic loss") is recoverable under a contract, but is not normally recoverable in tort. In the late 1970s and early 1980s, however, the House of Lords chose to depart from this long-standing rule in two important cases: *Anns v Merton LBC*[7] (which has now been overruled) and *Junior Books v Veitchi*[8] (which is nowadays unlikely to be followed). These cases were part of the general expansion of negligence liability during that period, discussed in Ch.2.

*The decision in Anns*

It will be recalled that *Anns* involved a claim against a local authority which, it was alleged, had failed properly to supervise the construction of a building, so that cracks appeared in the walls of the building. Lord Wilberforce took the unusual step of categorising these cracks as "damage to property",[9] apparently ignoring (or intending to displace) the distinction tort lawyers had always made between situations where a defect in a product *caused damage to*

3–009

3–010

---

[6] [1966] 1 Q.B. 569. See also *D Pride & Partners (A Firm) v Institute for Animal Health* [2009] EWHC 685. (Claims by farmers who suffered economic loss from restrictions on movement of livestock following an outbreak of foot and mouth had no real prospect of succeeding. This was so even though the restrictions had resulted in physical changes devaluing the livestock, which grew beyond its optimum profitable size.)

[7] [1978] A.C. 728.

[8] [1983] 1 A.C. 520.

[9] *Anns v Merton LBC* [1978] A.C. 728 at 759.

*other property*, and situations where the claim was for the cost of remedying the *defect itself*. The traditional position had been that if a defective building fell down, for example smashing furniture inside it, then a claim for replacing the furniture would be allowed (this would be a claim for "damage to property") but a tort claim for the cost of replacing the building itself would fail—it would be a claim for "defective product economic loss". Before *Anns*, a building that was defective, in the sense that it failed to meet the contract specification, could not properly be said to be "damaged". Lord Wilberforce, however, appeared to use that word in the very much looser sense that the building contained a defect which made it less valuable (i.e. in the sense that a lay person might complain that he or she has been supplied with "damaged goods"). As we shall see, in *Murphy v Brentwood DC*,[10] the House of Lords rejected this broad analysis, stating that the loss in *Anns* had been wrongly categorised, and restored the traditional distinction between defects in quality and "damage to property".

*The decision in Junior Books*

**3–011**     The decision in *Junior Books v Veitchi*,[11] which followed similar reasoning to that in *Anns*, marked the high point of the expansion of the duty to avoid causing economic loss by supplying a defective product. The plaintiffs entered into a contract with a firm of contractors ("the main contractors") for the construction of a factory. The factory needed a special floor to support heavy machinery, so the plaintiffs instructed the main contractors to sub-contract the flooring work to the defendants, who were flooring specialists. There was, therefore, a contract between the plaintiffs and the main contractors, and a contract between the main contractors and the defendants, but there was no contractual relationship between the plaintiffs and the defendants. The floor turned out to be defective and had to be rebuilt, necessitating a temporary closure of the plaintiffs' factory. For reasons which were unknown, the plaintiffs did not pursue their contractual remedy against the main contractors (who were perhaps insolvent), but instead brought a claim against the defendant sub-contractors, claiming the cost of re-laying the floor and lost profits while this was done.

In the House of Lords, it was observed (apparently without noticing any inconsistency with the way the loss had been categorised in *Anns*) that the claim in *Junior Books* was a claim for economic loss caused by the supply of a defective product. It was not a "damage to property" claim. Nor, indeed, was there any suggestion that the floor presented a danger to other property or a risk of personal injury (which might have made the plaintiffs' task a little easier). Regarding the case squarely as one of economic loss, their Lordships recognised that the question for the House was whether to extend the scope of the duty of care beyond a duty to prevent harm being done by faulty work, to a duty to avoid defects *being present in the work itself*. Normally, such a duty would only be owed in contract. By a 4:1 majority, the House of Lords held that the special circumstances of the case meant that the defendants owed such a duty in tort. Their Lordships gave a number of reasons why this should be so. The gist of their Lordships' argument was that Veitchi had "assumed responsibility" towards the plaintiffs for the quality of the floor, that the plaintiffs had "reasonably relied" on Veitchi's special skill, and that, because Veitchi were nominated sub-contractors, the relationship between the parties was "almost as close a commercial relationship . . . as it is possible to envisage short of privity of contract".[12]

---

[10] [1991] 1 A.C. 398.
[11] [1983] 1 A.C. 520.
[12] per Lord Roskill in *Junior Books v Veitchi* [1983] 1 A.C. 520 at 542.

Lord Roskill gave eight specific reasons why the plaintiffs should succeed:

"(1) The appellants were nominated sub-contractors. (2) The appellants were specialists in flooring. (3) The appellants knew what products were required by the respondents and their main contractors and specialised in the production of those products. (4) The appellants alone were responsible for the composition and construction of the flooring. (5) The respondents relied upon the appellants' skill and experience. (6) The appellants as nominated sub-contractors must have known that the respondents relied upon their skill and experience. (7) The relationship between the parties was as close as it could be short of actual privity of contract. (8) The appellants must be taken to have known that if they did the work negligently . . . the respondents would suffer financial or economic loss."[13]

His Lordship was careful to observe that the circumstances of *Junior Books* were to be distinguished from:

". . . the ordinary everyday transaction of purchasing chattels when it is obvious that in truth the real reliance was upon the immediate vendor and not upon the manufacturer."[14]

Thus, the reasoning in *Junior Books* did not mean, for example, that Mrs Donoghue should have been able to recover in tort the cost of a replacement bottle of ginger beer. It should be noted, however, that Lord Roskill's justification for excluding "everyday transactions" from the scope of *Junior Books* makes use of a legal fiction—the truth of the matter is that there are many occasions on which a consumer will walk into any nearby shop and buy a particular brand of product, putting his or her faith in the product's manufacturer, rather than in the shop. Clearly, then, Lord Roskill's interpretation of "reliance" was heavily influenced by policy considerations, namely the need to avoid widespread liability.

Lord Brandon dissented, arguing that the majority's decision created, between parties who were not in a contractual relationship, the sort of liability that should only arise in the law of contract. We shall see that it has proved very difficult to extract the *ratio* of *Junior Books*, and that the case has met with considerable judicial criticism. In *D. & F. Estates Ltd v Church Commissioners*,[15] for example, Lord Bridge gave his support to Lord Brandon's dissenting view, stating that his Lordship had enunciated principles of "fundamental importance" and that the decision in *Junior Books* could not be regarded as laying down any principle of general application.[16] Although *Junior Books* has never been overruled, it is nowadays regarded as having turned on its own special facts, and is unlikely to be followed.

The liberal approach to economic loss, then, exemplified by *Junior Books* and *Anns*, was short-lived. The courts quickly came to see that those decisions threatened to undermine the principles of contract law. Moreover, they were concerned that the prospect of widespread local authority liability raised by *Anns* might lead to an unacceptable drain on the public purse. These matters are considered below.

[13] [1983] 1 A.C. 520 at 546.
[14] [1983] 1 A.C. 520 at 547.
[15] [1989] A.C. 177.
[16] [1989] A.C. 177 at 202.

## THE "ACTIVITY" CASES: PRINCIPLES OF THE MODERN LAW

**3–012**   The courts now adopt a more restrictive approach to economic loss. Although the law is complex, it is possible clearly to identify three guiding principles which limit the scope of the duty of care. These principles, which all concern the problem of drawing a boundary between contract law and tort law, can be summarised as follows:

- economic loss is not generally recoverable in tort where this would undermine contractual intentions;

- "defective product economic loss" is not generally recoverable;

- a claimant cannot generally recover in respect of damage to property unless he or she has a proprietary interest in the property which is damaged.

Each principle is examined below.

## (1) No recovery where contractual intentions are undermined

**3–013**   There are a number of good reasons why tort law should not be allowed to circumvent the expressed intentions of contracting parties. First, it is arguable that allowing the parties, through contracts, to determine where liability will fall if things go wrong makes for economic efficiency. This is because the parties may choose to allocate risk to the person who can absorb that risk at least cost, perhaps by obtaining the cheapest insurance policy. Certainly, where all of the risk is allocated to a main contractor, who then employs sub-contractors, the transaction costs involved in taking out multiple insurance policies are avoided. Secondly, it is obvious that the quality of a product must be related to the price a person has paid for it. It makes little sense for the law of tort to regulate the quality of products (except to prevent them causing personal injury or damage to other property) because this is a matter for the market and for the rules of contract law. Freedom of contract exists precisely to allow the parties to trade off quality against price. If tort law begins to impose obligations to supply goods of a certain quality, it interferes with this process of bargaining, rendering the rules of contract law redundant.

*Contracts (Rights of Third Parties) Act 1999*

**3–014**   In *Junior Books*, tort law was used, in effect, to circumvent the strict rules of privity of contract. If the case were to arise today, there is a possibility that a court might impose liability via an alternative route that does not require recourse to the tort of negligence. This is because the rules of privity have been reformed. The Contracts (Rights of Third Parties) Act 1999 provides that where a third party is *expressly identified* in a contract (either by name or as a member of a class) and that contract either:

- expressly states that its terms are enforceable by the third party, *or*

- purports to confer a benefit on the third party, and, on a proper construction of the contract, it appears that the parties intend the contract to be enforceable by the third party,

the third party may sue on the contract as if he had been a party to it.[17]

---

[17]  Contracts (Rights of Third Parties) Act 1999 s.1.

It seems probable that Junior Books would have been identified in the contract between the main contractor and Veitchi. It is uncertain, however, whether on a proper construction of that contract, a court would feel able to say that the parties to the contract intended that it should be enforceable by Junior Books. It is important to note that the provisions of the Act place the emphasis firmly on the intentions of the contracting parties. The Act does not allow the courts to *impose* obligations on contracting parties in spite of their intentions. Arguably, this was what happened in *Junior Books*. In a line of subsequent cases, however, the Court of Appeal has repeatedly affirmed that it will not permit tort law to be used in this way.

### The retreat from Junior Books

In *Muirhead v Industrial Tank Specialities*,[18] an enterprising fishmonger conceived a plan to **3–015** buy lobsters during the summer months, when they were cheap, and resell them on the lucrative Christmas market. In order to store the lobsters, he contracted with the first defendants to build him a tank. The lobsters were stacked in the tank and kept alive in a semi-refrigerated immobile state. Sea-water had to be re-circulated through the tank in order to oxygenate it. This was achieved using a number of pumps which, though installed by the defendants, had been supplied to them by a third party. Because the motors driving the pumps had been made in France and were unsuitable for United Kingdom mains voltage, the pumps failed, causing the death of the lobsters.

Mr Muirhead successfully sued the first defendants for breach of contract, but they went into liquidation and were unable to satisfy the judgment. He therefore brought a claim in tort against the manufacturer of the pumps, claiming compensation for a number of things including: (1) the loss of the lobsters in the tank; (2) loss of profit consequent on loss of those lobsters; (3) expenditure incurred in trying to correct the fault with the pumps; (4) the cost of the pumps. The Court of Appeal, following the reasoning in *Spartan Steel*, held that Mr Muirhead could recover only for the damage to his property (the dead lobsters) and for the loss of profits consequent on that damage. He could not recover for the cost of the pumps or for the expenditure wasted in trying to fix them.

Relying on *Junior Books*, Mr Muirhead had argued that he had placed "reliance" on the manufacturer of the pumps and that the manufacturer had "assumed responsibility" for their quality. Robert Goff L.J., however, confessed difficulty in understanding the ratio of *Junior Books*. His Lordship said that the majority in *Junior Books* appeared to have stated that Veitchi had accepted a direct responsibility towards Junior Books for the quality of the floor, but pointed out that this proposition was very difficult to reconcile with the facts of the case—in fact, the parties had, through their contracts, deliberately structured their relationships so that Veitchi assumed responsibility only towards the main contractor, and the main contractor then assumed responsibility towards Junior Books.[19] Clearly, the parties *could* have structured their contractual relationships in such a way that Veitchi would have been directly responsible to Junior Books, but they had chosen not to do so. Thus, it was difficult to accept an argument based on "assumption of responsibility".

In any event, Robert Goff L.J. found it impossible to say that Mr Muirhead had relied on the manufacturer of the pumps in the same way that Junior Books had relied on Veitchi—he had not nominated the manufacturer to supply the pumps. On the contrary, he had never even heard of the pump manufacturer at the time the pumps were supplied. Here, therefore, there

---

[18] [1986] Q.B. 507.
[19] [1986] Q.B. 507 at 528.

was no close, quasi-contractual relationship. In the light of these difficulties, the Court of Appeal thought that the safest course of action was to treat *Junior Books* as a decision confined to its own facts. The decision in *Muirhead*, then, reflected a policy shift towards reaffirming the sharp distinction between contractual and tortious obligations—only contract would provide a remedy for "defective product economic loss".

This policy shift was further evidenced by the Court of Appeal's decision in *Greater Nottingham Co-operative Society v Cementation Piling Ltd.*[20] Here, the plaintiffs had employed contractors to build an extension to one of their buildings and the defendants were nominated sub-contractors, responsible for pile driving. They did this negligently so that completion of the building was delayed, causing the plaintiffs economic loss. Although there was a collateral contract between the plaintiffs and the defendants, the Court of Appeal was not prepared to find liability under *Junior Books*. Woolf L.J. stated:

> "Where, as here, the sub-contractor has entered into a direct contract and expressly undertaken a direct but limited contractual responsibility to the building owner, I regard the direct contract as being inconsistent with any assumption of responsibility beyond that which has been expressly undertaken."[21]

The contract, in setting out which materials were to be used and the design of the piles, therefore set out the sum total of the obligations which the defendants intended to assume towards the plaintiffs. This restrictive approach may also be seen in the Court of Appeal decisions in *Simaan v Pilkington Glass Ltd (No.2)*[22] and *Pacific Associates v Baxter.*[23] In both these cases, the courts held that in view of the way in which the parties had structured their contractual relationships, liability in tort would be inappropriate. The court in *Simaan* rejected the argument that a sub-contractor who had failed to provide the correct shade of glass should be liable to the plaintiffs, who, as main contractors, had suffered economic loss when their client refused to pay.[24] Dillon L.J. dismissed arguments that the principles of *Junior Books* should apply to allow the plaintiffs to sue a sub-contractor for supplying a defective product: "I find it difficult to see that future citation from the *Junior Books* case can ever serve any useful purpose".[25]

Similarly, in *Pacific Associates v Baxter*, the Court of Appeal rejected a claim by the plaintiffs, who had been employed to undertake certain dredging work, against an engineer who had been retained by their employer to supervise the work. The substance of the claim was that the engineer had failed to certify that the plaintiffs were entitled to extra payments when they met with hard material in the course of dredging which made the work more difficult. The Court of Appeal held that in the light of the way the parties had structured their contractual relationships—there was no contract between the engineer and the plaintiffs; his contract was with the employers and contained a general disclaimer of liability[26]—it would be

---

[20] [1989] Q.B. 71.
[21] [1989] Q.B. 71 at 106.
[22] [1988] 2 W.L.R. 761.
[23] [1990] 1 Q.B. 993.
[24] The client (Sheikh Al-Oteiba) had specified that panels of green glass should be incorporated into the curtain wall of the building; green being the colour of peace in Islam. The panels, on arrival, were found to contain shades of red.
[25] *Simaan v Pilkington Glass Ltd (No.2)* [1988] 2 W.L.R. 761 at 778.
[26] Compare *J. Jarvis & Sons Ltd v Castle Wharf Developments Ltd* [2001] EWCA Civ 19; [2001] Lloyd's Rep P. N. 308.

inconsistent to hold that the engineer owed a duty in tort to avoid causing the plaintiffs economic loss. All of these decisions, then, show that under the modern law the courts are unwilling to allow economic loss claims where to do so would interfere with expressed contractual intentions.[27]

## (2) "Defective product economic loss" generally not recoverable

We have seen that in *Muirhead* the cost of replacing the pumps was not recoverable in tort. This was a claim for "defective product economic loss"—whilst the pumps had caused damage to *other property* (the lobsters), they were not themselves "damaged" in the tort lawyers' sense of the word; they were simply defective. The issue of "defective product economic loss" has arisen most frequently in relation to defective buildings (i.e. where the "product" in question is a building). We have seen that in the 1970s, the House of Lords was prepared to allow such a claim in *Anns*. In subsequent cases, however, their Lordships were reluctant to apply the principles in *Anns* with a broad brush, eventually overruling their decision in that case.

**3–016**

In *D. & F. Estates Ltd v Church Commissioners*,[28] the plaintiffs brought an action against sub-contractors who had negligently plastered the walls of a flat. They claimed for the cost of renewing the plaster and for the consequent disruption and loss of rent while the work took place. The House of Lords held that the claim failed because it was for economic loss, which was only recoverable in contract. A number of important points emerged from the decision. First, their Lordships saw a clear difference between, on the one hand, situations where a latent (undiscovered) defect materialised, causing damage to other property or personal injury, and, on the other hand, situations where a dangerous defect is discovered by the building owner before any such damage has occurred. In the latter case, the cost of remedying the defect—even where this is necessary in order to obviate an immediate threat of personal injury or damage to other property—was to be regarded as non-recoverable economic loss. This observation, although obiter to the decision in *D. & F. Estates*, did much to settle previous debate about whether a duty of care could be owed in respect of defects that posed an imminent danger, but had not yet caused any damage. The approach suggested in *D. & F. Estates* was subsequently applied in *Murphy v Brentwood DC*. The second point of importance was their Lordships' reference to what has become known as the "complex structure theory". (This is dealt with in a separate section below.)

On the question of whether tort law should be used to impose obligations of a contractual nature, their Lordships were clear: the plasterers could not be liable to the plaintiffs, with whom they had no contractual relationship, simply for a defect in the quality of their workmanship. Lord Oliver stated that, in English law, there were no such things as "transmissible warranties" of quality,[29] and Lord Bridge did not consider that tort should be used to impose ". . . the obligation of one who warranted the quality of the plaster as regards materials,

---

[27] This is also now the position adopted in Canada. See *Design ServicesLtd v Canada* [2008] 1 S.C.R. 737, 2008 SCC 22. Note that the reverse does not necessarily apply. See *Riyad Bank v Ahli United Bank (UK) Plc* [2006] EWCA Civ 780; [2006] 2 Lloyd's Rep. 292. (The absence of a contractual relationship does not necessarily mean there can be no assumption of responsibility, even where contractual responsibility is assumed by another party.)

[28] [1989] A.C. 177.

[29] [1989] A.C. 214. Note that "transmissible warranties" are now, of course, provided for under the Contracts (Rights of Third Parties) Act 1999.

workmanship and fitness for purpose."[30] Dealing with *Anns*, Lord Oliver commented that the "underlying logical basis" of the case was "not entirely clear".[31]

The leading case is now *Murphy v Brentwood DC*.[32] Here, Brentwood Council, relying on the negligent advice of its consulting engineers, approved the building plans for a house. There were certain errors in the design of the foundations which made them defective. Mr Murphy subsequently bought the house, and, while he was in occupation, the foundations cracked, causing extensive damage. The gas, water and sewage pipes underneath the house began to rupture, posing a danger to Mr Murphy and his family and forcing them to move out. Instead of repairing the house, Mr Murphy sold it to a builder for considerably less than he had paid for it. He then sued the council for his financial loss.

The claim failed. The House of Lords held that Mr Murphy could not recover his economic loss. On the question of whether the law would allow claims for damage to "other property" caused by a defective building, their Lordships held that, whilst a local authority (or a builder) might be liable in tort if a *latent* (undiscovered) defect suddenly materialised, causing personal injury, or damage to property other than the building itself, no duty of care was owed in respect of damage caused by a defect that had become *apparent*. "Apparent", in this context, meant that the defect had already been discovered by the claimant, or that he or she ought reasonably to have discovered it. The cost of replacing "other property" damaged by an apparent defect was, like the defect itself, to be regarded as economic loss.

*Apparent defects: exceptions to the general rule*

**3–017**   There appear to be two exceptions to the principle stated in *Murphy* that there can be no liability in tort for damage caused by a defect in a building once that defect has been discovered. One of these exceptions arises from the subsequent decision of the Court of Appeal in *Targett v Torfaen BC*.[33] Another arises from certain observations made in *Murphy* itself:

*(i)  A claimant may recover for injury caused by an apparent defect where it is unreasonable to expect the claimant to repair the defect or vacate the building*

**3–018**   In *Targett v Torfaen BC* a council tenant was injured when he fell down some steps that had been poorly designed and were not adequately lit. When he sued the council, the defence was raised that because the defect in the steps was apparent, it was a matter of economic loss—the tenancy was simply less valuable than it might have been. It was argued that, because there was no liability for the defect, it followed that that there could be no liability for the injury it had caused. To put it another way, the tenant should be regarded as the author of his own misfortune by failing either to remedy the defect or to vacate the property.

The Court of Appeal rejected the council's argument, holding that *Murphy* did not lay down any absolute rule to the effect that a claimant who suffered personal injury because of a defect

---

[30]  [1989] A.C. 177 at 207.

[31]  [1989] A.C. 177 at 216.

[32]  [1991] 1 A.C. 398. The reasoning in *Murphy* was applied in *Department of Environment v Thomas Bates & Son Ltd* [1991] A.C. 499, an opinion handed down on the same day. For examples of how *Murphy* has subsequently been applied, see *Blaxhall Securities Ltd v Sheard Walshaw Partnership* [2001] B.L.R. 36; *Payne v John Setchell Ltd* [2002] B.L.R. 489 and also *Robinson v PE Jones (Contractors) Ltd* [2011] EWCA Civ 9

[33]  [1992] 3 All E.R. 27.

was automatically barred from recovery because of his or her knowledge of the defect.[34] In the case of many householders, it would be quite unrealistic to expect them to vacate their homes for fear of being injured by a relatively small defect. Therefore, liability should be decided by reference to whether, in the circumstances, it was reasonable to expect the householder to remain in the building.

*(ii) A claimant may recover where the defect is a potential source of liability to neighbouring landowners*

In *Murphy*, Lord Bridge suggested that:                                                                     **3–019**

> ". . . if a building stands so close to the boundary of the building owner's land that after discovery of the dangerous defect it remains a potential source of injury to persons or property on neighbouring land or on the highway, the building owner ought, in principle, to be entitled to recover in tort from the negligent builder the cost of obviating the danger . . . so far as that cost is necessarily incurred in order to protect himself from potential liability to third parties."[35]

His Lordship did not explain the reasoning behind this exception to the general rule, but it has been suggested that it might be explained on the basis that such a building would also constitute a nuisance, entitling the neighbouring land-owner to an injunction ordering that it be demolished or made safe.[36] It is possible, of course, that his Lordship's intention was to create a general exception, going beyond the case of neighbouring land-owners, to the effect that any expenditure in repairing a defective building might be recoverable where it was necessary to avoid liability to a third party. This is unlikely, however, because the implications of such a rule would be, for example, that Mr Murphy could have recovered the cost of repairing his house by arguing that this was necessary to protect himself from a law suit by his family or his visitors.

*The "complex structure theory"*

In *D. & F. Estates*, Lords Bridge and Oliver, seeking to distinguish *Anns*, appeared to suggest   **3–020** that the decision might be explained on the basis of the "complex structure theory". Before we consider this, it is important to emphasise that, in the light of *Murphy*, the theory has no application where a defect in property has already been discovered.[37] Rather, the theory may be advanced as a way of explaining how damage to some parts of a building (or product), caused by an undiscovered defect materialising, might be recoverable, even though the cost of replacing the defect itself is not.

According to the "complex structure" theory, it might be possible to regard the constituent parts of a building as *separate items of property*, instead of regarding the whole building as a distinct and indivisible entity. On this basis, their Lordships in *D. & F. Estates* thought it might be possible to say that the defective foundations in *Anns* were separate from the rest of the

---

[34] Such a proposition would have been inconsistent with the Court of Appeal's decision in *Rimmer v Liverpool City Council* [1985] Q.B. 1, which had not been referred to in *Murphy*.

[35] *Murphy v Brentwood DC* [1991] 1 A.C. 398 at 475.

[36] Rogers, *Winfield & Jolowicz on Tort* (18th edn, Sweet & Maxwell, 2010) p.479.

[37] This proposition, of course, is subject to the reasoning in *Targett v Torfaen BC* [1992] 3 All E.R. 27, viz. that there might be liability for damage caused by an apparent defect which the householder cannot reasonably be expected to fix. It is unclear, however, whether the reasoning in *Targett* would be extended to cover cases of property damage.

building, and that they had caused damage to "other property", namely the walls. It followed that there would be no objection to liability for the cost of repairing the walls, and, of course, to repair the cracked walls properly it would be necessary to rebuild the building, replacing the defective foundations themselves.

In *Murphy*, however, the House of Lords rejected the "complex structure theory" as an explanation for *Anns*—it was wholly unrealistic to view a building as distinct from its foundations. Lords Keith, Bridge and Jauncey did not, however, rule out the application of a limited version of the theory in appropriate cases. Thus, in a case where a defective central heating boiler (unexpectedly) exploded and damaged a house, or where a defective electrical installation set a house on fire, Lord Bridge thought that the owner of the house could recover damages against a builder on the basis that damage had been caused by one piece of property (for example, the boiler) to "other property" (the house).[38] Lord Jauncey, whilst agreeing that the theory could apply to the examples given by Lord Bridge, went further, stating that the theory might operate where:

> ". . . one integral component of the structure was built by a separate contractor and where a defect in such a component had caused damage to other parts of the structure, e.g. a steel frame erected by a specialist contractor which failed to give adequate support to floors and walls."[39]

In Lord Jauncey's example, then, the presence of a separate contractor is the crucial feature which brings the theory into play. The limits of the theory, however, remain unexplored.[40]

*Defective Premises Act 1972*

3–021    It is appropriate here to mention the Defective Premises Act 1972. At the same time that the judges had been considering liability for defective premises at common law, the matter was being considered by the Law Commission, whose conclusions led to the passing of the Act. In the more recent cases, therefore, the courts, in developing this area of law, have been concerned not to create liability that is wider than that provided for by Parliament. The Act provides for the liability of builders and other professionals involved in the construction of "dwellings", but the extent of their liability is much more restricted than that which had been envisaged in *Anns*. For a time, the decision in *Anns* had the effect of making the Act something of a dead letter, but the decision in *Murphy* restored its importance.

Under the Act, persons who undertake work for, or in connection with, the provision of a dwelling have a statutory duty to see that the work is done in a workmanlike or professional manner and with proper materials so that, as regards that work, the dwelling will be fit for habitation when completed.[41] The duty is imposed not only on the builders of dwellings, but also, for example, on the architects, surveyors and sub-contractors involved. Moreover, the

---

[38] *Murphy v Brentwood DC* [1991] 1 A.C. 398 at 478.

[39] *Murphy* [1991] 1 A.C. 398 at 497.

[40] See, however, *Aswan Engineering Establishment Co v Lupdine Ltd* [1987] 1 All E.R. 135, where defective containers caused damage to the proofing compound they contained. Lloyd L.J. was of the "provisional view" that the proofing compound was "other property", even though it had been bought in the containers from the same supplier. But see also *Bacardi-MartiniBeverages Ltd v Thomas Hardy Packaging Ltd* [2002] EWCA Civ 549, and note Mance L.J., at para.18, who points out that this pre-*Murphy* case does little to resolve borderline cases of complex structure.)

[41] Defective Premises Act 1972 s.1. See also *Bole v Huntsbuild Ltd* [2009] EWCA Civ 1146.

duty is owed not only to a person commissioning the work, but also to every person who later acquires an interest (whether legal or equitable) in the dwelling. The Act provides a remedy for mere defects in quality (provided they make the house unfit for habitation) without the claimant having to show an imminent danger of personal injury or damage to other property.

For many years, the effect of the Act was substantially curtailed. This was because the Act does not apply to houses protected by an "approved scheme". Most newly constructed dwelling houses are built under a scheme operated by the National House Building Council (NHBC), and until the late 1980s, the NHBC scheme was an "approved scheme", so that most new houses were not covered by the Act. But now that the NHBC no longer submits its scheme for approval by the Secretary of State, the Act has a wider field of application.[42] Under the Act, however, a claimant's position is much less favourable than under the common law as it was developed in *Anns*. This is because a six-year limitation period begins to run when the dwelling is completed.[43] If the common law in *Anns* had remained unchanged, the claimant could have taken advantage of a limitation period that started to run only when symptoms of the defect became reasonably discoverable.[44]

## (3) No recovery unless claimant has proprietary interest in damaged property[45]

The principles enunciated in *Cattle, Weller*, and *Spartan Steel* remain an important feature of the modern law. Thus, in *The Mineral Transporter*,[46] one ship, the Mineral Transporter, collided with another, the Ibaraki Maru, because of the negligence of the Mineral Transporter's crew. The first plaintiffs, who were in fact the owners of the Ibaraki Maru, had let it on a charterparty to the second plaintiffs. The second plaintiffs had then re-let it back to the first plaintiffs. When the first plaintiffs—not in their capacity as *owners* but as *charterers* of the ship—sued for economic loss caused while the ship was being repaired, the Privy Council held that they had no cause of action, re-affirming the principle established in *Cattle v Stockton Waterworks* that a person cannot sue in respect of damage to property in which he or she has only a contractual interest.

In *Leigh and Sillivan Ltd v Aliakmon Shipping Co Ltd (The Aliakmon)*,[47] the plaintiffs had contracted to buy a cargo of steel coils to be shipped from Korea. The arrangements between the plaintiffs and the sellers of the coils were such that, although the *risk* in the cargo had passed to the plaintiffs, the *ownership* of the coils had not. When the coils were damaged at sea by the defendant shippers' negligence, the plaintiffs, who had to pay for the damaged

**3–022**

---

[42] It should be noted, however, that the NHBC scheme generally provides superior cover in comparison with the Act because claims for major structural defects may be made for up to 10 years.

[43] Defective Premises Act 1972 s.1(5).

[44] The Latent Damage Act 1986 made the claimant's position more favourable in building cases at common law by providing a limitation period of three years running from the date damage was reasonably discoverable. The Act is now a dead letter in this regard, however, because, under *Murphy*, claimants have no cause of action in the first place.

[45] Contrast the position in Canada: *The Norsk (Canadian National Railway Co v Norsk Pacific Steamship Co)* (1992) 91 D.L.R. (4th) 289; *Bow Valley Husky (Bermuda) v Saint John Shipbuilding Ltd* (1998) 153 D.L.R. (4th) 385. Note also *Colour Quest Ltd v Total Downstream UK Plc (aka Shell UK Ltd v Total UK Ltd)* [2010] EWCA Civ 180. (Joining a legal owner to proceedings in respect of property damage will suffice to enable a beneficial owner of that property to recover.)

[46] *Candlewood Navigation Corp. Ltd v Mitsui O.S.K. Lines (The Mineral Transporter)* [1986] A.C. 1.

[47] [1986] A.C. 785. Applied in *Homburg Houtimport BV v Agrosin Private Ltd (The Starsin)* [2003] 2 W.L.R. 711.

goods, sought to recover their financial loss from the negligent shippers. The loss to the plaintiffs was clearly foreseeable, and in arrangements for the carriage of goods by sea, situations where the party likely to suffer loss is not the owner of the cargo are quite common. Nevertheless, the House of Lords denied the plaintiffs a remedy, holding that because they had had only a contractual interest in the coils at the time they were damaged, they were unable to recover.[48] This resulted in the somewhat bizarre situation that the person who had suffered the loss had no remedy, whilst the person who had a remedy (the owner of the coils) had suffered no loss (he had been paid for the damaged goods). As we shall see below, however, in the context of solicitors drafting wills, it is precisely this dilemma that has prompted the House of Lords to allow disappointed beneficiaries to recover economic loss.

## THE "WILL DRAFTING" CASES

**3–023**     There is one type of "activity" case that defies analysis in terms of the principles we have so far examined. The courts have held that a solicitor, in preparing a will for a testator, owes a duty of care to intended beneficiaries of the will to prevent them from suffering economic loss.

### The decision in *Ross v Caunters*

**3–024**     In *Ross v Caunters*,[49] the defendant solicitor failed to tell a testator that if his will was witnessed by the spouse of a beneficiary, any gift to that beneficiary would be void. The plaintiff, whose husband had witnessed the will, sued the solicitor for the loss of her gift under the will. Sir Robert Megarry V.C. held that the solicitor owed the plaintiff a duty of care and was liable. His Lordship found assistance in the decision of the High Court of Australia in *Caltex Oil (Australia) Pty Ltd v Dredge "Willemstad"*.[50] In that case, the owner of a dredger, which fractured a submerged oil pipeline, was held liable to an oil company. The oil company was not the owner of the pipeline, but it had the right to receive oil through it, and therefore incurred expense in transporting the oil by other means while the pipeline was being repaired. Mason and Gibbs JJ. were prepared to depart from the rule against recovery for damage to property belonging to others because, in this case, the negligence in question affected only a single clearly foreseeable plaintiff—it followed that the "floodgates" objection to economic loss claims did not apply. Applying similar reasoning, Sir Robert Megarry V.C. was prepared to say that liability in *Ross v Caunters* should follow, either by an extension of the *"Hedley Byrne* principle" (discussed later in this chapter), or by a direct application of the principle of *Donoghue v Stevenson*.[51] In any event, the decision was not likely to lead to indeterminate liability, because the specific intended beneficiaries would be persons known to the solicitor who was supposed to draft the will, and the sums of money at stake would be ascertained and finite.

---

[48] Note that the Carriage of Goods by Sea Act 1992 introduced certain amendments to the law which would nowadays enable claimants to recover.
[49] [1980] Ch.297.
[50] (1976) 136 C.L.R. 529.
[51] [1932] A.C. 562.

After the decision in *Ross v Caunters*, a number of cases seemed to cast doubt on whether it had been correctly decided. In *The Aliakmon*, for example, Robert Goff L.J., in the Court of Appeal, confessed difficulty in accepting the principle put forward in the *Caltex Oil* case, on which Sir Robert Megarry V.C. had relied. Similarly, in *The Mineral Transporter* (discussed above), the Privy Council considered the *Caltex* case, but were unable to extract any clear ratio from it and declined to apply it. In *White v Jones*, however, the House of Lords (employing different reasoning) upheld the decision in *Ross v Caunters*.

## The decision in *White v Jones*

In *White v Jones*,[52] a testator had quarrelled with his two daughters and had made a will **3–025** cutting them out of their inheritance. Subsequently, he became reconciled with them, so he instructed the defendants to prepare a new will under which they were to be left £9,000 each. The defendants failed to act promptly on these instructions. The solicitor dealing with the matter arranged to meet the testator three times, but failed to keep the appointments. He then went on holiday. When he returned, he made a further appointment to see the testator, but unfortunately the testator, who was 78, died three days before the meeting. The estate was distributed according to the old will, depriving the daughters of their intended legacies. They brought an action against the defendants, claiming £9,000 each in damages.

By a bare majority, the House of Lords upheld the daughters' claims. Lord Goff was content to decide the case by a very broad application of the principle laid down in *Hedley Byrne v Heller & Partners* (discussed below), but declined to follow the reasoning in *Ross v Caunters*, stating that that case had raised a number of conceptual difficulties. Lords Browne-Wilkinson and Nolan held that the defendants had assumed responsibility for the task of preparing the new will and that, as a matter of law, this meant that they had *assumed responsibility to the plaintiffs*. Lord Nolan also thought that the plaintiffs could be said to have *relied* on the defendants, who were acting as family solicitors. Lords Keith and Mustill dissented. Lord Keith stated that to allow the claim would, in effect, be to give the plaintiffs the benefit of a contract (between the testator and the defendants) to which they were not parties.

The overriding factor that seemed to influence the decisions in *Ross v Caunters* and *White v Jones* was the need to do practical justice in the circumstances. In such cases, the courts are faced with an exceptional situation where the only people who suffer loss (the intended beneficiaries) would, on traditional principles, be denied a remedy, but the only person who has a traditional remedy (the estate) suffers no loss. This situation leaves, as Lord Goff put it in *White v Jones*, "a lacuna in the law which needs to be filled".[53] It is interesting to note, however, that the decisions in these cases produce, arguably, injustice of a different kind. This is because those legally entitled to the deceased's estate receive a windfall, in the sense that the deceased does not intend that the money should go to them, while those to whom the money *should* have gone recover from the negligent solicitor. It may be argued that a truly coherent legal system should find a way of giving effect to the testator's intentions without causing this enrichment of the estate—after all (as we can see from the early behaviour of the testator in *White v Jones*) an intention to deprive may sometimes be just as important as an intention to bequeath!

---

[52] [1995] 2 A.C. 207.
[53] [1995] 2 A.C. 207 at 260.

## The limits of the *"Ross v Caunters* principle"

**3–026**   Subsequent cases have made it clear that the ratios of *Ross v Caunters* and *White v Jones* are limited in a number of respects. First, it is unlikely that the cases have any application to gifts made between living persons.[54] Thus, in *Hemmens v Wilson Browne*,[55] a certain Mr Panter, who was having an affair with the plaintiff, instructed his solicitors to draft a document that would entitle her to call upon him for the sum of £110,000 at any time in the future. The solicitors drafted a document which had no legal effect—it was not a deed (because it was not under seal) and it was not a contract (because there was no consideration). When the plaintiff asked Mr Panter to fulfil his promise, he refused to pay, having gone back to his wife. Unable to enforce the terms of the document, the plaintiff sued the solicitors, arguing that their negligent drafting had caused her to lose her gift. It was held that the special policy considerations which had dictated the outcomes in *Ross v Caunters* and *White v Jones*[56] did not apply here— Mr Panter, being still alive, would be able to rectify the situation, if he so wished, by instructing a solicitor to re-draft the document properly.

Secondly, it has been held that the *Ross v Caunters* principle can only be invoked in situations where the claimant has exhausted his or her other remedies. Thus, in *Walker v Geo. H. Medlicott & Son*,[57] the claimant sued solicitors who had been instructed to include a gift to him in a client's will, but had negligently failed to do so. The circumstances were such that the claimant was entitled to have the will rectified under s.20 of the Administration of Justice Act 1982. The Court of Appeal held that he could not bring an alternative claim in negligence.[58]

In *Worby v Rosser*[59] an attempt was made to apply the *Ross v Caunters* principle in a novel context. The testator had made a will in 1983, leaving money to the plaintiffs. Subsequently, he came under the influence of an associate who acted fraudulently in persuading him to make a new will, in 1989, under which the associate stood to benefit substantially. The plaintiffs successfully contested the new will, and it was refused probate, the 1983 will being admitted in its place. The plaintiffs brought an action against the solicitor who had drafted the new will, seeking to recover the legal costs they had incurred in disproving it. They argued that the solicitor had been negligent in failing to realise that the testator had lacked testamentary capacity and had been acting under undue influence. The Court of Appeal held that the *Ross v Caunters* principle could not be extended to cover such a situation. There was no authority to suggest that a solicitor owed a duty of care to beneficiaries of an earlier will. Moreover, the special circumstances in *Ross* and *White* were not present here. The expense of contesting the new will was a loss suffered by the *estate*, which it could recover from the solicitor. Therefore it could not be said that the person suffering the loss had no remedy.

---

[54] Although both Sir Donald Nicholls V.C. in the Court of Appeal in *White v Jones* [1995] 2 A.C. 207 (at 227) and Sir Robert Megarry V.C. in *Ross v Caunters* [1980] Ch.297 (at 322) thought that the principle could be applied to inter vivos gifts.

[55] [1993] 4 All E.R. 826.

[56] *White v Jones* was a Court of Appeal decision at the time.

[57] [1999] 1 W.L.R. 727.

[58] Compare *Horsefall v Haywards* [1999] 1 F.L.R. 1182. (There can be no objection to a negligence action where there is little likelihood that rectification will succeed.)

[59] *The Times*, June 9, 1999; [1999] Lloyd's Rep. P.N. 972.

# Economic Loss Caused by Negligent Statements and Services

The law on negligent misstatement has developed differently from the law relating to negli-   **3–027**
gent activities (although certain concepts were borrowed by the latter during its development).
This divergence in the law produces a somewhat uneasy result. For example, a surveyor who
negligently advises on the purchase of a defective house may, as we shall see, be liable for
economic loss caused as a result of his advice, whilst a builder who causes economic loss by
constructing a house negligently may escape liability.[60] It must be admitted that it is almost
impossible to reconcile the two branches of the law, more especially because, as we point out
in the conclusion to this chapter, the distinction between "activity" and "statement" cases is
often extremely fine. The lack of clarity in the law is compounded by the fact that, as we shall
see, the House of Lords has been prepared to extend the principle developed in negligent
misstatement cases to cases involving the negligent provision of services.

## The old law

In 1951, the Court of Appeal decided *Candler v Crane Christmas & Co*.[61] Here, the defend-   **3–028**
ants, a firm of accountants, prepared the accounts of a company knowing that the figures they
produced would be relied on by the plaintiff in deciding whether to invest in the company. The
accounts were prepared negligently, causing the plaintiff financial loss. The majority of the
Court of Appeal reaffirmed existing precedent, holding that liability for a careless (as opposed
to fraudulent) statement could only arise where the maker of the statement had a contractual
or fiduciary relationship with the plaintiff. Denning L.J. dissented. In his Lordship's view,
existing precedent was inapplicable, because it was based on the idea that the existence of a
contractual relationship would prevent a duty of care from being owed to third parties—and
this was a myth that had been exploded by the decision in *Donoghue v Stevenson*. Denning
L.J.'s dissenting view, then, paved the way for the change in the law that was to take place in
*Hedley Byrne & Co v Heller & Partners*.[62]

## The "*Hedley Byrne* principle"

The facts of *Hedley Byrne* were set out in Ch.2. It will be recalled that the claim was in respect   **3–029**
of a negligently given banking reference (accompanied by a disclaimer) on which the plaintiffs relied, suffering financial loss. The House of Lords held that, in view of the disclaimer,
the defendants had not accepted any legal responsibility towards the plaintiffs, so the claim
failed. What is important, however, is that their Lordships went on to consider what the position would have been in the absence of the disclaimer, holding that there was no reason in
principle why a duty of care should not be owed in respect of careless statements. Their
Lordships held that the majority in *Candler* had wrongly decided that case, and that the view
of Denning L.J. was to be preferred.

---

[60] For further discussion of this anomaly, see Stapleton (1991) 107 L.Q.R. 249 and Markesinis and Deakin (1992) 55
M.L.R. 619.
[61] [1951] 2 K.B. 164.
[62] [1964] A.C. 465.

The decision in *Hedley Byrne* represented a radical change in the law, because it was the first time that the duty of care had been extended to cover pure economic loss. The House of Lords was not, however, prepared to decide the case simply by extending the principle of *Donoghue v Stevenson*. Their Lordships noted that because statements may be repeated, and then relied on by an unlimited number of people, the effects of negligent statements have a much greater propensity to spread throughout society than do the effects of negligently manufactured products. In the case of statements, therefore, the law had to impose tighter controls on the scope of liability. Accordingly, their Lordships laid down two requirements which a claimant will need to satisfy to establish a duty of care in respect of a statement. These may be summarised as follows:

- the existence of a "special relationship" between the claimant and the defendant, involving an "assumption of responsibility" by the defendant;

- "reasonable reliance" by the claimant.

Taken together, these factors may be referred to as the *"Hedley Byrne* principle". We have seen that the factors in question were used to establish liability in *Junior Books*. We have also seen that in *Muirhead*, and in subsequent "careless activity" cases, the courts were critical of the way they had been applied in *Junior Books*, pointing out that where contracts exist, setting out the nature of the relationships between parties, it is inappropriate to talk about "special relationships" existing independently of those contracts. In negligent misstatement cases, however, the *"Hedley Byrne* principle" has continued to be regarded as important, although it is noteworthy that it has not escaped academic criticism.[63] In particular, it has been pointed out that in *Hedley Byrne*, the plaintiffs, in effect, were given the benefit of a contractual warranty for which they had not paid—there was nothing to stop the plaintiffs from protecting themselves in law by entering into a contract with the defendant bank for the supply of the advice, but instead they sought to "free-load" on the bank's advice, and then to impose a contractual type of liability when the advice proved wrong. Below, we explore each element of the *"Hedley Byrne* principle" in turn.

## (1)  "Special relationship" and "assumption of responsibility"

3–030     The ideas of "special relationship" and "assumption of responsibility" cannot really be examined in isolation from one another, because both phrases are ways of saying the same thing, namely that there is a sufficient degree of "proximity" between the claimant and the defendant. This is a rather complex area of the law, but it can be broken down into a number of discrete issues, which are considered below.

*When will a "special relationship" normally arise?*

3–031     In *Hedley Byrne*, Lord Reid thought that a "special relationship" would arise where:

> "it is plain that the party seeking information or advice was trusting the other to exercise such a degree of care as the circumstances required, where it was reasonable for him to do that, and where the other gave the information or advice when he knew or ought to have known that the inquirer was relying on him".[64]

---

[63] See, e.g. Weir [1963] C.L.J. 216.
[64] [1964] A.C. 465 at 486.

His Lordship went on to say that a reasonable man, when asked for advice, and realising that his skill and judgment might be relied on, would have three options open to him: he could keep silent; he could give an answer with a clear qualification that he accepted no responsibility for it (a disclaimer); or he could simply answer without any such qualification. A person who chose the last option would be held to have assumed responsibility for his or her answer being given carefully, and therefore would owe a duty of care to the recipient of the advice.

Whether a special relationship exists in any given circumstance is essentially decided by an evaluation of the particular facts of a case. Thus, for example, in *Patchett v Swimming Pool & Allied Trades Association Ltd*[65], where a trade association had made a statement on its web site, the Court of Appeal decided that it could not fairly be said that the association had "assumed responsibility" for the accuracy of that statement, given that the web site itself urged browsers to make further enquiries.

*Can a "special relationship" arise in a purely social context?*

Lord Reid, in *Hedley Byrne*, made it clear that a "special relationship" could only arise where    **3–032**
the statement was made in a "business connection". There would be no liability for statements made on purely social occasions. This was because, as his Lordship observed:

> "Quite careful people often express definite opinions on social or informal occasions even when they see that others are likely to be influenced by them; and they often do that without taking that care which they would take if asked for their opinion professionally or in a business connection."[66]

Interestingly, the Court of Appeal seemed to depart from this fundamental principle in *Chaudhry v Prabhakar*.[67] Here, a family friend agreed to help the plaintiff find a second-hand car, telling her that she could rely on him and that she need not have the car inspected by a mechanic. The defendant, through his negligence, advised the plaintiff to buy a car which, it turned out, was unroadworthy and practically worthless. Before the trial, the defendant conceded that he owed a duty of care to the plaintiff. A majority of the court held that this concession had been rightly made, and that the plaintiff was able to recover her economic loss. May L.J., however, dissented. His Lordship doubted that any duty of care was owed. In May L.J.'s view, to impose liability in such a situation was undesirable, because it would make social relations between friends unnecessarily hazardous.

What makes the decision in *Chaudhry v Prabhakar* so extraordinary is that there was no suggestion that the defendant, Mr Prabhakar, was securing any benefit to himself by offering the free advice—he offered his services on a purely gratuitous basis. Thus, the situation is to be contrasted with *Hedley Byrne*, where the bank, although not of course paid for the advice, nevertheless supplied it to further their general business interests. As Lord Devlin observed, in *Hedley Byrne*:

> "It may often be material to consider whether the adviser is acting purely out of good nature or whether he is getting his reward in some indirect form. The service that a bank performs in giving a reference is not done simply out of a desire to assist commerce. It

---

[65] [2009] EWCA Civ 717.
[66] [1964] A.C. 465 at 482.
[67] [1989] 1 W.L.R. 29.

would discourage the customers of the bank if their deals fell through because the bank had refused to testify to their credit when it was good."[68]

The majority of the Court of Appeal in *Chaudhry v Prabhakar* did not appear to think it relevant that the defendant was acting "purely out of good nature". Reading between the lines, however, it might be possible to explain the decision on the basis that Mr Prabhakar's conduct clearly involved a risk of injury to Miss Chaudhry.

*Must the defendant be "in the business of giving advice"?*

3–033     The Privy Council, in *Mutual Life and Citizens' Assurance Co v Evatt*,[69] took a somewhat restricted view of the circumstances in which a "special relationship" could arise. Here, the plaintiff sought advice from his insurance company about the wisdom of investing in a company with which it was associated. He was given certain information that turned out to be false, and sought to recover the money he lost on his investment. The majority held that the *Hedley Byrne* principle should be confined to cases involving defendants whose profession includes the giving of advice, such as accountants, surveyors and lawyers. Since the defendants were in the business of providing insurance cover, not investment advice, they could not be liable. Lords Reid and Morris, however, dissented, holding that it was sufficient for the *Hedley Byrne* principle to apply if the advice was sought from a business person in the course of business. It is this minority view in *Mutual Life* which has found favour with the courts. Thus, in *Esso v Mardon*[70] (discussed below), Ormrod L.J. remarked that if the majority opinion were accepted, "the effect of *Hedley Byrne* would be so radically curtailed as to be virtually eliminated",[71] and in *Howard Marine and Dredging Co Ltd v Ogden & Sons Ltd*[72] (discussed later), both Lord Denning M.R. and Shaw L.J. made it clear that they preferred the minority view.

In *Esso v Mardon*, the plaintiff leased a filling station on the strength of Esso's advice that he could expect to sell at least 200,000 gallons of petrol a year. This forecast had been based on an assumption that the petrol pumps would be located at the front of the filling station on the main road. It then transpired that the local planning authority in fact required the pumps to be at the back of the filling station, where they would attract much less passing trade. Esso failed to revise its forecast in the light of that fact. The plaintiff sold only 78,000 gallons in 15 months, and sued Esso for his financial loss. In allowing the claim, the Court of Appeal held that Esso had assumed responsibility for the accuracy of its forecast and that it had been reasonable for Mr Mardon to rely on Esso's skill in predicting likely petrol sales.

*Employment references*

3–034     The decision in *Spring v Guardian Assurance Plc*[73] makes it clear that a "special relationship" will exist between an employer and an employee who asks for a job reference. Here, the

---

[68] [1964] A.C. 465 at 529.
[69] [1971] A.C. 793.
[70] [1976] 1 Q.B. 801.
[71] [1976] 1 Q.B. 801 at 827.
[72] [1978] 2 All E.R. 1134.
[73] [1995] 2 A.C. 296. See also *Cox v Sun Alliance Life Ltd* [2001] I.R.L.R. 448. Compare *Kapfunde v Abbey National Plc* [1999] I.C.R. 1 (no duty owed by a doctor retained by a prospective employer who had no professional relationship with the plaintiff) and *Legal & General Assurance Plc v Kirk* [2002] I.R.L.R. 124 (no liability for negligent statements not amounting to a reference). Compare *Lennon v Commissioner of Police* [2004] EWCA Civ 130 (liability of a personnel officer who misled claimant about his employment rights.)

plaintiff, Mr Spring, had been employed by the defendants but subsequently dismissed. He sought work with one of the defendants' competitors, but received such a bad reference that he failed to get the job. The statements in the reference, although made honestly, had given a misleading impression of the circumstances surrounding Mr Spring's dismissal, and had been made without a proper investigation of the facts. The House of Lords held that the defendants owed a duty of care in preparing the reference and, accordingly, were liable. It made no difference that if Mr Spring had sued in defamation, the defendants would have had the defence of qualified privilege.[74] The existence of this defence did not prevent liability in negligence. Nor, apparently, did it matter that this was a case where, exceptionally, the plaintiff was seeking to recover in respect of a statement that had not been made to *him* but to someone else.

*Provision of services (the "extended Hedley Byrne principle")*[75]

In *Spring v Guardian Assurance Plc*, Lord Goff, with whom Lord Lowry agreed, stated that, **3–035** in appropriate cases, the *Hedley Byrne* principle should not be limited to the provision of advice, but could be applied more generally to situations involving the provision of services. The proper interpretation of *Hedley Byrne*, according to Lord Goff, was that:

> "where the plaintiff entrusts the defendant with the conduct of his affairs, in general or in particular, the defendant may be held to have assumed responsibility to the plaintiff . . ."[76]

His Lordship approved Lord Morris's assertion in *Hedley Byrne* that: "The fact that the service is to be given by means of or by the instrumentality of words can make no difference".[77]

This wider application of the *Hedley Byrne* principle was also seen in *Henderson v Merrett Syndicates Ltd*.[78] The action, which involved five appeals, arose in the following way: in the early 1990s, there were a number of unusually large claims made against the Lloyds insurance organisation. These losses had to be borne by people known as "Names", who invest in Lloyds by underwriting their insurance policies. The Names are grouped into syndicates. The plaintiffs alleged that the agents who had organised their syndicates had been negligent in handling their affairs.

Without having to refer to a specific statement or piece of advice, the House of Lords was able to say that a duty of care was owed because the agents had assumed responsibility for the financial welfare of the Names. Their Lordships also confirmed that the existence of a contractual relationship between the claimant and the defendant does not preclude the existence of a "special relationship", giving rise to liability in tort. Many of the Names had contracts with the defendant agents, but sought to sue in tort because the limitation period for actions in contract had expired. Their Lordships held that they were entitled to take advantage of a longer limitation period which (for reasons that do not concern us here) was applicable in tort.

---

[74] See Ch.14.
[75] This expression was used by Lord Steyn in *Williams and Reid v Natural Life Health Foods Ltd and Mistlin* [1998] 1 W.L.R. 830 at 835 et seq.
[76] *Spring v Guardian Assurance Plc* [1995] 2 A.C. 296 at 318.
[77] [1964] A.C. 465 at 503.
[78] [1995] 2 A.C. 145. See also *Welton v North Cornwall DC* [1997] 1 W.L.R. 570. The defendants' environmental health officer had imposed excessive hygiene requirements on a guest house. The claim was held to be well within the *Hedley Byrne* principle, even though it could not be described as a case involving negligent "advice".

*Pensions Advice*

**3–036**    In *Gorham v British Telecommunications Plc*,[79] the Court of Appeal was prepared to hold that the *Hedley Byrne* principle could, in appropriate cases, make providers of financial services liable to the dependants of a deceased person who had been wrongly advised about how to make provision for them. Mr Gorham had opted out of his employer's pension scheme and had sought the advice of the Standard Life Assurance Co, making it clear that his first priority was to make provision for his wife and children in the event of his death. The company negligently failed to advise him that his employer's pension scheme might provide superior cover, and instead sold him one of its personal pension plans. Some months later, the company admitted its mistake and correctly advised Mr Gorham that his employer's scheme was better. Unfortunately, however, Mr Gorham did not re-join his employer's scheme, mistakenly believing that he was already a member. This meant that his dependants were not provided for when he died. The court upheld an action by the wife and children for loss of the pension rights to which they would have been entitled had Mr Gorham been correctly advised in the first place and remained a member of his employer's scheme. Their Lordships took the view that the situation was directly analogous to that in *White v Jones* (discussed above) and that, just as a solicitor owed a duty to see that a testator's intentions were given effect so as to provide for beneficiaries, a company selling a pension plan had a duty not to give negligent advice to a customer which adversely affected the interests of his dependants as he intended them to be.

*How do the courts justify the "assumption of responsibility" doctrine?*

**3–037**    In recent cases, then, the courts have increasingly used the concept of "assumption of responsibility" to justify imposing a duty of care on the defendant to protect the claimant from economic loss. This concept lies at the heart of the decisions in *Henderson* and *Spring* (discussed above). Yet the concept has not escaped criticism. In *Henderson*, Lord Goff noted that there had been a tendency for the courts to criticise the notion of "assumption of responsibility" on the basis that it was inconsistent with contractual arrangements between the parties.[80] His Lordship noted that in *Smith v Eric Bush* (discussed later) Lord Griffiths had said that the idea was "unlikely to be a helpful or realistic test in most cases" and that in *Caparo v Dickman*, Lord Roskill had expressed a similar view. Lord Goff pointed out, however, that in those cases, the criticism had been made by their Lordships in an effort to contain the scope of liability under *Hedley Byrne* (i.e. to avoid opening the floodgates of litigation). His Lordship thought that in a case like *Henderson*, where there was no danger of liability to an indeterminate class of claimants, there was no reason why the idea of "assumption of responsibility" should not be applied.

A similar approach was taken by Lord Steyn in *Williams and Reid v Natural Life Health Foods Ltd and Mistlin*[81] (discussed later). Delivering the opinion of the House of Lords, his Lordship dealt specifically with academic criticism that had been levied against the principle of assumption of responsibility (on the basis that it rested on a fiction used to justify a conclusion

---

[79] [2000] 1 W.L.R. 2129. See also *Weldon v GRE Linked Life Assurance Ltd* [2000] 2 All E.R. (Comm.) 914 (Life insurance company liable for presenting a direct debit mandate to the wrong branch of a bank, so that premiums were not collected and the policy lapsed.) Compare *Precis (521) Plc v William M. Mercer Ltd.* [2005] EWCA Civ 114; [2005] P.N.L.R. 28. (No liability for preparation of an actuarial report on the status of a pension fund.)

[80] *Henderson v Merrett Syndicates Ltd* [1995] 2 A.C. 145 at 181.

[81] [1998] 1 W.L.R. 830.

that a duty of care existed)[82] and said: "In my view the general criticism is overstated. Coherence must sometimes yield to practical justice". Lord Steyn explained that *Hedley Byrne* and subsequent cases had been decided using the principle because of the restrictive nature of the doctrines of privity and consideration in English contract law, and concluded:

> "... while the present structure of English contract law remains intact the law of tort, as the general law, has to fulfil an essential gap-filling role. In these circumstances there ... is no better rationalisation for the relevant head of tort liability than assumption of responsibility."

The difficulty of finding a workable and meaningful test for determining precisely when a defendant can be said to have "assumed responsibility" was recently considered by the House of Lords in *Customs & Excise Commissioners v Barclays Bank*.[83] Here, Customs officials, who were seeking to recover outstanding tax payments from two companies, had obtained "freezing orders" on those companies' bank accounts. This meant that the defendant bank was prohibited by law from allowing any money in the accounts to be paid out. Through inadvertence, however, the bank allowed funds to be withdrawn from the accounts. The Customs officials sought to recover these funds from the bank, arguing that, on receipt of the freezing order, the bank had "assumed responsibility" to them for economic losses arising from the funds being withdrawn. In denying the claim, their Lordships noted that the bank could not in any meaningful sense be said to have *assumed* responsibility—it had no choice about complying with the freezing order. Therefore, as Lord Bingham noted, it would not be appropriate here for the law of tort to fill any gap left by the rigidity of contract law—the relationship between the parties was in no sense equivalent to contract, because "the essence of any contract is voluntariness, and the bank's position was wholly involuntary".[84] Their Lordships stressed that, in deciding this type of case, it was important to appreciate that the concept of "assumption of responsibility" (like the concepts of "proximity" and "fair, just and reasonable" to which it was inextricably linked) was inherently imprecise and could provide only limited assistance. What was required was a detailed consideration of the factual matrix of each case in the light of relevant policy considerations.

*Can there be an "assumption of responsibility" where the defendant expressly disclaims responsibility?*

Whilst the question of "assumption of responsibility" is decided by reference to things said or done by the defendant, it is clear, of course, that the term does *not* imply that the defendant has *expressly indicated* acceptance of legal responsibility. Liability is imposed on the basis of an objective test, to which the expressed intentions of the defendant are only partly relevant. It follows that although a disclaimer will normally work to absolve the defendant from liability (as in *Hedley Byrne*), there may be exceptional circumstances in which liability will be imposed in spite of an assertion that the defendant accepts no legal responsibility for the advice in question. Such was the case in *Smith v Eric Bush*.[85]     **3–038**

---

[82] [1998] 1 W.L.R. 830 at 837. His Lordship specifically refers to Barker (1993) 109 L.Q.R. 461; Hepple (1997) 50 C. L. P. 69 at 88, and Cane, *Tort Law and Economic Interests*, (2nd edn, 1996, OUP), pp.177 and 200.
[83] [2006] UKHL 28.
[84] [2006] UKHL 28 at para.14. See also Lord Mance at para.94.
[85] [1990] 1 A.C. 831.

Here, the House of Lords decided two appeals in which the plaintiffs had suffered economic loss as a result of negligent surveys. In the first appeal (which serves to illustrate the decision), the plaintiff, Mrs Smith, wished to buy a house, and approached a building society for a mortgage. The building society instructed the defendants, a firm of surveyors, to carry out a visual inspection of the house in order to confirm that it was worth at least the money which they were proposing to lend. The defendants' valuer noticed that two chimney breasts had been removed, but he failed to check whether the chimneys had been left adequately supported. His report stated that no essential repairs were necessary.

The mortgage application form and the valuation report contained a disclaimer of liability. Mrs Smith was also informed that the report was not a structural survey and she was advised to obtain independent professional advice. The building society, pursuant to an agreement with Mrs Smith, who had paid an inspection fee, supplied her with a copy of the report. She, like many purchasers of modest houses, relied on it and purchased the house without any further survey. The chimneys were not adequately supported and one of them subsequently collapsed.

When Mrs Smith sought to recover her financial loss, the defendants argued that the disclaimer exempted them from liability. The House of Lords, however, held that the disclaimer was invalid under s.2 of the Unfair Contract Terms Act 1977. It did not satisfy the requirement of reasonableness set out in s.11(3) of that Act. Since the valuer was a professional, whose services were paid for (albeit indirectly) by Mrs Smith, and since he was aware that Mrs Smith would probably purchase the house in reliance on his valuation without an independent survey, it would not be reasonable to allow the valuer to rely on the disclaimer. Accordingly, the valuer had assumed responsibility to Mrs Smith and was liable in negligence. Lord Griffiths observed:

> ". . . the phrase 'assumption of responsibility' can only have any real meaning if it is understood as referring to the circumstances in which the law will *deem* the maker of the statement to have assumed responsibility . . ."[86]

Faced with the familiar "floodgates" argument, their Lordships chose to confine the *ratio* of their decision to situations where a private purchaser was buying a modest house. Commercial purchasers, or purchasers of more expensive houses, could be expected to instruct their own independent surveyors. In this way, the decision would not expose surveyors to liability for very large losses, and would have only a small effect on their insurance premiums and the cost of surveys.

The decision in *Smith v Eric Bush* was subsequently applied in *Merrett v Babb*.[87] Here, the claimant applied to a building society for a mortgage, and the building society commissioned a survey from a firm of which the defendant was an employee. By the time the claimant discovered that the survey had been conducted negligently, causing her economic loss, the firm had gone into liquidation. However, by a majority, the Court of Appeal held that the negligent surveyor, by signing the mortgage valuation report for the building society, had assumed a *personal* responsibility to the claimant for its accuracy. A majority of the court was

---

[86] [1990] 1 A.C. 831 at 862. See also Lord Slynn, in *Phelps v Hillingdon LBC* [2001] 2 A.C. 619 at 654: "The phrase simply means that the law recognises that there is a duty of care. It is not so much that responsibility is assumed as that it is recognised or imposed by the law."
[87] [2001] Q.B. 1174.

prepared to hold that the claimant had reasonably relied on the surveyor's professional skill, even though the claimant was unaware of who had conducted the survey, because the copy of the survey she had been shown had omitted all references to the firm and the surveyor who had provided it. This decision seemed to produce a rather harsh result for the surveyor, and should be contrasted with the decision of the House of Lords in *Williams and Reid v Natural Life Health Foods Ltd and Mistlin*, discussed below.

*Policy considerations: the limits of the "assumption of responsibility" doctrine*

In *Williams and Reid v Natural Life Health Foods Ltd and Mistlin*,[88] the plaintiffs had **3–039** obtained a franchise from a company (the first defendant) to run a health food shop. They had relied on representations made in the company's literature about the likelihood of their shop being successful. In the event, the turnover of the shop proved to be substantially less that the company had predicted—in fact it traded at a loss for 18 months. The plaintiffs sought to recover their financial losses from the company, but the company went into liquidation, so they pursued their action against its managing director, Mr Mistlin. The plaintiffs argued that he had assumed personal responsibility towards them, because the company literature had made it plain that the predictions about profit were based on Mr Mistlin's personal expertise and experience in the health food trade. The House of Lords held, however, that nothing that had been said or done by Mr Mistlin showed that he had assumed responsibility towards the plaintiffs in a personal capacity. The representations on which they had relied had been made by the *company*. It was particularly important, in the context of small businesses, that the court should not be too ready to "lift the corporate veil" and undermine the protection of limited liability conferred by establishing a company.

A different policy consideration arose in *West Bromwich Albion Football Club Ltd v El-Safty*.[89] Here, a consultant orthopaedic surgeon had negligently advised one of the club's players to have an operation on his knee, instead of treating his injury more conservatively. The player had been put in touch with the surgeon by the club's in-house physiotherapist, and the surgeon's advice had been communicated both to the club and the player. As a result of the negligent advice, the player's career was brought to an end, and the club suffered economic loss. The Court of Appeal dismissed the club's claim, holding that an assumption of responsibility to the club would be inconsistent with the surgeon's role—he was (or ought to have been) concerned exclusively with the well-being of his patient, the player.

In *Caparo v Dickman*,[90] Lord Bridge examined the authorities and drew an important distinction between, on the one hand, cases like *Smith v Eric Bush* and *Hedley Byrne*, and, on the other hand, a case like *Caparo*. In *Caparo* the plaintiffs took over a company called Fidelity, relying on figures contained in an audit which had been prepared by the defendants, a firm of accountants. The plaintiffs alleged that the audit had been prepared negligently, causing them financial loss. The House of Lords held that the accountants owed them no duty of care. Lord Bridge made it clear that in deciding whether a sufficient relationship of proximity existed between the plaintiffs and the defendants, it was important to consider the *size of the class* to which the plaintiffs belonged. Here, although the plaintiffs were existing shareholders, for the purposes of the decision, they should be regarded as being in the same position as any other person who might wish to buy shares in Fidelity. In other words, they belonged to a class of persons the size

---

[88] [1998] 1 W.L.R. 830.
[89] [2006] EWCA Civ 1299; [2007] P.I.Q.R. P7.
[90] [1990] 2 A.C. 605.

of which could not be ascertained and which was potentially very large. It followed that making the accountants liable would set a precedent that would expose accountants to enormous liability.[91] (It was also important that, whilst the audit had been prepared for *one purpose*, it had been relied on by the plaintiffs for *another purpose*. This point is discussed later.)

Reading between the lines, we can see that their Lordships' decision in *Caparo* was underpinned by considerations of policy. If the case had been decided the other way, accountants' insurance premiums would have increased dramatically, leading to a rise in the cost of accounting. This in turn would have placed a great burden on businesses and might have had a depressing effect on the national economy.[92]

Dealing with *Hedley Byrne* and *Smith v Eric Bush*, Lord Bridge noted that, in those and similar cases:

> ". . . the defendant giving advice or information was fully aware of the nature of the transaction which the plaintiff had in contemplation, knew that the advice or information would be communicated to him directly or indirectly and knew that it was very likely that the plaintiff would rely on that advice or information in deciding whether or not to engage in the transaction in contemplation."[93]

His Lordship said that this was entirely different from the situation in a case like *Caparo*, where:

> ". . . a statement is put into more or less general circulation and may foreseeably be relied on by strangers to the maker of the statement for any one of a variety of different purposes which the maker of the statement has no specific reason to anticipate."[94]

To impose liability in the latter situation would subject the maker of the statement to indeterminate liability and would, as Lord Bridge put it:

> "confer on the world at large a quite unwarranted entitlement to appropriate for their own purposes the benefit of the expert knowledge or professional expertise attributed to the maker of the statement".[95]

Therefore, in order to limit the scope of the duty of care for negligent misstatement, it was necessary for the plaintiff to show a very high degree of "proximity" with the maker of the statement. In his Lordship's view, this could only be achieved where:

> ". . . the defendant knew that his statement would be communicated to the plaintiff, either as an individual or as a member of an identifiable class, specifically in connection

---

[91]  Compare *Law Society v KPMG Peat Marwick* [2000] 1 W.L.R. 1921, where the Court of Appeal upheld a preliminary ruling that accountants, in auditing solicitors' firms, owed a duty of care to the Law Society in respect of compensation payments made by the Society because the accountants had failed to detect fraud. Here, the scope of potential liability was limited and could arise only during the year for which the audit had been prepared.

[92]  Hoffmann J., in *Morgan Crucible Co v Hill Samuel & Co* [1991] 2 W.L.R. 655 at 662, said that ". . . if the decision in Caparo's case had gone the other way, firms of accountants below a certain size may have been deterred by insurance costs from competing for the audit work of public limited companies potentially liable to take-over bids. This would have driven such companies into the hands of the largest firms".

[93]  *Caparo v Dickman* [1990] 2 A.C. 605 at 620.

[94]  [1990] 2 A.C. 605 at 621.

[95]  [1990] 2 A.C. 605 at 621.

with a particular transaction or transactions of a particular kind . . . and that the plaintiff would be very likely to rely on it for the purpose of deciding whether or not to enter upon that transaction or upon a transaction of that kind."[96]

This formulation of the test for proximity (or "special relationship") may be taken to encapsulate the modern approach to applying the "*Hedley Byrne* principle".

The judgment of Hoffmann J., in *Morgan Crucible Plc v Hill Samuel & Co*,[97] provides a helpful insight into the policy reasons which influence the courts in negligent misstatement cases. *Morgan Crucible* was a case in which the accountants, directors and financial advisers of a target company were being sued by disappointed take-over bidders. Hoffmann J. undertook a comparison of the decisions in *Caparo* and *Smith v Eric Bush*. He started by noting the similarity between the cases. In both cases the statements in question had been prepared to fulfil a statutory purpose (under the Companies Act 1985 and the Building Societies Act 1986 respectively), and in both cases the person making the statement had had no wider purpose in mind. In both cases reliance on the statement by the defendant was regarded as highly foreseeable.

In answering the question why the House of Lords had felt able to find liability in *Smith v Eric Bush*, but not in *Caparo*, Hoffmann J. went on to identify a number of differences between the cases. First, in *Smith* the plaintiff had paid for the survey, but the plaintiffs in *Caparo* had not paid for the audit. Secondly, the plaintiff in *Smith* was a person of modest means making the most expensive purchase of her life, whilst the take-over bidders in *Caparo* were entrepreneurs taking high risks for high rewards. Thirdly, it was to be noted that the imposition of liability on surveyors would not be likely to result in a great increase in their insurance costs and in the cost of surveys. The same could not be said about the insurance costs of accountants if *Caparo* had been decided the other way. In Hoffmann J.'s view, then, the different results in the two cases could be justified in terms of the "different economic relationships between the parties and the nature of the markets in which they were operating".[98] His Lordship did point out, however, that "the courts do not have the information on which to form anything more than a broad view of the economic consequences of their decisions", and that consequently, "they are more concerned with what appears to be fair and reasonable than with wider utilitarian calculations".

## A summary of the current law

In *James McNaughton Paper Group v Hicks, Anderson & Co*,[99] Neill L.J., in the Court of Appeal, considered *Caparo* and provided a useful analysis of the modern law.[100] The case was brought against a firm of accountants that had been instructed to prepare the accounts of a company, knowing that they were going to be relied on by a take-over bidder. The accounts proved inaccurate and the take-over bidder suffered economic loss. In denying the existence

**3–040**

---

[96] [1990] 2 A.C. 605 at 621. Lord Bridge gives the example of "a prospectus inviting investment" as likely to give rise to a duty of care, as to which, see *Possfund Custodian Trustee Ltd v Diamond* [1996] 1 W.L.R. 1351, where the court refused to strike out a claim against those responsible for preparing a prospectus for general public circulation after the floatation of a company—it was arguable that the claimants' reliance might be reasonable if it could be shown that the authors of the prospectus intended the public to rely on it.

[97] [1991] 2 W.L.R. 655.

[98] [1991] 2 W.L.R. 655 at 662.

[99] [1991] 2 W.L.R. 641.

[100] [1991] 2 W.L.R. 641 at 651.

of a duty of care, Neill L.J. stated that the law was nowadays reluctant to extend the scope of the duty of care to protect claimants other than persons whom the maker of the statement *directly intended should rely on the statement*. His Lordship then said that, in deciding whether a duty of care existed, it was necessary to take into account all the circumstances of the particular case. Nevertheless, it was possible to identify certain matters that, in most cases, were likely to be of importance in deciding whether to impose a duty of care. His Lordship went on to enumerate six such matters:[101]

*(i)  The purpose for which the statement was made*

**3–041**      Where the primary purpose in making a statement is to advise the "advisee", it may be easy to conclude that he or she is owed a duty of care. However, in cases where a statement is made primarily for a *different* purpose, it becomes necessary to look carefully at the purpose for which the statement was *communicated* to the advisee and the purpose for which it was *used*.

*(ii)  The purpose for which the statement was communicated*

**3–042**      Under this heading, Neill L.J. observed:

> ". . . it will be necessary to consider the purpose of, and the circumstances surrounding, the communication. Was the communication made for information only? Was it made for some action to be taken and, if so, what action and by whom? Who requested the communication to be made? These are some of the questions which may have to be addressed."

*(iii)  The relationship between the adviser, the advisee and any relevant third party*

**3–043**      Where the statement is made primarily for the benefit of someone other than the advisee, the courts will consider the relationship between the parties in the case. In some cases, the advisee will receive information from an adviser via a third party (as in *Smith v Eric Bush*—where the valuer's advice was passed on by the building society). In such cases, the court must ask whether it is reasonable for the claimant to look *through the third party* to the adviser for advice.

*(iv)  The size of any class to which the advisee belongs*

**3–044**      Under this heading, his Lordship said:

> "Where there is a single advisee or he is a member of only a small class it may sometimes be simple to infer that a duty of care was owed to him. Membership of a large class, however, may make such an inference more difficult, particularly where the statement was made in the first instance for someone outside the class."

We have seen that in *Caparo v Dickman* the size of the class to which the plaintiffs belonged was a crucial factor in denying liability.

---

[101] His Lordship's headings are repeated in the text, whilst the gist of his Lordship's observations is presented in summary form. Compare Lord Oliver's distillation of the *Hedley Byrne* principle in *Caparo v Dickman* [1990] 2 A.C. 605 at 638.

*(v) The state of knowledge of the adviser*

According to Neill L.J., this is one of the most important matters to consider. When the state-    **3–045**
ment is made, does the adviser know, or ought he or she to know:

- the purpose for which the statement is being made?
- the purpose for which it may be communicated to the advisee?
- that the advisee will probably rely on the statement without obtaining independent advice?

Under this heading, his Lordship made it clear that a duty of care can be owed only in respect of transactions or types of transaction of which the adviser has knowledge.

*(vi) Reliance by the advisee*

Under this heading, the courts will consider whether the advisee did in fact rely on the state-    **3–046**
ment, as opposed to acting on his or her own judgement (even though this accorded with the advice given). They will also consider whether, and in what way, it was *reasonable* for the advisee to rely on the statement. These matters are considered below.

## (2) "Reasonable reliance"

There are two issues to consider here:    **3–047**

- was reliance reasonable in the circumstances?
- did reliance actually take place?

*Reliance must be reasonable*

The decision of the Court of Appeal, in *Howard Marine and Dredging Co Ltd v Ogden & Sons*    **3–048**
*Ltd*,[102] is a good example of how the question of whether a claimant's reliance on advice is "reasonable" in the circumstances can be a complex one, giving rise to judicial disagreement.

Ogden & Sons ("Ogdens") were about to put in a tender for dredging works, which involved carrying a large quantity of clay out to sea and dumping it. In order to carry the clay, they needed to hire a number of barges. In the course of negotiations with Howard Marine, they were on a number of occasions wrongly informed that the carrying capacity of the barges they intended to hire was greater than it actually was. Howard Marine's representative had based his answers to their questions on his recollection of a figure entered in Lloyd's Register. In fact, Lloyd's had made a mistake—the correct carrying capacity was stated in the ships' documents, written in German, which the representative had access to, but either did not consult or chose to disregard. Ogdens put in their tender in reliance on the defendants' advice, only to find that they had underestimated the expense involved in disposing of the clay. They sued for their financial loss.

---

[102] [1978] 2 All E.R. 1134. Compare *Fashion Brokers Ltd v Clarke Hayes* [2000] P.N.L.R. 473.

A majority of the Court of Appeal held that Howard Marine were liable. Lord Denning M.R. dissented, however, holding that in the circumstances the only duty which Howard Marine had owed in responding to Ogdens' inquiries was a duty to act honestly. Their representative had discharged this duty when he had quoted the carrying capacity of the barges from memory, twice on the telephone and once at a meeting. His Lordship pointed out that in *Hedley Byrne*, Lord Pearce had thought that for a duty of care to arise, the statement in question had to be made in the context of a business or professional transaction "whose nature makes clear the gravity of the inquiry and the importance and influence attached to the answer".[103] Similarly, in *Mutual Life v Evatt*, Lords Reid and Morris, whose dissenting opinions were to be preferred, had discussed liability in terms of situations where a plaintiff "makes it plain . . . that he is seeking considered advice and intends to act on it in a particular way".[104] In Lord Denning M.R.'s view, Ogdens had not done enough to emphasise that they intended to rely on the figures quoted by the representative. They could easily have made plain the "gravity of their inquiry", for example by asking him to put the figures in writing. It was therefore unreasonable for them to rely on the figures without making their own inquiries.

Bridge L.J., having reviewed the evidence given at the trial, concluded that Howard Marine's representative had, in fact, read the figures contained in the ships' documents and had not shown reasonable grounds for disregarding them and basing his advice on the Lloyd's Register figures instead. Accordingly, Howard Marine were liable under the Misrepresentation Act 1967, having made a false pre-contractual statement without reasonable grounds to believe it was true. Bridge L.J. found it unnecessary to decide the question of negligence liability, but doubted whether a duty of care arose in the circumstances. Shaw L.J. on the other hand, whilst agreeing with Bridge L.J. about liability for misrepresentation, thought that Howard Marine were also liable in negligence. On Shaw L.J.'s view, the carrying capacity of the barges was such an important and fundamental fact that the gravity of Ogdens' inquiries must have been obvious. Moreover, Howard Marine were in a better position than Ogdens to find out the carrying capacity of the barges. It followed that it was reasonable for Ogdens to rely on their advice without making inquiries of their own.

**3–049**     **The purpose for which the statement is made.**   Although the issue of "reasonable reliance" arises in all negligent misstatement cases, the courts have particularly focused on the issue in cases where the statement in question has been made for one purpose, but is relied on by the claimant for another purpose. Thus, in Caparo v Dickman, it was important that, whilst the accounts had been prepared for the purpose of fulfilling certain statutory duties placed on auditors for the benefit of shareholders (including the plaintiffs), the plaintiffs had relied on the accounts as a general guide to the performance of investments—a purpose for which they had not been designed. It followed that in the circumstances the plaintiffs' reliance on the accounts was unreasonable.

Similar reasoning was applied in *Reeman v Department of Transport*.[105] Here, the plaintiff was the owner of a fishing boat that required an annual certificate of seaworthiness from the Department of Transport. The boat had been covered by a certificate when Mr Reeman had bought it, but he later discovered that the surveyor who had inspected the boat had been

---

[103] *Hedley Byrne v Heller & Partners* [1964] A.C. 465 at 539.

[104] *Mutual Life v Evatt* [1971] A.C. 793 at 812.

[105] [1997] 2 Lloyd's Rep. 648. Consider also the purpose of the "statements" in, for example, *Customs & Excise Commissioners v Barclays Bank* [2006] UKHL 28, and *West Bromwich Albion FC v El-Safty* [2006] EWCA Civ 1299; [2007] P.I.Q.R. P7.

negligent. In fact, the boat was unseaworthy. The certificate should never have been issued and could not be renewed. This meant the boat was practically worthless. When Mr Reeman sued for his financial loss, the Court of Appeal, following *Caparo*, held that it had not been reasonable for him to rely on the certificate as a means of establishing the boat's commercial value. The certificate had not been provided for this purpose. It had been issued to promote safety at sea.

*Reliance must, in fact, take place*

Generally, a successful claimant must show that he or she has, in fact, relied on the defendant's advice or services (rather than acting in reliance on his or her own views or the views of another)—otherwise the advice or services cannot be said to be the cause of the claimant's loss.[106] The decision in *Abbott v Strong*[107] illustrates the idea that a claimant cannot be said to have placed reliance on a defendant unless the claimant knows (or acts reasonably in assuming) that the statement in question has been made *by the defendant*.[108] Here, the plaintiffs had been encouraged to invest in a company by a circular that had been sent to them by the company's directors. The circular contained inaccurate profit forecasts, and the company subsequently went into receivership. When the plaintiffs sued the accountants who had prepared the profit forecasts, it was held that the plaintiffs had not relied on the accountants, because, at the time they had acted on the information in the circular, they had thought that it had come solely from the directors of the company.

    The question of reliance was addressed by the House of Lords in *Customs & Excise Commissioners v Barclays Bank* (discussed above). Lord Bingham noted that the Customs officials could not "in any meaningful sense" be said to have relied on the bank to protect their economic interest in the frozen funds. This was because, as his Lordship put it, the concept of "reliance" in law "is usually taken to mean that if A had not relied on B he would have acted differently."[109] Here, nothing done (or not done) by the bank had had any effect on the commissioners' actions.

**3–050**

**The "will drafting" cases: an apparent exception.** It should be noted that in the "will drafting" cases (discussed earlier in this chapter), which represent an extension of the "Hedley Byrne principle" to cover negligent services, the fact of reliance does not seem to be a prerequisite of liability. Thus, a negligent solicitor may be liable to a disappointed beneficiary, even in cases where the beneficiary is not aware, at the time the negligence occurs, that but for the negligence he or she would be entitled to a legacy. In these circumstances it cannot be said that the disappointed beneficiary is "relying" on the skill of the solicitor, except in the very general sense that all members of society, some of whom may unknowingly be intended beneficiaries, rely on solicitors to get things right. The anomaly produced by the "will drafting" cases, however, may be explained on the basis that these cases fall into a special category where, for policy reasons, reliance is not regarded as important.

**3–051**

---

[106] *Bristol & West Building Society v Mothew* [1996] 4 All E.R. 698.

[107] [1998] B.C.L.C. 420.

[108] Note, however, that the claimant need not necessarily know the precise identity of the defendant. It may suffice if, as in *Merrett v Babb* (discussed above), the claimant reasonably assumes that the statement must have been prepared by a defendant of a particular type.

[109] *Customs & Excise Commissioners v Barclays Bank* [2006] UKHL 28, at para.14. See also the remarks of Lord Mance at para.112.

## Economic loss: conclusion

**3–052**     We have seen that, over the years, the courts have vacillated on the question of economic loss. This has resulted in a body of law that lacks coherence. It is convenient, for the purpose of learning the law, to distinguish, as we have done in this chapter, between the "activity" cases and the "statements and services" cases. However, the courts' extension of the "*Hedley Byrne* principle" into the realm of services—in cases like *Spring v Guardian Assurance, Smith v Eric Bush* and *Henderson v Merrett*—makes this distinction rather artificial. It should be remembered, therefore, that the outcomes of economic loss claims depend, not on their classification within an appropriate pigeon-hole, but on the different weight the courts accord to various issues in the unique factual matrix of each case. Detailed consideration of these issues leads the courts to form an overview or "impression" of whether or not, in the particular circumstances, there can sensibly be said to have been an "assumption of responsibility" (with sufficient "proximity" and "reliance") so that a duty of care can arise.

It is noteworthy that in Commonwealth jurisdictions, particularly in Australia, New Zealand and Canada, the United Kingdom's restrictive approach to economic loss has not been wholeheartedly embraced. Commonwealth courts have, for example, been more willing to allow recovery where the claimant has only a contractual interest in damaged property, and have taken a more liberal approach to the liability of builders and local authorities for defective premises.[110] Whilst (as we saw in Ch.2) the United Kingdom courts have rejected Lord Wilberforce's broad "two-stage test" for finding the duty of care, Commonwealth courts, in economic loss cases, have often chosen to apply it, in conjunction with a close examination of the economic and political relationships between the parties.[111] Academic commentators have pointed out that this approach makes much more sense, and that the incoherence of UK law has resulted from the courts' analysis of economic loss questions "not on the basis of common policy concerns but in pockets according to how the loss [has] been caused".[112] The reasoning of the House of Lords in *Customs & Excise v Barclays Bank*[113] (in which this commentary was specifically referred to[114]) indicates, perhaps, a new-found willingness to adopt a broad, flexible approach (rather than a "test-based" approach) when deciding economic loss claims. However, it remains to be seen whether this approach will succeed in providing clarity and consistency where a "test-based" approach has failed.

---

[110] See *Kamloops (City) v Nielsen* (1984) 10 D.L.R. 641 (Supreme Court of Canada); *Bryan v Maloney* (1994–5) 182 C.L.R. 609 (High Court of Australia); *Invercargill v Hamlin* [1996] A.C. 624 (Privy Council).

[111] In Canada, for example, the *Anns* test is still applied, although it has been "revisited". See *Cooper v Hobart* (2002) 206 D.L.R. (4th) 193 and *Edwards v Law Society of Upper Canada* (2002) 206 D.L.R. (4th) 211, but contrast the more flexible approach adopted by the High Court of Australia in *Perre v Apand Pty Ltd* (1999) 198 C.L.R. 180.

[112] See J. Stapleton (1991) 107 L.Q.R. 249, and more recently [2002] UCLA L Rev. 531.

[113] [2006] UKHL 28. Comment: J. Morgan (2006) 22 P.N. 206.

[114] By Lord Walker, at para.69.

# Chapter 4

# NEGLIGENCE: PSYCHIATRIC ILLNESS

## Introduction

This chapter deals with the circumstances in which a duty of care will be imposed to avoid   **4–001**
causing psychiatric illness. In *White v Chief Constable of South Yorkshire*,[1] a House of Lords
case that we shall examine in due course, Lord Steyn noted that the law in this area is "a patch-
work quilt of distinctions which are difficult to justify".[2] That case, like *Alcock v Chief Constable
of South Yorkshire*,[3] another important House of Lords authority, arose from events which
happened at the Hillsborough football stadium in April 1989, when police negligence caused the
overcrowding of spectator stands, crushing 95 people to death and injuring hundreds more.

   The claims in these cases were brought by people who, though not physically injured,
suffered psychiatric illness as a result of the tragedy. In *Alcock*, claims were brought by relatives who had witnessed or heard about the death or injury of their loved ones. In *White*,
claims were brought by police officers who had assisted in the aftermath of the disaster. In
deciding that no duty of care was owed to any of these plaintiffs, the House of Lords developed and applied a set of rules that are hard to justify in terms of logic and morality. The area
has been the subject of a report by the Law Commission, whose recommendations are
considered at the end of this chapter.

## Definition of "psychiatric illness"

It important to understand that the courts draw a distinction between claims in respect of *medi-*   **4–002**
*cally recognised psychiatric illness*[4] and claims for mere grief, sorrow and distress. The latter,
being unfortunate but commonplace symptoms of the human condition, are generally afforded
no remedy at law.[5] In psychiatric illness cases, successful claimants must establish that they

---

[1] [1999] 2 A.C. 455.
[2] [1999] 2 A.C. 455 at 500.
[3] [1992] 1 A.C. 310.
[4] For comprehensive discussion of the types of psychiatric illness that can found an action, see Law Com. 249
Part III (paras 3.1–3.33).
[5] Lord Denning M.R., in *Hinz v Berry* [1970] Q.B. 40 made it clear that "in English law no damages are awarded for
grief or sorrow caused by a person's death". Subsequent to that decision, however, a modest sum has become payable
for bereavement, in limited circumstances, under the Fatal Accidents Act 1976. (See Ch.17.)

are suffering from medical conditions such as "post-traumatic stress disorder (PTSD)",[6] "organic depression and a change of personality",[7] or "pathological grief disorder".[8] The law recognises that these conditions can be just as serious and debilitating as physical injuries. As we shall see, however, for policy reasons it limits the circumstances in which they can give rise to claims for compensation.

Until very recently, claims for psychiatric illness were described as claims for "nervous shock". This rather quaint terminology served to emphasise the idea that the law would only entertain such claims in cases where psychiatric illness resulted from the "sudden shock" of witnessing or participating in a *specific single event*. Although, in the modern law, the position remains uncertain,[9] it is generally thought that an element of "sudden shock" remains an essential ingredient of the cause of action. Thus, a person whose psychiatric illness is brought on by the cumulative effect of prolonged exposure to distressing circumstances (by caring for a brain-damaged accident victim, for example) will normally have no cause of action.[10]

Once the claimant has established that he or she is suffering from a psychiatric condition which the law will recognise as actionable, there are a number of additional hurdles that must be overcome in order to succeed. As in cases of economic loss, the law uses the concept of the duty of care as the mechanism to control the scope of liability. The nature of the hurdles which a particular claimant will have to overcome depends on the *type of situation* that has given rise to the psychiatric illness. The law divides claimants into a number of categories, with very different rules applying to each category.

## Types of Claimant

4–003    Broadly speaking, and in the light of the decision in *White v Chief Constable of South Yorkshire*, it can be said that there are nowadays three categories of claimant in psychiatric illness cases[11]:

- claimants who suffer psychiatric illness as a result of having been physically injured by the defendant's negligence;

---

[6] As in *White v Chief Constable of South York*shire [1999] 2 A.C. 455. Note that in *Ward v Leeds Teaching Hospitals NHS Trust* [2004] EWHC 2106, [2004] Lloyd's Rep. Med. 530 it was noted that the diagnostic criteria for PTSD required a shocking event of a particularly horrific nature. (The death of loved one in hospital would not normally meet this description.) This issue overlaps with the "sudden shock" requirement in *Alcock*, discussed later in this chapter.

[7] As in *McLoughlin v O'Brian* [1983] 1 A.C. 410 (per Lord Wilberforce at 417).

[8] As in *Vernon v Bosley (No.1)* [1997] 1 All E.R. 577.

[9] See the observations of Lord Slynn in *W v Essex CC* [2000] 2 All E.R. 237 at 240. See also *Vernon v Bosley (No.1)* [1997] 1 All E.R. 577 (where the claimant's condition results from a combination of grief and "sudden shock", the court will not attempt to draw a fine distinction between the two).

[10] See *Alcock v Chief Constable of South Yorkshire* [1992] 1 A.C. 310 at 396, 401 and 416. Note, however, that the position may be different where the defendant has a contractual relationship which requires him or her to exercise reasonable care in respect of the claimant's health. Thus, in *Walker v Northumberland CC* [1995] I.C.R. 702, discussed in Ch.7, an employer was liable for imposing an excessive work load which caused psychiatric illness.

[11] In addition to the three categories listed here, there are other situations where psychiatric illness may be recoverable in negligence. These include situations where psychiatric illness is induced by stress at work (discussed in Ch.7) and a group of situations which the Law Commission classified as "miscellaneous" (see Law Com. 249, para.2.51). These include: where a patient suffers psychiatric illness at the hands of a negligent psychiatrist; and where a prisoner suffers psychiatric illness as a result of ill-treatment in prison. Such cases, however, fall outside the traditional focus of psychiatric illness liability and are beyond the scope of this chapter.

- claimants who are put in physical danger, but who in fact suffer only psychiatric illness (these claimants are known as "primary victims"[12]);

- claimants who, though not in any physical danger themselves, suffer psychiatric illness as a result of *witnessing the death, injury or imperilment of another person* (known as the "immediate victim") with whom they have a close relationship of love and affection (these claimants are known as "secondary victims").

Arguably, there remains an additional category, namely claimants who suffer psychiatric illness as a result of witnessing the destruction of their property. Such a claim succeeded in *Attia v British Gas Plc*,[13] which is discussed later in this chapter. It should be remembered, however, that this decision was taken in the 1980s, at a time when the courts were in the last throes of expanding the duty of care in negligence, and before the modern rules relating to psychiatric illness had been clearly defined. It is therefore uncertain whether it would nowadays be followed.

## HISTORICAL DEVELOPMENT

### The old law

Unsurprisingly, perhaps, the law was slow to recognise claims for psychiatric illness. The approach of the courts in the nineteenth century is exemplified by the decision of the Privy Council in *Victorian Railway Commissioners v Coultas*.[14] Here, the defendants' gate-keeper had carelessly allowed a carriage to enter a railway crossing when a train was about to pass. Although no physical injury occurred, the plaintiff, who was pregnant and a passenger in the carriage, suffered severe shock—thinking she would be killed by the oncoming train—and subsequently miscarried her child. The Privy Council denied that there could be liability for psychiatric illness in the absence of physical injury. As Lord Hoffmann pointed out in *White*,[15] the main reason their Lordships gave for this restricted approach was the evidential difficulty of deciding on the causes of psychiatric illness at a time when so little was known about the workings of the mind. The Privy Council thought that opening the doors to psychiatric illness liability might have led to a large number of "imaginary claims".

**4–004**

### The "impact theory"

In 1901, however, the courts adopted a more liberal approach in deciding *Dulieu v White & Sons*.[16] Here, the plaintiff, a pregnant barmaid, was behind the bar in a pub when a negligently driven carriage came off the road and crashed into the pub, entering the room where she was standing. She suffered shock and a subsequent miscarriage. Kennedy J. upheld her claim. Dealing with *Victorian Railway Commissioners v Coultas*, Kennedy J. thought that the problem

**4–005**

---

[12] We use the term "primary victims" here in its "narrow" post-*White* sense. Contrast this with the sense in which it was used by Lord Oliver in *Alcock v Chief Constable of South Yorkshire* [1992] 1 A.C. 310 at 407.

[13] [1988] Q.B. 304.

[14] (1888) 13 App. Cas. 222.

[15] *White v Chief Constable of South Yorkshire* [1999] 2 A.C. 455 at 501.

[16] [1901] 2 K.B. 669.

of exaggerated or fraudulent claims was not a good enough reason for simply denying the existence of a duty of care in respect of psychiatric harm, observing:

> "Such a course involves the denial of redress in meritorious cases, and it necessarily implies a certain degree of distrust, which I do not share, in the capacity of legal tribunals to get at the truth in this class of claim".[17]

In allowing liability for psychiatric illness in negligence, Kennedy J. was influenced by the case of *Wilkinson v Downton*,[18] which had been decided four years earlier. Here, the defendant, in the exercise of what he regarded as a practical joke, had arrived at the plaintiff's front door and announced that her husband had been involved in a serious accident and had broken both his legs. When the plaintiff suffered shock, accompanied by vomiting and other physical symptoms, the defendant was held liable for the effect of his statement, on the basis that he had perpetrated an intentional act of wrongdoing. (Liability under the "rule in *Wilkinson v Downton*", as it is known, is discussed more fully in Ch.11. It should not be confused with liability in negligence.)

In *Dulieu v White & Sons*, then, and in a number of similar cases, the courts sought to control the scope of liability by using what became known as the "impact theory", according to which a plaintiff would be allowed to recover for psychiatric illness provided that this was caused by reasonable fear of being physically injured by the defendant's negligence.

## The law expands: *Hambrook v Stokes*

**4–006**     In later cases, the courts abandoned the "impact theory", extending the law to cover plaintiffs who had not been in danger, but had suffered psychiatric illness as a result of witnessing a loved one being injured or placed in peril by a defendant's negligence. (We now call such plaintiffs "secondary victims".)

Such was the case in *Hambrook v Stokes*.[19] Here, a pregnant mother had accompanied her three children part of the way on their journey to school and then, as usual, had left them to walk a short way by themselves along the bend of a road. The children had passed out of sight when, owing to the defendants' negligence, an out-of-control lorry came down a hill at speed and went round the bend. The mother was afraid that her children would be killed by the lorry (in fact, however, two of them were unharmed, whilst the third was taken to hospital with injuries). She suffered shock which led to a miscarriage with medical complications, causing her death. A majority of the Court of Appeal held the defendants liable. But in extending the law to cover this situation, Bankes L.J. was careful to point out that the ratio of the decision was to be confined to situations where the plaintiff suffered psychiatric illness because of fear for the safety of her children. The decision was not intended to overturn previous authority to the effect that a plaintiff could not recover in respect of psychiatric illness caused by witnessing physical injury to a person with whom the plaintiff had no relationship of love and affection.[20]

---

[17] [1901] 2 K.B. 669 at 681.
[18] [1897] 2 Q.B. 57.
[19] [1925] 1 K.B. 141.
[20] e.g. *Smith v Johnson & Co* (unreported, but considered in *Wilkinson v Downton* [1897] 2 Q.B. 57 and *Dulieu v White* [1901] 2 K.B. 669).

## No further expansion: *Bourhill v Young*

Nearly 20 years later, in *Bourhill v Young*,[21] the question of psychiatric illness liability came before the House of Lords for the first time. The facts of this case were noted in Ch.2. It will be recalled that it concerned a pregnant woman who, while descending from a tram, heard a road accident occur some distance away. She later attended the scene of the accident, saw blood on the road, and subsequently suffered a miscarriage produced by shock. As was noted in Ch.2, the House of Lords held, in effect, that the woman was not a "foreseeable claimant". In other words, she could not base her action on a wrong done to someone else.

4–007

In arriving at this conclusion, their Lordships considered a number of points. First, there was the question of whether the woman might be regarded as being peculiarly susceptible to psychiatric illness because of her pregnant condition (Lord Wright appeared to think this was likely). If so, then she could only recover if it could be said that, in the circumstances, psychiatric illness was reasonably foreseeable *in a person of ordinary fortitude*. On the facts, their Lordships did not think this was the case—ordinary people could be expected to withstand the rigours of witnessing injury to a stranger on the roads without suffering psychiatric illness. Secondly, there was the question of whether it mattered that the plaintiff had not feared for her own physical safety. A majority of their Lordships appeared to answer this question by resurrecting the "impact theory" and holding that she could not recover because she was outside the area of foreseeable physical impact. Their Lordships held that *Hambrook v Stokes* was to be regarded as a special case and was of limited application.

Initially, then, the courts took a narrow view of the decision in *Hambrook v Stokes*. In *King v Phillips*,[22] for example, the Court of Appeal denied recovery to a mother who suffered psychiatric illness when, from an upstairs window some 70 yards away, she saw her son's tricycle disappear under a reversing taxi and heard the boy scream. The decision in *Hambrook v Stokes* was distinguished on the basis that the mother in *King v Phillips* was too far away from the scene of the accident—like the plaintiff in *Bourhill v Young*, she was not, in effect, a "foreseeable claimant".

In the 1960s, however, the courts began to take a more liberal approach, holding in *Boardman v Sanderson*[23] that a plaintiff who suffered psychiatric illness when his son was involved in an accident could recover even though he had not seen the accident but had only heard it from some distance away, and had come to the scene of the accident shortly after its occurrence. This approach was developed a stage further by the House of Lords in 1982, when it decided the landmark case of *McLoughlin v O'Brian*.

## The emergence of the modern law: *McLoughlin v O'Brian*

In *McLoughlin v O'Brian*,[24] the plaintiff's husband and three of her children were involved in a serious road accident, caused by the defendants' negligence. The plaintiff did not witness the accident, being, at the time, at home about two miles away. About an hour after the accident, it was reported to her by a family friend that her 17-year-old son, George (who had been

4–008

---

[21] [1943] A.C. 92.
[22] [1953] 1 Q.B. 429.
[23] [1964] 1 W.L.R. 1317.
[24] [1983] A.C. 410.

driving the car), was dying. The friend then drove her to a local hospital where she was told that her three-year-old daughter had died. She could hear George shouting and screaming in an adjoining room. She saw her husband and seven year-old daughter, who were in a distressed state, covered with oil and mud. She was then taken to see George, who appeared to recognise her before lapsing into unconsciousness. These events caused her to suffer psychiatric illness.

In holding the defendants liable, the House of Lords extended the law to cover a situation where the plaintiff had not seen or heard the accident itself, but had come upon its "immediate aftermath". Their Lordships declined to say, in precise terms, what could constitute the "immediate aftermath" of an accident. But it was significant that the plaintiff in *McLoughlin v O'Brian* had seen her family within a fairly short time of the accident, and that, when she saw them, they had not been "cleaned up" and remained in more or less the same condition they had been in immediately after the accident. She had therefore witnessed scenes which went to "make up the accident as an entire event".[25] Lord Wilberforce thought that extending liability in these circumstances was "on the margin of what the process of logical progression [from previous authority] would allow".[26] His Lordship thought that the High Court of Australia's decision in *Chester v Waverly Municipal Council*,[27] where a child's body was found floating in a trench after a prolonged search, might "perhaps be placed on the other side of a recognisable line".[28] As we shall see, the question of what can constitute the "immediate aftermath" was considered again in *Alcock v Chief Constable of South Yorkshire*, but was left unresolved.[29]

The speech of Lord Wilberforce, then, laid the foundation for the modern approach of the courts in psychiatric illness cases. Whilst his Lordship thought that extending previous authority to assist the plaintiff was a "logical progression", he noted that, because psychiatric illness was capable of affecting such a large number of potential plaintiffs, there was "a real need for the law to place some limitation on the extent of admissible claims".[30]

*Lord Wilberforce's "control mechanisms"*

**4–009**    In *McLoughlin v O'Brian*, Lord Wilberforce identified three factors that would need to be considered in every case:

- the class of persons whose claims should be recognised;
- the proximity of such persons to the accident;
- the means by which the psychiatric illness was caused.

These three "control mechanisms" suggested by Lord Wilberforce were subsequently reformulated and applied by a unanimous House of Lords in *Alcock*.

In relation to the class of persons who might claim, Lord Wilberforce recognised that "the possible range is between the closest of family ties, of parent and child, or husband and wife, and the ordinary bystander". He noted that the law, as in *Bourhill v Young*, had always denied

---

[25] [1983] A.C. 410 at 422 (as in *Benson v Lee* [1972] V.R. 879, to which Lord Wilberforce referred).
[26] [1983] A.C. 410 at 419.
[27] (1939) 62 C.L.R. 1. Compare *Vernon v Bosley (No.1)* [1997] 1 All E.R. 577.
[28] [1983] A.C. 410 at 422.
[29] A point confirmed by Lord Slynn in *W v Essex CC* [2000] 2 All E.R. 237 at 244.
[30] [1983] A.C. 410 at 422.

recovery to mere "bystanders" who suffered psychiatric illness as a result of witnessing accidents. According to Lord Wilberforce, the law's justification for this approach was either that "such persons must be assumed to be possessed of fortitude sufficient to enable them to endure the calamities of modern life", or that "defendants cannot be expected to compensate the world at large".[31] His Lordship thought that cases brought by plaintiffs who did not have a very close family relationship with the "immediate victim" of the accident would have to be "very carefully scrutinised".

As regards proximity to the accident, this had to be "close in both time and space", but it would be impractical and unjust to insist that plaintiffs must be present at the scene of the accident. As regards the means by which the psychiatric illness was caused, his Lordship noted that there had thus far been no negligence case in which the law had compensated psychiatric illness brought about by mere communication to the plaintiff of distressing news. There was no justification for departing from this position. It followed that the psychiatric illness must arise through direct perception of the accident, or its immediate aftermath, by sight or hearing. Lord Wilberforce left open the question of whether "some equivalent of sight or hearing, e.g. through simultaneous television", would suffice. (This point, as we shall see, was subsequently considered by the House of Lords in *Alcock*.)

Although, as has been said, the "control mechanisms" suggested by Lord Wilberforce in *McLoughlin v O'Brian* were subsequently endorsed in *Alcock*, it was initially unclear whether they formed part of the ratio of the case. This was because other members of the House of Lords did not view them in the same way. Whilst Lord Wilberforce (with whom Lord Edmund-Davies agreed) appeared to think that the "control mechanisms" should be satisfied in addition to a test of reasonable foreseeability, Lords Bridge and Scarman appeared to think that liability for psychiatric illness should be decided by applying a broad test of foreseeability, and that, although the factors suggested by Lord Wilberforce were to be considered in applying that test, they did not exclusively define the circumstances in which psychiatric illness could be recoverable. (Lord Russell's opinion on the point was not clear.) This is why the plaintiffs in *Alcock* felt able to pursue their claims.

The House of Lords in *Alcock*, however, unanimously adopted Lord Wilberforce's approach. After *Alcock* came the important decision in *Page v Smith*,[32] a case involving a "primary victim" of psychiatric illness. Next came the case of *White v Chief Constable of South Yorkshire*.[33] The reasoning of the House of Lords in these three cases forms the core of the modern law and is considered, in a number of sections, below.

## ELEMENTS OF THE MODERN LAW

In this section, we examine certain elements of the modern law. We begin by dealing with the **4–010** position of claimants who suffer psychiatric illness as a result of suffering physical injury, or through witnessing damage to their property. The position of such claimants can be shortly stated, and should not be the focus of too much of our attention. Next, we examine the more important issue of the role of policy in psychiatric illness cases. Then, we consider the courts' use of "reasonable foreseeability" in establishing the duty of care.

[31] [1983] A.C. 410 at 422.
[32] [1996] A.C. 155.
[33] [1999] 2 A.C. 455.

## Psychiatric illness resulting from personal injury

**4–011**    Where a claimant has suffered bodily injury as a result of the defendant's negligence, the courts have no difficulty in allowing recovery in respect of psychiatric illness resulting from the injury. (Such claimants are sometimes referred to as "primary victims", although their position is conceptually distinct from that of the plaintiff in *Page v Smith*—discussed later— who did not suffer physical injury, though he had been placed in physical danger.) The ability of such claimants to recover for psychiatric illness follows from the fact that the law has traditionally allowed them to recover damages for pain and suffering consequent upon their injuries. Such damages were awarded, for example, in *Kralj v McGrath*,[34] where the negligence of a defendant obstetrician resulted in the plaintiff suffering psychiatric trauma and losing her baby shortly after its birth. (Woolf J. was careful to point out, however, that these damages were to be distinguished from damages awarded because of natural grief and sorrow resulting from the death of her child, which the law would not compensate.)

## Psychiatric illness resulting from property damage

**4–012**    In *Attia v British Gas Plc*,[35] the Court of Appeal was asked to decide, as a preliminary issue, whether a duty of care could arise where the plaintiff had witnessed the destruction of her home, as opposed to injury to a loved one. Their Lordships held that it could. The defendants, by negligently installing a central heating system, had caused a fire which destroyed the plaintiff's house. The plaintiff suffered psychiatric illness when she returned home one day to witness the blaze. Bingham L.J., holding that a duty of care could exist in such a situation, cited other possible examples, such as where "a scholar's life's work of research or composition were destroyed before his eyes as a result of a defendant's careless conduct".[36] The decision in *Attia*, however, is not considered in any of the three modern leading cases on psychiatric illness.[37] Therefore, as has already been noted, its status remains uncertain.[38]

## Policy considerations

**4–013**    In *White v Chief Constable of South Yorkshire*, Lord Steyn provided a useful summary of the main policy considerations that dictate that claims for psychiatric illness should be treated differently from claims for physical injury.[39] His Lordship identified four such considerations. First, there is the difficulty of drawing the line between acute grief and psychiatric illness.[40] It is difficult to draw this line because the symptoms of both conditions are often the same, but

---

[34] [1986] 1 All E.R. 54.

[35] [1988] Q.B. 304.

[36] [1988] Q.B. 304 at 320.

[37] The decision is not mentioned in *Alcock* or *White*, although in *Page v Smith* [1996] A.C. 155 at 179 it is referred to in passing by Lord Jauncey (dissenting) as an illustration of foreseeable damage.

[38] It has been suggested that the decisions in *Attia v British Gas* and in similar cases might be explained on the basis that a contractual relationship between the defendant and the claimant gave rise to an "assumption of responsibility" ' for the claimant's psychiatric well-being: see Deakin, Johnston and Markesinis, *Markesinis and Deakin's Tort Law* (6th edn, 2007), p.152.

[39] *White v Chief Constable of South Yorkshire* [1999] 2 A.C. 455 at 493. For further discussion of relevant policy considerations, see Law Com. 249, paras 6.5–6.8.

[40] See Hedley [1997] C.L.J. 254, to which his Lordship refers.

it is necessary to differentiate between them because, as we have noted, the law provides no compensation for the former. Lord Steyn pointed out that establishing psychiatric illness by expert evidence was a costly and time-consuming exercise, so that if claims for psychiatric illness were to be treated as generally on a par with physical injury cases there would be adverse economic implications for the administration of justice.

Secondly, Lord Steyn thought it was important to consider the effect on people who had witnessed gruesome events of increasing the availability of compensation. His Lordship did not have in mind fraudulent or bogus claims, saying that it ought to be possible for the courts to expose such claims. Rather, he thought that the prospect of compensation might sometimes be an *unconscious disincentive to rehabilitation*. His Lordship noted that in cases where there was generally no prospect of compensation for psychiatric illness, such as where injury had been sustained while playing sport, reports of psychiatric illness were uncommon. On the other hand, in industrial accident cases, where there was often a prospect of compensation, psychiatric illness was repeatedly encountered.

The third policy consideration was that relaxing the special rules governing compensation for psychiatric harm would greatly increase the class of persons who could recover damages in tort. (In other words, it would open the "floodgates of litigation".) Fourthly, his Lordship thought that expanding liability for psychiatric harm might result in liability which was disproportionate to the tortious conduct involved—perhaps only a momentary lapse of concentration, for example in a road traffic accident. (In other words, it would result in "crushing liability".)

Bearing these policy considerations in mind, we can now examine the various rules that the courts apply in order to limit the scope of the duty of care. The first of these, as may be expected, is the requirement that some harm (either physical or psychiatric, depending on the type of claim) must be reasonably foreseeable.

## Foreseeability of psychiatric illness

As in all negligence actions, reasonable foreseeability of damage is an essential ingredient of the duty of care in psychiatric illness cases. In this area of the law, however, the question of foreseeability can sometimes be a source of confusion. This is because different rules apply in relation to "primary victims" and "secondary victims".    **4–014**

*Foreseeability: primary victims*

In relation to "primary victims" (victims who are placed in physical danger), provided *physical harm* is reasonably foreseeable, *it is unnecessary to establish that psychiatric illness is reasonably foreseeable*. In *Page v Smith*,[41] the plaintiff was involved in a relatively minor car accident, but was not physically injured. Prior to the accident, he had for about 20 years suffered from a condition variously described as myalgic encephalomyelitis (ME), chronic fatigue syndrome, or post-viral fatigue syndrome. This had manifested itself from time to time with different degrees of severity. The illness had been in remission at the time of the accident and the plaintiff was expecting to return to work after a period of convalescence, but the crash triggered a recurrence of the disease, which became chronic and permanent, so that it was unlikely he would be able to take up full-time employment again.    **4–015**

---

[41] [1996] A.C. 155. On the application of the principle in *Page v Smith*, see *Donachie v Chief Constable of Greater Manchester* [2004] EWCA Civ 405 and *Simmons v British Steel Plc* [2004] UKHL 20.

In the Court of Appeal, it was held that the defendant driver was not liable, because he could not reasonably have foreseen that his negligence would cause psychiatric illness. A majority of the House of Lords, however, overturned this decision and held that reasonable foreseeability of psychiatric illness need not be established when physical injury was reasonably foreseeable. As Lord Lloyd put it:

"Since the defendant was admittedly under a duty of care not to cause the plaintiff foreseeable physical injury, it was unnecessary to ask whether he was under a separate duty of care not to cause foreseeable psychiatric injury".[42]

Lord Lloyd reasoned that if a plaintiff could recover for psychiatric illness in a case where he or she had *actually suffered* physical harm, it should follow that where the plaintiff had, by good luck, escaped reasonably foreseeable physical harm, he should not be deprived of compensation by the existence of this purely fortuitous fact.

The reasoning in *Page v Smith* is quite difficult to understand. In essence, however, their Lordships held that, where there is a danger of physical injury, the law should regard physical and psychiatric injury as the same kind of harm. Then, applying the so-called "eggshell skull rule", their Lordships reasoned that, because it was foreseeable that some (minor) harm of a relevant kind would be caused (being "shaken up" by the car crash), the defendant was liable for the full extent of the harm that was actually suffered. The "eggshell skull" rule is considered more fully in Ch.6. In summary, it provides that where an injured claimant suffers serious medical consequences, the defendant may be liable for *all* of those consequences, even though they could not all have been reasonably foreseen.

Lords Keith and Jauncey dissented in *Page v Smith*, on the basis that the defendant could not reasonably have foreseen that a person of ordinary fortitude would suffer psychiatric illness as a result of a minor car accident. Lord Jauncey appeared to think the "eggshell skull" rule was not relevant where what was in issue was the existence of a duty of care to avoid causing a particular kind of damage—it was only relevant to the *extent* of the damage which occurred, once an established duty of care had been breached.[43] Similar criticism of the approach of the majority in *Page v Smith* was articulated by Lord Goff in his dissenting judgment in *White v Chief Constable of South Yorkshire*. His Lordship observed that the "eggshell skull" rule was "a principle of compensation, not of liability"[44] and concluded that:

"Lord Lloyd appears to have taken an exceptional rule relating to compensation and treated it as being of general application, thereby creating a wider principle of liability".[45]

Lord Griffiths, in *White*, appeared to take the same view, stating:

"The law expects reasonable fortitude and robustness of its citizens and will not impose liability for the exceptional frailty of certain individuals. This is not to be confused with

---

[42] [1996] A.C. 155 at 187.
[43] [1996] A.C. 155 at 176. Lord Ackner, whilst approving Lord Lloyd's analysis, was content to decide the appeal on the basis that psychiatric illness (as opposed to physical injury) was reasonably foreseeable in the circumstances, and suggested (at 170) that consideration of the eggshell skull rule was "nothing to the point". In the light of Lord Ackner's position, then, it is unclear whether the extended application of the rule forms part of the true ratio of *Page v Smith*.
[44] *White v Chief Constable of South Yorkshire* [1999] 2 A.C. 455 at 470.
[45] [1999] 2 A.C. 455 at 476.

the 'eggshell skull' situation, where as a result of a breach of duty the damage inflicted proves to be more serious than expected".[46]

Despite these criticisms, the majority in *White* were content to accept that *Page v Smith* had been correctly decided.

The application of *Page v Smith* was considered by the House of Lords in *Rothwell v Chemical & Insulating Co Ltd*.[47] Here, a number of claimants had developed psychiatric illness as a result of finding out that they had pleural plaques (changes in their lung tissue) resulting from the fact that, in the past, they had been exposed to asbestos by their employer. The pleural plaques were completely harmless, and could not, therefore, found an action in negligence for personal injury (the claimants having suffered no injury). However, the presence of the plaques indicated past exposure to asbestos, and one of the claimants developed psychiatric symptoms through fear that this exposure might cause him to develop a serious lung disease in the future. Relying on *Page v Smith*, he argued that, given that the employer had exposed him to the risk of such disease (albeit that, fortuitously, that risk of physical harm had not materialised) the employer should be liable for the psychiatric harm that *had* materialised. The House of Lords rejected the claim, holding that the principle in *Page v Smith* should not be extended to cover the claimant's situation. Their Lordships' noted that the reasoning in *Page v Smith* had been controversial and had attracted much criticism, but declined to say that the case had been wrongly decided. Instead, they distinguished the claimant's case on its facts, and expressed the view that the *Page v Smith* principle should be confined to situations where (as Lord Rodger put it) claimants had been exposed to, but had escaped, "instant physical harm".[48]

*Foreseeability: secondary victims*

In relation to "secondary victims" (those suffering psychiatric illness because of *witnessing* an event, though they are not themselves in any danger), the claimant must establish that psychiatric illness was reasonably foreseeable. This involves showing that a person of ordinary fortitude or "customary phlegm"[49] might reasonably have suffered psychiatric illness in the circumstances. In other words, no duty of care is owed to avoid causing psychiatric harm to people who are "peculiarly susceptible" to such harm because they have a nervous or emotional disposition. (This is one of the reasons the plaintiff in *Bourhill v Young* did not succeed.)     **4–016**

In the case of "secondary victims", reasonable foreseeability of psychiatric illness to a person of ordinary fortitude *is part of the test for the existence of the duty of care*. But once it is shown that this duty exists, and has been breached, the defendant will be liable for all of the psychiatric illness that results, even though the precise nature and the seriousness of the claimant's particular illness may not have been foreseen. This means that a defendant who could reasonably foresee that his or her negligence might cause a person of ordinary fortitude to suffer from post-traumatic stress disorder, and require, say, two years off work to recuperate, cannot argue that his liability is limited to the cost of that period of recuperation when the claimant, because of     **4–017**

---

[46] [1999] 2 A.C. 455 at 463.

[47] [2007] UKHL 39; [2008] 1 A. C. 281.

[48] *Rothwell v Chemical & Insulating Co Ltd* [2007] UKHL 39, [2008] 1 A.C. 281, per Lord Rodger, at para.95. Comment: J Steele [2008] CLJ 28. *Rothwell* was applied in *Fryers v Belfast Health and Social Care Trust*. On the correctness of *Page v Smith*, see also the comments of Lord Neuberger in *Corr v IBC Vehicles* [2008] UKHL 13.

[49] This colourful phrase was coined by Lord Porter in *Bourhill v Young* [1943] A.C. 92 at 117.

his or her special susceptibility to psychiatric illness, will take 10 years to recover. Thus, in *Brice v Brown*,[50] where it was reasonably foreseeable that a mother of "customary phlegm" might suffer some psychiatric illness on witnessing injuries to her daughter, the plaintiff was able to recover for the full extent of her psychiatric illness even though the illness was made more severe by the fact that she had an underlying personality disorder.

## PRIMARY AND SECONDARY VICTIMS

**4–018**    We have, of course, already noted the distinction between "primary" and "secondary" victims of psychiatric illness. In this section, we consider in more detail how this distinction is drawn, and explore a little further the law relating to recovery by each type of claimant. This provides the background for detailed consideration of the law relating to "secondary victims" (examined in the next section) and for consideration of the law relating to certain claimants who, prior to the decision in *White v Chief Constable of South Yorkshire*, were traditionally regarded as "primary victims".

### "Primary victims"

**4–019**    The decision in *White* seems to make it clear that in order to qualify as a "primary victim", the claimant must establish that he or she has been placed in physical danger by the defendant's negligence (or at least has been put in reasonable fear for his or her physical safety). The position of "primary victims" is governed by the decision in *Page v Smith*, which has already been discussed. Thus, such a claimant may recover for *psychiatric* harm, even though the threatened *physical* harm does not materialise. This was established in the early case of *Dulieu v White & Sons* (discussed above) and was confirmed in *Page v Smith*.

It appears from the reasoning of the majority in *White*, that although physical imperilment is a precondition of qualifying as a "primary victim", it is not necessary to show that fear of physical harm is the *cause* of the primary victim's psychiatric illness. (Thus, where the primary victim is a "rescuer", although the element of physical danger—or reasonable fear thereof—must be present, the cause of the psychiatric illness may be witnessing the imperilment of those being rescued.)

The decision in *White* is important because, before that decision, it had been unclear whether the category of "primary victims" could be said to encompass a miscellaneous group of claimants, namely employees, rescuers and other "participants" in the circumstances of an accident who, *although placed in no physical danger*, were able to take advantage of liberal rules in recovering for psychiatric illness. *White* seems to make it clear that such claimants are not to be regarded as "primary victims".[51] This aspect of the decision is controversial, and its effects on the position of this group of claimants are discussed later. Here, however, two further points should be noted.

---

[50] [1984] 1 W.L.R. 997.

[51] Although this effect of *White* does not seem to have been wholly accepted by the courts. See, for example, the strange case of *Farrell v Avon Health Authority* [2001] Lloyd's Rep. Med. 458 where a claimant not in physical danger succeeded as "primary victim" and *Salter v UB Frozen and Chilled Foods Ltd*, 2003 S.L.T. 1011, where it was held that a claimant employee not in danger had an arguable case under *Dooley v Cammell Laird & Co Ltd* [1951] 1 Lloyd's Rep. 271 (discussed later), notwithstanding the way that case had been dealt with in *White*.

*There may be a requirement of "actual danger"*

In most cases, of course, a claimant's reasonable grounds for fearing for his or her safety will **4–020** derive from the fact that he or she is in actual danger. Nevertheless, it is possible to imagine a case where a claimant *reasonably thinks* that he or she is in danger when, as a matter of fact, no such danger exists. The position of such claimants is unclear because the two leading opinions in *White* do not deal with the point in the same way. Lord Steyn thought that an additional requirement of actual danger was not necessary, saying that it would be sufficient if a claimant had "objectively exposed himself to danger or reasonably believed that he was doing so".[52] According to Lord Hoffmann, however, claimants have to be "within the range of foreseeable physical injury"[53] to qualify as primary victims—it is unclear whether his Lordship meant by this that they must be in actual danger. The point therefore remains unresolved.[54]

*In any event, the claimant's fear for his or her own safety must be reasonable*

Whether or not there is a requirement of "actual danger", the decision of the Court of Appeal, **4–021** in *McFarlane v E.E. Caledonia*,[55] makes it clear that claimants who seek to qualify as "primary victims" because they have been put in fear for their physical safety must have some reasonable basis for that fear. Here, the plaintiff alleged psychiatric illness brought on by his involvement in the Piper Alpha oil rig disaster—the rig exploded, causing the death of many workers on board. His claim as a "primary victim" failed, however, because at the time of the disaster he had been working in a support boat about 50 yards away from the rig and it was obvious that the boat had never been in any danger. It followed that his fear for his safety was unreasonable. (The plaintiff could not recover as a "secondary victim", for reasons which are considered below.)

## "Secondary victims"

The position of "secondary victims" is governed by the decision in *Alcock v Chief Constable* **4–022** *of South Yorkshire*, which must now be examined in detail. The claims in *Alcock* (and in *White*) arose from the tragic events that took place during the 1989 F.A. Cup semi-final between Liverpool and Nottingham Forest. Tickets to the Hillsborough football stadium were sold out, and the match was being shown on live television. After six minutes of play, however, it had to be stopped because, owing to negligent crowd control, too many spectators had been allowed on to the terraces. It became apparent that some were being crushed against the high fences erected between the terraces and the pitch.

South Yorkshire police admitted that the death of 95 spectators, and injuries to a further 400, were caused by their negligence in allowing too many people into the stadium. Claims for physical injury and death were settled by the police, as were certain psychiatric illness claims by police officers who had dragged bodies from the scene of the danger, risking physical injury to themselves. Psychiatric illness claims were then brought by two groups of people who had not been in physical danger: relatives (and a fiancée) who had in various

---

[52] *White v Chief Constable of South Yorkshire* [1999] 2 A.C. 455 at 499.

[53] [1999] 2 A.C. 455 at 504, 505 and 509.

[54] Note that the Law Commission suggested that it should be a precondition of recovery by secondary victims that the immediate victim be in actual danger. See Law Com. 249, para.6.18 (discussed below).

[55] [1994] 2 All E.R. 1. See also *Fagan v Goodman* (2001) WL 1476185.

ways witnessed or heard about the death or injury of their loved ones (the plaintiffs in *Alcock*) and police officers who had assisted in the aftermath of the tragedy (the plaintiffs in *White*).

The question for the House of Lords in *Alcock* was whether the plaintiffs were owed a duty of care on the basis that their psychiatric illness was reasonably foreseeable, applying the reasoning of Lords Bridge and Scarman in *McLoughlin v O'Brian*, or whether, *in addition*, their claims should be governed by the "control mechanisms" which had been suggested by Lord Wilberforce in that case. *Alcock* was a test case in which the specific plaintiffs had been chosen because their situations—in terms of closeness of relationship to the dead and injured and proximity to the disaster in time and space—were similar to those of about 150 other people who also wished to claim for psychiatric illness. Their Lordships held that none of the plaintiffs could succeed. Each of the plaintiffs, in one way or another, failed to satisfy the stringent criteria that their Lordships laid down for recovery by "secondary victims".

## SECONDARY VICTIMS: THE *ALCOCK* "CONTROL MECHANISMS"

**4-023**  In *Alcock*, following the approach of Lord Wilberforce in *McLoughlin v O'Brian*, their Lordships held that "secondary victims" of psychiatric illness had to show not only that their injuries were reasonably foreseeable; they had to satisfy three additional "control mechanisms", designed to restrict the scope of liability, as follows:

- proximity of relationship with the "immediate victim";
- proximity in "time and space" to the events causing the psychiatric illness;
- the means by which the psychiatric illness is caused.

It should be noted that some elements of the second and third "control mechanisms" are sometimes called "proximity of perception". Each is considered in turn below.

### (1) Proximity of relationship

**4-024**  The plaintiffs in *Alcock* were parents, brothers, sisters, a brother-in-law, a grandparent and a fiancée of the immediate victims. Their Lordships refused to define rigid categories of relationship into which secondary victims of psychiatric illness must fall. Instead, they held that there must generally be a *close relationship of love and affection* between the "secondary victim" and the "immediate victim" of the accident. According to their Lordships, such a relationship could be *presumed* to exist in the case of spouses, parents and children. (But, of course, the presumption could be rebutted by evidence in an appropriate case, such as where the parties were estranged.) Lord Keith thought that the presumption relating to spouses should also extend to fiancé(e)s, or, at least, that it should be extended to the plaintiff in *Alcock* who had lost her fiancé, whom she had known for four years.[56] Siblings and other relatives

---

[56] *Alcock v Chief Constable of South Yorkshire* [1992] 1 A.C. 310 at 398.

(such as grandparents, uncles and aunts) would *not* normally be regarded as having the requisite closeness of relationship, unless they could show that, because of special factors, such a relationship did in fact exist. (For example, because they had brought up the immediate victim as their own child.) Dealing with the position of the plaintiff who had lost his brother in the disaster, Lord Ackner pointed out: "The quality of brotherly love is well known to differ widely".[57] It followed that this plaintiff did not satisfy the "close tie of love and affection" test in the absence of evidence that his relationship with his brother had been particularly close.

Whilst holding that closeness of relationship was an important factor to consider, their Lordships declined to hold that it was an absolute prerequisite of recovery in every case, leaving open the possibility that a mere "bystander" who witnessed a catastrophe which was *exceptionally horrifying* might be able to recover for psychiatric illness without showing any relationship at all with the immediate victim of the catastrophe. Lord Ackner gave the example of a bystander witnessing a petrol tanker careering out of control into a school in session and bursting into flames. Subsequent to the decision in *Alcock*, however, this point was tested in the Court of Appeal in *McFarlane v E.E. Caledonia Ltd*.[58] When his claim as a "primary victim" failed, the plaintiff, who had been in the support boat when the Piper Alpha oil rig had exploded, claimed to be a "secondary victim", on the basis that he had witnessed the death of fellow workers in exceptionally horrific circumstances. His claim failed. In holding that it was not reasonably foreseeable that a mere "bystander" would suffer psychiatric illness in such circumstances, Stuart-Smith L.J. noted that people's reactions to horrific events were "entirely subjective".[59] This meant that there were serious practical and policy objections to allowing recovery by mere bystanders. The reasoning in *McFarlane*, then, has probably excluded the possibility of such claims in the future.

## (2) Proximity in time and space

The various plaintiffs in *Alcock* had witnessed the injury or death of their loved ones in    **4–025**
different ways. Some had been in other stands inside the ground and had seen the disaster happen, others had only seen the events on television, or heard about them on the radio. After the disaster had occurred, some of the plaintiffs had gone to the ground to search for their relatives, or had identified their bodies in a mortuary.

Their Lordships held that, to succeed as a secondary victim, a plaintiff had to show a high degree of proximity to the accident in time and space. Thus, the plaintiff must normally witness the accident as it actually occurs, or must come upon its "immediate aftermath" within a very short space of time. Whilst conceding that subsequent identification of the body of an accident victim might, in some circumstances, be regarded as part of the "immediate aftermath", Lord Ackner thought that Mr Alcock, who had identified his brother-in-law in a bad condition in a mortuary some eight hours after the disaster, could not be described as having come upon its immediate aftermath.[60] The decision in *Alcock*, then, took the law on the

---

[57] [1992] 1 A.C. 310 at 406.
[58] [1994] 2 All E.R. 1.
[59] [1994] 2 All E.R. 1 at 14.
[60] *Alcock v Chief Constable of South Yorkshire* [1992] 1 A.C. 310 at 405. Compare the view of Lord Keith, at 397, who appears to endorse the view of Deane J. in *Jaensch v Coffey* (1984) 155 C.L.R. 549, viz. that the "immediate aftermath" will continue for as long as the victim remains in the state caused by the accident.

meaning of "immediate aftermath" little further than it had been taken in *McLoughlin v O'Brian*.

However, in *Galli-Atkinson v Seghal*[61] the Court of Appeal was prepared, on the facts, to take a more generous view of the circumstances in which a subsequent visit to a mortuary could constitute the "immediate aftermath" of an accident. Here, the claimant was a mother whose daughter had been involved in a road accident. The claimant arrived at the scene just over one hour later and was told by a police officer that her daughter had been killed. She then attended the mortuary and saw her daughter's body which, although it had been cleaned-up, had been badly disfigured by the accident. The trial judge had not been prepared to accept that the visit to the mortuary had formed part of the aftermath, and had disallowed the mother's claim because her psychiatric illness had resulted from what she had been told, rather than from witnessing the accident. In allowing her appeal, however, Latham L.J. thought that the visit to the mortuary was not, as it had been in *Alcock*, a separate event, taking place after the horror of the accident had unfolded. Rather, it was the last in a sequence of uninterrupted events which went to make up the entirety of the claimant's perception of the tragedy. His Lordship pointed out that the mortuary visit had been made not merely to identify the body, but to "complete the story so far as the appellant was concerned, who clearly at that stage did not want—and one can understand this—to believe that her child was dead".[62]

*Simultaneous live television*

**4–026**    If the plaintiffs had only seen *pre-recorded* television pictures of the disaster, they clearly would not have satisfied the requirement of temporal proximity. However, in *Alcock*, some of the plaintiffs had seen a simultaneous live broadcast of the disaster. The position of these plaintiffs required careful consideration. It will be recalled that in *McLoughlin v O'Brian*, Lord Wilberforce had left open the question of whether live television could sometimes be treated as the equivalent of being present at the scene of a disaster. Their Lordships held that, in the circumstances of the *Alcock* case, it could not. This was for two reasons. First, broadcasters had not shown the suffering of recognisable individuals—this was prohibited by their professional code of ethics. (If they had done this, then the broadcasters, rather than the police, might have been regarded as the legal cause of the plaintiffs' psychiatric illness.) Secondly, the pictures transmitted from Hillsborough had been taken by cameras from many different view points. They therefore showed a combination of scenes which no one individual present at the ground would have been likely to see. Their Lordships held, therefore, that it was normally a prerequisite of liability that claimants should perceive the events in question with their "own unaided senses". But they were reluctant to lay down an inflexible rule on this point, holding that there might be very exceptional circumstances where a simultaneous broadcast of a disaster would equate with direct perception. Lord Ackner (approving the example given by Nolan L.J. in the Court of Appeal) thought that this might be the case where a publicity-seeking organisation had made arrangements for children to go up in a hot air balloon, and the children's parents, watching a live broadcast of the event, suffered psychiatric illness on seeing the balloon suddenly burst into flames.[63]

---

[61] [2003] Lloyd's Rep. Med. 285.
[62] [2003] Lloyd's Rep. Med. 285 at para.26.
[63] *Alcock v Chief Constable of South Yorkshire* [1992] 1 A.C. 310 at 405.

## (3) The means by which the psychiatric illness is caused

In *Alcock*, Lord Jauncey observed:                                                4–027

> "The means by which the shock is caused constitutes a third control, although in these appeals I find it difficult to separate this from proximity."[64]

Despite their conceptual similarity to the requirements of "proximity in time and space" considered above, their Lordships chose to consider a number of additional points under this third heading.

*The "sudden shock" requirement*

It was reaffirmed in *Alcock* that the psychiatric illness in question must result from the sudden    4–028
psychological impact of witnessing a single event or its immediate aftermath, as opposed to being caused by subsequent reflection on an event,[65] or prolonged exposure to distressing circumstances. Thus, although two of the plaintiffs had been present at the ground and had witnessed obviously distressing scenes, their claims were rejected because their perception of the consequences of the disaster for their relatives was, as Lord Oliver put it, "gradual".[66] Similarly, those who had seen the disaster on television had not satisfied the "sudden shock" requirement because the psychological trauma in each case had not arisen purely from the impact of the transmitted images. Rather, it had been caused by a combination of two things: first, the plaintiffs had seen the images—which, as Lord Oliver put it, provided "the matrix for imagined consequences"—and secondly, they had had their worst fears confirmed by subsequently hearing about the death of a loved one or identifying his body.

The "sudden shock" requirement prevented recovery by the claimant in *Sion v Hampstead Health Authority*.[67] The claimant, a father whose son had been injured in a motorcycle accident, stayed by his son's bedside for 14 days, watching his son deteriorate, go into a coma and die. The Court of Appeal denied the father's claim, because his psychiatric illness had not resulted from the sudden appreciation of a horrifying event. (By the time the son died, his death was expected.) This decision should be contrasted with the Court of Appeal's approach in the more recent case of *North Glamorgan NHS Trust v Walters*.[68] Here, the claimant was a mother whose baby, following negligent treatment at a hospital, suffered an epileptic fit leading to a coma and, some 36 hours later, his death in his mother's arms. The Court of Appeal was prepared to hold that the 36 hours during which the claimant had been subjected to trauma could be regarded as a single event for the purpose of satisfying the sudden shock requirement.

*No liability where the claimant is merely informed about the accident*

In *Alcock*, their Lordships affirmed that a defendant who causes harm or imperilment to an    4–029
"immediate victim" will not be liable to a claimant who is merely informed about this by a

---

[64] [1992] 1 A.C. 310 at 420.
[65] Note, however, that in *W v Essex CC* [2000] 2 All E.R. 237 (discussed later in this chapter) the House of Lords refused to say that a claim in such circumstances would be unarguable.
[66] [1992] 1 A.C. 310 at 417.
[67] [1994] 5 Med. L.R. 170.
[68] [2003] P.I.Q.R. P16. Contrast *White v Lidl UK GmbH* [2005] EWHC 871. (No liability where minor injury to a wife from a car park crash barrier led to a husband's psychiatric illness when she committed suicide six months later.)

third party.[69] This rule, of course, may produce some bizarre results. Consider a claimant who, very shortly after an accident, is informed by a friend that his or her loved-one is dying in hospital. If the claimant suffers psychiatric illness there and then and faints on the spot, he or she will have no claim. But if the friend has the legal acumen to revive the claimant and take him or her to the hospital, the claimant may be compensated under the "immediate aftermath" doctrine, as was the plaintiff in *McLoughlin v O'Brian*. We shall see that the Law Commission has suggested that this restrictive rule, like many others, should be abolished.

It is important to understand that this rule does not mean that there can never be liability where a claimant suffers psychiatric illness as the result of hearing distressing news. The person who *communicates* the news (as opposed to the person who caused the harm the news is about) *may* be liable if the news is broken in a negligently insensitive manner. In *AB v Tameside and Glossop Health Authority*,[70] the defendants sent out letters warning former patients that they were at risk of having contracted HIV, because a health worker who had treated them had tested positive for the disease. The plaintiffs alleged they had suffered psychiatric illness as a result of hearing the news in this way, and argued that they should have been told face-to-face. The Court of Appeal held that the defendants had not been negligent in choosing to communicate the information by letter, but their Lordships made no comment on the fact that counsel in the case had conceded that a duty of care was owed.[71]

*Psychiatric illness caused by a defendant harming or imperilling himself or herself*

**4–030**     One further point was considered, obiter, in *Alcock*, but was left undecided. This was whether the law would allow a claim in circumstances where a defendant had caused psychiatric illness to a secondary victim by negligently placing *himself or herself* in danger, or causing *self-inflicted* harm. To take the example given by Lord Oliver, would a mother be able to bring a claim against her son for psychiatric illness caused by witnessing his imperilment when he negligently walked in front of an oncoming car? His Lordship thought that if such a claim were denied, the denial had to be based on policy rather than logic, because it would be difficult to imagine a case in which the elements of foreseeability of psychiatric harm and proximity were more clearly established. Whilst declining expressly to decide the point, Lord Oliver suspected that liability in such a situation would be barred as a matter of policy, noting that this view had been expressed by Deane J. in the Australian case of *Jaensch v Coffey*.[72]

The issue subsequently arose for consideration in the extraordinary case of *Greatorex v Greatorex*.[73] Here, the defendant, John Greatorex, had been out drinking with his friend and had then crashed his friend's car while driving on the wrong side of the road. He was trapped in the car, injured and unconscious, when the fire brigade arrived. By co-incidence, the leading fire-officer at the scene was Christopher Greatorex, the defendant's father. Christopher Greatorex suffered psychiatric illness as a result of witnessing his son's injuries, and so brought an action against his son. In denying the father's claim, Cazalet J. reasoned that, since the defendant's injuries were self-inflicted, to make him liable to those who witnessed the injuries would be

---

[69] Their Lordships doubted the correctness of *Hevican v Ruane* [1991] 3 All E.R. 65 and *Ravenscroft v Rederi AB Transatlantic* [1991] 3 All E.R. 73, which had appeared to decide that receiving news of a son's death could be an effective cause of psychiatric illness. (The latter decision was subsequently reversed by the Court of Appeal: [1992] 2 All E.R. 470.)

[70] [1997] 8 Med. L.R. 91.

[71] See also the reasoning of Morland J. in *CJD Group B Plaintiffs v Medical Research Council* [2000] Lloyd's Rep. Med. 161. Comment: Mullany (1998) 114 L.Q.R. 381.

[72] (1984) 155 C.L.R. 549.

[73] [2000] 1 W.L.R. 1970.

contrary to public policy. The policy consideration in question was that making a person liable in such a situation would restrict his or her right to self-determination—i.e. a person ought to be free to choose to incur personal risks, without exposing himself or herself to liability to others. (This point is considered further in the context of the Law Commission's proposals.) The issue was complicated by the fact that the claimant and defendant were father and son. On this point, Cazalet J. thought that an additional policy consideration precluded liability—causing distress to members of one's family was a normal part of family life, and for the law to allow a remedy for psychiatric illness caused by another family member would open the way for undesirable litigation within the family involving questions of relative fault as between its members. The gist of his Lordship's view was that, if such litigation were allowed, contrived and ill-founded claims might be used to prolong and aggravate family conflicts which might otherwise resolve themselves. Therefore, the law should only provide a remedy for psychiatric illness caused when a loved one is harmed by a defendant who is not a family member.

## THE IMPACT OF *WHITE*

The limits of the decision in *Alcock* were explored in *White v Chief Constable of South Yorkshire*. Here, as has been said, the plaintiffs were police officers who had suffered psychiatric illness as a result of their professional involvement in the Hillsborough disaster. Subsequent to the full height of the disaster, five of the six plaintiffs had assisted the injured and had worked to ensure that there was no further danger to those leaving the stadium. The sixth plaintiff had been on duty at a temporary mortuary which had been set up near the ground. None of the plaintiffs had been in physical danger. A majority of the Court of Appeal held that the five plaintiffs present at the stadium could recover in respect of their psychiatric illness.[74] This decision provoked outrage from the relatives of those killed and injured at Hillsborough, who had recently been refused compensation by the decision in *Alcock*. It was subsequently overturned by the House of Lords, which openly acknowledged the argument that the public would think it unacceptable to compensate police officers at the ground for psychiatric illness sustained simply in the course of doing their jobs, when compensation had been denied to the relatives in *Alcock*.

**4–031**

In the Court of Appeal, it was said that the police officers might be regarded as "primary victims" of the Chief Constable's negligence. This was because previous authority had suggested that the category of "primary victims" included plaintiffs who, though not in any physical danger, had *participated* in the events giving rise to their psychiatric illness. In *Alcock*, their Lordships had been content to divide psychiatric illness claimants into two broad categories—on the one hand, claimants who were *directly involved* in the accident (Lord Oliver thought that such claimants should be regarded as "primary victims") and, on the other hand, claimants who were only "passive and unwilling" witnesses of injury to others (who should be regarded as "secondary victims"). By the time the Court of Appeal came to decide *White*, however, the House of Lords, in *Page v Smith*, appeared to have suggested that only claimants who had been in physical danger could be regarded as "primary victims". This, as Henry L.J. recognised in the Court of Appeal, cast doubt on whether the police officers could be regarded as "primary victims".

---

[74] See *Frost v Chief Constable of South Yorkshire* [1998] Q.B. 254 (from which the appeal to the House of Lords in *White* was made).

The Court of Appeal thought, however, that even if there was doubt about their classification as "primary victims", the officers present at the stadium were entitled to succeed without needing to meet the *Alcock* criteria. Their Lordships drew this conclusion from previous authority (which we shall examine later) that appeared to establish that special rules applied where a psychiatric illness claimant was a "rescuer" or an employee, holding that the officers in question were both.[75] But the House of Lords in *White* took a very different approach, holding that no special rules applied to "rescuers" or employees. The police officers did not qualify as "primary victims"—this classification was to be reserved for people who had been placed in physical danger (or who reasonably believed themselves to be in danger). All other psychiatric illness claimants were "secondary victims", and had to bring themselves within the *Alcock* criteria in order to succeed. On the facts, these criteria had obviously not been met, not least because none of the officers at the scene had a close relationship of love and affection with the dead and injured.

Clearly, the decision in *White* has implications for the general law relating to employers' liability. It also appears to be contrary to the general attitude of the courts towards rescuers. The decision in *White* also leaves unresolved the law relating to so-called "unwitting agents"— that is to say, claimants who, because of the defendant's negligence, are placed in a position where they themselves bring about the death, injury, or imperilment of the "immediate victim". Below, then, we consider the implications of *White* for three types of claimant:

- employees
- unwitting agents
- rescuers

The general law of employers' liability is considered in Ch.7, so discussion of it here is omitted. The general law on rescuers, however, is considered here in some detail.

## (1) Employees

**4–032**  In *Dooley v Cammell Laird & Co Ltd*[76] (a case decided before *Alcock* and *White*), a crane driver was operating a crane at the docks where he worked when, through the fault of his employers, the sling connecting the load to the crane-hooks snapped, causing the load to fall into the hold of a ship where men were working. The crane driver suffered psychiatric illness, resulting from his fear that the falling load would injure or kill some of his fellow workmen. Donovan J., whilst drawing the inference that the men in the ship were friends of the plaintiff, was prepared to decide liability without requiring the plaintiff to establish any closer degree of relationship with the imperilled workers—the plaintiff's relationship of employment with the defendant created the necessary degree of "proximity" for his negligence action to succeed. Before the decision in *White*, it was thought that this case, and a number of similar decisions,[77]

---

[75] Technically, a police officer's relationship with a Chief Constable is not one of employment, but the courts were prepared to treat it as such in *White*.

[76] [1951] 1 Lloyd's Rep. 271.

[77] See *Galt v British Railways Board* (1983) 133 N.L.J. 870; *Wigg v British Railways Board, The Times*, February 4, 1986; *Mount Isa Mines Ltd v Pusey* (1970) 125 C.L.R 383.

might have established that an employee had a right to recover for psychiatric illness caused by witnessing or fearing injury to fellow workers as a result of an employer's negligence.

In *White*, however, their Lordships held that no such independent right existed. An employer's duty to safeguard employees from psychiatric harm was no different from the general duty of care owed by all people to others whom their conduct might affect. It followed that in cases where an employee suffered psychiatric illness through witnessing the death, injury or imperilment of others, the ordinary rules of tort applied, namely those laid down in *Alcock*. Therefore, there was no advantage to be gained by the police officers framing their action as a case of employers' liability. Their Lordships found little assistance in *Dooley v Cammell Laird & Co Ltd* and similar decisions. Dealing with these cases, Lord Hoffmann said:

> "I think that, on a fair reading, they were each regarded by the judges who decided them as raising one question of fact, namely whether psychiatric illness to the plaintiff was a foreseeable consequence of the defendant's negligent conduct. This was in accordance with the law as it was thought to be at the time. There was no reference to the control mechanisms, which had not yet been invented."[78]

## (2) "Unwitting agents"

Although *White* makes it clear that employees are not to be regarded as a special group of psychiatric illness claimants, what remains unclear is whether cases like *Dooley v Cammell Laird & Co Ltd* are still good authority for a different proposition, namely that special treatment should be given to claimants who, because of a defendant's negligence, are placed in circumstances where they accidentally cause the death, injury or imperilment of another through no fault of their own (or reasonably think that they have done so). In *White*, Lord Hoffmann acknowledged that "there may be grounds for treating such a rare category of case as exceptional and exempt from the *Alcock* control mechanisms".[79]    **4–033**

In this context, the decision of the House of Lords in *W v Essex CC*[80] should be noted. Here, an action for psychiatric illness was brought by foster parents against a local authority. The foster parents, who had four young children of their own, had made it clear to the authority that they would not be willing to foster a child who had a history of carrying out sexual abuse. Nevertheless, the authority placed such a child in their care. It was alleged that the child had perpetrated acts of indecency against the claimants' children. The substance of the foster parents' claim was that their psychiatric illness had been caused, not just by discovering the abuse, but also by feelings of guilt that they, by being parties to a decision to bring their children into contact with a child abuser, had unwittingly *caused* harm to their children.

The local authority applied to have the claim struck out as disclosing no cause of action, but the House of Lords refused to do this. Lord Slynn, delivering the unanimous opinion of the House, thought that although the claimants might have difficulty in succeeding, their claim could not be said to be unarguable. His Lordship observed: ". . . the categorisation of those

---

[78] *White v Chief Constable of South Yorkshire* [1999] 2 A.C. 455 at 507. Compare the analysis of Judge Gordon Reid Q.C. in *Salter v UB Frozen and Chilled Foods Ltd*, 2003 S.L.T. 1011.

[79] [1999] 2 A.C. 455 at 508.

[80] [2000] 2 All E.R. 237.

claiming to be included as primary or secondary victims is not as I read the cases finally closed".[81]

## (3) Rescuers

**4–034**   First, in this section, it is necessary to consider at some length the approach of the courts towards "rescuers" who suffer physical injury. This provides an understanding of the legal background against which the decision in *White* may seem controversial. We then go on to consider the implications of *White* for "rescuers" who suffer only psychiatric harm.

*Rescuers who suffer physical injury*

**4–035**   We have seen in Ch.2 that in English law there is generally no duty to go to the rescue of a person in peril. Here, we are considering a different point: if a person does go to the rescue of another, and suffers physical harm in attempting the rescue, can that person (the "rescuer") claim compensation from the defendant who negligently endangered the person being rescued?

In 1934, the courts answered this question in the affirmative, and they have done so ever since. The relevant case is *Haynes v Harwood*.[82] In Ch.2, we considered this case in the context of liability for creating a "source of danger" that is "sparked off" by the actions of a third party. Here, we consider it in a different context. The plaintiff was a police constable who was on duty inside a police station in a street where there were a large number of people, including children. The defendants had left their horses unattended in the street. A boy threw a stone at the horses and caused them to bolt ("sparking off" the danger). Seeing the defendants' horses coming down the street, the plaintiff rushed out of the police station and eventually stopped them, sustaining injuries in the process. The question for the Court of Appeal was whether, in the circumstances, physical harm to the plaintiff was reasonably foreseeable by the defendants. The court rejected arguments that rescuers were not, in effect, "foreseeable claimants", holding that a person who can reasonably foresee that his act or omission may imperil another will also be taken to foresee that it may imperil a rescuer. This idea is encapsulated by the well-known words of the American judge, Cardozo J., who, in *Wagner v International Railway Co*,[83] said: "Danger invites rescue. The cry of distress is a summons to relief".

Cardozo J.'s words were cited and approved by the Court of Appeal in *Baker v T.E. Hopkins and Son Ltd*,[84] a case which clearly illustrates the approach of the courts in this area. The defendant company was engaged to clean a well, and used a petrol-driven pump to clear out the water. The defendant's managing director realised that this would create carbon monoxide fumes inside the well, which could be a danger to his employees. He therefore instructed them not to go down the well until the next day, by which time, he assumed, the fumes would have dispersed. In fact, when the employees went down the well the next morning, the danger had not passed. They were overcome by the fumes and eventually died. The plaintiff, who was a

---

[81] [2000] 2 All E.R. 237 at 243. In *Salter v UB Frozen and Chilled Foods Ltd*, 2003 S.L.T. 1011, it was pointed out by counsel that in *W v Essex* the claimants' relationship with the local authority had a "contractual flavour". This might have allowed them to succeed as primary victims without being in physical danger (see *Walker v Northumberland C.C.* [1995] I.C.R. 702, discussed in Ch.7). See also *Monk v PC Harrington Ltd* [2008] EWHC 1879, where it was accepted in principle that in providing assistance, in circumstances where the claimant reasonably believed he had caused the accident, could establish sufficient proximity in the absence of physical danger.

[82] [1935] 1 K.B. 146.

[83] 232 N.Y. Rep. 176 at 180 (1921).

[84] [1959] 1 W.L.R. 966.

doctor, was summoned to the scene by concerned farm workers. People who had gathered at the top of the well urged him not to go down, and to wait for the arrival of the fire brigade, but he insisted, saying, "There are two men down there. I must see what I can do for them". Having tied a rope around his waist and asked the people at the top of the well to hold one end of it, and pull him up if he felt ill, he descended the well. He was heard to call up that there was nothing he could do for the men. He had started to climb up again when he was overcome by the fumes and collapsed. The people at the top tried to haul him up, but the rope became caught in a pipe or cross-member of the well and they were unable to raise him. Soon after-wards, the fire brigade arrived and the doctor was brought to the surface. He was unconscious, and died before reaching hospital.

The doctor's estate succeeded in its claim. The Court of Appeal (as it had done in *Haynes v Harwood*) rejected the suggestion that a rescuer, by intervening, should be regarded as having caused his or her own loss, or as having voluntarily accepted the risk of injury. Willmer L.J. made it clear that, provided the rescue attempt was not foolhardy or "wanton", the presence of a rescuer at the scene of an accident should be regarded as reasonably foreseeable. His Lordship cited with approval some additional words of Cardozo J. in *Wagner v International Railway Co*:

> "The risk of rescue, if only it be not wanton, is born of the occasion. The emergency begets the man. The wrongdoer may not have foreseen the coming of a deliverer. He is accountable as if he had".

The courts, then, have taken the view that as a matter of policy rescue attempts should be encouraged and rewarded. This has led them to hold that a duty may be owed to a rescuer even in circumstances where no duty is owed to the person being rescued. Such was the case in *Videan v British Transport Commission*.[85] Here, a two-year-old boy, who, being the son of a village stationmaster, lived in a house adjoining the platform, strayed on to the railway track. The stationmaster saw his son standing on the track and at the same time saw a power-driven trolley approaching on the track at considerable speed. He signalled to the driver of the trolley to stop, but the driver did not understand the signals and did not see the child until it was too late to pull up. In a desperate effort to rescue his son, the stationmaster leapt from the platform on to the track in front of the trolley, and in so doing was killed. (The child, though saved by this act, suffered severe injuries.)

In an action by the stationmaster's widow in respect of the death of her husband and on behalf her injured son, the court found that the trolley driver had been careless. He had driven too fast in wet conditions, and had failed to keep a proper look-out. The claim in respect of the child's injuries failed, because, at the time the case was decided, only very limited duties were owed to trespassers. This, however, did not prevent a successful claim in respect of the *station-master's* death. Harman and Pearson L.JJ. based their decision on the fact that, because the stationmaster had a duty to rescue trespassers on the line (even though he was off duty at the time), his presence on the track dealing with an emergency was reasonably foreseeable by the trolley driver. Lord Denning M.R. went a stage further, however, holding that the position would have been the same if the rescuer had been a mere passer-by and not the stationmaster rescuing his son—a person who negligently created a situation of peril should answer for it to anyone who attempted a rescue, whether or not the *victim rescued* had a cause of action.

---

[85] [1963] 2 Q.B. 650.

A number of additional points should be noted about rescuers. First, where a defendant negligently imperils *himself or herself*, as opposed to a third party, a rescuer who suffers *physical injury* will have a cause of action against the defendant,[86] although *Greatorex* suggests that this will not be the case where the rescuer suffers only psychiatric illness.[87] Secondly, it is clear that rescuers have a cause of action where what has been put in peril is not a person, but property. Thus, in *Haynes v Harwood*, it was accepted that the objects of the rescue were not only the people in the street who were endangered by the runaway horses, but the horses themselves. Similarly, in *Ogwo v Taylor*,[88] a fireman succeeded when he was injured trying to save the defendant's property from a fire. Where property is the object of the rescue, however, the question of whether it is reasonable for the rescuer to intervene and risk his own safety will have to be very carefully considered[89] (whereas, in the case of people, rescue attempts are normally regarded as reasonable, provided they are not reckless or "wanton"). Thirdly, the decision in *Ogwo v Taylor* confirmed that in English law there is no equivalent of the "firemen's rule" which obtains in some parts of the United States. This rule provides that, because members of the emergency services are employed to act as rescuers, defendants cannot be liable to them in respect of the very dangers they are paid to incur. In English law, however, (subject to the qualification that defendants are entitled to expect professional rescuers to use professional skill) professional rescuers are treated in the same way as public-spirited lay rescuers.

*Rescuers who suffer only psychiatric harm*

**4-036**    Prior to *White*, by way of an extension of their general approach to rescuers, the courts appeared to have developed a special approach to cases where rescuers suffered only psychiatric harm. The leading case here was *Chadwick v British Transport Commission*.[90] The case arose from the events of a serious train crash which occurred in December 1957 in Lewisham, South London. Mr Chadwick, who lived about 200 yards from the scene of the accident, went to the scene to do what he could to help, and worked all through the night giving assistance to the injured and dying. The key witness at the trial—a woman trapped in the wreckage who had been given an injection by Mr Chadwick at the request of a doctor, who was himself too large to enter the wrecked carriage—described the horrors of the tragedy to which Mr Chadwick had been exposed: there had been a "sea of bodies" and people had been screaming in pain and fear. Before the incident, Mr Chadwick had been a cheerful and active member of the local community and had run a successful window-cleaning business, but as a result of his involvement in the tragedy, he developed severe anxiety and neurosis. Waller J. held that the defendants (who admitted the train collision was caused by their negligence) were liable for Mr Chadwick's psychiatric illness.

Before *White*, it was widely thought that the decision in *Chadwick* meant that rescuers were to be given special treatment for the purposes of psychiatric illness claims. In particular, they did not need to establish that they had been in physical danger to qualify as "primary victims". Certainly, this was the view taken by the Law Commission in March 1998, who expressed concern about aspects of the Court of Appeal's reasoning in *McFarlane v E.E. Caledonia* that

---

[86] *Harrison v British Railways Board* [1981] 3 All E.R. 679.
[87] See *Greatorex v Greatorex* [2000] 1 W.L.R. 1970; the observations of Lord Oliver in *Alcock v Chief Constable of South Yorkshire* [1992] 1 A.C. 310 at 418 (discussed above); and Law Com. 249, para.6.18 (discussed below).
[88] [1998] A.C. 431.
[89] See *Hyett v Great Western Railway* [1948] 1 K.B. 345.
[90] [1967] 1 W.L.R. 912.

might have suggested otherwise.[91] We have seen that the majority of the Court of Appeal in *White* held that the police officers at the scene were entitled to recover for psychiatric illness as rescuers, even though they had not been in physical danger. By a bare 3:2 majority, however, the House of Lords disagreed. Whilst Lords Goff and Griffiths (dissenting) thought that rescuers were entitled to special treatment, the majority held that rescuers must either satisfy the "narrow" definition of "primary victims" (i.e. by being in physical danger) or must bring their claims as "secondary victims" and satisfy the *Alcock* criteria.

Lord Hoffmann gave two reasons why the law should not give special treatment to rescuers unless they had been placed in physical danger. The first was that, if the control mechanism of physical danger were removed, it would become difficult to define the concept of a "rescuer"— would the term then apply to a bystander who had rendered only some trivial assistance? The second (and in his Lordship's view more important) reason was that removing the control mechanism of physical danger would produce a result in *White* that would be "unacceptable", in the sense that it would offend against the ordinary person's notions of distributive justice. His Lordship said that the ordinary person:

> ". . . would think it wrong that policemen, even as part of a general class of persons who rendered assistance, should have the right to compensation for psychiatric injury out of public funds while the bereaved relatives are sent away with nothing".[92]

In *White*, then, the majority of the House of Lords distinguished *Chadwick* on its facts, saying that the situation of Mr Chadwick differed from the situation of the police officers at Hillsborough because Mr Chadwick, by entering wrecked train carriages, had been "within the range of foreseeable personal injury". This made him a "primary victim" (in the narrow *Page v Smith* sense). Lords Goff and Griffiths, however, disagreed with the majority about the ratio of *Chadwick*. Lord Goff pointed out that although Mr Chadwick had been exposed to some physical danger, "the trial judge [Waller J.] treated that as irrelevant".[93] Lord Steyn, on the other hand (speaking with the majority), thought that the fact that Mr Chadwick had been exposed to personal danger had influenced Waller J.'s decision, albeit that his Lordship had not held that fear of personal injury was the *cause* of Mr Chadwick's psychiatric illness.[94] Lord Hoffmann was also prepared to take a restricted view of *Chadwick*, stating that the case could be subjected to an "ex post facto rationalisation"[95] and should be regarded as one turning on the presence of physical danger.

In his powerful dissenting speech, Lord Goff clearly stated that he regarded the reasoning of the majority as contrary to the existing authority of *Chadwick*, and noted that introducing what his Lordship saw as a new requirement that rescuers had to be in physical danger could produce very unjust results. His Lordship put forward an extreme example to illustrate the point:[96]

> "Suppose that there was a terrible train crash and that there were two Chadwick brothers living nearby, both of them small and agile window cleaners distinguished by their

---

[91] See Law Com. 249, para.7.3.
[92] *White v Chief Constable of South Yorkshire* [1999] 2 A.C. 455 at 500.
[93] [1999] 2 A.C. 455 at 484.
[94] [1999] 2 A.C. 455 at 499.
[95] [1999] 2 A.C. 455 at 509.
[96] [1999] 2 A.C. 455 at 487.

courage and humanity. Mr. A. Chadwick worked on the front half of the train, and Mr. B. Chadwick on the rear half. It so happened that, although there was some physical danger present in the front half of the train, there was none in the rear. Both worked for 12 hours or so bringing aid and comfort to the victims. Both suffered P.T.S.D. in consequence of the general horror of the situation. On the new control mechanism now proposed, Mr. A. would recover but Mr. B. would not. To make things worse, the same conclusion must follow even if Mr. A. was unaware of the existence of the physical danger present in his half of the train. This is surely unacceptable."

Despite Lord Goff's objection, the decision of the majority of the House of Lords in *White* has effectively closed the door on future claims by rescuers who have not been placed in physical peril.[97] It remains to be seen, however, whether, in line with their general approach to rescue cases, the courts will adopt a liberal interpretation of this requirement in order to do justice in meritorious cases. In this context, it is interesting to note the (possible) combined effect of the decisions in *White* and *Page v Smith*. This is that if rescuers in physical peril are now to be regarded as "primary victims" (in the narrow *Page v Smith* sense), they may be able to take advantage of the "eggshell skull" reasoning in *Page v Smith* to establish a duty of care. Thus (arguably) in a case like *Chadwick*, provided it could be shown that some very minor personal injury to the claimant was reasonably foreseeable, the law would then proceed to regard personal injury and psychiatric injury as the same kind of damage. *Page v Smith* reasoning would then apply, so that the claimant could recover even if he or she were "peculiarly suscep-tible" to psychiatric illness. This consequence of their Lordship's interpretation of *Chadwick* has the effect of *widening* the scope of liability to rescuers for psychiatric illness—a point that does not appear to have been specifically addressed in *White*.[98]

## PSYCHIATRIC ILLNESS LAW: PROPOSALS FOR REFORM

**4–037**    In March 1998, the Law Commission published a report which recommended some important changes to the law.[99] In summary, the report concluded that, in relation to secondary victims, whilst the "control mechanism" of "close ties of love and affection" should remain, all of the other *Alcock* "control mechanisms" should be abolished. The Law Commission expressed the view that, with the decision in *Alcock*, the common law had in some respects "taken a wrong turn".[100] The Commission did not think it appropriate, however, to codify *all* of the common law on psychiatric illness—this was not a sensible option, because the flexibility of the common law would allow new areas of liability to develop incrementally, as experts learned more about psychiatric illness, and society further recognised its debilitating consequences. Therefore, the Commission proposed a strategy of minimal legislative intervention to modify and clarify the common law. A draft Bill forms part of the Law Commission's report. With the

---

[97] Thus, the fireman father in *Greatorex v Greatorex* [2000] 1 W.L.R. 1970, although a rescuer, could not succeed as a primary victim because he was not in physical danger.

[98] Although it is alluded to by Lord Goff at 479–480.

[99] "Liability for Psychiatric Illness" Law Com. 249 (available from *http://www.justice.gov.uk/lawcommission/index. htm* [Accessed April 15, 2011]). Compare the more recent report of the Scottish Law Commission No.196, "Damages for Psychiatric Injury" (2004) (discussed by D. Nolan (2005) 68 M.L.R. 983, who argues that the flexibility it envis-ages is a recipe for uncertainty.)

[100] "Liability for Psychiatric Illness" Law Com. 249; para.4.2.

help of consultants from the insurance industry, the Commission was able to estimate (very roughly and in relation to motor vehicle insurance only) that its proposals to expand the scope of liability might lead to an increase in insurance premiums of between 2 and 5 per cent.[101]

The most radical proposal, then, is that two of the *Alcock* "control mechanisms" should be abolished. Thus, it would no longer be necessary for secondary victims to show proximity to the accident in time and space,[102] or that they had perceived the accident or its aftermath by their "own unaided senses". This would mean that, provided they could show closeness of relationship with the "immediate victim" (see below), people in the position of the plaintiffs in *Alcock* would be able to succeed, as would claimants whose psychiatric illness resulted from merely being *told* about the accident. The requirement that the claimant's psychiatric illness must be produced by a "sudden shock" would be abolished. This would allow recovery, for example, by a long-term carer who developed psychiatric illness because of the emotional strain of looking after the victim of the defendant's negligence.

## "Close ties of love and affection": the "fixed list"

In deciding to retain the requirement of "close ties of love and affection" between a secondary victim and the immediate victim, the Commission noted that policy considerations dictated limits to recovery by secondary victims, and felt that the requirement operated as an appropriate control mechanism. It thought, however, that in *Alcock* the requirement had been too narrowly drawn. Under its proposals, therefore, the *rebuttable* common law presumptions governing spouses, parents and children would be replaced with *conclusive* statutory presumptions in respect of a wider class of relationships. Thus, there would be a statutory "fixed list" of relationships in which close ties of love and affection would be deemed to exist.[103] These relationships would be: parent, child, sibling, spouse, and cohabitant (whether heterosexual or homosexual) for a period of two or more years. (Thus, the list is wider than the categories of presumed close relationships in *Alcock*, because it includes siblings and cohabitants.) Persons outside the "fixed list" would remain in the hands of the common law. Thus, they would not be barred from making a claim, but would be required to establish the necessary ties of love and affection by evidence. (In this context, the Commission thought that the class of potential claimants might extend to non-relatives who could establish a "relationship of care"—such as might exist between a schoolteacher and a pupil.) The Commission saw no need for legislation relating to mere "bystanders", leaving their position to the common law (so the reasoning in *McFarlane v E.E. Caledonia* would probably prevent them recovering).

The Commission also recommended that legislation should provide that the requirement of a close relationship could be satisfied by the existence of such a relationship either at the time of the accident, *or* at the onset of the claimant's psychiatric illness. This provision would be necessary to accommodate, for example, the case of a carer who, whilst having no ties of love

4–038

---

[101] "Liability for Psychiatric Illness" Law Com. 249, para.1.13.

[102] At para.6.12, the report cites *Taylor v Somerset Health Authority* (1993) 4 Med. L.R. 34 and *Taylorson v Shieldness Produce Ltd* [1994] P.I.Q.R. P329 as examples where the requirement has produced unjust results.

[103] Note, however, as the report points out (at para.6.25), it would still be open to the court to hold that the absence of a de facto close relationship meant that psychiatric illness to the claimant was not reasonably foreseeable, as, for example, where a mother, who had abandoned her son at birth, suffered psychiatric illness on reading about his death in a newspaper many years later.

and affection with the victim at the time of the accident, subsequently developed such ties in the course of looking after the victim, and suffered psychiatric illness as a result of this task.

## The "just and reasonable" proviso

4–039    The report points out that the duty of care owed by a defendant to a secondary victim is an independent duty—its existence does not depend on a duty of care being owed to the immediate victim. (For example, where the immediate "victim" is placed in danger but not actually injured, there may be no tort committed against him or her.) The Law Commission recognised, however, that in certain circumstances it might be undesirable to impose liability on a defendant towards a secondary victim if the defendant would not be liable to the immediate victim (for example because the immediate victim had consented to the risk of injury). To accommodate such circumstances, the Commission proposed a legislative provision stating that defendants should not be liable to secondary victims in cases where the court considers that such liability would not be "just and reasonable".

Such a provision would also cover situations where the immediate victim was the defendant—in other words, where the defendant had injured or imperilled himself or herself, causing a secondary victim psychiatric illness. We have seen that, in *Alcock*, Lord Oliver thought that policy considerations would probably preclude the liability of such a defendant, and that in *Greatorex v Greatorex* such considerations formed part of the reasoning in denying liability. The Law Commission, however, thought that there was no good reason why, generally speaking, a defendant who injured or imperilled himself or herself should not owe a duty of care to others. The Commission was conscious, however, that the imposition of such a duty in all circumstances might severely restrict a person's right to self-determination. For example, it would mean that a person could not, without exposing himself or herself to potential liability, choose to engage in a dangerous sport, or refuse medical treatment for religious reasons. The Commission noted:

> "there is a difficult balance to be arrived at between respecting self-determination and requiring proper concern to be shown for the consequences for others of choosing to harm or incur the risk of harm to oneself".[104]

Regarding this as a matter for the courts, it proposed that, whilst the absolute bar to liability in such cases (if it existed) should be removed, the imposition of a duty should be qualified by a requirement that it must be "just and reasonable" in the circumstances.

## The "actual danger" proviso

4–040    The Law Commission noted that whilst it was not in doubt that, under existing law, a secondary victim who satisfied the *Alcock* criteria would be able to recover where the immediate victim had been *placed in danger* but had not actually been *injured*, some doubt existed as to whether a secondary victim could recover in a situation where he or she *reasonably believed* that the "victim" was in danger, whereas, as a matter of fact, he or she was not. The Commission thought that, if liability were allowed in such a situation, "the policy against opening the

---

[104] Law Com. 249, para.5.42.

floodgates of litigation would be undermined".[105] It therefore proposed that "legislation should draw the line at where the loved one has in fact been killed, injured or imperilled by the defendant". Thus, to take the Law Commission's example,[106] there would be no liability in a situation where a wife suffers psychiatric illness after watching evening news reports of a train crash, believing that her husband is on the train, when, in fact, he has been delayed at work and taken a later train, arriving home safely that night.

### Rescuers, "participants" and "unwitting agents"

The Commission's report (dated March 1998) suggested that the position of "rescuers" and "involuntary participants" should be left to the common law. The decision in *White* (in 1999) has, of course, settled the position of rescuers. However, in the light of Lord Hoffmann's remarks in that case (noted earlier) to the effect that "unwitting agent" cases may be exempt from the normal control mechanisms, there appears to remain some scope for the courts to develop the law in situations where the claimant is either an "unwitting agent" (the involuntary cause of the death, injury or imperilment of the immediate victim) or is otherwise intimately involved as a "participant" in the events which give rise to the harm to the immediate victim.   **4–041**

Such a claim succeeded in the Scottish case of *Salter v UB Frozen and Chilled Foods Ltd*.[107] Here, the claimant was a forklift-truck driver engaged in a stock-taking exercise in a warehouse whereby he drove along carrying his workmate in a cage at the top of the truck. The workmate was fatally injured when he failed to duck to avoid a roof-beam while checking stock on the upper shelves, and the claimant suffered psychiatric illness as a result of witnessing the incident. The claimant had not himself been in physical danger. In an action against his employer, however, he was able to succeed on the basis that he was so intimately involved in the incident that (unlike the police constables in *White*) he could be regarded as a "participant" in the tragic event. Judge Gordon Reid Q.C. pointed out that this was not the same as saying that he was the *cause* of the tragedy—the true cause was the employers' unsafe working practices (as it had been in *Dooley*).

### Defences

Finally, it should be noted that the Law Commission's proposals would preserve certain defences.[108] Thus, there would be no liability to a secondary victim who had voluntarily assumed the risk of suffering psychiatric illness, or in relation to whom a defendant had excluded his or her duty not to cause psychiatric illness (for example by a contract term[109]), or in situations where it would be unjust to allow the secondary victim to recover because he or she was involved in conduct that was illegal or contrary to public policy.   **4–042**

---

[105] Law Com. 249, para.6.18.
[106] Law Com. 249, para.6.69.
[107] 2003 S.L.T. 1011.
[108] Law Com. 249, para.6.42.
[109] Unfair Contract Terms Act 1977 s.2(1) prohibits the valid exclusion of negligence liability for personal injury and death where the liability in question is "business liability".

## Liability for psychiatric illness: conclusion

Clearly, the law on psychiatric illness, like the law on economic loss, suffers from a lack of    **4–0**
coherence. It is an emotionally charged area of liability which raises acute moral problems.
The rules developed in *Alcock* and *White* seem to deny liability to many genuinely deserving
claimants. Moreover, the application of those rules compounds the moral dilemma. As Lord
Hoffmann noted in *Alcock* (echoing the views of the Law Commission):[110]

> ". . . the spectacle of a plaintiff who has, ex hypothesi, suffered psychiatric illness in
> consequence of his brother's death or injury, being cross-examined on the closeness of
> their ties of love and affection and then perhaps contradicted by the evidence of a private
> investigator, might not be to everyone's taste."[111]

It is the prospect of such an undignified spectacle, of course, which has led the Law Commission
to recommend replacing the rebuttable common law presumptions of close ties of love and
affection with conclusive presumptions in statutory form.

In conclusion, we can do little more than endorse the sentiments of Lord Oliver, who stated
in *Alcock*: ". . . I cannot, for my part, regard the present state of the law as either entirely satisfactory or as logically defensible", and, after acknowledging that the answers in this area of
the law were to be found "not in logic but in policy", concluded that the relevant policy
considerations would be "much better accommodated if the rights of persons injured in this
way were to be enshrined in and limited by legislation".[112] Unfortunately, however, it seems
unlikely that this will happen in the near future. A Government consultation paper was issued
in May 2007, in the wake of the Law Commission's report.[113] The response to this consultation, published in July 2009, concluded:

> "On balance the Government continues to take the view that it is preferable for the
> courts to have the flexibility to continue to develop the law rather than attempt to impose
> a statutory solution."[114]

---

[110] Law Com. 249, para.6.24.

[111] *Alcock v Chief Constable of South Yorkshire* [1992] 1 A.C. 310 at 503. His Lordship also refers to J. Stapleton, "In
Restraint of Tort" in *The Frontiers of Liability* (1994, OUP), Vol.2, p.84, who says that a mother who suffers psychiatric illness after finding her child's mangled body in a mortuary "might wonder why the law rules her child's blood
too dry to found an action".

[112] *Alcock v Chief Constable of South Yorkshire* [1992] 1 A.C. 310 at 418 and 419.

[113] Government Consultation Paper, The Law of Damages, CP 09/07 (May 2007), Ch.3, para.97.

[114] Ministry of Justice, The Law of Damages: Response to Consultation CP9 (R) 9/7, 1 July, 2009.

# Chapter 5

# NEGLIGENCE: BREACH OF DUTY

## Introduction

Once it has been established that the defendant owes the claimant a duty of care, it must next **5–001** be established that the defendant has breached that duty. In practical terms, breach of duty is the most important element of the tort of negligence, because in everyday cases the existence of a duty of care and questions of causation and remoteness are rarely in issue.

Establishing breach of duty involves showing that the defendant's conduct has fallen below the *standard of care* required in all the circumstances. The standard set by the law is one of "reasonableness". The flexibility inherent in the concept of "reasonableness" is necessary to accommodate the infinite variety of cases that may arise. Thus, for example, the law says that motorists must drive with "reasonable care in all the circumstances" because it cannot possibly prescribe the precise speed at which motorists must drive in each and every possible set of road conditions. In the case of driving, of course, the law makes some attempt to reduce the requirement of "reasonableness" into a set of concrete "rules"—in the form of speed limits and the rules of the Highway Code—but generally speaking the courts have resisted attempts to boil down the requirement of "reasonableness" into a series of precise and definite obligations. Decisions in individual cases as to what amounts to "reasonable conduct" are regarded only as useful guides. To treat them otherwise would introduce a rigidity into the law that might produce injustice.

In this chapter, then, we are not concerned with learning a multiplicity of specific "rules" about what defendants must or must not do in various sets of circumstances. Although it is possible to enumerate a great number of fairly definite "rules" about what the law considers "reasonable" in specific situations (for example, when driving, looking after another's property, or carrying passengers on a ship), it is not usual to consider all of these rules in a book of this kind. The only specific obligations we do consider are those owed by an employer to an employee (see Ch.7) and by an occupier to persons on his or her premises (see Ch.8). This chapter deals with the *general principles* the courts employ in setting the standard of care. It begins by exploring these principles. It then discusses the extent to which the law expects special standards of care from special categories of defendant (for example from children, or professionals). Finally, it considers the problem of *proving* breach of duty.

## The "reasonable person"

**5–002**    The law's starting point in deciding breach of duty is to judge the defendant's conduct by the standard of the hypothetical "reasonable person" (in older cases referred to as the "reasonable man"). The most famous example of the "reasonable person" being used to define the standard of care comes from the judgment of Alderson B. in *Blyth v Birmingham Waterworks Co.*[1] His Lordship said:

> "Negligence is the omission to do something which a reasonable man, guided upon those considerations which ordinarily regulate the conduct of human affairs, would do, or doing something which a prudent and reasonable man would not do."

Two important points must be noted about the standard of the "reasonable person":

- the standard is objective

- the standard does not always reflect "average" behaviour

*The standard of care is objective*

**5–003**    The first point to note, then, is that the judgment as to whether the defendant has behaved like a "reasonable person" is an objective one. That is to say, the question for the court is not: "What could we have expected *this particular defendant* to do in the circumstances?" Rather, the question is: "What could we expect a 'reasonable person' to do?" Thus, a defendant who is unusually clumsy or slow-witted cannot succeed by arguing that his or her conduct amounts to an "incompetent best". The defendant will be judged according to the best efforts of the hypothetical "reasonable person".

The objective nature of the "reasonable person" test was explained by Lord Macmillan in *Glasgow Corp v Muir.*[2] Here, the manageress of the defendants' tea-room, to which access was obtained by way of a small shop, gave a picnic party permission to use the tea-room when rain prevented them from eating their food outside. She allowed two members of the party to carry a tea urn through the shop. Despite taking all due care, one of the carriers let go of the urn, so that tea was spilt, severely scalding several children who were buying sweets at the counter of the shop. The plaintiffs argued that the manageress had been negligent in giving permission for the tea urn to be brought in without first clearing the children out of the shop. On the facts, the defendants were not liable, because the risk of injury was not so high that a reasonable person would have done this in the circumstances. Dealing with the "reasonable person" standard, Lord Macmillan said:

> "The standard of foresight of the reasonable man is in one sense an impersonal test. It eliminates the personal equation and is independent of the idiosyncrasies of the particular person whose conduct is in question. Some persons are by nature unduly timorous and imagine every path beset with lions; others, of more robust temperament, fail to foresee or nonchalantly disregard even the most obvious dangers. The

[1] (1856) 11 Ex. 781 at 784.
[2] [1943] 2 A.C. 448.

reasonable man is presumed to be free both from over-apprehension and from over-confidence."[3]

His Lordship conceded, however, that the test for breach of duty does contain a certain subjective element. This is because the question for the court is: what would the reasonable person have done in the defendant's circumstances? However, although the defendant's conduct must be judged in the light of "all the circumstances of the case", it is important to distinguish between, on the one hand, external circumstances (for example, the defendant was acting in an emergency) and, on the other hand, "circumstances" which are personal characteristics of the particular defendant (for example, the defendant's "circumstances" were that he or she happened to be a novice). Whilst the law will adapt the standard of care to take account of external circumstances, it will not, generally speaking, take account of the defendant's personal characteristics.

The case of *Nettleship v Weston*[4] provides perhaps the most famous illustration of the objective standard of care. The defendant was a learner driver. The plaintiff, a family friend, had agreed to give her driving lessons. On her third lesson, when the car was moving very slowly, with the plaintiff moving the gear lever and the defendant steering, the defendant panicked. The car mounted the pavement and struck a lamp-post, causing the plaintiff to suffer a broken knee cap. He sued the defendant for personal injury.

The Court of Appeal held the defendant liable. The majority of the Court held that her conduct was not to be judged, as she argued, by the standard of a learner driver, but by the standard of a reasonably competent and experienced one. Lord Denning M.R. stated that, although the defendant was not *morally* at fault, she should be regarded as *legally* at fault. Since she was legally required to be insured, it made sense that she should bear the risk of her driving. Megaw L.J. pointed out that, once the law accepted the principle that the standard of care could be varied according to the experience of the particular defendant, it would be logically impossible to confine application of the principle to cases of driving. This would mean that in every negligence case, the court would be obliged to hear evidence about the level of competence to be expected of a reasonable person with the same level of experience as the defendant. Such an exercise would be costly and time-consuming and would undoubtedly produce unpredictability and uncertainty in the law. His Lordship concluded, therefore, that "the certainty of a general standard is preferable to the vagaries of a fluctuating standard".[5]

*The standard of care is a "hypothetical", not an "average" standard*

Although the "reasonable person" is sometimes personified as the "man on the Clapham omnibus",[6] or the "man on the Underground",[7] it is important to appreciate that the standard of care the law requires is sometimes a poor reflection of the standard such a man would probably, in fact, exercise. Whilst evidence of the fact that most people behave in a certain way may, in appropriate cases, be relevant in setting the legal standard of care, the law will not always regard such evidence as conclusive. This is because there are situations where, as a matter of policy, very high standards of care are imposed for the purpose of shifting losses

**5–004**

[3] [1943] 2 A.C. 448 at 457.
[4] [1971] 2 Q.B. 691.
[5] [1971] 2 Q.B. 691 at 707.
[6] per Greer L.J. in *Hall v Brooklands Auto Racing Club* [1933] 1 K.B. 205 at 224.
[7] per Lord Steyn in *White v Chief Constable of South Yorkshire* [1999] 2 A.C. 455 at 495.

on to defendants, with little regard for fault. In such cases, the idea of fault is subordinated to the objectives of compensation and loss distribution, discussed in Ch.1. Below, we discuss how this is achieved in the context of road traffic accidents, but the reader should also consider the issue in the context of the high standards of care required of employers, discussed in Ch.7.

Because the "reasonable person" is a mythical judicial creation, then, he or she may sometimes be credited with a level of skill and prudence that is seldom attainable in the real world. The Pearson Commission, which in 1978 reported on civil liability for personal injury, noted:

> "Even good drivers make mistakes. A study by the World Health Organisation in 1962 found that a good driver makes a mistake every two miles; and an American study in 1964 suggested that on average a good driver makes nine mistakes every five minutes."[8]

Yet, many of the "mistakes" good drivers make are regarded by the law as conduct falling below the standard expected of a "reasonable driver". This means, in effect, that the standard of care in relation to driving is so high that in certain situations there is almost strict liability (liability without fault) for driving. The reason why this is so has partly to do with historical accident (the rules on driving were developed when many fewer cars were on the roads), but it also has to do with particular policy considerations which apply in road traffic cases. The most important goal of tort law in the context of driving accidents is to provide compensation for victims. The issue of fault, therefore, is subordinated to achieving this goal. As was noted in Ch.1, the law is assisted in this regard by the availability of third party insurance, which is compulsory for motorists.

It should be noted, however, that whilst the standard of care in relation to driving is very high, the courts have stopped short of holding that liability for driving is entirely divorced from fault. In *Mansfield v Weetabix Ltd*,[9] the Court of Appeal held that a driver who becomes unable to control a vehicle will not be liable for damage caused by his or her loss of control if the driver is unaware (and should not reasonably have been aware) of a disabling condition from which he or she is suffering, which suddenly manifests itself, causing the loss of control. Prior to this decision, Neill J. had held, in *Roberts v Ramsbottom*,[10] that a driver who suffered a stroke at the wheel remained liable. His Lordship had suggested that this would be so even if the driver had been unaware that he had a medical condition likely to lead to a loss of control. In *Mansfield v Weetabix Ltd*, however, the Court of Appeal held that *Roberts v Ramsbottom* was wrongly decided on this point, although the decision could be supported on the alternative ground that the defendant had carried on driving when he felt strange and ought to have known that he was probably unfit to drive.

Now that we are familiar with the standard of the "reasonable person", it is appropriate to explore the various factors which the courts take into account in deciding whether this standard has been met.

---

[8] Report of the Royal Commission on Civil Liability and Compensation for Personal Injury, Vol.1, Ch.18, para.983.
[9] [1998] 1 W.L.R. 1263. Compare *C (A Child) v Burcome* [2003] C.L.Y. 3030 (liability imposed where a 70-year-old driver with a heart condition had been advised not to engage in strenuous activity, but continued to drive after pulling in to change a wheel).
[10] [1980] 1 All E.R. 7.

## FACTORS RELEVANT TO THE STANDARD OF CARE

The relevant factors can be stated as follows:                                          5–005

- foreseeability of harm;

- magnitude of the risk;

- burden of taking precautions;

- utility of the defendant's conduct;

- common practice.

Below, we consider each of these in turn. We then look at how some of them may be considered together in a quasi-mathematical way, using what is known as the "Learned Hand test".

### Foreseeability of harm

If the particular harm the claimant suffers is not foreseeable, the defendant will not be liable.   5–006
This is because, rather obviously, the "reasonable person" cannot be expected to take any precautions against unforeseeable risks. The point is illustrated by the decision of the Court of Appeal in *Roe v Minister of Health*.[11] In 1947, the plaintiff went into hospital for a minor operation. He suffered permanent paralysis as a result of being given a spinal anaesthetic which was contaminated with phenol. The contamination had occurred when glass ampoules containing the anaesthetic had been stored in the phenol, which was used as a disinfectant, and the phenol had seeped through invisible cracks in the glass. At the time, it was not known that contamination could occur in this way. The action came to trial in 1954, by which time the dangers had become known. The defendants were not liable. Denning L.J. made the point that, although in 1954 it would be regarded as negligent to store anaesthetic in phenol, the court "must not look at the 1947 accident with 1954 spectacles".[12]

Whilst the defendant will escape liability where the risk is unforeseeable, it does not follow that he or she will automatically be liable for all risks that are foreseeable. The law insists that a risk must be *reasonably* foreseeable before making a defendant liable. This point is explored below.

### The magnitude of the risk

The "reasonable person" does not take precautions against risks that are very small. Assessing the   5–007
"magnitude" of any risk involves consideration of two factors. First, there is the likelihood that harm will occur. Secondly, there is the question of how serious the consequences will be if harm *does* occur.

*(1)  The likelihood of harm*

In *Bolton v Stone*,[13] the plaintiff, who was standing outside her house on a quiet street, was hit   5–008
by a cricket ball which came from a nearby cricket ground. It was clear that the defendant

---

[11]  [1954] 2 Q.B. 66.
[12]  [1954] 2 Q.B. 66 at 84.
[13]  [1951] A.C. 850.

cricketers could have foreseen that a ball might be hit out of the ground, because this had happened before, but it was a very rare occurrence. The evidence established that cricket balls had been hit out of the ground on about six occasions in the previous 30 years. There was a fence around the ground which was seven feet high and, due to the slope of the ground, the top of the fence was some 17 feet above the level of the pitch. The fence was some 80 yards away from where the batsman stood. The House of Lords held that, in these circumstances, the chance of an injury occurring to someone who was standing in the position of the plaintiff was so slight that the defendants were not negligent in continuing to play cricket without taking additional precautions. Lord Oaksey said that:

> "an ordinarily careful man does not take precautions against every foreseeable risk. He can, of course, foresee the possibility of many risks, but life would be almost impossible if he were to attempt to take precautions against every risk which he can foresee".[14]

Similarly, Lord Radcliffe thought that a reasonable person, taking account of the chances against such an accident occurring, "would have done what the appellants did: in other words, he would have done nothing".[15]

It is useful to compare *Bolton v Stone* with the decision of Ashworth J. in *Hilder v Associated Portland Cement Manufacturers Ltd.*[16] Here, the defendants were the occupiers of some grassland on which they permitted some small boys to play football. One of the boys kicked the ball over a low wall into the adjoining road where it caused the plaintiff, a passing motorcyclist, to fall off his motorbike and suffer fatal injuries. The defendants were held liable. Because the risk of injury to a road user was much greater than the risk in *Bolton v Stone*—the land was only some 15 yards from the road—it was not a risk that the reasonable person would have disregarded.

In *Haley v London Electricity Board*,[17] the House of Lords was presented with detailed statistical evidence about the likelihood of harm occurring. The plaintiff, who was blind, fell into a hole in the pavement that had been dug by the defendants. As a result of the fall he became deaf. The precautions taken to guard the hole were sufficient for sighted people but were insufficient for the blind. Their Lordships considered evidence relating to the number of blind people who lived in the same London borough as the plaintiff, and concluded that the likelihood of a blind person falling into the hole was not so small that the defendants could ignore it. The case is authority for the proposition that the reasonable person must tailor his conduct in the light of the characteristics of the people whom he knows it might affect. Thus (as we shall see in Ch.7), a defendant employer has been held liable for causing psychiatric illness to an employee whom he ought to have known was likely to suffer a nervous breakdown,[18] but in other cases, where the risk of psychiatric illness to the particular employee could not reasonably have been known, employers have escaped liability.

---

[14] [1951] A.C. 850 at 863.
[15] [1951] A.C. 850 at 869.
[16] [1961] 1 W.L.R. 1434. *Bolton v Stone* was applied, for example, in *Zucchi v Waitrose Ltd* 2000 WL 345171 where the risk of customers being injured by a collapsing stack of plastic bottles was so small that the store had acted reasonably in disregarding it.
[17] [1965] A.C. 778.
[18] *Walker v Northumberland CC* [1995] 1 All E.R. 737.

*(2) The seriousness of the consequences*

The decision in *Bolton v Stone* does not mean that a reasonable person is *always* justified in **5–009** ignoring a very small risk. The risk of harm materialising must be weighed against other factors, including the seriousness of the consequences if the harm does materialise. The more serious the consequences, the greater the obligations of the defendant. This point is neatly illustrated by the decision in *Paris v Stepney Borough Council.*[19] The plaintiff, who was blind in one eye, was employed by the defendants in a garage. One day he was called upon to dismantle the chassis of a large vehicle and had to use a hammer to knock out a rusty bolt. A fragment of metal came off the bolt and hit him in his good eye, causing him to become totally blind. The risk of such an injury occurring was extremely small and did not justify the use of goggles by ordinary workers. Nevertheless, a majority of the House of Lords held that the defendants were liable for failing to provide this particular worker with goggles, knowing that he might suffer such serious consequences if the small risk materialised.

## The burden of taking precautions

The court will take account of the cost and practicality of taking precautions against a risk. **5–010** If the burden of taking steps to eliminate a risk is far greater than the benefit obtained by its elimination, then failure to take those steps will not generally amount to negligence. Thus, one factor which influenced the House of Lords in deciding *Bolton v Stone* was that the only practical way the defendant cricketers could have prevented balls from going out of the ground would have been to erect an extremely high fence—wind conditions made this very difficult, if not impossible. Alternatively, they could simply have stopped playing cricket. In either case, taking precautions against the risk would have placed a burden on the defendants that was out of all proportion to the risk the precautions would avoid.

The case most often cited in this context is *Latimer v AEC Ltd.*[20] Here, the floor of the defendants' factory was flooded by an exceptionally heavy rainstorm. As a result, an oily cooling mixture, which was normally contained in a channel in the floor, mixed with the flood waters. When the flood subsided, the floor was left in a slippery state. The defendants spread sawdust on the floor, but did not have enough sawdust to go round, so some areas were left untreated. The plaintiff, who was working in an area which had not been treated with sawdust, was attempting to load a heavy barrel on to a trolley when he slipped and injured his ankle. The House of Lords held that the defendants had not been negligent. They had done all that reasonable employers could be expected to do for the safety of their workers. The only way the defendants could have eliminated the risk entirely would have been to close the factory, and this would have been a precaution out of all proportion to the risk in question.

It is useful to compare *Bolton* and *Latimer* with the decision of the Privy Council in *The Wagon Mound (No.2)*.[21] Here, the defendants negligently discharged a quantity of furnace oil into the sea. The evidence in the case established that there was an extremely small risk that the oil might ignite in very unusual circumstances. (These circumstances are explained in Ch.6, because the incident also gave rise to another case—*The Wagon Mound (No.1)*—which is the leading authority on remoteness of damage.) The oil ignited, causing damage to the

---

[19] [1951] A.C. 367.
[20] [1953] A.C. 643.
[21] *Overseas Tankship (UK) v Miller Steamship Co Pty Ltd, The Wagon Mound (No.2)* [1967] 1 A.C. 617.

plaintiffs' ships. The defendants argued that, because the risk of damage was very small, they were justified in disregarding it. The Privy Council was unimpressed by this argument. The burden of eliminating the risk in this case was minimal—all the defendants had to do was ensure that the oil did not discharge into the harbour by keeping a tap turned off. Their Lordships pointed out that a reasonable person would not ignore even a very small risk "if action to eliminate it presented no difficulty, involved no disadvantage and required no expense".[22] In *The Wagon Mound (No.2)*, it was also relevant to a finding of liability that the defendants, in discharging the oil, were not doing anything worthwhile—they were committing an act of pollution. In other words, their act had no "utility". This issue is considered further elsewhere.

*The defendant's financial circumstances*

**5–011**  A difficult issue is whether the financial resources available to the defendant should be taken into account in deciding whether the defendant should take precautions against a risk. Where the defendant can be said to have a choice about whether or not to engage in the activity which creates the risk, he or she cannot argue lack of resources as a reason for failing to meet the standard of care. The Australian case of *P.Q. v Australian Red Cross Society*[23] serves as a vivid illustration. Here, the Australian court firmly rejected the argument that the standard to be expected of the Red Cross in testing blood donations for the AIDS virus should be determined in the light of the financial constraints of the charity. The charity had a choice. If it lacked adequate financial resources to collect blood donations properly, it should choose not to provide that service.

By contrast, there are situations where the defendant's lack of choice in pursuing a certain course of action justifies taking financial constraints into account. Such is the case where an occupier comes under an affirmative duty of care to prevent others being harmed by a natural hazard arising on his land.[24] Acting in an emergency may be regarded as another "no choice" situation in which the actor can only be expected to make use of the financial resources immediately available.

Decisions concerning the standard of care required of public authorities indicate that the financial resources available to the authority are a relevant consideration in setting the standard of care.[25] Thus, for example, in *Knight v Home Office*[26] it was held that the prison authorities were not negligent in failing to provide the same level of care for prisoners suffering from psychiatric illness that could be expected in a psychiatric hospital outside prison. Pill J., however, noted that there were limits to this approach. Lack of financial resources could not operate as a complete defence. Taking an extreme example, his Lordship said that:

> "if the evidence was that no funds were available to provide any medical facilities in a large prison there would be a failure to achieve the standard of care appropriate for prisoners".

---

[22] [1967] 1 A.C. 617 at 642.

[23] [1992] 1 V.R. 19.

[24] See *Goldman v Hargrave* [1967] 1 A.C. 645 and *Leakey v National Trust* [1980] Q.B. 485, discussed in Ch.10.

[25] At least, this appears to be so where the authority is in a "no choice" situation, in the sense that it is fulfilling a statutory duty rather than exercising a power. There is some obvious overlap here with the question of when the authority will owe a duty of care, which has been explored in Ch.2.

[26] [1990] 3 All E.R. 237.

## The utility of the defendant's conduct

The greater the social utility of the defendant's conduct, the less likely it is that the defendant will be held to be negligent. The classic case which illustrates this is *Daborn v Bath Tramways Motor Co Ltd*.[27] The relevant issue was whether, in wartime, the driver of a left-hand drive ambulance had been negligent in turning into a road without giving a hand signal. The Court of Appeal held that she was not liable. During wartime, it was necessary for many highly important operations to be carried out by means of vehicles with left-hand drives, and it was impossible for the drivers of such vehicles to give the warning signals which drivers might normally have been expected to give. Asquith L.J. noted that the utility of the defendant's act had to be weighed against the risks it created, saying:

> "... if all the trains in this country were restricted to a speed of five miles an hour, there would be fewer accidents, but our national life would be intolerably slowed down. The purpose to be served, if sufficiently important, justified the assumption of abnormal risk."[28]

His Lordship concluded that, because ambulance drivers were performing a valuable service in a time of national emergency, it would be demanding too high a standard of care from them to say: "Either you must give signals which the structure of your vehicle renders impossible or you must not drive at all".

Similar reasoning was adopted in *Watt v Hertfordshire CC*.[29] Here, the plaintiff was a fireman, who was injured when travelling to rescue a woman reported to have been trapped under a heavy lorry. In the haste of the rescue, the plaintiff's colleagues picked up a jack, which was needed to save the woman's life, and put it into the lorry in which they were travelling. The lorry was not equipped for carrying the jack and the plaintiff was injured when the driver of the lorry braked suddenly and the jack fell on him. It was held that the defendant employers were not negligent because the need to act speedily in an attempt to save the woman's life outweighed the risk to the plaintiff. It should be noted, however, that this decision does not mean that the emergency services will always escape liability for accidents occurring in the haste of a rescue. The court will have regard to all of the circumstances of the particular case. Thus, for example, in *Ward v London CC*[30] the driver of a fire engine was held to have been negligent in driving through a red traffic light.

*The Compensation Act 2006: the deterrent effect of potential liability*

Section 1 of the Compensation Act 2006 is designed to promote the idea that people and organisations who wish to undertake socially worthwhile activities should not be deterred from doing so by an unrealistic fear of negligence liability. It was passed in the light of certain government reports which had examined the question of whether there might be a growing "compensation culture" in the UK (i.e. whether society was becoming more litigious, with citizens believing they had a right to sue someone whenever they suffered a

5–012

5–013

---

[27] [1946] 2 All E.R. 333.
[28] [1946] 2 All E.R. 333 at 336.
[29] [1954] 1 W.L.R. 835.
[30] [1938] 2 All E.R. 341. See also *Nelson v Chief Constable of Cumbria* [2000] C.L.Y. 4217.

misfortune).[31] These reports had found that, as a matter of fact, this was not the case—the statistical evidence showed that people nowadays were not much more likely to sue than in former times. However, the reports identified that, despite the statistical reality, there was nevertheless a *perception* held by many organisations that they were at risk of being unfairly sued. This fear was leading to unduly cautious practices that were not in the public interest.

The sort of unduly cautious behaviour that Parliament had in mind was exemplified by the attitude adopted by the defendant local authority in *Tomlinson v Congleton BC*[32]— an important House of Lords case on occupiers' liability, considered in Ch.8. The local authority owned and managed a lake for the benefit of the public. Most visitors used the site responsibly, enjoying the sandy beaches and respecting the signs prohibiting them from swimming in the lake. A number of visitors, however, persistently disobeyed these signs. The local authority became concerned that it might be sued if one of these swimmers were to meet with an accident in the water. They therefore resolved to discolour and destroy the beaches by dumping ballast on them and planting vegetation—although this, of course, would have spoiled the enjoyment of the people who used the beaches responsibly.

The authority had not yet carried out this work when the claimant, a young man, severely injured himself by diving into the lake and hitting his head on the bottom. In denying his claim, the House of Lords reasoned that it would be extremely unjust to place the authority under a duty to people who disobeyed the signs and swam. There could be no duty to protect people from their own irresponsible behaviour, especially where this would mean destroying a socially desirable public amenity. Their Lordships expressed concern that, in setting the standard of care, the courts should not allow the fear of liability to deter local authorities and other organisations from engaging in or encouraging socially desirable activity. This sentiment is put on a statutory footing by section 1 of the Act:

"s.1. Deterrent effect of potential liability

A court considering a claim in negligence or breach of statutory duty[33] may, in determining whether the defendant should have taken particular steps to meet a standard of care (whether by taking precautions against a risk or otherwise), have regard to whether a requirement to take those steps might—

(a)  prevent a desirable activity from being undertaken at all, to a particular extent or in a particular way, or

(b)  discourage persons from undertaking functions in connection with a desirable activity."

---

[31] See Report of the Better Regulation Task Force (2004) and report of the Constitutional Affairs Committee (2006). For comment on the Compensation Act 2006, see R. Herbert [2006] 4 J.P.I. Law 337; K. Williams [2006] 4 J.P.I. Law 347.

[32] [2004] 1 A.C. 46 (reversed in part [2011] EWCA Civ 66).

[33] The reference in the Act to "breach of statutory duty" was thought necessary to cover claims under the Occupiers' Liability Acts (see Ch.8). However, the Act affects only statutory duties which involve a standard of care. It has no application where liability for breach is strict (see Ch.7).

These provisions will clearly provide reassurance, for example, to volunteer groups which organise outdoor pursuits, and schools wishing to take pupils on excursions. In reality, however, they do little to extend the common law.

The effect of s.1 was considered in *Uren v Corporate Leisure (UK) Ltd*,[34] where it was held that a balance had to be struck between the level of risk involved and the benefits the game conferred on the participants and thereby on society generally in a game at a 'health and fun day'. Field J. commented:

> "It is also to be noted that it was common ground that in the context of this case section 1 of the Compensation Act 2006 adds nothing to the common law.

(I should add that this accords with my own view of the effect of the section.)[35]

## Common practice

Failure to conform to a common practice of taking safety precautions is strong evidence of negligence because it suggests that the defendant did not do what others in the community regard as reasonable. It must be remembered, however, that such a failure is not conclusive evidence of negligence. This is because the claimant must also prove that the failure to adopt the safety precautions in question was the cause of his or her loss. Thus, in *Brown v Rolls Royce Ltd*,[36] the plaintiff contracted dermatitis from contact with grease during the course of her work. She claimed that this was caused by the negligence of her employers, who had not supplied a barrier cream which was commonly supplied by other employers to people doing the same type of work. However, whilst it was the common practice to use this cream, there was conflicting evidence about its efficacy. The plaintiff's action failed because she could not prove that, had the defendants supplied the cream, it would have prevented her from contracting dermatitis.

Conversely, where it can be shown that the defendant *has* complied with a common practice in relation to safety precautions, this is very good evidence that the defendant has not been negligent. Again, however, such evidence cannot be regarded as conclusive. This is because a particular course of conduct may be negligent despite its being common practice. As Lord Tomlin succinctly put it in *Bank of Montreal v Dominion Gresham*: "Neglect of duty does not cease by repetition to be neglect of duty".[37] The question of common practice assumes enormous significance in cases involving professional negligence and is discussed more fully in that context later in this chapter.

**5–014**

## The "Learned Hand" test

It is clear that in deciding breach of duty, the courts "balance" all of the factors we have considered above. In *United States v Carroll Towing Co*,[38] an American case, Learned Hand J. provided a useful insight into the way the courts may perform this "balancing act" in some

**5–015**

[34] [2010] EWHC 46.
[35] [2010] EWHC 46, at para.19.
[36] [1960] 1 W.L.R. 210.
[37] [1930] A.C. 659 at 666.
[38] 159 F. 2d 169 (1947).

cases. He suggested that some of the factors relevant to breach of duty might be given a notional statistical value, so that the problem could be approached in a quasi-mathematical way. Taking B as the "burden of taking precautions", P as the "probability that the risk will materialise", and L as the "loss which will occur if the risk does materialise", one can express the courts' approach in terms of two "equations":

$$B < P \times L = \text{Liability}$$
$$B > P \times L = \text{No Liability}$$

Expressed in words, these "equations" mean that, where the "burden" on the defendant (in terms of taking precautions) *is less than* the notional value achieved by multiplying the "probability" and the "loss", the court will be likely to find the defendant liable. Conversely, where the "burden" on the defendant *is greater than* the product of the "probability" and the "loss", a finding of no liability is likely.

We can see how these "equations" might work by analysing two cases—*Bolton v Stone* and *The Wagon Mound (No.2)*. In *Bolton*, a finding of no liability resulted from the fact that a low value could be given to the probability of the risk materialising (six times in 30 years) and a relatively low value could be given to the loss in question (at worst, injury of one individual). The burden on the defendants (giving up cricket) could be given a high value. By contrast, in *The Wagon Mound (No.2)*, whilst the probability of the risk materialising could also be given a low value, the loss in question (at worst, the complete destruction of Sydney Harbour) would have to be given a relatively high value, whilst the slight burden on the defendants (retaining the oil onboard ship) would obviously be given a very low value. Thus, a finding of liability resulted.

## SPECIAL STANDARDS OF CARE

5–016    There are certain types of defendant to whom additional special rules apply in determining the standard of care required of them. These are:

- children;

- defendants acting in an emergency;

- defendants engaged in sport;

- defendants claiming to have special or professional skill.

In this section, we consider the standard of care required of the first three of these special types of defendant. The standard of care required of professionals warrants more lengthy discussion and is dealt with in a later section.

### Children

5–017    The conduct of a child defendant is judged by reference to the standard of conduct that can be expected of a reasonable child of the defendant's own age. For many years, there was no English authority on the point, but it was assumed that the courts would adopt the reasoning of Kitto J. in the Australian case of *McHale v Watson*.[39] Here, the defendant was a 12-year-old boy. He threw a sharp rod which ricocheted off a post and hit a nine-year-old girl. The High Court of Australia declined to apply the standard of the "reasonable person" to cases involving children, and applied a lower standard which was appropriate to the defendant's age. Applying that standard, it was held that the boy was not negligent. It should be noted, however, that the standard of care applied to children remains an objective one. As Kitto J. remarked:

> "It is no answer for [a child], any more than it is for an adult to say that the harm he caused was due to his being abnormally slow-witted, quick tempered, absent minded or inexperienced".

In England, the same approach was adopted by the Court of Appeal in *Mullin v Richards*.[40] Here, the defendant and the plaintiff were 15-year-old schoolgirls. They were fencing with plastic rulers during a lesson, when one of the rulers snapped and a piece of plastic flew into the plaintiff's eye, causing blindness. It was held that the proper test to apply was whether an ordinarily careful and reasonable 15-year-old would have foreseen that the game carried a risk of injury. On the facts, the injury was held to be not reasonably foreseeable by such a child—the game was common and the girls had never been warned that it could be dangerous.

## Defendants acting in an emergency

Where the defendant is forced to act quickly "in the heat of the moment", the standard of care is relaxed to take account of the exigencies of the situation. This was established long ago in the case of *Jones v Boyce*[41] (a case concerned with contributory negligence). Here, the issue was whether a passenger on a coach had acted reasonably when, thinking that the coach was about to overturn, he jumped off in order to save himself, breaking his leg. The jury found in the man's favour, Lord Ellenborough C.J. having directed them that the man was not guilty of negligence just because he had selected the more perilous of two alternatives with which he was confronted in an emergency. It made no difference that, with the benefit of hindsight, it was obvious the man had made the wrong decision.

    A more modern example of the principle is the case of *Ng Chun Pui v Lee Chuen Tat*.[42] Here, the defendant was driving a coach on a dual carriageway when another vehicle cut in front of him without warning, forcing him to brake suddenly. The coach swerved and skidded across the central reservation, where it collided with a bus travelling in the opposite direction, injuring the plaintiffs, who were passengers on the bus. The Privy Council held that the driver's actions had been reasonable, given the emergency with which he was faced.

**5–018**

---

[39] [1966] A.L.R. 513.
[40] [1998] 1 W.L.R. 1304. *Mullin v Richards* was applied in *Etheridge v K* [1999] Ed. C.R. 550 where a teacher was injured by a basketball thrown by a 13-year-old boy. See also *Blake v Galloway* [2004] 1 W.L.R. 2844 and *Orchard v Lee* [2009] EWCA Civ 295. Comment: P Giliker (2009), 25 (2) P.N. 91–95.
[41] (1816) 1 Stark. 493.
[42] [1988] R.T.R. 298.

It appears from the decision in *Marshall v Osmond*[43] that where the police are chasing a suspected criminal, this may count as an emergency situation. Here, the plaintiff, a suspect, was injured when a police car drew up alongside the car from which he was attempting to run away. It was held that in these circumstances the actions of the police could not be judged by the same standard of care that would apply had there been time for reflection. This decision, however, should be compared with *Rigby v Chief Constable of Northamptonshire*.[44] Here, the police were held liable for fire damage to the plaintiff's shop when they fired a canister of CS gas into the shop to flush out a dangerous psychopath. The nature of the situation did not justify the police's failure to ensure that fire-fighting equipment was at hand.

## Participants in sport

**5–019**     It is clear that those engaged in sport owe a duty of care both to other competitors in the sporting event and to spectators. The courts have recognised, however, that a participant in sporting activity is in a similar position to a person faced with an emergency, in the sense that he or she may have to take a decision in the heat of the moment. The required standard of care takes account of this.

In the well-known case of *Wooldridge v Sumner*,[45] the Court of Appeal laid down a test for the sporting standard of care that meant that a participant in sport would only be liable to spectators if he or she had "acted in reckless disregard of the spectators' safety". This test, however, was subjected to severe academic criticism on the basis that the need to show "recklessness" seemed too favourable to the defendant. The courts appear to have responded to this criticism. Thus, in *Wilks v Cheltenham Cycle Club*,[46] the Court of Appeal applied the test suggested by Professor Goodhart in his commentary on *Wooldridge*, namely that there was negligence if injury was caused "by an error of judgment that a reasonable competitor, being the reasonable man of the sporting world, would not have made".[47] Applying this test, it was held that the defendant, a participant in a motorcycle scramble, was not negligent when his bike left the course and hit a spectator. The standard of care would be adjusted to take account of the fact that a competitor could reasonably be expected to "go all out to win", even if this meant exposing others to some risk. This did not mean, however, that it was acceptable for a competitor to expose others to danger by conduct that was "foolhardy".[48]

It is clear that the mere fact that a competitor has broken the rules of a game will not, of itself, provide a conclusive indication of negligence. This point is illustrated by the decision of the Court of Appeal in *Caldwell v Maguire*.[49] The claimant, a professional jockey, was injured when the defendants, two other jockeys, rode in such a way as to cause an accident. The defendants' conduct was investigated by the Jockey Club and found to amount to "careless riding" in breach

---

[43] [1983] Q.B. 1034. Compare *Nelson v Chief Constable of Cumbria* [2000] C.L.Y. 4217 (police driver causing a crash to be judged by the same standard as an ordinary driver unless in a situation of pursuit at speed) and see also *Henry v Chief Constable of Thames Valley* [2010] EWCA Civ 5.

[44] [1985] 1 W.L.R. 1242.

[45] [1963] 2 Q.B. 43.

[46] [1971] 1 W.L.R. 668.

[47] Goodhart (1962) 78 L.Q.R. 490 at 496.

[48] per Lord Denning M.R. at 670. Compare the behaviour of the defendant in *Condon v Basi* [1985] 1 W.L.R 866 who was liable for a rugby tackle made in a "reckless and dangerous manner".

[49] [2001] EWCA Civ 1054; [2002] P.I.Q.R. P6. The approach in *Caldwell v Maguire* was followed in the context of children's horseplay in *Blake v Galloway* [2004] 1 W.L.R. 2844. Comment: P. Charlish [2004] 4 J.P.I. Law 291.

of its rules. However, the Court of Appeal drew a distinction between a finding of carelessness by a regulatory body and a finding of negligence by a court of law. In the circumstances, it was not possible to characterise the defendants' momentary carelessness as negligence.

Where referees put competitors at risk by failing to enforce the rules of the game, they may be liable where this causes injury to the competitors. Thus, in *Vowles v Evans*[50] a rugby referee was held liable when a player was injured by a scrummage collapsing in circumstances where the referee should not have allowed the game to continue with contestable scrummages after the substitution of an untrained player. The court was careful to point out, however, that the threshold of referee liability should be a high one, and that the standard of care expected of referees depended on all the circumstances of the case. One of those circumstances was the nature of the game. Thus, in a fast-moving game, a referee could not be expected to avoid some oversight and error of judgment when supervising the game. Moreover, the standard of care demanded of a referee would depend on the grade of the referee and the level of the game in question. In other words, rather than apply the usual objective standard of care, the law would adopt the unusual practice of adjusting the standard of care in the light of the referee's qualifications. Clearly, the Court of Appeal thought that this approach was necessary so as not to discourage amateurs from volunteering as referees.

## THE PROFESSIONAL STANDARD OF CARE

In this section, we consider the standard of care demanded of people who, by following a particular trade or profession, hold themselves out as having special skills. In relation to such people, the question of breach of duty is decided by applying the so-called "*Bolam* test".   **5–020**

### The *Bolam* test

The case of *Bolam v Friern Hospital Management Committee*[51] (the facts of which we shall discuss later) confirmed the application of two important principles, which can be summarised as follows:   **5–021**

- Where the defendant purports to have a special skill, the defendant's conduct is judged according to the standard of a reasonable person having the skill the defendant claims to possess. It is not judged by the standard of the reasonable lay person.

- The law will not regard a professional defendant as having fallen below the required standard of care if it is shown that the defendant's conduct is regarded as proper by one responsible body of professional opinion. (Even though some other members of the defendant's profession may think the conduct is negligent.)

It is convenient to explore each principle in turn.

---

[50] [2003] 1 W.L.R. 1607. See also *Smolden v Whitworth* [1997] P.I.Q.R. P 133.

[51] [1957] 1 W.L.R. 582. For some examples of the application of the *Bolam* test, see: *B v South Tyneside Health Care Trust* [2004] EWHC 1169, [2004] Lloyd's Rep. Med. 505; *Bellarby v Worthing and Southlands NHS Trust* [2005] EWHC 2089, (2005) 86 B.M.L.R. 1; *E v Castro* [2003] EWHC 2066, (2004) 80 B.M.L.R. 14; *Kingsberry v Greater Manchester Strategic HA* [2005] EWHC 2253, (2006) 87 B.M.L.R.73.

*The standard of the "reasonable skilled person"*

**5–022**    This first element of the *"Bolam* test" is straightforward. The obvious point here is that the law expects a member of a trade or profession to live up to the standard of an ordinary skilled member of the trade or profession in question. As McNair J. put it in *Bolam*:

> "Where you get a situation which involves the use of some special skill or competence, then the test as to whether there has been negligence or not is not the test of the man on the top of the Clapham omnibus, because he has not got this special skill. The test is the standard of the ordinary skilled man exercising and professing to have that special skill."[52]

Accordingly, the law will not judge a surgeon performing an operation by the standard of a reasonable lay person performing that operation (to do so would be absurd) but by the standard of the "reasonable surgeon". Although most cases of interest in this area concern allegations of medical negligence, it should be remembered that the relevant principles apply equally in other contexts. Thus, a lawyer is judged by the standard of a "reasonable lawyer", an accountant by the standard of a "reasonable accountant", and so on. Similarly, in *Gates v McKenna*,[53] Paul McKenna, the well-known stage hypnotist, was judged by the standard of a "reasonably careful exponent of stage hypnotism".

It is important to note that the relevant issue is not whether the defendant is in fact a member of a trade or profession, but whether, in all the circumstances, by undertaking a particular task, the defendant has held himself or herself out as possessing a trade or professional skill. There are cases, however, where the fact that the defendant is *not* a member of a relevant trade or profession has been seen as important in determining whether the defendant has held himself or herself out as possessing a particular level of skill. In *Philips v William Whitely Ltd*,[54] for example, it was held that the plaintiff, who had had her ears pierced by the defendants, who were jewellers, could not expect them to exercise the same degree of care and skill that would be exercised by a qualified surgeon. Similarly, in *Wells v Cooper*,[55] where the plaintiff suffered injury when a door handle came off in his hand, it was held that, although householders who decide to carry out work on their property involving carpentry skills must achieve the standards of a reasonably competent amateur carpenter, the safety of their work was not to be judged by reference to the contractual obligations that might be owed by a professional carpenter working for reward, since this would be too high a standard.[56]

In *Wilsher v Essex Area Health Authority*[57] it was confirmed that the standard of care to be expected from a professionally qualified defendant is to be determined by considering the nature of his or her "post" and the tasks which it involves. The professional standard of care is objective in the sense that the same standard of care will be required of all professionals holding the same "post". In *Wilsher*, therefore, where a number of medical professionals professed expertise in the care of premature babies, the Court of Appeal held that each of them

---

[52]   [1957] 1 W.L.R. 582 at 586.
[53]   [1998] Lloyd's Rep. Med. 405. See also *Bhamra v Dubb (t/a Lucky Caterers)* [2010] EWCA Civ 13. (Standard of care of caterers at a Sikh wedding.)
[54]   [1938] 1 All E.R. 566.
[55]   [1958] 2 Q.B. 265.
[56]   [1958] 2 Q.B. 265 per Jenkins L.J. at 271. On the standard of care owed by a jobbing labourer, see *James v Butler* [2005] EWCA Civ 1014.
[57]   [1987] Q.B. 730. The facts of *Wilsher* are considered in Ch.6. The case eventually went to the House of Lords and is important in the context of causation.

could be expected to exercise a degree of care and skill appropriate to the tasks usually under-taken by a person holding his or her post. The defendant's "post" was to be distinguished from the defendant's "rank" or "status". This meant that, where a junior doctor was filling a "post" involving the performance of tasks more usually undertaken by someone more senior, the junior doctor would be judged by exactly the same standards as a senior doctor. Dealing with the argument that this placed too great a burden on young doctors, Mustill L.J. commented:

> "To my mind, it would be a false step to subordinate the legitimate expectation of the patient that he will receive from each person concerned with his care a degree of skill appropriate to the task which he undertakes, to an understandable wish to minimise the psychological and financial pressures on hard-pressed young doctors."[58]

The apparent harshness of this rule, however, is mitigated to some extent by the Court of Appeal's assertion in *Wilsher* that where an inexperienced doctor is called upon to perform a task in which he or she lacks expertise, it is sufficient for the doctor to discharge the duty of care to the patient if he or she seeks and acts on the advice of a more senior colleague.

In this context, it should also be noted that a doctor or other professional may, in certain circumstances, discharge the duty of care by simply refusing to act. In certain professions, the position is straightforward. Barristers, for example, have a professional duty to decline cases that are beyond their competence. In the context of the medical profession, however, the posi-tion is more complicated. Junior doctors on duty in casualty departments, for example, cannot, without breaching their duty of care, decline to treat patients whose conditions call for exper-tise they do not possess. On the other hand, it is clear that a general practitioner, unskilled in open heart surgery, can and should decline to perform that task.

*The relevance of common practice and professional opinion*

The second element of the "*Bolam* test"—namely that a professional will escape liability if his or her conduct accords with one view of responsible common practice—has proved contro-versial. Before considering the nature of this controversy, it is useful to explore the facts of *Bolam*, which neatly illustrate the problem which this part of the test was designed to solve.     **5–023**

Mr Bolam was a mental patient suffering from acute depression. One of the accepted forms of treatment for this condition was (and still is today) to administer electro-convulsive therapy (ECT). The treatment involves the patient being given a brief but severe electric shock. An unfortunate side effect, however, is that the shock causes muscle spasms. These can some-times be of such magnitude as to break the patient's bones. Mr Bolam suffered a fractured pelvis during a bout of ECT treatment. He contended that the doctor who administered the treatment had been negligent in a number of respects. First, he argued that he should have been given relaxant drugs prior to the treatment. Secondly, he argued that a restraining sheet should have been used to hold him down whilst the shock was being given. His third argument related not to the way in which the treatment was administered, but to the doctor's failure to warn him of the danger of broken bones so that he could decide for himself whether or not to undergo the treatment. (The issue of whether doctors have a duty to disclose the risks of treatment is considered in more detail later.)

At the trial, the expert evidence given showed a marked difference of opinion within the medical profession as to the correct procedure for administering ECT. It became clear that

[58] [1987] Q.B. 730 at 751.

some doctors favoured relaxant drugs, whilst others preferred not to use them because they could depress the respiratory system, causing the patient to stop breathing. Whilst some doctors favoured restraining sheets, others preferred to leave the limbs free during the treatment (as the doctor in this case had done), arguing that if bones were trapped under a sheet, they were, in fact, more likely to break.

In summing up the case for the jury (the case was decided when juries were used in negligence trials), McNair J. pointed out that ECT was a "progressive science", on which responsible medical opinion differed. His Lordship stated that, according to the law, a doctor will not be liable in negligence if, "he has acted in accordance with a practice accepted as proper by a responsible body of medical men skilled in that particular art". He went on to say that a professional person would not be liable "merely because there is a body of opinion which would take a contrary view".[59] Unsurprisingly, in the light of this direction, the jury in *Bolam* returned a verdict in favour of the defendant doctor.

The controversial aspect of the approach taken in *Bolam*, which has been followed in subsequent cases, is that, to a great extent, it allows the professions to be "self-regulating"—if the conduct required of a doctor is to be determined, not by a judge, but by evidence of what some other doctors do, then it can be argued that doctors are not truly answerable to their patients through the courts, because they are allowed to set their own standards of care.[60] We shall see, however, that there are limits to the extent to which doctors and other professionals can place themselves "above the law" in this way. These limits were re-affirmed by the House of Lords in the important case of *Bolitho v City and Hackney Health Authority*.[61] Nevertheless, the "*Bolam* test*" makes it very difficult for a claimant to prove negligence against a professional person.

It is important to recognise that the "*Bolam* test" means that a judge is not normally permitted to substitute his or her own views for the views of the defendant's responsible expert witnesses. In other words, even though a judge, as a lay person in medical (or other professional) terms, may strongly prefer a form of practice advocated by the claimant's expert witnesses, and may instinctively feel that the defendant's way of doing things was wrong, he or she must resist the temptation to choose between two competing "responsible" schools of professional thought.

This point is clearly illustrated by *Maynard v West Midlands Health Authority*.[62] Here, the defendants carried out a diagnostic procedure, in the nature of a biopsy, on the plaintiff's throat. The procedure was performed with all due care and skill, but it carried a small risk of damage to the vocal chords. This risk materialised, and the plaintiff brought a negligence action alleging that the biopsy had been unnecessary. The defendants contended that they had acted properly in deciding to perform the procedure, because it was required in order to exclude the possibility (albeit remote) that the plaintiff was suffering from Hodgkin's Disease. The trial judge preferred the view of the plaintiff's experts—who would have waited for the results of blood tests to come through instead of carrying out a biopsy—and held the defendants liable. His Lordship's judgment, however, was overruled by the Court of Appeal and the House of Lords. Lord Scarman said:

[59] *Bolam v Friern Hospital Management Committee* [1957] 1 W.L.R 582 at 587–588.
[60] See Grubb [1988] C.L.J. 12.
[61] [1998] A.C. 232. On the application of *Bolitho*, see: *Zarb v Odetoyinbo* [2006] EWHC 2880, (2007) 93 B.M.L.R. 166; *Gouldsmith v Mid Staffordshire General Hospitals NHS Trust* [2007] EWCA Civ 397.
[62] [1984] 1 W.L.R. 634. It is important to distinguish this type of case from a case such as *Penney v East Kent Health Authority* [2000] Lloyd's Rep. Med. 41 where the expert witnesses agree that the defendant's conduct was wrong but give conflicting opinions about whether it is "excusable". See de Prez (2001) 17 P.N. 75.

"a judge's 'preference' for one body of distinguished professional opinion to another also professionally distinguished is not sufficient to establish negligence in a practitioner".

The practical result of Lord Scarman's approach, then, is that it is extremely difficult for a claimant to prove professional negligence—he or she must effectively show that no responsible body of professional opinion would have supported what the defendant did. Whilst showing this may be difficult, however, it is not always impossible. This is because the cases have repeatedly made it clear that a judge is only obliged to accept the views of the defendant's experts if those views are "responsible".

*The limits of the "Bolam principle"*

As we have already noted, the fact that the defendant has conformed with common practice **5–024** cannot be regarded as *conclusive* evidence that he or she has met the standard of care, because the common practice in question may itself be negligent. Thus, in *Edward Wong Finance Co Ltd v Johnson, Stokes & Master*,[63] the Privy Council held that a conveyancing practice which involved a risk to the client was negligent, despite its widespread adoption by the legal profession in Hong Kong. The courts clearly have a part to play in setting standards of professional conduct. Were it otherwise, certain professionals might persist with outdated or clearly indefensible practices, and escape justice by saying that are only doing what some other professionals do. This would amount to an abuse of their position in society.

In *Bolam* itself, McNair J. made it clear that "mere personal belief that a particular technique is best is no defence unless that belief is based on reasonable grounds".[64] His Lordship went on to explain that it had long been the law, for example, that a doctor who obstinately refused to use anaesthetics or antiseptics could not escape liability simply by calling as witnesses colleagues who took a similarly stubborn and irrational view. More recently, in *Bolitho v City and Hackney Health Authority*,[65] Lord Browne-Wilkinson, delivering the opinion of a unanimous House of Lords, took the opportunity to clarify the circumstances in which a court was entitled to reject the professional opinions of the defendant's experts.

*Bolitho* is a rather complicated case, because it involves issues of causation as well as issues of breach of duty. It is further considered in Ch.6. For present purposes it is sufficient to note that the case concerned a two-year-old boy who was admitted to hospital suffering from breathing difficulties. In the events which happened, the boy suffered cardiac arrest leading to brain damage, and his mother brought a negligence action on his behalf. One of the questions for the court was whether the doctor in charge should have intubated the child (put a tube down his throat to assist his breathing) or whether, given the boy's symptoms, she would have been justified in taking no such action. At the trial, the judge heard evidence from eight different experts. Five of them (called for the plaintiff) said that, in the circumstances, any competent doctor should have intubated the boy. Three of them (called for the defendant doctor) said that intubation would not have been appropriate, and referred to the fact that intubation carried a very small risk of injuring the child's throat. The trial judge held that the doctor was not liable. Although, having listened to the experts, as a lay person he felt persuaded that intubation would have been the right course of action, he felt bound to hold that the defendant escaped liability because her failure to intubate was endorsed by *one* responsible

[63] [1984] A.C. 296.
[64] *Bolam v Friern Hospital Management Committee* [1957] 1 W.L.R 582 at 587.
[65] [1998] A.C. 232. Comment: R. Heywood (2006) 22(4) P.N. 225–235.

body of medical opinion. To hold otherwise would amount to substituting his own views for the views of the defendant's expert witnesses, and the "*Bolam* test" did not allow him to do this.

The House of Lords confirmed the judge's approach as correct. What is important to note, however, is that Lord Browne-Wilkinson made it clear that in some circumstances a judge *would* be entitled to reject the opinions of professional experts, if he or she felt that their opinions had no *logical basis*. Thus, where (as in this case) the expert evidence was concerned with the question of weighing up the risks presented by different forms of treatment, the experts, in order to have their evidence accepted, had to show that they had directed their minds to this question and had reached a conclusion that was logically defensible.

On one view, it can be argued that Lord Browne-Wilkinson's approach entails a slight modification of the "*Bolam* test". That is to say, whilst McNair J. had made it clear in *Bolam* that expert evidence could be rejected *if the person giving it* was not "responsible", *Bolitho* now makes it clear that expert evidence, even when given by a responsible and respected expert, can be rejected *if the evidence itself* is not "responsible", in the sense that it does not withstand logical analysis. The distinction between the credibility of the evidence and the credibility of the person giving it is, of course, an extremely fine one. This point did not escape Lord Browne-Wilkinson, who thought that, in most cases, the fact that an opinion was held by a responsible medical expert would, in itself, demonstrate that the opinion was a reasonable one. His Lordship was careful to point out that, this being the case, it would be only in very rare cases that a judge would be justified in rejecting professional expert opinion as unreasonable.

Lord Browne-Wilkinson went on to conclude that the case before him was not, in fact, one of these rare cases. On the facts of *Bolitho*, the trial judge had been right in accepting the defendant's expert evidence, because the experts had given a logical justification for their opinion that intubating the child was not appropriate—namely that intubation involved a small risk of injury. Accordingly, because the defendant doctor's failure to intubate had been endorsed by one body of reasonable medical thought, she escaped liability.

It is clear from *Bolitho*, then, that a doctor cannot escape liability for his or her conduct unless that conduct has a rational justification. But the limits of this rule remain untested.[66] In particular, one thorny problem remains to be directly addressed by the courts: suppose the defendant's experts say that he or she was justified in withholding a very expensive drug from a patient, on the basis that it is common medical practice to have regard to budgetary constraints in administering treatment. Would a judge be entitled to reject this view because, in the words of Lord Browne-Wilkinson, it "does not withstand logical analysis"?[67]

## Disclosure of the risks of treatment

**5–025**    Here, we consider the extent to which the standard of care expected of doctors requires them to disclose to a patient the risks of treatment, so that the patient can make an informed choice

---

[66] See, however, *Wisniewski v Central Manchester Health Authority* [1998] P.I.Q.R. P324, where the Court of Appeal rejected a finding by the trial judge that because the defendant's witness failed to give oral evidence at the trial, his view was not logically supported.

[67] Note that in *Hucks v Cole (1968)* (1993) 4 Med. L.R. 393 the court was prepared to say that the relatively low cost of administering penicillin to prevent septicaemia was a relevant reason for rejecting the defendant's evidence that it was reasonable not to administer the drug—but this, of course, is a slightly different issue.

about whether to consent to that treatment. (It will be recalled that this was one of the issues in *Bolam*.) Where the treatment in question involves physical contact (as opposed to taking a drug orally, for example), absence of consent on the part of the patient may render the doctor liable in the tort of battery. This issue is discussed in Ch.11, where we shall see that so long as the claimant has given consent to the procedure in broad terms, no action in battery will lie. Here, we are concerned with liability in negligence.

The leading case is *Sidaway v Bethlem Royal Hospital Governors*.[68] The plaintiff, who was suffering from pain in her neck and shoulders, was advised by her surgeon to have an operation on her back. The surgeon did not warn her that there was a very small risk (around 1 per cent) of damage being done to her spine, due to the fact that he would be operating within less than three millimetres of her spinal cord. The plaintiff consented to the operation and it was performed with all due care and skill. But the risk of injury materialised, leaving the plaintiff disabled. She claimed that the surgeon had been negligent in failing to tell her about the risk, and that had she known about it, she would not have agreed to the operation.

The House of Lords (Lord Scarman dissenting) held that the surgeon was not liable. Lords Diplock and Bridge, who gave the leading speeches for the majority, both thought that the "*Bolam* test" applied in this context. Accordingly, because the surgeon had conformed with a responsible body of medical opinion which would not have disclosed the risk, he escaped liability. Lord Bridge was careful to point out, however, that the decision did not amount to handing over to the medical profession complete control over the practice of disclosure. His Lordship said that a judge:

> ". . . might in certain circumstances come to the conclusion that disclosure of a particular risk was so obviously necessary to an informed choice on the part of the patient that no reasonably prudent medical man would fail to make it".[69]

As an example of the type of case he had in mind, Lord Bridge referred to an operation involving "a substantial risk of grave adverse consequences, as for example the 10 per cent risk of a stroke".

In *Sidaway*, then, the majority declined to adopt a strict doctrine of "informed consent". The reasons for this refusal were clearly enunciated by Lord Bridge:

> "The doctor cannot set out to educate the patient to his own standard of medical knowledge of all the relevant factors involved. He may take the view, certainly with some patients, that the very fact of his volunteering, without being asked, information of some remote risk involved in the treatment proposed, even though he describes it as remote, may lead to that risk assuming an undue significance in the patient's calculations."[70]

According to the majority in *Sidaway*, then, it is for doctors to decide whether, and how much, information to reveal to a patient, having regard to the best interests of the particular patient. Lord Scarman, however, took a different view. His Lordship thought that the question of

---

[68] [1985] A.C. 871.
[69] [1985] A.C. 871 at 900. On the issue of facts relevant to an informed choice, see *A v Leeds Teaching Hospitals NHS Trust (aka In Re Organ Retention Group)* [2005] Q.B. 506. (In obtaining consent for a post mortem, a duty was owed to explain what it involved, including the fact that organs might be retained.)
[70] *Sidaway v Bethlem Royal Hospital Governors* [1985] A.C. 871 at 899.

disclosure should be decided by the courts, using an objective test. On Lord Scarman's view, doctors should be placed under a duty to disclose all "material" risks, and the question for the judge (in deciding whether a risk was "material") would be whether or not a reasonable person in the patient's position would be likely to attach significance to the risk. If the answer to this question was "yes", then a doctor who failed to disclose that risk would be in breach of duty.

Lords Bridge and Templeman, in *Sidaway*, placed great emphasis on the fact that Mrs Sidaway had not specifically asked the surgeon about the risks of the operation. Lord Bridge thought that, in a case where a doctor was questioned specifically by the patient, the doctor would be obliged to answer "both truthfully and as fully as the questioner requires".[71] This principle was applied in *Chester v Afshar*.[72] The claimant, who was considering an operation on her spine, specifically asked her consultant about the risks inherent in the operation. The defendant was held to be in breach of duty when, instead of explaining that the operation carried a small but inherent risk, he merely gave the light-hearted reply: "Well, I have never crippled anybody yet".

It should be noted that (even in cases where the patient does not ask about the risks) the modern law may well place doctors under a more stringent duty to disclose risks than some of the dicta in *Sidaway* might suggest. This is for a number of reasons. First, the medical profession has now subscribed to guidelines requiring the disclosure of small but significant risks which would affect a patient's ability to make a balanced judgment about whether to consent to an operation.[73] Secondly, there has, since *Sidaway* was decided, been a cultural shift in favour of greater risk disclosure and the patient's "right to know". Thus, although there is no doubt that the issue of disclosure is still governed ultimately by the *Bolam* test, it will, perhaps, be in only the most exceptional cases that the courts (or expert witnesses) will accept that there are special reasons for failing to disclose risks. Moreover, under the modern law, the threshold of what constitutes a "significant risk" may well be considerably lower than the "10 per cent risk of a stroke" suggested by Lord Bridge. This cultural shift in favour of disclosure was noted by Lord Steyn in *Chester v Afshar*:

> "In modern law medical paternalism no longer rules and a patient has a prima facie right to be informed by a surgeon of a small, but well established, risk of serious injury as a result of surgery."[74]

## Policy issues in medical negligence cases

5–026    It is possible to discern a number of policy considerations underlying the decisions we have examined in this section. First, the courts are concerned that their decisions should not encourage the practice of "defensive medicine", i.e. medical care which involves a "belt and braces" approach to treating patients, motivated by the desire to avoid negligence liability.[75] There is some concern in the United States that doctors are adopting this sort of approach, which is not always in the best interests of the patient.

---

[71] [1985] A.C. 871 at 898.

[72] [2005] 1 A.C. 134. This case is important in the context of causation and is further considered in Ch.6.

[73] See: Royal College of Surgeons, *Good Surgical Practice* (2002), Ch.4 (referred to by Lord Steyn in *Chester v Afshar* [2005] 1 A.C. 134, at para.26), now superseded by *Good Surgical Practice* (2008).

[74] *Chester v Afshar* [2005] 1 A.C. 134, per Lord Steyn at para.16. See also *Birch v University College London Hospital NHS Trust* [2008] EWHC 2237 and R. Heywood [2009] C.L.J. 30.

[75] See Fanning (2008) 24 P.N. 93.

In *Whitehouse v Jordan*,[76] Lord Denning M.R., in the Court of Appeal, warned of the dangers of following the American example. The case involved an allegation of negligence against a senior registrar who, it was argued, had wrongly persisted in delivering a baby by forceps when a Caesarean section was called for. In holding the defendant not liable, Lord Denning M.R. expressed the view that if too high a standard of care were demanded of doctors, experienced practitioners might refuse to treat certain patients, and young people might be deterred from entering the medical profession because of the high insurance premiums that would be required to meet professional negligence claims.

In the factual context of *Whitehouse v Jordan*, the gist of Lord Denning's argument is that a finding of liability might have led doctors to "err on the side of caution" when delivering babies, and opt for Caesarean section, even where this was not in the best interests of the mother or the child. It should also be noted that the practice of "defensive medicine" is expensive, because it requires the administration of "precautionary" tests and treatments to exclude remote risks. The courts' attempts to contain the scope of liability for medical negligence may reflect concern about the proper allocation of scarce NHS resources.

The second policy issue to note is that the courts may be anxious not to encourage a "culture of litigation" in medical cases, because of the harm that unjustified allegations of negligence can do to a defendant's reputation. It was noted in Ch.1 that a professional person's fear of having his or her reputation tarnished by a negligence action may serve as a deterrent to negligent conduct. But it must be remembered that, because many people may take the view that there is "no smoke without fire", a professional's reputation may be unjustly tarnished by a mere allegation of negligence, even though the professional is eventually absolved of fault.

This problem was recognised by Kilner Brown J. in *Ashcroft v Mersey Regional Health Authority*.[77] Here, an allegation was made against a much respected senior surgeon, who had carried out an operation on the plaintiff's inner ear involving a small risk of injury to her facial nerve. This injury materialised despite his having performed the operation with all due care and skill. In holding him not liable, Kilner Brown J. stated the case for no-fault compensation in cases of medical mishap. His Lordship observed:

> ". . . this claim reveals a disgraceful state of affairs. Where an injury is caused which never should have been caused, common sense and natural justice indicate that some degree of compensation ought to be paid by someone. As the law stands, in order to obtain compensation an injured person is compelled to allege negligence against a surgeon who may, as in this case, be a careful, dedicated person of the highest skill and reputation. If ever there was a case in which some reasonable compromise was called for, which would provide some amount of solace for the injured person and avoid the pillorying of a distinguished surgeon, this was such a case."[78]

## PROOF OF BREACH

Although the claimant bears the burden of proving breach of duty, there are certain circum-  **5–027** stances in which special rules will assist in discharging this burden.

[76] [1980] 1 All E.R. 650, CA. The decision was subsequently upheld by the House of Lords at [1981] 1 W.L.R. 246.
[77] [1983] 2 All E.R. 245, affirmed on appeal [1985] 2 All E.R. 96.
[78] [1983] 2 All E.R. 245 at 246.

## Civil Evidence Act 1968

**5–028**    Section 11(1) of the Civil Evidence Act 1968 provides that, in a civil trial, proof that a person has been convicted of a criminal offence shall be taken as proof that he or she committed the offence, unless the contrary is proved. What this means in the context of a negligence trial is that, if the claimant shows that the defendant has been convicted of an offence arising out of the same facts as those in issue at the trial, the burden of proof is reversed, so that the defendant will have to disprove negligence. Thus, in *Wauchope v Mordecai*,[79] the plaintiff was injured by being knocked off his bicycle when the defendant suddenly opened the door of a parked car. The defendant was convicted of an offence arising out of the incident. The Court of Appeal held that the effect of s.11 of the 1968 Act was to shift the burden of proof to the defendant. Since the defendant had failed to prove that he had *not* been negligent, the trial judge had been wrong to dismiss the plaintiff's case on a finding that the plaintiff had not proved negligence.

## Res ipsa loquitur

**5–029**    The maxim res ipsa loquitur means "the thing speaks for itself". Where the maxim applies, the court is prepared to draw an inference that the defendant has been negligent without requiring the claimant to bring evidence about the precise way in which the negligence occurred. This idea originates from the judgment of Erle C.J. in *Scott v London and St Katherine Docks Co*,[80] a case which provides a good example of when the maxim will apply.

The plaintiff was passing the defendants' warehouse when six bags of sugar, which were being hoisted by the defendant's crane, fell on him. The plaintiff could not prove *how* and *why* this happened—the only thing he could prove was that the bags fell and caused him injury. It was held, however, that these facts were sufficient to give rise to an inference of negligence. Bags of sugar do not usually fall from a crane unless someone *has* been negligent, so the fact of negligence "spoke for itself". Since the defendants had failed to provide an innocent explanation of how the incident had occurred, they were held liable.

*When does the maxim apply?*

**5–030**    There are three conditions which must be satisfied before res ipsa loquitur can apply:

*(1) The occurrence must be one that will not normally happen without negligence*

This requirement was clearly met on the facts of *Scott v London and St Katherine Docks*— there was no obvious alternative explanation why the bags fell off the crane. Similarly, in *Byrne v Boodle*[81] the maxim was held to apply when a barrel of flour fell on the plaintiff as he was passing underneath the defendant's window. The cases in which the requirement has been met are many and varied. In *Chaproniere v Mason*,[82] for example, the court was prepared to infer negligence when a stone was found in a bun, and in *Ward v Tesco Stores Ltd*,[83] negli-

---

[79] [1970] 1 W.L.R. 317.
[80] (1865) 3 Hurl. & C. 596. For a modern example of the application of the doctrine, see *George v Eagle Services Ltd.* [2009] UKPC 21. Comment: K. Williams (2009) 125 LQR. 567.
[81] (1863) 2 Hurl. & C. 722.
[82] (1905) 21 T.L.R. 633.
[83] [1976] 1 W.L.R. 810. Applied in *Dobson v Asda Stores* [2002] C.L.Y. 4551 and *Hall v Holker Estate Co. Ltd.* [2008] EWCA Civ 1422.

gence was inferred when the plaintiff slipped on a spillage of yoghurt on a supermarket floor, which the defendants had failed to clean up.

As the reliability of machines has improved, the courts have become increasingly willing to conclude that accidents involving machines are more probably due to the negligence of their operators than to mechanical failure. Thus, the courts have been willing to invoke the maxim in road traffic cases where cars skid,[84] or veer on to the pavement[85] or into the opposite carriageway.[86] In a medical context, res ipsa loquitur has been applied, for example, to a case where a surgeon left a swab inside a patient's body.[87] It has also been applied in the context of failed treatment. Thus, in *Cassidy v Ministry of Health*,[88] as Denning L.J. put it, the plaintiff was entitled to say:

> "I went into hospital to be cured of two stiff fingers. I have come out with four stiff fingers and my hand is useless. That should not happen if due care had been used. Explain it if you can".

*(2) The defendant must have control of the thing which causes the harm*

This requirement can be illustrated by comparing two cases involving railway accidents. In *Gee v Metropolitan Railway*,[89] the plaintiff was injured when he fell out of an underground train, having leaned against a door. Because the train had only just left the station, it could be inferred that the defendants, who clearly had a duty to see that the door was closed before the train departed, had been in control of the door at the time it flew open. By contrast, in *Easson v London and North Eastern Ry. Co*,[90] where a four-year-old boy fell through an unsecured train door, it was held that res ipsa loquitur did not apply. At the time of the accident, the train was seven miles beyond its last stopping place. In these circumstances, although the accident *might* have been due to the defendants' negligence, it was not appropriate to infer that it was, because the door might have been opened by a passenger, rather than by one of the defendants' employees.

5–031

*(3) The cause of the occurrence must be unknown to the claimant*

This requirement is not of any great practical significance. All it means is that, where the facts are sufficiently known, there is no need to invoke the maxim because the claimant can prove what actually happened. Thus, in *Bolton v Stone*,[91] the maxim was held to have no application, because it was obvious that the cricket ball must have been hit over the fence by the batsman. In *Barkway v South Wales Transport Co Ltd*,[92] where a burst tyre on a bus caused an accident, it was held that the maxim should not be applied. There was some evidence that the bus company might have prevented the accident if it had told its drivers to report incidents involving blown tyres, and it had failed to do so. Accordingly, the plaintiff was required to investigate this issue, rather than rely on res ipsa loquitur.

5–032

---

[84] *Richley v Faull* [1965] 1 W.L.R. 1454.
[85] *Ellor v Selfridge & Co Ltd* (1930) 46 T.L.R. 236.
[86] *Ng Chun Pui v Lee Chuen Tat* [1988] R.T.R. 298.
[87] *Mahon v Osborne* [1939] 2 K.B. 14.
[88] [1951] 2 K.B. 343 at 365.
[89] (1873) L.R. 8 Q.B. 161.
[90] [1944] 2 K.B. 421.
[91] [1951] A.C. 850
[92] [1950] 1 All E.R. 392.

*What is the effect of the maxim?*

**5–033**    There has been some debate about whether the effect of res ipsa loquitur is to reverse the legal burden of proof, or whether it places only an *evidential* burden on the defendant to rebut the inference of negligence.[93] In most cases, the point is of little practical importance, but in one circumstance it may be significant. Suppose that, after hearing the defendant's explanation, the judge finds that the balance of probabilities is *equal* as between a negligent and an innocent explanation of the occurrence in question. Who should win the case? If the effect of the maxim is to reverse the legal burden of proof, the claimant should win, because the defendant has not proved, on the balance of probabilities, that he or she has *not* been negligent. On the other hand, if the burden of proof stays with the claimant, the defendant should win, unless the claimant can adduce further evidence to tip the scales in his or her favour.

In *Colvilles Ltd v Devine*,[94] Lord Donovan in the House of Lords said that the maxim had no effect on the legal burden of proof. However, a year later, the House of Lords appeared to take a different approach in the case of *Henderson v Henry E. Jenkins & Sons*.[95] Here, the plaintiff's husband was killed when the brakes of the defendants' lorry failed. The failure was caused by corrosion of a brake fluid pipe. In answer to the plaintiff's claim of res ipsa loquitur, the defendants gave evidence that they had maintained the lorry in accordance with common practice. They had had the lorry regularly inspected, but the pipe in question could only be fully inspected by removing it from the lorry, and this was not recommended by the manufacturers until the lorry had done a certain mileage. In spite of this, the House of Lords held that the defendants had failed to rebut the inference of negligence—they should have gone on to show that there was nothing in the history of the lorry that would have caused abnormal corrosion and required a special inspection. Thus, although the point was not entirely clear, their Lordships appeared to say that it was for the *defendants* to prove that they were *not* negligent. As Lord Pearson put it, the defendants lost the case because "their answer was incomplete".[96]

More recently, however, in *Ng Chun Pui v Lee Chuen Tat*,[97] the Privy Council has reasserted that in res ipsa loquitur cases the burden of proof does not switch to the defendant. Here, a coach veered across a central reservation into the opposite carriageway, where it collided with oncoming traffic. This fact alone would have justified a finding of negligence, so the plaintiff called no evidence. The defendants, however, explained that a car had suddenly cut across the driver's path, causing him to brake suddenly and skid. In the light of this explanation, the Privy Council held that there could be no inference of negligence, because the driver's actions in such an emergency had not been negligent. What is important is that, rather than saying that the defendants *had discharged the burden of proof*, their Lordships said, in effect, that the explanation had tilted the balance of probabilities against the plaintiff. The burden of proof remained with the plaintiff, who was entitled to bring further evidence to show that the defendants had been negligent. But since he could not do so, he lost the case. Lord Griffiths, delivering the opinion of the Privy Council, said that it was misleading to talk of the burden of proof shifting to the defendant in a res ipsa loquitur situation. The burden of proving negligence rests throughout the case on the plaintiff. Although *Ng Chun Pui v Lee*

---

[93]  See, e.g. P.S. Atiyah (1972) 35 M.L.R. 337.
[94]  [1969] 1 W.L.R. 475.
[95]  [1970] A.C. 282. A similar approach was taken by the Court of Appeal in *Ward v Tesco Stores Ltd* [1976] 1 W.L.R. 810.
[96]  [1970] A.C. 282 at 303.
[97]  [1988] R.T.R. 298.

*Chuen Tat* is a Privy Council decision, and therefore not technically binding, it is probable that this approach will be followed in future cases.

## Breach of duty: conclusion

We have seen that breach of duty is in most respects a relatively straightforward element of the tort of negligence, but one where policy nevertheless plays an important part in the courts' decisions. In Chs 7 and 8, we shall explore breach of duty again in the specific contexts of employers' liability and occupiers' liability. First, however, it is appropriate to examine two further elements of the tort of negligence, namely causation and remoteness.     **5–034**

# Chapter 6

## CAUSATION AND REMOTENESS

### Introduction

This chapter deals with the question of whether the defendant's actions can be said to be the legal cause of a claimant's loss. Essentially, in answering this question, two separate issues need to be considered. First, there is the issue of whether what the defendant did was the factual cause of the defendant's loss (or whether the loss was caused by something else). Secondly, there is the issue of whether, in certain cases, although the claimant's loss is the factual result of the defendant's actions, the law should nevertheless say that the defendant is not liable because that loss is too "remote"—in the sense that it is too unusual or "far removed" a consequence of the defendant's actions. We explore each of these issues in turn.

6–001

### FACTUAL CAUSATION

Factual causation is a difficult subject. It divides into a number of separate issues, but there is a considerable degree of conceptual overlap between these issues. Often, when a court focuses on one particular issue, it is merely selecting one particular approach from a number of alternatives. In some cases, a number of approaches are adopted concurrently, and it may be difficult to classify a given case as turning on one issue rather than another.[1] The root of all the confusion is the difficult nature of causation as a philosophical problem. We begin by examining this problem and noting, in general terms, the law's response to it.

6–002

#### The pragmatic approach

The relationship between "cause" and "effect" is complex. Philosophically speaking, every "effect" is produced by the coming together of many different "causes". Moreover, all of these "causes" will, in truth, themselves be "effects" produced by other "causes". Take an example: I light a cigarette and carelessly discard my lighted match in your waste paper basket, which results in a fire burning down your house. Who is to blame? Legally speaking, the answer is

6–003

---

[1] For more detailed discussion of causation, see Hart and Honoré, *Causation in the Law* (2nd edn, Oxford: Clarendon Press, 1985). For a perspective on the modern law, see Hoffmann (2005) 121 L.Q.R. 592.

pretty obvious—it is my carelessness that has caused the fire. But philosophically speaking, the fire has many causes. A philosopher might say that there are many "conditions" without which the fire might not have happened. It might not have happened had you not allowed the waste paper basket to become so full with paper. It certainly would not have happened without your inviting me to your house in the first place, and allowing me to smoke there. Do these factors mean that you are the cause of your own loss? Alternatively, we might say that there would have been no fire if I were not an addicted smoker. Therefore, can we not blame the person who offered me my first cigarette? Ultimately, if I had not been born, your house would not have burned down. Does this mean we can blame my parents? How about fixing the blame on my distant ancestors? Clearly, the law cannot take a philosophical approach to causation. If it did, nobody could ever be said to have caused *anything*. Defendants could always "pass the buck", or, as a lawyer might say, fix responsibility on a person or an event further back in the "chain of causation". Therefore, the law takes a pragmatic, or "common sense" view of causation. As Lord Wright put it, in *Yorkshire Dale Steamship Co Ltd v Minister of War Transport*: "Causation is to be understood as the man in the street, and not as either the scientist or the metaphysician, would understand it".[2] But this approach, of course, can leave us in a position where the reasoning in the cases defies analysis in terms of logical principle. Another unfortunate consequence of the "common sense" approach is that, in causation cases, legal language is particularly apt to produce confusion. For example, judges and writers may say that a defendant is not liable unless he has "caused" the damage; on the other hand, they may say that a defendant is not liable for all of the damage that he has "caused". Qualifying the word "cause" with adjectives such as "legal", "proximate" or "remote" does little to unravel the mysteries of the topic.[3]

In most cases, the application of the "man in the street" approach reveals that there is only one activity or event that can be sensibly regarded as the cause of the claimant's loss, so the issue is straightforward. In a small minority of cases, however, the law must somehow choose between two or more competing causes of the claimant's loss. These problematic cases are the focus of this chapter. We shall consider them once we have examined in more detail the test the courts apply in straightforward cases.

## The "but for" test

**6–004**   The law's starting point in determining causation is to apply the "but for" test.[4] In other words, to ask the question, "Can it be said that 'but for' the defendant's conduct, the claimant's loss would not have occurred?" Another way of putting this is to ask, "Would the claimant's loss have occurred *in any event*, even without the defendant's conduct?" If the answer to this question is "yes", then the defendant will not have caused the claimant's loss. The classic illustration of the application of the "but for" test is the case of *Barnett v Chelsea and Kensington Hospital Management Committee*.[5] Here, a man went to a casualty department feeling unwell after having drunk some tea. The doctor in charge sent him away without treatment, telling him to see his own doctor. He subsequently died from arsenic poisoning. It was held that the doctor was in breach of his duty of care in failing to examine the man, but expert evidence indicated that,

---

[2] [1942] A.C. 691 at 706.
[3] *Hepple and Matthews' Tort: Cases and Materials* (6th edn, OUP, 2008) p.343.
[4] *Cork v Kirby MacLean Ltd* [1952] 2 All E.R. 402.
[5] [1969] 1 Q.B. 428.

having drunk the arsenic, the man was beyond help when he arrived at the hospital and would have died in any event. Therefore, the doctor's breach of duty had not caused the man's death.

In applying the "but for" test, the courts take into account not only *existing* causes that might have produced the claimant's loss (for example, the arsenic in *Barnett*), but also *hypothetical* causes that might have produced the loss. For example, in *McWilliams v Sir William Arrol Ltd*,[6] a steel erector fell to his death at work. The defendants were in breach of their statutory duty in failing to provide him with a safety harness, but the evidence was that he had rarely used such a harness in the past. In the House of Lords, the defendants successfully argued that this meant he would not have worn a harness even if one had been provided. This being the case, it followed that the defendants were not liable because the man would probably have died in any event.

*Bolitho v City and Hackney Health Authority*[7] (considered in Ch.5) was another case in which the House of Lords had to consider the causal effect of a hypothetical omission. Here, a two-year-old boy was admitted to hospital suffering from breathing difficulties and was kept under observation. His condition deteriorated and on two occasions a nurse contacted the doctor in charge, asking her to attend, but she failed to do so. The child subsequently suffered cardiac arrest leading to brain damage. The doctor had clearly been negligent in failing to attend, but the doctor argued that her non-attendance had not caused the child's death. She maintained that, given the child's symptoms, even if she had attended and examined the child, she would not have taken any action, but would have left the child for a further period of observation. The plaintiff countered this argument by saying that such a course of action would have been negligent—given the symptoms, a competent doctor should have "intubated" (inserted a tube) to assist the child's breathing.

As was noted in Ch.5, the House of Lords held that the doctor's failure to intubate would not have been negligent, because her reasons for not doing so were supported by a body of responsible medical opinion. What is relevant here, however, is to note that in deciding the question of causation, the House of Lords was prepared to ask not simply, "Would the doctor have intubated if she had attended?", but "*Should* the doctor have intubated in such circumstances?" As Lord Browne-Wilkinson put it:

> "A defendant [who is in breach of duty] cannot escape liability by saying that the damage would have occurred in any event because he would have committed some other breach of duty thereafter."[8]

## Problems with the "but for" test

The "but for" test works well enough in the majority of cases, but in cases where there are "multiple causes" it runs into problems. The celebrated example is that of two fires—Fire A and Fire B—both started negligently on different pieces of neighbouring land, which each are capable of burning down the claimant's house.[9] The fires converge and destroy the house. If the claimant sues the creator of Fire A, the creator of Fire A can argue that the loss would have happened in any event, because of the existence of Fire B. If the creator of Fire B is sued, he can employ a similar argument. Thus, applying the "but for" test, neither defendant is liable. It

**6–005**

---

[6] [1962] 1 All E.R. 623.
[7] [1998] A.C. 232. For further discussion of *Bolitho*, see Giliker (1998–99) 9 K.C.L.J. 109 and Scott (1998) 148 N.L.J. 64.
[8] *Bolitho v City and Hackney Health Authority* [1998] A.C. 232 at 240.
[9] See P. Cane, *Atiyah's Accidents, Compensation and the Law* (7th edn, Cambridge University Press, 2006), 5.2.4.

is doubtful that the courts would countenance such an unjust result. They would (probably) treat the case as one involving "cumulative causes" (discussed below), making both defendants jointly liable for the full extent of the damage.[10]

In the sections below, we consider the courts' approach to different types of cases involving multiple causes. It is traditional to classify such cases under a number of headings. But this classification, and the traditional accompanying analysis of the various "rules" governing each class of case, can give the misleading impression that causation is a rather "technical" or "evidential" branch of the law, in which policy plays only a minor role. It should not be forgotten that, as in other areas of tort law, the rules are flexible. We shall see that they have often been stretched to accommodate policy concerns. Indeed, they have sometimes been stretched so far that they cease to withstand clear analysis.

## CONCURRENT CAUSES

**6–006**     Certain cases are traditionally described as involving "concurrent causes", by which is meant simply that the causes in question occur more or less simultaneously, as opposed to one after another. As a means of classification, the expression is rather inadequate, because, as we shall see, it might equally be applied to certain cases traditionally described as involving "consecutive causes", in which the causes occur at different times but their effects operate at the same time. Nevertheless, it is traditional to consider the so-called "concurrent cause" cases separately.

"Concurrent cause" cases can be divided into two groups, as follows:

*"Indeterminate cause"*

**6–007**     In these cases, there is more than one defendant, but there is only one "operative cause" of the claimant's loss, it being unclear which of the defendants' acts produced this cause. Such is the case, for example, where a claimant has *one* bullet in his leg, but several defendants have been negligent in shooting their guns in the claimant's direction. (As in *Cook v Lewis* and *Summers v Tice*, considered below.)

*"Cumulative cause"*

**6–008**     In these cases, there is more than one "operative cause" of the claimant's loss, each produced by the act of a different defendant, but the problem is, these causes have combined inextricably to produce the same damage. Such is the case, for example, where a claimant has *two* bullets in his leg, each fired by a different defendant, and as a result of this predicament has to have his leg amputated.

We consider each type of case in turn.

### "Indeterminate cause"

**6–009**     The relevant principles here can be understood by considering the Canadian case of *Cook v Lewis*[11] and the American case of *Summers v Tice*.[12] Both cases involved hunting accidents in

---

[10] Alternatively, the courts might apportion liability equally between the two defendants.

[11] [1951] S.C.R. 830.

[12] 119 P.2d 1 (1948).

which the plaintiff had been shot by *one* bullet, fired by one of two defendants, each of whom had been careless in aiming his gun in the plaintiff's direction. The evidence could not establish from whose gun the shot had been fired. The courts adopted the pragmatic approach of reversing the burden of proof. Thus, in the absence of evidence from either defendant that he had *not* been responsible for the bullet, both defendants were held liable as joint tortfeasors.[13] Joint tortfeasors are each potentially liable for the whole of the claimant's loss. Each defendant can then seek a contribution from the other, but that is a separate question relating to damages rather than to liability (see Ch.17).

In *Sindell v Abbott Laboratories*,[14] another American case, the court adopted a more radical solution. The case concerned the liability of manufacturers for a defective pregnancy drug which caused cancer in the female children of mothers who had taken it. The problem did not become apparent until the children had reached puberty and it was then impossible to show which of several hundred manufacturers had produced the particular drug taken by the plaintiffs' mothers. It was known, however, that the drug was inherently defective, so that any one of the manufacturers could have been responsible. The court rejected the solution of imposing joint liability, as in *Summers v Tice*, because only a few of those potentially responsible were defendants before the court and it was unfair to make them responsible to the full extent. Instead, the court held each defendant liable according to the degree of its share of the market for the drug at the relevant time, on the basis that this was the best approximation that could be made of each defendant's likely responsibility.

In the cases discussed above, the courts had to decide which of two human actions produced the claimant's loss. The solutions adopted in these cases, however, have not been favoured by the English courts in cases where the fault of one defendant is competing with one or more "innocent" or "natural" explanations for the claimant's loss. The leading authorities here are *Wilsher v Essex Area Health Authority*,[15] *Hotson v East Berkshire Area Health Authority*[16] and *Gregg v Scott*.[17] In these cases, the courts have not been prepared to make a defendant liable unless the claimant can show that, on the balance of probabilities, his or her loss was caused by the defendant's fault rather than by a natural occurrence. In such cases, the standard of proof required of the claimant assumes enormous significance. For this reason, these cases are worthy of separate consideration and are discussed in a later section of this chapter, under the heading "proof of causation".

## "Cumulative cause"

We have already considered a good example of a "cumulative cause" situation—that of two    **6–010**
negligently started fires, each capable of burning down the claimant's house, which converge and destroy the house. We have noted that in such situations, applying the "but for" test would result in neither defendant being liable. Therefore, the usual approach of the courts is to say that, because either negligent act would have produced the same damage, each defendant is

---

[13] In the UK, the HL unsuccessfully attempted to impose several (rather than joint) liability in this type of situation. See *Barker v Corus UK Ltd* [2006] 2 A.C. 572, reversed by the Compensation Act 2006 (discussed later in this chapter).

[14] 607 P.2d 924 (1980).

[15] [1988] A.C. 1074.

[16] [1987] A.C. 750.

[17] [2005] 2 A.C. 176.

liable for the whole of the damage.[18] This is what happened in *The Koursk*,[19] where two ships collided because both were simultaneously subject to negligent navigation.

In the example above, we have made the assumption that the act of one defendant alone would have given rise to the whole of the damage. If we cast aside this assumption, however, we are left with a slightly different and more complex type of "cumulative cause" case. This is the sort of case where one defendant (the "first defendant") commits a tortious act, and then, very shortly afterwards, and before the force of that act is spent, a second defendant commits an act which *combines* with it, producing a single result that might not have occurred without the operation of the second act. In such cases, both the first and the second defendant may be liable for the result produced. Take an example: negligent driver A causes his vehicle to obstruct the highway, and subsequently negligent driver B crashes into it, causing injury to a bystander, C. Here, driver A may be held to have caused C's injuries, and may be jointly liable with driver B.[20] This is so, even though it cannot be said that driver A's negligence alone would have caused the accident.

One of the best known examples of this type of "cumulative cause" case is *Fitzgerald v Lane*.[21] Here, the plaintiff was crossing a pelican crossing when the lights showed green for cars, but red for pedestrians. He was hit by a car driven negligently by the first defendant. The force of the collision threw him up on the bonnet and propelled him into the middle of the road. He was then hit by a car driven negligently by the second defendant. He suffered severe injuries to his spine resulting in tetraplegia. At the trial, the evidence could not establish whether his tetraplegia resulted from impact with the first car or from impact with the second car. Moreover, it was impossible to say whether the tetraplegia had only one (indeterminate) cause, or whether it was the result of the combined effect of being hit by both cars. It was clear, however, that the plaintiff had himself been careless in crossing when the lights were against him. The judge held that all three parties involved had been negligent and that, since it was impossible to say that one of the parties was more or less to blame than the other, the responsibility should be borne equally by all three. Therefore, both defendants were held liable and the plaintiff was held contributorily negligent.

## CONSECUTIVE CAUSES

**6–011**     In so-called "consecutive cause" cases, the key issue is whether, where one act succeeds another, there are circumstances where the effect of the first act can be said to have become "overtaken" or "obliterated" by the effect of the second act, in such a way that the first act ceases to be a cause of the claimant's loss. The classic illustration of this sort of situation is

---

[18] Note, however, that where the evidence shows that one defendant is more responsible than another, the court will apportion liability between them in proportion to their fault. See *Holtby v Brigham & Cowan (Hull) Ltd* [2000] 3 All E.R. 421 and *Allen v British Rail Engineering Ltd* [2001] I.C.R. 942. See also *Environment Agency v Ellis* [2008] EWCA Civ 1117. (It was not appropriate to apply the cumulative cause principle to a case involving a subsequent fall, after a back injury at work.)

[19] [1924] P. 140.

[20] See *Rouse v Squires* [1973] Q.B. 889 per Cairns L.J. at 898, but see also *Wright v Lodge* [1993] 4 All E.R. 299 (discussed below) for a restriction on the application of this principle, namely that subsequent "reckless" conduct by the second driver will exculpate the first driver.

[21] [1987] Q.B. 781, CA. There was an appeal to the House of Lords, but only on the question of apportionment of damages, which is discussed in Ch.17.

this: Imagine that a man is about to set out on a journey across the desert. He has a lethal dose of poison put into his water bottle by one of his enemies. Later, the bottle is emptied by a second enemy. Ignorant of these events, he sets out on his journey during the course of which he dies of thirst.

Now, in theory we might absolve the second enemy by pointing to the fact that, if the water bottle had not been emptied, the man would have died in any event from poison. But we could also absolve the poisoner by pointing out that, if the water had not been poisoned, the man would still have died of thirst. Thus, applying the "but for" test makes nobody liable. This sort of situation, however, is different from the example of the converging fires, where the law, unable to determine which action caused the loss, may make both actors liable. Here, the factual cause of the traveller's death is clear—he died of thirst and not of poison. In cases of this sort, then, we might say that the effect of the poisoner's act was "overtaken" or "obliterated" by the act of the second enemy. In other words, in the light of what the second enemy did, the act of the poisoner had no effect.

Situations like that in the example above, however, must be distinguished from cases where the effect of the first wrongful act is said to continue, in spite of the effect of the second. Such was the case in *Performance Cars v Abraham*.[22] The plaintiff's Rolls-Royce was involved in two collisions in the space of a fortnight. After the first collision, the car was in need of a respray. It was then hit by a second driver (the defendant), sustaining the sort of damage that would also necessitate a respray. In an action against the second driver, the Court of Appeal rejected the owner's claim for the cost of a respray on the grounds that the loss did not flow from the defendant's wrongdoing—at the time of the second collision, the vehicle was already in need of a respray. Here, then, rather than saying that effect of the first tort was obliterated by the second, the court applied exactly the opposite sort of reasoning: the second tort had no effect, given the continuing effect of the first.

Broadly similar reasoning was applied by the House of Lords in *Baker v Willoughby*.[23] The plaintiff was run down by the defendant's negligent driving, suffering a stiff leg which caused him loss of mobility and a consequent reduction in his earning capacity. Before the action came to trial, the plaintiff was shot in the same leg by armed robbers, after which the leg had to be amputated. The defendant driver argued that his liability should be limited to the loss caused by the original injury up to the date of the robbery—any loss of mobility and reduction in earning capacity thereafter had been caused, not by him, but by the amputation of the leg. In other words, it was argued that the effect of the original injury had been submerged or obliterated by the second. The defendant also argued that, because, in assessing the amount of damages, it is the courts' practice to discount the award to take account of the hypothetical "vicissitudes of life" that a claimant may suffer in the future, it followed that where these "vicissitudes" had become actual, the damages should be reduced accordingly.

The House of Lords rejected these arguments. Treating the case as one where the plaintiff's continuing loss of amenity had *concurrent* causes, Lord Reid, speaking for the majority, held the defendant liable for *all* of the consequences of the first injury, just as if the second injury had not occurred. In Lord Pearson's view, this result was necessary in order to avoid "manifest injustice" and could be achieved by taking a "comprehensive and unitary view of the damage caused by the original accident".[24] In other words, as Lord Reid put it:

---

[22] [1962] 1 Q.B. 33.
[23] [1970] A.C. 467.
[24] [1970] A.C. 467 at 496.

"A man is not compensated for the physical injury: he is compensated for the loss which he suffers as a result of that injury".[25]

Because the second injury had not diminished the loss the plaintiff would continue to suffer, it could not be regarded as having "submerged" or "obliterated" the effects of the first injury.

Their Lordships were influenced by the need to do practical justice. The thieves who had shot the plaintiff could not be found, and even if they could be found and sued in tort, it would be unlikely that they would be able to pay compensation. Moreover, if the thieves were sued in tort, they would be entitled to "take their victim as they found him". This meant that they could not be liable for the whole of the plaintiff's loss of amenity, but only for the extent to which they had made his condition worse. In this light, it would be very unfair to say that the first tortfeasor could not be fully liable either, because this would leave the plaintiff under-compensated. He would "fall between two defendants". Policy therefore dictated that a first tortfeasor should remain liable for the continuing effects of his or her tort, even where a second tort produced the same (or worse) effects.

The decision in *Baker v Willoughby* should be contrasted with that in *Jobling v Associated Dairies Ltd*.[26] In *Jobling*, the defendant employers had been responsible for injuring the plaintiff's back, causing him loss of mobility and reduced earning capacity. Before the action came to trial, the plaintiff succumbed to a crippling back disease, completely unrelated to his accident, which rendered him totally unfit for work. As in *Baker*, the House of Lords had to decide whether, in the light of a supervening event giving rise to the same loss, the defendants could remain liable for the plaintiff's reduced earning capacity in the future. Here, however, the supervening event in question was a disease rather than a tort. Their Lordships reached the opposite conclusion from that in *Baker*. Taking account of the aim of an award of damages, their Lordships held that the plaintiff would be over-compensated if he were able to recover from the defendants. It was held, therefore, that the defendants' liability ceased at the time of the onset of the disease.

In *Jobling*, Lord Bridge felt unable to accept the approach that had been adopted in *Baker*. His Lordship pointed out that the decision in *Baker* appeared to ignore the fundamental principle that the aim of a damages award in tort is to put the claimant in the same position he or she would have been in had the tort not occurred. On Lord Bridge's analysis of *Baker*, it could be said that, had the first tort not occurred, the plaintiff would have suffered the same sort of loss *in any event* when he was shot by the thieves. Thus, the outcome of the decision was one which actually put him in a *better* position than he would have been in had the first tort never occurred.[27] Arguably, however, on the facts of *Baker*, this analysis is not entirely accurate: the only reason why the plaintiff happened to be where he was when he was shot—sorting scrap metal in a yard—was that he was forced to accept such a menial job by the first tortfeasor's negligence, which had rendered him unfit for other types of work. But for the first tort, therefore, he might never have been shot.

Lord Edmund-Davies, acknowledging academic criticism of the decision in *Baker*,[28] pointed out that the decision had appeared to overlook the fact that the plaintiff could be compensated under the Criminal Injuries Compensation Scheme in respect of the actions of the thieves. This meant that the "injustice" the decision sought to avoid "did not, at least in its

---

[25]  [1970] A.C. 467 at 492.
[26]  [1982] A.C. 794.
[27]  [1982] A.C. 794 at 820.
[28]  See Atiyah (1969) 85 L.Q.R. 475.

full dimensions, exist".[29] Both Lord Edmund-Davies and Lord Wilberforce thought that the decision in *Baker* could not be properly analysed in terms of legal principle and that the case had been decided on policy grounds. Lord Edmund-Davies concluded:

> "My Lords, it is a truism that cases of cumulative causation of damage can present problems of great complexity. I can formulate no convincing juristic or logical principles supportive of the decision of this House in *Baker v Willoughby*, and none were there propounded."[30]

Although, in *Jobling*, their Lordships criticised the decision in *Baker*, they were not prepared to overrule it and accepted that the case might have been correctly decided on its facts. Lords Keith and Russell drew a distinction between a supervening illness, which would obliterate the effect of a previous tortious act, and a supervening tort, which might not.[31] This distinction is hard to justify. At bottom, it must be admitted that the decisions in *Baker* and in *Jobling* cannot be satisfactorily reconciled. The decisions show us that the answers to causation questions are heavily dependent on a pragmatic, policy-driven approach.

What might be discerned, however, is a tendency in the modern law to prefer the *Jobling* approach in this type of case. Thus, in *Gray v Thames Trains Ltd*[32] one of the issues which arose was whether a claim for continuing loss of earnings could be made after the claimant had been sentenced for a crime. Although the loss of earnings was initially caused by the defendant's negligence, the House of Lords held that the principle in *Jobling* prevented such a claim—after the claimant had been sentenced, the effective cause of his continuing lost earnings was to be regarded as his incarceration, rather than the defendant's tort.

## PROOF OF CAUSATION

In this section we are concerned with the difficult question of how, in cases where the defend-    **6–012**
ant's conduct competes with other possible explanations of the claimant's loss, the courts approach the question of requiring the claimant to prove that the defendant's breach is the cause of his or her loss. The nature of the approach the courts will take depends on the type of case with which they are concerned, and here, again, we can see that the courts' decisions seem heavily influenced by policy considerations. A number of different approaches can be discerned. These approaches may be described as:

- the "all or nothing" approach;
- the "vindication of rights" approach;
- the "material increase in risk" approach.

Like the different approaches taken in *Jobling* and *Baker*, which we have just examined, the different approaches in the "proof of causation" cases are not possible to reconcile with one

---

[29] *Jobling v Associated Dairies* [1982] A.C. 794 at 807.
[30] [1982] A.C. 794 at 808.
[31] In *Heil v Rankin* [2001] P.I.Q.R. Q3 the Court of Appeal affirmed that there was no absolute rule that the effect of a supervening tort would obliterate the effect of a previous tort.
[32] [2009] UKHL 33; [2009] 1 A.C. 1339.

another on the basis of coherent principle. Each is simply a pragmatic response to what the courts perceive as the broad demands of justice in particular circumstances.

## The "all or nothing" approach

6–013    The "all or nothing" approach is the approach that will be applied in most cases. It takes as its starting point the proposition that the claimant, who bears the burden of proof in a civil trial, must discharge that burden by meeting the normal civil standard of proof. Thus, the claimant must show that, on the balance of probabilities, it was the defendant's breach (rather than some other event) that caused the loss. This is known as an "all or nothing" approach because, where a claimant succeeds in showing that it is probable (at least 51 per cent likely) that the breach caused the loss, the law will treat this probability as a certainty, so the claimant will win the case and be compensated for all of the loss. If, on the other hand, a claimant can only show, say, a 25 per cent likelihood that the breach caused the loss, the claimant will lose the case and leave court with nothing. As we shall see, difficulites have arisen in applying this seemingly straightforward approach to cases where the loss in question is a claimant's lost chance of recovery, following negligent medical treatment. The approach of the courts is exemplified by the decisions of the House of Lords in *Hotson v East Berkshire Area Health Authority*,[33] *Gregg v Scott*[34] and *Wilsher v Essex Area Health Authority*,[35] all of which were cases where medical negligence was alleged to be the cause of the plaintiffs' loss.

In *Hotson*, the plaintiff, when aged 13, fell while climbing a tree and sustained injury to his hip. He was taken to hospital, but his injury was not correctly diagnosed or treated for five days. In the event, he suffered avascular necrosis—a condition that left him with severe and permanent disability by the time he was 20. Had the hospital treated him promptly when he was first admitted, the plaintiff would have had a 25 per cent chance of making a full recovery, but the effect of the delay in treatment was that the plaintiff lost that 25 per cent chance.

The trial judge (Simon Brown J.) awarded the plaintiff a sum in damages which reflected 25 per cent of the damages which might have been awarded had the hospital's negligence been the only possible cause of his disability. This decision was affirmed by the Court of Appeal, but was reversed by the House of Lords. The key finding of the House of Lords was that the plaintiff had failed to prove his case on the balance of probabilities. Simon Brown J., assessing the medical evidence, had found, of course, that there had been a 75 per cent chance that avascular necrosis would have resulted *in any event*, even if the plaintiff had been treated promptly. This meant, in their Lordships' view, that on the balance of probabilities the plaintiff's disability had been caused when he fell out of the tree. In these circumstances, Simon Brown J. had been wrong to embark on a "quantification" of the loss caused by the defendant—the issue of quantifying the loss could only arise once the hurdle of causation had been overcome, and this the plaintiff had failed to do.

Whilst their Lordships did not rule out the possibility that damages in medical negligence cases could sometimes be awarded for "loss of a chance", they did not think that the circumstances of *Hotson* warranted such an approach. This was because the evidence as to when the plaintiff's disability occurred was clear—when he fell from the tree, he was, on the balance of

---

[33]  [1987] A.C. 750.
[34]  [2005] 2 A.C. 176.
[35]  [1988] A.C. 1074.

probabilities, disabled; the law would treat this probability as a factual certainty, which meant that, by the time the plaintiff arrived at the hospital he was *as a matter of decided fact* already disabled. Thus, in effect, at this point in time the plaintiff had had no chance to lose.[36]

The strict approach to causation exemplified in *Hotson* was subsequently followed by a majority of the House of Lords in *Gregg v Scott*.[37] Here, the defendant, a GP, negligently failed to refer the claimant to hospital to be tested for cancer, so that there was a delay of nine months before his condition was diagnosed. According to the accepted statistical evidence, when the claimant had originally gone to see his GP, he had had a 42 per cent chance of making a full recovery with prompt treatment (and, of course, a 58 per cent chance of *not* doing so). The effect of the negligent delay was to reduce the claimant's chance of recovery to 25 per cent.

The claimant felt able to bring his case because, in their decision in *Fairchild v Glenhaven Funeral Services Ltd*[38] (discussed below) the House of Lords had recently ruled that the "all or nothing" approach could be modified in certain circumstances, where the demands of justice made it right to do so. In *Gregg v Scott*, however, their Lordships declined to extend the reasoning in *Fairchild* (which had involved a risk of industrial disease) to cover the claimant's case. By a 3:2 majority, their Lordships held that the traditional rules of causation should apply. Thus, the claimant lost his case because the "but for" test was not satisfied—he could not show, on the balance of probabilities, that the fact that he had failed to make a full recovery was due to the GP's negligence. The probability (58 per cent) was that he would have failed to make a full recovery *in any event*.

The reasoning in *Gregg v Scott* reveals a stark division of opinion between the Law Lords about the correct approach to be taken in medical negligence cases involving loss of a chance of recovery. The key issue is whether justice demands that the tort of negligence should abandon its strict causation rules in this type of case, and, instead, compensate claimants for lost chances that (even though less than 50 per cent) were of real and substantial value to them. Lord Nicholls, in a powerful dissenting judgment, said that if the law failed to do this, it would be "irrational and indefensible".[39] His Lordship went on to say:

> "The law should be extremely slow to disregard medical reality . . . In these cases a doctor's duty to act in the best interests of his patient involves maximising the patient's recovery prospects, and doing so whether the patient's prospects are good or not so good. In the event of a breach of this duty the law must fashion a matching and meaningful remedy . . . It cannot be right to adopt a procedure having the effect that, in law, a patient's prospects of recovery are treated as non-existent whenever they exist but fall short of 50%. If the law were to proceed in this way it would deserve to be likened to the proverbial ass."[40]

Baroness Hale, however, speaking in the majority, explained the difficulty the courts would face if they recognised claims for loss of a (less than 50 per cent) chance of recovery. Such recognition would, as her Ladyship put it, require "that personal injury law should transform

---

[36] For further consideration of all these issues, see J. Stapleton (1988) 104 L.Q.R. 389 and H. Reece (1996) 59 M.L.R. 188.

[37] [2005] 2 A.C. 176.

[38] [2003] 1 A.C. 32.

[39] *Gregg v Scott* [2005] 2 A.C. 176 per Lord Nicholls at para.6.

[40] [2005] 2 A.C. 176 per Lord Nicholls at paras 42 and 43. Compare the approach adopted in Australia, see e.g. *Rufo v Hosking* [2004] NSWCA 391.

itself".[41] If a claimant who had lost, say, a 40 per cent chance of recovery, were entitled to a "proportionate" sum representing that loss, where would be the justice in allowing a claimant who had lost a 51 per cent chance of recovery (thereby satisfying the standard of proof) to leave court with 100 per cent of the damages? Surely the idea of proportionate compensation would cut both ways, allowing defendants, if it suited them, to reformulate the gist of the action against them as "loss of a chance". This would lead to the strange proposition (to borrow her Ladyship's example) that, where it is shown that there is a 90 per cent chance that my negligence broke your leg, I am entitled to require the court to reduce your damages by 10 per cent, to reflect the chance that your leg might have become broken in any event. This proposition would create an unwelcome complication in the great majority of personal injury cases, and would make recovery of compensation much less predictable for defendants and for the insurance market. For these reasons, then, it was not desirable that the court should view Mr Gregg's loss in a case like *Gregg v Scott* as a "lost chance".[42] Rather, it should be viewed as an *outcome* (i.e. after the negligent treatment, he was unlikely to get better)—and on this basis, of course, the *outcome* of the defendant's negligence had placed the claimant in *no different a position* from the position he had been in before the negligence had occurred, meaning, in effect, that he had suffered no actionable loss.

The "all or nothing" approach taken in *Gregg v Scott* reflects the approach that had been taken by the House of Lords in an earlier case—*Wilsher v Essex Area Health Authority*. In *Wilsher*, the plaintiff was a premature baby who suffered from oxygen deficiency. In monitoring the levels of oxygen in his blood, one of the doctors employed by the defendants negligently failed to notice that a catheter had been wrongly placed into a vein instead of an artery. This meant that the monitoring equipment gave a misleading reading, resulting in the plaintiff being given too much oxygen. The plaintiff developed retrolental fibroplasia (RLF)—a condition permanently affecting his retina—which left him almost totally blind. The expert evidence suggested that excess oxygen was a possible cause of RLF. But RLF was a condition that occurred even in premature babies who did not receive oxygen, and there was a causal link between RLF and at least five conditions that were very common in premature babies.

The trial judge and the Court of Appeal (relying on the House of Lords' decision in *McGhee v National Coal Board*—discussed below) had held the defendants liable on the basis that, by supplying excess oxygen, they had "materially increased the risk" that the plaintiff would succumb to RLF. The House of Lords, however, rejected this liberal approach to causation and substituted the "all or nothing" approach, holding that the plaintiff had failed to establish, on the balance of probabilities, that his RLF had been produced by the excess oxygen, rather than by one of the five other possible common causes of RLF. Lord Bridge, who delivered the unanimous opinion of the House of Lords, acknowledged that the application of the "all or nothing" approach had produced a harsh result for the plaintiff. His Lordship said:

> "Many may feel that [ordering a retrial] serves only to highlight the shortcomings of a system in which the victim of some grievous misfortune will recover substantial

---

[41] [2005] 2 A.C. 176 per Baroness Hale at para.222.

[42] Compare the approach of the courts in cases where the lost chance is one of financial gain. See, e.g. *Allied Maples Group Ltd v Simmons and Simmons* [1995] 1 W.L.R. 1602. It is difficult to distinguish such cases from *Gregg v Scott*, save (as Baroness Hale did in *Gregg* at para.220) on the basis that the claimant's loss is different in quality: "There is not much difference between the money one expected to have and the money one expected to have a chance of having: it is all money. There is a difference between the leg one ought to have and the chance of keeping a leg one ought to have."

compensation or none at all according to the unpredictable hazards of the forensic process. But, whether we like it or not, the law, which only Parliament can change, requires proof of fault causing damage as the basis of liability in tort. We should do society nothing but disservice if we made the forensic process still more unpredictable and hazardous by distorting the law to accommodate the exigencies of what may seem hard cases."[43]

Despite continued assertions by some members of the House of Lords that the rules of causation should not be displaced to accommodate "hard cases", this is precisely what appears to have happened recently in two types of case we examine below. In both types of case, the House of Lords was prepared to relax the strict requirements of causation in order to produce what was perceived as a just result.

## The "vindication of rights" approach: *Chester v Afshar*

*Chester v Afshar*[44] is a 3:2 majority decision, taken by a House of Lords that was differently    **6–014** constituted from the House that decided *Gregg v Scott* (also a 3:2 majority decision). Here, the claimant, who was suffering from chronic back pain, went to see the defendant, an eminent neurosurgeon. He advised her to have surgery, but failed, in response to her questioning, to warn her that there was a very small risk (1 or 2 per cent) of complications with the surgery. Ignorant of this risk, the claimant consented to the surgery. Unfortunately, the risk materialised, leaving her with pain and disability, for which she sued the defendant in negligence.

It was clear that the defendant had been in breach of duty by failing to warn the claimant of the risk (see Ch.5). The difficulty, however, was that the claimant was unable honestly to say that, if she had known about the risk, she would not have consented to the surgery—the most she could say was that she would not have had the operation immediately, but would have taken time for reflection, and perhaps sought a second opinion, before, perhaps, having the operation (with the same associated risk) at a later date. She could not prove, therefore, that "but for" the negligent failure to warn, her disability would never have arisen. Despite this difficulty, the Court of Appeal upheld her claim, as did the House of Lords (but for different reasons).

The Court of Appeal, taking a robust and pragmatic approach, held that the claimant could succeed by applying conventional causation principles. Thus, it could be said that the claimant's disability had resulted from having a particular operation at a particular time. If the defendant had warned her about the risks, she would not have had that particular operation— she would have had an operation (with the same risks) at a later date. If she had had this later operation, in all probability, the very small risk of disability would not have materialised. On this basis, it could be said that the defendant's failure to warn had resulted in the claimant's disability.

The House of Lords did not find this approach attractive. As Lord Hoffmann put it, the approach of the Court of Appeal was:

"... about as logical as saying that if one had been told, on entering a casino, that the odds on the number 7 coming up were only 1 in 37, one would have gone away and come back next week or gone to a different casino. The question is whether one would have

---

[43]  [1988] A.C. 1074 at 1092.
[44]  [2005] 1 A.C. 134. Comment: J. Stapleton (2006) 122 L.Q.R. 426.

taken the opportunity to avoid or reduce the risk, not whether one would have changed the scenario in some irrelevant detail."[45]

In the House of Lords, both the majority and the minority rejected the reasoning of the Court of Appeal and held that the claimant could not succeed in proving causation on conventional principles. For the minority (Lords Hoffmann and Bingham), this was sufficient to dispose of the case. However, the majority went on to state that, for policy reasons, the traditional rules of causation ought to be relaxed to allow the claimant to succeed. Central to their Lordship's reasoning was the need to give effect to the right of a patient to make an informed choice about whether and when to undergo medical treatment. In law, this right was underpinned by a doctor's duty to warn the patient about any significant risks involved in the treatment. It would therefore be unjust if a breach of this duty did not give rise to a remedy. If the doctor were not made liable for such a breach, the duty to inform the patient about significant risks would, as Lord Hope put it, be a "hollow one". His Lordship said:

> "The function of the law is to enable rights to be vindicated and to provide remedies when duties have been breached. Unless this is done the duty is a hollow one, stripped of all practical force and devoid of all content. It will have lost its ability to protect the patient and thus to fulfil the only purpose which brought it into existence. On policy grounds therefore I would hold that the test of causation is satisfied in this case."[46]

The effect of the decision in *Chester v Afshar*, then, is that, for policy reasons, the law requires that a doctor who negligently fails to warn a patient about a complication from treatment must compensate the patient for the consequences of that complication occurring. Lord Steyn thought that such a proposition was sound because it reflected "the reasonable expectations of the public in contemporary society".[47] The approach in *Chester*, however, is very difficult to reconcile with the approach taken in *Gregg* (above). If the claimant in *Chester* is said to have a "right" (to self-determination) that must be "vindicated" by a modification of causation principles, what about Mr Gregg's "right" to be promptly advised about treatment that would maximise his chances of surviving cancer? It is difficult to draw a distinction between the two, because, in both cases, what is in issue is the dignity of the patient, which is supported by a doctor's duty to act in the patient's best interests.[48]

*Chester v Afshar* was not a case where the defendant's negligent conduct had increased the risk that the claimant would suffer loss—the risk of complications from an operation would have been the same, whether or not she had been told about them beforehand. In the cases we examine next, however, the position is slightly different. Although the reasoning in these cases sometimes reflects the "vindication of rights" approach, there is an additional element that the courts can point to in justifying a relaxation of the "but for" test—the defendant's conduct, though not the proven cause of the claimant's loss, has probably increased the risk of the claimant suffering such loss.

---

[45] [2005] 1 A.C. 134 per Lord Hoffmann at para.31.
[46] [2005] 1 A.C. 134 per Lord Hope at para.87.
[47] [2005] 1 A.C. 134 per Lord Steyn at para.25.
[48] On the issue of the "mixed messages" sent by the HL in *Gregg* and *Chester*, see S. Maskery Q.C. and W. Edis (who were opposing counsel in *Gregg*) [2005] 3 J.P.I. Law 205.

## The "material increase in risk" approach

In *McGhee v National Coal Board*,[49] the plaintiff contracted the skin disease dermatitis from    **6–015**
the presence of abrasive brick dust on his skin. Some exposure to brick dust was an inevitable
part of his job—he worked in brick kilns. It was accepted that the defendants were not negligent in exposing him to brick dust during his working day. The plaintiff's argument, however,
was that because no washing facilities were provided at his place of work, throughout his
working life he had had to cycle home each day with his skin coated with the dust. He argued
that, without this additional and unnecessary exposure to the dust, he would not have contracted
dermatitis. The defendants admitted that they had been negligent in failing to provide washing
facilities, but they argued that their negligence was not the cause of the plaintiff's disease. The
medical evidence established that exposure to brick dust caused dermatitis, but the experts
were unable to say that, on the balance of probabilities, the *additional* negligent exposure to
brick dust had been the cause of plaintiff's condition—it might have occurred in any event,
given that he was daily exposed to the "innocent" dust.

The House of Lords held the defendants liable. Their Lordships did not expect the plaintiff
to establish, on the balance of probabilities, that the absence of washing facilities was the
*actual cause* of his dermatitis. It was sufficient that, by failing to provide washing facilities,
the defendants had "materially increased the risk" of the plaintiff contracting the disease.
Their Lordships justified this conclusion in different ways. Thus, at the time *McGhee* was
decided, it was not altogether clear what the ratio of the case was, or in what other factual
circumstances its liberal approach to proof of causation might apply. According to Lord
Wilberforce, in *McGhee*, the outcome was dictated by policy. The defendants, by their negligence, had created a risk of a particular kind of damage, and when damage of that very kind
materialised, they should not be allowed to escape liability because of the claimant's "evidential difficulties" in proving causation. In appropriate cases, where such difficulties became
apparent they should, as a matter of policy and justice, be borne by the person who created the
risk. As his Lordship put it:

> ". . . it is a sound principle that where a person has, by breach of a duty of care, created a
> risk, and injury occurs within the area of that risk, the loss should be borne by him unless
> he shows that it had some other cause."[50]

The logical objection to Lord Wilberforce's approach, of course, was that it appeared to ignore
the fundamental principle that the claimant must prove his case. There was really no evidence
to suggest that the plaintiff's damage materialised "within the area of risk" created by the
defendants' negligence. (It might have materialised within the area of risk created by his doing
his job, for which it was accepted that the defendants could not be liable.) Clearly, Lord
Wilberforce's attempt to elide what were, in fact, two distinct "areas of risk" owed much to
the broad policy consideration that, as a matter of justice, large employers should be made to
compensate their employees for all injuries and diseases occurring in the workplace.

When the House of Lords came to decide *Wilsher*, Lord Bridge, no doubt mindful of this
logical objection, sought to explain the decision in *McGhee* by saying that the case had "laid

---

[49] [1973] 1 W.L.R. 1. For a detailed and entertaining account of the case, see Lord Hope of Craighead, [2003]
C.L.J. 587.
[50] [1973] 1 W.L.R. 1 at 6.

down no new principle of law whatever"—on a proper interpretation, it was simply a case where their Lordships had, in the light of the evidence, felt able to draw a "legitimate inference of fact",[51] namely that the absence of washing facilities had *actually been one of the causes* contributing to the plaintiff's dermatitis. In *Fairchild v Glenhaven Funeral Services Ltd*,[52] however, the House of Lords rejected this explanation of *McGhee*, stating that there had been no evidence in the case from which their Lordships could have legitimately inferred that the defendant's conduct was an *actual cause* of the dermatitis—all the defendants had done was to create an *increased risk* of dermatitis. Accordingly, the decision in *McGhee* should indeed be seen as having laid down a new principle of law, namely that, in appropriate cases, a claimant will succeed by merely establishing a "material increase in risk".

The approach in *McGhee* was followed in *Fairchild v Glenhaven Funeral Services Ltd*. This was a case concerning a number of claimants who had contracted mesothelioma (a lung tumour) as a result of exposure to asbestos, over a lifetime of work for different employers. All the employers admitted they were in breach of their duty of care to protect the claimants against exposure to asbestos. The problem for the claimants, however, was that they could not establish which of their different employers had exposed them to the particular asbestos that had caused their disease. The medical evidence was that the disease did not necessarily build up gradually with continued exposure to asbestos, but could be triggered suddenly at any time, perhaps by one single fibre causing a cell to become malignant. It followed that, while all the employers could be said to have increased the *risk* of mesothelioma, it was not possible to say that all of them had been responsible for *cumulatively causing* the disease. And, of course, it was not possible to say which of them had been responsible for the particular fibre(s) that had suddenly triggered the disease.

The solution adopted by the House of Lords was to make all of the employers liable, on the basis that each had increased the risk of mesothelioma, without requiring the claimants to prove which of the employers had been responsible for causing it. Their Lordships affirmed the principle laid down in *McGhee* that, in appropriate cases, merely establishing a "material increase in risk" would be sufficient to discharge the claimant's burden of proving causation.

## Contribution between defendants: The Compensation Act 2006

**6–016**     The House of Lords in *Fairchild*, whilst making it clear that all of the employers should be liable, gave no guidance as to how that liability should be shared between them. This omission gave rise to academic criticism[53] and left lawyers to presume that the effect of *Fairchild* was to impose "joint liability". Where this sort of liability is imposed, each defendant is potentially liable for the *whole amount* of the loss—the defendants are then left to argue amongst themselves as to who should contribute how much to the claimant's compensation award, but, at the end of the day, the award must be paid in full by one or more of them. This sort of liability has a clear advantage for the claimant—should one or more of the defendants be insolvent or untraceable, the claimant is entitled to look to the remaining defendant(s) to satisfy judgment.

---

[51] [1988] 1 A.C. 1074 at 1090.
[52] [2003] 1 A.C. 32.
[53] See, for example, J. Stapleton (2002) 10 Torts L.J. 276.

After *Fairchild* had been decided, however, the House of Lords decided *Barker v Corus UK Ltd*,[54] a case dealing with three appeals concerning asbestos and mesothelioma. Their Lordships held that the sort of liability that should be imposed on employers in cases like *Fairchild* was "several liability", and not "joint liability". This meant that liability to pay compensation was to be apportioned among the various defendants according to their relative degree of contribution to the risk of the claimant contracting the disease. Although their Lordships declined to be specific on the point, it was clear that these contributions would normally be worked out by reference to the length of time each defendant had exposed the claimant to asbestos, the intensity of that exposure, and (where quantifiable) the potency of the type of asbestos in question. This approach was thought necessary in order to be fair to the defendants in these cases. As Lord Hoffmann put it, apportionment of liability would "smooth out the roughness" of the justice created by joint liability.[55] His Lordship took the view that apportionment was appropriate because the fault of each defendant lay in *creating a percentage risk* of mesothelioma. It could not be said that any of the defendants had *actually caused* the mesothelioma.[56] (Indeed, the whole point of the *Fairchild* principle was that it applied where the cause could not be determined.)

The result of the decision in *Barker*, therefore, was that the risk that one or more defendants would be insolvent or untraceable fell on the claimants. In many cases, this meant that claimants' compensation would be substantially reduced, because much of their exposure to asbestos had occurred long ago, and the companies that had employed them were no longer in existence. Moreover, in practice, claimants would have to trace all relevant defendants, so far as possible, before apportionment could be carried out and any compensation at all could be paid. The practical implication of this was that claims would take much longer to conclude, so claimants and their families, who were already under considerable stress, would have a lengthy wait before receiving any compensation.[57]

When these implications of *Barker* became apparent, there was a public and parliamentary outcry. The government moved swiftly to pass legislation reversing the effect of the decision. As David Anderson MP put it in the House of Commons:

"... if we do not overturn the *Barker* decision, the reality will be that of a man facing a firing squad armed with five guns. A bullet pierces his heart. Nobody knows which gun fired the bullet, so nobody is found guilty. But the truth is that they should all be found guilty."[58]

The effect of *Barker* was therefore reversed by s.3 of the Compensation Act 2006. This provides that, where a defendant, through negligence or breach of statutory duty, has exposed a claimant to asbestos, and that claimant contracts mesothelioma, the defendant is liable "for the whole of the damage caused to the victim by the disease". Liability is declared to exist "jointly and severally" with any other persons responsible for asbestos exposure.

---

[54] [2006] 2 A.C. 572.

[55] [2006] 2 A.C. 572 at para 43.

[56] The other members of the House of Lords did not go as far as Lord Hoffmann on this point. Baroness Hale, although with the majority on apportionment, agreed (at para.120) with Lord Rodger (who dissented) that the "gist" of the harm was the mesothelioma itself, not the risk of causing it.

[57] See Compensation Act 2006, Explanatory Notes, para.14.

[58] *Hansard*, June 8, 2006.

## When will the "material increase in risk approach" apply?

**6–017**    First, it must be remembered that the *Fairchild* principle will have no application in cases where evidence can be produced to show that particular defendants are responsible for making *distinct and quantifiable causal contributions* to the claimant's loss. In such cases, the courts will apportion liability to each defendant in accordance with his or her degree of fault. This is what happened in *Holtby v Brigham & Cowan (Hull) Ltd.*[59] Here, the claimant contracted asbestosis. Unlike mesothelioma, asbestosis is a disease that can get progressively worse the more a person is exposed to asbestos. The claimant had been exposed to asbestos for most of his working life, but had only been employed by the defendants for about half that time. The medical evidence stated that if the claimant's exposure to asbestos had been limited to that caused by the defendants, his condition would not be so bad. The Court of Appeal therefore reduced the claimant's damages, holding that the defendants could only be liable to the extent that their fault had made a causal contribution to the claimant's condition. The *Fairchild* principle is therefore reserved for the sort of exceptional circumstance that occurred in the case itself, namely where it is established that the whole of the damage results from a single event (e.g. exposure to an asbestos fibre) at a specific time in the past, yet the limits of scientific knowledge mean that it is impossible to say which event, out of a number of identical events, has actually caused the damage.

It is clear from the decision of the Supreme Court in *Sienkiewicz v Greif*[60] that the *Fairchild* principle will now apply in mesothelioma cases where only a single defendant has negligently exposed the claimant to asbestos. In contrast to the situation in *Fairchild* and *Barker*, where a number of defendants had negligently exposed the victim to asbestos and thereby materially increased the risk of the employee developing mesothelioma, in *Sienkiewicz*, there was only one defendant, and evidence that the victim had been at risk in any event of developing the disease from low-level exposure to asbestos in the general atmosphere. Seven Justices of the Supreme Court unanimously provided that the *Fairchild* approach would also apply where a single defendant had negligently exposed the victim to asbestos. Although the claimant could only establish an increased risk of 18 per cent arising from the defendant's negligence, such a risk was material: a risk would only be regarded as immaterial if the negligent exposure had been too insignificant to be taken into account, having regard to the overall exposure. This was a matter for the judge on the facts of the particular case. The Supreme Court did warn, however, that the rule in *Fairchild* and *Barker* had been adopted to cater for an evidential gap that had existed at the time of those decisions about the causes of mesothelioma.[61] This did not preclude the courts from reverting to the conventional approach of balance of probabilities should advances in medical science in relation to the disease make such a step appropriate.

In cases where the *Fairchild* principle applies, it sits rather uncomfortably alongside the approach adopted by the House of Lords in *Wilsher*. If the claimants in *Fairchild* could succeed simply by showing that exposure to asbestos had *increased the risk* of mesothelioma,

---

[59] [2000] 3 All E.R. 421. See also *Allen v British Rail Engineering Ltd* [2001] P.I.Q.R. Q10. Consider also *Bonnington Castings Ltd v Wardlaw* [1956] A.C. 613 (Comment: S.H. Bailey (2010) 30 L.S. 167.) See also Janet Smith L.J. "Causation—the seach for principle" (2009) J.P.I. Law 101.

[60] [2011] UKSC 10.

[61] See Lord Phillips, President at para 18: "The special rule of causation applied to mesothelioma was devised because of ignorance about the biological cause of the disease. It was accepted in *Fairchild* and *Barker* that this rendered it impossible for a claimant to prove causation according to the conventional "but for" test and this caused injustice to the claimants."

why was it that the plaintiff in *Wilsher* could not succeed by showing that exposure to excess oxygen had increased the risk that he would contract RLF? Their Lordships in *Fairchild* were content to say that *Wilsher* had been correctly decided, the majority basing this assertion on the factual differences between that case and cases like *McGhee* and *Fairchild*. The key difference is that, in the *Fairchild* type of case, there is only one "causal agent" of the claimant's injury (brick dust in *McGhee* and asbestos in *Fairchild*) whereas, in a case like *Wilsher*, there are many competing "causal agents" (oxygen and the other possible natural causes of RLF).

This approach to distinguishing *Wilsher* was adopted by the Court of Appeal in *Bailey v Ministry of Defence*.[62] Here, the claimant suffered brain damage when she choked on her own vomit whilst in a weakened state, after undergoing an operation. The issue was whether this occurrence had been caused by a medical condition (pancreatitis) or by the negligent post-operative care she had received. Both factors had made her weak, as of course had the operation itself. Treating the case as one of "cumulative causes" which combine to produce the harm, which was indivisible, the Court of Appeal held that in a case where medical science cannot establish the evidence needed to apply the 'but for' test, it would suffice to show that the defendants' negligence materially contributed to the injury, that is, made a contribution which is more than negligible. *Wilsher* was distinguished on the basis that it was not a case involving cumulative causes, but one involving "distinct causes" which operated in different ways, and the claimant could not establish which cause had either "caused or contributed" to his injury.

These rather technical distinctions, based on the number of "causal agents" or "distinct causes" present in a case, do not provide a very satisfying or coherent justification for adopting different approaches to causation. They may, however, be necessary on policy grounds. Certainly, the distinctions can prevent the *Fairchild* principle from creating widespread negligence liability where the causes of damage are indeterminate. For example, as Lord Hoffmann pointed out in *Barker*, the "single agent rule" means that the *Fairchild* principle cannot apply to a case where the claimant suffers from lung cancer, which may have been caused by exposure to asbestos, but may also have been caused by smoking, and it cannot be proved which is more likely to have been the causative agent.[63]

We have seen that in *Gregg v Scott* the House of Lords declined to adopt a broad interpretation of the *Fairchild* principle in the context of medical negligence, and so refused to apply a "material increase in risk" approach to the fact of Mr Gregg's untimely diagnosis and treatment. More recently, however, Waller L.J. in *Bailey*[64] asserted that a distinction should not be drawn between cases of industrial diseases and medical negligence so that, if a case is regarded as involving cumulative causes producing one outcome, the "but for" test can be modified, and the claimant will succeed by showing that the negligent cause merely made a material contribution (i.e. less than 51 per cent) to that outcome. It may be questioned whether the approach in *Bailey* is entirely consistent with the authority of *Gregg v Scott*,

---

[62] [2008] EWCA Civ 883; [2009] 1 W.L.R. 1052.

[63] *Barker v Corus UK Ltd.* [2006] 2 A.C. 572 per Lord Hoffmann at para.24. In *Barker*, Lord Hoffmann revised the view he had expressed in *Fairchild*, and agreed with Lord Rodger's opinion in *Fairchild* that it was not strictly necessary for there to be a sole causative agent for the *Fairchild* principle to apply; it would be sufficient if the all possible causes of the damage "operated in substantially the same way". (See *Fairchild v Glenhaven Funeral Services* [2003] 1 A.C. 32 at 118.)

[64] [2008] EWCA Civ 883; at para.46.

however, and the implications of the case, in terms increased claims against the NHS[65] remain to be seen.[66]

## NOVUS ACTUS INTERVENIENS

**6–018**    In certain circumstances, where one act follows another, the law will say that the second act (the "new intervening act") is to be regarded as the true cause of the damage, because it has "broken the chain of causation" and has extinguished the effect of the first act. This idea, known as the doctrine of novus actus interveniens, is explored here. It should be noted that the essence of the doctrine overlaps not only with the reasoning in "consecutive cause" cases, which we have already examined, but with other areas of the law—in particular, the question of whether a person owes a duty to prevent a third party from causing damage (considered in Ch.2) and the defences of act of God, volenti non fit injuria, and act of stranger, which are considered in later chapters. Each area of the law simply represents a different way of determining liability. The fact that some cases are decided using the concepts of "duty" or "defence", rather than causation, is sometimes the result of historical accident in the way the law has developed, and sometimes the product of a judicial search for clarity.

It should also be noted that many writers and judges treat the idea of novus actus interveniens as part of the test for "remoteness of damage".[67] This is mainly because, as we shall see later, the test for "remoteness" is whether the kind of damage in question is reasonably foreseeable, and the same issue arises when considering whether a defendant is liable in spite of an intervening act. Some writers, on the other hand (ourselves included), reserve the phrase "remoteness of damage" for a slightly different problem, namely, where, on any sensible view, there is only one true cause of the claimant's loss, but where the loss caused seems too bizarre or "far removed" to be recoverable. This problem is explored in a later section.

It is convenient to place the relevant cases into two groups—intervening act of a third party and intervening act of the claimant.

### Intervening act of a third party

**6–019**    It is useful to draw a distinction between three different ways in which a third party may interfere with a course of events—natural (or "instinctive") intervention; negligent intervention; and intervention in the form of intentional wrongdoing. We consider each type of intervention in turn.

---

[65] The case was brought against the Ministry of Defence because the claimant was being treated in a military hospital, but the relevant principles would, of course, apply in the context of NHS treatment.

[66] The approach in *Bailey* has been followed in *Ingram v Williams* [2010] EWHC 758 and *Canning-Kishver v Sandwell and West Birmingham Hospitals NHS Trust*. For commentary on the implications of *Bailey*, see M Stauch [2009] C.L.J. 27; S Green (2009) 125 L.Q.R. 44.

[67] See, e.g. the terminology used by the Court of Appeal in *Lamb v Camden LBC* [1981] Q.B. 625.

*Natural or "instinctive" intervention*

The classic example of "instinctive" human conduct failing to amount to a novus actus inter-   **6–020**
veniens is the very old case of *Scott v Shepherd*.[68] Here, the defendant threw a lighted firework
into a market place. It landed on a stall belonging to a third party, A, who threw it on so that it
landed on the stall of a fourth party, B, who reacted in a similar way. The firework ultimately
hit the plaintiff and injured him. It was held that neither the intervening act of A or B broke the
causal connection between the defendant's act and the subsequent damage. Both A and B had
acted in an instinctive and natural way to avoid damage to themselves and their property.

It is clear from *Scott v Shepherd*, then, that a third party's intervention will not break the
chain of causation where it is an involuntary reaction in the "heat of the moment". But the
same sort of reasoning appears to apply in cases where the third party has some opportunity to
reflect before taking action. Consider, for example, *The Oropesa*.[69] Here, because of the
defendants' negligence, a ship of that name collided with a ship called the Manchester
Regiment. The captain of the Manchester Regiment set out in a life boat to consult the captain
of The Oropesa about how best to save his crew. The life boat capsized, causing the death of
many of those aboard. The captain's intervention did not break the chain of causation.

*Negligent intervention*

It is impossible to state with clarity the circumstances in which the negligent conduct of a third   **6–021**
party will break the chain of causation. Where A commits a tort, and B commits a subsequent
tort, the key question is whether the nature of B's tort is so powerful that it ought to be
regarded as rendering A's tort merely part of the surrounding historical circumstances—the
backdrop against which B's tort occurred. Thus, negligent conduct will not always break the
chain of causation. For example, in *Roberts v Bettany*[70] the defendant negligently started an
underground fire, and was ordered by the council to extinguish it. He failed to comply with
this order, so the council intervened to extinguish the fire. Unfortunately, owing to the council's negligence in so doing, subsidence occurred under the claimant's house. The Court of
Appeal held that the council's negligence did not break the chain of causation, so the defendant
was liable for the subsidence. The defendant's having started the fire could not be said to be
merely part of the "surrounding circumstances" of the council's negligence—it being the
direct cause of the council's foreseeable and necessary intervention.

Some flavour of the courts' approach can be gained by considering a number of cases
involving negligent driving. In *Knightley v Johns*,[71] for example, the defendant negligently
overturned his car in a tunnel. A police inspector then arrived at the scene to take charge of the
situation, and negligently ordered a police motorcyclist to secure the closure of the tunnel by
riding against the traffic towards its entrance. The motorcyclist collided with the plaintiff's
oncoming car. In holding the defendant not liable for this accident, the Court of Appeal stated
that the relevant question to ask was whether the whole sequence of events was a natural and
probable consequence of the defendant's negligence, so that it should have been reasonably
foreseen by the defendant, or whether the events were foreseeable only as a mere possibility.
In answering this question, it was helpful to consider whether the third party's negligent
intervention had involved a deliberate choice to do a positive act, as opposed to an error of

[68] (1773) 2 Wm. Bl. 892.
[69] [1943] P. 32.
[70] [2001] EWCA Civ 109; [2001] N.P.C. 45.
[71] [1982] 1 All E.R. 851.

judgment in the course of performing an act in which the third party was already engaged. Here, the conduct of the police had taken the form of a deliberate positive act, and was not reasonably foreseeable by the defendant.

It is useful to compare *Knightley v Johns* with the decision in *Rouse v Squires*.[72] Here, the defendant lorry driver negligently caused an accident which blocked two lanes of a motorway. The plaintiff, who was assisting at the scene, was killed when a second lorry driver negligently drove into the obstruction. The Court of Appeal held that the defendant was 25 per cent to blame. The negligent driving of the second lorry driver did not break the chain of causation between the original accident and the plaintiff's death—a driver who caused an obstruction could be taken reasonably to foresee that a further accident might be caused by other drivers negligently colliding with the obstruction.

Whilst an act of *negligent* driving may not break the chain of causation, then, *reckless* driving may amount to a novus actus interveniens, because such driving is not normally foreseeable. Such was the case in *Wright v Lodge*.[73] Here, the second defendant was driving her Mini at night along a dual carriageway. It was foggy and the road was unlit. The Mini broke down and came to a stop in the near side lane. A few minutes later, as she was trying to restart her car, it was hit from behind by an articulated lorry being driven at 60 mph by the first defendant. After hitting the Mini, the lorry careered across the central reservation. It ended up on its side, blocking the opposite carriageway, and four oncoming vehicles collided with it. One driver died of his injuries and another was seriously injured. The Court of Appeal accepted that the Mini driver had been negligent in failing to push her car off the road before trying to restart it—which she could easily have done with the help of her passengers—but held that the lorry driver's dangerous driving was to be regarded as the true cause of the plaintiffs' injuries.

A particularly difficult question is whether, when a claimant is injured by a defendant's negligence and subsequently undergoes negligent medical treatment, the latter can be regarded as a novus actus interveniens. This should not be confused with the more straightforward question of whether a defendant remains liable when non-negligent medical treatment makes a claimant's position worse because of the claimant's pre-disposition to respond adversely to treatment. This point is discussed in a later section.

The circumstances in which negligent treatment will break the chain of causation cannot be stated with certainty. Assistance, however, may be found from the decision of the House of Lords in *Hogan v Bentinck West Hartley Collieries (Owners) Ltd*.[74] The case concerned a miner who injured his thumb at work. He was taken to hospital, where, initial treatment having failed to relieve his pain, doctors negligently decided to amputate part of his thumb. This reduced his earning capacity, because it left him able to do only light work. The question before the House of Lords was whether the man's incapacity resulted from the original injury or the operation. The case was complicated by the fact that the man had a congenital abnormality (an additional top joint to his thumb) for which amputation in the event of pain was considered a reasonable form of treatment. By a 3:2 majority, their Lordships held that the amputation amounted to a novus actus interveniens, absolving the defendant employers from liability. Lord Reid, however, in a powerful dissenting speech, thought that subsequent

[72] [1973] Q.B. 889.
[73] [1993] 4 All E.R. 299.
[74] [1949] 1 All E.R. 588. The case decided a claim under the Workmen's Compensation Act 1925. It is only of persuasive authority in the tort of negligence.

medical treatment should only break the chain of causation where there was a "grave lack of skill and care" on the part of the doctors. It should not do so in this case, because it was not abundantly clear that an alternative form of treatment would have cured the plaintiff of his condition. It has been suggested that, nowadays, only where the treatment in question is "so grossly negligent as to be a completely inappropriate response to the injury inflicted by the defendant" should it operate to break the chain of causation.[75]

*Intentional acts of wrongdoing*

Where a third party's intervention takes the form of a deliberate act of wrongdoing, the courts      **6–022** are very reluctant to hold a defendant liable, and will usually say that the third party's act has broken the chain of causation. However, much will depend on the particular circumstances of the case. In *Att-Gen of the British Virgin Islands v Hartwell*[76] an emotionally disturbed police officer in the British Virgin Islands, whom the defendant police authority had given access to a gun, deserted his post and travelled to a bar where he shot and injured a British tourist. The Privy Council, whilst conceding that the case was a "closely balanced" one, held that this action did not break the chain of causation. The defendant authority was liable for the tourist's injuries. The standard of diligence expected of the authority in supervising the use of firearms was a high one, in view of the grave risks involved. Moreover, given that the authority knew about the officer's disturbed emotional state, his actions were sufficiently foreseeable.

The case of *Home Office v Dorset Yacht Co Ltd*[77] (discussed in Ch.2) is a further example of a situation where criminal intervention did not break the chain of causation. Its outcome was justified on the basis that the wrongful intervention of the Borstal boys was extremely foreseeable by the defendants—there was a close relationship between the negligent guards and the boys, and their actions were the "very kind of thing" that was likely to happen if the guards allowed them to escape.

The "foreseeability-based" approach to liability for the criminal acts of third parties caused some difficulty for the Court of Appeal, however, in *Lamb v Camden LBC*.[78] This case suggests that the issue is ultimately one of pure policy. Here, a burst water main, for which the defendant council was responsible, had caused the plaintiff's house to become flooded. The plaintiff, who was living abroad at the time, moved her furniture out of the house and made arrangements for repairing the damage. Whilst the house was left unoccupied, squatters moved in and caused extensive damage to the house. The plaintiff's action in respect of this damage failed. The council was not liable for the squatters' antisocial and criminal behaviour. This was so even though (according to the majority) in modern times the actions of the squatters could be regarded as highly foreseeable.

In *Lamb*, their Lordships arrived at their decision by slightly different routes. Lord Denning M.R. thought that, as a matter of policy, the responsibility for keeping the squatters out lay with the plaintiff and not the council and that the loss they had caused should be borne by the plaintiff's insurers. (We can see at work here the economic and political consideration that loss should not be transferred from a private insurance arrangement to a publicly funded

---

[75] *Clerk & Lindsell on Torts* (20th edn, 2010), para.2–115. See also *Webb v Barclays Bank Plc* [2002] P.I.Q.R. P8; *Mitchell v Rahman* (2002) 209 D.L.R. (4th ) 621; *Conley v Strain* [1988] I.R. 628.

[76] [2004] 1 W.L.R. 1273.

[77] [1970] A.C. 1004.

[78] [1981] Q.B. 625. Compare *Clark Fixing Ltd v Dudley Metropolitan Borough Council* [2001] EWCA Civ 1898 (discussed in Ch.2).

authority.) His Lordship thought that in *Home Office v Dorset Yacht* Lord Reid had been wrong to decide the question of novus actus interveniens using a test of foreseeability, and that it was not helpful to attempt to distinguish between different degrees of foreseeability. To illustrate the point, Lord Denning M.R. put forward an example: Suppose a prisoner escapes and steals a car. He then drives many miles, abandons the car, breaks into a house to steal a change of clothes, gets a lift in a lorry and continues with his criminal activities. On Lord Reid's test of "very likely to happen", none of the prisoner's intervening acts would break the chain of causation, so that the Home Office would be liable for all of the damage caused by escaped convicts. As a matter of policy, this was unacceptable.

Oliver L.J., on the other hand, was content to say that the squatters' intervention was not reasonably foreseeable (although it was foreseeable as a mere possibility). Watkins L.J. thought that, in addition to foreseeability, the court should consider a number of other factors, including:

> "the nature of the event or act, the time it occurred, the place where it occurred, the identity of the perpetrator and his intentions and responsibility, if any, for taking measures to avoid the occurrence and matters of public policy".[79]

The authorities suggest that the nature of the relationship between the defendant and the third party is an important consideration for the courts. In *Lamb*, the third parties were strangers to the defendant, whereas in *Dorset Yacht* there was a relationship of supervision and care. The relationship between the defendant and the claimant may also be important. Thus, in *Stansbie v Troman*[80] (considered in Ch.2), the decorator who had impliedly agreed to look after the plaintiff's house was liable for the actions of the thief who broke in—the thief's action did not amount to a novus actus interveniens. Applying both of these "relationship" considerations, we can explain why, for example, in *Topp v London Country Bus (South West) Ltd*[81] the defendants were not liable when a bus driver, for whose actions the defendants were responsible, left his bus unattended with the keys in the ignition and it was stolen by a third party whose careless driving caused injury to the plaintiff.

In the final analysis, it seems that both "relationship" and "degree of foreseeability" play a part in the courts' reasoning in these cases. Both concepts are the servants of policy, judicial "common sense" and judicial "instinct". (Thus, in *Lamb v Camden*, Watkins L.J. famously concluded: "I have the instinctive feeling that the squatters' damage is too remote".)[82] Given that policy considerations are so fundamental to the courts' assessment of when a defendant will be liable for the intervening act of a third party, the question, as we have suggested in Ch.2, is perhaps better framed as one relating to the scope of the duty of care owed by the defendant.[83] Arguably, this allows the relevant policy concerns to be accommodated with greater coherence.

## Intervening act of the claimant

**6–023**  In appropriate circumstances, the actions of the claimant can break the chain of causation, so that he or she, rather than the defendant, is to be regarded as the operative cause of his or

---

[79] [1981] Q.B. 625 at 647.
[80] [1948] 2 K.B. 48.
[81] [1993] 1 W.L.R. 976.
[82] *Lamb v Camden LBC* [1981] Q.B. 625 at 647.
[83] See Lord Goff's analysis of the problem in *Smith v Littlewoods* [1987] A.C. 241, considered in Ch.2.

her own loss. This question overlaps with the question of when a claimant can be regarded as having caused his or her own loss by accepting the risk of injury. This idea, known as the defence of volenti non fit injuria, is considered in Ch.16. The question also overlaps with the rules on "contributory negligence" (also discussed in Ch.16) under which a claimant can have his or her damages award reduced because he or she has been partly to blame.

It should be noted that the "all or nothing" approach to causation, which depends on the balance of probabilities, sits somewhat uneasily alongside the fact that a claimant may be regarded by the law as so contributorily negligent that his or her damages are reduced by an amount greater than 50 per cent. Where this is so, why does the law not regard the claimant, rather than the defendant as the true cause of the loss? There is no clear answer to this question, save to say that the law places the question of contributory negligence in a separate "conceptual compartment" from factual causation, and sees it as a matter relating to the quantification of damages, rather than as a matter relating to the determination of liability in the first place.[84]

The courts' general approach to deciding whether a claimant's own act breaks the chain of causation can be illustrated by comparing two cases: *McKew v Holland and Hannens and Cubitts (Scotland) Ltd*[85] and *Wieland v Cyril Lord Carpets Ltd*.[86]

In *McKew*, the plaintiff suffered a slight injury to his leg as a result of the defendant's negligence, so that it had a tendency to give way when he was walking. Shortly afterwards, he went with his family to look at a flat. He descended a steep staircase with no handrail, ahead of his family, and holding a child by the hand. His injured leg gave way and he fell, fracturing his ankle. The House of Lords held that the plaintiff's unreasonable behaviour was a novus actus interveniens. He, not the defendant, had caused his injury by descending the staircase without waiting for the assistance of his wife or brother-in-law, knowing that his leg might give way at any moment.

A claimant's act will only break the chain of causation when it is unreasonable. Thus, in *Wieland v Cyril Lord Carpets Ltd*, although the facts were similar to those in *McKew*, the court reached a different conclusion. The plaintiff suffered an injury to her neck, caused by the defendant's negligence. Shortly after this, the plaintiff, who wore bi-focal spectacles, returned to the hospital where she had originally been taken and was fitted with a surgical collar. The position of her neck in the collar deprived her of her usual ability to use her bi-focals—she could not easily adjust the position of her head. After leaving the hospital, the plaintiff was in a nervous state because of the trauma of the visit, and this, together with the problem with her bi-focals, made her unsteady on her feet. She went to her son's office to ask him to take her home. He accompanied her down the stairs of the office building, but when she neared the bottom she fell and injured her ankles. Eveleigh J. held that these injuries were caused by the defendant's negligence, which had impaired her ability to negotiate the stairs. Her actions in descending the stairs had been reasonable and could not be regarded as a novus actus interveniens.

---

[84] See, e.g. *Stapley v Gypsum Mines* [1953] A.C. 663 where the damages were reduced by 80 per cent because of contributory negligence. See also P.S. Atiyah (1965) 43 Can. Bar. Rev. 609.

[85] [1969] 3 All E.R. 1621.

[86] [1969] 3 All E.R. 1006.

More recently, the same principle was applied in *Spencer v Wincanton Holdings Ltd.*[87] Here, the claimant had his leg amputated as a result of the defendant's negligence. He was fitted with a prosthesis, but pending further adaptations to his car, this could not be worn whilst he was driving. He pulled into a filling station, and, without the aid of his prosthesis or walking sticks, got out of his car and filled it with petrol, using the car for support. As he was returning to the driver's door, he tripped and fell, sustaining a further injury which confined him to a wheelchair. The Court of Appeal upheld the trial judge's finding that the claimant's actions were not so unreasonable as to break the chain of causation. He had made a misjudgement in running a risk by not using his prosthesis or sticks, but this was properly reflected in a finding of contributory negligence.

In a number of cases, the question has arisen whether a claimant's taking his or her own life will break the chain of causation. The courts' approach has been to hold that where the defendant's negligence creates a risk of psychiatric illness leading to suicide, the suicide does not constitute a novus actus interveniens. Thus, in *Corr v IBC Vehicles Ltd,*[88] the claimant suffered a head injury at work as a result of his employer's negligence. He succumbed to severe depression and eventually killed himself. In an action by his widow, it was held that his suicide did not break the chain of causation.

A similar conclusion was reached by the House of Lords in *Reeves v Metropolitan Police Commissioner.*[89] Here, the deceased was in police custody. Taking advantage of the police officers' inadvertence in leaving the flap of his cell door open, he hanged himself by tying his shirt through the spy hole on the outside of the door. It had been noted in police records that the deceased was a suicide risk, having made two previous attempts to kill himself whilst in custody. The doctor who had examined him on his arrival at the police station, whilst finding no evidence of psychiatric illness, had noted that he should be kept under frequent observation in the light of his previous suicide attempts. By a 3:2 majority, the House of Lords held that the suicide, although a deliberate and informed act, could not be regarded as having broken the chain of causation, given that the police were under a specific legal duty to guard against the commission of that very act.

## REMOTENESS OF DAMAGE

**6–024**    Here, we are not concerned with whether the claimant's loss may have an alternative cause. Rather, the question is whether the law will deny recovery on the basis that the loss in question is a very unusual result of the defendant's conduct.

### The old law

**6–025**    Before 1961, the law was dominated by the decision of the Court of Appeal in *Re Polemis and Furness, Withy & Co,*[90] in 1921. Here, a ship had been loaded with a quantity of petrol, which,

---

[87] [2009] EWCA Civ 1404. Comment: K. Hughes (2010) C.L.J. 228.
[88] [2008] UKHL 13. See also *Pigney v Pointer's Transport Services Ltd* [1957] 1 W.L.R. 1121; *Kirkham v Chief Constable of Greater Manchester* [1990] 2 Q.B. 283.
[89] [2000] 1 A.C. 360.
[90] [1921] 3 K.B. 560.

unbeknown to any of the parties, had leaked, causing the hold of the ship to fill with vapour. A dock worker employed by the defendants negligently allowed a wooden plank to drop into the hold, where it somehow caused a spark that ignited the petrol vapour, causing the ship to be lost by fire. The Court of Appeal held the defendants liable. Whilst the worker could not have foreseen that the falling plank would cause a fire, he could have foreseen that it might cause some damage to the ship (such as a scratch on the paint work). Given that this was so, the defendants were liable for all of the damage that was a direct factual consequence of the worker's negligence.

The exact ratio of *Re Polemis* is a matter of some confusion. It is often argued that there are two possible interpretations of the decision. On the first interpretation, their Lordships appear to have held that because *some* damage *of the relevant kind* was reasonably foreseeable, the defendants were liable for all damage *of that kind*. In other words, they were liable for the fire because "damage to a ship", whether by fire or by a scratch in the paintwork, was the same kind of damage—damage to property. According to this interpretation, then, all that their Lordships did in *Re Polemis* was to draw a distinction between "damage to property" on the one hand, and other "kinds" of damage (economic loss and personal injury) on the other. The second, wider, interpretation of the case, however, is that so long as *some* damage (of whatever "kind") was the foreseeable result of the defendant's conduct, he or she would be liable for any damage that was a "direct" consequence of his or her conduct (including damage of a different "kind", and even damage to an "unforeseeable claimant").

In the subsequent case of *The Wagon Mound (No.1)*, which is now the leading authority on remoteness of damage, the Privy Council appeared to treat *Re Polemis* as authority for this second, wider, proposition. Their Lordships held that the "rule" in the case—that a defendant was to be liable for all the direct consequences of his or her actions—was wrong, because, if it were right, it would mean that a defendant could be liable even for damage that could not be reasonably foreseen.[91] Such a proposition could not be reconciled with important cases that had been decided after *Re Polemis*, not least of which was *Donoghue v Stevenson*.

## The modern law: *The Wagon Mound (No.1)*

The decision in *Overseas Tankship (UK) Ltd v Morts Dock & Engineering Co Ltd*[92] is known **6–026** as *The Wagon Mound (No.1)* because it is the first of two cases involving a ship of that name. It will be recalled that the second of these cases—*The Wagon Mound (No.2)*—has already been considered in Ch.5 as a case involving breach of duty. It is important not to confuse the two cases. The difference between them lies in the fact that, whereas in *The Wagon Mound (No.2)* the evidence before the court showed there was a foreseeable risk (albeit a small one) that the oil would ignite, in *The Wagon Mound (No.1)*—the case we are now concerned with— the evidence was that the oil catching fire was unforeseeable. This rather surprising difference is explained by the fact that, at the time *The Wagon Mound (No.1)* was brought to trial in New South Wales, contributory negligence was a complete defence. This meant that the plaintiffs in *The Wagon Mound (No.1)* did not dare allege that it was reasonably foreseeable that the oil might catch fire, for fear that they might be held contributorily negligent in continuing with their welding operations.

---

[91] *The Wagon Mound (No.1)* [1961] A.C. 388 at 398. See also Dias [1962] C.L.J. 178.
[92] [1961] A.C. 388.

It will be recalled that in the *Wagon Mound* litigation the defendants negligently allowed some furnace oil to spill on to the sea while their ship was in Sydney Harbour. In *The Wagon Mound (No.1)*, the plaintiffs were ship repairers. The oil was washed by the tide so that it fouled the plaintiffs' slipways, causing them to stop work. However, having been assured that there was no chance of the oil igniting, the plaintiffs resumed their welding operations. It was not clear what happened next, but it was assumed that some cotton waste, which was floating on the water, was ignited by a fragment of molten metal from the welding operations. The cotton waste, acting as a sort of wick, allowed the oil to ignite, and the plaintiffs' wharf and equipment were extensively damaged in the ensuing blaze. As has been said, the important finding of fact, on which the Privy Council based its decision, was that the occurrence of the fire was not reasonably foreseeable. But it *was* reasonably foreseeable, of course, that the oil might cause *some* damage to the plaintiffs' wharf by fouling it.

The Privy Council held that the defendants were not liable. Declaring *Re Polemis* to have been wrongly decided, their Lordships held that the proper test for remoteness of damage was whether the defendant could have reasonably foreseen the *kind of damage* for which the plaintiffs were suing. Their Lordships thought that "damage by fire" should be regarded as a different "kind" of damage from "damage by fouling", and since the former could not have been foreseen, the defendants were not answerable for it. Viscount Simonds explained the basis for the decision, saying:

> "It does not seem consonant with current ideas of justice or morality that for an act of negligence, however slight or venial, which results in some trivial foreseeable damage the actor should be liable for all consequences however unforeseeable and however grave . . ."[93]

It may be argued, of course, that his Lordship's explanation is not wholly satisfactory. It views the matter exclusively from the defendant's point of view, and imports into tort law the penal idea that the "punishment" should fit the wrong, ignoring the idea that the traditional role of tort is to compensate the victim. It has been rightly asked: why should the claimant, who has not been to blame, be made to shoulder the whole loss rather than the defendant, who has been to blame at least in some degree?[94] Such considerations have doubtless influenced the courts in their interpretation of the decision in *The Wagon Mound (No.1)*, especially in the context of personal injury cases. This we explore below.

The principle in The *Wagon Mound (No.1)* contains a number of elements, which (as in the following sections) are traditionally considered in turn. It should be noted, however, that the elements overlap considerably. We shall see that this area of the law is beset with uncertainty and contains many decisions that are quite hard to reconcile.

*Foreseeability of the "kind of damage"*

6–027    In *Hughes v Lord Advocate*,[95] the Post Office, in breach of its duty, left a manhole open in the street during the course of its work on some telephone cables. The manhole was covered with a tent and, in the evening, left unguarded but surrounded by warning paraffin lamps. The plaintiff was an eight-year-old boy who had picked up one of the lamps and clambered down

---

[93] [1961] A.C. 388 at 422.
[94] *Clerk & Lindsell on Torts* (19th edn, 2006), para.2–120.
[95] [1963] A.C. 837. Applied in *Pearson Education Ltd v Charter Partnerships Ltd* [2007] EWCA Civ 130.

the manhole. Because of a very unusual set of scientific circumstances, an explosion occurred, causing him severe burns. The House of Lords held that the Post Office was liable, even though it could not reasonably have foreseen that anyone might be burned by an explosion in the manhole. It was sufficient to found liability that there was a reasonably foreseeable risk of the boy being burned by the paraffin lamp. In other words, "damage by burning" was the "kind" of damage in question, there being no distinction between burning caused by the flame of the lamp and burning caused by an unforeseeable explosion.

Similar reasoning was applied in *Bradford Corp v Robinson Rentals Ltd.*[96] Here, the plaintiff suffered frostbite when he was sent on a journey by his employer in a van without a heater. It was held that, although frostbite was a rather unusual consequence in the circumstances (it was practically unheard of in Britain), it was nevertheless "of the type and kind of injury which was reasonably foreseeable".[97]

Both of these cases, then, suggest that the courts are happy to view personal injury as a single and indivisible "kind" of damage. Whilst the decision in *The Wagon Mound (No.1)* shows us that the courts will subdivide "damage to property" into different "kinds" of damage—such as "damage by fire" and "damage by fouling"—the courts appear not to apply the same sort of reasoning in personal injury cases. The difference in approach can be explained in terms of policy. First, the law has always been more anxious to protect physical wellbeing than to protect property. Secondly, if "damage to property" were regarded as a single, indivisible "kind" of damage, defendants might be exposed to "crushing liability" for very large amounts of loss. By contrast, in personal injury cases, losses are generally likely to be less expensive to compensate.

There is one well-known case, however, that appears to conflict with a general proposition that personal injury is an indivisible "kind" of damage. In *Tremain v Pike*[98] the plaintiff was a herdsman employed by the defendants, who were farmers. The farm became infested with rats and the plaintiff contracted Weil's disease—a rare disease that is caught by coming into contact with rats' urine. Payne J. held that, even on the assumption that the defendants had been negligent in failing to control the rat population, the plaintiff could not succeed. His Lordship thought that Weil's disease was both unforeseeable and "entirely different in kind" from the foreseeable consequences of contact with rats, such as food poisoning or the effects of a rat-bite. The status of *Tremain v Pike* is uncertain, especially in the light of *Parsons v Uttley Ingham* (discussed later), where the Court of Appeal implicitly rejected its reasoning.

So far as property damage is concerned, whilst it is clear that *The Wagon Mound (No.1)* allows the courts to subdivide property damage into different "kinds" of damage, the limitations (if any) on their ability to do so remain unclear. Analysis of the issue is difficult for a number of reasons. First, the answer to the question: "what is the kind of damage in suit?" is inextricably bound up with the problems (considered below) of whether the *extent* of the damage, and the *way it is caused*, have to be foreseeable. Secondly, the issue is often difficult to separate from the issue of the *measure of damages* necessary to compensate a foreseeable kind of loss. It is well established that if a defendant injures a person with a high earning capacity, or damages a valuable piece of property, he or she cannot object to paying damages on the basis that the cost of compensation is greater than it might have been if the person had had a low income, or if the property had been less valuable.[99] But, suppose that (for some

[96] [1967] 1 W.L.R. 337.
[97] [1967] 1 W.L.R. 337 per Rees J. at 344.
[98] [1969] 3 All E.R. 1303.
[99] *Smith v London & South Western Railway Co* (1870) L.R. 6. C.P. 14.

reasonable purpose) you leave a priceless Ming vase on your coffee table and I negligently break it. In such bizarre circumstances, can I not argue that, whilst "damage to a household ornament" might have been a foreseeable consequence of my negligence, "damage to a price-less antique" is an unforeseeable "kind" of damage? Or will the court say that "damage to a vase" was the foreseeable "kind" of damage, and that it matters not that the cost of replacing the vase is much greater than I could have expected?

To make matters worse, all of these issues are difficult to separate from the questions of whether, and how, the "eggshell skull" rule applies in the context of property damage (consid-ered in a later section). In the final analysis, one is left with the suspicion that the courts are reluctant to rule authoritatively on the subdivision of property damage into different "kinds", so as to preserve the flexibility necessary to do justice whilst containing the scope of liability in appropriate cases.

*Foreseeability of the "way the damage is caused"*

**6–028**  In *Hughes v Lord Advocate* it was held that the precise manner in which the damage was caused did not have to be reasonably foreseen. So long as the defendant could reasonably foresee damage of the relevant "kind", the damage would not be too remote. In *Hughes*, there-fore, the Post Office was liable even though it could not have foreseen the scientific circum-stances which led to an underground explosion injuring the plaintiff. The same approach was adopted in *The Trecarrell*.[100] Here, the defendants were held liable when one of their employees, whilst working in a ship yard, carelessly dropped a drum of inflammable lacquer. The drum fell on a temporary electricity cable and severed it, causing a short circuit which ignited the lacquer. The plaintiffs' ship was damaged in the resulting blaze.

There are, however, two cases where precisely the opposite reasoning has been applied—the defendants were not liable because they could not have foreseen harm caused in such an unusual way. In *Doughty v Turner Manufacturing Ltd*,[101] workmen employed by the defend-ants had allowed an asbestos cover to drop into a vat of very hot liquid. The cover slid in at an angle and did not cause a splash. A few minutes later, however, chemical changes in the asbestos brought about by the high temperature caused an eruption of the liquid, which splashed out of the vat, burning the plaintiff. The possibility of an eruption occurring in this way was unknown at the time. The Court of Appeal, following *The Wagon Mound (No.1)*,[102] held that the defendants were not liable. *Hughes* was distinguished on the basis that, in *Doughty*, the risk which materialised was very substantially different from any that could be foreseen.

This narrow view of risk was also adopted by the Divisional Court in *Crossley v Rawlinson*.[103] Here, the defendant had stopped his lorry when, as a result of his negligence, a tarpaulin covering the body of the lorry had caught fire. The plaintiff, an AA patrolman, who was on duty at a nearby AA service centre, saw the fire and ran out to assist. Whilst running towards the lorry on a rough path, he caught his foot in a concealed hole and fell. His claim for personal injury was dismissed on the basis that his being injured in this way was not reason-ably foreseeable. The court drew a fine distinction between injury occurring during the course of tackling the fire (which was foreseeable) and injury occurring on the way to tackle the fire (which was not). Bearing in mind that the plaintiff was a rescuer, and that rescuers usually

---

[100]  [1973] 1 Lloyd's Rep. 402.
[101]  [1964] 1 Q.B. 518.
[102]  [1961] A.C. 388.
[103]  [1982] 1 W.L.R. 369.

receive more sympathetic treatment from the courts, this seems a particularly harsh decision which has received considerable criticism.[104]

The validity of such reasoning must now be questioned in the light of the House of Lords' decision in *Jolley v Sutton LBC*.[105] Here, a 14-year-old boy had been severely injured when a boat, abandoned on council land, had fallen upon him, breaking his back. He and his friend had been attempting to repair the boat to take it to Cornwall to sail it. Although the council, as occupier, owed him a duty of care, the Court of Appeal had rejected his claim on the basis that whilst it was foreseeable that children playing on the boat might suffer some minor injuries, it was *not* foreseeable that a teenager would attempt to reconstruct the boat. The House of Lords disagreed. *Hughes* required the court to judge foresight according to the nature of the risk which ought to have been foreseen. Here, in view of the known ingenuity of children in finding unexpected ways of doing mischief to themselves, and the fact that the council had conceded that it was under a duty to remove the boat to avoid the risk of minor injuries— which would have cost it no more than removing it to avoid the injuries that actually occurred[106]—their Lordships adopted a broad view of risk: was it foreseeable that children would meddle with the boat causing some physical injury? On this basis, the council was found liable for the claimant's injuries.

Their Lordships in *Jolley*, then, adopted a far more generous interpretation of risk than that seen in *Doughty* and *Crossley* above, although they did stress that much would depend on the individual facts of each case. Nevertheless, Lord Nicholls, delivering the opinion of the Privy Council in *Att-Gen of the British Virgin Islands v Hartwell*,[107] doubted whether the reasoning in *Doughty* would find favour with modern courts, and suggested that courts now take a more liberal approach in determining whether the way in which the damage is caused is foreseeable.

*Foreseeability of the "extent" of the damage*

In *Hughes v Lord Advocate*, Lord Reid made it clear that a defendant can be liable even when the damage caused is greater in extent than was reasonably foreseeable. Only where the damage is different in "kind" can the defendant escape liability.[108] This approach was followed in *Vacwell Engineering Co Ltd v BDH Chemicals Ltd*.[109] The defendants manufactured and supplied a chemical that was liable to explode in contact with water, but they gave no warning of this hazard to the plaintiffs. The plaintiffs bought a quantity of the chemical and a scientist who worked for them put the ampoules containing the chemical in the sink. A violent explosion resulted, causing extensive damage to the plaintiffs' premises. Rees J., whilst holding that an explosion of the magnitude which occurred was not reasonably foreseeable, thought that, given that a *small* explosion was foreseeable, the damage was not too remote. The damage was of a foreseeable kind, and it did not matter that it was greater in extent than could have been foreseen.

**6–029**

---

[104] For example, Jones, *Textbook on Torts* (OUP, 8th edn, 2002) p.269 finds the decision "arbitrary and inconsistent with *Hughes*".

[105] [2000] 1 W.L.R. 1082. This decision concerns occupiers' liability and will be considered further in Ch.8. The principles of causation and remoteness are the same, however, for common law negligence and under the occupiers' liability statutes.

[106] See Lord Hoffmann [2000] 1 W.L.R. 1082 at 1093,

[107] [2004] 1 W.L.R. 1273.

[108] *Hughes v Lord Advocate* [1963] A.C. 837 at 845.

[109] [1971] 1 Q.B. 88.

Similarly, in *Parsons v Uttley Ingham & Co Ltd*,[110] the defendants installed a feed hopper for the plaintiffs' pigs, but negligently failed to leave open the ventilator, so that the nuts stored inside became mouldy. On eating the nuts, the pigs contracted a rare disease and a number of them died. The Court of Appeal held that, provided *some* damage of the relevant kind was reasonably foreseeable (in the form of mild illness of the pigs), the plaintiffs could recover for the more serious and unforeseeable consequence resulting from the defendants' negligence.

## THE "EGGSHELL SKULL" RULE

**6–030**     Before the decision in *The Wagon Mound (No.1)*, it was established law that where an injured claimant suffered from some peculiar hypersensitivity which exacerbated his or her loss, then, provided the defendant could reasonably foresee *some* injury to a *normal* claimant,[111] the defendant would be liable for the full extent of the loss. Thus, in *Dulieu v White & Sons*,[112] Kennedy J. stated:

> "If a man is negligently run over or otherwise negligently injured in his body, it is no answer to the sufferer's claim for damages that he would have suffered less injury, or no injury at all, if he had not had an unusually thin skull or an unusually weak heart."[113]

The "eggshell skull" rule is sometimes also referred to as the maxim that "the defendant must take his victim as he finds him".

For a short time, it was uncertain whether the reasoning in *The Wagon Mound (No.1)* had displaced the rule. The matter was quickly settled, however, by the decision in *Smith v Leech Brain & Co Ltd*.[114] The plaintiff's husband was burned on the lip at work by a splash of molten metal. At the time of the accident, it was not known that he had a form of pre-malignant cancer. The burn triggered the onset of the cancer, from which he died three years later. Lord Parker C.J. stated that, in *The Wagon Mound*, whilst the Privy Council had held that a defendant must foresee the kind of damage in suit, their Lordships had not meant to hold that the extent of the damage had to be foreseeable. It followed that the "eggshell skull" rule had not been displaced. Thus, apparently regarding "damage by burning" and "damage by cancer" as the same "kind" of damage (personal injury caused by an accident at work), his Lordship held the defendants liable.

It is clear that the rule will apply in cases where the particular characteristics of the claimant act in combination with surrounding circumstances (including the reasonable action of a third

---

[110] [1978] Q.B. 791. The action was for breach of contract but was decided on the basis that the rules of remoteness being considered were equally applicable in tort.

[111] It should be remembered that the rule does not come into play unless the claimant first establishes that a duty of care was owed and breached. Thus, in *Bourhill v Young* [1943] A.C. 92 Lord Wright, at 109, correctly stated: "One who suffers from the terrible tendency to bleed on slight contact, which is denoted by the term 'a bleeder', cannot complain if he mixes with the crowd and suffers severely, perhaps fatally, from being merely brushed against. There is no wrong done there." In the context of psychiatric illness, however, consider Lord Lloyd's reasoning in *Page v Smith* [1996] A.C. 155 (explored in Ch.4).

[112] [1901] 2 K.B. 669.

[113] [1901] 2 K.B. 669 at 679. Note, however, that his Lordship's reference to "no injury at all" seems inconsistent with the modern approach to the rule.

[114] [1962] 2 Q.B. 405.

party) to exacerbate the claimant's loss. Thus, in *Robinson v Post Office*,[115] owing to the defendant's negligence, the plaintiff slipped and wounded his leg at work. He was subsequently given an anti-tetanus injection and developed encephalitis because of an unforeseeable reaction to the serum. The defendants were held liable for this consequence.

What is less clear is whether the "eggshell skull" rule applies to claims in respect of damage to "hypersensitive" property as well as to hypersensitive people. It has been convincingly suggested that it should. Thus, for example, where a defendant drops a lighted cigarette on an unexpectedly "hypersensitive" carpet, which catches fire and is destroyed, he or she should be liable for the full extent of the damage, even though the reasonably foreseeable damage is no more than a small hole. It has been suggested that to hold otherwise would present the impossible difficulty of determining the extent of the "foreseeable" damage in circumstances where that damage has been "swallowed up" by events—if the carpet is completely destroyed, how can a court quantify the damage which would have been caused by a mere hole? Damages would have to be awarded by guesswork, rather than to compensate losses proved to have been suffered by the claimant.[116]

It is also unclear whether the "eggshell skull" rule can be properly thought of as applying to situations where the claimant's loss is exacerbated *only by surrounding circumstances*, rather than by *inherent* hypersensitive characteristics of the claimant's person or property. Some writers and judges appear to think that such cases can be analysed in terms of the rule.[117] Others tend to classify such cases as turning on the elements of the *Wagon Mound* principle we have considered above.[118] Analysis of certain cases in terms of the "eggshell skull" rule, however, gives us the broad proposition that "the defendant takes as he finds them, not only the physical state of the damaged person or property, but also the surrounding external physical circumstances".[119] On this basis, a case like *Great Lakes Steamship Co v Maple Leaf Milling Co*[120] can be explained by reference to the rule. Here, because of the defendant's negligence in failing to lighten a ship, it settled on a submerged anchor. The defendants were held liable for the full extent of the damage, even though they could not have known the anchor was there. Having created a risk of foreseeable damage of the relevant kind (the ship hitting the bottom), they had to take all the circumstances as they found them. The decision in *Parsons v Uttley Ingham & Co Ltd* (considered above) can also be explained using this version of the "eggshell skull" rule.

Until recently, however, the courts refused to apply the "eggshell skull" rule to losses which were caused by the claimant's own lack of funds. In *Liesbosch Dredger v SS Edison*,[121] the House of Lords had restricted the plaintiffs' claim for losses caused by the sinking of their dredger due to the defendants' negligence, to exclude the additional costs incurred by hiring a replacement dredger at an exorbitant rate to fulfil an existing contract. Their Lordships awarded the lesser cost of buying a comparable dredger, and refused to recognise that, due to the plaintiffs' impecuniosity, such a purchase had been a financial impossibility. The additional costs

---

[115]  [1974] 1 W.L.R. 1176.
[116]  *Clerk & Lindsell on Torts* (20th edn, 2010), para.2–165.
[117]  See, e.g. Murphy, *Street on Torts* (12th edn, 2007).
[118]  See, e.g. *Clerk & Lindsell on Torts*.
[119]  Murphy, *Street on Torts* (12th edn, 2007), p.165.
[120]  (1924) 41 T.L.R. 21 This was a contract case, but it is generally accepted that the relevant principle may apply in tort.
[121]  (*The Liesbosch*) [1933] A.C. 449.

incurred in hiring a replacement vessel had an "extraneous cause",[122] namely the plaintiffs' financial circumstances, and were therefore too remote.

This decision received considerable academic criticism,[123] and subsequent courts sought to distinguish it. For example, in *Dodd Properties (Kent) Ltd v Canterbury CC*,[124] it was held that *The Liesbosch* did not govern a situation where the claimant, because of "commercial prudence" rather than impecuniosity, made a decision not to undertake prompt repairs to damaged property. In view of such criticism, the House of Lords in *Lagden v O'Connor*[125] in 2003 finally accepted that *The Liesbosch* should no longer be viewed as good law. In the words of Lord Hope:

> ". . . the law has moved on, and . . . the correct test of remoteness today is whether the loss was reasonably foreseeable. The wrongdoer must take his victim as he finds him . . . This rule applies to the economic state of the victim in the same way as it applies to his physical and mental vulnerability."[126]

## Causation and remoteness: conclusion

**6–031**     In concluding, it is important to note that although the law we have examined in this chapter has developed as part of the tort of negligence (and most of the cases we have discussed are negligence cases), the rules relating to factual causation are applicable to all torts (except, of course, those actionable per se, where no damage need be proved) and the rules relating to remoteness are applicable to most.[127]

We have seen that causation and remoteness are difficult areas, where the courts, in a sense, are faced with the tricky problem of "what to do when the rules run out". The apparent absence of logical rules leaves one with the impression that in many cases the judges adopt a practice of "reasoning backwards". In other words, they decide what is a fair and just outcome for the case at hand, and then select an appropriate set of rules to justify that decision.

---

[122] [1933] A.C. 449 per Lord Wright at 460.

[123] See, for example, Coote [2001] C.L.J. 511.

[124] [1980] 1 W.L.R. 433. See also *Mattocks v Mann* [1993] R.T.R. 13.

[125] [2004] 1 A.C. 1067. Comment: B. Coote (2004) 120 L.Q.R. 382.

[126] [2004] 1 A.C. 1067 at para.61.

[127] Note that usual rules on remoteness do not apply, e.g. to the tort of deceit (see *Doyle v Olby (Ironmongers) Ltd* [1969] 2 Q.B. 158; *Shelley v Paddock* [1980] Q.B. 348). Uncertainty about the application of *The Wagon Mound (No.1)* to the rule in *Rylands v Fletcher* has been removed by the decision of the House of Lords in *Cambridge Water Co Ltd v Eastern Counties Leather Plc* [1994] 2 A.C. 264 (considered in Ch.10).

# Chapter 7

# EMPLOYERS' LIABILITY

## Introduction

Injury in the workplace is a significant problem. The Health and Safety Executive reported    **7–001**
that, in 2008–09, 180 people in Great Britain lost their lives at work.[1] The legal response to
such injury takes a number of forms. For many injured employees, the simplest option is to
turn to social security, which provides specific benefits for industrial injuries. Since 1948,[2]
such compensation has been part of the welfare state. Therefore, victims who suffer personal
injury due to an industrial accident[3] are entitled to claim benefits from the Department for
Work and Pensions. Such benefits are inevitably not as high as any tort award and are subject
to restrictions, but for many victims provide a simpler and cheaper way of gaining compensation. Readers are advised to consult textbooks on labour law generally for employers' liability
outside tort law[4] and in particular should consider the provisions of the Health and Safety at
Work etc. Act 1974, which applies to all persons at work in Great Britain, and recent regulations such as the Management of Health and Safety at Work Regulations 1999[5] and the
Provision and Use of Work Equipment Regulations 1998.[6]

We concentrate here on an employer's liability in tort. This can take three forms:

- personal liability in negligence;
- liability for breach of statutory duty;

---

[1] Health and Safety Executive, *HSE Statistics* (*http://www.hse.gov.uk/statistics* [Accessed April 20, 2011]). In 2008–09,
there were over 130,000 non-fatal injuries reported and an estimated 1.2 million people suffered from ill health which
they believed had been caused or made worse by current or past work.

[2] Industrial benefits first appeared in 1897 (see Workmen's Compensation Acts 1897, 1925 and 1943), but the
changes in 1948 led to industrial benefits being integrated into the welfare state.

[3] This includes certain industrial diseases.

[4] See, e.g. S. Deakin and G.S. Morris, *Labour Law* (5th edn, Hart, 2009) or G. Pitt, *Employment law* (7th revised edn,
Sweet & Maxwell, 2009).

[5] SI 1999/3242, which replace the Management of Health and Safety at Work Regulations 1992. These are part of
significant EU developments to improve workplace conditions. Note, in particular, the amendments made by the
Management of Health and Safety at Work and Fire Precautions (Workplace) (Amendment) Regulations SI 2003/2457
(as amended by SI 2006/438) which now permit employees to bring civil claims against their employers where they
are in breach of duties imposed by the 1999 Regulations (but as respects claims by non-employees the exclusion of
civil liability for breach of duties imposed by the 1999 Regulations remains).

[6] SI 1998/2306, as amended.

- vicarious liability for the torts of employees committed in the course of their employment.[7]

Employers are popular targets for tort claims. As insurance is compulsory,[8] claimants know that if they succeed, the employer is likely to be able to meet their claim and may, for the sake of labour relations or to avoid adverse publicity, be willing to settle. Although we examine all three forms of liability below, we spend more time discussing vicarious liability, which plays a significant role in distributing loss and ensuring that claimants receive adequate compensation.

First of all, we examine the historical development of employers' liability. In seeking to understand the current law, it is particularly important to understand its historical background and why the rules have developed in their present form. For example, it may be questioned why there are three forms of liability and not simply one head of employers' liability. The answer lies in the historical development of the law, which we outline below.

## The development of employers' liability

7–002    The law on employers' liability reflects the economic and political trends of the last 200 years. Courts have always been aware, even if this has not been admitted openly, that their decisions affect the relationship between employers and employees and, more bluntly, the amount of money employers will have to spend on employee protection. It is perhaps unsurprising that in the early nineteenth century, at a time of increasing industrialisation, and with the insurance industry still embryonic, the courts were not prepared to impose a heavy burden of liability on employers and strove instead to urge employees to take responsibility for their own safety. In *Priestley v Fowler*,[9] the Court of Exchequer introduced what became known as the doctrine of common employment. This prevented an employee from suing his or her employer for injury negligently caused by a fellow employee. The courts held that it was implied in the employee's contract of employment that he or she would assume the risk of injury caused by the negligence of fellow employees, provided they had been selected with due care by the employer.[10] Liability was further restricted by the fact that contributory negligence at that time was an absolute bar to any claim in negligence[11]—however minimal the negligence of the claimant—and the fact that the courts were willing to apply the defence of voluntary assumption of risk to tasks undertaken in the workplace.[12] The result of this "unholy trinity" was very limited liability on the employer.

However, as the century progressed (and insurance began to develop by which employers could protect themselves against legal claims), attitudes changed. The judiciary and legislature began to take note of the hardship suffered by employees injured by new machinery and

---

[7] These heads impose specific duties on employers in tort. This is, of course, in addition to any general liability in tort, e.g. for negligence or nuisance.

[8] Employers' Liability (Compulsory Insurance) Act 1969. Regulation 3 of the Employers' Liability (Compulsory Insurance) Regulations 1998 (SI 1998/2573) (as amended) raises the sum to be insured to not less than £5 million.

[9] (1837) 3 M. & W. 1; 150 E.R. 1030. B.A. Hepple and M. Matthews, *Tort: Cases and Materials* (4th edn., Butterworths, 1991) p.566, report that in addition to losing his case, Priestley spent some years in a debtors' prison because he could not pay the costs of his unsuccessful action.

[10] See *Bartonshill Coal Co v Reid* (1858) 3 Macq. 266; *Johnson v Lindsay & Co* [1891] A.C. 371.

[11] See *Senior v Ward* (1859) 1 El. & El. 385; 120 E.R. 954.

[12] This is discussed more fully in Ch.16.

the introduction of the railways. New concepts were developed to circumvent the obstacles to recovery. Vicarious liability continued to grow,[13] but this could not overcome the obstacle of the doctrine of common employment. The courts therefore developed the idea of a personal duty on the employer which was non-delegable, i.e. responsibility could not be displaced onto another party. Personal liability allowed claimants to sue the employer for damages, even if the injury had been caused by another employee, and provided a means of circumventing the barriers to liability. *Groves v Lord Wimborne*[14] also established that the doctrine of common employment did not apply to the tort of breach of statutory duty, and therefore boosted the use of this tort to permit an injured employee to sue for an award of damages.

Unsurprisingly, in the twentieth century, the three barriers to employers' liability came under attack. The doctrine of common employment was abolished under the Law Reform (Personal Injuries) Act 1948, and the Law Reform (Contributory Negligence) Act 1945 permitted the courts to apportion liability where the claimant had been contributorily negligent.[15] In *Smith v Charles Baker & Sons*,[16] the House of Lords had already expressed its reluctance to apply the defence of voluntary assumption of risk to employees, and so by 1948, all three obstacles had either been abolished or tightly confined.

Despite these changes, the distinction between personal and vicarious liability remains,[17] although personal liability and breach of statutory duty are obviously less important nowadays than in the past. Having considered the historical development of liability, we shall now consider the three forms of tortious liability in turn.

## PERSONAL LIABILITY

To understand the nature of the employer's personal liability, it is necessary to remember that it was developed to circumvent the doctrine of common employment. As a result of this doctrine—which prevented claims against the employer in respect of a fellow employee's negligence—where an employee (X) brought an action against his employer (Y) for negligent injury in the workplace, X ran the risk that Y could simply claim that he was not liable because:    **7–003**

(a) the injury was caused by the action of a fellow employee; and

(b) Y had taken reasonable care in choosing the employee in question.

Having delegated the duty, Y would therefore not have been responsible for how this duty was carried out. The victim would be left with an action against a fellow employee, which would be difficult to establish and in all probability worthless. The leading case of *Wilson and Clyde Coal Co v English*[18] resolved this difficulty by making the duty on the employer

---

[13] See D. Ibbetson, *A Historical Introduction to the Law of Obligations* (Oxford, 1999), pp.181–184.

[14] [1895–99] All E.R. Rep. 147.

[15] See Ch.16.

[16] [1891] A.C. 325, HL, unless the job of necessity involved risk. For full discussion, see Ch.16.

[17] See *Staveley Iron & Chemical Co v Jones* [1956] A.C. 627. This has nevertheless been the subject of extensive academic debate—see G. Williams (1957) 72 L.Q.R. 522 and F.H. Newark (1954) 17 M.L.R. 102—and the distinction is not always clearly expressed by the judiciary—see, for example, Lord Hobhouse in *Lister v Hesley Hall Ltd* [2001] UKHL 22; [2002] 1 A.C. 215.

[18] [1938] A.C. 57. See G. Williams [1956] C.L.J. 180, 190–192.

non-delegable. "Non-delegable" here does not mean that the employer cannot delegate its health and safety tasks (this would simply be impracticable in modern employment conditions), but that it cannot delegate *responsibility* at law. It is no excuse that the employer has taken care to ensure a competent fellow employee deals with safety: if the employee is injured due to lack of care, the employer is liable.

The facts of *Wilson and Clyde Coal Co v English*[19] illustrate this point. A miner had been crushed in a mining accident, and had sued the mine-owners, on the basis that a safe system of work had not been adopted. The defendants argued that they had delegated pit safety to a qualified manager, as required by statute, and should not be held liable. Lord Wright, in the House of Lords, held that it was not enough for an employer to entrust the fulfilment of its duty of care to its employees, even when they had been selected with due care and skill.[20] The employer retained responsibility to provide a competent staff, adequate plant and equipment and effective supervision. If these were not provided with reasonable care and skill, the employer would be liable. Here, the system of working had not been reasonably safe and so the employers were liable.

## The nature of the duty

7–004    In this section, we shall examine the nature of the non-delegable duty placed on the employer.[21] An employer's personal duty is a duty to see that reasonable care is taken.[22] This will also apply to analogous relationships, for example the relationship between the Chief Constable of Police and police officers, although the courts do consider the demands of public policy in this context.[23] To comply with this duty, case law indicates that the employers should take care in the provision of:

- competent staff;

- adequate plant and equipment;

- a safe place of work;

- a safe system of work.

Each of these matters will be examined in more detail below.

*(1) Provision of competent staff*

7–005    This was obviously important when the doctrine of common employment barred the employer's liability for the negligence of fellow employees. It meant that the employer would be

---

[19] [1938] A.C. 57

[20] [1938] A.C. 57 at 78. See also Lord Herschell in *Smith v Baker* [1891] A.C. 325 at 362.

[21] Other analogous duties may also be non-delegable e.g. the duty to undertake a risk assessment under the Management of Health and Safety at Work Regulations 1999: see *Uren v Corporate Leisure (UK) Ltd* [2011] EWCA Civ 66.

[22] As stated in Ch.5, readers should note the distinction between the employer's duty of care and breach of that duty. The duty is to see that reasonable care is taken. Breach of duty can be shown by evidence that the employer had failed to take reasonable steps to provide competent staff or a safe system of work.

[23] See *W v Commissioner of Police for the Metropolis* [2000] 1 W.L.R. 1607 and *Mullaney v Chief Constable of West Midlands Police* (CA) [2001] EWCA Civ 700; *Independent*, July 9, 2001, where the courts continue to take note of the policy factors discussed in *Hill v Chief Constable of West Yorkshire* [1989] 1 A.C. 53 discussed in Ch.2. Consider also *Mulcahy v Ministry of Defence* [1996] Q.B. 732 (no duty on Ministry of Defence to maintain a safe system of work in battle situations).

personally responsible for providing such incompetent staff. It still has some modern relevance, however. A good example is *Hudson v Ridge Manufacturing Co*.[24] An employee had for nearly four years persistently engaged in practical jokes, such as tripping up fellow employees, and had been reprimanded many times. His employers were found to be personally liable when he tripped up the plaintiff and caused him injury. They had failed to exercise reasonable care to put an end to such conduct, which was a potential danger to other employees.[25] Equally an employer may find itself liable for failing to prevent a campaign of sustained bullying when it was in its power to do so.[26]

## (2) Provision of adequate plant and equipment and a safe place of work

The employer should take reasonable care to ensure that the employee's place of work is safe, **7–006** which extends to access to the premises.[27] In addition, the employer must take reasonable care to provide all necessary equipment and to maintain it in a reasonable condition. An interesting point was raised by *Davie v New Merton Board Mills*.[28] In this case, the plaintiff lost the sight in his left eye when a particle of metal chipped off a tool he was using, due to a fault in its manufacture. The tool had been provided by his employers, who had bought it from a reputable supplier, and the defect could not be detected by reasonable inspection. The House of Lords held that his employers were not liable. Although they had a duty to take reasonable care to provide a reasonably safe tool, this had been discharged[29]—they had bought the tool from a reputable source and they had no means of discovering that it contained a latent defect. The court held that if liability was imposed in such circumstances, any employer "employing another and supplying him with tools for his job acts at his peril".[30]

This decision, which obviously favoured employers, was reversed by the Employer's Liability (Defective Equipment) Act 1969. Section 1 provides that where an employee is injured in the course of his or her employment in consequence of a defect in equipment provided by the employer for the purposes of the employer's business, and the defect is due (wholly or partly) to the fault of a third party, then the injury will be attributed to the fault of the employer. This applies regardless of whether the third party is identified or not and extends to plant, machinery, vehicles, aircraft and even clothing.[31] This provision is obviously intended to make it easier for an employee to sue. He or she is no longer required to pursue a manufacturer[32] who may be overseas, but can sue his or her employer. The employee must nevertheless show that:

---

[24] [1957] 2 Q.B. 348. See also *Smith v Crossley Brothers Ltd* (1951) 95 Sol. Jo. 655 and Sir Nicolas Browne-Wilkinson V.C. in *Wilsher v Essex Area Health Authority* [1987] Q.B. 730, CA at 778: "In my judgment, a health authority which so conducts its hospital that it fails to provide doctors of sufficient skill and experience to give the treatment offered at the hospital may be directly liable in negligence to the patient".

[25] The employer here is unlikely to be vicariously liable for the "playful" activities of such an employee as it is doubtful whether a court would find such conduct to be in the course of his or her employment.

[26] See *W v Commissioner of Police for the Metropolis* [2000] 1 W.L.R. 1607 (breach of duty found to be arguable).

[27] See *Ashdown v Samuel Williams & Sons Ltd* [1957] 1 Q.B. 409, CA.

[28] [1959] A.C. 604.

[29] The court held that the employer could not be found to have delegated its duty of care to the manufacturer.

[30] Viscount Simonds [1959] A.C. 604 at 618. See C.J. Hamson [1959] C.L.J. 157.

[31] *Coltman v Bibby Tankers Ltd (The Derbyshire)* [1988] A.C. 276 even extended the Act to a ship which had sunk off the coast of Japan with the loss of all hands. See also *Knowles v Liverpool City Council* [1993] 1 W.L.R. 1428 (not restricted to tools and plant and could include flagstone which broke injuring workman laying the pavement).

[32] The employee still has a right to sue the manufacturer. Liability of manufacturers in tort will be discussed in Ch.9.

(1) a defect in equipment caused the accident; and

(2) the defect, on the balance of probabilities, was due to some fault in its manufacture.

These matters are not always easy to prove. The Act also provides that the rules relating to contributory negligence still apply.

*(3) Provision of a safe system of work*

**7–007**    This is difficult to define, but essentially refers to decisions adopted by the employer on the method of working.[33] Employers are required to take reasonable steps to organise and supervise the work of their employees, and to give proper instructions and guidance to employees and check that it is adhered to. Employers must take account of the fact that employees are often heedless of their own safety and so the system of work adopted should, so far as possible, minimise the danger of the employee's own foreseeable carelessness. For example, in *General Cleaning Contractors v Christmas*,[34] there was an obvious danger that if window cleaners stood on the sill to clean the outside of the window, they might suffer injury if the window closed. By failing to instruct the window cleaners to take precautions, their employers had failed to provide a safe system of work. Particular care must be taken if the work is complex or involves a large number of personnel.

## The modern scope of personal liability

**7–008**    It can be seen that the personal liability of an employer in negligence differs from the ordinary duty of care we have examined earlier in this book. Rather than being a duty to take care, it is perhaps more accurately described as a duty to see that reasonable care is taken. This duty extends not only to the actual work of employees, but to all such acts as are normally and reasonably incidental to a day's work, such as making a cup of tea or going to the toilet.[35] Yet, apart from this, the ordinary rules of negligence apply. The employee must show that the duty of care has been breached and that breach caused the loss suffered. The duty is owed to the individual employee. We have seen in Ch.5 that the particular characteristics of an employee may require extra care to be taken. In *Paris v Stepney BC*,[36] the court held that the employer was required to undertake extra safety precautions in respect of a one-eyed employee. The defendants were therefore liable for not providing safety goggles, even though they were not required to provide them to two-eyed employees.

Case law suggests that the courts are prepared to adopt a very generous approach towards the personal liability of employers. In *McDermid v Nash Dredging and Reclamation Co Ltd*,[37] the plaintiff was an employee of the defendants, which were a wholly-owned subsidiary of a Dutch company, Stevin. The function of the defendants was to provide and pay the staff engaged in Stevin's operation in Sweden. The plaintiff had been injured whilst working on the

---

[33] Consider *McGhee v National Coal Board* [1973] 1 W.L.R. 1 discussed in Ch.6 (failure to provide adequate washing facilities).
[34] [1953] A.C. 180, see in particular Lord Oaksey at 189–190. See, more recently, *Ammah v Kuehne & Nagel Logistics Ltd* [2009] EWCA Civ 11.
[35] *Davidson v Handley Page Ltd* [1945] 1 All E.R. 235.
[36] [1951] A.C. 367.
[37] [1987] A.C. 906. For a discussion of the case, see JD Fleming [1988] C.L.J. 11. Consider also *Johnstone v Bloomsbury Area Health Authority* [1992] Q.B. 333 (although this was only a striking-out case and so weak authority).

deck of a tug owned by Stevin, due to the negligence of one of Stevin's employees. The question was whether the defendants (the subsidiary company) could be liable in such circumstances. The House of Lords held that the defendants could not effectively delegate the task of providing a safe system of work to the Dutch company and its employees and therefore retained personal responsibility for any lack of care which injured the plaintiff.

This decision stretches personal liability very far, but may be explained by the close connection between the Dutch company and the defendants. It should also be noted that the House of Lords was quite happy to base a failure to provide a safe system of work on a negligent failure to devise such a system or negligence in its operation.[38] It has been observed that this represented an extension of existing legal principles.[39]

*Stress in the workplace*

A similarly generous approach was adopted in the context of psychiatric illness in *Walker v* **7–009**
*Northumberland CC.*[40] In this case, Colman J. held that there was no logical reason for excluding the risk of psychiatric damage from the scope of an employer's duty to provide a safe system of work. Here, the plaintiff, the defendants' area social services manager, suffered a second nervous breakdown due to stress and pressure at work. The plaintiff had suffered an earlier breakdown due to stress at work and it was therefore reasonably foreseeable that a failure to lessen his work load might lead to a second breakdown.

Colman J. in *Walker* applied the ordinary principles of employers' liability. No mention was made of the House of Lords' decision in *Alcock v Chief Constable of South Yorkshire*[41] (discussed in Ch.4) which stipulated that a restrictive approach should be taken towards psychiatric damage. The status of *Walker* has therefore been questioned, particularly in the light of the more recent case of *White v Chief Constable of South Yorkshire*,[42] where the House of Lords held that police attending the victims of the Hillsborough disaster could not claim against their employers for psychiatric illness suffered as a result.[43] Although the majority of the House of Lords expressed no clear view on *Walker*, some comments were made. Lord Hoffmann suggested that a distinction may be drawn between claims arising from the work itself and claims due to witnessing injury to others in the course of work.[44] Lord Steyn, however, did seem to advocate that the ordinary rules of tort, which restrict recovery for psychiatric damage, should apply to all employee claims.

---

[38] See also *Mullaney v Chief Constable of West Midlands Police* [2001] EWCA Civ 700; *Independent,* July 9, 2001 (failure to operate a safe system of work where distress calls from a police officer had not been monitored as instructed with the result that the officer received severe head injuries from an assailant).

[39] See E. McKendrick (1990) 53 M.L.R. 770 at 773–774 who remarks that the effect of the decision is as if vicarious liability had been imposed.

[40] [1995] I.C.R. 702; [1995] 1 All E.R. 737. Comment: D. Nolan (1995) 24 I.L.J. 280. Contrast *Petch v Customs and Excise Commissioners* [1993] I.C.R. 789. See also *Young v Post Office* [2002] I.R.L.R. 660 and *W v Commissioner of Police for the Metropolis* [2000] 1 W.L.R. 1607. This generous approach does not seem to extend to economic loss: see *Reid v Rush and Tompkins Group Plc* [1990] 1 W.L.R. 212, CA, although contrast the generous use of implied terms in *Scally v Southern Health and Social Services Board* [1992] 1 A.C. 294. The Court of Appeal in *Crossley v Faithful & Gould Holdings Ltd* [2004] EWCA Civ 293; [2004] 4 All E.R. 447, while approving *Scally*, regarded it as a specific exception and refused to imply a general term into every contract of employment that an employer should take reasonable care of an employee's economic well being.

[41] [1992] 1 A.C. 310.

[42] [1999] 2 A.C. 455.

[43] By a majority of 4 to 1, Lord Goff dissenting. Nevertheless, the Law Commission (Law Commission Report No. 249 *Liability for Psychiatric Illness* (1998), para.7.22) had found that *Walker* represented "a just development in the law".

[44] See Lord Hoffmann [1999] 2 A.C. 455 at 506.

Subsequent case law has confirmed the status of *Walker* and attempted to clarify exactly when employers will find themselves liable for psychiatric injury arising from stress or harassment in the workplace. The leading decision is that of *Sutherland v Hatton*.[45] In this case, the Court of Appeal, dealing with four conjoined appeals, sought to give employers guidance. It distinguished:

(a) cases where the harm suffered was the reasonably foreseeable product of specific breaches of a contractual duty of care between the defendant and a known primary victim (e.g. the employee in *Walker*);

(b) cases where the relationship was only in tort (e.g. *Page v Smith*,[46] *Alcock v Chief Constable of South Yorkshire Police*[47]) and

(c) cases where there was a contractual claim by a secondary victim (e.g. the police officer witnessing the Hillsborough disaster in *White v Chief Constable of South Yorkshire*).

The control mechanisms of *White* and *Alcock* would only apply under (b) and (c), and not where the employee was a primary victim under (a). This seems a rather fine distinction and is clearly introduced to maintain the *Walker* line of authority for potential claimants. Nevertheless, *Hatton* has been welcomed by employers primarily due to its acceptance that an employer is entitled, unless he knows otherwise, to assume that the employee can cope. This is obviously in the employer's favour.[48] Only if the employer knows, or should know, of some particular problem or vulnerability will the employer be liable. This will require the court to look at a number of relevant factors, including the nature and amount of work undertaken by the employee (is the employee overworked or placed under unreasonable pressure?) and signs of stress in the employee. The indications that a person is about to suffer harm from stress at work must be plain enough for any reasonable employer to realise something should be done about it. Even if the risk of harm is foreseeable, the court must in every case examine what the employer could and should have done, bearing in mind the size and scope of the operation, its resources, whether it is in the public or private sector, and other demands placed upon it.[49] The "threshold question" is whether this kind of harm to this particular employee was reasonably foreseeable.[50]

In the case of *Hatton*, Mrs Hatton had suffered a stress-related psychiatric illness whilst teaching at a comprehensive school. However, like many people, she had struggled to cope and did not complain to her superiors or ask for help. Yet, the fact that she had struggled on without complaint led the court to conclude that there was no clear indication that she was likely to suffer from psychiatric injury and that the school should not be liable.[51] In contrast,

---

[45] [2002] EWCA Civ 76; [2002] 2 All E.R. 1. Applied in *Foumeny v University of Leeds* [2003] EWCA Civ 557; [2003] E.L.R. 443. Hale L.J. at para.20 cited *Walker* and Lord Hoffmann's judgment in *White* above with approval.

[46] [1996] A.C. 155.

[47] [1992] 1 A.C. 310.

[48] See N.J. Mullany "Containing claims for workplace mental illness" (2002) 118 L.Q.R. 373.

[49] Note that this is a more subjective test than that used in ordinary negligence claims (discussed in Ch.5).

[50] See Hale L.J. [2002] EWCA Civ 76; [2002] 2 All E.R. 1 at para.23. Her Ladyship lists 16 practical propositions at para.43 which aim to provide clear guidance for employers in future.

[51] See also *Pratley v Surrey CC* [2003] EWCA Civ 1067, [2004] I.C.R. 159 (foresight of risk of illness arising from continuing overwork in the future not sufficient).

in the conjoined case of *Barber v Somerset County Council*,[52] another school teacher, Mr Barber, had been forced to take three weeks off school, which had been certified by his GP as due to depression and stress, and could point to several meetings in which he had expressed concern as to his workload and its effect on his health. Although these meetings had taken place before the summer vacation ("usually a source of relaxation and recuperation for hard-pressed teachers") and his actual breakdown had taken place the following November, the House of Lords (on appeal) overturned the view of the Court of Appeal that "it is expecting far too much to expect school authorities to pick up the fact that the problems were continuing without some such indication."[53]

Although the Court of Appeal guidelines in *Hatton* were not appealed,[54] Lord Walker, giving the leading judgment in *Barber*, appeared to favour a more "employee-friendly" approach. His Lordship found that although the *Hatton* guidelines provided practical assistance, the overall test remains "the conduct of the reasonable and prudent employer, taking positive thought for the safety of his workers in the light of what he knows or ought to know."[55] On this basis, although this case was close to the borderline, the school had been negligent in failing to make ongoing inquiries as to Mr Barber's health and in not taking any measures to ease the problem.

The more recent Court of Appeal decision in *Hartman v South Essex Mental Health and Community Care NHS Trust*,[56] involving six conjoined appeals, sought to quash any fears of inconsistency between *Hatton* and *Barber*. Scott-Baker L.J., giving judgment for the court, found that Lord Walker was not disagreeing with the *Hatton* guidelines, but simply sounding a word of caution that no two cases were alike and that the test must be applied to each new set of facts.[57] The decisions reached in *Hartman* indicate that the courts will continue generally to require some specific signs to be evident to the reasonable employer that a problem exists.[58] In *Hartman* itself, the claim of a hard-working nursing auxiliary dealing with children with learning difficulties failed. The Court of Appeal rejected the argument that such a job required a higher degree of alertness from employers. Equally, knowledge of an earlier nervous breakdown disclosed in confidence to the Occupational Health Department would not be attributed to the employer. This decision may be contrasted with the sixth appeal, *Melville v Home Office*. Here, the Home Office had conceded that the job of health care officer in a prison, which included the recovery of the bodies of prisoners who committed suicide, might cause injury to health and had undertaken to provide support following any such incident. Mr Melville unfortunately had been unable to access this support. The Court of Appeal distinguished ordinary claims for stress in the workplace from a situation where the employer

---

[52] [2004] UKHL 13; [2004] 1 W.L.R. 1089, HL; [2002] 2 All E.R. 1, CA.

[53] [2004] UKHL 13 at para.59.

[54] Lord Walker, giving the leading judgment, describes them at paras 63 and 65 as "a valuable contribution to the development of the law" and "useful practical guidance, but . . . not . . . having anything like statutory force".

[55] Quoting Swanwick J. in *Stokes v Guest, Keen and Nettlefold (Bolts and Nuts) Ltd* [1968] 1 W.L.R. 1776, 1783. His judgment is heavily criticised by Lord Scott dissenting for setting an unrealistically high standard of care on the school.

[56] [2005] EWCA Civ 6; [2005] I.C.R. 782. Comment: C. McIvor (2005) 21 P.N. 123.

[57] [2005] EWCA Civ 6; [2005] I.C.R. 782 at para.10.

[58] For example, in *Garrod v North Devon NHS Primary Care Trust* [2006] EWHC 850, [2007] P.I.Q.R. Q1, a health visitor had already had a breakdown due to pressure of work. Nevertheless, on her return, she was repeatedly put under pressure to the detriment of her health. See also *Dickins v O2 Plc* [2008] EWCA Civ 1144; [2009] I.R.L.R. 58. Contrast *Harding v Pub Estate Co Ltd* [2005] EWCA Civ 553, [2005] N.P.C. 62 (heart attack due to stress treated under the *Hatton* principles).

foresaw that a specific task might lead to mental injury and devised a system to deal with this. In such circumstances, a negligent failure to implement this system would lead to liability.[59] It nevertheless cautioned that the mere fact that an employer offered an occupational health service should not lead to the conclusion that the employer had foreseen the risk of injury due to stress at work.

As may be seen, complaints to one's employer will often form the basis for any claim for liability. Yet, few employees in such circumstances will wish to alert their superiors to the fact that they are not doing their job properly. The Court of Appeal in *Hatton* recognised this, but insisted that it is difficult in such circumstances to blame the employer for failing to act. Any stricter regime would be better implemented by way of regulations imposing specific statutory duties.[60]

## BREACH OF STATUTORY DUTY

**7–010**    This is a tort in its own right.[61] Although, as we shall see below, breach of statutory duty is not confined to the employment context, its main application is in the employment field, particularly in relation to matters of industrial safety.[62] It therefore forms a part of the potential liability of employers in tort and it is appropriate to deal with it in this chapter. The tort of breach of statutory duty gives a remedy for breach of certain statutory duties where the legislature intended that, in addition to any criminal or administrative penalties, the injured party should have a right to sue in tort. The House of Lords, in *Lonrho Ltd v Shell Petroleum Co Ltd (No.2)*,[63] declined to accept the broader notion that liability could arise whenever damage results from a contravention of a statutory duty. The question, therefore, is when does Parliament intend such a right to exist? Unfortunately, very few statutes expressly deal with this issue.[64] In the absence of an express right to sue[65] (or an express exclusion from suing),[66] the courts are left to construe the statute, and to infer whether Parliament intended to provide a right to damages in tort. This gives the courts a considerable amount of discretion, in the

---

[59] "It is illogical to argue that when an employer has foreseen a risk of psychiatric injury to employees exposed to certain traumatic incidents, such injury is not foreseeable": Scott-Baker L.J. in *Hartman v South Essex Mental Health and Community Care NHS Trust* [2005] I.C.R. 782 at para.134.

[60] Hale L.J. [2002] 2 All E.R. 1 at 9–10. The Court of Appeal further indicated that should the employer set up a confidential advice service, with referral to appropriate counselling or treatment services, it would be unlikely to be found liable, but see now *Daw v Intel Corp (UK) Ltd* [2007] EWCA Civ 70; [2007] 2 All E.R. 126 (counselling services were not a panacea by which employers could discharge their duty of care in all cases. It was a question of fact. Here the claimant's problems could only have been dealt with by management reducing her workload).

[61] Although there are arguments to the contrary, most notably the argument of statutory negligence forwarded by E.R. Thayer (1914) 27 Harv. L.R. 317. It should be noted that the tort of breach of statutory duty is distinct from statutes which place liability in negligence in statutory form such as the Occupiers' Liability Acts which are discussed in Ch.8. See, generally, K.M. Stanton et al, *Statutory Torts* (Sweet and Maxwell, 2003), R.A. Buckley (1984) 100 L.Q.R. 204 and K.M. Stanton (2004) 120 L.Q.R. 324.

[62] See G. Williams (1960) 23 M.L.R. 233.

[63] [1982] A.C. 173 at 187, rejecting the majority judgment in *Ex p. Island Records Ltd* [1978] Ch.122.

[64] Despite the plea by Lord du Parcq in *Cutler v Wandsworth Stadium Ltd* [1949] A.C. 398 at 410 that Parliament should state explicitly whether it intended that there should be a civil remedy or not. See also *McCall v Abelesz* [1976] Q.B. 585.

[65] e.g. see Consumer Protection Act 1987 s.41.

[66] e.g. Health and Safety at Work etc. Act 1974 s.47(1)(a) which provides that the general duties under the Act do not give rise to civil liability. Section 47(2) provides, however, that breach of a duty imposed by the health and safety regulations shall, so far as it causes damage, give rise to civil liability except in so far as the regulations provide otherwise. See also Guard Dogs Act 1975 s.5 and Railways Act 2005 s.44.

exercise of which they will consider the purpose of the statute and whether, in all the circumstances, individuals such as the claimant could have been intended to have a civil remedy.

The first question in dealing with breach of statutory duty is therefore to look at the wording of the particular statutory provision which has been breached: construing it according to the guidelines established by the courts, does it give a remedy in tort to individuals who suffer harm as a result of its breach? If this is established, there are four further matters to consider:

- Is the duty owed to this particular claimant?

- Has the defendant breached his or her statutory duty?

- Did the breach cause the damage in question?

- Was the injury of the kind which the statute intended to prevent?

Only if all five questions are answered in the affirmative will an action lie for breach of statutory duty. It must be stated that much turns on the interpretative powers of the courts and whether or not they are willing to accept that a regulatory statute was intended to place an additional burden on defendants to pay civil damages. Generally, the courts have shown themselves willing to adopt such a construction in relation to employee safety, but have adopted a more restrictive view in other contexts. In considering the employment cases, it should be borne in mind that until 1948, breach of statutory duty formed one of the ways of circumventing the doctrine of common employment. Policy considerations have therefore been influential in deciding when to allow a remedy for breach of statutory duty—arguably this is inevitable when the courts are given a broad interpretative discretion. The Law Commission, in 1969,[67] attempted to limit this discretion by recommending the enactment of a general statute that would have created a presumption that a civil remedy was intended unless the contrary was stated. This did not become law. Such a provision would have greatly increased the role of this tort, in a way which does not reflect the current restrictive view taken outside industrial safety.

Although the courts exercise discretion in such cases, this discretion is not without limits. The courts have developed guidelines which they use in deciding whether a civil remedy was intended. These are examined below.

## Construing Parliamentary intention

The courts have identified a number of factors which indicate whether Parliament intended a    **7–011**
remedy to lie for breach of statutory duty. The leading case of *Lonrho Ltd v Shell Petroleum Co Ltd (No.2)*[68] highlights the most significant factors. The case concerned the supply of oil in breach of certain sanctions following the unilateral declaration of independence by Southern Rhodesia in 1965. Lonrho brought an action for breach of statutory duty, alleging that it had suffered heavy losses when (unlike its competitors) it had complied with the

---

[67] See Law Commission Report No. 21, *The Interpretation of Statutes* (1969) para.38. This proposal did form part of the Interpretation of Legislation Bill 1980, but this was subsequently withdrawn. R.A. Buckley (1984) 100 L.Q.R. 204 at 231–232 argues that this provision would not, in any event, have resolved all the problems involved in construing statutes.

[68] [1982] A.C. 173 at 185.

sanctions. Lord Diplock, giving the leading judgment, held that the action failed. Whilst confirming that the overall test was one of identifying whether the purpose of the Act was to give the claimant a civil remedy, his Lordship identified a number of factors which assisted the courts in construing statutory provisions. His Lordship held that the courts should generally take a restrictive view where the Act provided its own penalties, but that there were two main exceptions to this rule. The first exception was where the claimant could show that the statute had been enacted for the benefit or protection of a particular class of individuals. The second exception was where the statute conferred a public right and a particular member of the public suffered special damage.[69] Neither exception was applicable in *Lonrho*. The sanctions had been imposed, as a matter of state policy, to destroy the illegal UDI regime and were not intended either to benefit a particular class of individuals, nor to establish a public right. Lonrho therefore had no valid claim for breach of statutory duty.

Whilst the considerations which influence the courts in construing Parliamentary intention are elusive, and difficult to examine in isolation, it is possible to identify and discuss a number of relevant points:

- whether the statute protects a specific "class" of individuals;

- the nature of the legislation;

- whether alternative remedies exist at law.

Each of these points will be examined below.

*(1) Protection of a class*

**7–012**   There is clear authority that if the statute is passed for the protection of a limited class of the public, rather than for the benefit of the public as a whole, a court will be more inclined to find that a civil remedy was intended.[70] Thus, in *Atkinson v Newcastle Waterworks Co*,[71] the Court of Appeal rejected the claim of a householder whose premises had burnt down. The defendants had been in breach of their statutory duty to maintain water pressure in their pipes. As a result, when the fire broke out, there was insufficient water to extinguish it. Lord Cairns L.C. held that it would be a startling proposition to place an additional burden on a company supplying a town with water by making it liable to householders whose properties were damaged by fire.[72] The statutory scheme was for the benefit of the public as a whole and not individual householders, otherwise the company would be practically insuring householders against damage by fire.[73]

However, the fact that a particular provision refers to a certain class of individuals will not of itself give rise to an action in tort. As Lord Browne-Wilkinson stated in *X v Bedfordshire CC*:

---

[69] His Lordship's second exception is contentious and it is fair to say that it has not been taken up by the courts. The best example of liability in such circumstances is that of public nuisance (discussed in Ch.10) which is clearly not statutory.

[70] See *X v Bedfordshire CC* [1995] 2 A.C. 633 at 731 and *O'Rourke v Camden LBC* [1998] A.C. 188 at 193. But note criticism of this approach by Atkin L.J. in *Phillips v Britannia Hygienic Laundry Co* [1923] 2 K.B. 832 at 841.

[71] (1877) 2 Ex.D. 441. This marked a change from the more liberal approach first adopted by the courts, see *Couch v Steel* (1854) 3 E. & B. 402; 118 E.R. 1193.

[72] (1877) 2 Ex. D. 441 at 445–446.

[73] See also *Thames Trains Ltd v Health and Safety Executive* [2003] EWCA Civ 720; (2003) 147 S.J.L.B. 661, CA (duty owed by Health and Safety Executive to anyone affected by the railway being unsafe did not give rise to individual rights for passengers and train operators).

"a private law cause of action will arise if it can be shown, as a matter of construction of a statute, that the statutory duty was imposed for the protection of a limited class of the public *and* that Parliament intended to confer on members of that class a private right of action."[74]

The *purpose* of the statute remains important. For example, in *Cutler v Wandsworth Stadium Ltd*,[75] s.11(2) of the Betting and Lotteries Act 1934 required the owner of a dog-racing track to provide space for bookmakers. The House of Lords held that although bookmakers were indeed an identifiable class, they could not sue for damages when excluded from the track. The purpose of the statute was to regulate the conduct of race tracks, and not to protect the livelihood of bookmakers, who might benefit incidentally from such regulation.

Similarly, in the more recent case of *R. v Deputy Governor of Parkhurst Prison, Ex p. Hague*,[76] the House of Lords held that the Prison Rules 1964 were intended to regulate the administration of prisons and the management and control of prisoners. They did not give rise to any private rights for prisoners if they were breached.

*(2) The nature of the legislation*

This also seems to be significant in recent years. Where a statute has a "social welfare" goal, **7–013** the courts have resisted imposing the burden of civil liability on usually a public authority defendant. It may be recalled that in the House of Lords decision in *X v Bedfordshire CC*[77] (discussed in Ch.2) the plaintiffs brought actions against local authorities concerning the negligent performance of their statutory duties relating to education and child welfare. Actions were also brought for breach of statutory duty. The plaintiffs were unsuccessful in their claims in negligence and, unsurprisingly, their Lordships were also reluctant to impose liability for breach of statutory duty. Lord Browne-Wilkinson held that although the legislation was designed to protect children at risk and ensure adequate educational provision, it was never-theless not Parliament's intention to allow individual children or their families to sue for damages. The plaintiffs were told to pursue their claims in administrative law, rather than the law of torts. In the later case of *Phelps v Hillingdon LBC*,[78] Lord Slynn reiterated that, despite the existence of a valid claim for negligence, no remedy would lie for breach of statutory duty where the purpose of the legislation was one of social welfare:

"The general nature of the duties imposed on local authorities in the context of a national system of education and the remedies available by way of appeal and judicial review indicate that Parliament did not intend to create a statutory remedy by way of damages."[79]

---

[74] [1995] 2 A.C. 633 at 731 (emphasis added).

[75] [1949] A.C. 398.

[76] [1992] 1 A.C. 58. Hague was more successful in his alternative claim in public law. The House of Lords held that prisoners' rights were adequately protected by alternative claims in public law and in the torts of misfeasance in public office, trespass to the person and negligence. For the significance of alternative remedies, see below. Note also the restrictive approach in *Morrison Sports Ltd v Scottish Power Plc* [2010] UKSC 37; [2010] 1 W.L.R. 1934 (legis-lative scheme pointed against individuals having private right of action, an argument reinforced by the fact it was difficult to identify any limited class of the public for whose protection the Electricity Supply Regulations 1988 had been enacted).

[77] [1995] 2 A.C. 633.

[78] [2001] 2 A.C. 619.

[79] [2001] 2 A.C. 619 at 652. See also *Carty v Croydon LBC* [2005] EWCA Civ 19, [2005] 1 W.L.R. 2312 at para.19.

A similar position was taken in *O'Rourke v Camden LBC*[80] in relation to the local authority's statutory duty to house homeless persons. Lord Hoffmann in *O'Rourke* set out the reasoning of the court:

> ". . . the Act is a scheme of social welfare, intended to confer benefits at the public expense on grounds of public policy. Public money is spent on housing the homeless not merely for the private benefit of people who find themselves homeless but on grounds of general public interest: because, for example, proper housing means that people will be less likely to suffer illness, turn to crime or require the attention of other social services. The expenditure interacts with expenditure on other public services such as education, the National Health Service and even the police. It is not simply a private matter between the claimant and the housing authority."[81]

On this basis, the statutes in both cases were passed for the benefit of society in general, and not for the benefit of individuals. This indicator is therefore perhaps better analysed as a particular example of (1) above: the courts rejecting liability where the statute is not for the benefit of a specific class of the public, but for the public at large. The courts are also very conscious of the wide discretion exercised by public authorities in such cases, and are reluctant to regulate this discretion through the law of tort. As Lord Hoffmann commented in *O'Rourke*:

> "the existence of all these discretions makes it unlikely that Parliament intended errors of judgment to give rise to an obligation to make financial reparation. Control by public law remedies would appear much more appropriate".[82]

### (3) Alternative remedies

**7–014**  This overlaps with (2) in that the courts are influenced by the fact that public authorities are accountable in administrative law.[83] Moreover, where the statute sets up a system of fines, the court will be reluctant to assume that Parliament intended the additional burden of civil liability, unless, as stated by Lord Diplock in *Lonrho*,[84] it is apparent that the duty was imposed for the benefit or protection of a particular class.[85] In contrast, if there is no stated remedy for

---

[80] [1998] A.C. 188. See R. Carnwath [1998] P.L. 407.

[81] [1998] A.C. 188 at 193.

[82] [1998] A.C. 188 at 194.

[83] See *X v Bedfordshire C.C.* [1995] 2 A.C. 633 and *Phelps v Hillingdon LBC* [2001] 2 A.C. 619.

[84] *Lonrho Ltd v Shell Petroleum Co Ltd (No.2)* [1982] A.C. 173 at 185.

[85] This may be unclear on the facts. Compare, for example, the Court of Appeal decisions of *Todd v Adams (The Maragetha Maria)* [2002] EWCA Civ 509; [2002] 2 Lloyd's Rep 293 (CA) and *Ziemniak v ETPM Deep Sea Ltd* [2003] EWCA Civ 636; [2003] 2 Lloyd's Rep 214, which both concerned breach of safety rules pursuant to the Merchant Shipping Act 1995. In *Todd*, the court somewhat reluctantly found that breach of rules made under the Act concerning the safety of fishing vessels did not give a right of action following a tragic fishing accident with the loss of all crew. The rules had specifically provided criminal sanctions and penalties and established a certification scheme which rendered civil liability inappropriate. However, in *Ziemniak* breach of rules in a different part of the Act did provide a civil remedy for a claimant seriously injured during a lifeboat test in harbour. Here, the claim was treated as one of safety in the workplace, thereby meriting the more generous treatment given to such claims. The rules did contain criminal sanctions, although they did not cover the accident in question. *Todd* was doubted, but nevertheless distinguished.

breach and there is an intention to protect a limited class, the court is more likely to hold that the statute gives rise to a civil action.[86]

Similarly, if adequate remedies are provided by the common law, or by other statutory provisions, this will indicate that no additional civil action exists. This, however, begs the question as to what is meant by "adequate". In *McCall v Abelesz*,[87] adequate remedies were said to exist against the harassment of tenants, which justified the refusal of liability, but it may be questioned whether this was in fact the case. The court in *Issa v Hackney LBC*[88] held that the adequacy of alternative remedies should be assessed at the date of enactment of the statute in question, and in that case refused to take account of the fact that the protection of tenants had diminished since the enactment of the Public Health Act 1936.

The common law position can impact in a further way. As well as suggesting that no liability should exist where there is an alternative remedy at law, it also indicates that no liability should exist where it is for a type of damage irrecoverable at common law. The case of *Pickering v Liverpool Daily Post*[89] illustrates this point. Here, the plaintiff (a convicted murderer and sex offender) wished to prevent a newspaper from publishing information about his application to a mental health review tribunal to be discharged from a mental hospital. The House of Lords held that any breach of the Mental Health Review Tribunal Rules did not grant him a right to a civil remedy. There is no tort of breaching privacy in English law,[90] and, at that time the court held that the defendants' actions were not capable of causing the plaintiff loss of a kind for which the law affords a remedy.[91] The courts also, in line with the common law position, seem far more willing to award damages for personal injury than for economic loss.[92]

The considerations discussed above are subject to the underlying policy decisions of the courts. As stated earlier, the courts have shown a notable leniency in finding civil liability for breaches of statutes involving industrial safety.[93] The questionable case of *Monk v Warbey*[94] is also a good example of the influence of policy on the courts. Despite clear authority that road-users did not form an identifiable class,[95] the court held that civil liability would be imposed on the owner of a vehicle who had allowed an uninsured driver to use it, contrary to s.35(1) of

---

[86] See *Cutler v Wandsworth Stadium Ltd* [1949] A.C. 398 and *Kirvek Management & Consulting Services Ltd v Attorney General of Trinidad and Tobago* [2002] UKPC 43; [2002] 1 W.L.R. 2792, PC. However, this did not assist the plaintiff in *R. v Deputy Governor of Parkhurst Prison Ex p. Hague* [1992] 1 A.C. 58.

[87] [1976] Q.B. 585 (the case concerned s.30(2) of the Rent Act 1965 which is no longer applicable) See also *Cullen v Chief Constable of the Royal Ulster Constabulary* [2003] UKHL 39; [2003] 1 W.L.R. 1763 (HL(NI)): adequate public law remedies justified denying the claimant a private law claim when refused a reason for denial of access to solicitor in custody (note the strong dissent of Lords Bingham and Steyn concerning adequacy).

[88] [1997] 1 W.L.R. 956.

[89] [1991] 2 A.C. 370.

[90] *Wainwright v Home Office* [2003] UKHL 53; [2004] 2 A.C. 406, but see Ch.15.

[91] "[T]hough [publication] may in one sense be adverse to the patient's interest" per Lord Bridge at 420. This is applied very narrowly in *Cullen v Chief Constable of the Royal Ulster Constabulary* [2003] 1 W.L.R. 1763 (HL(NI)). Privacy law has since developed following the implementation of the Human Rights Act 1998: see *Campbell v Mirror Group Newspapers Ltd* [2004] UKHL 22; [2004] 2 A.C. 457.

[92] See *Richardson v Pitt-Stanley* [1995] Q.B. 123 at 130 and 132.

[93] See, e.g. *Groves v Lord Wimborne* [1898] 2 Q.B. 402 and *Black v Fife Coal Co Ltd* [1912] A.C. 149.

[94] [1935] 1 K.B. 75, CA.

[95] See *Phillips v Britannia Hygienic Laundry Co* [1923] 2 K.B. 832.

the Road Traffic Act 1930.[96] This was obviously an attempt to ensure that the victim received compensation. Nowadays such a problem is dealt with by the Motor Insurers' Bureau (see Ch.1), although *Monk* remains good law.[97] A contrasting approach was taken by the Court of Appeal, however, in the more recent case of *Richardson v Pitt-Stanley*.[98] In this case, the plaintiff, who had been injured at work, had successfully sued his employers only to find that the company which employed him was in liquidation and unable to pay, and had failed to comply with its obligation under the Employers' Liability (Compulsory Insurance) Act 1969 to obtain insurance against liability. He therefore brought an action against the directors of the company for breach of statutory duty. The majority of the Court of Appeal rejected his claim. *Monk* was distinguished on a number of technical grounds.[99] Stuart-Smith L.J. also held, controversially, that the purpose of the Act was not solely to ensure injured employees could be compensated, but to protect employers from the risk of a heavy claim or loss.[100] Such a construction undoubtedly masked a policy decision not to render employers liable in tort for failing to comply with the insurance provisions of the Act.

It is therefore impossible to divorce the decisions of the courts from the influence of policy. In fact, the whole task of finding whether Parliament intended civil liability has been dismissed by many writers as a fiction.[101] It is unlikely in many cases that parliamentary drafters actually considered whether a remedy should exist in tort and it might be suspected that, even if the issue was considered, it would have been avoided as politically contentious. This leaves a considerable amount of discretion with the courts. While this may be thought undesirable, the courts have little option until parliamentary drafters deal with the question of civil liability for breach of statutory obligations on a more regular basis. The law at present is unpredictable and reflects the policy choices of the court. It is important, however, not to over-exaggerate these problems. In practice, the number of claims made for breach of statutory duty is small and the significance of such problems is minimal.

## Further considerations

**7–015**    If the statute is one for which the courts are prepared to find civil liability, then this is not the end of the matter. The claimant has to satisfy four further hurdles:

- Is the duty owed to this particular claimant?

- Has the defendant breached his or her statutory duty?

---

[96] Now the Road Traffic Act 1988 s.143. See also *Roe v Sheffield City Council* [2003] EWCA Civ 1; [2004] Q.B. 653. The duty, however, is limited to third party insurance against liability for death or bodily injury or damage to property and liability will not arise in relation to claims for pure economic loss: see *Bretton v Hancock* [2005] EWCA Civ 404; [2006] P.I.Q.R. P1 (rejecting a claim by joint tortfeasor that, due to the failure to insure, he was unable to recover a contribution to damages payable).

[97] See *Norman v Ali (Limitation Period)* [2000] R.T.R. 107 where the MIB required, pursuant to s.5(1)(d) of the Uninsured Drivers' Agreement 1988, that the claimant should bring the car-owner (Aziz) into the action, on a *Monk v Warbey* type action, for permitting Ali to drive the car when uninsured against third party risks. The limitation period for such actions is that of personal injury claims, namely, three years (see Ch.16).

[98] [1995] Q.B. 123 (Sir John Megaw dissenting).

[99] Which have been described as "less than compelling": see J. O'Sullivan [1995] C.L.J. 241 at 242.

[100] [1995] Q.B. 123 at 131.

[101] G. Williams (1960) 23 M.L.R. 233 at 244 describes it as "this process of looking for what is not there".

- Did the breach cause the damage concerned?

- Was the damage of the kind which the statute intended to prevent?

These will be examined below.

*(1) Is the duty owed to this particular claimant?*

The claimant must show that he or she is within the class of persons intended to benefit under **7–016**
the statute. This goes back to the construction of the statute. In *Knapp v Railway Executive,*[102]
for example, a breach of regulations in maintaining a level crossing, which led to a gate
swinging back to injure the driver of an oncoming train, was held not to be actionable.
Although the statutory provisions did give a remedy at common law, they were only for the
benefit of road-users and did not benefit persons travelling on the train.

*(2) Has the defendant breached his or her duty to the claimant?*

The defendant must have acted in breach of his or her duty as set out in the statute. Again, we **7–017**
must turn back to the wording of the statute and examine just what the defendant was required
to do or not to do. Is the duty one of reasonable care or does the statute impose strict liability?
The courts will examine the exact wording of the statute and, again, in the industrial context,
have interpreted legislation in a pro-employee manner. For example, the provision that the
employer must act "so far as is reasonably practicable" has been interpreted to place the legal
burden on the employer to establish that it was not reasonably practicable to take the precautions in question.[103] However, the courts do respect the strict wording of the statute. In
*Chipchase v British Titan Products Co Ltd,*[104] a regulation required every working platform
from which a person could fall more than six feet six inches to be at least 34 inches wide. The
plaintiff fell from a platform that was nine inches wide, but only six feet from the ground. On
this basis, no claim could arise under statute and the plaintiff was left to pursue a claim in
ordinary negligence.

*(3) Did the breach cause the damage concerned?*

Causation must be proved, and a similar approach is taken to that adopted for the tort of negli- **7–018**
gence, which we discussed in Ch.6.[105] One particular problem which has arisen is where the
statutory duty is placed on both the employer and the employee, and although the employer
has taken all reasonable steps, the conduct of the employee has caused the accident. In such
cases, the courts are reluctant to find the employer liable for the employee's own breach of
statutory duty. In *Boyle v Kodak Ltd,*[106] the plaintiff had been injured when he fell off a ladder
which was required by law to be secured. Previous authority demonstrated that civil liability
arose from breach, but the House of Lords held that it was not prepared to find the employer
liable if only the plaintiff had been at fault. Lord Reid stated that "it would be absurd if,
notwithstanding the employer having done all he could reasonably be expected to do to ensure

---

[102] [1949] 2 All E.R. 508, CA.
[103] *Nimmo v Alexander Cowan & Sons Ltd* [1968] A.C. 107, HL (admittedly by a slim majority of 3 to 2).
[104] [1956] 1 Q.B 545, CA.
[105] See, in particular, *McWilliams v Sir William Arrol Ltd* [1962] 1 All E.R. 623 which concerns breach of
statutory duty.
[106] [1969] 1 W.L.R. 661; [1969] 2 All E.R. 439. See also *Ginty v Belmont Building Supplies Ltd* [1959] 1 All E.R. 414
at 423–424 and *Anderson v Newham College of Further Education* [2002] EWCA Civ 505; [2003] I.C.R. 212.

compliance, a workman, who deliberately disobeyed his employer's orders and thereby put the employer in breach of a regulation, could claim damages for injury caused to him solely by his own wrongdoing".[107] On the facts, however, the court found that the employers had failed to show that the accident was solely due to the fault of the plaintiff and so liability would be divided 50:50, due to the contributory negligence of the plaintiff. The limitations of *Boyle* should be noted. Only if the duty is placed both on the employer and employee and the employee is the only person at fault will the courts refuse liability.

*(4) Is the damage of the kind which the statute intended to prevent?*

**7–019**   This, again, is a question of construction. The courts will examine the statute, and if the claimant has suffered an injury different from that mentioned in the statute, then the claimant will not be able to recover. It will therefore depend on how the court interprets "damage". In *Gorris v Scott*,[108] the Court of Exchequer adopted a strict line. Here, the Act in question required that animals be transported in pens to prevent the spread of contagious diseases. In violation of the Act, the plaintiff's sheep had been transported without pens and had been washed overboard in bad weather. The court held that such damage was "something totally apart from the object of the Act of Parliament"[109] and rejected the plaintiff's claim. Nowadays it is unlikely that a court would take such a strict approach. The courts (in line with the approach taken in *The Wagon Mound*) will simply examine whether the damage suffered is of the kind that the statute was designed to prevent.[110]

## Defences

**7–020**   These will be discussed in more detail in Ch.16. It is worth noting at this stage that there is some indecision as to whether the defence of voluntary assumption of risk (or volenti non fit injuria) applies to breach of statutory duty. The House of Lords in *ICI v Shatwell*[111] held that the defence would apply where the employer was not at fault and was only liable vicariously for the acts of its employees. Lords Reid and Pearce stressed that the defence should not apply if the employer is in some way at fault in failing to comply with the duty.[112]

   Although the principle of contributory negligence clearly applies to the tort of breach of statutory duty,[113] there is some authority that it will be applied leniently towards employees injured in the course of their employment. In *Caswell v Powell Duffryn Associated Collieries*,[114] it was held that the courts should take account of any continual noise, strain and risk to which

---

[107] [1969] 1 W.L.R. 661 at 665–666.

[108] (1874) L.R.9 Exch.125.

[109] (1874) L.R.9 Exch.125 at 129–130 per Kelly C.B. See also *Fytche v Wincanton Logistics Plc* [2004] UKHL 31; [2004] 4 All E.R. 221 (boots provided under Regulations were to protect against impact injury, not frostbite due to leak in boots).

[110] *Donaghey v Boulton & Paul Ltd* [1968] A.C. 1 at 26 per Lord Reid, HL (who draws a clear comparison with the position in negligence under *The Wagon Mound* [1961] A.C. 388 discussed in Ch.6).

[111] [1965] A.C. 656.

[112] Lord Pearce, [1965] A.C. 656 at 687, extends this to where the employer is vicariously in breach of statutory duty through the neglect of some person who is of superior rank to the claimant and whose commands the claimant was bound to obey.

[113] See Law Reform (Contributory Negligence) Act 1945 s.4.

[114] [1940] A.C. 152 at 166. It should be noted that this case was decided before the Law Reform (Contributory Negligence) Act 1945 when contributory negligence was an absolute defence to the employee's claim which may have encouraged a more generous approach.

employees were exposed which might lead to their failure to take reasonable care. This seems to be another example of the preferential treatment given to industrial injury claims.

## Breaches of European legislation (the "Eurotort")

This is an area of increasing importance, which we mentioned in our introductory chapter.     **7–021**
Claimants have a right to a remedy in national law for a number of breaches of European law, and the House of Lords in *Garden Cottage Foods Ltd v Milk Marketing Board*[115] held that such remedies would arise under the tort of breach of statutory duty. Under s.2(1) of the European Communities Act 1972, the State has an obligation to ensure that national law should be consistent with EU law and, therefore, if it acts in breach of Treaty provisions, it can be said to "breach" this duty. The right to a national remedy has increased in recent years, with ground-breaking decisions such as *Francovich v Italian Republic*[116] and *Brasserie du Pêcheur v Germany; R. v Secretary of State for Transport, ex p. Factortame (No.4)*.[117] Reference should be made to works on EU law for detailed discussion of such developments,[118] but it should be noted that these developments in European law have led to a right to damages which is far wider than that provided by the traditional English tort of breach of statutory duty. In the leading case of *Brasserie du Pêcheur v Germany; R. v Secretary of State for Transport, Ex p. Factortame (No.4)*,[119] the European Court of Justice indicated the scope of the right to damages in national law:

> "Community law confers a right to reparation where three conditions are met: the rule of law infringed must be intended to confer rights on individuals; the breach must be sufficiently serious; and there must be a direct causal link between the breach of the obligation resting on the state and the damage sustained by the injured parties."[120]

The first and third conditions are very similar to those of breach of statutory duty.[121] However, the second condition does differ. It is not intended to be a test of fault, but whether the State[122]

---

[115] [1984] A.C. 130. See also Mann J. in *Bourgoin S.A. and Others v Ministry of Agriculture, Fisheries and Food* [1986] Q.B. 716 at 733 and Lords Nicholls, Walker and Mance in *Sempra Metals Ltd v Inland Revenue Comrs* [2007] UKHL 34; [2008] 1 A.C. 561 at paras 69, 162 and 225 respectively.

[116] (C6/90) [1991] E.C.R. I-5357; [1993] 2 C.M.L.R. 66.

[117] (C46/93 and C48/93) [1996] Q.B. 404; [1996] 1 C.M.L.R. 889. See A. Downes (1997) 17 L.S. 286 and P. Craig (1997) 113 L.Q.R. 67.

[118] See P. Craig and G. de Burca, *EU law: Text, Cases and Materials* (4th edn, Oxford, 2007) Ch.9, especially 328–342 and T. Tridimas (2001) 38 C.M.L.R. 301.

[119] [1996] Q.B. 404.

[120] [1996] Q.B. 404 at 499, para.51. See also *Norbrook Laboratories Ltd v Ministry of Agriculture, Fisheries and Food* [1998] 3 C.M.L.R. 809 paras 106–111; *R. v H.M. Treasury Ex p. British Telecommunications* [1996] 2 C.M.L.R. 217 para.39; *R. v MAFF Ex p. Hedley Lomas* [1996] 2 C.M.L.R. 391, para.25, and *Dillenkofer and Others v Germany* [1996] 3 C.M.L.R. 469 para.24. See W. van Gerven (1996) 45 I.C.L.Q. 507. The court also warned at 503 (para.87) that a more flexible approach towards compensation might be required, notably in relation to damages for loss of profit. However, the Court of Appeal in *Devenish Nutrition Ltd v Sanofi-Aventis SA* [2008] EWCA Civ 1086, [2009] Ch 390 recently held that purely compensatory damages were sufficient for the purpose of safeguarding the rights of private persons under art.81 of the EC Treaty (now art.101, TFEU) and rejected a claim for restitutionary damages.

[121] For a recent example, see *Poole v HM Treasury* [2007] EWCA Civ 1021; [2008] 1 All E.R. (Comm) 1132: Council Directive 73/239 did not intend to grant rights to Lloyds underwriting names.

[122] Recent case law has stated that State liability will also arise due to violations of EU law by national courts of last instance: see *Köbler v Austria (C224/01)* [2004] Q.B. 848 (ECJ) and *Traghetti del Mediterraneo SpA (In Liquidation) v Italy* (C-173/03) [2006] All E.R. (EC) 983; [2006] 3 C.M.L.R. 19 (ECJ).

has shown a manifest and grave disregard to the limits of its discretion.[123] Where such conditions exist, States must provide remedies which are no less favourable than rules applying to similar claims based on national law, and the rules must not be such as in practice to make it impossible or excessively difficult to obtain reparation.[124] Subject to these principles of equality and effectiveness, it remains for the national court to find the facts, decide whether the breach of European law is sufficiently serious[125] and determine whether there is a direct causal link between the breach and the damage suffered.[126] There is no precondition that the claimant should have exhausted all domestic remedies before relying on this cause of action.[127]

It remains a moot point how this fits into the tort of breach of statutory duty. Three main options exist. Either breach of European legislation should be treated as a tort in its own right (which is unlikely), breach of statutory duty should evolve as a tort according to the demands of European law, or breach of European legislation should be treated as a separate category of liability within breach of statutory duty, whose rules should remain unchanged. At present, the third option seems to be adopted.[128] *R. v Secretary of State for Transport Ex p. Factortame (No.7)*[129] confirms that, for limitation purposes at least, the action will be treated as a claim for breach of statutory duty, although Judge Toulmin Q.C. remarked that:

> "[i]t may well be that the term 'Eurotort' is apt to describe the particular characteristic in *Brasserie du Pêcheur* to -differentiate it from the somewhat different requirements under English domestic law."[130]

The court rejected the argument that such claims could be classified as misfeasance in public office.[131]

## VICARIOUS LIABILITY

**7–022**  This is a different concept from the two forms of liability examined above. It is not a tort in its own right, but a rule of responsibility which renders the defendant liable for the torts committed by another. The commonest example is that of an employer for its employees. It therefore fits

---

[123] See *Brasserie du Pêcheur v Germany; R. v Secretary of State for Transport Ex p. Factortame (No.4)* [1996] Q.B. 404 and *R. v Secretary of State for Transport Ex p. Factortame (No.5)* [2000] 1 A.C. 524.

[124] [1996] Q.B. 404 at 504, para.90.

[125] See *R v Secretary of State for Transport Ex p. Factortame (No.5)* [2000] 1 A.C. 524, where the House of Lords found that the Government's breach of EC law in enacting the Merchant Shipping Act 1988 which prevented foreign nationals from fishing in British waters was "sufficiently serious".

[126] The national courts may also determine whether the European legislation provides individual rights provided that the interpretation amounts to an acte clair: *Three Rivers District Council v Bank of England (No.3)* [2003] 2 A.C. 1.

[127] *Spencer v Secretary of State for Work and Pensions* [2008] EWCA Civ 750; [2009] Q.B. 358.

[128] For criticism, see Stanton (2004) 120 L.Q.R. 324, 329–330: "The Eurotort [should] simply . . . be classified as a tort in domestic proceedings and the repeated references to breach of statutory duty are a redundancy."

[129] [2001] 1 W.L.R. 942, QBD (T & CC), Judge Toulmin Q.C. See also *Spencer v Secretary of State for Work and Pensions* [2008] EWCA Civ 750: action accrues from the time that claimants suffered personal injuries—Limitation Act 1980 s.2 applies.

[130] [2001] 1 W.L.R. 942, para.176.

[131] See the now leading case on this intentional tort: *Three Rivers District Council v Bank of England (No.3)* [2003] 2 A.C. 1, which imposes liability for a deliberate abuse of power by a public official. See also *Watkins v Secretary of State for the Home Department* [2006] UKHL 17; [2006] 2 A.C. 395 (requires proof of damage) and, more generally, Ch. 11.

neatly into this chapter and will be dealt with solely in this context. Other examples of vicarious liability include the liability of a firm for the torts of partners.[132]

Vicarious liability is essentially a rule of convenience. It does not mean that the tortfeasor (X) is not personally liable for his negligence, but that the claimant has the choice to sue X or his employer (Y) and generally, the claimant will sue Y, because Y has the deeper pocket. The House of Lords has confirmed that the employer may seek to recover damages from the employee who committed the tort,[133] but in practice, this does not happen. Employers' liability insurers have entered into a "gentlemen's agreement" not to pursue actions against employees except where there has been evidence of collusion or wilful misconduct.[134] This, of course, contradicts completely the idea of corrective justice, discussed in Ch.1, that only those at fault should pay compensation in tort.

Yet, the vicarious liability of an employer is limited in application. It is confined first to "employees", and secondly to acts committed in the course of employment. An employer is not responsible if the employee's negligent act does not relate to his or her position, for example, where the employee (X) negligently crashes his car into the claimant whilst driving home from work. This has led to subtle distinctions, which will be discussed below.

To establish vicarious liability against an employer,[135] the claimant must show all three of the following:

- The employee committed a tort;

- The existence of an employer/employee relationship;

- The employee acted in the course of his or her employment when committing the tort in question.

We examine these requirements below.

## (1) The employee committed a tort

This may be considered obvious, but is worth noting. If the employee is not liable in tort, **7–023** then it is pointless suing the employer, as there is nothing for the employer to be vicariously liable for. The claimant must therefore prove that the employee's conduct satisfies all the requirements of the tort in question.

---

[132] Partnership Act 1890 s.10. See *Dubai Aluminium Co Ltd v Salaam* [2002] UKHL 48; [2003] 2 A.C. 366 (HL): firm of solicitors liable for partner's dishonest participation in a fraud. Section 10 covers both common law and equitable wrongs. Vicarious liability has also been linked with the concept of agency. For an attempt to use agency to extend the liability of an (insured) car owner, see *Morgans v Launchbury* [1973] A.C. 127, HL. In exceptional circumstances, where the owner of the vehicle retains control and has an interest in the purpose for which the vehicle is being used, the courts have been prepared to find the owner of the vehicle liable for the torts of the driver: see *Ormrod v Crosville Motor Services Ltd* [1953] 1 W.L.R. 1120 (CA), confirming the judgment of Devlin J. [1953] 1 W.L.R. 409.

[133] This may occur either for breach of an implied term in the contract of employment to use reasonable care and skill (*Lister v Romford Ice and Cold Storage Co* [1957] A.C. 555), or, because vicarious liability is treated as joint and several liability, under the Civil Liability (Contribution) Act 1978 which entitles the employer to seek a contribution from the employee with respect to his or her responsibility for the damage caused. This Act is discussed in more detail in Ch.17.

[134] See G. Gardiner (1959) 22 M.L.R. 652. Also R. Lewis (1985) 48 M.L.R. 275, 281–282.

[135] See, generally, P.S. Atiyah, *Vicarious Liability in the Law of Torts* (Butterworths, 1967) and P. Giliker, *Vicarious Liability in Tort: A Comparative Perspective* (CUP 2010).

## (2) The existence of an employer/employee relationship

7–024    This has caused some confusion, which is aggravated by the fact that most cases on the employer/employee relationship do not arise in tort, but usually in relation to employment and tax law disputes.[136] It is not enough to say that the tortfeasor was employed by the defendant. The courts draw a distinction between, on the one hand, a contract *of* service[137] or employment—where the person employed is an "employee", and, on the other hand, a contract *for* services—where the person employed is an "independent contractor". Generally, an employer is not vicariously liable for the actions of independent contractors. So, if I employ a workman to fix the reception on my television, I have entered a contract for services with an independent contractor and I would not be liable for his torts. Unfortunately, this distinction is not always so easy to draw. In recent times, the nature of employment has changed, with workers far more insecure than they have been in the past. Workers may be employed on a casual basis, or via an employment agency, or on a government scheme, and it is difficult to ascertain their exact status.[138] This difficulty is compounded by the various arrangements undertaken by workers to limit their tax liability, frequently by labelling themselves as independent contractors for this purpose. The courts, therefore, face a real challenge in distinguishing between contracts of employment and contracts for services. A number of factors can be identified as important to the courts in deciding this question, but it is fair to state that the courts generally adopt a "broad brush" approach, dependent on the facts of each particular case.[139]

*Factors identifying "employees"*[140]

7–025    **The terms of the contract.**    The courts have clearly stated that they will not be governed by the wording of the contract, but will examine the substance of the contract. In *Ferguson v Dawson*,[141] for example, it had been agreed between the parties that workers employed on a building site would be "self-employed labour only sub-contractors". By this means, the workers avoided the deduction of income tax and national insurance contributions from their weekly payments.[142] The plaintiff, who worked on the defendants' building site, argued when

---

[136]    See E. McKendrick (1990) 53 M.L.R. 770 and R. Kidner (1995) 15 L.S. 47, who both argue that the courts should recognise that the status of workers may vary according to the context in question.

[137]    Readers will find reference to employees as "servants" in case law. We prefer to avoid this old-fashioned term, and, for the sake of clarity, we use the term "employee".

[138]    See, for example, *Brook Street Bureau (UK) Ltd v Dacas* [2004] EWCA Civ 217; [2004] I.C.R. 1437 and *Cable & Wireless Plc v Muscat* [2006] EWCA Civ 220; [2006] I.R.L.R. 354, in which the Court of Appeal struggled to ascertain the status of workers hired via employment agencies, but working for one particular employer for a long period of time. In *Dacas*, for example, a local authority had contracted out its cleaning services and employed Mrs Dacas through the Brook Street agency as a cleaner for over four years. In such circumstances, the court advised that an implied contract of employment might exist between the "end user" and the worker. Subsequent decisions have adopted a cautious approach towards the implication of such a contract: see *James v Greenwich LBC* [2008] EWCA Civ 35; [2008] I.R.L.R. 302 and *Cairns v Visteon UK Ltd* [2007] I.C.R. 616 (EAT).

[139]    The question of the existence of a contract of employment will, in most cases, be considered a mixed question of law and fact for the trial judge, and an appeal court will be reluctant to intervene in the absence of an error of law or perversity: see Lord Hoffmann in *Carmichael v National Power Plc* [1999] 1 W.L.R. 2042.

[140]    Chief Constables will be vicariously liable for the torts of police officers even though they are not strictly employees: see Police Act 1996 s.88(1). Due to the discretion given to police officers, such liability may be more extensive than that of the ordinary employer, provided that the police officer in question was at least apparently acting in the capacity of a police officer: see *Weir v Bettison* [2003] EWCA Civ 111; [2003] I.C.R. 708.

[141]    [1976] 1 W.L.R. 1213. See also *Mersey Docks and Harbour Board v Coggins and Griffith (Liverpool) Ltd* [1947] A.C. 1.

[142]    The plaintiff further ensured his avoidance of PAYE tax by giving the false name "Goff".

injured that he was an employee and therefore able to sue for breach of statutory duty. The court held that in reality the relationship was indeed one of employer and employee. The defendants could dismiss the workmen, move them between sites, tell them what work to do and had provided them with tools. These factors indicated that they were employees and not independent contractors.

However, the courts have experienced some disquiet in allowing a worker, who deliberately chooses to be employed as an independent contractor to avoid tax, to turn to the courts when he or she wishes to obtain the benefit of employee protection legislation.[143] The Court of Appeal in *Young and Woods v West*[144] was sympathetic to such concerns, but maintained that the court should look to the realities of the situation in the belief that "the Inland Revenue would [not] fail to discharge their statutory duty".[145]

**Control.** In the past, the control test was the primary indicator used by the courts.[146] An **7–026** employer/employee relationship was held to exist when an employer could tell an employee what work to undertake and how it should be done. While this test is still used, it is clearly outdated in relation to modern work practices.[147] In an advanced technological age, employees are frequently expected to be able to exercise discretion and initiative in their performance. Professionals with skill and experience do not expect to be told what to do and how to act during each working day. A good example is that of a doctor in the Accident and Emergency department of a hospital.[148] It is clearly impossible for any employer to tell the doctor how to perform his or her duties. The doctor will be expected to exercise a large amount of discretion in deciding how to deal with patients. As Cooke J. commented in *Market Investigations v Minister of Social Security*[149]:

> "the most that can be said is that control will no doubt always have to be considered, although it can no longer be regarded as the sole determining factor".

**The relationship as a whole.** This is the modern approach, which encompasses the two **7–027** earlier points. The cases reveal a number of factors which the courts will consider in deciding whether an employer/employee relationship exists.[150] These include, in addition to the terms of the contract and the control test:

- the payment of wages and National Insurance contributions, etc., on a regular basis;
- an indefinite term of employment;
- a fixed place and time of performance;

---

[143] Lawton L.J. dissenting in *Ferguson v Dawson* [1976] 1 W.L.R. 1213 at 1227 held that it was contrary to public policy to allow a worker to change his or her status in such a manner and that the worker should be held to the initial bargain. See also comments in *Massey v Crown Life Assurance* [1978] 1 W.L.R. 676, CA.

[144] [1980] I.R.L.R. 201.

[145] [1980] I.R.L.R. 201 at 207 per Stephenson L.J.

[146] Originating in the judgment of Bramwell L.J. in *Yewens v Noakes* (1880) 6 Q.B.D. 530.

[147] See O. Kahn-Freund (1951) 14 M.L.R. 504 who criticises the control test as old-fashioned.

[148] See *Cassidy v Ministry of Health* [1951] 2 K.B. 343, CA.

[149] [1969] 2 Q.B. 173 at 185.

[150] See, notably, Cooke J. in *Market Investigations Ltd v Minister of Social Security* [1969] 2 Q.B. 173, 184–185 ("the matter had never been better put than by Cooke J.": Lord Griffiths in *Lee Ting Sang v Chung Chi-Keung* [1990] 2 A.C. 374 at 382, PC).

- the provision of equipment or materials by the employer;
- the degree of financial risk and investment taken by the worker;
- whether the worker can profit from his or her performance;
- whether the worker must hire his or her own assistants or replacements;
- whether the work is integrated into the business or accessory to it;[151]
- whether there are mutual obligations on both parties. (A contract of employment is indicated where there is an obligation on the employer to provide and pay for work and an obligation on the worker to be ready and willing for work).[152]

Recent cases in employment law have stressed that mutuality of obligation and control, interpreted broadly in the light of modern employment practice, should form the "irreducible minimum" of any contract of employment.[153] In the words of Elias J., in *Stephenson v Delphi Diesel Systems Ltd,*

> "The significance of mutuality is that it determines whether there is a contract in existence at all. The significance of control is that it determines whether, if there a contract in place, it can properly be classified as a contract of service, rather than some other kind of contract."[154]

On this basis, in *Market Investigations v Minister of Social Security,*[155] part-time interviewers working under short-term contracts for a market research company were held to be employees. Their employers exercised extensive control over their work and Cooke J. held that the limited discretion given to employees to decide when they would work, and the ability to work for others during the relevant period, were not inconsistent with the existence of a series of contracts of employment. In contrast, in *Ready Mixed Concrete (South East) Ltd v Minister of Pensions and National Insurance,*[156] McKenna J. held that arrangements to deliver ready-mixed concrete by "owner-drivers", paid at fixed mileage rates, were not contracts of employment. This difficult case illustrates the problem often facing the court where there are indications both ways. Against a contract of employment was the fact that the drivers had to buy their own vehicles, which were maintained at their own expense, and the fact that the drivers were described in the contracts as independent contractors. Yet in favour of a contract of employment was the high level of control exercised by the company. Vehicles were bought on hire purchase from a company associated with the defendants and had to be painted in the company's colours. The drivers were obliged to wear the company uniform and comply with the company's rules, including a prohibition on using the vehicles for any other business. Nevertheless, McKenna J.

---

[151] See Denning L.J. in *Stevenson, Jordan and Harrison Ltd v Macdonald and Evans* [1952] 1 T.L.R. 101 at 111, although it is questionable whether this does any more than restate the question.
[152] Compare the application of this test in *Nethermere (St Neots) Ltd v Taverna and Gardiner* [1984] I.C.R. 612 and *O'Kelly v Trusthouse Forte* [1984] 1 Q.B. 90.
[153] See *Nethermere (St Neots) Ltd v Taverna and Gardiner* [1984] I.C.R. 612 at 623 per Stephenson L.J., approved in *Carmichael v National Power Plc* [1999] 1 W.L.R. 2042 at 2047 per Lord Irvine L.C. and *Montgomery v Johnson Underwood Ltd* [2001] I.C.R. 819 (CA).
[154] [2003] I.C.R. 471, para.11.
[155] [1969] 2 Q.B. 173.
[156] [1968] 2 Q.B. 497.

felt that ownership of the vehicles, and the fact that the drivers took the chance of profit and bore the risk of loss, indicated that the drivers were in reality independent contractors.[157]

**Lending an employee.** One particular problem which arises is the status of employees who are hired out to work for a different company. Do such employees remain the employees of their general employer, or do they become the employees of the hirer? This will of course determine who is vicariously liable for the employees' torts. The leading case is that of *Mersey Docks and Harbour Board v Coggins and Griffith (Liverpool) Ltd.*[158] Here, the harbour board employed Newall as a crane driver. The board hired the crane, together with Newall, to a firm of stevedores on terms which stipulated that Newall was the employee of the firm, although the board continued to pay his wages and retained a power of dismissal. In loading a ship, Newall negligently injured one of the firm's employees and the question was who was liable for his actions. The House of Lords held that the harbour board remained liable. At the time of the accident, although the company instructed Newall in what work to do, they had no control as to how Newall operated the crane. Looking at all the circumstances of the case, the facts that the harbour board retained authority to control how the crane was driven and paid the wages of Newall indicated that they were still his employers. Further, it was held that the courts would generally assume that the general or permanent employer would remain the employer of the tortfeasor. Only in exceptional circumstances would the heavy burden of proof be satisfied to find the hirer liable.[159]

7–028

Lord Porter indicated that in future cases, courts should consider a number of factors, including who pays the worker's wages, who has power of dismissal, how long the alternative work lasts and the complexity of the machinery used.[160] The more complex the machinery, the more unlikely that the employee will be deemed to work for the company hiring his or her services. In contrast, where the employee is unskilled and loaned out on a labour-only contract, then the stronger the possibility that the hirer may be found vicariously liable for his or her torts. Therefore, in *Hawley v Luminar Leisure Ltd*,[161] a nightclub was found to be vicariously liable for a doorman hired under a contract for the provision of security services where the doorman could be shown to be acting under the orders of the nightclub manager.

One further alternative exists. In 2005, the Court of Appeal in *Viasystems (Tyneside) Ltd v Thermal Transfer (Northern) Ltd*[162] rejected the previously held assumption that the court must choose between employers and found the general and temporary employers jointly liable. In so doing, the court clarified that, in this situation, the role of the court was to determine who should bear responsibility for the employee's tortious acts. Where both employers exercised some form of control over the employee, then both might be liable. Here, a fitter's mate, Strang, had negligently caused a flood in a factory in which he was working. Strang and the fitter had been supplied to the subcontractors on a labour-only basis. At the time of the accident, Strang was acting on the instructions of the fitter, but both were under the

[157] See also *Todd v Adams (The Maragetha Maria)* [2002] EWCA Civ 509; [2002] 2 Lloyd's Rep 293 where the Court of Appeal held that an arrangement whereby remuneration of the crew of a fishing vessel depended solely on a share of the profits (or losses) of each trip should be characterised as a joint venture rather than a contract of service.
[158] [1947] A.C. 1.
[159] But see *Interlink Express Parcels Ltd v Night Trunkers Ltd* [2001] R.T.R. 23, CA, where the court stressed the question of control.
[160] [1947] A.C. 1 at 17.
[161] [2006] EWCA Civ 18; [2006] P.I.Q.R. P17. See also *Gibb v United Steel Companies* [1957] 1 W.L.R. 668.
[162] [2005] EWCA Civ 1151; [2006] Q.B. 510. See R. Stevens (2006) 122 L.Q.R. 201.

supervision of the subcontractors' employee, Horsley. The Court of Appeal found dual liability. Such liability is joint and several and the court found that, despite the discretion under the Civil Liability (Contribution) Act 1978 (see Ch.17), a 50/50 division would be close to a logical necessity.[163]

The court therefore has three alternatives, outlined by Rix L.J. in *Viasystems*:[164]

- The general employer is liable. Here the employee is still recognisably his employee, acting in the general employer's own sphere of operations and using his equipment, despite working for another.

- The temporary employer is liable. In this situation, an employee will be seconded to the temporary employer, usually for a substantial period of time, to perform a role embedded in that employer's organisation.

- Both employers are jointly liable. Here, the employee is likely to be contracted-out labour, selected and possibly trained by his general employer and hired out as part of his business, but employed at the temporary employer's site, using the temporary employer's equipment and subject to the temporary employer's orders.

It is still assumed that in most cases the courts will continue to find the general employer solely liable for the acts of the lent employee.[165] This was confirmed by Stanley Burnton LJ in *Biffa Waste Services Ltd v Maschinenfabrik Ernst Hesse GmbH*,[166] who emphasised that the mere right to supervise did not, without more, amount to a power to control.

## (3) The employee acted in the course of employment

**7–029**    The employer will be liable for torts committed "in the course of employment".[167] This phrase has caused considerable problems in interpretation. It has been established that the employer cannot simply argue that the employee was not employed to commit torts and was therefore acting outside the course of his or her employment. This would effectively undermine the whole concept of vicarious liability. A broader test is therefore applied. The employee is held to be acting in the course of employment if his or her conduct is authorised by the employer, or is considered to be an unauthorised means of performing the job for which he or she is employed. Whilst it is obvious that an employer will be liable for actions it has authorised,[168] the second category has proven more difficult to explain. It has now been interpreted as covering actions closely connected to the job for which the tortfeasor is employed.[169] The

---

[163] But contrast the approach of the Supreme Court of Canada in *Blackwater v Plint* (2005) 258 DLR (4th) 275, noted by J. Neyers (2006) 122 L.Q.R. 195.

[164] [2005] EWCA Civ 1151; [2006] Q.B. 510 at para.80.

[165] [2005] EWCA Civ 1151; [2006] Q.B. 510 at para.46 per May L.J.

[166] [2008] EWCA Civ 1257; [2009] Q.B. 725. Joint vicarious liability was also rejected in *Various Claimants v The Catholic Child Welfare Society; Institute of the Brothers of the Christian Schools* [2010] EWCA Civ 1106.

[167] To be actionable all necessary features of the tort must be committed in the course of employment: see *Credit Lyonnais NV v Export Credits Guarantee Department* [2000] 1 A.C. 486, HL.

[168] Although arguably the employer is primarily liable for such actions: see Lord Millett in *Lister v Hesley Hall Ltd* [2001] UKHL 22; [2002] 1 A.C. 215.

[169] See *Lister v Hesley Hall Ltd* [2001] UKHL 22; [2002] 1 A.C. 215.

"course" or "scope" of employment will depend on the facts of each particular case, but we outline below a selection of case law indicating the approach adopted by the courts.

Generally, the courts have taken a generous approach to this question. For example, in *Century Insurance v NI Road Transport Board*,[170] a driver of a petrol lorry was held to be acting in the course of his employment when he discarded a lighted match, which he had used to light a cigarette, while delivering petrol. This led to an explosion which damaged the tanker, a car, and several nearby houses. Lighting a cigarette was held to be an act of comfort and convenience which would not be treated as outside the scope of employment.

An equally broad approach was taken by the House of Lords in *Smith v Stages*.[171] This case raised the problem whether employees driving to and from work were acting within the scope of their employment. The court held that generally this will not be the case unless special circumstances exist, for example the employee is required under the contract of employment to use the employer's transport to work.[172] Equally, if the employee's job requires travel, for example because he or she is a sales rep or a gas-fitter, then such travel will be deemed to be within the course of his or her employment. However, a deviation or interruption from a journey taken in the course of employment will, unless incidental, take the employee out of the course of employment for the time being. This last point is illustrated by two cases involving tortfeasors employed to drive a horse and cart for their employers. In *Whatman v Pearson*,[173] the employee had, against strict instructions, chosen to travel home for dinner by horse and cart. His employers were held liable for the damage caused when the horse escaped due to the employee's negligence. Byles J. held that the employee was clearly acting within the general scope of his authority in dealing with the horse and cart during the day. In contrast, in *Storey v Ashton*,[174] the court held that an employee who, after business hours, had driven to a friend's house, was not in the course of employment. The trip had nothing to do with his employment and his employer was thus not held liable for the injuries suffered by the plaintiff due to the employee's negligent driving. We can see from these cases that the question is therefore one of degree.

The facts of *Smith v Stages* raised a different issue. Here, two employees who normally worked in Staffordshire had been sent to South Wales to undertake certain emergency works. They had been paid their ordinary salary to travel to and from Wales, together with their travel expenses. The employees decided to work non-stop and so return to Staffordshire earlier than anticipated. They drove back immediately on completion of the job without any sleep. A crash occurred in which both men were seriously injured. As the driver (Stages) was uninsured, his passenger sued their employer, claiming that the employer was vicariously liable for Stages' negligent driving.

The court held that the employer was vicariously liable. The employer had paid the men their wages and not merely a travel allowance for the time taken on the journey. This meant that the men were still acting in the course of their employment. This was despite the fact that the employer did not provide the car and left the mode of transport to the discretion of the

---

[170] [1942] A.C. 509. See also *Bayley v Manchester, Sheffield and Lincolnshire Ry Co* (1873) L.R. 8 C.P. 148: railway porter mistakenly pulling passenger from what he believed to be the wrong train just after the train had started to leave the station found to be in the course of his employment.

[171] [1989] A.C. 928.

[172] See Lord Goff [1989] A.C. 928 at 936–937 and Lord Lowry [1989] A.C. 928 at 955–956. This is subject, of course, to any express arrangements between employer and employee.

[173] (1868) L.R. 3 C.P. 422.

[174] (1869) L.R. 4 Q.B. 476.

men. This seems to be a policy decision ensuring that, in the absence of insurance, and in circumstances where the Motor Insurers' Bureau will not provide cover,[175] the victim is fully compensated.

The line distinguishing conduct within and outside the scope of employment can be extremely fine. A good illustration is *Staton v NCB*.[176] Here, an employee at a colliery was held to be within the course of his employment while cycling across his employer's premises at the end of the working day to collect his wages from the pay office. Finnemore J. held that it was an act incidental to his employment and, if performed negligently, his employer would be vicariously liable.

*Prohibited and criminal conduct by employees*

**7–030**     Even if the conduct in question has been expressly prohibited by the employer, this does not mean that the employee has acted outside the scope of his or her employment. Whilst this may seem unfair to employers, it would be wrong if the employer could escape liability by simply prohibiting the commission of torts in the course of employment. The test is therefore whether the prohibition limits the scope of employment (as opposed to simply directing how the employee does his or her job). This is not particularly clear, and the courts' decisions provide limited assistance.

If the prohibited conduct can be found to benefit the employer in some way, then there is authority that the courts will be willing to find the employer vicariously liable. For example, in *Limpus v London General Omnibus Co*,[177] the company's instructions not to race with, or obstruct, other buses had been disobeyed by one of its drivers who had obstructed a rival bus. This led to a collision with the plaintiff's bus, which overturned. The court found the company vicariously liable for the driver's negligent actions, on the basis that the employee's actions were simply an improper and unauthorised mode of doing an act which he was authorised to do, namely promoting the company's bus service.

More difficult are the cases where the driver of a company vehicle, contrary to express instructions, gives a lift to an unauthorised passenger. Will the employer be vicariously liable for any injury to the passenger in such circumstances? The courts' approach has not been particularly consistent. In *Twine v Bean's Express Ltd*,[178] Lord Greene M.R., arguably influenced by the fact that trespassers were owed a minimal duty of care in 1946 (see Ch.8), held that giving a lift to a hitchhiker was an act which the driver was not employed to perform. A different approach was taken by the majority of the Court of Appeal, however, in *Rose v Plenty*.[179] Here, a milkman had been warned by his employer not to allow children to assist him, nor to allow passengers on his float. In breach of these instructions, he engaged the plaintiff, aged 13, to help him. The plaintiff was injured due to the milkman's negligent driving. The majority held that if the purpose of the prohibited act was to further the employer's business, the act was in the course of employment. Scarman L.J. distinguished *Twine v Bean's*

---

[175] Lord Lowry [1989] A.C. 928 at 939 comments that the case arose because the driver was uninsured and the time limits under the Motor Insurers' Bureau agreement had not been complied with.

[176] [1957] 1 W.L.R. 893.

[177] (1862) 1 Hurl. & C. 526; 158 E.R. 993. See also *Ilkiw v Samuels* [1963] 1 W.L.R. 991 and *Kay v ITW Ltd* [1968] 1 Q.B. 140, but contrast *Beard v London General Omnibus Co* [1900] 2 Q.B. 530 (bus conductor not in the course of employment when driving bus).

[178] (1946) 62 T.L.R. 458; 175 L.T. 131. Comment: F.H. Newark (1954) 17 M.L.R. 102, 114. See also *Conway v George Wimpey & Co Ltd* [1951] 2 K.B. 266.

[179] [1976] 1 W.L.R. 141. See J. Finch (1976) 39 M.L.R. 575.

*Express Ltd* on its facts. In that case, giving a lift to another had not been a mode of doing something which the driver was employed to do. We can perhaps share the doubts of Lawton L.J. (dissenting) as to the clarity of this distinction in practice,[180] especially where there is clear authority that an act is not required to benefit an employer to be in the course of employment.[181] The answer possibly lies in the comment of Denning L.J., in *Rose v Plenty*, that following the introduction of compulsory insurance in 1972, such cases are unlikely to arise in future. This does suggest a policy decision to ensure that the injured boy obtained compensation. It must be questioned whether *Rose v Plenty* leaves the law in a satisfactory state.

Further confusion may be found in relation to the question of vicarious liability for criminal acts by employees. Whilst vicarious liability may seem surprising in this context, it should be remembered that crimes such as assault, theft and fraud are also torts, and employers have been found liable in such circumstances. In *Poland v John Parr and Sons*,[182] for example, the defendants were found liable for their employee assaulting a boy whom he believed had stolen a bag of sugar from his employer's wagon. The court held that the employee had implied authority to make reasonable efforts to protect his employer's property, and that the violence was not so excessive as to take the act outside the scope of his employment. Equally, in *Lloyd v Grace, Smith & Co*,[183] a firm of solicitors was found vicariously liable for the fraudulent activities of its managing clerk, who had defrauded a widow of her property. However, the courts have stressed that for fraudulent misrepresentation, employers will only be liable if they have given the employee actual or ostensible authority to make the statements and this authority is relied upon by the claimant.[184] There is also authority that an employer may be vicariously liable for the theft by an employee of goods entrusted to his or her care.[185] The House of Lords in *Lister v Hesley Hall Ltd*[186] reviewed the application of vicarious liability in the context of serious criminal conduct amounting to an intentional tort. Here, the warden of a home for boys with emotional and behavioural difficulties had been found guilty of systematic sexual abuse of some of the boys under his care. In the earlier case of *Trotman v North Yorkshire County Council*,[187] the Court of Appeal had refused to accept that similar miscon-

---

[180] His Lordship comments [1976] 1 W.L.R. 141 at 146 that "fine distinctions of that kind should have no place in our law, particularly in a branch of it which affects so many employers and their insurers".

[181] See *Lloyd v Grace, Smith & Co* [1912] A.C. 716 overturning *Barwick v English Joint Stock Bank* (1867) L.R. 2 Ex. 259 on this point.

[182] [1927] 1 K.B. 236. See also *Dyer v Munday* [1895] 1 Q.B. 742 and FD Rose (1977) 40 M.L.R. 420 who argues for a more liberal approach. The fact that the boy in *Poland* had fallen and had his leg amputated as a result of the injury might have encouraged a more generous approach.

[183] [1912] A.C. 716. See also *Uxbridge Permanent Benefit Building Society v Pickard* [1939] 2 K.B. 248 and *Noel v Poland* [2001] 2 B.C.L.C. 645.

[184] See *Armagas Ltd v Mundogas SA (The Ocean Frost)* [1986] A.C. 717, HL and *Kooragang Investments Pty v Richardson & Wrench* [1982] A.C. 462 (PC), but see *Dubai Aluminium Co Ltd v Salaam* [2002] UKHL 48; [2003] 2 A.C. 366.

[185] Although the Court of Appeal in *Morris v Martin* [1966] 1 Q.B. 716 found an employer liable for the employee's theft on the basis of the principles of bailment for reward, it has been suggested that this case could simply have been decided on the basis that the act was in the course of the thief's employment. In *Lister v Hesley Hall Ltd* [2001] UKHL 22; [2002] 1 A.C. 215, for example, Lord Steyn at para.19 viewed the case as "the classic example of vicarious liability for intentional wrongdoing". The fact that the employee had been entrusted with the care of the fur was considered to strengthen the argument that the theft could be considered in the course of his employment. See also *Frans Maas (UK) Ltd v Samsung Electronics (UK) Ltd* [2004] EWHC 1502; [2004] 2 Lloyd's Rep 251 and *Brink's Global Services Inc v Igrox Ltd* [2010] EWCA Civ 1208.

[186] [2001] UKHL 22; [2002] 1 A.C. 215. Comment P. Giliker (2002) 65 M.L.R. 269 and C.A. Hopkins [2001] C.L.J. 458.

[187] [1999] L.G.R. 584.

duct—the antithesis of what a carer was employed to do—could be deemed to be "in the course of his employment". The House of Lords took a different view. Where the intentional tort was closely connected to the work the perpetrator was employed to do, it would be fair and just to find his employer vicariously liable.[188] The warden in *Lister* had been employed to provide a home for the boys and supervise them day-to-day in circumstances where he and his disabled wife were often the only members of staff on the premises. Such close contact was sufficient to satisfy the court that there was a close connection between what he had been employed to do and the acts of abuse committed. If, however, the acts of abuse had been committed by a groundsman, there would have been no close connection between his job and the torts in question.

To establish this connection, then, the court will examine the nature and purpose of the job and the circumstances and context in which the acts took place. Their Lordships maintained, however, that this would not affect existing authority that private acts of passion, resentment or spite were outside the scope of employment.[189]

*The application of Lister*

7–031    *Lister* has been followed by a number of cases in which the "close connection" test has been applied. In *Dubai Aluminium Co Ltd v Salaam*,[190] work undertaken by a solicitor for a client which assisted a fraud was found by the House of Lords to be closely connected to his work. Lord Nicholls, in a helpful judgment, set out a general test in the light of the different formulations used in *Lister*:

> "Perhaps the best general answer is that the wrongful conduct must be so closely connected with acts the partner or employee was authorised to do that, for the purpose of the liability of the firm or the employer to third parties, the wrongful conduct *may fairly and properly be regarded* as done by the partner while acting in the ordinary course of the firm's business or the employee's employment."[191]

This formulation has been supported in subsequent decisions,[192] and continues to be interpreted generously. In *Mattis v Pollock (t/a Flamingo's Nightclub)*[193] the Court of Appeal found vicarious liability when a guest at a nightclub had been rendered paraplegic when stabbed by the bouncer outside the club. Although the act was one of revenge for injuries and humiliation inflicted on the bouncer some time earlier in the club by the victim's group of friends, the court

---

[188] The House noted that a test of "close connection" had been used by the Supreme Court of Canada in *Bazley v Curry* (1999) 174 D.L.R. (4th) 45 and *Jacobi v Griffiths* (1999) 174 D.L.R. (4th) 71, noted by P. Cane (2000) 116 L.Q.R. 21.

[189] See, for example, *Irving v Post Office* [1987] I.R.L.R. 289—Post Office not liable for postman writing racially offensive message on the back of an envelope addressed to his neighbours—and compare *Deatons Pty Ltd v Flew* (1949) 79 C.L.R. 370, HC Aus (beer and glass thrown in customer's face by barmaid found not to be in course of employment) with *Petterson v Royal Oak Hotel Ltd* [1948] N.Z.L.R. 136 where, in similar circumstances, the barman was found to be in the course of his employment.

[190] [2002] UKHL 48; [2003] 2 A.C. 366. Contrast *JJ Coughlan Ltd v Ruparelia* [2003] EWCA Civ 1057; [2004] P.N.L.R. 4, CA (no close connection between promotion of "preposterous" fraudulent scheme promising risk-free investment with return of 6,000 per cent per annum and ordinary course of solicitor's business).

[191] [2002] UKHL 48; [2003] 2 A.C. 366 at para.23 (his Lordship's emphasis).

[192] See, for example, *Bernard v Attorney General of Jamaica* [2004] UKPC 47; [2005] I.R.L.R. 398, *Brown v Robinson* [2004] UKPC 56, *Majrowski v Guy's and St Thomas' NHS Trust* [2006] UKHL 34, [2007] 1 A.C. 224 and *Gravil v Carroll* [2008] EWCA Civ 689; [2008] I.C.R. 1222.

[193] [2003] EWCA Civ 887; [2003] 1 W.L.R. 2158 (leave to appeal to HL refused: [2003] 1 W.L.R. 2838).

held that since the employee had been encouraged by his employer to keep order by violent behaviour, the employer would be vicariously liable for an assault linked to the incident in the club.[194] Here, much would seem to turn on the court's condemnation of the employer's behaviour. He had known of and encouraged the violent tendencies of the bouncer and so the court was able to find a close connection between the attack and what the bouncer had actually been employed to do.[195] The decision does, however, throw doubt on earlier cases such as *Warren v Henlys Ltd*[196] where the courts were more ready to classify acts of personal vengeance as outside the scope of employment. It may be argued that a preferable approach in such circumstances would be to focus on the primary liability of the employer towards the victim. This may be seen in *Att-Gen of the British Virgin Islands v Hartwell*[197] where a policeman had abandoned his post and duties, entered a crowded bar where his partner was working as a waitress, and shot at her and her companion in a fit of jealous rage with his police service revolver. The Privy Council found the police authorities were not vicariously liable for his vendetta. In the words of Lord Nicholls, "Laurent's activities had nothing whatever to do with any police duties, either actually or ostensibly."[198] The authorities were nevertheless primarily liable for entrusting a man, known to be unreliable from previous incidents, with a dangerous firearm. The public authorities owe to the public at large a duty to take reasonable care to see that police officers are suitable persons to be entrusted with dangerous weapons lest by any misuse of them they inflict personal injury, accidentally or intentionally, on other persons.

However, where the option of primary liability does not exist, the courts continue to be willing to find vicarious liability to ensure that the victim obtains damages. The recent House of Lords case of *Majrowski v Guy's and St Thomas' NHS Trust*[199] permitted a claim for vicarious liability under the Protection from Harassment Act 1997, regardless of the fact that the Act focused on the impact of the perpetrator's conduct on the victim. The court saw no reason to distinguish between breach of statutory duty and other tortious conduct—all would be subject to the "close connection" test unless vicarious liability was expressly or impliedly excluded by the statute in question.

It must be questioned, however, despite the explanation of Lord Nicholls above, how easy this test is to apply in practice. Lord Nicholls himself commented in *Dubai* that:

> "This 'close connection' test focuses attention in the right direction. But it affords no guidance on the type or degree of connection which will normally be regarded as sufficiently close to prompt the legal conclusion that the risk of the wrongful act occurring,

---

[194] Even where the employee in question had been chased out of the club by the group of friends, gone to his nearby home to fetch a knife and then had returned to the club to wreak revenge.

[195] The court was even, in such circumstances, prepared to find the employer primarily liable for the attack.

[196] [1948] 2 All E.R. 935. (Assault by garage attendant following argument over payment for petrol. Customer had called the police and told the garage attendant that he would report him to his employers, whereupon the attendant hit him.) See similar decision in *Keppel Bus v Sa'ad bin Ahmad* [1974] 1 W.L.R. 1082, PC (Comment: F.D. Rose (1975) 91 L.Q.R. 17): Bus passenger who criticised the conductor for being rude to an elderly female passenger was insulted and then struck in the eye with the ticket punch. Conductor acting outside the course of his employment. Doubt was also expressed on *Daniels v Whetstone Entertainments Ltd* [1962] 2 Lloyd's Rep 1.

[197] [2004] UKPC 12; [2004] 1 W.L.R. 1273. Contrast *Bernard v Attorney General of Jamaica* [2005] I.R.L.R. 398, PC (police authorities vicariously liable when policeman shot Bernard after announcing that he was a policeman where the employer had furthermore created the risk of shooting by giving officer revolver for use at home) and *Brown v Robinson* [2004] UKPC 56 (vicariously liable for security guard shooting unruly member of crowd).

[198] [2004] UKPC 12 at para.17.

[199] [2006] UKHL 34, [2007] 1 A.C. 224. Applied in *Green v DB Group Services (UK) Ltd* [2006] EWHC 1898, [2006] I.R.L.R. 764 (QBD).

and any loss flowing from the wrongful act, should fall on the firm or employer rather than the third party who was wronged. . . . This lack of precision is inevitable, given the infinite range of circumstances where the issue arises."[200]

In each case, therefore, the courts will face the difficult question whether the employee can "fairly" and "properly" be said to be acting in the course of employment. Some guidance may be obtained from pre-existing authority, but ultimately it will be a question of policy for the courts dependent on the extent to which they consider victims should receive the protection of vicarious liability. Unfortunately, as Longmore LJ commented in the recent case of *Maga v Birmingham Roman Catholic Archdiocese Trustees*[201] these policy rationales remain unclear:

> "Is it that the law should impose liability on someone who can pay rather than someone who cannot? Or is it to encourage employers to be even more vigilant than they would be pursuant to a duty of care? Or is it just a weapon of distributive justice. Academic writers disagree and the House of Lords in *Lister* did not give any definitive guidance to lower courts."

## Summary

**7–032**  We have seen that employers may find themselves liable for the tortious acts of their employees if they are deemed to be acting in the course of their employment. It is not necessary that the employee acts for the benefit of his or her employer, although this will support the conclusion that the employee is acting in the course of his or her employment, and not "on a frolic of their own".[202] If, however, the tortfeasor is not an employee, but an independent contractor, the employer will not generally be liable for his or her actions, unless the independent contractor has been taken on to perform a task for which the employer is directly responsible and cannot delegate responsibility. The extent of such liability will be examined below.

## Liability for the actions of independent contractors[203]

**7–033**  Whilst an employer cannot be vicariously liable for the actions of independent contractors, employers may nevertheless find themselves liable for the actions of independent contractors if they place the employer in breach of a non-delegable duty to the claimant, or the employer has authorised the independent contractor to commit a tort.[204] Examples of such non-delegable duties include the employer's duty of care to its employees (discussed above), liability under the rule in *Rylands v Fletcher* (discussed in Ch.10), and liability for works

[200] [2003] 2 A.C. 366 at 377–378. See also Judge L.J. in *Mattis* [2003] EWCA Civ 887; [2003] 1 W.L.R. 2158 at 2164: "a deceptively simple question".
[201] [2010] EWCA Civ 256; [2010] 1 W.L.R. 1441 at para.81 (Court of Appeal holding Trustees vicariously liable for sexual abuse by priest of boy who was not a member of the congregation or even a Catholic, but encouraged to do odd jobs in the church). Comment: P Giliker (2010) 126 L.Q.R 521.
[202] See Parke B. in *Joel v Morrison* (1834) 6 C. & P. 501; 172 E.R. 1338. See, for example, the recent Scottish case of *Wilson v Exel UK Ltd* 2010 S.L.T. 671: supervisor pulling pursuer's ponytail as a prank treated as "frolic" and not within course of employment.
[203] See, generally, G. Williams [1956] C.L.J. 180.
[204] *Ellis v Sheffield Gas Consumers Co.* (1853) 2 E. & B. 767; 118 E.R. 955.

conducted on or over the highway, such as occurred in the odd case of *Tarry v Ashton*,[205] where a householder was found strictly liable when a lamp attached to his house, which was adjacent to the highway, fell on a person walking past.[206] On this basis, an employer will be liable to an employee if reasonable care is not taken in providing a safe place of work, even though the problem has been created by the negligence of an independent contractor.

It should be noted, however, that the courts are not prepared to find the employer liable, even when a non-delegable duty is owed, for collateral or casual negligence by the independent contractor which is unconnected with the job the independent contractor was engaged to perform.[207] The leading example is that of *Padbury v Holliday and Greenwood Ltd*.[208] Here, a sub-contractor, engaged to place casements in windows on a building site, had negligently placed an iron tool on a window sill. The tool fell and injured a passer-by. The Court of Appeal held that placing the tool on the sill was not an action taken in the ordinary course of doing the work he was employed to do, but was an act of collateral negligence for which the defendants were not liable. The case therefore limits the scope of the employer's duty to guard against risks which are not created by the work itself. This should be contrasted with the courts' more liberal treatment of the "scope of employment", discussed above.

## Can vicarious liability be justified?

So far we have discussed the various criteria used by the courts to impose vicarious liability. In this section, we address a different issue: should we have a rule of vicarious liability in English law? It is plainly inconsistent with any idea that the person at fault should pay the claimant damages, and with the concept of corrective justice (see Ch.1). It also diminishes the deterrent effect of tort law. Why should I take care at work if any harm I cause will be paid for by my employer?[209] A number of arguments have been put forward to justify vicarious liability.[210] It has been suggested that the employer has, in effect, caused the accident by setting the whole incident in motion by negligently employing a careless employee. Alternatively, the employer takes on the employee in the pursuit of profit, and one of the "costs" of employing the employee is his or her potential to cause harm.[211] Little credit is given now to early ideas

**7–034**

---

[205] (1876) 1 Q.B.D. 314. Contrast the two Court of Appeal decisions in *Salsbury v Woodland* [1970] 1 Q.B. 324 and *Rowe v Herman* [1997] 1 W.L.R. 1390, which adopt a narrow interpretation of this category.

[206] Other examples include withdrawal of support from neighbouring land: *Bower v Peate* (1876) 1 Q.B.D. 321 and cases involving extra-hazardous acts: *Honeywill & Stein v Larkin Bros* [1934] 1 K.B. 191. Although *Honeywill* is still good law, it is more often distinguished than applied and it has been questioned whether the House of Lords would continue to accept an authority resting on the subtle distinction between what is or is not "extra-hazardous": see Brooke L.J. in *Bottomley v Todmorden Cricket Club* [2003] EWCA Civ 1575; [2004] P.I.Q.R. P18. Stanley Burnton LJ in *Biffa Waste Services Ltd v Maschinenfabrik Ernst Hesse GmbH* [2008] EWCA Civ 1257 remarked at para. 78 that the *Honeywill* case "is so unsatisfactory that its application should be kept as narrow as possible, It should be applied only to activities that are exceptionally dangerous whatever precautions are taken."

[207] But note the criticisms of this rule by Sach L.J. in *Salsbury v Woodland* [1970] 1 Q.B. 324 at 348.

[208] (1912) 28 T.L.R. 494. See also comments of Denning L.J. in *Cassidy v Ministry of Health* [1951] 2 K.B. 343 at 365. But contrast *Holliday v National Telephone Co* [1899] 2 Q.B. 392.

[209] Apart from the fact that failing to take care is unlikely to boost my employment prospects! Arguably, however, vicarious liability will encourage employers to take greater measures to prevent such accidents occurring in the first place.

[210] See P.S. Atiyah, *Vicarious Liability in the Law of Torts* (Butterworths, 1967), Ch.2 and the excellent article of G. Williams (1957) 20 M.L.R. 220, 228–235 and 437.

[211] See Lord Nicholls in *Dubai* [2002] UKHL 48; [2003] 2 A.C. 366 at para.21.

that vicarious liability rested on the fact that the employee's acts were impliedly authorised, or that the employee should have been controlled by the employer.

The most realistic explanation, perhaps, rests with the two factors of compensation and insurance.[212] Professor Glanville Williams has commented:

> "However distasteful the theory may be, we have to admit that vicarious liability owes its explanation, if not its justification, to the search for a solvent defendant".[213]

Vicarious liability ensures that the claimant sues a defendant with means, and that losses are spread efficiently via the network of compulsory employer insurance. Employers are free to spread the cost of insurance either through the price of their goods or by controlling other fixed costs, such as the level of wages.

The courts themselves have shown no particular willingness to pin down the rationale behind vicarious liability. Scarman L.J. famously in *Rose v Plenty* commented that:

> "It [is] important to realise that the principle of vicarious liability is one of public policy. It is not a principle which derives from a critical or refined consideration of other concepts in the common law".[214]

Lord Nicholls in the recent case of *Majrowski*[215] confirms the differing policy ideas which influence the courts in their decision whether or not to find vicarious liability:

> "Whatever its historical origin, this common law principle of strict liability for another person's wrongs finds its rationale today in a combination of policy factors ... Stated shortly, these factors are that all forms of economic activity carry a risk of harm to others, and fairness requires that those responsible for such activities should be liable to persons suffering loss from wrongs committed in the conduct of the enterprise. This is 'fair', because it means injured persons can look for recompense to a source better placed financially than individual wrongdoing employees. It means also that the financial loss arising from the wrongs can be spread more widely, by liability insurance and higher prices. In addition, and importantly, imposing strict liability on employers encourages them to maintain standards of 'good practice' by their employees. For these reasons employers are to be held liable for wrongs committed by their employees in the course of their employment."

## Employers' liability: conclusion

7–035    Employers' liability is a large subject. Tort law forms only a part of the potential liability of an employer. Nevertheless, it is important, particularly in the form of vicarious liability which

---

[212] See Lord Millett in *Lister* [2001] UKHL 22; [2002] 1 A.C. 215 at para.65 who comments that vicarious liability "is best understood as a loss-distribution device." Note also his Lordship's comment in *Dubai* [2002] UKHL 48; [2003] 2 A.C. 366 at para.107.

[213] G. Williams (1957) 20 M.L.R. 220 at 232. See also H.J. Laski (1916) 26 Yale L.J. 105.

[214] [1976] 1 W.L.R. 141 at 147. See also Lord Pearce in *ICI v Shatwell* [1965] A.C. 656 at 685: "The doctrine of vicarious responsibility has not grown from any very clear, logical or legal principle, but from social convenience and rough justice."

[215] [2006] UKHL 34, [2007] 1 A.C. 224 at para.9.

plays a significant role in ensuring compensation in the law of torts. Although, following the abolition of the doctrine of common employment, the employer's personal liability is no longer as important, it is still a noteworthy part of negligence liability in tort. Breach of statutory duty is a limited remedy, and until statutory drafters undertake to provide some clarity in this area of law, or a clear policy stance is taken by the Government—such as that suggested by the Law Commission in 1969—this will continue to be a confusing area of law.

# Chapter 8

## OCCUPIERS' LIABILITY

### Introduction

An occupier of premises may be liable in tort to a claimant who, whilst on those premises, suffers personal injury or property damage because the premises are in a defective or dangerous condition.[1] As in a common law negligence action, the claimant must prove the existence of a duty of care, breach of that duty, causation, and that the loss suffered is not too remote. Occupiers' liability, therefore, may be thought of simply as an aspect of the tort of negligence. The important difference, however, is that in this area of the law the question of whether or not a defendant owes a duty of care, and the question of the standard of care required of him or her are answered by reference to two statutes, namely the Occupiers' Liability Act 1957 and the Occupiers' Liability Act 1984. In summary, the 1957 Act regulates the duties owed by an occupier to "visitors" to his or her premises, whilst the 1984 Act applies to "others" who enter premises. Usually, these "others" will be trespassers.

    This chapter examines both of these statutes in detail, beginning with the Occupiers' Liability Act 1957. Before considering this Act, however, it is appropriate to give an outline of the common law which prevailed before it was passed. The old law relating to occupiers' liability was complex and uncertain. It is useful to have some understanding of the problems associated with the old law, in order to appreciate the purpose of the modern legislation. Reference to the old law is also necessary to explain some of the terminology which the modern legislation employs.

**8–001**

### The old law

Prior to the Occupiers' Liability Act 1957, the common law had distinguished between four categories of persons who entered premises. Each category of entrant was owed a different standard of care by the occupier. The distinctions between these categories were extremely fine. The basic idea, however, was that the greater the benefit which accrued to the occupier by the person's presence on the premises, the higher would be the standard of care

**8–002**

---

[1] Liability of non-occupiers for defective premises, at common law and under the Defective Premises Act 1972, is discussed in Ch.3.

owed to that person. The four categories of entrant recognised by the common law were as follows:

*(1) Contractual entrants*

**8–003**    The highest standard of care was owed to persons who entered premises in accordance with the terms of a contract made with the occupier, for example guests staying in a hotel. The occupier had a duty to see that the premises were as safe as reasonable care and skill could make them for the purposes contemplated by the contract.

*(2) Invitees*

**8–004**    Invitees at common law were persons who entered premises to pursue some "common interest" with the occupier, for example customers entering the occupier's shop. Here, the occupier was obliged to use reasonable care to protect the invitee from unusual dangers of which he or she knew or ought to have known.[2]

*(3) Licensees*

**8–005**    Where the entrant could not be said to be pursuing any "common interest" with the occupier, but the occupier had simply given his or her permission (express or implied) for the entrant to be on the premises, the entrant was classified as a licensee. Friends invited to dinner by an occupier, for example, were classified as licensees at common law. Here, the occupier merely had a duty to warn the licensee about any trap or concealed danger on the premises of which he or she had actual knowledge.

*(4) Trespassers*

**8–006**    The lowest standard of care was owed to trespassers (i.e. those entering without the permission of the occupier). Trespassers generally entered premises at their own risk. The only duty which an occupier had was a duty to refrain from any deliberate act intended to cause bodily harm to the trespasser (firing a shotgun, for example) or done with reckless disregard for the presence of the trespasser (setting a man-trap, for example).[3]

## The need for reform

**8–007**    The four categories of entrant described above were regarded by the common law as exhaustive, so that all entrants had to be classified as falling into one category or another. The case law, as it developed, presented a very muddled picture. In particular, the courts experienced difficulty in distinguishing between invitees, who had a "common interest" with the occupier, and licensees, who did not. The legalistic distinction between invitees and licensees eventually appeared artificial and unworkable. The need to revise the old rules prompted the government to appoint a Law Reform Committee, whose report was published in 1954.[4] The committee recommended that the fine distinctions under the old law should be abolished, in favour of a uniform standard of care owed to all *lawful* visitors to premises.[5] The tough attitude towards trespassers, however, was maintained, and it was not until the Occupiers'

---

[2]  See *Indermaur v Dames* (1866) L.R. 1 C.P. 274 per Willes J. at 288.

[3]  *Robert Addie & Sons (Collieries) Ltd v Dumbreck* [1929] A.C. 358.

[4]  *Occupiers' Liability to Invitees, Licensees and Trespassers*, Cmnd 9305 (1954).

[5]  *Occupiers' Liability to Invitees, Licensees and Trespassers*, Cmnd 9305 (1954), paras 78(i) and (ii).

Liability Act 1984 that unlawful entrants were given statutory protection. The committee's recommendations were given legal force in the Occupiers' Liability Act 1957.

# OCCUPIERS' LIABILITY ACT 1957

Under the Occupiers' Liability Act 1957,[6] an occupier owes a single duty to all lawful visitors, irrespective of their purpose in entering the premises. Thus, s.2(1) of the Occupiers' Liability Act 1957 states:    **8–008**

> "An occupier of premises owes the same duty, the 'common duty of care', to all his visitors . . ."

Section 2(2) goes on to define the "common duty of care", and the sections which follow set out various matters which are relevant in deciding whether the common duty of care has been discharged. Before we embark on a detailed analysis of those sections, however, it is appropriate to make a number of general observations.

## The scope of the 1957 Act

*(1) The Act covers damage to property as well as personal injury*

Like the common law which it replaced, the Act covers both personal injury caused to a visitor and damage to his or her property. The Act also applies in respect of damage to property lawfully on the premises, even where that property does not belong to a visitor.[7] Thus, if a tile falls from the roof and damages a visitor's borrowed car parked on the premises, the owner of the car may sue for that damage. The Act does not, however, apply to property which is outside the boundaries of the premises. Mocatta J., in *AMF International Ltd v Magnet Bowling Ltd*,[8] remarked that, where property was damaged, there was no reason in principle why consequential economic loss should not be recoverable.[9]    **8–009**

*(2) Liability under the Act may be limited by an express term of a contract, or by a notice given to visitors*

It should be appreciated at the outset that, to a certain extent, the Act allows an occupier to limit his or her liability to visitors. An occupier can do this by displaying a notice on the premises, or, where visitors enter under a contract, by including a term in that contract which sets the standard of care he or she owes. These matters are considered more fully towards the end of this chapter.    **8–010**

*(3) The Act is thought to apply only to the "occupancy duty"*

It is unlikely that every careless act or omission which causes loss to a visitor on an occupier's premises will give rise to a claim under the Act. Thus, if a visitor is walking up the occupier's    **8–011**

---

[6] See, generally, D. Payne, "The Occupiers' Liability Act" (1958) 21 M.L.R. 359.
[7] s.1(3)(b).
[8] [1968] 1 W.L.R. 1028.
[9] [1968] 1 W.L.R. 1028 at 1049 (on the basis that the Act makes no attempt to quantify or limit the damages recoverable).

drive and is injured by a carelessly driven car, he or she will not sue under the Act, but in ordinary common law negligence. This is because the duty of care he or she is owed has nothing to do with the fact that the accident happened on the occupier's premises.

The old common law had distinguished between situations where the claimant suffered loss because he or she fell foul of some defect in, or dangerous object on, the premises (tripping over a loose floorboard, for example, or being electrocuted by a badly wired plug) and situations where the claimant's loss was caused by some *activity* carried out on the premises (the claimant was knocked down by a car, for example). The former situation was governed by the special rules of occupiers' liability, which laid down the "occupancy duty". This duty arose where the claimant's loss could be said to result from the *state of the premises*. The latter situation, however, was governed only by the ordinary rules of negligence, which laid down the "activity duty".

It is unclear whether this distinction has survived the 1957 Act. The wording of the Act does not make it clear whether the Act regulates only the "occupancy duty", or whether it also regulates the "activity duty", and the issue has been the subject of academic debate. The problem is that there are two relevant sections of the Act, each of which appears to give a conflicting answer to the question. Section 1(2) of the Act provides that the Act shall ". . . regulate the nature of the duty imposed by law in consequence of a person's occupation or control of premises". This implies that the Act covers only the "occupancy duty". Section 1(1), on the other hand, provides that the Act shall apply ". . . in respect of dangers due to the state of the premises or to things done or omitted to be done on them". This, then, implies that the modern law of occupiers' liability also covers situations where the claimant's loss is caused by a breach of the "activity duty".

Most academic commentary suggests that the 1957 Act applies only to the "occupancy duty".[10] In other words, it covers only those situations where the claimant's loss is due to the defective or dangerous state of the premises. It appears, however, that where an activity on premises gives rise to a continuing source of danger (use of the premises for motor racing, for example), the Act may apply.[11] The true position remains undecided by the courts because, whilst the debate may be of academic interest, the principles applied in a common law negligence action arising from a harmful activity on premises are so similar to those applied under the 1957 Act that nothing turns on the distinction between the "activity duty" and the "occupancy duty" under the modern law.

Having gained some appreciation of the general scope of the Act, then, our next task must be to examine its precise wording. It is this wording that provides the mechanism by which the interest of an occupier, in maintaining the premises as he or she wishes, is to be balanced against the safety of his or her visitors. It has been said that, under the Act, an "occupier" of "premises" owes a "common duty of care" to all his "visitors". These key terms require clarification.

## Definition of "occupier"

**8–012**      Section 1(2) of the Act states that an "occupier" is simply a person "who would at common law be treated as an occupier". We must therefore examine the relevant case law. What

---

[10] A view endorsed by the Law Commission in Report No.75 *Report on Liability for Damage or Injury to Trespassers and Related Questions of Occupiers' Liability*, Cmnd 6428 (1976), para.23, cited by Neill L.J. in *Revill v Newbery* [1996] 2 W.L.R. 239 at 245. See also Stephen-Brown L.J, obiter, in *Ogwo v Taylor* [1988] A.C. 431 at 438.

[11] Law Commission Report No.75 (above).

emerges is that the courts have taken a broad approach, holding that a person will be an "occupier" if he or she has a *sufficient degree of control over the state of the premises*. A person need not have a legal estate in land to be the "occupier" of that land, nor need he or she have a right to exclusive possession.[12]

The leading case is *Wheat v E. Lacon & Co Ltd*.[13] The defendants, a brewery, owned a public house. They allowed the publican and his wife, Mr and Mrs Richardson, to live in accommodation above the pub, not as tenants, but as mere licensees. The brewery had given Mrs Richardson permission to take in paying guests in part of the upstairs accommodation, access to which was gained by an outside staircase. The staircase was dangerous because its handrail did not go all the way to the bottom, and because it was unlit. One evening, the plaintiff's husband, who was a paying guest, fell down the staircase and was fatally injured. The plaintiff sued the brewery under the 1957 Act, and the question arose whether the brewery were "occupiers" of the private part of the building.

The House of Lords held that, in the circumstances, the brewery had retained sufficient control over the upstairs part of the premises to be regarded as occupiers. Although they had granted Mr and Mrs Richardson a licence to occupy the upstairs part of the premises, they had retained the right to access that part themselves. This meant that they could still exercise some control over the state of that part of the premises. Their Lordships found that the publican, his wife and the brewery were all "occupiers" under the Act. The standard of care required of each, however, was defined by the extent to which each had control over the premises. On the facts, neither the Richardsons nor the brewery had fallen below their respective standards of care. The short handrail did not by itself make the staircase unreasonably hazardous, and they were not responsible for a stranger having caused it to become unlit by removing a light bulb.

Two important points, then, emerge from the decision in *Wheat v E. Lacon & Co Ltd*:

- There can be more than one occupier of premises;

- Where the owner of premises licenses others to occupy those premises, but retains the right to enter the premises, he or she remains an "occupier" for the purposes of the Act. This is to be contrasted with a situation where the owner grants a tenancy conferring on others exclusive possession of the premises. Here, the landlord will normally have given up control of the premises, so that he or she cannot be regarded as an occupier.

In all cases, the key question for the courts is not whether a person is in actual occupation of the premises, but whether he or she exercises control over the premises. This is clear from the decision in *Harris v Birkenhead Corp*.[14] The defendant was a local authority which had made a compulsory purchase order on a house. It then served on the owner of the house, and on a tenant who occupied it, a notice of entry under the Housing Acts, which entitled it to take possession of the house within 14 days. The local authority did not in fact take possession of the house after that time, and the tenant remained there for many weeks. Eventually the tenant departed, leaving the house uninhabited, but the local authority took no steps to assert its

---

[12] *Humphreys v Dreamland (Margate) Ltd* (1930) 144 L.T. 529; *Hartwell v Grayson Rollo and Clover Docks Ltd* [1947] K.B. 901.

[13] [1966] A.C. 552. Compare *Bailey v Armes* [1999] E.G.C.S. 21 (no occupation of a flat roof to which children gained access without the defendants' knowledge.)

[14] [1976] 1 W.L.R. 279. See also *Vodden v Gayton* [2001] P.I.Q.R. P4. (Where a private right of way ran over land, owners of the servient and dominant tenement were both occupiers for the purposes of the 1984 Act.)

possession of the house. A four and a half year-old child entered the house through an unsecured door and was injured when he fell from a second floor window.

In the Court of Appeal, the local authority argued that before it could be regarded as the "occupier" of the house, there must have been an actual or symbolic taking of possession of the house on its behalf, and that its mere *right* to take possession was insufficient. This argument was rejected. On the facts, the Court of Appeal held that the local authority became the occupier as soon as the premises were vacated. Although it could not be said that in every case a person with an immediate right to take possession of premises would be an "occupier", in these particular circumstances, actual physical possession of the premises was not necessary before the local authority could be regarded as having control of the premises.

Where an independent contractor enters premises to undertake work, whether or not this contractor becomes an occupier of the premises depends on the nature and scale of the work being undertaken. Thus, a contractor undertaking a large building development would become the occupier of the site, whilst a decorator painting a house would not.[15] Later in this chapter we shall see that where a visitor suffers loss because of a contractor's negligent work, an occupier can sometimes escape liability by arguing that he or she had delegated the work to a contractor. It does not follow, however, that entrusting work to a contractor automatically makes that contractor an occupier.

## Definition of "premises"

**8–013**    There is no explicit definition of "premises" in the Act. Section 1(3)(a), however, states that the Act regulates the obligations of persons occupying or having control over "any fixed or moveable structure, including any vessel, vehicle or aircraft". Case law has established that "premises" covers not only land and buildings, but also such structures as lifts, ladders, diving boards, scaffolding and even large digging machines.[16]

## Definition of "visitor"

**8–014**    Section 1(2) of the Act provides that a "visitor", under the Act, is simply someone who would have been either an "invitee" or a "licensee" at common law before the Act was passed. The position of contractual entrants is governed by s.5 of the Act. To a limited extent, an occupier is free to set his or her own standard of care in relation to contractual entrants, but where he or she does not do so, such entrants are treated in the same way as visitors and are owed the "common duty of care".[17] As has been said, the Act gives no protection to trespassers. It should also be remembered, of course, that the Act has no application to persons who are outside the premises.

Under the Act, the troublesome distinction between invitees and licensees is replaced by a single test: has the occupier given the entrant permission to be on the premises? In cases where the occupier has expressly given permission to enter, the matter is straightforward. In other cases, the law will sometimes say that an occupier has given *implied permission* for a person

---

[15] *Page v Read* (1984) 134 N.L.J. 723.
[16] See *Haseldine v Daw* [1941] 2 K.B. 343; *Wheeler v Copas* [1981] 3 All E.R. 405; *Ewa Perkowski v Wellington Corp.* [1959] A.C. 53; *Bunker v Charles Brand* [1969] 2 Q.B. 480.
[17] Occupiers' Liability Act 1957 s.5(1).

to be on the premises. In addition, there are certain rules which govern the status of particular types of entrant. The issues which arise may be considered under the following headings:

*Persons entering by authority of law*

By s.2(6) of the Act, persons entering premises in the exercise of a right conferred by law, for **8–015** example firemen attending a fire, or policemen executing a warrant, are treated as if they had been given permission to enter by the occupier. Strictly speaking, such cases are not cases of implied permission, but of *deemed* permission, because these persons are treated as visitors even where the occupier expressly states that he or she does not want them on the premises.

*Persons exercising rights of way*

Persons entering land in the exercise of a public[18] or private[19] right of way, or in the exercise **8–016** of a statutory right to access land for recreational purposes (conferred under the National Parks and Access to the Countryside Act 1949, or the Countryside and Rights of Way Act 2000) are not "visitors" under the Act.[20] Persons exercising private rights of way are owed a duty under the Occupiers' Liability Act 1984, which is discussed later in this chapter. Those exercising a *public* right of way, however, are only owed the limited duty which had been established at common law. Thus, the occupier is not under a duty to maintain the natural features of public rights of way which run over his or her land.[21]

*Implied permission*

It is clear that a person who enters premises in order to communicate with the occupier will be **8–017** treated as having the occupier's implied permission to be on the premises. Thus, a postman or other individual has implied permission to walk up the occupier's drive to use the letterbox, or to call at the front door, unless he or she knows, or ought to know, that this is expressly forbidden (for example, by a sign posted on the gate).[22]

Much of the case law on implied permission, however, must nowadays be seen in the context of the state of the common law when it developed. As has been noted, the common law was harsh in its treatment of trespassers. Many judges felt that the rules could produce injustice. They therefore sought to avoid the rigours of the common law in hard cases by classifying trespassers as implied licensees. This often entailed a strained interpretation of the facts.

In *Lowery v Walker*,[23] for example, the plaintiff was using a short-cut across a farmer's field when he was attacked by a horse. The farmer knew that the short-cut had been regularly used

---

[18] *Greenhalgh v British Railways Board* [1969] 2 Q.B. 286; *McGeown v Northern Ireland Housing Executive* [1995] 1 A.C. 233. See J. Murphy, "Public Rights of Way and Private Law Wrongs" [1997] Conv. 362.

[19] *Holden v White* [1982] 2 Q.B. 679.

[20] Occupiers' Liability Act 1957 s.1(4). (As amended by Countryside and Rights of Way Act 2000 s.13.)

[21] This position is now reflected in the Occupiers' Liability Act 1984 s.1(6A) (inserted by the Countryside and Rights of Way Act 2000). Persons exercising rights of way conferred by the 2000 Act are owed no duty in respect of dangers arising from natural features of the landscape or when passing through walls, fences, etc. *except* when making proper use of gates and stiles. (There may therefore be a duty to maintain gates and stiles. The existence of such a duty might be consistent with the reasoning in *McGeown v Northern Ireland Housing Executive* [1995] 1 A.C. 233, but now needs to considered in the light of s.1A. of the 1984 Act.) The Marine and Coastal Access Act 2009 inserts s.1(6AA), extending the provisions of s.1(6A) to coastal land.

[22] *Robson v Hallett* [1967] 2 Q.B. 939. For an interesting application of this principle, see *R. (on the application of Fullard) v Woking Magistrates* [2005] EWHC 2922 (2005 WL 3605690). In insisting that revocation of implied permission must be clear, to what extent does the law discriminate against the inarticulate?

[23] [1911] A.C. 10.

by the public for the past 35 years, and had protested about this, although he had never brought legal proceedings. Despite these protests, it was held that the farmer had given implied permission for people to use the short-cut. The plaintiff could therefore be classified as an implied licensee and was able to succeed in his claim. Similarly, in *Glasgow Corp v Taylor*,[24] a council's failure to fence off a poisonous plant near a children's playground made it liable in respect of a seven-year-old child who died after eating berries from the plant. The berries looked like cherries or large blackcurrants and were tempting to children. Even though the boy had no right to take the berries, or even to approach the bush, and an adult doing so might have been treated as a trespasser, the boy was treated as an implied licensee.

Now that trespassers are afforded greater protection under the Occupiers' Liability Act 1984 than was the case at common law, there is less need for the courts to resort to the idea of implied permission to do justice in hard cases. The earlier authorities, therefore, are unlikely to be followed unless the court feels that, in a particularly meritorious case, even the protection afforded by the Occupiers' Liability Act 1984 would be insufficient.

*Limitations on permission*

**8–018**    The permission given by an occupier, whether express or implied, may be limited in three ways. First, the occupier may permit a person to be in some parts of the premises but not others. Secondly, the occupier may permit the person to remain on the premises only for a certain period of time. Thirdly, the occupier may permit the person to be on the premises only for certain purposes. It is clear that where a person enters premises with permission, but that permission is subsequently expressly revoked, the law will allow a reasonable time to leave the premises, during which he or she will still be treated as a visitor.[25]

Difficulties arise when visitors stray from the permitted area. In *Gould v McAuliffe*,[26] for example, a customer in a pub, looking for an outside lavatory, wandered through an unlocked gate into a private part of the premises where she was attacked by a dog. The argument that she had become a trespasser was rejected. It was held that where an occupier wishes to exclude a visitor from an area into which visitors are likely to wander, he or she must take reasonable steps to inform the visitor that the area is out of bounds. On the facts, because there was no notice informing the plaintiff that the area beyond the gate was private, this had not been done. Whether it is necessary to post a notice excluding visitors from a particular area will, of course, depend on the facts of each case. Such a notice will not be necessary in respect of a part of the premises to which no one would reasonably expect a visitor to go.[27]

In determining whether or not a person is a visitor, it is relevant to consider the purpose for which that person is permitted to be on the premises. As Scrutton L.J. put it, in *The Carlgarth*[28]:

> "When you invite a person into your house to use the staircase, you do not invite him to slide down the banisters."

---

[24] [1922] 1 A.C. 44. Compare *Edwards v Railway Executive* [1952] A.C. 737.
[25] *Robson v Hallett* [1967] 2 Q.B. 939; *Kay v Hibbert* [1977] Crim. L.R. 226; *R. (on the application of Fullard) v Woking Magistrates* [2005] EWHC 2922 (2005 WL 3605690).
[26] [1941] 2 All E.R. 527, CA.
[27] *Mersey Docks and Harbour Board v Procter* [1923] A.C. 253.
[28] [1927] P. 93 at 110. For a real life scenario closely analogous to Scrutton L.J.'s example, note the facts of *Keown v Coventry Healthcare NHS Trust* [2006] 1 W.L.R. 953, discussed later in this chapter.

Thus, where a person is invited for one purpose (to sleep in a bed) and starts to pursue an activity unrelated to that purpose (jump up and down on the mattress), that person may cease to be a visitor, even though he or she has not strayed from the permitted area. To understand why this is so, it must be remembered that the Act treats as "visitors" people who were, under the old law, licensees or invitees. A licence to be on premises will almost always have implied conditions. When a person breaches one of these conditions, he or she ceases to be a licensee. It therefore follows that he or she ceases to be a "visitor". It should be noted that the permission to use the premises for the purposes in question must be given *by the occupier*.[29] Permission given by someone else is not sufficient.

## The "common duty of care"

Section 2(2) of the Act defines the "common duty of care" as follows:                   **8–019**

> "The common duty of care is a duty to take such care as in all the circumstances of the case is reasonable to see that the visitor will be reasonably safe in using the premises for the purposes for which he or she is invited or permitted by the occupier to be there."

It should be noted that it is the *visitor*, rather than simply the *premises* which must be reasonably safe. It follows that if the occupier invites or permits, say, a blind man to come onto the premises, he or she must take greater care for that visitor's safety than would be the case in relation to a sighted person.[30] In this regard, it should be noted that liability under the Act can arise where an occupier merely *fails to protect* a visitor from a danger on the premises. The occupier does not need to have created that danger in order to be liable. Thus, the Act imposes liability for mere omissions in a way which is unusual in English law. It imposes on an occupier a duty to his or her visitor which is very different from the duty owed at common law by a bystander to a stranger. It will be recalled that Lord Keith, in *Yuen Kun Yeu v Att-Gen of Hong Kong*,[31] made it clear that there is no liability at common law "on the part of one who sees another about to walk over a cliff with his head in the air, and forbears to shout a warning". This is because, although the danger is foreseeable, there is insufficient "proximity" (closeness of relationship) between the claimant and the defendant. In cases of occupiers' liability, however, the position is different. The fact that the occupier has invited or permitted the claimant to be on the premises creates the necessary degree of proximity. Therefore, the occupier must protect the visitor from danger, even though he or she has not caused the danger by any positive act.

## Discharging the common duty of care

In deciding whether or not the occupier is in breach of the common duty of care, the courts    **8–020** will have regard to the same general factors which would be considered in a common law negligence action. These general factors were discussed in Ch.5. They include the likelihood

---

[29] See Occupiers' Liability Act 1957 s.2(2), discussed below.
[30] See e.g. *Atkins v Butlins Skyline Ltd* [2006] 1 C.L. 510 (Taunton County Court). (The defendant holiday camp operators were liable to a blind visitor who was trapped by closing lift doors that were safe for sighted visitors.)
[31] [1988] A.C. 175 at 192 (see Ch.2).

of a risk materialising, the magnitude of the loss if the risk does materialise, and the cost and practicality of taking precautions.[32] In addition, however, the Act expressly refers to a number of more *specific* factors which are to be considered when deciding the question of breach of duty. In particular, the Act contains a provision relating to warnings, and another governing the extent to which an occupier will be liable for dangers created by independent contractors. These provisions are discussed later in the chapter. First, we must examine the extent to which an occupier can rely on a visitor to look after his or her own safety on the premises.

Section 2(3) of the Act provides that, in deciding whether the common duty of care is discharged, it is relevant to consider "the degree of care, and of want of care, which would ordinarily be looked for in such a visitor". For good measure, however, that subsection goes on to refer to two specific types of visitor—children and professionals—and makes it clear what degree of vigilance for their own safety an occupier should expect from each type of visitor. It is convenient to deal with each type of visitor in turn.

## Children[33]

**8–021**    Section 2(3)(a) of the Act provides:

> "an occupier must be prepared for children to be less careful than adults."

Children often fail to appreciate dangers that are obvious to adults. Their natural curiosity often leads them into dangerous situations. In discharging his or her duty of care, therefore, an occupier must bear in mind that children tend to be attracted to certain objects, unaware that they are dangerous. This, of course, was what happened in *Glasgow Corp v Taylor*[34] (discussed above) where the poisonous berries, which looked like blackcurrants, were said to be an "allurement" to small children. Similarly, in *Jolley v Sutton LBC*,[35] the council was held to be in breach of its duty of care by allowing an old wooden boat, which was an enticing play area for children, to be left abandoned on its land. A 13-year-old boy (Jolley) and his friend had attempted to repair the boat to take it to Cornwall to sail, and Jolley had been injured when the boat, which had been jacked up, fell on him. Overturning the Court of Appeal decision which had held the activities of the boys too remote a consequence of breach,[36] the House of Lords took the view that the courts should not underestimate the ingenuity of children in finding unexpected ways of doing mischief to themselves and others.[37] On this basis, their Lordships restored the view of the trial judge that the type of accident and injury which occurred was reasonably foreseeable in the context of teenage boys attracted to an obviously abandoned boat.

---

[32] Cases therefore tend to turn on their own particular facts. For some modern examples of various factual scenarios, see: *Cole v Davis-Gilbert* [2007] EWCA Civ 396, (2007) 151 S.J.L.B. 335; *Lewis v Six Continents Plc* [2005] EWCA Civ 1805; *Wattleworth v Goodwood Road Racing Co Ltd* [2004] EWHC 140, [2004] P.I.Q.R. P25; *Moores v Snow Dome Ltd* [2005] C.L.Y. 4195; *Tedstone v Bourne Leisure Ltd (t/a Thoresby Hall Hotel & Spa)* [2008] EWCA Civ 654.

[33] See R. Kidner, "The Duty of Occupiers towards Children" (1988) 39 N.I.L.Q. 150.

[34] [1922] 1 A.C. 44.

[35] [2000] 1 W.L.R. 1082, HL; [1998] 1 W.L.R. 1546, CA.

[36] On remoteness generally, see Ch.6.

[37] Compare, however, the approach of the CA in *Keown v Coventry Healthcare NHS Trust* [2006] 1 W.L.R. 953. (Where the danger is obvious to a child, the court should not ignore a child's choice to incur that danger just because he is a child.)

The decision in *Jolley*, then, makes it clear that the courts will apply the rules of occupiers' liability generously towards children, particularly in relation to serious personal injury.[38] However, an occupier will not be liable for every action of a child on his or her premises. This is especially true in the case of very young children, for whom even the most innocuous objects on premises may present a danger. An occupier cannot be expected to ensure that his or her premises are as safe as a nursery for any visiting toddler. If some provision were not made in law to limit the scope of an occupier's duty to very young visitors, the occupier might be apt to exclude them from the premises for fear of liability. Such a solution would not be socially acceptable. The law therefore provides that an occupier is entitled to assume that the behaviour of very young children will be supervised by a responsible adult. The leading case is *Phipps v Rochester Corp.*[39]

In *Phipps*, the plaintiff was a five-year-old boy. Accompanied by his sister, aged seven, he went out collecting blackberries on a large open space and fell into a deep trench, breaking his leg. The trench, which would have been an obvious danger to an adult, had been dug by the defendants, who were developing the site. Devlin J., after reviewing the relevant authorities, concluded that where children of "tender years" were concerned, an occupier was entitled to consider how a prudent parent or guardian of the child should behave. As Devlin J. remarked:

> "it would not be socially desirable if parents were, as a matter of course, able to shift the burden of looking after their children from their own shoulders to those of persons who happen to have accessible bits of land".[40]

Prudent adults would not have allowed two small children to roam over the site unaccompanied. In the circumstances, therefore, the occupiers of the site escaped liability. Their only duty to very young children was to ensure that they were reasonably safe on the site when accompanied by a responsible adult, and on the facts, this duty had been discharged.

Whether or not an occupier is entitled to expect that very young children on his or her premises will be accompanied by an adult depends on the facts of any given case. Essentially, two matters are relevant, namely the age of the child and the nature of the premises. Thus, a prudent parent should realise that whilst only very young children will be at risk in a playground, a building site, such as that in *Phipps*, would present dangers to older children if unaccompanied. It appears from the decision in *Simkiss v Rhondda BC*,[41] however, that an occupier is required to take account of the social habits of the neighbourhood in which his or her premises are situated. Thus, where a piece of land becomes locally recognised as a playground for unaccompanied small children, an occupier must ensure that these children are reasonably safe.

## Professional visitors

Section 2(3)(b) of the Act provides:    **8–022**

---

[38] Justin Jolley had suffered serious spinal injuries rendering him paraplegic.

[39] [1955] 1 Q.B. 450.

[40] [1955] 1 Q.B. 450 at 472.

[41] (1983) 81 L.G.R. 460. See also *Bourne Leisure Ltd (t/a Briish Holidays) v Marsden* [2009] EWCA Civ 671. (Owner of a holiday site under no obligation to draw parents' attention to precise location of a pond that was an obvious danger to small children. Giving the parents a plan showing the pond was sufficient.)

"an occupier may expect that a person, in the exercise of his calling, will appreciate and guard against any special risks ordinarily incident to it, so far as the occupier leaves him free to do so."

This subsection gives statutory force to the position which had been established at common law.[42] An occupier may expect that a skilled visitor, employed to undertake work on the premises, will take appropriate precautions against risks ordinarily associated with his or her work. The subsection does not, of course, cover risks not normally associated with the job. Thus, in *Eden v West & Co*[43] the defendants were liable where a carpenter removed a window and the brickwork above it collapsed on him—the risk of this happening in a modern property was extraordinary and the defendants ought therefore to have warned him that the brickwork was not properly supported.

The leading case is *Roles v Nathan*.[44] (This is also an important case on warnings, discussed below.) Two chimney sweeps had been engaged to clean the flue of a boiler and to seal up some vent holes in the flue so that it would operate more efficiently. The defendant's heating engineer had repeatedly warned the sweeps about the dangers of being overcome by carbon monoxide fumes if they worked on the flue while the boiler was lit. He gave evidence, however, that the sweeps had been inclined to dismiss his warnings, taking the view that *they* were the experts and could look after themselves. The sweeps completed most of their work, telling the man in charge of the boiler room that they would return to finish the job the following day. In fact, the sweeps returned later that evening, by which time the boiler had been lit, and were overcome by fumes while working in the flue.

A majority of the Court of Appeal held that the occupiers were not liable for the death of the sweeps. As Lord Denning M.R. put it:

"When a householder calls in a specialist to deal with a defective installation on his premises, he can reasonably expect the specialist to appreciate and guard against the dangers arising from the defect. The householder is not bound to watch over him to see that he comes to no harm."[45]

This view accords with common sense—an occupier would not receive a warm reception if he or she began to tell a specialist contractor all about the usual risks involved in his or her job. Therefore, since it would be inappropriate for the occupier to give a warning of those risks, the occupier should not be liable if the risks materialise. Both Harman L.J. and Pearson L.J. agreed with Lord Denning's statement of principle, although Pearson L.J., who dissented, took a different view of the facts. On his Lordship's view, the risk of the boiler being lit was not a risk which was "ordinarily incident" to the sweeps' calling. Rather, it was a special and unusual risk. This was shown by the fact that the defendants had felt it necessary to give repeated warnings about its occurrence.

Sometimes, professional visitors will suffer injury as a result of a danger on the premises, even though they have exercised all due care and skill in taking care of their own safety. In

---

[42] See *Christmas v General Cleaning Contractors* [1952] 1 K.B. 141, affirmed [1953] A.C. 180, and *Bates v Parker* [1953] 2 Q.B. 231.
[43] [2003] P.I.Q.R. Q2.
[44] [1963] 1 W.L.R. 1117.
[45] [1963] 1 W.L.R. 1117 at 1123.

such cases, the courts have held that the mere fact that the visitor is possessed of special skill will not, by itself, entitle the occupier to escape liability. The essential point to grasp is this: the fact that the visitor has special skill does not mean that he or she has *voluntarily assumed the risks* associated with the task, it simply means that he or she is expected to take greater care than would be taken by a lay person in relation to those risks. Thus, in *Ogwo v Taylor*,[46] a fireman injured whilst fighting a fire in a confined space was able to recover from an occupier who had negligently started the fire on the premises. The House of Lords held that whilst an occupier was entitled to expect that the fireman would use his professional skill in tackling a fire, if, despite exercising all due skill, the fireman suffered injury, the occupier would be liable. (It should be noted that *Ogwo v Taylor* was decided on the basis of common law negligence principles. The key finding was that the occupier had put the fireman at risk by negligently *creating* a danger on his premises.)

## Giving a warning of the danger

Section 2(4)(a) of the Act provides that in deciding whether or not an occupier has discharged the common duty of care, the fact that he or she has warned visitors of the danger is a relevant consideration. The subsection goes on to state, however, that:    **8–023**

> "the warning is not to be treated without more as absolving the occupier from liability, unless in all the circumstances it was enough to enable the visitor to be reasonably safe."

Thus, a distinction must be drawn between a mere warning of the danger, which offers no assistance as to how to avoid the danger, and a warning which *enables the visitor to be reasonably safe*. Under the Act, only the latter type of warning will completely discharge the common duty of care. Again, the leading authority is *Roles v Nathan*,[47] in which Lord Denning M.R. explained the position as follows:

> "Supposing, for instance, that there was only one way of getting into and out of premises, and it was by a footbridge over a stream which was rotten and dangerous. According to [the old law] the occupier could escape all liability to any visitor by putting up a notice: 'This bridge is dangerous', even though there was no other way by which the visitor could get in or out, and he had no option but to go over the bridge. In such a case, s.2(4) makes it clear that the occupier would nowadays be liable. But if there were two footbridges, one of which was rotten, and the other safe a hundred yards away, the occupier could still escape liability, even today, by putting up a notice: 'Do not use this footbridge. It is dangerous. There is a safe one further upstream'. Such a warning is sufficient because it does enable the visitor to be reasonably safe."

The chimney sweeps in *Roles v Nathan* had been given clear warnings of the danger by the defendant's heating engineer. According to Lord Denning M.R., with whom Harman L.J. agreed, these warnings enabled the sweeps to be reasonably safe, by making it clear that the danger could be avoided if they desisted from working in the flue when the boiler was alight.

---

[46] [1988] A.C. 431, HL, approving *Salmon v Seafarer Restaurants Ltd* [1983] 3 All E.R. 729.
[47] [1963] 1 W.L.R. 1117 at 1124.

Pearson L.J, however, took a different view, holding that the warnings were of little value to the sweeps, given that the defendant's agents had themselves ignored the advice of the heating engineer and had lit the boiler before the sweeps had completed their work.

Not only must the warning tell the visitor what to do in order to avoid the danger, it must be given in terms which are comprehensible to the visitor. It is recognised that children do not always give warnings the attention they deserve, so that an occupier may be required to take other steps, such as the erection of a barrier, to discharge the common duty of care.

A number of other points should be noted about s.2(4)(a). First, the section refers to a warning given *by the occupier*.[48] Strictly speaking, it must follow that a warning given by someone other than the occupier is prima facie insufficient to discharge the occupier's duty of care, even if it enables the visitor to be reasonably safe. This being said, a warning given to a visitor by a third party will, of course, form part of "all the circumstances of the case" and as such (according to s.2(2) of the Act) will be a relevant consideration. Secondly, it should be noted that the words "without more" raise the possibility that a warning which does not by itself enable the visitor to be reasonably safe might be regarded as sufficient to discharge the common duty of care when taken together with some other factor in the case (the presence of a guard rail, for example). Thirdly, note that a sign stating that "visitors enter at their own risk" is not a warning at all, but an attempt to invoke the defence of voluntary assumption of risk. Similarly, a sign declaring that "no responsibility is accepted for any loss or damage on the premises" is not a warning, but an attempt to exclude liability. These matters are discussed towards the end of this chapter.

Above, we have dealt with the effect of a warning in situations where the occupier has decided to give one. But warnings can be important in a different context: sometimes, the claimant's case is that the defendant's breach of the common duty of care consists of *failing to give a warning* in circumstances where one should have been given. In such cases, the courts have repeatedly stressed that an occupier has no duty to warn visitors about *obvious* risks. Thus, in *Darby v National Trust*[49] where the claimant drowned in a pond of deep murky water, the defendants were under no duty to place notices around the pond warning of this risk—there were no hidden dangers in the pond, and the risk of drowning in deep murky water was one which would have been obvious to any adult who went into the pond. Similarly, in *Blackpool and Fylde College v Burke*,[50] when a pile of badly stacked classroom chairs fell on a student, the college was under no duty give warnings and instructions about how to stack the chairs, because the way the chairs should be stacked was obvious, as was the risk of their collapsing if this was not properly done.

## Entrusting work to independent contractors

**8–024**      We have seen the extent to which independent contractors, who are possessed of special skill, can be expected to look after their own safety while they are on the premises. Here, we are concerned with a different situation, namely where a visitor (other than the independent

---

[48] In *Roles v Nathan* [1963] 1 W.L.R. 1117, this requirement was satisfied because the heating engineer who gave the warnings was the defendant's agent.

[49] [2001] P.I.Q.R. P27. See also: *Mills-Davies v RSPB* [2005] C.L.Y. 4196 (QBD); *Clare v Perry (t/a Widemouth Manor Hotel)* [2005] EWCA Civ 39, (2005) 149 S.J.L.B. 114.

[50] [2001] EWCA Civ 1679. See also *Poppleton v Trustees of the Portsmouth Youth Activities Committee* [2008] EWCA Civ 646; *Evans v Kosmar Villa Holiday Plc* [2007] EWCA Civ 1003.

contractor) suffers loss because of the independent contractor's negligence in carrying out work for the occupier. The visitor's loss may result from the manner in which the contractors conduct themselves whilst on the premises (the visitor trips over a toolbox left in a corridor), or it may result from a defect in the premises left by poor workmanship (the visitor falls down a staircase negligently erected by the contractors). Under the doctrine of vicarious liability (discussed in Ch.7) an employer is not normally responsible for the negligent actions of independent contractors. Can an occupier therefore escape all blame for dangers created by independent contractors on the premises? The House of Lords decision in *Thomson v Cremin*,[51] in 1941, had suggested that an occupier would usually remain personally responsible for the shortcomings of contractors employed on the premises, but this decision was criticised by the Law Reform Committee in 1954. The committee's recommendations were given statutory force in s.2(4)(b) of the Act.

In summary, s.2(4)(b) provides that where a visitor suffers damage due to "the faulty execution of any work of construction, maintenance or repair"[52] by an independent contractor, the occupier is not normally liable if, in all the circumstances of the case:

- it was reasonable to entrust the work to an independent contractor;

- the occupier took reasonable steps to satisfy himself or herself that the contractor was competent; and

- the occupier took reasonable steps to satisfy himself or herself that the work had been properly done.

The first of these requirements has posed few problems for the courts, who appear to have taken the view that it will be reasonable to entrust work to a contractor whenever that work is of a type which is normally undertaken by contractors. As to the second requirement, a contractor will usually be taken to be competent unless the occupier is aware of facts which suggest incompetence (faulty work carried out in the past, for example). In some circumstances, however, it may be appropriate for an occupier to check a contractor's competence by seeing that he or she is a member of a relevant trade association, holds relevant qualifications, is suitably experienced and is insured. Such circumstances arose in *Bottomley v Todmorden Cricket Club*,[53] where the defendants were held liable for the activities of independent contractors providing a fireworks display—the hazardous nature of the activity placed the defendants under a duty to take positive steps to check the competence of the contractors, and, in particular, to check whether they were insured. In *Gwilliam v West Hertfordshire NHS Trust*[54] the defendant hospital had engaged a contractor to operate a "splat-wall" at a fund-raising event. (A "splat-wall" is an amusement whereby participants stick themselves to a wall with Velcro by bouncing off a trampoline.) The hospital had selected the contractor's name from the phone

---

[51] (1941) [1953] 2 All E.R. 1185.

[52] The courts have interpreted these words broadly. It was held in *Ferguson v Welsh* [1987] 1 W.L.R. 1553, for example, that the section is applicable to demolition work, even though this is, of course, the complete antithesis of "construction, maintenance and repair".

[53] [2003] EWCA Civ 1575, [2004] P.I.Q.R. P18.

[54] [2003] Q.B. 443. But see *Naylor v Payling* [2004] EWCA Civ 560, [2004] P.I.Q.R. P36. (The duty to ensure that contractors carry public liability insurance is not a general "free-standing" duty. It only arises in special circumstances such as those in *Bottomley* and *Gwilliam*, where the defendant is organising a one-off event and enquiries about the contractor's insurance position are a reasonable means of assessing whether the contractor is likely to be competent.). See also *Glaister v Appleby-in-Westmorland Town Council* [2009] EWCA Civ 1325.

book, and had paid him an extra £100 to operate the amusement, so as to benefit from his public liability insurance. The claimant was injured by the contractor's negligence, and it turned out that his public liability insurance had expired four days before the event. In an action against the hospital, a majority of the Court of Appeal held that, whilst the hospital had been under a duty to inquire into the contractor's insurance position, it would have been unreasonable for them to actually check his insurance certificate. Therefore, by accepting the contractor's assurances that he was insured, the hospital had discharged its duty of care to the claimant.[55]

Some difficulty for the courts has arisen in deciding whether and when it will be reasonable for an occupier to inspect a contractor's work personally, to see that it has been properly done. Two matters are relevant, namely the nature of the work undertaken and the character of the occupier. Thus, the more complex and technical the work, the less reasonable it is for the occupier to inspect it in person. Where, however, the occupier is a specialist company or a local authority, a more detailed inspection may be called for than would be required of a lay person. Two cases, both decided prior to the 1957 Act, illustrate the principles which the courts will apply.

In *Woodward v Mayor of Hastings*,[56] a pupil was injured when he slipped on a snow-covered step at school. The local authority was not able to escape liability by claiming that it had delegated the task of cleaning the step to the school cleaner who, it was argued, was an independent contractor.[57] The cleaning of the step was not a specialist task, and the danger was obvious. The occupiers therefore had a duty to inspect the cleaner's work to see that it had been properly done. This seems a particularly harsh decision, but perhaps may be explained due to the obvious risk of danger to children on an icy day requiring the school to check that such work was properly done, and the courts' sympathy towards child visitors.

In *Haseldine v Daw*,[58] on the other hand, the plaintiff was fatally injured when a lift in a block of flats fell to the bottom of its shaft, due to the negligence of independent contractors employed to repair the lift. It was held that the occupier had discharged his duty to visitors by engaging an apparently competent firm of engineers to maintain the lift. Because the work carried out on the lift was of a technical nature, the occupier could not be expected to ensure that it had been properly done. It was reasonable for him to leave the maintenance of the lift to an expert. Scott L.J. observed that, if the occupier were made liable in such circumstances, this would effectively make him the insurer of the contractor's negligence.[59] Such a decision would be inconsistent with the principle discussed in Ch.1 that the law of tort operates most efficiently when it places liability on the party who is able to avoid the risk at least cost.

A few words must be said about the limits of the decision in *Haseldine v Daw*. Clearly, it is authority for the proposition that where the work in question involves complex or technical tasks, the occupier cannot be expected personally to see whether these tasks have been properly performed. It is far from certain, however, that the decision will allow an occupier to wash his or her hands of all responsibility simply by arguing that the work requiring special skill has been delegated to a contractor. Whatever may have been the position when the case was

---

[55] Sedley L.J., whilst agreeing with the majority as to the result of the case, thought that there should be no duty on the part of an occupier to check the insurance position of contractors.

[56] [1945] 1 K.B. 174.

[57] The court in fact found that the cleaner was the agent of the local authority rather than an independent contractor.

[58] [1941] 2 K.B. 343.

[59] [1941] 2 K.B. 343 at 356.

decided, it must be remembered that the 1957 Act requires an occupier to take reasonable steps to check the work. Thus, if contractors were to remove a lift (a specialist task) but were to leave the entrance to the shaft unguarded, it would be difficult for the occupier to escape liability, because the danger would be obvious, even to a lay person. Where the occupier is a commercial concern, and the work in question is especially complex (such as the construction of a large building or ship), the occupier's duty to check each part of the work, as it is completed, may be onerous. In some cases, he or she may even have to engage independent experts to supervise the contractor's work.[60]

It is to be noted that s.2(4)(b) employs the past tense. It requires an occupier to "satisfy himself . . . that the work *had* been properly done". It follows from this that the section does not require an occupier to supervise a contractor's working practices on a day-to-day basis. However, an occupier may be held in breach of his or her duty to supervise the contractor's activities, not by virtue of s.2(4)(b), but because of a general breach of the "common duty of care", which requires an occupier to do what is reasonable "in all the circumstances of the case". Thus, an ordinary householder will not be expected to supervise the technical aspects of a contractor's day-to-day activities,[61] but may be under a duty to safeguard visitors against obvious dangers created by those activities.

It is clear from the House of Lords decision in *Ferguson v Welsh*[62] that an occupier has no general duty to supervise the system of work used by a contractor so as to protect the contractor's employees from harm. Their Lordships stated that in very exceptional cases, an occupier who becomes aware that the contractor's employees are obviously in danger might be under a duty to ensure that dangerous working practices are stopped. Lord Goff, however, doubted whether an ordinary householder could really be expected to challenge the working practices of, for example, an electrician sent to work on his premises, even if he or she knew that those working practices were dangerous.[63]

## Exclusion of liability

It was noted at the beginning of this chapter that an occupier may limit or exclude his or her liability under the Act. This is clear from the wording of s.2(1) of the Act, which imposes the "common duty of care" on an occupier "except in so far as he is free to and does extend, restrict, modify or exclude his duty . . . by agreement or otherwise". An occupier may exclude or limit his or her liability either by displaying a notice on the premises, or by an express term of a contract governing a visitor's entry. Both of these methods, however, are subject to the restrictions on exclusion of liability contained in the Unfair Contract Terms Act 1977. Before considering that Act, it is convenient to deal with each method of exclusion in turn. **8–025**

*(1) Displaying a notice on the premises*

It has been noted that exclusion notices are conceptually distinct from warning notices. Although it is not uncommon to see notices which combine exclusion of liability with an element of warning, in such cases, each element of the notice should be treated separately. **8–026**

---

[60] *AMF International Ltd v Magnet Bowling Ltd* [1968] 1 W.L.R. 1028. Compare *Gray v Fire Alarm Fabrication Services Ltd* [2006] EWCA Civ 1496, [2007] I.C.R. 247.
[61] *Ferguson v Welsh* [1987] 1 W.L.R. 1553 per Lord Goff at 1564; *Green v Fibreglass Ltd* [1958] 2 Q.B. 245.
[62] [1987] 1 W.L.R. 1553.
[63] [1987] 1 W.L.R. 1553 at 1564.

The fact that the 1957 Act permits an occupier to exclude liability by a notice is a reflection of the position which had been established under the common law. In *Ashdown v Samuel Williams & Sons Ltd*,[64] a licensee was injured while using a short-cut over the defendants' land. The defendants were not liable because they had posted notices on the land stating that no person on the land would have any claim against the defendants for any injury whatsoever. The Court of Appeal held that, provided occupiers took reasonable steps to bring the exclusion of liability to the attention of persons on the premises, they were free to dictate their own terms of entry. The decision reflected the idea that "an Englishman's home is his castle"—it was based on the assumption that if the law allowed an occupier to exclude a person altogether from his or her premises, it followed that the occupier would be entitled to attach whatever conditions he or she liked to a person's permission to enter.

In *Ashdown*, the conflict between the freedom of an occupier to exclude liability and the right of a visitor to claim compensation for injury was resolved in favour of the occupier. Under modern law, however, this conflict is often resolved in favour of the visitor. Thus, if the case were decided today, the defendant would be unable to rely on the notice to exclude liability for personal injury, because the notice would be void under s.2(1) of the Unfair Contract Terms Act 1977. The relevant provisions of this Act are considered more fully below. Despite its title, the Act does not apply just to exclusion clauses in contracts, it also applies where the defendant attempts to restrict his or her liability in tort by displaying a notice. Section 1(1)(c) of the Unfair Contract Terms Act 1977 expressly states that the Act applies to notices excluding or limiting the common duty of care under the 1957 Act.

*(2) An express term of a contract*

8–027    Where a visitor enters premises in accordance with a contract governing his or her entry, occupiers may include in that contract an express term which specifies the standard of care owed to their visitor. This standard may be lower (or higher) than the "common duty of care".[65] Where the contract in question contains no express term providing for a standard of care (or where it contains an express term which is void under the Unfair Contract Terms Act 1977, discussed below), s.5(1) of the Act operates to imply into the contract the "common duty of care". Thus, an occupier cannot argue that there is an implied term in the contract to the effect that the standard of care he or she owes is lower than the standard in the 1957 Act. Conversely, in the absence of an express term, the visitor cannot argue for the existence of an *implied* term to the effect that he or she is owed a *higher* contractual standard of care than the standard in the Act. Thus, in *Maguire v Sefton MBC*[66] the claimant contracted to use a leisure centre run by the defendants, and was injured when one of the exercise machines malfunctioned. The Court of Appeal held that, since that contract was silent on the standard of care owed, the trial judge had been wrong to imply into the contract a strict term amounting to a warranty that the machine would be safe to use—in the absence of an express term, the only standard of care that could be implied was the standard demanded by the 1957 Act.

8–028    **The contract's effect on third parties.**    It is important to note the effect of s.3 of the 1957 Act. The wording of this section is rather complex, but its effect is simple. The section deals with a situation where: (1) an occupier enters into a contract with A, under which the occupier permits

---

[64] [1957] 1 Q.B. 409.
[65] e.g. such a term may exclude or limit liability for damage to the visitor's property.
[66] [2006] 1 W.L.R. 2550.

A to use his or her premises, *and* (2) the contract contains an express term setting a standard of care in relation to A, *and* (3) the occupier agrees, by the terms of the contract, to let B enter the premises (even though the occupier has no contract with B). This situation may arise, for example, where a landlord occupier lets a room to A on terms which allow B to visit him.

In such cases, s.3 provides that if the relevant term of the contract sets a standard of care *lower* than the standard set in the 1957 Act, then that term does not apply to B. This is a straightforward application of privity of contract. Instead, B is owed the "common duty of care" under the Act. The section also provides, however, that if the term in question sets a *higher* standard of care than the Act demands, B is entitled to the benefit of the term, unless the contract expressly provides to the contrary. Thus, if a person, while visiting a tenant, suffers loss because of some defect in a part of the building over which the landlord retains occupational control (the stairway, for example), he or she can sue the landlord irrespective of any exclusion clause in the lease, but will also be able to sue if he or she suffers injury because the landlord has not provided security lighting as promised in the lease.

## The Unfair Contract Terms Act 1977

Section 2 of the Unfair Contract Terms Act 1977 provides that where the liability in question **8–029** is "business liability", notices or contract terms which attempt to exclude liability for personal injury or death are void.[67] Notices or contract terms which attempt to exclude liability for other matters (damage to property, for example) are valid only if they are "reasonable".[68] The main difficulty, then, is to decide whether the occupier is attempting to exclude "business liability". Section 1(3) of the Act defines "business liability" as liability for the breach of an obligation arising from "things done . . . in the course of a business[69] . . . or . . . from the occupation of premises used for business purposes of the occupier". Clearly, then, an ordinary householder, unless he or she is using their house for business purposes, will not be affected by the 1977 Act. It is equally clear that where the occupier makes a personal profit by charging the visitor for admission, the Act will apply.

The Act's rather vague definition of "business liability", however, gave rise to uncertainty in cases where the occupier used his or her land for a business purpose (farming or forestry, for example) but allowed people to access that land for a purpose unrelated to the business (to view an ancient monument, for example). This uncertainty was resolved by s.2 of the Occupiers' Liability Act 1984. That section amended the definition of "business liability" to make it clear that in such cases the 1977 Act does not generally apply. According to the amended definition, liability to persons accessing premises for "recreational or educational purposes" is not "business liability" unless those persons are also accessing the premises for the business purposes of the occupier. Thus, a farmer can exclude liability to persons viewing an ancient monument on his land (unless he or she charges them a fee). It should be noted, however, that in such cases the occupier is only free to exclude liability resulting from the dangerous or defective state of the premises (i.e. liability for breach of the "occupancy duty"). The occupier cannot exclude liability for breach of the "activity" duty. Thus, if the visitor were hit by a negligently driven tractor, the 1977 Act would apply to prohibit exclusion of liability.

It remains unclear how far the words "recreational . . . purposes" can cover a situation where the occupier allows his or her premises to be used for charity fund-raising events. It is

---

[67] s.2(1).
[68] s.2(2). For the test of reasonableness, see s.11 and Sch.2.
[69] "Business" includes the activities of professionals, government departments and local authorities: s.14.

noteworthy that the word "charitable" is omitted from the description of purposes for which exclusion of liability is permitted. It is also noteworthy that the definition of "business" in s.14 of the 1977 Act includes activities which would not normally be thought of as "business", namely the activities of government departments and local authorities. This suggests that the courts would have little difficulty in extending the definition of "business" to cover charitable activities. "Professional fund raising", where only a proportion of the proceeds are donated to charity, is clearly a business activity, so the 1977 Act's prohibitions on excluding liability will apply. But do these prohibitions also apply even in cases where the use of the premises is wholly for a charitable purpose? The point is undecided, although some assistance may be derived from the pre-1977 decision in *White v Blackmore*.[70] Here, the plaintiff was killed because of defective barrier ropes at a charity motor-racing event. A majority of the Court of Appeal held that the organisers had effectively excluded liability by posting a notice outside the premises. The fact that the premises were being used for a charitable purpose, however, forms no part of the ratio of the case. Only Lord Denning M.R. (dissenting) refers to the point. In his view, the court should not be "over-anxious" about imposing liability on a charity where that liability is covered by insurance.

In cases where the Unfair Contract Terms Act 1977 does not prohibit exclusion of liability, it is unclear whether the occupier is entitled to exclude liability altogether, or whether he or she will always owe his or her visitors some minimum standard of care, such as the lesser duty owed to trespassers, discussed below. Certainly, the 1957 Act does not entitle an occupier to exclude liability where he or she would not have been allowed to do so under the pre-Act common law. Thus it has been suggested that there can be no exclusion of the common duty of care in relation to persons who enter premises under authority of law.[71] It is unlikely that a court would allow an occupier ever to exclude the duty of "common humanity"[72] because, as a matter of policy, this represents a minimum standard of care owed to all, and should therefore be unexcludable. The real question, then, is whether the higher standard of care owed under the 1984 Act is excludable. This, again, is unlikely. Unlike the 1957 Act, the 1984 Act does not expressly allow an occupier to modify or restrict the duty of care. The point remains undecided, however, because, in practice, it is quite easy to *discharge* the duty (rather than *exclude* it) by giving a warning of the danger.[73]

## LIABILITY TO NON-VISITORS

**8–030**    We have seen that the 1957 Act applies only to "visitors", but that certain persons who enter premises are not "visitors", either because they were not invitees or licensees at common law, or because the Act specifically excludes them from its scope. All of these persons, however, with the exception of individuals exercising a public right of way,[74] are owed a duty under the Occupiers' Liability Act 1984.

---

[70] [1972] 3 All E.R. 158.

[71] W.H. Rogers, *Winfield & Jolowicz on Tort* (18th edn, Sweet and Maxwell, 2010), p. 464.

[72] See the House of Lords in *British Railways Board v Herrington* [1972] A.C. 877.

[73] For further discussion, see Gower (1956) 19 M.L.R. 536, Jones (1984) 47 M.L.R. 713 and Buckley [1984] Conv. 413.

[74] *McGeown v Northern Ireland Housing Executive* [1995] 1 A.C. 233. As to persons exercising the "right to roam" under the Countryside and Rights of Way Act 2000, see Occupiers' Liability Act 1984 s.1A. See M. Stevens-Hoare and R. Higgins, "Roam free?" (2004) 154 N.L.J. 1846.

The 1984 Act, then, applies to people who are on the premises without the occupier's permission. Usually, such people are trespassers, although it should be noted that a person who, for example, falls on to premises from other premises, is not, technically, a trespasser, because the tort of trespass requires that a defendant must intend to be on the land. It should also be noted that, especially in the case of children, it is not true to say that all trespassers are committing a moral wrong. People can become trespassers by accident if they wander on to an occupier's land not realising they need permission to be there.

Sometimes, a person enters premises as a visitor, but becomes a trespasser when he or she breaches some express or implied condition of his or her licence to be there. Thus, a visitor who strays from the permitted area, outstays his welcome, or begins to pursue some purpose unauthorised by the occupier will lose his protection under the 1957 Act and will be protected only by the 1984 Act.

## The old law

In order to appreciate the scope of the 1984 Act, it is necessary to refer to the position at **8–031** common law before it was passed. This is useful not only by way of background, but because much of the reasoning of Lord Diplock in *British Railways Board v Herrington*,[75] the leading pre-Act case, has recently been approved by the Court of Appeal when interpreting the Act's provisions.

The law as it stood in 1929 was shortly stated by Lord Hailsham in *Robert Addie & Sons (Collieries) Ltd v Dumbreck*[76]:

> "The trespasser comes on to the premises at his own risk. An occupier . . . is liable only where the injury is due to some wilful act involving something more than the absence of reasonable care. There must be some act done with the deliberate intention of doing harm to the trespasser, or at least some act done with reckless disregard of the presence of the trespasser."

This approach reflected the idea that, as a matter of policy, an occupier should not be bound to protect a wrongdoer who violated his or her property rights by entering without permission. But the rule could produce some harsh results. In *Addie* itself, for example, a child trespasser, playing in a field owned by the colliery, got caught in the machinery and died. The boy could not, as in *Glasgow Corp v Taylor*,[77] be classified as an implied licensee, because he had been repeatedly warned not to go into the field. The colliery therefore escaped liability.

In 1954, the Law Reform Committee, whose proposals formed the basis of the 1957 Act, stated that although it felt that the existing law relating to trespassers could be harsh when applied to children, it could find no adequate way of providing for child trespassers without imposing too great a burden on occupiers.[78] Trespassers were therefore omitted from the 1957 Act. In 1972, however, the law underwent a fundamental change with the decision in *British Railways Board v Herrington*.[79]

---

[75] [1972] A.C. 877.
[76] [1929] A.C. 358 at 365.
[77] [1922] 1 A.C. 44.
[78] *Occupiers' Liability to Invitees, Licensees and Trespassers*, Cmnd 9305 (1954), para.80.
[79] [1972] A.C. 877.

In *Herrington*, a six-year-old boy climbed through a gap in a fence beside an electrified railway line and was severely injured when he came into contact with the live rail. The defendants knew that children had been using the gap in the fence as a short-cut, but had taken no steps to deter them. The House of Lords held that the defendants were liable, observing that the policy considerations which had formed the basis of the old law on trespassers were no longer persuasive. Society's attitude towards trespassers had changed, so *Addie* was no longer good law. Their Lordships held that occupiers owed a duty of "common humanity" to trespassers. This was more than a duty to refrain from causing deliberate harm, but lower than the duty imposed by the 1957 Act. The precise scope of the duty, however, was unclear, because each of the Law Lords appeared to regard the matter slightly differently. In 1976, the Law Commission reported that it could not extract from the decision any single clear principle, and that legislation was required.[80] Eventually, this came in the form of the Occupiers' Liability Act 1984.

## OCCUPIERS' LIABILITY ACT 1984

8–032   It is convenient to speak of the 1984 Act applying to "trespassers", because this covers the majority of cases, although, as explained above, technically it can apply to other people as well. In summary, the Act provides that an occupier must take reasonable care to see that a trespasser does not suffer personal injury on his or her premises.[81] No duty is owed in respect of a trespasser's property.[82] According to s.1(3), the duty in respect of personal injury is owed if:

- the occupier is aware of the danger, or has reasonable grounds to believe it exists; and

- the occupier knows or has reasonable grounds to believe that a trespasser is in the vicinity of the danger, or may come into that vicinity; and

- the risk of personal injury is one against which, in all the circumstances of the case, the occupier may be expected to offer the trespasser some protection.

An occupier may discharge his or her duty to trespassers either by giving a warning of the danger, or by taking other reasonable steps to discourage trespassers from encountering the danger,[83] for example by securing the premises behind a locked gate. Note that, in contrast to the 1957 Act, there is no requirement that the warning must enable the entrant to be reasonably safe. Thus, the duty can be discharged by a notice posted on the premises which gives a simple warning of the danger (for example "Danger–Rotten Footbridge"). The notice need not inform trespassers how to use the premises safely.

In applying these provisions, the courts have been anxious not to impose too onerous an obligation on occupiers. They have often held that there is no liability, either because no duty is owed under the Act, or because the duty has been discharged, or because the claimant voluntarily assumed the risk and is the author of his or her own misfortune. All three of

---

[80] Law Commission Report No. 75, Cmnd 6428 (1976).
[81] s.1(4).
[82] s.1(8), but see *Tutton v Walter* [1986] Q.B. 61.
[83] s.1(5).

these factors found favour with the House of Lords in *Tomlinson v Congleton Borough Council*[84] to produce a finding of no liability. It was noted in Ch.5 that the reasoning in this case gave rise to, and is reflected in, s.1 of the Compensation Act 2006. This provides that, in considering whether a defendant is in breach of a duty of care, courts should have regard to whether imposing liability might deter potential defendants from carrying out desirable activities.

In *Tomlinson*, the defendant council was in charge of a piece of recreational land on the site of a disused quarry. A lake had formed in part of the old quarry, which attracted many visitors in hot weather. The defendant council had placed notices around the lake, reading: "Dangerous water: no swimming", and had employed rangers to warn visitors of the dangers of swimming in the lake. However, visitors would frequently swim in the lake, ignoring the notices, and were often rude to the rangers when asked to get out of the water. Following a number of serious incidents in which visitors nearly drowned, the council had resolved to make the beaches of the lake less attractive by dumping ballast on the shore to discolour the sand, and by planting vegetation at the lakeside, but, owing to financial constraints, this had not been done at the time of the claimant's accident. The claimant was an 18-year-old man, who entered the water, and, from a standing position in the shallows, executed a dive.[85] He hit his head on the sandy bottom, suffering severe injury which rendered him tetraplegic.

The House of Lords held that the risk of the claimant suffering injury had not arisen from the "state of the premises, or things done or omitted to be done on them" within the meaning of the 1984 Act. Rather, it had arisen from the claimant's own misjudgment in attempting to dive into shallow water. It followed that the risk was not one against which the Act obliged the council to offer him any protection. According to Lord Hoffmann,[86] there was "an important question of freedom at stake" in the case. The Court of Appeal had held that the council, having been aware of the number of accidents suffered by irresponsible visitors swimming in the lake, was under a duty to safeguard those visitors by implementing its resolution to destroy the beaches. Lord Hoffmann pointed out, however, that the majority of people at the lakeside were behaving quite properly, enjoying themselves in a way which posed no risk to themselves or to others, and continued:

> "It is unjust that the harmless recreation of responsible parents and children with buckets and spades on the beaches should be prohibited in order to comply with what is thought to be a legal duty to safeguard irresponsible visitors against dangers which are perfectly obvious."[87]

Accordingly, the "social cost" involved in denying responsible visitors access to recreational facilities should have been taken into account in deciding whether it was reasonable for the council to have destroyed the beaches in order to discourage irresponsible visitors from harming themselves. In their Lordships' view, this "social cost" could not be justified.

---

[84] [2004] 1 A.C. 46. See also *Donoghue v Folkestone Properties* [2003] Q.B. 1008; *Rhind v Astbury Water Park Ltd* [2004] EWCA Civ 756, (2004) 148 S.J.L.B. 759, [2004] N.P.C. 95; *R. (on the application of Hampstead Heath Winter Swimming Club) v London Corp.* [2005] 1 W.L.R. 2930.

[85] There was some indecision as to whether he had become a trespasser by so doing—it was "swimming" that was prohibited by the notices, not entering the water.

[86] *Tomlinson v Congleton Borough Council* [2004] 1 A.C. 46 at 85.

[87] [2004] 1 A.C. 46 at 85.

The approach in *Tomlinson* was followed in *Simonds v Isle of Wight Council*.[88] Here, the claimant, a five-year-old child, broke his arm when he fell from a swing near to a playing field being used for a school sports day. It had been argued that the school was under a duty to immobilise the swings, or at least to place a cordon around them to discourage children from using them. In denying that the school was under such a duty, Gross J., referring to *Tomlinson*, pointed out that the result of a finding of liability might be that pleasurable sporting events such as the one in question would cease to be held, because of the high cost of liability insurance.

The general principles the courts adopt in applying the Act are adequately illustrated by the reasoning in *Tomlinson*. There are few other noteworthy cases on the 1984 Act. This is largely because, as Lord Steyn observed in *Jolley v Sutton LBC*,[89] cases on occupiers' liability are "invariably very fact-sensitive". In other words, because the statutes (particularly the 1984 Act) are framed in such broad terms, the question of whether or not they produce liability in any given situation will depend heavily on the particular factual circumstances of each case. One interesting point of law, however, has arisen in respect of the words "has reasonable grounds to believe". The decision in *White v St Albans City and District Council*[90] made it clear that where an occupier erected a fence around the premises, this did not necessarily mean that he or she had "reasonable grounds" to expect trespassers, but uncertainty remained about how the words should be interpreted.

In *Herrington*, Lord Diplock had expressed the view that no duty to trespassers could arise unless an occupier had actual knowledge of facts as to the condition of his or her land, and actual knowledge of facts which suggested the likely presence of trespassers. An occupier was under no duty to make inquiry as to the state of the premises for the benefit of trespassers.[91] Under the 1984 Act, it was unclear whether this remained the position, or whether the words "reasonable grounds to believe" meant, for example, that an occupier who had no actual knowledge of a dangerous object on the premises could be liable in circumstances where a reasonable occupier *ought* to have known about its presence. However, in *Swain v Natui Ram Puri*[92] and *Ratcliff v McConnell*,[93] the Court of Appeal has expressly endorsed Lord Diplock's views, suggesting that, on a proper construction of the Act, an occupier must actually know the primary facts (from which a reasonable occupier would conclude that there was a danger, or a likelihood of trespassers) before he or she can be liable. The judgment in *Ratcliff* also endorses Lord Diplock's view that the financial resources of the particular occupier are relevant in deciding what level of protection he or she can reasonably be expected to offer to trespassers.

In *Swain*, a child trespasser had been seriously injured when, having scaled a seven foot fence and wall covered with barbed wire to reach a roof, he fell through a skylight. It was argued that although the occupier did not know of trespassers in the vicinity, he should have known that a large unoccupied factory, adjacent to an inner city council estate where many

---

[88] [2004] E.L.R. 59. See also *Poppleton v Trustees of the Portsmouth Youth Activities Committee* [2008] EWCA Civ 646; *Baldacchino v West Wittering Estate Plc* [2008] EWHC 3386.

[89] [2000] 1 W.L.R. 1082 at 1089.

[90] *The Times*, March 12, 1990. On the application of s.1(3) generally, see *Donoghue v Folkestone Properties* [2003] Q.B. 1008; *Higgs v WH Foster* [2004] EWCA Civ 843; *Maloney v Torfaen CBC* [2005] EWCA Civ 1762, [2006] P.I.Q.R. P21.

[91] [1972] A.C. 877 at 941.

[92] [1996] P.I.Q.R. P442, CA,

[93] [1999] 1 W.L.R. 670

children lived, would be bound to attract child trespassers. The Court of Appeal rejected this view. A duty would only arise under the 1984 Act when the occupier had actual knowledge[94] of the relevant facts (here, that children would climb on the roof) or had known facts which gave reasonable grounds for this belief (e.g. had known about gaps in the barbed wire over the perimeter fence). Constructive knowledge would not suffice.

Although the Court of Appeal approved Lord Diplock's views in *Ratcliff*, the case itself turned on the defence of voluntary assumption of risk. In *Ratcliff*, the occupiers of a college swimming pool were not liable when a student trespasser broke into the pool and dived head first into the water, suffering severe injuries. The Court of Appeal held that the student had voluntarily assumed the risk of his activities. He knew that the pool was closed for the winter and had been partially drained, and ought to have realised that it was dangerous to dive into shallow water.

It should be noted that although the 1984 Act refers to liability for "things done or omitted to be done" on premises,[95] the decision in *Revill v Newbery*[96] makes it clear that the Act applies only to liability for the state of premises. It does not regulate the "activity duty". Thus, in considering whether the defendant was liable for accidentally injuring a trespasser, when firing a shotgun towards him intending to frighten him off, the Court of Appeal held that the provisions of the 1984 Act were not, strictly speaking, relevant, although they assisted greatly in determining the nature of the duty owed at common law, which was virtually identical to that owed under the Act.

Finally, it is worth remembering that, because the 1984 Act imposes liability for "the state of the premises",[97] there can be no liability in a situation where non-dangerous premises cause injury simply because of the unorthodox way the trespasser has chosen to use them. (This, of course, was what happened in *Tomlinson*—the lake was not dangerous per se.) The point is illustrated by *Keown v Coventry Healthcare NHS Trust*.[98] Here, an 11-year-old boy fell while, in effect, using the underside of a fire escape as climbing frame. The defendant hospital escaped liability. In the circumstances, the boy had been aware of the danger, and in any event, the risk arose not from the state of the fire escape (which was just as one would expect it to be) but from the fact that the boy had chosen to trespass on it in such an unusual way.

## DEFENCES

The various defences generally applicable to actions in negligence apply in the same way to actions brought under the Occupiers' Liability Act 1957 and the Occupiers' Liability Act 1984. In practice, voluntary assumption of risk is the most important defence in occupiers' liability cases (see *Ratcliff v McConnell*, noted above). This defence is expressly preserved in both Acts.[99] It is discussed, together with other defences, in Ch.16.

**8–033**

---

[94] This would extend to "shut eye" knowledge, that is, facts which are obvious but which the occupier chooses to ignore.

[95] s.1(1)(a).

[96] [1996] 2 W.L.R. 239.

[97] Occupiers' Liability Act 1984 s.1(1)(a).

[98] [2006] 1 W.L.R. 953. See also *Siddorn v Patel* [2007] EWHC 1248 (QB). (No liability where the claimant danced on a flat roof and fell through a skylight.)

[99] Occupiers' Liability Act 1957 s.2(5) and Occupiers' Liability Act 1984 s.1(6).

## Contributory negligence

**8–034**   There is no explicit reference to the Law Reform (Contributory Negligence) Act 1945 in either the 1957 or the 1984 Act. This is surprising, because the matter was expressly mentioned in the Law Reform Committee's recommendations which led to the passing of the 1957 Act.[100] Nevertheless, the courts have regularly applied the principle of contributory negligence in deciding cases under both Acts.[101]

[100]  *Occupiers' Liability to Invitees, Licensees and Trespassers*, Cmnd 9305 (1954), para.78(ix).
[101]  See, e.g. *Stone v Taffe* [1974] 1 W.L.R. 1575 and *Bunker v Charles Brand* [1969] 2 Q.B. 480 where in both cases damages were reduced by 50 per cent. See also *Kiapasha v Laverton* [2002] EWCA Civ 1656. For the 1984 Act, see *Revill v Newbery* [1996] 2 W.L.R. 239.

# Chapter 9

# STRICT LIABILITY STATUTES

In this chapter, we will examine two forms of strict liability imposed by statute: for defective **9–001** products under the Consumer Protection Act 1987 and for damage caused by animals under the Animals Act 1971. In both cases, these forms of liability are in addition to the existing common law. The first part of this chapter will deal with the important provisions relating to defective products. This will be followed by a brief discussion of the Animals Act 1971.

## (1) CONSUMER PROTECTION ACT 1987

### Introduction

In this section, we examine liability for defective products in the law of torts, that is, products **9–002** which are faulty and cause damage to individual victims. At common law, this is simply part of the tort of negligence, with which we should now be familiar. It should not be forgotten that *Donoghue v Stevenson*[1] involved an allegation that Mrs Donoghue's ginger beer bottle contained a snail, or, in other words, that Mrs Donoghue had been the victim of a defective product. The case is therefore not only the classic example of the duty of care in negligence, but the classic example of liability for a defective product. However, the common law has now been supplemented by the enactment of the Consumer Protection Act 1987, which was introduced to comply with EC Directive 85/374 on liability for defective products. The aim of the Act is to assist consumers in their claims against manufacturers of defective products by rendering the manufacturer (and associated parties) strictly liable, that is, liable without the need to prove fault. However, until recently, this change in the law has had less impact in practice than may have been expected.

We shall proceed by considering, first of all, the position at common law. This is of interest in highlighting why reform of this area of law was necessary and, more significantly, in understanding the position in law when the provisions of the 1987 Act do not apply. It is important to remember that the 1987 Act supplements the common law—it does not replace it. Secondly, we shall examine the provisions of the 1987 Act and the extent to which it imposes strict liability on manufacturers of products and on associated parties.

---

[1] [1932] A.C. 562.

## THE COMMON LAW POSITION

**9-003**     Prior to *Donoghue v Stevenson*, tort law provided little assistance to persons injured by a defective product. Most claimants were forced to rely on contract law, provided, of course, that they could establish the necessary contractual relationship. There are a number of benefits in bringing a contractual claim. First, the claimant is not required to show the fault of the seller, but simply that the seller is in breach of a term of the contract. The seller is therefore strictly liable for his or her breach. Secondly, contract law has no problem in awarding compensation for personal injury and property damage caused by the supply of a defective product[2] and will also award compensation for the cost of replacing the defective product itself. The buyer's position is further improved by the existence of implied terms. For example, under the Sale of Goods Act 1979, it is implied that, where the seller sells the goods in the course of a business, the goods must be of satisfactory quality[3] and be fit for their purpose.[4] On this basis, the buyer can sue for breach of contract if the goods fail to satisfy these terms.

There are, however, a number of disadvantages in bringing a claim in contract law. First, there must be a term (express or implied) in the contract which provides that the product should not be defective. Secondly, subject to the provisions of the Contract (Rights of Third Parties) Act 1999,[5] the rules of privity of contract only allow the parties to the contract to take the benefit of such terms.[6] Thirdly, the seller may exclude or limit liability for breach, although this will be subject to the provisions of the Unfair Contract Terms Act 1977 and Unfair Terms in Consumer Contracts Regulations 1999. Fourthly, although the chain of contracts between the manufacturer and the buyer will ultimately pass liability back up the chain to the manufacturer, this chain is easily broken, for example, by exclusion clauses or the insolvency of one of the parties. Liability may therefore fall arbitrarily on one party in the chain, regardless of the fact that the fault is solely that of the manufacturer.

As stated earlier, prior to 1932, tort law had a very limited application to defective products. A manufacturer would only be liable in tort if the product was classified as "dangerous" (for example, dynamite) or was actually known to the manufacturer to be dangerous, in which case he or she would then be obliged to warn the product's recipient of the danger. The distinction between "dangerous" and "non-dangerous" products was not particularly helpful and indeed made little sense. As Scrutton L.J. famously commented:

---

[2] Subject of course to the rules of remoteness stated in *Hadley v Baxendale* (1854) 9 Ex 341. See *Grant v Australian Knitting Mills Ltd* [1936] A.C. 85 where the plaintiff sued the retailer under the contract of sale for the skin disease he suffered as a result of the defective state of the product sold.

[3] s.14(2) of the Sale of Goods Act 1979 (as amended by the Sale and Supply of Goods Act 1994).

[4] s.14(3) of the Sale of Goods Act 1979 (as amended by the Sale and Supply of Goods Act 1994). See also the Supply of Goods and Services Act 1982.

[5] s.1(1) provides that a third party may be able to enforce a term of a contract in his or her own right if either (a) the contract expressly provides for this or (b) the parties intend by a term of the contract to confer a benefit on him or her. The third party must be expressly identified in the contract by name, as a member of a class or as answering a particular description: s.1(3). These requirements will limit the number of possible claims under the Act.

[6] Unless, of course, the purchaser sues for his or her own loss, which includes that arising from the injury of a third party. For example, in *Frost v Aylesbury Dairy* [1905] 1 K.B. 608, the purchaser sued to recover the expenses to which he had been put by the illness and death of his wife due to typhoid fever caught from the milk supplied by the defendants.

"Personally, I do not understand the difference between a thing dangerous in itself, as poison, and a thing not dangerous as a class, but by negligent construction dangerous as a particular thing. The latter, if anything, seems the more dangerous of the two; it is a wolf in sheep's clothing instead of an obvious wolf".[7]

The courts' reluctance to adopt a general principle of negligence liability and their adherence to the "privity of contract fallacy" (by which the contract between the manufacturer and the retailer was deemed to obstruct any other form of liability in favour of third parties)[8] prevented the emergence of a general defective product action in tort.

In *Donoghue v Stevenson*,[9] the majority of the House of Lords overturned the questionable distinction between dangerous and non-dangerous chattels and discarded the "privity of contract fallacy". The court saw no reason why the same set of facts should not give one person a right in contract and another a concurrent right to sue in tort.[10] It will be recalled that the case concerned the decomposed remains of snail, alleged to have been found in an opaque bottle of ginger beer that had been bought by Mrs Donoghue's friend. The existing rules of tort law seemed to preclude Mrs Donoghue's claim. A ginger beer bottle is not dangerous in itself and it was not known to contain a noxious substance. Mrs Donoghue had no contractual relationship with any of the parties and so could not rely on any implied terms as to quality. Nevertheless, the majority of the House of Lords held that where a manufacturer sells goods in such a manner that he intends them to reach the ultimate consumer in the form in which they have left him, with no reasonable possibility of intermediate examination, then the manufacturer will be liable for the absence of reasonable care in manufacturing the products.[11]

Three points may be noted about the decision in *Donoghue v Stevenson*. First, no distinction is drawn between different types of products. Logically, however, in assessing breach of duty (i.e. whether the manufacturer has exercised reasonable care), greater care would be required in the manufacture of explosives than in the manufacture of ginger beer. Indeed, the standard of care required for particularly dangerous products may be so high as practically to amount to a guarantee of safety.[12] Secondly, it should be noted that the manufacturer must intend the goods to reach the consumer intact. A reasonable possibility of intermediate examination would appear to exclude liability. Thirdly, the case deals with the manufacture of products and not with design. Design defects in products are of particular concern. Whereas a problem with manufacture may be limited to a particular batch, a design defect will affect many more products, thereby increasing the possibility of harm. We shall have to consider how *Donoghue v Stevenson*[13] applies to defects in design and what protection it gives to potential claimants.

---

[7] *Hodge & Sons v Anglo-American Oil Co* (1922) 12 Lloyd's Rep. 183 at 187.
[8] See *Winterbottom v Wright* (1842) 10 M. & W. 109; 152 E.R. 402, discussed in Ch.2.
[9] [1932] A.C. 562.
[10] [1932] A.C. 562 per Lord Macmillan at 610.
[11] [1932] A.C. 562 per Lord Atkin at 599. Contrast Lord Buckmaster's strong dissenting judgment at 577–8.
[12] [1932] A.C. 562 per Lord Macmillan at 612.
[13] [1932] A.C. 562.

## The scope of *Donoghue v Stevenson*

**9–004**     The burden will be on the claimant to satisfy the ordinary rules of negligence, i.e. to establish a duty of care, breach, causation and remoteness. Their application to defective product claims will be discussed below.

*The duty of care*

**9–005**     This is the ordinary common law duty of care, discussed in Ch.2. It is not confined to the relationship between manufacturers and ultimate consumers. Makers of component parts, repairers, fitters, erectors, assemblers and even distributors may find themselves liable to the consumer for their failure to exercise reasonable care in dealing with a product. Equally, the range of claimants has extended beyond the ultimate consumer to parties coming into contact with the product. In *Stennett v Hancock and Peters*,[14] for example, a decision which followed shortly after *Donoghue*, the plaintiff suffered injury when part of a wheel from a passing lorry flew off and struck her on the leg. The lorry had recently been repaired by the second defendants, who were found to have re-attached the wheel negligently. The court rejected the claim against the owners of the lorry, but the claim against the second defendants succeeded. *Donoghue v Stevenson* was held to extend to repairers where a person suffered injury on the road as a result of their negligence. Moreover, it is clear that the duty may extend beyond the product itself to include its container, packaging, and directions or instructions for use.[15]

*Breach*

**9–006**     Whether the defendant has exercised reasonable care will obviously depend on the particular facts of each case, to which the general principles relating to breach will be applied. Obviously, once the manufacturer knows of the defect, he or she will be negligent if production and marketing of the unsafe product continues.[16] It has been held that even when using component parts, a manufacturer should exercise care in purchasing suitable parts and should not simply assume that the component part is sound.[17] It is a more difficult question whether the manufacturer's duty extends to taking steps to recall products found to be defective after the products have gone into circulation. The best view, perhaps, is that the manufacturer may find himself or herself liable for failing to recall products already in circulation, particularly if the products have just entered the market, and should recall the product line in question as soon as practicable. As Sir Michael Ogden Q.C. commented in *E. Hobbs v Baxenden Chemical Co*[18]:

> ". . . a manufacturer's duty of care does not end when the goods are sold. A manufacturer, who realises that omitting to warn past customers about something might result in injury to them, must take reasonable steps to attempt to warn them, however lacking in negligence he may have been at the time the goods were sold".

---

[14] [1939] 2 All E.R. 578. See also *Haseldine v Daw* [1941] 2 K.B. 343 where a visitor using a lift in a block of flats was allowed to sue the repairers of the lift when the lift fell to the bottom of its shaft.

[15] *Watson v Buckley, Osborne, Garrett & Co* [1940] 1 All E.R. 174.

[16] *Wright v Dunlop Rubber Co Ltd* (1972) 13 K.I.R. 255 at 272.

[17] *Winward v T.V.R. Engineering* [1986] B.T.L.C. 366.

[18] [1992] 1 Lloyd's Rep. 54 at 65. See also *Hamble Fisheries Ltd v L Gardner & Sons Ltd* [1999] 2 Lloyd's Rep. 1 at 9 per Mummery L.J.; *Hollis v Dow Corning* (1996) 129 D.L.R. (4th) 609; *Carroll v Fearon* [1998] P.I.Q.R. P416.

Breach will generally not cause the claimant particular problems.[19] Although there is some authority that the res ipsa loquitur rule (see Ch.5) does not apply to defective products,[20] the courts have shown themselves willing to infer the absence of reasonable care from the fact a defect exists. For example, in *Grant v Australian Knitting Mills Ltd*,[21] Dr Grant claimed that he had suffered a skin disease from wearing underpants manufactured by the defendants, because they contained an excess of sulphites. The fact that the manufacturers had specifically adopted precautions against excess sulphite did not assist them. Lord Wright inferred that, in such circumstances, the chemicals could only be present in the garment if someone had been at fault. The plaintiff was not required to identify the exact person responsible for the breach, or to specify what he or she did wrong. The burden was therefore on the manufacturer to rebut the inference of negligence with sufficient evidence. This sort of approach lightens the claimant's burden considerably. It would, for example, have been very difficult for Mrs Donoghue to specify exactly what was so wrong with the manufacturing process that a snail could have entered a ginger beer bottle. Equally, in *Mason v Williams & Williams Ltd*,[22] the court was prepared to infer negligence where a plaintiff had been injured using a chisel which was too hard for its purpose. The chisel had come straight from the manufacturers and the court was prepared to find that the undue hardness must have been produced by carelessness in the course of manufacture, rather than by anything that had happened at the plaintiff's place of work. Finnemore J. stated that showing that the chisel was defective was "as far as any plaintiff can be expected to take his case". It should be noted, however, that his Lordship was careful to distinguish this approach from the doctrine of res ipsa loquitur. It should also be noted that the approach has only been applied in relation to manufacturing defects and appears to have little application to design defects.

*Causation and remoteness*

The ordinary rules of negligence apply and reference should be made to the principles outlined        **9–007**
in Ch.6. The ordinary "but for" test will apply. Note, however, that particularly in medical cases, it may be difficult to differentiate between different possible causes of the injury.

*The type of loss recoverable*

In defective product cases, the type of loss recoverable is limited by the same rules that apply        **9–008**
in other negligence cases. A claimant, therefore, may recover foreseeable personal injury and property damage, but will not succeed in recovering pure economic loss. In *Murphy v Brentwood DC*,[23] the House of Lords emphasised that the cost of replacing a defective product will be classified as pure economic loss, and is therefore non-recoverable. It was noted in Ch.3 that a claim for loss of profits is unlikely to succeed unless that loss of profits is consequential on property damage caused by the defective product supplied.[24] Whilst the "complex

---

[19] Note, however, the particular situation of defective equipment in the workplace. Whereas at common law, employers will not be found negligent for supplying defective tools if they have taken reasonable care to purchase the tools from a reputable supplier (*Davie v New Merton Board Mills Ltd* [1959] A.C. 604), the Employer's Liability (Defective Equipment) Act 1969 imposes strict liability on employers providing defective equipment for the purposes of their business. See, further, Ch. 7

[20] Lord Macmillan in *Donoghue v Stevenson* [1932] A.C. 562 at 622: "There is no presumption of negligence in such a case at present, nor is there any justification for applying the maxim *res ipsa loquitur*".

[21] [1936] A.C. 85 at 101. See also *Carroll v Fearon* [1998] P.I.Q.R. P416.

[22] [1955] 1 W.L.R. 549. See also *Hill v Crowe* [1978] 1 All E.R. 812.

[23] [1991] 1 A.C. 398; [1990] 2 All E.R. 908.

[24] *Spartan Steel & Alloys Ltd v Martin & Co (Contractors) Ltd* [1973] Q.B. 27, CA.

structure theory" was discussed in Ch.3 in relation to defective buildings,[25] its relevance to defective products generally must be considered here.[26] Component parts installed at the time of manufacture will be considered part of the product supplied.[27] In contrast, it appears that replacement parts, such as a replacement wheel, will be regarded as a separate product.[28] The decision of the Court of Appeal in *M/S Aswan Engineering Establishment Co v Lupdine Ltd*[29] highlights the difficulties of applying the complex structure idea to products. The plaintiffs in this case had shipped a consignment of a waterproofing compound (Lupguard) to Kuwait in plastic pails. The pails, which had been selected by the sellers of the compound, had collapsed in the high temperatures of Kuwait with the result that the entire consignment had been lost. As the seller of the compound was in liquidation, Aswan brought an action against the manufacturers of the pails for the loss suffered. The Court of Appeal dismissed the claim on the basis that the loss was not reasonably foreseeable, but Lloyd L.J. expressed the provisional view that there was damage to "other property", namely the Lupguard, which would be recoverable even though the compound had been purchased in the pails.[30] Whilst finding such reasoning logical, Nicholls L.J. expressed reservations as to a rule which would impose liability on the maker of a container—such as a bag, carton or bucket—for loss of its contents.[31]

## Particular problems relating to defective products

### (1) What is a product?

**9–009**    In *Donoghue v Stevenson*, Lord Atkin restricted himself to consideration of articles of common household use, where everyone, including the manufacturer, would know that the articles would be used by persons other than the actual ultimate purchaser.[32] The courts have been prepared to interpret "product" quite broadly to include tombstones,[33] hair dye,[34] industrial chemicals,[35] lifts[36] and motor cars.[37]

### (2) Has there been intermediate examination or interference?

**9–010**    This is, in a sense, a question of causation. To find the defendant liable, the court must be satisfied that he or she caused the defect, and that it was not due to the fault of another party

---

[25] See *D & F Estates v Church Commissioners* [1989] A.C. 177.

[26] See A. Tettenborn [2000] L.M.C.L.Q. 338.

[27] See, for example, *The Rebecca Elaine (Hamble Fisheries Ltd v L Gardner & Sons Ltd)* [1999] 2 Lloyd's Rep. 1 (defective pistons in an engine where the manufacturer of the engine was sued) cf. *Nitrigin Eireann Teoranta v Inco Alloys* [1992] 1 W.L.R. 498, May J.

[28] See *M/S Aswan Engineering Establishment Co v Lupdine Ltd* [1987] 1 W.L.R. 1 at 21.

[29] [1987] 1 W.L.R. 1.

[30] Fox L.J. in agreement.

[31] [1987] 1 W.L.R. 1 at 29. See also Mance L.J. in *Bacardi-Martini Beverages Ltd v Thomas Hardy Packaging Ltd* [2002] EWCA Civ 549, [2002] 2 Lloyd's Rep 379 at para.18, who doubted the authority of this case in that it preceded *Murphy v Brentwood DC* and "occurred when the star of *Junior Books Ltd v Veitchi Co Ltd* [1983] 1 A.C. 520 was still high in the sky".

[32] [1932] A.C. 562 at 583.

[33] *Brown v Cotterill* (1934) 51 T.L.R. 21.

[34] *Watson v Buckley, Osborne, Garrett & Co* [1940] 1 All E.R. 174.

[35] *Vacwell Engineering Co v BDH Chemicals* [1971] 1 Q.B. 88.

[36] *Haseldine v Daw* [1941] 2 K.B. 343.

[37] *Andrews v Hopkinson* [1957] 1 Q.B. 229 at 237.

in the supply chain (or even the claimant). In *Grant v Australian Knitting Mills Ltd*,[38] it was argued that the mere possibility that the goods might be tampered with after they had left the factory should enable the manufacturer to escape liability. The defendants claimed that because the garments had been wrapped in paper packets to allow shopkeepers to sell each garment separately, there was a possibility of interference with the goods, and this meant the defendants should not be liable. The Privy Council dismissed this argument. Interference was a question of fact, and here it was beyond question that the garment had reached Dr Grant subject to the same defect as when it left the manufacturer.

Where, however, there is a reasonable possibility or probability[39] of interference, the court will take a different line. In *Evans v Triplex Safety Glass Co Ltd*,[40] Mr Evans had bought a car which had been fitted with a "Triplex Toughened Safety Glass" windscreen. One year later, the windscreen shattered whilst Mr Evans was driving the vehicle, injuring himself, his wife and his son. In an action against the manufacturers of the safety glass, Porter J. held that Mr Evans had not given sufficient evidence to satisfy the court that the manufacturers were at fault. His Lordship suspected that the real fault lay with the fitting of the windscreen into its frame. In addition, Mr Evans had owned the car for a year before the accident and either he or his supplier might reasonably have inspected the windscreen prior to the accident.

The question of inspection or examination may be a difficult one, particularly where one party in the contractual chain, other than the manufacturer, has had the opportunity to examine the product but chooses not to do so. There is no general obligation at law on such parties to subject all goods to exhaustive examination. The manufacturer will therefore remain liable where he or she has no reason to contemplate that the defect will be discovered before the product reaches the consumer. There may be circumstances, however, when the manufacturer may reasonably expect a third party to examine the product and, if such examination would have revealed the defect, assert that it is the third party's failure to examine the product adequately (rather than defective manufacture) which has caused the injury. In such circumstances, it will be the third party and not the manufacturer who is liable to the claimant.

This question did not arise in *Donoghue*. The ginger beer bottle was opaque and had been sealed, so no-one could have examined its contents prior to consumption. In *Andrews v Hopkinson*,[41] however, a second-hand car dealer, who did have the opportunity to check cars for defects, was held liable for failing to inspect his cars for obvious defects. In this case, which involved a hire purchase agreement for a second-hand car, the plaintiff brought an action against the dealer for injuries resulting from an accident due to the defective steering mechanism of the car. The car was around 18 years old and had been in the dealer's possession for a week. The court heard evidence that the steering mechanism was a particular danger in an old car, which could have been discovered on inspection. In such circumstances, McNair J. was in no doubt that the defendant was liable for failing to examine the vehicle, or at least for failing to warn the claimant that no examination had been carried out. Similarly, in *Vacwell*

---

[38] [1936] A.C. 85.
[39] Goddard L.J. in *Haseldine v Daw* [1941] 2 K.B. 343 at 376 suggested that the word "probability" is more accurate. In that case, the engineers repairing the lift could not have reasonably contemplated any immediate inspection and so owed a duty to any person who, in the ordinary course of events, would be expected to make use of the thing repaired.
[40] [1936] 1 All E.R. 283.
[41] [1957] 1 Q.B. 229 at 237. See also *White v Warwick* [1953] 1 W.L.R. 1285; *Griffiths v Arch Engineering Co Ltd* [1968] 3 All E.R. 217.

*Engineering Co v BDH Chemicals*,[42] a party supplying chemicals was expected to inform himself about the potential hazards and warn the recipient accordingly.

The real question is whether the defendant can reasonably expect a third party or the consumer to undertake an inspection in the circumstances. For example, in *Griffiths v Arch Engineering Co Ltd*,[43] a sub-contractor, who had hired a portable grinding tool which was in a dangerous condition, was not liable to an injured workman for failing to examine the tool. It was clear that the tool had been hired for immediate use, and because the plant hire company had no reason to suppose that an examination would be carried out, they would be liable. The defendant can secure his or her position by attaching a warning to the product that it must be examined prior to use. This places a duty on the third party to examine the product and, of course, renders intermediate examination reasonably probable. By this means, the seller of a dangerously defective car in *Hurley v Dyke*,[44] who had warned that the car was sold "as seen and with all its faults", avoided liability to a claimant, who had been injured in a subsequent accident caused by the car's defective condition.

### (3) The manufacture/design distinction

**9–011**    The cases we have discussed so far have been concerned with manufacturing defects where, due to a problem at the manufacturing stage, the product contains a particular defect which has injured the claimant. This is distinct from a design defect, which arises from the very nature of the product itself. The latter is obviously more potentially damaging. Whilst a bad batch of goods will affect a number of consumers, a design defect will affect every consumer of the product and may be impossible to discover on inspection or examination. In considering liability for defective goods, design defects must be given particular attention.

The case law, however, is primarily concerned with manufacturing defects. There are a number of reasons for this. First, *Donoghue*, the main precedent in this area of law, concerns a manufacturing defect. Secondly, and more fundamentally, liability for design defects is more difficult to establish on the common law rules of negligence, and presents particular problems for litigants. As shown above, the courts are prepared to infer negligence in respect of manufacturing defects, placing the burden on the defendant to rebut this inference by giving evidence that the defect has been caused by the fault of another party, or that its manufacturing system operates in a reasonable manner. This imposes a considerable burden on the defendant, which has been held to be close to strict liability. In contrast, the same reasoning does not apply to design defects. If a person develops cancer after taking drug X, which has been manufactured without fault, this may be caused by a multiplicity of different factors, for example, the claimant's genetic makeup, or environmental pollution. It will be for the claimant to establish that (a) a design fault in drug X causes cancer and (b) the design fault was a material cause of his or her cancer. This is a far from easy task and is rendered more difficult if the person is taking other drugs, or undertaking other medical treatment. The claimant will only be able to obtain disclosure of the relevant design documentation after he or she has commenced the claim and incurred considerable costs. Without a clear admission by the manufacturer, or inside information, it will be difficult to bring a claim in the first place. In contrast where a person bites into a bar of chocolate and finds a lump of metal in it, the court will infer that the metal can only be present due to the fault of someone in the manufacturing process and, in the

---

[42] [1971] 1 Q.B. 88.
[43] [1968] 3 All E.R. 217.
[44] [1979] R.T.R. 265, HL. See also *Kubach v Hollands* [1937] 3 All E.R. 907.

absence of evidence of interference, or a duty to inspect, will turn to the manufacturer to meet this claim.

The problems arising from design defects were only too apparent in the thalidomide cases.[45] Thalidomide was a drug used by mothers to counter morning sickness, but with appalling side-effects, in that between 1959 and 1962 an estimated 10,000 children were born with physical deformities. This was a classic example of a design defect. Yet, when the parents brought claims in negligence, they experienced difficulty in showing that the manufacturers had failed to take reasonable care in producing the drug. The manufacturer's conduct is judged by reference to what was reasonable at the time the product was put into circulation.[46] The manufacturer will not be judged with hindsight if the dreadful consequences were not foreseeable by the reasonable manufacturer at the time the product was put in circulation.[47]

## The need for change?

Whilst the common law has reached a fairly satisfactory position in relation to manufacturing defects—with the courts willing to infer negligence and adopt a flexible approach towards liability–the thalidomide tragedy focused attention on the problems litigants might experience in relation to design defects. This led to demands for a change in the law. At this time (the 1970s), the concept of strict liability as a means of ensuring loss distribution and compensation was particularly fashionable (see the Report of the Pearson Commission in 1978, discussed in Ch.1). It was suggested that manufacturers should be strictly liable for defects in their products for the following reasons:

- The manufacturer created the product and therefore the hazard. Since this risk was created in the pursuit of profit, it was reasonable to expect the manufacturer to accept liability for the hazards caused;

- The manufacturer was best placed to insure against the risk, and the price of insurance could be distributed via the price of the product; and

- Liability would give the manufacturer a greater incentive to take safety precautions.

Such arguments are not without problems. For example, where individuals have contents insurance for their personal property, forcing manufacturers to take out insurance against product liability would lead to double cover, which is economically inefficient. The Law Commission in its 1977 Report, *Liability for Defective Products*,[48] suggested that this could be dealt with by limiting strict liability to claims for personal injury and death, but this has not been implemented. A manufacturer is also likely to disagree fundamentally with the first argument which arguably penalises the manufacturer's initiative in placing a product on the market which may have enormous social benefits and responds to consumer choice.

Nevertheless, growing pressure for reform, combined with EC initiatives to harmonise the rules on defective products in Member States, resulted in a change in the law. EC Directive 85/374 of July 25, 1985 required Member States to bring into force, within three years,

9–012

---

[45] See the excellent book by H. Teff and C. Munro, *Thalidomide: the legal aftermath* (Saxon House, 1976).
[46] See *Roe v Minister of Health* [1954] 2 Q.B. 66: "We must not look at the 1947 accident with 1954 spectacles".
[47] The legal issues were never decided as the thalidomide litigation was settled.
[48] Report No.82, Cmnd 6831.

changes in their national laws to comply with the Directive.[49] The UK, on March 1, 1988, brought into force Part 1 of the Consumer Protection Act 1987, s.1(1) of which states that:

> "This Part shall have effect for the purpose of making such provision as is necessary in order to comply with the product liability Directive and shall be construed accordingly".

Therefore, if the wording of the Act appears to conflict with the Directive, this conflict should be resolved in favour of the Directive and any dispute settled by the European Court of Justice.

## CONSUMER PROTECTION ACT 1987

**9–013**    The Product Liability Directive, in its preamble, states:

> ". . . liability without fault on the part of the producer is the sole means of adequately solving the problem, peculiar to our age of increasing technicality, of a fair apportionment of the risks inherent in modern technological production".

Part 1 of the Consumer Protection Act 1987 ("the Act") therefore seeks to make the manufacturer of a product (and others dealing with it) liable without proof of fault for personal injury and property damage caused wholly or partly by a defect in a product. The provisions of the Act and the way in which they operate are set out below. It should be noted, however, that by granting the manufacturer certain defences and failing to give a precise definition of "defect", the Act has led many to question how "strict" the liability imposed by the Act actually is.[50]

### Who can sue?

**9–014**    This obvious question is not dealt with expressly by the Act. However, reading ss.2(1) and 5(1), it clearly allows litigants to sue if they suffer damage as a result of a defective product.

### Who is liable?

**9–015**    Reference should be made here to s.1(2) and s.2 generally. The Act includes not only manufacturers (or "producers"), but extends to own-branders and parties importing goods into the European Union. Suppliers are not generally liable, except under the special provisions of s.2(3). However, the Act does not, of course, prevent a supplier from being sued for breach of contract.

---

[49] Art. 19. See [1985] OJ L210, 29.
[50] See, for example, J. Stapleton (1986) 6 OJLS 392 and *Product Liability* (Butterworths, 1994) and C. Newdick (1987) 103 L.Q.R. 288. For a more recent appraisal, see S. Whittaker, *Liability for products: English law, French law and European Harmonization* (OUP: 2005).

*(1) Producer—ss.1(2) and 2(2)(a)*

Section 1(2) gives three different meanings for a "producer". The first and simplest is that of a manufacturer of a product.[51] It should be noted that a manufacturer of a component part of the product is equally classified as a producer, so that if the product fails due to a malfunction of a component part, both the manufacturer of the final product and the manufacturer of the component part will be liable.[52]    **9–016**

The second and third meanings relate to goods which have not been manufactured. If the defendant has "won or abstracted" the product[53] (for example, mined coal), or has carried out an industrial or other process on the goods to which the essential characteristics of the goods are attributable[54] (as in the case of canned peas or frozen fish, for example), he or she will be classified as a producer. This last category is not particularly clear and leaves a number of important questions (such as what are the "essential characteristics" of the goods) to the discretion of the court. Those involved in packaging will not be affected unless the packaging alters the essential characteristics of the product.

*(2) Own-brander—s.2(2)(b)*

Section 2(2)(b) states that liability may attach to:    **9–017**

> "any person, who, by putting his name on the product or using a trade mark or other distinguishing mark in relation to the product, has held himself out to be the producer of the product".

The important question here is whether the person has held himself out as the producer. This will not be so in the case of a product in a supermarket marked "made for Sainsco", but will be so where a product is marketed as "Sainsco baked beans".

*(3) Importer into EU—s.2(2)(c)*

This is a provision to save claimants the time and expense of pursuing defendants outside the European Union. Thus, the subsection provides that:    **9–018**

> "any person who has imported the product into a member State from a place outside the member States in order, in the course of any business of his, to supply it to another"

will be liable. This provision is confined to the importer into the EU. It does not affect those who import from one EU country to another, where liability will remain with the first importer. The product must be imported for supply "in the course of any business of his" and so if person X imports a car from Japan privately for his own use, he will not be liable under the Act to any person who is injured when it explodes due to a defect in its manufacture.

*(4) Supplier—s.2(3)*

The supplier is not generally liable under the Act. However, s.2(3) deals with the situation where the consumer has bought defective goods which do not indicate the identity of the    **9–019**

---

[51]  s.1(2)(a).
[52]  s.2(5). Liability is "joint and several". This is discussed in Ch.17.
[53]  s.1(2)(b).
[54]  s.1(2)(c).

producer. Where damage has been caused wholly or partly by a defect in a product, the supplier will be liable if:

- the claimant has requested the supplier to identify the producer/own-brander or importer of the product;

- the request is made within a reasonable period after the damage has occurred and at a time when it is not reasonably practicable for the person making the request to identify those persons; and

- the supplier fails within a reasonable period after receiving the request either to comply with the request or to identify the person who supplied the product to him.

The consumer can therefore trace the producer through the chain of supply. The supplier will be able to pass on liability, provided, of course, he or she has maintained proper records of his or her dealings. It should be noted that the mere supply of the end product does not mean that the supplier is deemed to have supplied all the component parts.[55] This means that the supplier will not be liable for failing to identify the producers of all the component parts.

Liability under the Act therefore extends beyond the manufacturer, but it should be noted that it is nevertheless not as wide as the common law, which extends to repairers, fitters, erectors and assemblers.

## What is a product?

**9–020**     This is defined by s.1(2) to include any goods[56] or electricity and includes a product which is comprised in another product, whether by virtue of being a component part or raw material or otherwise. From December 4, 2000, "product" includes all primary agricultural products (that is, food sold in its raw state such as meat or vegetables) and game. Although these products were previously excluded from the Act,[57] it became desirable in the wake of the BSE crisis to include these products and "help restore consumer confidence in the safety of agricultural products".[58] Accordingly, following Directive 1999/34/EC, the Act has been modified.[59]

Buildings are not covered by the Act, although individual goods from which they are built (for example, bricks and beams) are covered. The Act is additionally not intended to extend to pure information, except in the case of printed instructions or warnings for a product, which will render the producer (not the printer) liable for errors or omissions in the instructions or warnings which make the product unsafe. The Government guidance on the Act[60] indicates

---

[55] s.1(3).

[56] s.45(1) defines "goods" to include substances, growing crops and things comprised in land by virtue of being attached to it and any ship, aircraft or vehicle. It does not seem to include the land itself.

[57] Art.15(1)(a) of the 1985 Directive rendered it optional to include primary agricultural produce and game within the definition of "product". Solely Greece, France, Luxembourg, Finland, Sweden and Austria (with respect to GMOs) chose to include such products.

[58] Recital 5 to Directive 1999/34/EC [1999] OJ L/1.

[59] See Consumer Protection Act 1987 (Product Liability)(Modification) Order 2000 (SI 2000/2771). Unfortunately, no corresponding alteration has been made to the definition of "producer" in s.1(2), although agriculture will no doubt often involve some form of "industrial process".

[60] *Guide to the Consumer Protection Act 1987* (HMSO, 2001), p.5.

that in relation to computer software supplied as an intrinsic part of a product, liability will rest on the producer of the product and not on the consultant who designed the package.

## What is a defect?

This is the key concept in the Act.[61] The defendant is liable for damage caused wholly or in part by a "defect" in a product. Section 3 defines a defect as existing when "the safety[62] of the product is not such as persons generally are entitled to expect". The standard is thus set by "persons generally". This ambiguous term has led to some difficulty. It would appear to include the expectations not only of consumers, but also of the manufacturing community. Manufacturers, however, are likely to have lower expectations than those of consumers, who may view themselves as entitled to a product perfect in every way, despite its low market price. The manufacturers' view will inevitably reflect a cost/benefit analysis, whereby the product is only "defective" if the magnitude of the danger inherent in the product, and the cost of preventing the danger, outweighs its utility. It is not clear from the section which form of reasoning a court should utilise in deciding whether a product is "defective" under the Act. Subsequent case law has, by reference to the wording of the Directive and its preamble, specified that the standard is "the safety which the public at large is entitled to expect".[63]

A further question is *what* the public are entitled to expect. For example, a knife, due to its very nature, has an obvious risk of danger, but it nevertheless provides a useful tool. It would clearly be unrealistic if the public could legitimately expect to be protected from any harm due to its sharp blade. Certain practical limits are therefore necessary in applying the "public expectation" test.

This test will ultimately be applied by the court. Section 3(2), does, however, provide that in assessing whether a defect exists, the court should take all the circumstances into account, including:

(a) (i) the manner in which and purposes for which the product has been marketed;
    (ii) the get-up (or packaging) of the product;
    (iii) the use of any mark (for example the "kite mark") in relation to the product;
    (iv) any instructions for, or warnings with respect to doing or refraining from doing anything with or in relation to the product;

(b) what might reasonably be expected to be done with or in relation to the product; and

(c) the time when the product was supplied by its producer to another. It is irrelevant that products supplied after that time are generally safer than the product supplied to the claimant.

**9–021**

---

[61] See A. Stoppa (1992) 12 L.S. 210.

[62] "Safety" is defined to include safety with respect to products comprised in that product and safety in the context of risks of damage to property, as well as in the context of risks of death and personal injury: s.3(1).

[63] See *Abouzaid v Mothercare (UK) Ltd* [2000] All E.R. (D) 2436; *The Times*, February 20, 2001, where Pill L.J. relied on Recital 6 to the Directive, and *A v National Blood Authority* [2001] 3 All E.R. 289 at 334: "the court will act as ... the appointed representative of the public at large".

For many years, however, it was difficult, due to the absence of reported cases, to consider how this test would be applied in practice. Since 1999, a number of cases have been reported, which give valuable assistance in assessing the meaning of "defect" under the Act. Initially, the courts adopted an approach similar to that used in negligence (discussed in Ch.5). In *Richardson v LRC Products*,[64] for example, Mrs Richardson brought an unsuccessful action under the Act when she became pregnant when a condom used by her husband failed. In the absence of any convincing explanation for its failure, the judge examined the care taken by the manufacturer in producing the goods and noted that its standards exceeded the relevant British Standard. It is difficult to reconcile such concerns with a regime of strict liability. A better approach would be that the public do not expect condoms to be 100 per cent effective and, on this basis, the product could not be said to be defective.

The Court of Appeal in *Abouzaid v Mothercare (UK) Ltd*,[65] in its first full judgment on the Act, was critical of such fault-based reasoning. In this case, a child of 12 had been injured when attempting to fasten a sleeping bag manufactured by the defendants to the back of a pushchair. The buckle on the elastic fastenings had sprung back, hitting him in the eye. As a result, the child suffered a significant loss of vision in his left eye. The Court of Appeal adopted a strict view of "defect". In examining the safety which the public at large is entitled to expect, Pill L.J. found that, although this was a borderline case, the severe consequences of injury indicated that the product was defective.[66] It was irrelevant whether this defect should have reasonably come to the manufacturer's attention. The fact that the court found that the defendants would not have been liable in negligence highlighted the distinction between fault-based liability and liability under the Act.

This distinction is further reinforced by the judgment of Burton J. in *A & Others v National Blood Authority*.[67] This was a class action brought by over 100 claimants who had been infected with the virus Hepatitis C through blood transfusions which had used blood or blood products obtained from infected donors. It was alleged that, although the risk of the virus had been known since at least the 1970s, it was, at the time of infection, impossible to detect. Screening for the virus was available only from September 1991. On that basis, the defendants argued that the most that the public could have legitimately expected up to that date was that all reasonable precautions would be carried out, not that the blood would be 100 per cent clean. In the view of the judge, this was a blatant attempt to re-introduce fault-based ideas which were contrary to the purpose of the Directive. Section 3 would be confined to *relevant* circumstances,[68] and the steps taken by the manufacturer to avoid the risk would not be relevant in a no-fault regime. On this basis, "avoidability" of the harmful characteristic would be ignored,[69] as would the impracticality, cost or difficulty of taking precautionary measures. Burton J. equally refused to take account of the fact that the defendants were obliged to supply

---

[64] [2000] Lloyd's Rep. Med. 280. See also *Worsley v Tambrands Ltd* [2000] P.I.Q.R. P95 (toxic shock syndrome resulting from use of tampon), the highly questionable decision of *Foster v Biosil* (2001) 59 B.M.L.R. 178 (CC (Central London)) (ruptured breast implant) and *Sam B v McDonald's Restaurants Limited* [2002] EWHC 490 (QBD) (spillage of hot drinks). See R. Freeman [2001] J.P.I.L. 26.

[65] [2000] All E.R. (D) 2436; *The Times*, February 20, 2001, CA, also known as the "Cosytoes" case.

[66] "Members of the public were entitled to expect better from the appellants": at para.27.

[67] [2001] 3 All E.R. 289. Comment: C. Hodges (2001) 117 L.Q.R. 528; G. Howells and M. Mildred (2002) 65 M.L.R. 95.

[68] This is not obvious from the wording of s.3(2), which states that "all the circumstances shall be taken into account": see C. Hodges (2001) 117 L.Q.R. 528, 530.

[69] "Indeed . . . had it been intended that it would be included as a derogation from, or at any rate a palliation of [the purpose of the Directive] then it would certainly have been mentioned" [2001] 3 All E.R. 289 at 336.

blood to hospitals and patients as a service to society. There was no necessary reason why a public body should receive preferential treatment where a product was unsafe.[70] The public at large were entitled to expect that the blood transfusion would be free from infection. There was no publicity or information to make them consider otherwise.[71]

This would suggest that the courts will in future take a stricter view of what will be deemed "defective" under the Act. Burton J. drew a distinction between two categories of product—standard and non-standard. "Standard" products are those which perform as the producer intends. Any defect will thus show up in every product produced. A "non-standard" product, in contrast, is a rogue product, which differs from the normal product manufactured for use by the public, for example, a chocolate bar containing a piece of metal. Where a product is "non-standard", Burton J. noted that it will be easier to establish that it is defective unless it can be shown that the public have accepted its non-standard nature (for example, due to warnings, its presentation or publicity). In the judge's view, infected blood fell into the "non-standard" category.[72] It differed from the norm intended for use by the public. Further, the public (unlike the medical profession) had not been aware of the risk of Hepatitis C and could not be said to have accepted its non-standard nature.

**9–022**

In contrast, a standard product will raise more complex issues. The courts will be forced to consider, and take expert evidence on, the relevant factors under s.3(2) and the nature of comparable products in the market (and their price) to ascertain the product's safety for foreseeable use.

The cases subsequent to *A* continue to demonstrate uncertainty as to the operation of this test in practice. The Court of Appeal in *Tesco Stores Ltd v Pollard*[73] was prepared to accept that dishwasher powder with a child resistant closure cap (CRC), which was less safe than that specified in the British Standard certificate, was not defective.[74] In the view of Laws L.J., the public were only entitled to expect that the bottle would be more difficult to open than if it had an ordinary screw-top.[75] Such an approach, in which the Court of Appeal expressly rejected the argument that the Act effectively provides a warranty of the safety of products by the producer,[76] contrasts with the purposive analysis of the courts in *Abouzaid* and *A*. In these cases, the courts favoured a policy of consumer protection in a no-fault regime, and Burton J. in *A* cast doubt on earlier decisions such as *Richardson*.[77] It remains to be seen whether the approach in the *Pollard* case is followed or the stricter approach of *A* and *Abouzaid* maintained.

The factors expressly mentioned in s.3(2) will continue to be of assistance. For example, the use of warnings may still provide a means to avoid liability. In *Worsley v Tambrands Ltd*,[78] the

**9–023**

---

[70] [2001] 3 All E.R. 289 at 318.

[71] Burton J. questioned at 338 whether, in any event, even express warnings would have been sufficient or whether they would have been ruled out as an attempt to exclude or limit liability which, under s.7, is not permitted.

[72] Burton J. [2001] 3 All E.R. 289 at 337 rejected the view that blood with a risk of virus could be treated as a "standard" product as too "philosophical".

[73] [2006] EWCA Civ 393; (2006) 150 S.J.L.B. 537.

[74] For criticism, see M. Mildred [2006] J.P.I.L. C130, who argues that there may be good common sense grounds for tying the public expectation test to that of the British Standard. Contrast *Palmer v Palmer* [2006] EWHC 1284 (QBD (Admin)): "Klunk Klip" device, which introduced slack into seat-belts to make them more comfortable, was defective.

[75] [2006] EWCA Civ 393 at para.18.

[76] [2006] EWCA Civ 393, at para.17 per Laws L.J.

[77] See Burton J. in *A v National Blood Authority* [2001] 3 All E.R. 289, 319.

[78] [2000] P.I.Q.R. P95.

fact that the risk of toxic shock syndrome had been mentioned on the packaging of the product, and in detail on a leaflet which accompanied the product which the purchaser was advised to read and keep, led to a finding of no liability. It will be a question for the court whether the warning is sufficient. In *Worsley*, for example, the claimant suffered a near-fatal illness, but the risk of such an event was very small. The courts are likely to be particularly demanding in relation to products aimed at children or other vulnerable parties.

Further, s.3(2)(c) ensures that defendants are not discouraged from making improvements in product safety. This subsection prevents the claimant from arguing that the very act of improving the product amounts to an admission that it was defective in the past. The product is judged at the time that it is supplied by the producer, not when it is received by the claimant. On this basis, the producer will not be liable for ordinary wear and tear to goods which may have lingered on the shelves for months or even years. It will not protect the producer, however, where safety expectations and the product design have not changed in the intervening years.[79]

## What damage?

**9–024**    Section 5(1) provides that death and personal injury[80] are covered by the Act. The Act is more restrictive, however, in relation to property damage,[81] and does not include pure economic loss. This is consistent with the common law position, which excludes liability for pure economic loss resulting from a defective product. Section 5(2) excludes loss or damage to the product itself and loss or damage to the whole or any part of the final product which has been supplied with the product as a component. On this basis, if the windscreen of a vehicle shatters due to a defect and causes the vehicle to crash, the claimant cannot sue for the cost of the windscreen or the vehicle itself. If, however, the driver had purchased a replacement tyre for the vehicle, which burst due to a defect and caused the car to crash, the driver would be able to recover for damage to the car. The tyre was not supplied with the vehicle when purchased, and so recovery is not excluded by s.5(2).

Property claims are further excluded if the loss or damage suffered, excluding interest, does not exceed £275 (s.5(4)). By this means, the courts avoid having to consider very small claims. Claims are also excluded if the property at the time it is lost or damaged is not of a description ordinarily intended for private use, occupation or consumption, and not intended to be so used (s.5(3)). The Act therefore gives primary protection to the consumer. Again, there will be definitional problems. For example, if a lecturer buys a computer for use in his or her research, but also for the family to play games and surf the net, can it be viewed as property ordinarily intended for private use and intended to be so used?

The UK government chose not to implement an option in the Directive to set a maximum level of damages for which a defendant could be liable. Article 16(1) of the Directive states that the producer's total liability for damage resulting from death or personal injury caused by the product and identical items with the same defect may be limited to an amount not less than €70 million. This has only been implemented in Germany, Spain and Portugal.

---

[79]  See *Abouzaid v Mothercare (UK) Ltd* [2000] All E.R. (D) 2436; *The Times*, February 20, 2001.
[80]  s.45(1) defines "personal injury" to include any disease and any other impairment of a person's physical or mental condition.
[81]  Which includes damage to land: s.5(1).

# Defences

Section 4, or more specifically s.4(1)(e), of the Act has caused the most controversy and has **9–025** even led to a reference to the European Court of Justice challenging the United Kingdom's implementation of the Product Liability Directive. Section 4 gives the defendant six possible defences. It is important to recognise that the mere existence of defences does not mean that the Act does not impose strict liability on the defendant. The aim of strict liability is simply to remove from the claimant the burden of proving that the defendant has been at fault.

Let us examine the defences in turn.

*(a) The defect is attributable to compliance with a requirement imposed by law*

This is obviously necessary, because otherwise the defendant would be torn between complying **9–026** with two conflicting legal provisions. However, compliance with a legal requirement will only absolve a producer from liability if the defect was an inevitable result of compliance.[82]

*(b) The defendants did not at any time supply the product to another*

This protects the defendants if they have not put the product in circulation, for example, the **9–027** product is stolen or a counterfeit copy, and found to be defective. It should be noted, however, that "supply" is defined quite generously under the Act.[83]

*(c) Supply by the defendants was not in course of their business*

Defendants can take advantage of this defence if the only supply of the product was not in the **9–028** course of their business and either:

(i) section 2(2) does not apply (i.e. they are only suppliers), or

(ii) they are within s.2(2) (i.e. they are producers, own-branders or importers into the EC), but are not acting at the time with a view to profit.

This is somewhat confusing and is best illustrated by examples. If I make a cake and sell it at the local craft fair, I am not acting in the course of business, but I am a producer and acting with a view to profit.[84] I cannot therefore use the defence. If, however, I wish to get rid of my old lawnmower and sell it to my neighbour for £50, I am not acting in the course of business and I am not a producer, own-brander or importer and so can rely on the defence if the lawnmower proves to be defective. It is irrelevant whether I have profited from the transaction or not.

*(d) The defect did not exist in the product at the relevant time, i.e. when it was put into circulation*[85]

This makes the simple point that if the defect is due to wear and tear resulting from use of the **9–029** product after the product has been put into circulation, the defendant will not be liable. As a

---

[82] *Guide to the Consumer Protection Act 1987* (HMSO, 2001).

[83] "Supply" is defined in s.46 to include selling, hiring out or lending goods, entering into a hire-purchase agreement to furnish the goods, the performance of any contract for work and materials to furnish the goods or even giving the goods as a prize or otherwise making a gift of the goods.

[84] Query the situation if I sold it at the school fête for charity.

[85] s.4(2) defines the "relevant time" to signify (a) if the defendant is within s.2(2), the time when he supplied the product to another, or (b) if the defendant is not within s.2(2) (for example, a supplier), the time when the product was last supplied by a person to whom s.2(2) does apply.

defence, the burden will be on the defendant to establish this. The defence was raised recently in *Piper v JRI (Manufacturing) Ltd.*[86] Here, the claimant had undergone a total hip replacement operation. Unfortunately, after an apparently successful operation, the prosthesis implanted into his right hip sheared in two. Piper alleged that the prosthesis was defective. However, the manufacturer alleged that the defect had not existed when the product had been supplied to the hospital. The Court of Appeal found that, on the evidence, the manufacturer had discharged the burden of proving the defence by showing that any defect would have been picked up by their inspection system.

### (e)  The development risk defence

**9–030**   This defence is optional to Member States (see art.15(1)(b)), although it has generally been implemented within the European Union.[87] Its implementation in English law has, however, proved controversial.[88] Section 4(1)(e) provides a defence where:

> ". . . the state of scientific and technical knowledge at the relevant time was not such that a producer of products of the same description as the product in question might be expected to have discovered the defect if it had existed in his products while they were under his control".

This may be contrasted with the wording of art.7(e) of the Directive, which the Act seeks to transpose into English law:

> ". . . the state of scientific and technical knowledge at the time when [the producer] put the product into circulation was not such as to enable the existence of the defect to be discovered".

At first sight, there appears to be a substantive difference between the two provisions. Whilst the Directive suggests that the producer must establish, objectively, that the knowledge available at the time of circulation would not have alerted the defendant to the particular risk, s.4(1)(e) appears more generous. Its wording suggests that the producer need only show that a "reasonable producer", i.e. another producer in the same market, would not have known of the risks in question. Such a test is reminiscent of the *Bolam* test for breach of duty, discussed in Ch.5, and is hardly indicative of strict liability on the producer. Indeed, it seems to suggest simply that the defendant will not be liable if he or she can demonstrate that he or she has exercised the care of a "reasonable producer" in the market in assessing the risks associated with the product.[89]

---

[86]  [2006] EWCA Civ 1344, (2006) 92 B.M.L.R. 141.

[87]  Except in Finland and Luxembourg. Spain excludes the defence for food and medicinal products and France excludes the defence for products derived from the human body. Germany has permitted liability for development risks in the area of pharmaceutical products since 1978.

[88]  The United Kingdom's implementation of the defence may be contrasted with the view of the Law Commission, in their 1977 report, *Liability for Defective Products* No.82, Cmnd 6831 para.105, that if the product was found to be defective, in the light of the thalidomide case, the injured person should be compensated by the producer however careful the producer had been. The report of the *Royal Commission on Civil Liability and Compensation for Personal Injury*, Cmnd 7054 (1978), Vol.1, para.1259 also recommended that the defence should not be allowed.

[89]  This provoked a considerable academic debate: see, for example, J. Stapleton, *Product Liability* (Butterworths, 1994) and C. Newdick [1988] C.L.J. 455.

The possible conflict between these two provisions was examined by the European Court of Justice in *European Commission v United Kingdom*.[90] The European Commission had initiated infringement proceedings against the UK in April 1989, alleging that the Act did not properly transpose the Directive into English law, as required by Art.19 of the Directive. It was argued that s.4(1)(e) was broader than the defence in art.7(e). The European Court of Justice rejected this claim. It held that art.7(e) imposed an objective test on the producer as to the state of scientific and technical knowledge at the time the product was put in circulation, which would include the most advanced level of knowledge in the relevant field. The producer would be presumed to possess such knowledge, and it was not a question of the producer's subjective state of knowledge or the particular practices and safety standards of the producer's industrial sector. However, the Court was not prepared to go so far as to presume that the producer would be acquainted with *all* relevant scientific knowledge at the time the product was put into circulation. It approved the view of Advocate General Tesauro that the knowledge in question must be accessible. It would thus be unfair to expect the producer to be familiar with research carried out by an academic in Manchuria who published in a local scientific journal in Chinese, which was not circulated outside the boundaries of the region. If the relevant scientific research is accessible, however, it will not be a valid excuse to argue that it represents an isolated opinion: the producer is expected to keep note of, and consider, all relevant research.

In the view of the court, there was no clear indication that s.4(1)(e) was inconsistent with a proper interpretation of the Directive. Whilst the section could be interpreted in a broader sense, the court held that its wording did not suggest that the availability of the defence depended on the subjective knowledge of the producer. There was, in any event, no English decision which indicated that the English courts would interpret s.4(1)(e) in a way which would conflict with their duty, stated in s.1(1) of the Act, to construe the Act in accordance with the Directive. The Advocate General suggested that, in this light, the Commission's application had been "overhasty, to say the least". **9–031**

One might consider that, due to the absence of case law, English law had a fortunate escape, but the legacy of this case is that, in future, s.4(1)(e) will be interpreted in a manner consistent with the comments of the European Court of Justice. Indeed, in the leading case of *A & Others v National Blood Authority*,[91] Burton J. referred not to the sections of the Act, but to the Directive itself, in considering this defence. It is clear from this decision that the courts will, in future, adopt a strict approach to this defence and reject any approach based on fault.

As stated above, *A & Others v National Blood Authority* concerned a class action by over 100 claimants who had been infected with Hepatitis C through blood transfusions. At the time of infection, the relevant defendants had been aware of the risk of the disease, but did not possess the requisite technology to identify infected blood until a later date. They therefore sought to rely on the "development risk" defence on the basis that the state of scientific and technical knowledge was such that the existence of the defect in the product itself was undetectable. Burton J. adopted a firm line. The defendants did know of the possible existence of a defect in blood generally. Their absence of knowledge related to the ability to devise a test to identify which blood was infected. In such circumstances, it would be inconsistent with the

---

[90] [1997] All E.R. (EC) 481; [1997] 3 C.M.L.R. 923. Comment: C. Hodges (1998) 61 M.L.R. 560.
[91] [2001] 3 All E.R. 289. Comment: C. Hodges (2001) 117 L.Q.R. 528; G. Howells and M. Mildred (2002) 65 M.L.R. 95.

purpose of the Directive if the producer, knowing of a risk, continued to supply the product without liability simply because he or she could not identify in which of his products the defect would occur:

> "If there is a known risk, i.e. the existence of the defect is known or should have been known in the light of . . . accessible information, then the producer continues to produce and supply at his own risk. It would, in my judgment, be inconsistent with the purpose of the directive if a producer, in the case of a known risk, continues to supply products simply because, and despite the fact that, he is unable to identify in which if any of his products that defect will occur or recur".[92]

This firm line was also adopted by the Court of Appeal in *Abouzaid v Mothercare (UK) Ltd.*[93] It had been argued that since the defendants had been unaware of the potential problems with the buckle fastening, and no record of any comparable incident had been recorded by the Department of Trade and Industry accident database, the state of scientific and technical knowledge did not indicate a problem at the relevant time. The Court of Appeal gave this argument short shrift. The defence was present to deal with technical advances, not to deal with problems which no-one had thought about. A simple practical test would have identified how a buckle would spring back if extended. Equally, Pill L.J. doubted whether a DTI database fell within the category of "scientific and technical knowledge".[94]

The strict line taken in these cases would seem finally to allay fears that s.4(1)(e) has re-introduced negligence into the Act with a reversed burden of proof on the manufacturer.

*(f) The defect was a defect in a finished product (X) in which the product in question had been comprised AND was wholly attributable to the design of X or to compliance with the producer of X's instructions*

**9–032** This protects the defendant who has supplied a component part of a product, and risks being found to be jointly and severally liable, under s.2(5), when a defect is found in the finished product. It is essentially a denial of causation: my product has no causal link with the injury caused to the claimant. The defence is somewhat complicated and best illustrated by an example. A instructs B to supply tyres which are suitable for a family car, which A decides would be ideal in constructing his new racing car. A is wrong, and the tyres burst at 100 mph, causing A to crash. B will be able to rely on this defence to deny liability. If, however, B was aware of the purpose for which A was purchasing the tyres (for which they were clearly deficient), it is likely that B would be liable in negligence for failing to warn A that they were not suitable for racing cars. Equally, if the tyres burst not because they were used for the wrong purpose, but because they were defectively manufactured, the defence would not apply. The defect must be wholly attributable to A's conduct and the burden will be on the component producer to prove this to the court.

[92] [2001] 3 All E.R. 289 at 340.
[93] [2000] All E.R. (D) 2436; *The Times*, February 20, 2001.
[94] para.29.

## Contributory negligence

Section 6(4) ensures that the principle of contributory negligence is also available to the **9–033** defendant.[95] This may appear somewhat odd. The defendant is liable without proof of fault, but the claimant's damages may be reduced if the claimant's fault has increased the damage suffered by him or her. Section 1(1) of the Law Reform (Contributory Negligence) Act 1945 states that the defence applies "where any person suffers damage as the result partly of his own fault and partly of the fault of any other person", but "fault" is interpreted broadly by s.4 of that Act to include any "act or omission which gives rise to a liability in tort". The defendant, if liable, is therefore presumed to be at "fault", and the claimant's actual fault is balanced against the responsibility of the defendant. This again gives rise to concern as to the intrusion of fault into a strict liability statute. It should also be noted that the claimant's contributory negligence, for example in using a product in an unreasonable way, may indicate that the product is not defective, in any event, under the criteria set under s.3(2) (see, in particular, s.3(2)(b)).

## Exclusion clauses

In view of the aim of the Act to protect claimants from injury due to defective products, s.7 **9–034** provides that such claims "shall not be limited or excluded by any contract term, by any notice or by any other provision". This avoids the technicalities of the Unfair Contract Terms Act 1977 and sends a clear message to defendants that exclusion clauses are not an adequate response to potential liability.

## Limitation periods

These are discussed in Ch.16. A limitation period indicates the time period within which a **9–035** claimant must bring a claim. If a claim is brought after this period, however good the claim, the courts will refuse to allow the claim to proceed. By this means, the courts avoid dealing with stale claims and claimants are encouraged to act promptly when the evidence is fresh. The Limitation Act 1980 contains the main provisions. Section 11A deals specifically with actions in respect of defective products. In relation to claims for personal injury or property loss, the claim must be brought within three years from the date on which the cause of action accrued.[96] The cause of action will accrue either when the damage is caused or, if later, when the damage is reasonably discoverable[97] by the claimant. Section 11A(3) provides that an action under Part 1 of the 1987 Act shall not be brought after the expiration of the period of 10 years from the time the product was put into circulation. This long-stop provision will serve to protect defendants from claims in respect of design defects which come to light long after products have been in circulation.

The recent *O'Byrne* litigation has highlighted tensions existing between national limitations rules and the Directive. Declan O'Byrne had been vaccinated in 1992 and subsequently

---

[95] s.6 also renders the Fatal Accidents Act 1976 and the Congenital Disabilities (Civil Liability) Act 1976 applicable.

[96] s.11A(4).

[97] The date of knowledge is defined in Limitation Act 1980 s.14.

suffered severe brain damage. It was alleged that the vaccine was defective. An action had mistakenly been brought against the defendant's English subsidiary. Realising the mistake, the claimant applied to substitute as defendant the parent company and manufacturer of the vaccine (Limitation Act 1980 s.35, granting a discretion to the court to substitute a new party), however after the 10 year long-stop period had expired. The English High Court, at the request of both parties, made a preliminary reference to the European Court of Justice (ECJ) which, in *O'Byrne v Sanofi Pasteur MSD Ltd*,[98] ruled that a product was put into circulation for the purposes of s.11A(3)

> "when it leaves the production process operated by the producer and enters a marketing process in the form in which it is offered to the public in order to be used or consumed . . . in the case of a wholly owned subsidiary of the [producer], it is necessary to establish whether it is a consequence of that link that that entity is in reality involved in the manufacturing process of the product concerned".[99]

The question of the substitution of parties after the 10 year long-stop was considered to be a matter for the national court to decide: "it is as a rule for national law to determine the conditions in accordance with which one party may be substituted for another in the context of such an action. A national court . . . must, however, ensure that due regard is had to the personal scope of Directive 85/374, as established by articles 1 and 3 thereof".[100] The matter was then referred back to the English courts.

This less than straightforward statement resulted in a second reference to the European Court of Justice in 2008.[101] The ECJ was asked, bluntly, did the Directive, which sought to harmonise limitation periods for defective products, nevertheless permit national legislation which allowed the substitution of one defendant for another after the expiry of the 10 year long-stop period? The Grand Chamber in 2009[102] held that where national legislation allowed for substitution of parties, it should *not* be applied in a way which permitted the producer to be sued after the expiry of the limitation period even though the action had been begun within time, albeit against the wrong defendant. It did accept, however, that where the proceedings had been issued within time against a wholly-owned subsidiary of the producer, the Product Liability Directive did not prevent the national court from substituting the producer for that subsidiary if it found that the putting into circulation of the product had been determined by the producer.

Applying this ruling, the Supreme Court in *O'Byrne v Aventis Pasteur MSD Ltd*[103] held in 2010 that a new party could not be substituted in this case, despite the fact that the manufacturer wholly-owned its English subsidiary. The ECJ's core ruling had been that a national rule allowing substitution should not be invoked against a producer after expiry of the 10 year period. The exception for wholly-owned subsidiaries was interpreted narrowly to indicate a situation where, as a matter of fact, a distribution subsidiary was so closely involved with the parent producer that they could, in effect, also be regarded as a producer. This was not the case

---

[98] (C127/04) [2006] 1 W.L.R. 1606 (ECJ).
[99] (C127/04) [2006] 1 W.L.R. 1606 (ECJ) at paras 27–29. The term "put into circulation" was not defined in the Directive as it was considered self-explanatory. As this rather unclear definition indicates, this is far from the case.
[100] At para.39.
[101] *OB v Aventis Pasteur* [2008] UKHL 34; [2008] 3 C.M.L.R. 10.
[102] *O'Byrne v Aventis Pasteur SA* (C-358/08) [2010] 1 W.L.R. 1375.
[103] [2010] UKSC 23; [2010] 1 W.L.R. 1412, reversing Court of Appeal in [2007] EWCA Civ 966.

here. O'Byrne, therefore, finally lost his battle for compensation some 18 years after the vaccination had taken place.

## Causation and remoteness

There are no specific rules in the Act and so the ordinary rules described in Ch.6 of this **9–036** book will apply. The Act gives the claimant no further assistance in what, as stated earlier, may be a difficult task, particularly in cases of illness and disease.[104] This was illustrated in *X v Schering Health Care Ltd*[105] in relation to the third generation oral contraceptive pill. In a trial lasting three months and hearing the conflicting evidence of 10 experts, Mackay J. concluded, in a judgment of 200 pages, that there was insufficient evidential basis to establish that an increased risk of cardio-vascular injury was caused by the product. On this basis, there was therefore no need to examine the law under the Act.

## ASSESSMENT OF THE IMPACT OF THE ACT

## Continuing practical problems

Whilst it took almost 12 years from the introduction of the Act for a claimant to bring a **9–037** successful claim,[106] the two important cases of *Abouzaid* and *A* have done much to allay fears that the Act provided little addition to the common law.[107] The ruling of the European Court of Justice in *European Commission v United Kingdom*[108] has proved a significant milestone in affirming the objectives of the Directive and its goal in providing consumer protection. Nevertheless, as seen in the cases discussed above, litigation will often prove an expensive and lengthy process, particularly if complex medical evidence is involved. Further, the claimant receives no assistance in proving causation, which may be an onerous task. The claimant's position is moreover weakened by the strict time limitations on his or her action. It is entirely probable that it would take more than 10 years for certain injuries resulting from design defects to become apparent, and yet the long-stop provision bars the litigant's claim absolutely. The inclusion of primary agricultural products in the Directive is therefore unlikely to assist persons suffering vCJD as a result of eating beef infected with BSE, due to the long incubation period of the illness.

---

[104] See, for example, *Ide v ATB Sales Ltd* [2008] EWCA Civ 424 where two alternative explanations for the cause of Mr Ide's accident were put before the court. The court indicated, however, that in Consumer Protection Act cases, it was unnecessary to ascertain the cause of the defect: the question was whether the claimant could prove on the balance of probabilities that the defect caused the damage sustained.

[105] [2002] EWHC 1420, (2003) 70 B.M.L.R. 88. See M. Mildred [2002] J.P.I.L. 428 and A. McAdams (2002) 146 S.J. 900.

[106] Our first edition in 2000 noted only one reported case which was directly in point: *European Commission v United Kingdom* [1997] 3 C.M.L.R. 923.

[107] See E. Deards and C. Twigg-Flesner (2001) 10 Nott L.J. 1.

[108] [1997] All E.R. (EC) 481; [1997] 3 C.M.L.R. 923, discussed above.

## Standard and non-standard products

9–038    It would seem that the different treatment of manufacture and design defects has survived the Act, although Burton J. in *A* preferred the similar, but not identical, terms of "standard" and "non-standard" product. In defining a "standard" product as one which performs as the producer intended, there is an obvious link with design defects. Equally, a clear example of a "non-standard" product would be a product subject to a manufacturing defect. Burton J. conceded that it would be easier to prove a defect in a non-standard product and that it would be more difficult to apply the "development risk defence" to non-standard products. Such a product may at most qualify once, i.e. where the problem, which led to an occasional defective product, was not known. Once the problem can be discovered by virtue of accessible information, the defence will no longer apply. Standard products, however, are likely to give rise to more complex litigation in ascertaining exactly what level of safety the public is entitled to expect. This mirrors the position at common law, where, it may be recalled, the courts are more willing to infer negligence in relation to manufacturing defects. The real deficiency in the common law lay in relation to claims for design defects, and it would appear that, despite the tough line taken by Burton J., the practical difficulties in bringing a claim for design defects will not disappear. It remains to be seen whether the English courts will succeed in addressing the questions of defects in standard products and the degree of warning necessary to avoid liability without reference to cost/benefit analysis. For example, is it possible to ascertain what safety the public can legitimately expect from a product without considering what precautions the producer could have taken at the time it was put into circulation? The difficulties caused by the "standard"/"non-standard" distinction have already led two leading academics to question the merits of this distinction and what it positively contributes to our understanding of this area of law.[109]

## Use of settlements

9–039    It is likely to remain the case that most litigation under the 1987 Act will be settled out of court. Despite evidence that the Directive is now being used in all Member States and the delivery by the ECJ of a number of judgments since 2001, there are still few reported cases to be found.[110] It is therefore difficult to assess the impact of the Act, particularly as settlements will frequently require the parties not to publicise the terms of the agreement. In contrast, in the United States, s.37 of the Consumer Product Safety Act obliges producers to announce cases involving defective products and notify the Consumer Product Safety Commission (CPSC).[111] If the product which has allegedly caused death or grievous bodily injury is the subject of at least three civil cases in a two-year period, producers (and importers as well) have to notify the Commission of the circumstances of the case as soon as the cases have been settled, either by a ruling in favour of the claimant, or as the result of an out of court

---

[109]    See G. Howells and M. Mildred (2002) 65 M.L.R. 95, 101.

[110]    See *Third Report on the application of Council Directive 85/374 on the approximation of laws, regulations and administrative provisions of the Member States concerning liability for defective products*, COM (2006) 496, final.

[111]    This is an independent federal regulatory agency created in 1972 to "protect the public against unreasonable risks of injuries and deaths associated with consumer products". It covers about 15,000 types of consumer products used in home, schools and recreation, but does not regulate on-road motor vehicles, boats, aircraft, cosmetics, pesticides, alcohol, tobacco, firearms and medical devices. See *www.cpsc.gov/*.

agreement.[112] There is no equivalent provision in the United Kingdom. Arguably, it would be in the public interest for greater information to be available on such settlements, which would enable a clearer assessment to be made of the impact of the Act on UK law. Certainly, it would assist the European Commission in its review of the operation of the Product Liability Directive within the European Union. Such measures, however, are likely to be opposed by manufacturers, who are far from willing to allow their competitors access to such information.

## BREACH OF STATUTORY DUTY

Part II of the Consumer Protection Act 1987 provides for the Secretary of State to make safety    **9–040** regulations prescribing rules as to design, manufacture and packaging of certain classes of goods. This replaced earlier legislation in the Consumer Safety Act 1978. Although breach of such regulations generally incurs only criminal liability, s.41 expressly provides that an individual injured by a defect in a product resulting from breach of safety regulations has an action for breach of statutory duty. This provides a further option for litigants, although it should be noted that the regulations only cover a limited class of goods.[113]

## REFORM OF THE PRODUCT LIABILITY DIRECTIVE[114]

The European Commission is required to undertake a review of the Product Liability Directive    **9–041** every five years.[115] In July 1999, it published a Green Paper on Liability for Defective Products,[116] in which it outlined the Commission's proposals to consult interested parties to assess the impact of the Directive on victims and on the sectors of the economy concerned, and to reflect on the need for reform. In particular, it sought views on:

- the burden of proof imposed on victims;
- the operation of the "development risks" defence;
- the existence of minimum and maximum values for claims and their justification;
- the 10-year deadline and the effects of a possible modification of this;
- assessment of the insurability of risks deriving from defective production;
- improved information on the settlement of cases concerning defective products;

---

[112] See 15 USC Sec. 2084, "Information reporting".

[113] See s.11(7).

[114] Details of European Commission documents on defective products, including all three reports on the Directive and the Green Paper, may be found at: *http://ec.europa.eu/enterprise/policies/single-market-goods/documents/liability/ index_en.htm* [Accessed April 20, 2011.

[115] The Commission has to report regularly to the Community institutions on the state of the application of the Directive. Art. 21 of the Directive stipulates that it must report every 5 years on the general application of the Directive. arts 15(3) and 16(2) stipulate that it must report every 10 years after notification of the Directive on development risks and financial limits.

[116] COM (1999) 396, final.

- the supplier's liability;

- the type of goods and damage covered.

In its report of January 2001,[117] the Commission resolved that in view of the belated transposition of the Directive in certain countries,[118] the possibility given to the Member States to apply their own national law, and the lack of available data, it would again not recommend any change to the Directive.[119] Nevertheless, the Commission resolved actively to seek further information for future reforms. This included setting up a study to analyse and compare the practical effects of the different systems applicable in EU Member States regarding the procedural aspects of claims for defective products,[120] and launching a study into the economic impact of the development risk defence.[121] In 2006, a further review took place.[122] It concluded that by and large the Directive worked in a satisfactory way and that there was as yet no need for amendments. It expressly rejected a proposal that the Directive be modified to allow for national rules on liability of suppliers to be based on the same grounds as the liability system concerning producers.[123] A number of topics were, nevertheless, highlighted as requiring close and regular monitoring:

- the burden of proof

- the concept of defect

- the development risks defence

- the minimum threshold for liability

- the possibility, argued for strongly by the pharmaceutical industry, of a defence of regulatory compliance, that is, no liability should be imposed for a product whose safety is closely regulated if these regulations are complied with

- whether strict liability should continue to apply to novel products, design defects or injuries arising from a failure to warn.

---

[117] COM (2000) 893, final.

[118] For example, France only implemented the Directive on May 23, 1998 (see Act No. 389–98 of May 19, 1998). Its legislation was successfully challenged twice by the European Commission for failing to implement the Directive correctly: see *EC Commission v France* (C-52/00) [2002] E.C.R. I-3827 and *EC Commission v France* (C-177/04) [2006] E.C.R. I-2461. The final amended provisions now constitute Arts 1386–1 to 1386–18 of the French Civil Code. See P. Shears [2007] J.B.L. 884.

[119] This is the second report of the Commission. In its first report of December 1995 (COM (1995) 617, final), the Commission concluded that, on the basis of the limited information available as to the operation of the Directive, it was not appropriate to submit any proposals for amendments.

[120] Lovells, *Product liability in the European Union* (2003).

[121] Fondazione Rosselli, *Analysis of the economic impact of the development risk clause as provided by Directive 85/374/EEC on liability for defective products* (2004). Two working groups were also created—one of experts designated by national authorities and another of stakeholders—to assist the Commission in its task of keeping existing legislation under constant review.

[122] *Third Report on the application of Council Directive 85/374 on the approximation of laws, regulations and administrative provisions of the Member States concerning liability for defective products*, Com (2006) 496, final. For a critical assessment, see D. Fairgrieve and G. Howells (2007) 70 M.L.R. 962.

[123] Requested by Council Resolution of 19 December 2002 ([2003] OJ C26/2–3).

As may be seen, there is some overlap with the issues identified in 1999. Uncertainty as to the meaning of defect is raised in the context of mainly English case law, which has, as seen above, demonstrated over the years an inconsistent approach to this concept.[124] The last two questions highlight the impact of the ongoing lobbying by producers seeking to minimise the impact of the Directive on their businesses. It is clear that product liability will continue to be contentious, particularly as it is transposed in new European States. One of the foremost priorities identified by the Commission is to continue to follow closely developments in the practical application of product liability in Member States.[125]

# (2) ANIMALS ACT 1971

In this last part of the chapter, we will look briefly at the liability imposed by the Animals Act 1971. This was brought in to replace the rather complicated existing common law provisions which imposed strict liability on those responsible for wild and domestic animals.[126] The Act imposes strict liability for damage done by animals under the care of another. It should be noted that the Act applies in addition to ordinary common law principles. Therefore, an owner of a dog may still find himself or herself liable under occupiers' liability for injuries caused (see Ch.8),[127] liable in nuisance (for example, for the smell caused by his or her pigs: see Ch.10)[128] or liable in trespass (for example, for allowing hounds to stray onto another's land: see Ch.11).[129] Owners may equally find themselves liable under the ordinary rules of negligence where they have failed to exercise reasonable care to prevent their pet causing foreseeable harm to another.[130]                **9–042**

We set out below the main provisions of the 1971 Act. We do not deal with liability for injuries committed by dogs to livestock (s.3)[131] or liability for damage caused by straying livestock (s.4),[132] which are not considered in most law courses.

## Dangerous/non-dangerous species

The fundamental distinction in the Act is between wild animals (or dangerous species) and domestic animals (non-dangerous species). For example, a tiger will be classified as the former, a cat the latter. Different provisions apply according to the classification of the animal in question. Liability will be imposed on the "keeper" of the animal in both cases. "Keeper" is                **9–043**

---

[124] Contrast, for example, the approach in *A* with that of *Richardson v LRC Products*.

[125] Third report at p.8. The fourth report is due in 2011.

[126] See s.1. Note the 1967 Report of the Law Commission, *Civil liability for animals* (Law Com No 13) on which the Act is based and the classic work of P.M. North, *The Modern Law of Animals* (Butterworths: 1972).

[127] See *Gould v McAuliffe* [1941] 1 All E.R. 515.

[128] See *Wheeler v JJ Saunders Ltd* [1996] Ch.19. Note also *Leeman v Montague* [1936] 2 All E.R. 1677.

[129] See *League against Cruel Sports v Scott* [1986] Q.B. 240 (owner responsible for the damage caused if he or she intended animals to enter the claimant's land or, knowing that there was a real risk that they would enter, failed to take reasonable care to prevent their entry.)

[130] See *Fardon v Harcourt-Rivington* (1932) 146 L.T. 391, HL, *Draper v Hodder* [1971] 2 Q.B. 556 and *Whippey v Jones* [2009] EWCA Civ 452. A further action may lie for a compensatory award from the Criminal Injuries Compensation Authority if the victim can establish that a criminal offence has taken place: see *Re C [CICA: Liability: 2002]* December 3, 2002; [2003] 7 C.L.10 (horses straying onto the highway amounting to a criminal offence under the Highways Act 1980, s.155).

[131] See also ss.5(4) and 9.

[132] See also ss.5(5), 5(6), 7 and 8.

defined in s.6(3)[133] as the owner of the animal, someone who has it in his possession, or the head of a household where a minor under 16 owns or possesses the animal.[134]

*Dangerous species*

**9–044**   These are defined in s.6(2) of the Act.

> "A dangerous species[135] is a species—
>
> (a) which is not commonly domesticated in the British Islands; and
> (b) whose fully grown animals normally have such characteristics that they are likely, unless restrained, to cause severe damage or that any damage they may cause is likely to be severe".

This will therefore include animals such as tigers, elephants[136] and lions. As noted in the leading case of *Mirvahedy v Henley*,[137] cases will generally arise in the context of escapes from circuses or zoos. Section 2(1) provides that the keeper of the dangerous animal will be strictly liable for any damage caused by such an animal, subject to the defences outlined below. Liability will be regardless of fault and irrespective of any awareness of the animal's dangerous propensities. This appears to be entirely sensible. It is no excuse that your pet tiger escaped despite your reasonable efforts to fence it in. The risk of injury lies firmly on the keeper of any such animal.

*Non-dangerous species*

**9–045**   This is rather more complicated. It concerns domesticated animals and here liability is limited to circumstances where the keeper knows of the danger and severe injury is likely to arise due to the particular characteristics of the animal. Section 2(2) sets three conditions for liability which must all be satisfied:

> "(a) the damage is of a kind which the animal, unless restrained, was likely to cause or which, if caused by the animal, was likely to be severe; and
>
> (b) the likelihood of the damage or of its being severe was due to characteristics of the animal which are not normally found in animals of the same species or are not normally so found except at particular times or in particular circumstances; and
>
> (c) those characteristics were known to that keeper or were at any time known to a person who at that time had charge of the animal as that keeper's servant or, where that keeper is the head of a household, were known to another keeper of the animal who is a member of that household and under the age of sixteen".

---

[133] See also s.6(4): "Where an animal is taken into and kept in possession for the purpose of preventing it from causing damage or of restoring it to its owner, a person is not a keeper of it by virtue only of that possession".

[134] It should be noted that there may be more than one keeper: see *Flack v Hudson* [2001] Q.B. 698 where an action was brought on behalf of the person with possession of the horse against its owner. The Court of Appeal held that there was nothing in the Act to prevent one keeper suing another.

[135] "Species" includes sub-species and variety: s.11.

[136] See *Behrens v Bertram Mills Circus Ltd* [1957] 2 Q.B. 1 (Devlin J.) in which it was held to be irrelevant that the elephant in question was a trained circus animal rather than a wild animal. See also *Filburn v People's Palace and Aquarium Co* (1890) L.R. 25 Q.B.D. 258.

[137] [2003] UKHL 16, [2003] 2 A.C. 491 at para.135 per Lord Walker.

The courts will generally consider each matter in turn. The first two conditions set an objective test. First of all, was the type of damage foreseeable? "Likely" has been interpreted as "to be reasonably expected".[138] It does not require probability, but equally a mere possibility will not suffice. Secondly, did the relevant characteristic of the animal cause the harm suffered? The third condition is subjective: did the keeper know of this characteristic? This requires actual knowledge of the potential danger by the keeper.[139] It does not, however, require the keeper to have actual knowledge of the particular circumstances in which the injury arose. It is enough that the keeper knows that animals of the relevant species would behave in that way in those circumstances.[140]

The application of these conditions has caused problems in practice, largely due to their wording, which has been described as giving rise to "several difficulties",[141] "remarkably opaque",[142] "somewhat tortuous",[143] and "inept".[144] The real difficulty arises in interpreting s.2(2)(b). The first limb is fairly straightforward: you will be liable if your animal has charac-teristics which other animals of the same species do not possess, for example, it is more vicious than usual. These have been called "permanent characteristics".[145]

The second limb deals with "temporary characteristics" and has been described by the House of Lords itself as "ambiguous" and "opaque". It contains a double negative: characteristics not normally found except at particular times or in particular circumstances. Does this mean:

(a) Normal characteristics which arise at particular times or in particular circumstances? or;

(b) Abnormal characteristics which only manifest themselves at particular times?

The House of Lords in the leading case of *Mirvahedy v Henley*[146] by a bare majority (3:2) chose the first explanation. On this basis, normal characteristics which only manifest them-selves at particular times or on particular occasions might give rise to liability if the other two conditions are met. As Lord Nicholls indicated, as a matter of social policy, the choice is between placing the burden of liability on those who care for the animals and undertake any associated risks or forcing the public in general to accept that animals inevitably bring with them a risk of injury.[147] In adopting a broad interpretation of s.2(2)(b), the majority ensured that it would be easier in future to bring a claim under the 1971 Act without the necessity to show that the animal at that time was acting abnormally.

---

[138] Lord Scott in *Mirvahedy v Henley* at para.95. See also Neill L.J. in *Smith v Ainger The Times*, June 5, 1990: "such as might happen" and "such as might well happen".

[139] It is not enough that the keeper ought to have known of the danger: see *Hunt v Wallis* [1994] P.I.Q.R. P128.

[140] See *Welsh v Stokes* [2007] EWCA Civ 796, [2007] P.I.Q.R. P27 at para.71 per Dyson L.J. Contrast *McKenny v Foster (t/a Foster Partnership)* [2008] EWCA Civ 173 (escape by "extraordinarily agitated" cow in a manner which was not a normal characteristic of breed and was not known to defendant).

[141] Lord Denning M.R. in *Cummings v Grainger* [1977] Q.B. 397 at 404.

[142] Ormrod L.J. in *Cummings v Grainger* at 407.

[143] Slade L.J. in *Curtis v Betts* [1990] 1 W.L.R. 459 at 462.

[144] Nourse L.J. in *Curtis v Betts* [1990] 1 W.L.R. 459 at 468.

[145] See Stuart-Smith LJ in *Curtis v Betts* [1990] 1 W.L.R. 459 at 469.

[146] [2003] 2 A.C. 491. Comment: K. Amirthalingam (2003) 119 L.Q.R. 563. For an overview of the post-*Mirvahedy* case law, see R. Harris (2008) 158 N.L.J. 945.

[147] [2003] 2 A.C. 491 at para.6, although his Lordship indicated that where the law in question was governed by statute, such policy decisions must be deemed to have been dealt with by Parliament and it was not for the courts to intervene.

**9–046**    The case itself concerned a car accident caused by an alarmed horse bolting onto a busy dual carriageway. Mirvahedy suffered serious personal injuries and his car was badly damaged. The owners of the horse had taken reasonable care to fence in the horse and were not found to be liable on the basis of common law negligence. The case rested on the interpretation of s.2(2) of the Act. It was accepted that there was nothing abnormal in a horse bolting when frightened. It was entirely normal.[148] However, a horse would only bolt in particular circumstances, here where it had been terrified by some unknown event into escaping. The owners of the horse would therefore be strictly liable for the damage caused.

In reaching its decision, the majority affirmed the approach taken in two earlier Court of Appeal decisions in *Cummings v Grainger*[149] and *Curtis v Betts*.[150] In *Cummings*, the plaintiff was attacked and seriously injured by an untrained Alsatian guard dog let loose in the defendant's scrap yard. But for certain defences discussed below, the plaintiff would have succeeded in her claim under the second limb of s.2(2)(b). This was not a ferocious dog possessed of characteristics not normally possessed by Alsatians, but just a typical guard dog which would be likely to attack any intruder into its territory. This was enough to establish the second limb.

Equally, in *Curtis v Betts*,[151] a bull mastiff named Max attacked a 10-year-old child in the street while being transferred from the defendants' house to a Land Rover to be taken to the local park for exercise. The judge found that bull mastiffs[152] have a tendency to react fiercely at particular times and in particular circumstances, namely when defending the boundaries of what they regard as their own territory. Slade L.J. remarked that:

> "The mere fact that a particular animal shared its potentially dangerous characteristics with other animals of the same species will not preclude the satisfaction of requirement (b) if on the particular facts the likelihood of damage was attributable to characteristics normally found in animals of the same species at times or in circumstances corresponding with those in which the damage actually occurred".[153]

On this basis where an animal is only aggressive in particular circumstances, for example, a dog guarding its territory or, if a bitch, when it has a litter of pups,[154] the keeper may be found liable under s.2(2). Equally, in *Welsh v Stokes*,[155] a "sensible" horse with no history of misbehaviour which reared up and threw its rider could be regarded as displaying a normal characteristic (rearing as a reaction to fear) in the particular circumstances of the case. However, the mere fact that a horse is heavy and capable of inflicting serious

---

[148] "Normal" is defined in the later case of *Welsh v Stokes* [2007] EWCA Civ 796; [2007] P.I.Q.R. P27 as "conforming to type", that is, behaving in the same manner as any other type of animal of the species. Dyson L.J. advised at para.46 that the best evidence of such a characteristic is that it is usually found in such animals.

[149] [1977] Q.B. 397.

[150] [1990] 1 W.L.R. 459.

[151] [1990] 1 W.L.R. 459.

[152] The species here is treated as that of a "bull mastiff" rather than dogs in general. See also *Hunt v Wallis* [1994] P.I.Q.R. P128 (comparison with other border collies). From the case law, this only seems to apply to breeds of dogs (except mongrels: *Smith v Ainger, The Times*, June 5, 1990). Other animals are treated generally, e.g. horses.

[153] [1990] 1 W.L.R. 459 at 464.

[154] See *Barnes v Lucille Ltd* [1907] L.T.R. 680.

[155] [2007] EWCA Civ 796, [2007] P.I.Q.R. P27. See also *Collings v Home Office* [2006] 12 C.L. 22: the fact that the dog, which bit its handler, was in pain, was a circumstance within s.2(2)(b).

damage to a vehicle is not a characteristic giving rise to liability under s.2(2)(b).[156] As Sedley L.J. indicated in *Clark v Bowlt*,[157] the Act does not aim to render the keepers of domesticated animals routinely liable for damage. Some particular characteristic must be relied upon.

## Defences

As we saw in relation to the Consumer Protection Act 1987, strict liability does not prevent defences arising. These are listed primarily in s.5 of the Act, although s.10 does provide a defence of contributory negligence.      **9–047**

### (i)  Fault of the victim

Section 5(1) provides that the keeper will not be liable where the damage suffered is due wholly to the fault of the person suffering it, for example the claimant is bitten by a dog he has just kicked.    **9–048**

### (ii)  Voluntary acceptance of risk

Section 5(2) provides that the keeper will not be liable under s.2 where the victim has voluntarily accepted the risk of injury or damage,[158] that is, the victim has fully appreciated the risk and nevertheless exposed himself to it.[159] There is some possible overlap with s.5(1). For example, a person who tries to escape despite being warned that a police dog will be released may be found to be at fault and to have voluntarily accepted the risk of being bitten.[160]      **9–049**

### (iii)  The victim is a trespasser

Section 5(3) is divided into two limbs. Under the first limb, the keeper will not be liable for any damage caused by an animal kept on the premises to a trespasser if it is proved that the animal was not kept there for the protection of persons or property. If it is kept there for protection, the keeper will not be liable if it is kept for a purpose which is not unreasonable.      **9–050**

The operation of these defences is illustrated in *Cummings v Granger*.[161] Here, the plaintiff had been bitten when entering a scrap yard at night as a trespasser. Here, the Court of Appeal found s.2(2) to be satisfied, but that the defendant had good defences under s.5(2) and 5(3). Section 5(1) was not satisfied as the incident had not solely been due to the plaintiff's fault. However, she had known that there was a fierce guard dog in the yard and could be taken to have knowingly accepted the risk of injury, satisfying s.5(2). Further it was held that a defence existed under s.5(3) as well: "Old scrap and bits of spares for motor cars are fair game in most

---

[156] *Clark v Bowlt* [2006] EWCA Civ 978, [2007] P.I.Q.R. P12: No liability when Chance, a 600 lb horse, moved and hit the front nearside of Clark's car. See also Lord Nicholls in *Mirvahedy v Henley* [2003] 2 A.C. 491 at para.46.
[157] [2006] EWCA Civ 978; [2007] P.I.Q.R. P12 at para.24.
[158] Note also s.6(5): "Where a person employed as a servant by a keeper of an animal incurs a risk incidental to his employment he shall not be treated as accepting it voluntarily".
[159] *Cummings v Grainger* [1977] Q.B. 397; *Freeman v Higher Park Farm* [2008] EWCA Civ 1185.
[160] See *Dhesi v Chief Constable of West Midlands, The Times*, May 9, 2000.
[161] [1977] Q.B. 397.

parts of the country to anybody who is minded to steal that kind of thing. I do not think that it was in the least unreasonable to keep a guard dog in the yard".[162]

## Conclusion

**9–051**   As a result of *Mirvahedy*, it will be easier to establish liability under the 1971 Act. Owning a pet is therefore not only a privilege, but a potential basis for liability.

---

[162] Ormrod L.J. [1977] Q.B. 397 at 408. This is now subject to the Guard Dogs Act 1975, which regulates the use of guard dogs.

# Chapter 10

## NUISANCE AND THE RULE IN *RYLANDS V FLETCHER*

### Introduction

So far, we have examined torts which seek to protect the individual from harm inflicted negligently. The only exception has been liability under certain statutes which, as discussed in Ch.9, impose a form of strict liability on the producer of a defective product or the keeper of an animal. In this chapter, we consider the torts of nuisance and the rule in *Rylands v Fletcher*.[1] These torts have a different role from that discussed in earlier chapters. Private nuisance, for example, seeks to protect the claimant's ability to use and enjoy his or her land freely without undue interference by the defendant. Here, fault plays only a limited role. The main concern of the courts is to protect the claimant's rights in land. This chapter examines the rules governing the different types of nuisance recognised at law, the tensions between them, and their relationship with the rule in *Rylands v Fletcher*—which deals only with isolated cases of interference with the claimant's land. It also considers the impact of the House of Lords' judgments in *Hunter v Canary Wharf Ltd*[2] and *Cambridge Water Co v Eastern Counties Leather Plc*,[3] which have had a dramatic effect on the law of private nuisance and the rule in *Rylands v Fletcher*. This is a developing area of law, impacting on the lives of ordinary individuals and the protection of the environment as a whole.[4] The continuing role of these torts, and their difficult relationship with negligence, will be discussed in this chapter. We begin by considering the role of nuisance in the law of torts, before considering liability under the rule in *Rylands v Fletcher*.

10–001

---

[1] (1865) 3 H & C 774 (Court of Exchequer); (1866) 1 LR 1 Ex 265 (Court of Exchequer Chamber), (1868) LR 3 HL 330 (House of Lords).

[2] [1997] A.C. 655.

[3] [1994] 2 A.C. 264. See also *Transco Plc v Stockport MBC* [2003] UKHL 61; [2004] 2 A.C. 1.

[4] There is, of course, a limit to what the private action of nuisance or *Rylands v Fletcher* liability can do to protect the environment and such protection is perhaps more efficiently dealt with on a national or international level by legislation in favour of the public at large. The role of tort in protecting the environment is discussed in *Environmental Protection and the Common Law* (J. Lowry and R. Edmunds eds.) (Hart, 2000).

## Nuisance

**10–002**   There are three main types of nuisance, which should be distinguished:

- Private nuisance
- Public nuisance
- Statutory nuisance

Private nuisance is generally defined as an "unlawful interference with a person's use or enjoyment of land, or some right over, or in connection with it."[5] Consideration of this tort will form the main body of this chapter. Public nuisance, in contrast, is both a crime and a tort. An individual can bring an action where he or she has suffered particular harm from a nuisance which has materially affected the reasonable comfort and convenience of life of a sufficiently large number of citizens who come within the sphere or neighbourhood of its operation. Although the courts frequently draw comparisons between private and public nuisance, they are in reality very different torts, which seek to protect different interests. Whilst private nuisance seeks to protect private rights, public nuisance is primarily a crime, and acts as a general measure of public protection. Whilst the claimant may seek in his or her Statement of Case to allege that both torts have been committed,[6] it is important to recognise that in character, they have little in common bar their name.

Both private and public nuisance are distinct from statutory nuisances, which are nuisances which operate by virtue of particular statutes. The best example perhaps is that of Pt III of the Environmental Protection Act 1990, which is primarily concerned with matters of public health. As statutory nuisances are unlikely even to provide a claim for breach of statutory duty,[7] they are not dealt with in this book. Readers are advised to consult specialist texts.[8]

## Private Nuisance

**10–003**   There are three main forms of private nuisance:

- Physical injury to land (for example, by flooding or noxious fumes);
- Substantial interference with the enjoyment of land (for example smells, dust and noise);
- Encroachment on a neighbour's land (for example, by spreading roots or overhanging branches).[9] This is of minor significance, but will be considered further in the section on remedies.

---

[5] W.V.H. Rogers, *Winfield & Jolowicz on Torts* (18th edn, Sweet and Maxwell, 2010), 14–04. Winfield (1930–32) 4 C.L.J. 189 at 190.

[6] See, e.g. *Halsey v Esso Petroleum* [1961] 1 W.L.R. 683.

[7] *Issa v Hackney LBC* [1997] 1 W.L.R. 956.

[8] See, e.g. S. Bell and D. McGillivray, *Environmental Law* (7th edn, OUP, 2008).

[9] See *Lemmon v Webb* [1895] A.C. 1, *Delaware Mansions Ltd v Westminster City Council* [2001] UKHL 55; [2002] 1 A.C. 321 and *L.E. Jones (Insurance Brokers) Ltd v Portsmouth CC* [2002] EWCA Civ 1723; [2003] 1 W.L.R. 427. The rules of causation are the same as for negligence: did the tree roots materially contribute to the damage? (*Loftus-Brigham v Ealing LBC* [2003] EWCA Civ 1490; 103 Con. L.R. 102).

All three forms seek to protect the claimant's use and enjoyment of land from an activity or state of affairs for which the defendant is responsible. A fourth form of nuisance exists which is generally discussed in works on land law, namely where the defendant has interfered with a particular proprietary right the claimant possesses over the land, for example a right of way. Such interference is generally treated by analogy to trespass, in that provided a substantial degree of interference can be shown, the tort will be actionable per se.[10] By this means, the claimant's rights over land are vindicated, although where the right in question is simply a right to support, damage must be shown.[11]

The main distinction drawn by the courts is between physical damage to property and interference with one's enjoyment of land or personal comfort. The main impact of this distinction is that the courts are more willing to find a nuisance where physical damage to property has been caused. Mere personal discomfort will be treated with latitude unless the interference is such that it is "materially interfering with the ordinary comfort physically of human existence, not merely according to elegant or dainty modes and habits of living".[12] On this basis, loss of a view from one's property is a loss of "elegant" living and not such as to interfere with the ordinary comfort of human existence.[13] So, while the courts are willing to protect the claimant's personal comfort, they are more willing to protect the claimant's property. Thus, there is clear House of Lords authority that matters such as the nature of the locality will not be relevant where there has been material injury to property.[14]

## What amounts to a private nuisance?

It must be self-evident that not every interference with the claimant's use and enjoyment of land can amount to a private nuisance. For example, I enjoy playing the piano, but of necessity must practise. Can my neighbour complain (a) because I play at all; or (b) because he or she enjoys fine music and the sound of my bad playing is unbearable? If either of the above were actionable, I would be severely limited in my ability to play the piano. My neighbour would be given the power to veto my choice of activity. However, if in a fit of enthusiasm, I decide to practice my scales between 02.00 and 04.00 every morning, my neighbour would appear to have legitimate grounds for complaint.[15] The tort of nuisance must balance my rights against those of my neighbour. Whilst it may be easy to say that noxious fumes which destroy every plant in my garden should be actionable, it is far more difficult to weigh up the complaints of a resident in an industrial area that lorries travelling to a factory cause noise and dust which affect his or her property. The test is one of "reasonable user", balancing the interest of the defendant to use his or her land as is legally permitted against the conflicting interest of the claimant to have quiet enjoyment of his or her land. The ordinary use of your home will not

**10–004**

---

[10] *Nicholls v Ely Beet Sugar Factory Ltd* [1936] 1 Ch.343.

[11] *Midland Bank v Bardgrove Property Services* [1992] 37 E.G. 126.

[12] Sir Knight-Bruce V.C. in *Walter v Selfe* (1851) 20 LJ Ch 433 at 435.

[13] *Aldred's Case* (1610) 9 Co. Rep. 57b.

[14] *St Helen's Smelting Co v Tipping* (1865) 11 HLC 642 at 651.

[15] The neighbour might in practice prefer to rely on the procedures under Pt III of the Environmental Protection Act 1990, ss.79–80 (duty on the local authority to abate a statutory nuisance where, inter alia, noise is prejudicial to health or a nuisance) and, if available, under the Noise Act 1996 (duty on local authorities to investigate complaints of excessive levels of noise from a dwelling house at night). See, further, texts on environmental law and F McManus (2000) 20 L.S. 264.

amount to a nuisance, even if it discomforts your neighbour due to poor soundproofing or insulation.[16] As Lord Wright stated in the leading case of *Sedleigh-Denfield v O'Callaghan*[17]:

> "A balance has to be maintained between the right of the occupier to do what he likes with his own, and the right of his neighbour not to be interfered with".

## "Reasonable user"

**10–005**    The first point to stress is that this is not a standard of reasonable care as in negligence. The rule is one of give and take. I do not expect my neighbours to be perfect or to exist in hermit-like silence and isolation, but neither do I expect my neighbours to use their property in such a way as to render my existence unbearable: I therefore expect them to use it reasonably. However, as in negligence, what is "unreasonable" is difficult to define. It does not require that the defendant's actions must be deliberate. Equally, it is clearly established that, in nuisance, the defendant's use of land can be "unreasonable" even though he or she has taken all reasonable care to prevent the nuisance occurring.[18] The courts' approach is therefore results-based: is the result of the defendant's conduct such that it is likely to cause unreasonable interference with the claimant's use and enjoyment of land? It is not a question of blaming the defendant, but of protecting the claimant's interest. There is, predictably, no set formula for determining what results are unreasonable. It is possible to list a number of circumstances which are clearly relevant to the courts' decisions in particular cases, the answer will vary according to the circumstances of each case.

## Factors determining reasonable user

**10–006**    The following factors are considered in turn below:

- The nature of the locality;
- The duration and frequency of the defendant's conduct;
- The utility of the defendant's conduct;
- Abnormal sensitivity of the claimant;
- Malice on the part of the defendant.

*(1)  The nature of the locality*

**10–007**    As stated above, this is not relevant where material physical damage has been suffered by the claimant. Where the claimant has suffered personal discomfort and inconvenience, however, it is relevant. The classic quotation is that of Thesiger L.J. in *Sturges v Bridgman*: "What

---

[16] *Southwark LBC v Mills; Baxter v Camden LBC (No.2)* [2001] 1 A.C. 1; approving Court of Appeal in *Baxter v Camden LBC (No.2)* [1999] 1 All E.R. 237. See J. O'Sullivan "Nuisance, local authorities and neighbours from hell" [2000] C.L.J. 11.

[17] [1940] A.C. 880 at 903.

[18] *Rapier v London Tramways Co* [1893] 2 Ch.588.

would be a nuisance in Belgrave Square would not necessarily be so in Bermondsey".[19] Therefore, in considering whether noise from a local factory causes a nuisance to local residents, the courts will examine the nature of the locality, and if it is an industrial area, will be less likely to find an actionable nuisance.

The nature of the locality may change over time from industrial to residential, and therefore the courts must have regard to the locality as it is today. Change may happen naturally, or may be due to deliberate development of the locality, as seen with the development of the London Docklands, which was classified as an urban development area. Indeed, in *Gillingham BC v Medway (Chatham) Dock Co Ltd*,[20] Buckley J. held that planning permission to develop a disused naval dockyard as a 24-hour commercial dock had changed the character of the neighbourhood. Local residents therefore could not complain about the serious disruption caused to them by its operation. The question, however, is one of fact, not law. Planning permission is not a defence to nuisance. Where planning permission was given to expand a pig farm adjacent to holiday accommodation, this did not change the nature of the locality, and did not excuse the nuisance caused to the plaintiffs by the smell of the pigs.[21]

*(2) Duration and frequency*

It is a matter of common sense that the claimant will have to endure *some* inconvenience in his or her enjoyment of land. What is unreasonable is when it occurs frequently and for long periods of time.[22] Therefore, my neighbour undertaking DIY on Sunday morning must be endured, but my neighbour drilling for 24 hours, or every day between 00.00 and 02.00, is unreasonable.

**10–008**

Again, the courts will use a largely common-sense approach to this factor. In *De Keyser's Royal Hotel Ltd v Spicer Bros Ltd*,[23] the court was willing to grant an injunction for a temporary interference when it consisted of pile-driving in the middle of the night, but confined the injunction to forbidding work between 22.00 and 06.30. An action for physical damage to property is likely to succeed even where the nuisance is temporary, but in such a case the court will only award damages rather than an injunction. In *Crown River Cruises Ltd v Kimbolton Fireworks Ltd*,[24] the plaintiffs' vessels had suffered substantial fire damage caused by falling debris from a fireworks display to celebrate the fiftieth anniversary of the Battle of Britain. The display had only lasted about 20 minutes, but it was found to be inevitable that debris, some of it hot and burning, would fall on nearby property of a potentially flammable nature. The plaintiffs were therefore awarded damages.

Much ink has been spilt analysing whether an isolated escape can amount to an actionable nuisance. It is true that it is easier to obtain an injunction where the interference is continuous or recurrent, but this does not necessarily exclude an isolated escape of sufficient gravity. The

---

[19] (1879) 11 Ch.D. 852 at 865. See also Veale J. in *Halsey v Esso Petroleum* [1961] 1 W.L.R. 683 and *Miller v Jackson* [1977] Q.B. 966 at 986.

[20] [1993] Q.B. 343.

[21] *Wheeler v J.J. Saunders Ltd* [1996] Ch.19. See also *Watson v Croft Promo-Sport Ltd* [2009] EWCA Civ 15; [2009] 3 All E.R. 249.

[22] See *Andreae v Selfridge* [1938] Ch.1 at 5–6 per Lord Greene M.R. The Court of Appeal in *Clift v Welsh Office* [1999] 1 W.L.R. 796 held that there is no reason, however, why the law should expect the neighbour to put up with actual physical damage to his property, as opposed to discomfort and inconvenience, because the nuisance is temporary in nature (claim under Compulsory Purchase Act 1965 s.10).

[23] (1914) 30 T.L.R. 257.

[24] [1996] 2 Lloyd's Rep. 533.

court in *SCM (United Kingdom) Ltd v W.J. Whittal & Son Ltd*[25] accepted that such liability could arise where the plaintiff was affected by the state of the defendant's land or activities upon it, but excluded liability for a single negligent act, which it held would only found an action in negligence. Isolated escapes may, of course, be actionable in any event under the rule in *Rylands v Fletcher*, which will be considered later in this chapter.

### (3) Utility of the defendant's conduct

**10–009**    This is not generally an important consideration. Private nuisance is concerned with the results of the defendant's conduct on the claimant and not on the community as a whole. It has been argued, however, that it should influence the court in exercising its equitable jurisdiction whether to grant an injunction, and will therefore be considered further in the section on remedies.

### (4) Abnormal sensitivity

**10–010**    The result of the defendant's conduct must be such as to unreasonably affect the ordinary citizen. Discomfort resulting from personal sensitivity to noise or heat which would not affect the ordinary citizen will not found an action in nuisance. The leading case is *Robinson v Kilvert*,[26] where the defendant operated a business in the lower part of a building, which required hot and dry air. As a result, the temperature of the floor of the plaintiff's premises above rose to 80 °F, which diminished the value of the brown paper stored there. The heat was not such as to affect ordinary paper or to cause discomfort to the plaintiff's workforce. The Court of Appeal refused the plaintiff damages. He had undertaken an exceptionally delicate trade and had not shown an actionable nuisance. This must be correct. It cannot be just to impose a burden on the defendant to compensate all claimants for interference, no matter how sensitive they are. This would unduly interfere with the defendant's own freedom to enjoy his or her property. It should be noted, however, that once an actionable nuisance is shown, the claimant may recover the full extent of his or her losses, even where they result from interference with an exceptionally delicate use of the land.[27]

**10–011**       Yet it may be difficult to determine what we would now regard as "unduly sensitive". It is clear that a person who cannot stand any noise or odours is more sensitive than normal. Does this extend, however, to the avid television viewer, which encompasses about 97 per cent of the population? Unfortunately, there are dicta suggesting exactly that. The root of the problem lies with the decision of Buckley J. in *Bridlington Relay v Yorkshire Electricity Board*.[28] The court in that case was unimpressed with the claim of a company, which relayed sound and television broadcasts, that its business would be interfered with by the erection of two pylons within 250 feet of its mast. Buckley J. refused an injunction because the defendants had given an assurance that the interference could be remedied, but his Lordship went further and doubted whether interference with a primarily recreational activity could ever found an actionable nuisance. This decision has been dismissed as out-of-date,[29] and Buckley J. expressly stated that he was not laying down an absolute rule. As our use of land changes with the advent of modern technology, it would be strange

---

[25] [1970] 1 W.L.R. 1017 at 1031—point not considered on appeal [1971] 1 Q.B. 337. See also *British Celanese v Hunt* [1969] 1 W.L.R. 959 at 969 (liability for the way in which metal foil was stored on land) and *Colour Quest Ltd v Total Downstream UK Plc* [2009] EWHC 540 (Comm); [2009] 2 Lloyd's Rep. 1 at para.421.

[26] (1889) 41 Ch.D. 88. See also *Heath v Mayor of Brighton* (1908) 98 L.T. 718.

[27] *McKinnon Industries Ltd v Walker* (1951) 3 D.L.R. 577 at 581, PC

[28] [1965] Ch.436.

[29] See *Nor-Video Services v Ontario Hydro* (1978) 84 D.L.R. (3d) 221.

if an activity enjoyed by the majority of the population would not be regarded as an ordinary and natural use of one's premises. Nevertheless, the House of Lords in *Hunter v Canary Wharf Ltd*[30] gave no clear indication as to whether the case would be decided differently today, and Lords Goff, Hoffmann and Cooke expressly left the question open for future decision.

In the more recent decision of *Network Rail Infrastructure Ltd v Morris (t/a Soundstar Studio)*,[31] however, the Court of Appeal adopted a more considered approach. Here the claimant was complaining about electromagnetic interference from a section of Railtrack's signalling system to the music created by electric guitars in his recording studio. The court recognised that, although this might have been dismissed as "extra-sensitive" in the past, the use of electric and electronic equipment was now a feature of modern life. It thus focused on what was reasonable in the circumstances of the case. Buxton L.J. also went further to question the continued utility of *Robinson v Kilvert* when loss, in any event, must be reasonably foreseeable to be actionable in nuisance (see Remoteness below). It is to be hoped that the courts will in future take a more generous view of what can be regarded as actionable in nuisance.

### (5) Malice

In assessing whether the defendant's use of his or her land is reasonable, regard will be had to his or her frame of mind. This can be criticised for judging the defendant's conduct, which is not the role of nuisance, but there seems good authority for the fact that malice will encourage the courts to find an unreasonable user. The case of *Christie v Davey*[32] is the leading authority. The plaintiff was a music teacher who gave lessons at her home. The defendant, her neighbour, found the noise irritating and chose to express his displeasure by knocking on the party wall, beating trays, whistling and shrieking. The plaintiff succeeded in her claim for an injunction. North J. held that

> ". . . what was done by the defendant was done only for the purpose of annoyance and in my opinion, it was not a legitimate use of the defendant's house".[33]

*Christie* was followed in *Hollywood Silver Fox Farm Ltd v Emmett*,[34] where Macnaghten J. granted an injunction against a defendant who had deliberately fired guns on his own land near its boundary with the plaintiffs' land. The plaintiffs carried on the business of breeding silver foxes on their land, and evidence was given that the discharge of guns during breeding time would frighten the vixens leading them to refuse to breed, miscarry, or kill their young. Although the use of land for breeding foxes was obviously sensitive, the presence of malice was sufficient to overcome this objection.

Such authority should be contrasted with that of the House of Lords in *Bradford Corp v Pickles*.[35] The defendant had deliberately drained his land, with the intention of diminishing the water supply leading into the plaintiffs' land, and thereby forcing them to purchase his land. The House of Lords did not, however, grant an injunction, and refused to take note of the alleged malice of the defendant. This decision can nevertheless be distinguished from *Christie*

10–012

---

[30] [1997] A.C. 655.
[31] [2004] EWCA Civ 172; [2004] Env. L.R. 41.
[32] [1893] 1 Ch.316.
[33] [1893] 1 Ch.316 at 327.
[34] [1936] 2 K.B. 468.
[35] [1895] A.C. 587.

in a number of ways. First, the plaintiffs in *Bradford* had no right to receive the water, and therefore no right had been interfered with on which to found the nuisance. Secondly, at least from the laissez-faire perspective of the nineteenth century, the defendant had done no more than exercise his right to appropriate or divert underground water to obtain a better deal from the plaintiffs. Could this really be regarded as malicious?

Malice will therefore be considered relevant by the courts in applying the test of "reasonable user". Caution should be adopted, however, towards comments in the leading case of *Hunter v Canary Wharf Ltd* (see below)[36] by Lord Cooke, who suggested that malicious erection of a structure for the purpose of interfering with television reception should be actionable in nuisance. These comments were based on Lord Cooke's minority belief that the interference caused by building the Canary Wharf tower was actionable, but could be justified on the ordinary principles of give and take. On this basis, malice (as in *Christie*) would be capable of converting a reasonable user into an unreasonable user. This was not, however, the majority view. On the majority view, as seen above, the claimant has no right to complain in such circumstances. The appropriate analogy would therefore be that of *Bradford Corp v Pickles*: the defendant had a right to build the tower; the claimant had no right which had been interfered with, and so malice would be irrelevant.

## Who can sue?

**10–013**   The aim of private nuisance is to protect the claimant's use and enjoyment of land. It is therefore logical that the claimant must have some land which has been unreasonably interfered with. The more difficult question is: what link must the claimant have with the land? Does the law of tort demand an interest in land, as defined by property law, or simply some substantial link with the land? The traditional view was that an interest in land had to be shown. In *Malone v Laskey*,[37] the Court of Appeal refused the plaintiff's action for damages for personal injury when vibrations emitted from the defendant's premises caused an iron bracket supporting a cistern to fall upon her. She was a mere licensee without any interest in land, and so had no cause of action.

This position was challenged, however, by Dillon L.J. in *Khorasandjian v Bush*.[38] In this case, Miss Khorasandjian had been subjected to a campaign of harassment by a former boyfriend, for which he had spent some time in prison. She sought an injunction to prevent him "harassing, pestering or communicating" with her, particularly by means of persistent and unwanted telephone calls to her mother's home where she lived. Miss Khorasandjian, in common with Mrs Malone, had no proprietary interest in the home, but Dillon L.J. held that "the court has at times to reconsider earlier decisions in the light of changed social conditions" and therefore supported her claim in private nuisance.

*Khorasandjian* was in turn rejected by the majority of the House of Lords in the leading case of *Hunter v Canary Wharf Ltd*.[39] In this case, a number of local residents, who included homeowners, their families and other licensees, had complained about the Canary Wharf tower, which forms part of the Docklands development in London. The tower is nearly 250 metres in height and over 50 metres square, with a metallic surface, and, when erected, was found to interfere with the television reception of neighbouring homes. Two preliminary questions arose:

---

[36] [1997] A.C. 677.
[37] [1907] 2 K.B. 141. See also *Read v Lyons* [1947] A.C. 156 at 183.
[38] [1993] Q.B. 727 at 735, relying on the Canadian case of *Motherwell v Motherwell* (1976) 73 D.L.R. (3d) 62.
[39] [1997] A.C. 677.

(1) Did an actionable nuisance exist?
The House of Lords held that the interference with television reception by the erection of a **10–014**
building did not amount to an actionable nuisance. It was held, by analogy to cases which
refused liability for blocking a view,[40] that the defendants were free to build what they wanted
on their land, subject to planning controls and proprietary restrictions, such as easements, over
the land. Complaints could thus only be made at the planning stage and not by means of the
tort of private nuisance.[41]

(2) If an actionable nuisance existed, who could sue?
Their Lordships reasserted the traditional view stated in *Malone v Laskey*[42] and held that only **10–015**
claimants with an interest in land or exclusive possession could bring an action for nuisance.
In the words of Lord Goff: ". . . on the authorities as they stand, an action in private nuisance
will only lie at the suit of a person who has a right to the land".[43] This represented a return to
the historical roots of private nuisance as a tort to land. In so doing, the majority of the House
of Lords (Lord Cooke dissenting) rejected the opportunity given in *Khorasandjian* to develop
the tort to protect the personal interests of anyone occupying the land.

*Rights in the land*

These were defined by the House of Lords in *Hunter* as consisting of interests in land or exclusive **10–016**
possession. On this basis, if you are a landowner, tenant, grantee of an easement or profit à prendre,
or simply have a right to exclusive possession of the land, you may sue, but any lesser right will
not suffice. This division was justified by Lord Hoffmann in *Hunter*:

"Exclusive possession distinguishes an occupier who may in due course acquire title
under the Limitation Act 1980 from a mere trespasser. It distinguishes a tenant holding a
leasehold estate from a mere licensee. Exclusive possession de jure or de facto, now or
in the future, is the bedrock of English land law".[44]

The importance of exclusive possession may be seen in the Court of Appeal decision in
*Pemberton v Southwark LBC*.[45] In this case, a "tolerated trespasser", that is a former secure
tenant, against whom an order for possession had been obtained but suspended whilst she
continued to occupy the property and pay rent,[46] was allowed to sue for nuisance when her flat
became infested with cockroaches. As stated by Roch L.J.:

"Possession or occupation by the tolerated trespasser may be precarious, but it is not
wrongful and it is exclusive. . . . In those circumstances, in my judgment, the tolerated
trespasser does have a sufficient interest in the premises to sustain an action in nuisance."[47]

[40] See *Dalton v Angus* (1881) 6 App Cas 740.
[41] However, in *Hunter*, due to the fact that the Secretary of State for the Environment had designated the area an
enterprise zone, planning permission was deemed to have been granted for any form of development and no application for permission had to be made.
[42] [1907] 2 K.B. 141.
[43] [1997] A.C. 677 at 692, relying heavily on the classic article of Professor Newark "The Boundaries of Nuisance"
(1949) 65 L.Q.R. 480.
[44] [1997] A.C. 655 at 703.
[45] [2000] 1 W.L.R. 1672 (leave to appeal denied by the House of Lords: [2001] 1 W.L.R. 538).
[46] The term comes from *Burrows v Brent LBC* [1996] 1 W.L.R. 1448.
[47] [2000] 1 W.L.R. 1672 at 1682.

You will not be able to claim, however, if you are simply a member of the landowner's family, a guest, lodger or employee. This does not, of course, stop you seeking alternative remedies in negligence, occupiers' liability, or resorting to the Protection from Harassment Act 1997 (which will be discussed further in Ch.11) providing you can satisfy the necessary requirements to establish liability.

*Losses incurred prior to acquisition of a right to land*

**10–017**    It should be noted that, provided the nuisance is continuing, there is authority that the claimant may sue for his or her losses even if they began prior to acquisition of the premises. In *Masters v Brent LBC*,[48] Talbot J. held that the plaintiff was able to recover the losses incurred by him in remedying damage caused by encroaching tree roots, which caused subsidence to the house he had recently acquired. He could show a continuing actionable nuisance and so could recover the total cost of the works necessary to remedy the damage caused by the tree roots to the property. In *Delaware Mansions Ltd v Westminster City Council*,[49] the House of Lords approved this approach. Here, the roots of a tree on council land had caused damage to an adjoining building. Although most of the damage had occurred prior to the claimant's purchase of the property, their Lordships found that where there was a continuing nuisance of which the defendant knew or should have known, the purchaser would be able to recover reasonable remedial expenditure. The claimant was thus able to recover the cost of underpinning works which amounted to over £570,000. It should be noted that in both *Masters* and *Delaware*, there was no possibility of double recovery. Where, for example, the previous owner has incurred some remedial expenditure, a court would apportion the damages awarded between the two parties.

*Landlords*

**10–018**    A landlord whose property is leased retains only a "reversionary interest" in the premises, namely his or her right to possession at the end of the term of the lease. The landlord can only sue where the nuisance has harmed this interest in a permanent way, i.e. the value of the property will be diminished when the landlord comes back into possession.[50] Examples include vibrations which affect the structure of the property, and nuisances where there is a risk of the perpetrator gaining a legal right to commit the nuisance by prescription (see below). In contrast, the landlord cannot sue if the interference is of a temporary nature, such as noise or smoke which is unlikely to have any permanent effect on the land. In these circumstances, the action can only be brought by the tenant. The landlord can do nothing if the tenant decides instead to leave, or demands a decrease in rent.

*The Human Rights Act 1998*

**10–019**    It has been questioned whether the test in *Hunter v Canary Wharf* confining the right to sue to those with rights to land is compatible with the Human Rights Act 1998. For example, Professor Wright in her book, *Tort Law and Human Rights*, suggests that:

> "it is time for English law to move beyond the straitjacket of the forms of action, so that the boundaries of private nuisance are determined by the link with one's home."[51]

---

[48]    [1978] Q.B. 841, although the close connection between the former owner (the plaintiff's father) and the plaintiff had placed doubt on the scope of this decision.

[49]    [2001] UKHL 55; [2002] 1 A.C. 321. Comment: B. Parker [2002] C.L.J. 260.

[50]    See *Jones v Llanrwst UDC* [1911] 1 Ch.393 at 404.

[51]    (Hart, 2001), p.194.

The difficulty would seem to lie with art.8(1) of the European Convention on Human Rights. This states that "Everyone has the right to respect for his private and family life, his home and his correspondence."[52] This has been interpreted by the European Court of Human Rights in a broad sense, thereby permitting parties without rights in the home to sue.[53] For example, in *Khatun v United Kingdom*[54]—an appeal from part of the *Hunter* litigation in which the applicants had complained of dust arising from construction of the Limehouse Link Road—the European Commission of Human Rights found that:

> "in domestic proceedings, a distinction was made between those applicants with a proprietary interest in the land and those without such an interest. For the purposes of Article 8 (Art 8) of the Convention, there is no such distinction. 'Home' is an autonomous concept which does not depend on classification under domestic law. Whether or not a particular habitation constitutes a 'home' . . . will depend on the factual circumstances, namely, the existence of sufficient and continuous links."[55]

This suggests that in a suitable case, a court would be able to challenge the limitation in *Hunter* in favour of a test based on a sufficient link with the land. In *McKenna v British Aluminium Ltd*,[56] for example, Neuberger J. in a striking-out decision was prepared to contemplate such a move. Here, over 30 children from a number of households had brought actions for private nuisance and under the rule in *Rylands v Fletcher*, alleging that emissions and noise from the defendants' neighbouring factory had caused them mental distress, physical harm and an invasion of privacy. The judge rejected the defendants' argument that their claims should be struck out unless they could point to a proprietary right.

> "There is obviously a powerful case for saying that effect has not been properly given to Article 8.1 if a person with no interest in the home, but who has lived in the house for some time and had his enjoyment of the home interfered with, is at the mercy of the person who owns the home, as the only person who can bring proceedings."[57]

It remains to be seen whether the courts are prepared to change the rule in *Hunter* and ignore the evident intention of the House of Lords to provide a straightforward rule which sets out the boundaries of the tort and facilitates negotiated settlements of claims. It should also be noted that art.8 is a qualified right and interference may, under art.8.2, be justified on the basis that it is:

> "necessary in a democratic society in the interests of national security, public safety or the economic well-being of the country, for the prevention of disorder or crime, for the protection of health or morals, or for the protection of the rights and freedoms of others."

---

[52] See Sch.1, Pt 1 of the Human Rights Act 1998.

[53] See, for example, H. Fenwick, *Civil Liberties and Human Rights* (4th edn, Routledge-Cavendish, 2007).

[54] (1998) 26 E.H.R.R. CD 212. The applicants complained that the work disrupted their rights under art.8 (home and family life) and art.14 (discrimination on the grounds of poverty in that due to the low value of their homes, any diminution of the market value was minimal).

[55] (1998) 26 E.H.R.R. CD 212 at 215.

[56] [2002] Env LR 30, Birmingham District Registry.

[57] Neuberger J. left open the question whether the common law should be extended by reference to the law of nuisance, the rule in *Rylands v Fletcher*, negligence or a common law tort analogous to nuisance.

On the facts of *Khatun*, the Commission ruled that the defendants' activities could be justified as pursuing a legitimate and important aim, given the importance of the public interest in developing the Docklands area of London and the limited interference to the applicants' homes.[58] The proposed change would alter the fundamental character of the tort, and, over ten years after the implementation of the Human Rights Act 1998, the courts have yet to overturn *Hunter* on this point.

## Who can be sued?

10–020    The most obvious defendant is the person who created the nuisance. This is not contentious, but it is important to recognise that the liability of the creator of the nuisance is not dependent on occupation of the land. Even if the defendant no longer occupies the land, and cannot therefore abate (or "stop") any nuisance, he or she may still be liable.[59] However, if the creator cannot be traced or it is not financially viable to sue the creator, a number of other defendants exist:

- The occupier of the land;
- The landlord.

We deal with each of these potential defendants in turn.

*(1) The occupier of the land*

10–021    The occupier may find himself or herself liable for nuisances occurring during the period of occupancy even where he or she is not the creator. This will occur in four particular instances.

10–022    **(i) The occupier exercises control over the creator:**    The occupier will be liable for a nuisance created by its employees in the course of their employment (under the principles discussed in Ch.7), which will extend to independent contractors where the duty not to create a nuisance is non-delegable. Liability for independent contractors has caused some problems, and the concept of a non-delegable duty has been interpreted broadly. In *Matania v National Provincial Bank*,[60] the occupier of two floors of a building brought an action for nuisance against the occupier of the first floor in respect of the dust and noise caused by the work of his independent contractors. The Court of Appeal held that the employer in such circumstances is liable for the damage occasioned by its independent contractors when their operations, by their very nature, involve a risk of damage to the claimant.

10–023    **(ii) The occupier has adopted or continued a nuisance created by a trespasser:**    Here, the defendant is rendered liable for his or her omissions in failing to deal with a nuisance created by a trespasser. Liability is, however, far from strict. The defendant is only liable if he or she (i) adopts the nuisance, i.e. uses the state of affairs for his or her purposes or (ii) continues the nuisance, i.e. with actual or presumed knowledge of the nuisance, fails to take reasonably

---

[58] The Commission additionally rejected the claim under art.14, on the basis that there were no other persons in "relevantly" similar situations to the applicants.

[59] See *Thompson v Gibson* (1841) 7 M. & W. 456; 151 E.R. 845.

[60] [1936] 2 All E.R. 633. See also *Bower v Peate* (1876) 1 Q.B.D. 321 and *Spicer v Smee* [1946] 1 All E.R. 489.

prompt and efficient steps to abate it. The same rule applies to private and public nuisance.[61] The leading case is the House of Lords decision of *Sedleigh-Denfield v O'Callaghan*.[62] A local authority, without the defendant's permission (and therefore as a trespasser), had placed a drainage pipe in a ditch on the defendant's land, with a grating designed to keep out leaves. The grating had not been fixed in the correct position, with the result that during a heavy rainstorm the pipe became choked with leaves and water overflowed onto the plaintiff's land. The House of Lords held the defendant liable. He had adopted the nuisance by using the drain for his own purposes to drain water from his land. He had also continued the nuisance because his manager should have realised the risk of flooding created by the obstruction and taken reasonable steps to abate it.

The rule can be justified as one of good sense and convenience. The occupier is best placed to deal with the nuisance, and the House of Lords rejected the idea that it was enough to give the claimant the right to enter on to the land to abate the nuisance. The Court of Appeal has more recently decided that there is no relevant distinction between a nuisance caused by the state of the property and one caused by the activities of trespassers upon it. Therefore, in *Page Motors Ltd v Epsom and Ewell BC*,[63] the local authority was found liable for failing to take reasonable steps to evict travellers whose activities had been harming the plaintiffs' businesses.

**(iii) The occupier has adopted or continued a nuisance created by an act of nature:**   **10–024**
Until *Goldman v Hargrave*,[64] the courts had drawn a distinction between nuisances created by third parties and those resulting from acts of nature. Occupiers were under no duty to abate the latter, although they would have to allow their neighbours reasonable access to abate the nuisance. The Privy Council in *Goldman* refused to maintain this distinction, and held that the House of Lords decision in *Sedleigh-Denfield* should be applied equally to situations where the nuisance had been created by an act of nature. In *Goldman*, a 100 feet high redgum tree, growing in the centre of the defendant's land, was struck by lightning and caught fire. The defendant quite properly cut down the tree, but left it to burn itself out when he could have simply eliminated any risk of fire by dousing the smouldering sections of the tree with water. The wind later picked up and rekindled the fire, which spread, causing damage to the plaintiff's land. In a significant judgment, Lord Wilberforce held that the defendant was liable for not acting against the foreseeable risk of fire.

The Court of Appeal approved Lord Wilberforce's judgment in *Leakey v National Trust*.[65] In this case, it was found that there was no valid distinction between an act of nature affecting something on the land and one deriving from the state of the land itself. In 1976, an exceptionally dry summer, followed by a very wet autumn, had led to subsidence of a hill above the plaintiffs' properties, causing damage to the properties. There was evidence that the defendants had been aware of this potential problem, indeed they had been warned by the plaintiffs, but

---

[61] See *Attorney General v Tod Heatley* [1897] 1 Ch.560, *R. v Shorrock* [1994] Q.B. 279 (liability for rave held on defendant's field) and *Wandsworth LBC v Railtrack Plc* [2001] EWCA Civ 1236; [2002] Q.B. 756 (Railtrack liable for failing to abate public nuisance caused by pigeons roosting under its railway bridge). It is not clear, however, whether the measured duty of care (see below) applies to public nuisance. *Wandsworth* states the law in objective terms and states that nothing in the later authorities should throw doubt on the law as stated in *Tod Heatley* in 1897. However, it also found that Railtrack had the means to abate the nuisance and, in view of its small cost of £9,000, liability would have been found in any event.
[62] [1940] A.C. 880.
[63] (1982) 80 L.G.R. 337.
[64] [1967] 1 A.C. 645.
[65] [1980] 1 All E.R. 17.

had refused to act. The Court of Appeal held that they were liable. Megaw L.J. found that it would be a "grievous blot on the law"[66] if the law did not impose liability on the defendants in such circumstances.

**10–025**   **The measured duty of care:**   In finding liability in *Goldman*, Lord Wilberforce, however, made it clear that the defendant's conduct should be judged in the light of his or her resources and ability to act in the circumstances:

> "The law must take account of the fact that the occupier on whom the duty is cast has, ex hypothesi, had this hazard thrust upon him through no seeking or fault of his own. His interest, and his resources, whether physical or material, may be of a very modest character either in relation to the magnitude of the hazard, or as compared with those of his threatened neighbour. A rule which required of him in such unsought circumstances in his neighbour's interest a physical effort of which he is not capable, or an excessive expenditure of money, would be unenforceable or unjust . . . In such situations the standard ought to be to require of the occupier what it is reasonable to expect of him in his individual circumstances."[67]

Where, therefore, the defendant is poor, and abatement will require vast expense, the defendant will not be considered liable.[68] Equally, less will be expected of the infirm than of the able-bodied. This subjective approach would seem to extend to situations where the occupier is liable for the act of a trespasser or for a failure to support his or her neighbour's land. In *Page Motors Ltd v Epsom and Ewell BC*,[69] for example, the Court of Appeal applied and extended the test to include consideration of the particular character of the defendant. In that case, the defendant was a local authority. The court, in deciding whether it had failed to take reasonable steps, therefore considered the responsibilities of the local authority to the public at large, for example, for the problems likely to be produced by moving the travellers to another site in the borough. Whilst this would justify it acting more slowly than a private individual, permitting the nuisance to continue for five years was clearly excessive. Equally, in *Holbeck Hall Hotel Ltd v Scarborough BC (No.2)*,[70] the Court of Appeal applied the test to a local authority sued for loss of support. Here, a massive landslip in 1993 had led to the collapse of part of the four star Holbeck Hall Hotel, which was situated at the top of a cliff overlooking the North Sea. As a result, the hotel had to be demolished. The hoteliers sued the local council, which owned the land forming the undercliff between the hotel and the sea, for loss of support, claiming that they should have taken measures to prevent the damage caused. The council had been aware of the danger of landslips due to marine erosion, and had undertaken works in the past, but had not foreseen a landslip of this magnitude. The Court of Appeal rejected the claim. The

---

[66] [1980] 1 All E.R. 17 at 35. See also *Bybrook Barn Garden Centre Ltd v Kent County Council* [2001] Env L.R. 30, CA and *Green v Lord Somerleyton* [2003] EWCA Civ 198; [2004] 1 P. & C.R. 33 (applied to naturally flowing water). The House of Lords in *Marcic v Thames Water Utilities Ltd* [2003] UKHL 66; [2004] 2 A.C. 42, however, distinguished an ordinary occupier of land from statutory occupiers where the law of nuisance must be careful not to impose obligations inconsistent with the statutory scheme under which they operate.

[67] [1967] 1 A.C. 645 at 663.

[68] Although contrast *Abbahall Ltd v Smee* [2002] EWCA Civ 1831; [2003] 1 W.L.R. 1472, (no allowance made for elderly flat-owner reliant on state benefits), although this may be distinguished on its facts—cost of repairs to communal roof to be shared equally amongst flat-owners.

[69] (1982) 80 L.G.R. 337.

[70] [2000] Q.B. 836. Comment: M.P. Thompson [2001] Conv 177 and C.A. Hopkins [2000] C.L.J. 438.

Wilberforce test would apply to claims for loss of support,[71] but the council could not be found liable for failing to undertake measures which only a geological expert could have identified as necessary. The defendant would thus not be liable where he or she was unable to foresee the extent of the loss suffered. In any event, even if the loss had been foreseeable, in view of the extensive and expensive nature of the works necessary:

> "the scope of the duty may be limited to warning neighbours of such risk as they were aware of or ought to have foreseen and sharing such information as they had acquired relating to it."[72]

This subjective test may be contrasted with the objective standard of care adopted in negligence (discussed in Ch.5). We may also note the more restrictive test of remoteness employed in *Holbeck Hall* in comparison to the more generous *Wagon Mound* test discussed in Ch.6. The test is confined, however, to circumstances in which the defendant has not created the nuisance.

One final point of comparison may be drawn between *Sedleigh-Denfield* liability, and the duty of care imposed on landowners in negligence for omissions discussed in Ch.2. It will be recalled that in *Smith v Littlewoods*,[73] the occupier was held not to be liable to adjoining occupiers for the acts of vandals who had set fire to a derelict cinema on its land. The court held that the occupier would not be responsible where it was no more than a merely foreseeable possibility that trespassers would gain access to land and cause damage to the property of neighbouring owners.[74]

**(iv) The creator is the occupier's predecessor in title:** Liability in this context is limited. It **10–026** can only arise where the nuisance was created by a predecessor in title to the occupier and the occupier knew or ought reasonably to know of the existence of the nuisance.[75] In this sense, it strongly resembles the *Sedleigh-Denfield* principle. Although there is no authority that the subjective standard of care applies, it would be illogical not to apply it in such a case.

*(2) The landlord*

On the grant of a lease, the tenant will be in possession and will be liable for any nuisance he **10–027** or she creates. However, there may be circumstances where an alternative action lies against the landlord. There are three main situations where this may occur.

**(i) Where the landlord expressly or impliedly authorises the nuisance:**[76] To establish **10–028** whether the landlord has authorised the tenant to commit the nuisance, the courts will examine the

---

[71] Thereby overturning previous authority which indicated that there was no positive duty in such circumstances to provide support: *Sack v Jones* [1925] Ch.235; *Macpherson v London Passenger Transport Board* (1946) 175 L.T. 279. *Holbeck Hall* was applied in *Rees v Skerrett* [2001] 1 W.L.R. 1541, CA where the owner of a terraced house had, when demolishing the house, failed to take reasonable steps to protect the party wall where it was reasonably foreseeable that, if not properly weatherproofed, the wall would suffer damage.

[72] See Stuart-Smith L.J. [2000] Q.B. 836 at 863. See also *Lambert v Barratt Homes Ltd* [2010] EWCA Civ 681; [2010] 33 E.G. 72 where the court expressly recognised that most local authorities operate under a degree of financial pressure and held that the measured duty of care involved, here, only a duty to co-operate in a solution which involved the construction of suitable drainage.

[73] [1987] A.C. 241. See B.S. Markesinis (1989) 105 L.Q.R. 104.

[74] See Lord Griffiths [1987] A.C. 241 at 251.

[75] *St Anne's Well Brewery Co v Roberts* (1929) 140 L.T. 1; *Wilkins v Leighton* [1932] 2 Ch.106.

[76] See *Harris v James* (1876) 45 L.J.Q.B. 545.

purpose for which the premises are let. The landlord will be liable if the necessary consequence of the letting is that an actionable nuisance will be produced. *Tetley v Chitty*[77] is a good example of such liability. The local authority had let a parcel of its land in a residential area to a go-kart club, in the full knowledge that the club intended to use and develop the land for go-karting. The local residents complained, however, at the noise which came from the track. The court found the local authority liable for the nuisance. The noise was the natural and necessary consequence of that activity, and by granting a lease for this purpose, the authority had given express or at least implied consent to the nuisance.

Such liability did not lie, however, in *Smith v Scott*.[78] Here, a dwelling house had been let to a family known by the landlord to be likely to cause a nuisance. The tenants proceeded to cause damage to the neighbouring property of an elderly couple, and caused such a nuisance that the couple were obliged to leave their home and seek other accommodation. The landlord had inserted in the tenancy agreement a clause expressly prohibiting the committing of a nuisance. The insertion of this covenant countered any arguments of implied authorisation, so that it could not be said that the nuisance was a necessary consequence of the letting.

This decision was approved by the Court of Appeal in *Hussain v Lancaster CC*.[79] Here, the claimants were shopkeepers in a council housing estate, who had been subjected to racial harassment and vandalism by other council tenants. Some individuals were prosecuted, but a total of 106 people had been involved in these actions. The council was held not to be liable for the racial harassment of the shopkeepers by its tenants on the estate. The council's standard form tenancy agreement included a clause instructing the tenant "not to discriminate against or harass any residents or visitors". In the circumstances, the council could not be said to have specifically authorised these acts. Equally, in *Mowan v Wandsworth LBC*,[80] the Court of Appeal struck out a claim against the council on the basis that it could not be said to have authorised the conduct of a tenant suffering from a mental disorder, who lived above the home of the claimant. Reasonable foresight of the nuisance is not sufficient to impose liability on the landlord. As stated by the House of Lords in *Southwark LBC v Tanner*:

> "It is not enough for [landlords] to be aware of the nuisance and take no steps to prevent it. They must either participate directly in the commission of the nuisance or they must be taken to have authorised it by letting the property."[81]

This would seem to let the landlord off fairly easily.[82] In *Smith v Scott*, for example, it was obvious that the tenants would not respect this clause, but foresight was not enough to establish liability. In reality, the courts are being asked to deal with difficult social problems through the imperfect medium of the tort of private nuisance. In *Hussain*, the Court of Appeal clearly regarded this as a matter for police and other agencies rather than the civil courts. Issues such as anti-social behaviour, racial harassment and care in the community cannot realistically be dealt with by the courts alone, and the test of express or implied authorisation thus masks a

---

[77] [1986] 1 All E.R. 663.
[78] [1973] Ch.314.
[79] [2000] Q.B. 1.
[80] (2001) 33 H.L.R. 56.
[81] [2001] 1 A.C. 1 at 22 per Lord Millett, relying on *Malzy v Eichholz* [1916] 2 K.B. 308 (for criticism, see I. Loveland [2005] J.P.L. 405).
[82] See M. Davey [2001] Conv 31 and J. Morgan [2001] C.L.J. 382.

refusal by the courts to intervene. This provides little consolation, however, to those suffering as a result of these problems.[83]

The courts are, however, willing to make such judgments where the defendant is not the landlord, but a licensor of the premises. For example, in *Lippiatt v South Gloucestershire CC*,[84] the Court of Appeal was prepared to find a licensor liable for the acts of licensees on its property. In this case, travellers on the council's land had undertaken a number of acts which harmed the land of neighbouring farmers. Such activities included frequent acts of trespass, stealing timber, gates and fences, dumping rubbish and damaging crops. *Hussain* was distinguished on the basis that the licensor, unlike the landlord, retains control over the premises, and that licensees may be moved on more easily than tenants. The local authority was thus found liable for failing to exercise its powers to evict travellers from its land at an earlier stage. One may question this distinction. The treatment of travellers raises social issues not so different from those outlined in relation to landlords, rendering such a distinction artificial in practice.[85] Equally, the justification that the claimant may also sue the tenant directly, whilst he or she may have difficulties pursuing a licensee, ignores the problems in identifying the tenant in question (consider *Hussain*) or potential difficulties in obtaining a remedy against a particular tenant (for example, in *Mowan*, the court was not convinced that an injunction would be awarded against a person suffering from a mental disorder).[86] It must be questioned whether this distinction can be justified in practice.

It has been suggested that the claimants in the above cases may now be able to invoke art.8 of the European Convention on Human Rights, namely the right to respect for their private and family life and their home.[87] However, it remains questionable how useful it will be in this context. Although art.8 imposes a positive duty on local authorities to ensure that this right is respected, it is a qualified right, and subject to the discretion of the court, which will consider any other remedies available.[88] In *Mowan*, Peter Gibson L.J. rejected the argument on the basis of art.8 where the complainant had an alternative action for judicial review of the local authority's decision not to take the neighbour into care or against the tenant herself, despite some misgivings as to the likely success of any such action. Equally, it has been conceded that provided the local authority adopts a decision-making process which satisfies proportionality and does not impose a disproportionate burden on the complainants, it may escape liability.[89]

**(ii) The landlord knew or ought to have known of the nuisance before letting:** There is **10–029** authority that where the nuisance consists of lack of repair, the landlord cannot avoid liability by simply inserting into the lease a covenant that the tenant must undertake the repairs. As Sachs L.J. commented in *Brew Bros Ltd v Snax (Ross) Ltd*[90]:

---

[83] See S. Bright and C. Bakalis [2003] C.L.J. 305.

[84] [2000] Q.B. 51.

[85] The distinction is equally blurred by cases such as *Chartered Trust Plc v Davies* (1998) 76 P. & C.R. 396, where a landlord was found liable for continuing the nuisance where it had retained control over the common parts in which the nuisance created by its tenant had taken place.

[86] See *Wookey v Wookey* [1991] Fam 121.

[87] D. Rook [2002] Conv 316.

[88] See s.8 of the Human Rights Act 1998.

[89] See D. Rook [2002] Conv 316 at 340.

[90] [1970] 1 Q.B. 612 at 638–9. Contrast, however, the principle of caveat lessee whereby the tenant cannot sue the landlord for nuisance on the basis that, on taking a lease of the property, he or she takes the property as he or she finds it: *Baxter v Camden LBC (No.2)* [2001] Q.B. 1 and *Jackson v JH Watson Property Investment Ltd* [2008] EWHC 14 (Ch).

"As regards nuisance of which [the landlord] knew at the date of the lease, the duty simi-larly arises by reason of his control before that date. Once the liability attaches I can find no rational reason why it should as regards third parties be shuffled off merely by signing a document which as between owner and tenant casts on the latter the burden of executing remedial work. The duty of the owner is to ensure that the nuisance causes no injury, not merely to get someone else's promise to take the requisite steps to abate it."

**10–030**  (iii) **The landlord covenanted to repair, or has a right to enter to repair:**  This may be express or implied.[91] Liability is based on the fact that the landlord has retained a degree of control over the condition of the premises. One particular example of implied retention of control is through ss.11 and 12 of the Landlord and Tenant Act 1985. If a dwelling house is let for a term of less than seven years, there is an implied and non-excludable covenant to keep in repair the structure and exterior of the house and certain installations for the supply of water, gas, sanitation and electricity. This is supplemented by negligence liability under s.4 of the Defective Premises Act 1972. Section 4(1) provides that:

"Where premises are let under a tenancy which puts on the landlord an obligation to the tenant for the maintenance or repair of the premises, the landlord owes to all persons who might reasonably be expected to be affected by defects in the state of the premises a duty to take such care as is reasonable in all the circumstances to see that they are reasonably safe from personal injury or from damage to their property caused by the relevant defect."[92]

This duty is owed only if the landlord knows of the defect (whether as the result of being noti-fied by the tenant or otherwise) or ought in all the circumstances to have known of the relevant defect.[93] It is a duty to repair, not a statutory warranty that the premises are reasonably safe.[94]

## Must the nuisance emanate from the defendant's land?

**10–031**  Lord Goff commented in *Hunter v Canary Wharf Ltd* that the nuisance would generally arise from something emanating from the defendant's land.[95] He did, however, recognise that there were exceptions to this rule. Injunctions have been granted against brothels and "sex centres", where the complaint has been about the presence of prostitutes and clients visiting the premises, rather than an "emanation" from the land.[96] Some confusion has been caused, however, by the case of *Hussain v Lancaster CC*,[97] where the Court of Appeal rejected a claim for nuisance on the basis that the actions complained of did not involve a use of the defendants' land. This case was distinguished, however, by the Court of Appeal in the

---

[91]  See *Mint v Good* [1951] 1 K.B. 517.

[92]  "Relevant defect" is defined in s.4(3).

[93]  s.4(2). See also s.4(4), which extends the duty to situations where the landlord has reserved the right to enter the premises to carry out any description of maintenance or repair of the premises.

[94]  *Alker v Collingwood Housing Association* [2007] EWCA Civ 343; [2007] 1 W.L.R. 2230.

[95]  [1997] A.C. 655 at 685–686.

[96]  *Laws v Florinplace* [1981] 1 All E.R. 659, *Thompson-Schwab v Costaki* [1956] 1 All E.R. 652 and *Church of Jesus Christ of the Latter-Day Saints v Price* [2004] EWHC 3245 (QB).

[97]  [2000] Q.B. 1.

subsequent decision in *Lippiatt v South Gloucestershire CC*,[98] where the court held that when the land on which the trespassers resided was used as a "launching pad" for repeated acts of damage, the council would be liable. *Hussain* was distinguished as relating to individual acts by perpetrators who happened to live in council property. Their conduct was in no sense linked to, nor did it emanate from, their homes. Whilst Evans L.J. suggested that there had thus been an "emanation" in *Lippiatt*—namely the travellers themselves—Staughton L.J. was less convinced:

> "It seems to me that there is not a great difference in such a case whether the offending act of the defendant takes place on his land, or on the public road outside his gate. But we need not rule on that today."[99]

The question was therefore left open and we must await another occasion when an authoritative statement may be produced by the House of Lords.

## Relevant defences

There are a number of defences which apply to an action for nuisance. The general defences **10–032** of voluntary assumption of risk and contributory negligence apply, but will be discussed in more detail in Ch.16. It should be noted that although the Law Reform (Contributory Negligence) Act 1945 does not expressly mention nuisance, its provisions are generally accepted to apply. We confine our examination here to defences which are peculiar to nuisance. These are:

- Statutory authority;
- 20 years prescription;
- Inevitable accident;
- Act of a stranger.

The most significant defence is that of statutory authority.

### (1) Statutory authority

Many nuisances are caused by activities undertaken by local authorities or other bodies **10–033** acting under statutory powers. If their actions are within the scope of the statute (or intra vires), they are authorised by Act of Parliament and cannot be challenged by the courts. Parliament is presumed to have considered the competing interests, and to have determined which is to prevail in the public interest and whether or not compensation is to be paid to those adversely affected. It is important to distinguish this defence from planning permission, by which the applicant is given permission to construct a particular building. This does not mean that his or her actions have been authorised by Parliament. Planning permission is, at most, a matter to be considered in identifying the nature of the locality of the nuisance. The question here is very different: does the defendant have statutory authority to commit the nuisance?

---

[98] [2000] Q.B. 51.
[99] [2000] Q.B. 51 at 65.

The vital question is whether the operations causing the alleged nuisance are within the authority given by statute. Generally, this will be the case if the statute expressly or by necessary implication authorises the nuisance, or the nuisance is the inevitable consequence of the performance of the authorised operations. The leading case on statutory authority is *Allen v Gulf Oil Refining Ltd.*[100] Gulf Oil had obtained its own private Act of Parliament to authorise its expansion in Milford Haven, South Wales. The Act provided specifically for the acquisition of all necessary land and the construction of a refinery, but no express provision was made for the use and operation of the refinery once it had been built. Local residents complained about the noise and vibrations emitted by the refinery and *Allen* was brought as a test case. The House of Lords took the question to be one essentially of statutory construction. Was the nuisance authorised, expressly or implicitly, by the relevant statute? If so, the defendant would not be liable. The burden was, however, on the defendant to satisfy the court that this was in fact so. The court held, by a majority of four to one, that the operation of the refinery was implicitly authorised by the Act, the nuisances were inevitable, and so Gulf Oil had a good defence to the plaintiffs' action. The plaintiffs would only have a remedy to the extent to which any nuisance exceeded the statutory immunity.

The nuisance will not be inevitable if it has been caused by the negligence of the defendant. "Negligence" here is used in a special sense to mean a failure by the undertaker to carry out the work and conduct the operation with all reasonable regard and care for the interests of other persons.[101] It should be noted that an inevitable nuisance, even when committed without negligence, is unlikely to be considered authorised if the statute contains a "nuisance clause" providing that nothing in the Act shall exonerate the undertaker from liability for the nuisance.[102] Equally, if the defendant has a choice how to exercise a statutory power, and chooses an option which creates a nuisance when there are other options which would not have raised such problems, it is unlikely to be found to be authorised.[103]

The Human Rights Act 1998 may, additionally, have some impact on this defence. Section 3(1) of the Act provides that:

"So far as it is possible to do so, primary legislation and subordinate legislation must be read and given effect in a way which is compatible with the convention rights."

It is possible that conduct authorised by statute may conflict with an individual's rights, for example, in relation to art.8 (right to private and family life). The House of Lords' decision in *Ghaidan v Godin-Mendoza*[104] indicates that the courts do possess broad interpretative powers to avoid all such conflicts without resorting to a declaration of incompatibility.

*(2)  20 years' prescription*

**10–034**  Prescription provides a means by which the defendant obtains a legal right to act in a certain way, which would ordinarily be contrary to the law, due to the passage of time. In this context,

---

[100] [1981] A.C. 1001.

[101] See *Wildtree Hotels Ltd v Harrow L.B.C.* [2001] 2 A.C. 1 at 13 per Lord Hoffmann.

[102] See *Department of Transport v N.W. Water Authority* [1983] 3 W.L.R. 105 at 109, approved [1984] A.C. 336 at 359. This only applies to statutory powers and will not apply to statutory duties.

[103] *Metropolitan Asylum District v Hill* (1881) 6 App. Cas. 193.

[104] [2004] UKHL 30; [2004] 2 A.C. 557 (Millett dissenting): interpretation of the Rent Act 1977 SCh.1 para.2 to comply with arts 8 and 14. See also *R. v A (No.2)* [2001] UKHL 25; [2002] 1 A.C. 45 (interpretation of s.41(3), Youth Justice and Criminal Evidence Act 1999 to comply with art.6), and A. Kavanagh (2006) 26 O.J.L.S. 179.

it will be a valid defence for the defendant to show that the nuisance complained of had interfered with the claimant's interest in land for more than 20 years. It should be noted, however, that this applies only to private nuisance. It does not apply to public nuisance, on the basis that length of time should not legitimise a crime. The period is judged carefully, because the law does not easily diminish property rights, and starts from the time at which the nuisance is known by the claimant to affect his or her interests. The difficulties faced in successfully relying on this defence were shown in *Sturges v Bridgman*.[105] Here, a confectioner had used large pestles and mortars at the back of his premises for more than 20 years. His premises were adjacent to the garden of a doctor, who made no complaint until he decided to build a consulting room at the end of his garden. Then, for the first time, he found that the noise and vibration materially interfered with the pursuit of his practice. The court granted him an injunction, despite the fact that the noise and vibrations had existed for over 20 years and that he had chosen to build in his garden in the full knowledge of the defendant's operations (it was no defence that the plaintiff came to the nuisance—see below).

*(3) Inevitable accident*

The defence of inevitable accident is based on the fact that the damage suffered by the claimant    **10–035**
occurred despite the exercise of all reasonable care by the defendant. On this basis, this defence can only be relevant to torts where the exercise of reasonable care is necessary for liability. It therefore plays a minimal role in the tort of nuisance and is only relevant where liability is dependent upon proof of negligence. Reference should be made to Ch.16.

*(4) Act of a stranger*

This defence is subject to the principle in *Sedleigh-Denfield v O'Callaghan*.[106] Reference    **10–036**
should therefore be made to the earlier part of this chapter.

## Ineffective defences

The following are defences which have been rejected by the courts:                              **10–037**

- The claimant came to the nuisance;
- The defendant's conduct has social utility;
- *Jus tertii*;
- The nuisance is due to many.

*(1) Coming to the nuisance*

It is a well-established rule that the claimant may sue even though the nuisance was, to his or    **10–038**
her knowledge, in existence before he or she arrived at the premises. By upholding such a rule, the courts clearly favour the right of the claimant to freely enjoy his or her land. The claimant is able to attack the status quo on the basis of his or her own personal interests, despite the fact it may result in the closing down of established businesses, or put an end to activities which

---

[105] (1879) 11 Ch.D. 852.
[106] [1940] A.C. 880.

benefit the community as a whole. The classic case is that of *Bliss v Hall*,[107] in which the defendant's business of manufacturing candles gave off offensive smells. It was no defence to the plaintiff's action that the business had already been in existence for three years before the plaintiff moved in nearby. In more recent times, the rule has been criticised as being unduly favourable to the claimant. In *Miller v Jackson*,[108] the defendants had used a cricket ground for over 70 years. In 1972, the land to the north of the cricket ground was sold to developers, who built a line of semi-detached houses there. The plaintiffs bought one of these properties and complained that despite the fence around the ground (which was increased in height in 1975) cricket balls had been struck into their garden or against their house on a number of occasions. The Court of Appeal was sympathetic to the club. If the plaintiffs were granted an injunction, the club would be closed down at the instigation of parties who had chosen to move to a property adjoining a cricket club. Nevertheless, the majority held that *Sturges v Bridgman*[109] was still good law, and they were bound to hold that it was not a good defence that the plaintiffs had come to the nuisance. As Geoffrey Lane L.J. explained, ". . . it is not for this court as I see it to alter a rule which has stood for so long."[110] This did not prevent the majority ruling that it would not be equitable to award an injunction in such circumstances, thereby confining the plaintiffs' remedy to an award of damages. This case will be discussed further in the section on remedies below.

### (2) Utility

**10–039**    The courts will not accept a defence that the nuisance caused by the defendant has a benefit to the public at large. This is a further example of the law's support for the property rights of the individual, as is clearly seen in the case of *Adams v Ursell*.[111] The defendant ran a fried fish shop in a residential part of a street. The court granted an injunction restraining the defendant from carrying on his fried fish business on the premises, and rejected the argument that the closure of the shop would cause great hardship to the defendant and to his customers, for whom it was a cheap source of nourishment.

### (3) Jus Tertii

**10–040**    This rests on the allegation that a third party has a better title to the affected land than the claimant, and that the third party should therefore be bringing the action. It has been rejected in a number of cases.[112] It seems correct that where the claimant must show an interest in land or right to exclusive possession, this should be sufficient to found his or her claim.

### (4) Due to many

**10–041**    It is no excuse that the defendant was simply one of many causing the nuisance in question. This will be so even if his or her actions in isolation would not amount to a nuisance. In *Lambton v Mellish*,[113] the plaintiff sought an injunction against two rival businessmen who operated merry-go-rounds accompanied by music on their premises. The combined noise was found to be

---

[107] (1838) 4 Bing. N.C. 183 at 185, 132 E.R. 758 at 759.
[108] [1977] Q.B. 966.
[109] (1879) 11 Ch.D. 852.
[110] [1977] Q.B. 966 at 987.
[111] [1913] 1 Ch.269.
[112] *Nicholls v Ely Beet Sugar Factory* Ltd [1936] 1 Ch.343.
[113] [1894] 3 Ch.163.

"maddening". Chitty J. was not prepared to excuse one of the defendants on the basis that his contribution to the noise was slight:

> "if the acts of two persons, each being aware of what the other is doing, amount in the aggregate to what is an actionable wrong, each is amenable to the remedy against the aggregate cause of complaint."[114]

Again, this seems to be a rule of convenience in favour of the claimant, although it may be justified on the basis that the defendant's conduct should be considered in the light of all the surrounding circumstances, including the conduct of others. Therefore, an act which would have been reasonable in isolation may, in the light of all the circumstances, amount to an unreasonable interference with the claimant's use and enjoyment of land.

## RELATIONSHIP BETWEEN PRIVATE NUISANCE AND OTHER TORTS

It is important to distinguish private nuisance from other torts, such as negligence and tres-    **10–042**
pass, which are commonly claimed in the same action. The relationship between private and
public nuisance has already been dealt with above.

### The relationship between private nuisance and negligence[115]

This has caused the most controversy over the years, primarily due to a number of cases which    **10–043**
focus on negligence in determining whether the defendant has committed an actionable
nuisance. The clearest example of this is the group of cases on continuing or adopting a
nuisance. In *Goldman v Hargrave*,[116] Lord Wilberforce remarked that:

> "The present case is one where liability, if it exists, rests upon negligence and nothing
> else; whether it falls within or overlaps the boundaries of nuisance is a question of
> classification which need not here be resolved".

However, Megaw L.J. in *Leakey v National Trust*[117] described the claim as one in nuisance,
and, as stated earlier, such cases are distinct from ordinary claims in negligence in that (a) they
impose liability for an omission, and (b) they impose a subjective standard of care.
    The accepted position is that the two torts are conceptually distinct, and this was empha-
sised by the House of Lords in *Hunter v Canary Wharf Ltd*[118] and *Cambridge Water Co v
Eastern Counties Leather Plc*.[119] The central concept of private nuisance is that of "reasonable
user". This is distinct from negligence. There is clear authority that the defendant may be

[114] [1894] 3 Ch.163 at 166.
[115] See C. Gearty (1989) 48 C.L.J. 211; M. Lee (2003) 119 L.Q.R. 298; P. Giliker in *Environmental Protection and the Law* (Hart, 2000).
[116] [1967] 1 A.C. 645 at 657. Consider, also, defences such as act of stranger (10–036 and 10–061).
[117] [1980] Q.B. 485.
[118] [1997] A.C. 655.
[119] [1994] 2 A.C. 264.

liable in spite of exercising reasonable care and skill.[120] As stated above, the concept of reason-able user is results-based: is the result of the defendant's conduct such that the claimant suffers unreasonable interference with the use and enjoyment of his or her property? This is a very different approach from that in negligence. For example, the classic case of negligence is that of a road traffic accident caused by the negligent driving of a motorist. The court does not consider the degree of injury suffered by the particular claimant, and weigh this against the right of the particular motorist to drive his or her car without restriction. Rather, it draws on case law which has established that the motorist owes a duty of care to pedestrians and other road-users, and ascertains whether he or she has driven below the standard of the ordinary reasonable driver, thereby causing the accident.

A further distinction is that while negligence primarily protects against personal injury, private nuisance seeks to protect interests in land. This is forcefully stated by the majority of the House of Lords in *Hunter*. The role of private nuisance is to remedy undue interference with rights in land—hence the only parties who can sue are those with an interest in land or exclusive possession which has been interfered with. Their Lordships, in *Hunter* and *Transco*, went further, suggesting that only negligence was capable of protecting against personal injury, as this is not the concern of private nuisance. The implications of this will be consid-ered further in our section on remedies.

It is clear, therefore, that while the torts overlap, and the fact that the defendant's actions were committed negligently may encourage a court to find liability, the torts are distinct. This is not to deny that the growth of negligence in the twentieth century has influenced the development of the older tort of private nuisance. This influence may be seen in relation to the continuation or adoption of a nuisance and the fact that the rules of remoteness set out in *The Wagon Mound (No.1)*[121] are common to negligence, private and public nuisance.[122] This does not signify, however, that the courts will not continue to distinguish between the two different torts.

## The relationship between private nuisance and trespass to land

10–044    Both torts have the common aim of protecting those with an interest in or exclusive possession of land. Trespass will be discussed in more detail in our next chapter: Ch.11. For the moment, it should be noted that trespass involves an intentional and direct act which interferes with the land. It is actionable without proof of damage. In contrast, nuisance involves an indirect act which is only actionable on proof of damage. The distinction is historical, and results from the old rigid forms of action, which required that a claim had to be made in a certain form or not at all. Although the forms of action were abolished in the nineteenth century, the distinction between direct and indirect forms of interference with land persists. The distinction may be illustrated by the following classic example: I throw a log onto your land—this is a direct interference and therefore I am liable in trespass even if it does not cause you injury or prop-erty damage. (Obviously more damages will be recovered if it crashes through your green-house!) Alternatively, I pile up some logs on my land and one of them rolls off the pile and onto your land. Here, the interference is indirect and it will only be actionable in nuisance if you can show that it has caused some injury to your rights in the land.

---

[120]  *Rapier v London Tramways Co* [1893] 2 Ch.588.
[121]  [1961] A.C. 388.
[122]  See *The Wagon Mound (No.2)* [1967] 1 A.C. 617. See below.

## PUBLIC NUISANCE[123]

It is important, before examining the rule in *Rylands v Fletcher*, to give an overview of the **10–045** operation of public nuisance. It has a minor role to play in the law of torts and therefore this section will seek to give the reader a general idea of its impact, whilst acknowledging that its role has been largely overtaken by statute. The classic definition may be found in Romer L.J.'s judgment in *Att-Gen v PYA Quarries Ltd*:[124]

> "any nuisance is 'public' which materially affects the reasonable comfort and conven-
> ience of life of a class of Her Majesty's subjects. The sphere of the nuisance may be
> described generally as 'the neighbourhood'; but the question whether the local commu-
> nity within that sphere comprises a sufficient number of persons to constitute a class of
> the public is a question of fact in every case".

It is not necessary to show that every member of the class has been affected, but the nuisance must be shown to injure a representative cross-section of the class.

More recently, the House of Lords in *R. v Rimmington; Goldstein*[125] examined the applica-tion of public nuisance in modern law. In *Rimmington*, the defendant had sent over 500 racially abusive letters and packages to different individuals all over the country. In *Goldstein*, the defendant, as a joke, had sent an envelope containing salt to a friend, which backfired completely when it leaked out in the postal sorting office and triggered an anthrax scare. Neither defendant was found guilty of public nuisance. In the first case, their Lordships emphasised that a section of the community must be affected.[126] It was not enough to incon-venience selected individuals. Mr Goldstein was equally not guilty of a public nuisance where it could not be shown that he knew or reasonably should have known that a public nuisance would occur as a consequence of his actions.[127]

As Lord Denning remarked in *Southport Corp v Esso Petroleum Co Ltd*,[128] "the term 'public nuisance' covers a multitude of sins, great and small". The tort has indeed been used to deal with a variety of situations including pollution from oil and silt, pigeon droppings, bogus bomb alerts, pirate radio broadcasting and raves. Its most common use, however, is in relation to claims for unreasonable interference with the claimant's use of the highway. Obviously, in such cases, it will be difficult to bring a claim in private nuisance unless the interference affects the use and enjoyment of the claimant's land, and here the complaint will generally relate to the claimant's right to pass along the highway.

---

[123] See J. Spencer [1989] C.L.J. 55, who, at 59, describes it as "a ragbag of odds and ends".

[124] [1957] 2 Q.B. 169 at 184. See also Denning L.J. at 190–191.

[125] [2005] UKHL 63; [2006] 1 A.C. 459. Although these are criminal cases, Lord Bingham expressly stated that the ingredients of public nuisance as a crime or a tort were the same: para.7.

[126] "A core element of the crime of public nuisance is that the defendant's act should affect the community, a section of the public, rather than simply individuals": Lord Rodger [2005] UKHL 63; [2006] 1 A.C. 459, at para.47. See also *DPP v Fearon* [2010] EWHC 340 (Admin): single act of soliciting not a public nuisance.

[127] Following *R. v Shorrock* [1994] Q.B. 279 (see para.10–023).

[128] [1954] 2 Q.B. 182 at 196.

## Obstructions on the highway

**10–046**    Whilst complaints as to the condition of the highway itself will now largely be covered by the Highways Act 1980, the claimant may wish to bring an action relating to unreasonable obstructions on the highway. As noted in *Dymond v Pearce*,[129] some obstructions are inevitable. It is generally acceptable for vehicles to stop on the highway to deliver goods or to park in a lay-by, but a prima facie nuisance would be created where a vehicle is left for a considerable period without any valid justification. Equally, whilst it is reasonable for a person to put up scaffolding for works on his or her house which obstructs the highway on a temporary basis, a nuisance would be created if the erection of the scaffolding was unreasonable in size or duration.[130] It is a matter of degree. It is still unclear whether fault is necessary to establish that the obstruction is unreasonable. Certainly the majority in *Dymond* were prepared to contemplate liability where an action for negligence would fail, despite statements to the contrary in *The Wagon Mound (No.2)*.[131] Lord Denning M.R. attempted a compromise in *Southport Corp v Esso Petroleum Co Ltd*[132] by suggesting that for public nuisance, unlike negligence, once the nuisance was proved, the legal burden would fall on the defendant who caused it to justify or excuse himself or herself. This would serve to keep the torts logically distinct, but as the House of Lords on appeal did not deal with this matter, the view of Lord Denning M.R. is not authoritative. The courts still experience difficulty in separating the question whether there is a nuisance (i.e. an unreasonable obstruction of the highway) from the question of fault.

## Projections over the highway

**10–047**    There is further confusion whether fault is relevant when the claimant's injuries are caused by an object projecting onto the highway from the defendant's land. In *Tarry v Ashton*,[133] an occupier had been found liable when a heavy lamp, attached to the front of his building on the Strand, fell on a passer-by. The occupier was held to owe a positive, continuing and non-delegable duty to keep the premises in repair so as not to prejudice the public. In *Noble v Harrison*,[134] however, the court held that the defendant could only be liable if he or she knew, or should have known, of the circumstances which caused the injury. Here, a branch of a beech tree growing on the defendant's land, which overhung the highway, had suddenly broken and damaged the plaintiff's vehicle. The fracture had been due to a latent defect which could not have been detected by reasonable and careful inspection. Rowlatt J. held that the defendant was not liable and distinguished the earlier decision of *Tarry v Ashton*[135] on the basis that it applied to artificial rather than natural objects.

The Court of Appeal in *Wringe v Cohen*[136] continued to follow *Tarry* as imposing a rule of strict liability in respect of artificial structures projecting onto the highway:

---

[129] [1972] 1 All E.R. 1142.
[130] *Harper v Haden* [1933] Ch.298.
[131] *Overseas Tankships (UK) Ltd v Miller Steamship Co Pty* [1967] 1 A.C. 617.
[132] [1954] 2 Q.B. 182 at 197.
[133] (1876) 1 Q.B.D. 314.
[134] [1926] 2 K.B. 332.
[135] (1876) 1 Q.B.D. 314.
[136] [1940] 1 K.B. 229 at 233.

". . . if, owing to want of repair, premises on a highway become dangerous and, there-fore, a nuisance and a passer-by or an adjoining owner suffers damage by their collapse, the occupier, or owner if he has undertaken the duty of repair, is answerable whether he knew or ought to have known of the danger or not."

This line of authority was followed by the Court of Appeal in *Mint v Good*.[137] As a result of these decisions, the courts apply different rules depending on whether the projection onto the highway is artificial or natural. This distinction is difficult to justify on principle, but, as may be seen above, owes more to the court's willingness in *Noble* to distinguish a line of authority it preferred not to follow.

However, in practice, the distinction between the different rules is not great. The court in *Wringe v Cohen* recognised two defences which had been mentioned by Blackburn J. in *Tarry*: (i) where the danger had been caused by the unseen act of a trespasser, and (ii) where the damage is due to a "secret and unobservable operation of nature" (a latent defect) of which the occupier does not know or ought not to have known. Such defences largely undermine the idea of strict liability for projections on the highway and clearly inject an element of fault. Here, once again, we can observe the influence of negligence on the development of the tort of nuisance. It should also be noted that the Court of Appeal in *Salsbury v Woodland*[138] refused to extend *Tarry* to work undertaken near the highway in circumstances where, if care was not taken, injury to passers-by might be caused. The court held that no such category of strict liability existed, and that the ordinary rules of negligence would apply. The occupier would, however, have been strictly liable for the actions of his independent contractors if the work had been inherently dangerous (see our earlier discussion of this point under Private Nuisance, above).

## Particular damage

It is not enough for the claimant to show that he or she is a member of the class whose reasonable comfort and convenience has been materially affected by the defendant. To bring an action in tort, the claimant must show that he or she has suffered "special" or "partic-ular" damage in excess of that suffered by the public at large.[139] This is largely a measure to limit the number of claims and avoid the defendant being deluged with claims from every member of the class affected. Such special damage must be direct and substantial and includes personal injury, property damage, loss of custom or business and, it is claimed, delay and inconvenience. The latter category is contentious, and it has been suggested that the claimant must also show pecuniary loss due to the delay.[140] If the individual cannot prove special damage, the only other basis on which an action may be brought in tort is in the name of the Attorney-General by means of a relator action (for example, see *PYA Quarries* above). This is seldom used. Alternatively, the local authority may be persuaded to exercise its power under s.222 of the Local Government Act 1972 to bring proceedings for an injunction when it

**10–048**

---

[137] [1951] 1 K.B. 517.
[138] [1970] 1 Q.B. 324 at 345, CA.
[139] See G. Kodalinye (1986) 2 L.S. 182.
[140] See *Winterbottom v Lord Derby* (1867) L.R. 2 Ex. 316 at 321–322.

considers it "expedient for the promotion or protection of the interests of the inhabitants of their area".[141]

## THE RULE IN *RYLANDS V FLETCHER*

**10–049**    So far, we have considered the way in which nuisance protects the claimant's ability to exercise his or her rights over land without undue interference by the defendant. In this section, we consider a particular cause of action which protects an occupier against interference due to an isolated escape from his or her neighbour's land. The particular rules relating to this cause of action, and its relationship with nuisance, will be considered below. First, let us examine the case which provides both the principle and the name for this cause of action: *Rylands v Fletcher*.[142]

The defendant was a millowner, who had employed independent contractors to build a reservoir on his land to provide water for his mill. During the course of building, the independent contractors discovered some old shafts and passages of an abandoned coalmine on the defendant's land, which appeared to be blocked. When the reservoir was filled, the water burst through the old shafts, which were subsequently found to connect with the plaintiff's mine. As a result, the plaintiff's mine was flooded and he sought compensation.

Although the independent contractors had clearly been negligent in failing to ensure that the mine shafts were blocked off securely, the plaintiff's action was against the millowner. The millowner had not been shown to be negligent. The plaintiff also faced the added obstacle that the courts had severe doubts whether an isolated escape, as opposed to a continuous state of affairs, could found an action in nuisance. This did not prevent his action succeeding. The case was finally resolved at House of Lords level, but the classic statement of principle was given by Blackburn J. in the Court of Exchequer Chamber:

> "We think that the true rule of law is that the person who for his own purposes brings on his lands and collects and keeps there anything likely to do mischief if it escapes, must keep it in at his peril, and, if he does not do so, is prima facie answerable for all the damage which is the natural consequence of its escape."

This was approved by the House of Lords, although Lord Cairns added the term "non-natural user" in explaining the principle.

---

[141] See, for example, *Stoke-on-Trent City Council v B & Q (Retail) Ltd* [1984] A.C. 754. In *Wandsworth LBC v Railtrack Plc* [2001] EWCA Civ 1236; [2002] Q.B. 756, the local authority was able to complain about the damage caused by pigeons roosting under the defendant's railway bridge under s.222 and, because the nuisance affected those using the highway when passing under the bridge, by virtue of s.130 of the Highways Act 1980 (highway authority empowered to bring legal proceedings in their own name to protect the public's right to use and enjoy the highway). There is no obstacle to the local authority bringing an action under both provisions in highway cases: *Nottingham City Council v Zain* [2001] EWCA Civ 1248; [2002] 1 W.L.R. 607. *Zain* additionally raises the interesting question as to what extent a local authority should be permitted to use s.222 to enforce criminal law, for example, by excluding a drug dealer from a housing estate. Such a use was found to be arguable in this case. The House of Lords in *R. v Rimmington* [2005] UKHL 63; [2006] 1 A.C. 459 warned, however, that public nuisance should not be used to undermine the intention of Parliament where it had made express provision for certain offences.

[142] (1865) 3 H. & C. 774 (Court of Exchequer); (1866) 1 L.R. 1 Ex. 265 (Court of Exchequer Chamber); (1868) L.R. 3 H.L. 330 (House of Lords).

## What is the significance of *Rylands v Fletcher?*

This has caused some controversy. Blackburn J. reasoned by analogy to existing examples of **10–050** liability, such as cattle trespass and nuisance, and clearly did not believe himself to be laying down any new principle of law. Liability under the rule is therefore closely related to these torts. However, in the first part of the twentieth century, *Rylands v Fletcher* liability developed as a separate "rule" with its own requirements, which will be outlined below. It has been suggested that the rule can be explained as a decision to impose strict liability on persons conducting ultra-hazardous activities. Certainly this idea has received support in the United States. The Draft of the Restatement (3d) on Torts imposes strict liability for abnormally dangerous activities,[143] when

> "(1) the activity creates a foreseeable and highly significant risk of physical harm even when reasonable care is exercised by all actors; and (2) the activity is not one of common usage."[144]

This idea was not, however, accepted in England. The Law Commission, in its 1970 Report, *Civil Liability for Dangerous Things and Activities*,[145] expressed doubts as to its usefulness, finding that any benefits provided by its relative simplicity and flexibility would be outweighed by difficulties in application. The House of Lords sounded the death-knell for strict liability for ultra-hazardous activities in *Read v Lyons*,[146] where their Lordships clearly rejected this as an explanation of *Rylands v Fletcher* liability. (This case is discussed below). Lord Goff in *Cambridge Water* took the view that, as a general rule, strict liability for operations of high risk would be more appropriately imposed by statute than the courts and that, in any event, *Read v Lyons* served to preclude any such development.[147]

A further suggestion has been that the rule should be absorbed into the law of negligence. Whilst this may seem an odd suggestion, the High Court of Australia in *Burnie Port Authority v General Jones*[148] decided exactly that in 1984. The court held, by a majority of five to two, that the occupier was liable for fire damage caused by the negligence of his independent contractors under the ordinary rules of negligence, due to the existence of a non-delegable duty of care. The reasoning in this case, which relies heavily on the concept of non-delegable duties, is somewhat strained and, despite the growing influence of negligence in the twentieth century, has received little support in England.

---

[143] para.20, replacing para.519 of the Second Restatement. See, generally, K.N. Hylton "The Theory of Tort Doctrine and the Restatement (Third) of Torts" (2001) 54 Vanderbilt Law Review 1413 and K.W.Simons, 'The Restatement Third of Torts and Traditional Strict Liability: Robust Rationales, Slender Doctrines' (2009) 44 Wake Forest Law Review 1355.

[144] This is a modification of para.520 of the Second Restatement.

[145] Law Commission Report No. 32 (1970), Pt III. However, the idea did receive some support in the report of the Pearson Commission in 1978 (*Report of the Royal Commission on Civil Liability and Compensation for Personal Injury*, Cmnd 7054 (1978), Vol.1, Ch.31, para.1651) which recommended a statutory scheme making the controller of any listed dangerous thing or activity strictly liable for death or personal injury resulting from its malfunction. As discussed in Ch.1, the broad views of the Pearson Commission on liability have never been adopted in this country.

[146] [1947] A.C. 156 at 167, 181, 186 (liability rejected in respect of a high explosive shell which exploded and injured a munitions inspector).

[147] [1994] 2 A.C. 264 at 305.

[148] (1994) 120 A.L.R. 42. For a discussion of the case, see R.F.V. Heuston and R.A. Buckley (1994) 110 L.Q.R. 506.

The English courts have questioned, however, the relationship between the rule in *Rylands v Fletcher* and private nuisance. Lord Goff in *Cambridge Water Co v Eastern Counties Leather Plc*,[149] relying on historical analysis,[150] commented that:

> "it would . . . lead to a more coherent body of common law principles if the rule were to be regarded as essentially an extension of the law of nuisance to isolated escapes from land".

**10–051**   The 2003 House of Lords ruling in *Transco Plc v Stockport MBC*[151] confirmed that the rule should be treated as a sub-species of private nuisance.[152] In this case, their Lordships took the opportunity to review the scope and application in modern conditions of the rule in *Rylands v Fletcher*. It therefore provides helpful guidance as to the future application of this tort. In particular, the court:

- Rejected the suggestion that it should be absorbed into the tort of negligence or fault-based principles, as in Australia and Scotland[153];

- Rejected the suggestion of a more generous application of the rule. Their Lordships favoured a more restrictive approach, confining the rule to exceptional circumstances where the occupier has brought some dangerous thing onto his land which poses an exceptionally high risk to neighbouring property should it escape, and which amounts to an extraordinary and unusual use of land; and

- Clarified that only those with rights to land could sue.

This decision ends a long period of speculation as to the relationship between this tort and private nuisance. It serves also to emphasise the residuary role of the rule in modern society where statutes and regulations largely cover the area of dangerous escapes which the rule once covered e.g. the discharge of water is now regulated by s.209 of the Water Industry Act 1991.[154] It remains to be seen, following such a review, how useful such a limited claim will now be.[155]

## Liability under the rule in *Rylands v Fletcher*

**10–052**   There are four requirements which must be established for the claimant to sue under the rule. The first two derive from Blackburn J.'s statement of principle. The third derives from Lord Cairns in the House of Lords. The fourth requirement, namely foreseeability of the kind of

---

[149] [1994] 2 A.C. 264 at 306.

[150] Particularly, the article of F.H. Newark, "The Boundaries of Nuisance" (1949) 65 L.Q.R. 480.

[151] [2003] UKHL 61; [2004] 2 A.C. 1.

[152] For criticism, see D. Nolan (2005) 121 L.Q.R. 421 (who favours abolition of the rule) and J. Murphy (2004) 24 O.J.L.S. 643 (who defends the rule (at 669) as "a useful residual mechanism for securing environmental protection by individuals affected by harmful escapes from polluting heavyweight industrialists").

[153] See *RHM Bakeries (Scotland) Ltd v Strathclyde Regional Council*, 1985 S.L.T. 214.

[154] See also Environmental Protection Act 1990 s.73(6) (pollution by escape of waste) and Nuclear Installations Act 1965 s.7 (radio-active matter).

[155] Lord Hoffmann commented [2003] UKHL 61; [2004] 2 A.C. 1 at para.39 that "It is perhaps not surprising that counsel could not find a reported case since the second world war in which anyone had succeeded in a claim under the rule." It is then somewhat ironic that a mere two years after this judgment, liability was found for the escape of fire from industrial premises in *LMS International Ltd v Styrene Packaging & Insulation Ltd* [2005] EWHC 2065; [2006] T.C.L.R. 6 (QBD (TCC)), which also suggested, at para.26, that there were cases which could have been cited in *Transco*.

damage suffered, is of more recent origin and comes from the leading judgment of Lord Goff in *Cambridge Water Co v Eastern Counties Leather Plc.*[156]

*(1) The defendant brings on his lands for his own purposes something likely to do mischief*

This requires a voluntary act of bringing something on the land. What is "likely to do mischief" is an interesting question. In *Rylands* itself, water was held to be within this category, and other case law has referred to electricity, oil, vibrations, noxious fumes and even a flagpole or a fairground ride.   **10–053**

This requirement seems to have been toughened up by *Transco*. Lord Bingham remarked that:

> "I do not think the mischief or danger test should be at all easily satisfied. It must be shown that the defendant has done something which he recognised, or judged by the standards appropriate at the relevant place and time, he ought reasonably to have recognised, as giving rise to an *exceptionally high risk of danger* or mischief if there should be an escape, however unlikely an escape may have been thought to be."[157]

This again will serve to restrict the application of the rule.

*(2) If it escapes*

This is one of the key features of liability. The rule in *Rylands v Fletcher* deals with isolated escapes and therefore proof of an actual escape is vital. The leading case is the House of Lords decision in *Read v Lyons*,[158] where their Lordships took the opportunity to review the law and establish clear rules of liability. In the case itself, an inspector of munitions had been injured by an explosion of a shell whilst inspecting the defendants' munitions factory. Their Lordships held that there had not been an "escape" within the rule. An escape would only occur when the object moved from the defendant's premises to a place which was outside his occupation or control.   **10–054**

There is some debate whether an intentional release of an object is capable of being regarded as an "escape". Taylor J. in *Rigby v Chief Constable of Northamptonshire*[159] held that trespass would seem to be the correct action for the intentional and direct infliction of harm. However, this was questioned by Potter J. in *Crown River Cruises Ltd v Kimbolton Fireworks Ltd*,[160] at least where the intentional release was not deliberately aimed in the direction of the claimant, or with the intention of impinging on his or her property. With respect, Taylor J.'s view is probably more consistent with the traditional division between nuisance and trespass, and with Lord Goff's return to the traditional view of these torts in *Cambridge Water* and *Hunter v Canary Wharf*.

*(3) Non-natural user*

Blackburn J. in *Rylands v Fletcher* referred to the defendant bringing onto the property something "which was not naturally there", which Lord Cairns in the House of Lords interpreted as a "non-natural use". On this basis, thistledown, blowing from the defendant's land onto the   **10–055**

---

[156] [1994] 2 A.C. 264.
[157] [2003] UKHL 61; [2004] 2 A.C. 1 at para.10 (emphasis added).
[158] [1947] A.C. 156.
[159] [1985] 2 All E.R. 985 at 996.
[160] [1996] 2 Lloyd's Rep. 533.

plaintiff's land, has been held not to found an action.[161] Over time, however, the "non-natural" use requirement came to be interpreted as "non-ordinary" use, so as to limit the application of the rule in *Rylands v Fletcher*. As Professor Newark has remarked, "the result as applied in the modern cases is, we believe, one which would have surprised Lord Cairns and astounded Blackburn J."[162] The result has been unpredictability and confusion, and many would sympathise with Viscount Simon in *Read v Lyons*, who commented:

> "I confess to finding this test of 'non-natural' user (or of bringing on the land what was not 'naturally there', which is not the same test) difficult to apply".[163]

The classic definition, however, is that of Lord Moulton in *Rickards v Lothian*[164]:

> "It is not every use to which land is put that brings into play [the *Rylands v Fletcher*] principle. It must be some special use bringing with it increased danger to others, and must not merely be the ordinary use of the land or such a use as is proper for the general benefit of the community."

This broad definition has allowed the courts to conclude that domestic water, electricity and gas supplies could be regarded as a "natural" use of land. "Natural user" has even controversially been extended to the manufacture of explosives during war-time,[165] although this was doubted in *Transco*.[166] Essentially, "natural" has been interpreted as any ordinary use of land. Whilst what is ordinary will change with time (for example keeping a car was "non-natural" in 1919,[167] but would not be so regarded today), interpreting the rule in this way clearly gives the courts considerable discretion in deciding whether to apply the rule to a given set of facts.

The meaning of "non-natural user" must now be viewed in the light of Lord Goff's comments in *Cambridge Water Co v Eastern Counties Leather Plc*[168] and the House of Lords ruling in *Transco Plc v Stockport MBC*.[169] Lord Goff remarked in *Cambridge Water* that ". . . the storage of substantial quantities of chemicals on industrial premises should be regarded as an almost classic case of non-natural use".[170] His Lordship held that this was regardless of any benefit the factory may give to the public by means of increased employment (thereby criticising the "general benefit of the community" test of Lord Moulton). Equally, his Lordship refused to accept that storing chemicals in industrial premises might be regarded as an "ordinary" use of such premises.

---

[161] *Giles v Walker* (1890) 24 Q.B.D. 656.

[162] F.H. Newark (1961) 24 M.L.R. 557 at 571.

[163] [1947] A.C. 156 at 166.

[164] [1913] A.C. 263 at 280.

[165] *Read v Lyons* [1947] A.C. 156 at 174, 176.

[166] See Lords Bingham [2003] UKHL 61; [2004] 2 A.C. 1 at para.11 and Walker at para.105. Note also criticism of this decision by Lord Goff in *Cambridge Water Co v Eastern Counties Leather Plc* [1994] 2 A.C. 264 at 308 and contrast *Rainham Chemical Works v Belvedere Fish Guano Co* [1921] 2 A.C. 465 where the manufacture of explosives during the First World War was regarded as "non-natural".

[167] *Musgrove v Pandelis* [1919] 2 K.B. 43.

[168] [1994] 2 A.C. 264.

[169] [2003] UKHL 61; [2004] 2 A.C. 1.

[170] [1994] 2 A.C. 264 at 309. See also *LMS International Ltd v Styrene Packaging & Insulation Ltd* [2005] EWHC 2065; [2006] T.C.L.R. 6 (QBD (TCC)): flammable material stored in factory premises.

The House of Lords in *Transco* approved Lord Goff's judgment and expanded upon it. The case itself was primarily concerned with the nature of the "non-natural user" test. Stockport MBC were the owners of a block of flats and an adjacent disused railway embankment. A water pipe serving the flats leaked and the water percolated to the surface and onward into the embankment through a crack in the ground. There was no evidence that this was due to negligence. The embankment collapsed as a result of having become saturated with water, and the void left by the collapse exposed a high pressure gas main owned by British Gas (now Transco). The claimants wisely acted promptly to prevent a potential fracture of the pipe, incurring costs of around £94,000. The question arose whether the storage of water in pipes was a "non-natural" use of the land.

The House of Lords agreed with the Court of Appeal that the provision of a water supply to a block of flats by means of a connecting pipe was a natural use of land. This is consistent with prior authority. However, the tests used indicate that the "non-natural user" requirement will be more difficult to satisfy than previously. The court sought to find the creation of a special hazard constituting an extraordinary use of land, and noted the link between the first requirement (something likely to do mischief) and the question of non-natural use. All five judges sought some use which was extraordinary and unusual according to contemporary standards.[171] This clearly did not exist on the facts. It was a routine function which would not have struck anyone as raising any special hazard. Lord Hoffmann suggested that:

> "A useful guide in deciding whether the risk has been created by a 'non-natural' user of land is therefore to ask whether the damage which eventuated was something against which the occupier could reasonably be expected to have insured himself."[172]

If it is, then the use is classified as ordinary and the test is not satisfied.

### (4) Foreseeability of damage of the relevant type

This requirement comes from the review undertaken by the House of Lords of liability under the rule in *Cambridge Water Co v Eastern Counties Leather Plc*.[173] In this case, the defendants had used a chemical called perchloroethene (PCE) for degreasing pelts at their tannery. There were regular spillages, which gradually seeped into and built up under the land. The chemical seepage was such that it contaminated the plaintiffs' water supply 1.3 miles away, forcing them to find another source at a cost of nearly £1 million. The plaintiffs sued in negligence, nuisance and under the rule in *Rylands v Fletcher*. By the time the case reached the House of Lords, only liability under the latter head was in issue.

The House of Lords held that the defendants were not liable. It was not foreseeable to the skilled person that quantities of chemical would cause damage to the plaintiffs' water, and foreseeability of damage was a requirement of liability under the rule in *Rylands v Fletcher*.[174]

**10–056**

---

[171] Although Lord Bingham [2003] UKHL 61; [2004] 2 A.C. 1 at para.11 warned against a too inflexible approach. A use might be extraordinary and unusual at one time or place, but not so at another.

[172] [2003] UKHL 61; [2004] 2 A.C. 1 at para.46.

[173] [1994] 2 A.C. 264.

[174] See also *Savage v Fairclough* [2000] Env L.R. 183, CA where pollution of a private water supply, which had arisen due to nitrate contamination from a neighbour's farm, was not considered foreseeable by a "hypothetical good farmer" running a farm such as the one in question. Note also *Hamilton v Papakura DC* [2002] UKPC 9; *The Times*, March 2, 2002, where the Privy Council held that damage caused to crops due to the presence of a herbicide in the town water supply (which remained fit for human consumption) did not lead to foreseeable loss.

Lord Goff justified his conclusion by analogy to nuisance, and by reference to Blackburn J.'s statement of principle in *Rylands* itself, namely that the rule referred to "anything likely to do mischief if it escapes".

There has been some discussion as to how far this test of foreseeability goes. Must the escape also be foreseeable? Although Lord Goff's judgment is not entirely clear, the best view is that the escape need not be foreseeable. As Lord Goff commented:

> "the principle is one of strict liability in the sense that the defendant may be held liable notwithstanding that he has exercised all due care to prevent the escape from occurring".[175]

This is certainly the interpretation adopted by Judge Peter Bowsher Q.C. in *Ellison v Ministry of Defence*,[176] although his comments were obiter on the facts.

Lord Goff also considered the position in relation to the continuing contamination by PCE. The problem had been identified. Could the defendants be liable for such ongoing damage now it was clearly foreseeable? His Lordship found this argument to be ill-founded. The chemical was now beyond the control of the defendants, and to impose liability would be to adopt a stricter position than that adopted in nuisance or negligence.

## Who can sue?

**10–057**  Before the House of Lords' decision in *Transco*, it had been unclear in light of *Cambridge Water* and *Hunter* whether it was necessary to have an interest in land or exclusive possession to sue. Non-occupiers had in the past recovered damages under this head;[177] although this line of authority had been criticised in the leading case of *Read v Lyons*.[178] Yet, in view of Lord Goff's comment in *Cambridge Water* that the focus of both torts is the same—namely the protection of rights to land—logically, only claimants with a right to land should be able to sue.[179] *Transco* confirms the force of Lord Goff's logic: only parties with rights over land may bring an action under the rule in *Rylands v Fletcher*.

## Who can be sued?

**10–058**  The occupier of land will be liable if he or she satisfies the requirements for establishing the tort. Therefore, if you have accumulated the mischief which has escaped, etc., you may be liable. There is clear authority that licensees may be sued.[180] Indeed, in *Rylands* itself, although the millowner was treated as the owner of the land, on the facts of the case, the millowner had

---

[175]  [1994] 2 A.C. 264 at 302.

[176]  (1996) 81 B.L.R. 101.

[177]  See, e.g. dicta in *Shiffman v Order of the Hospital of St John of Jerusalem* [1936] 1 All E.R. 557 (although decided on negligence) and *Perry v Kendricks Transport Ltd* [1956] 1 W.L.R. 85 at 92.

[178]  [1947] A.C. 156 at 173 (per Lord Macmillan) and at 186 (per Lord Uthwatt). See also Widgery J. in *Weller & Co v Foot and Mouth Disease Research Institute* [1966] 1 Q.B. 569 at 588.

[179]  Such reasoning convinced Neuberger J. in *McKenna v British Aluminium Ltd* [2002] Env LR 30, Birmingham District Registry.

[180]  See *Rainham Chemical Works v Belvedere Fish Guano Co* [1921] 2 A.C. 465 at 479 per Lord Sumner, who cited *Eastern and South African Telegraph Co v Cape Town Tramways Cos Ltd* [1902] A.C. 381 at 392; *Midwood v Manchester Corp* [1905] 2 K. B. 597; *Charing Cross Electricity Supply Co v Hydraulic Power Company* [1914] 3 K. B. 772.

built the reservoir to serve his mill on land belonging to a certain Lord Wilton (with his Lordship's permission) and was therefore strictly only a licensee.

## Defences

There are a number of relevant defences:       **10–059**

- Claimant's default;
- Unforeseeable act of a stranger;
- Act of God;
- Statutory authority;
- Consent.

The first three derive from the judgment of Blackburn J. in *Rylands*.

*(1) Claimant's default*

It is a valid defence that the escape was due wholly or partially to the claimant's fault. In    **10–060** *Ponting v Noakes*,[181] the plaintiff's horse had died when it had reached over the fence and eaten leaves from a poisonous tree on the defendant's land. The defendant was not found to be liable when the harm suffered was due to the horse's own conduct. (There had equally been no "escape"). Reference should also be made to the Law Reform (Contributory Negligence) Act 1945 s.1.

*(2) Unforeseeable act of stranger*

This is a well-established defence. In *Box v Jubb*,[182] the court again faced the consequences of    **10–061** a reservoir overflowing onto the plaintiff's land, but this time the defendant was not liable. The overflow had been due to the actions of another neighbouring reservoir owner, over which the defendant had no control, and of which he had no knowledge. In such circumstances, the defendant was not held liable for the flooding.

This approach was followed in *Rickards v Lothian*.[183] Here, the plaintiff's premises had been flooded due to a continuous overflow of water from a sink on the top floor of the building. The overflow had been caused by a water tap being turned on full, and the wastepipe plugged, by the deliberate act of a third party. The defendant escaped liability as he could not reasonably have known of the act so as to prevent it.

The act of the third party must be unforeseeable. If the defendant should have foreseen the intervention, the defence will not be established. For example, in *North Western Utilities Ltd v London Guarantee Co*,[184] it was held to be foreseeable that works undertaken by a third party near the defendants' gas mains might damage their mains and require remedial work. It was therefore no defence to claim that the gas leak, which caused the fire destroying the

---

[181] [1894] 2 Q.B. 281.
[182] (1879) 4 Ex. D. 76.
[183] [1913] A.C. 263. See also *Perry v Kendricks Transport Ltd* [1956] 1 W.L.R. 85.
[184] [1936] A.C. 108.

plaintiff's hotel, was due to damage to the mains by the acts of a third party. The defendants had left the matter to chance, and this was not sufficient to excuse them from liability.

Three points of contention remain. First, and simplest, there has been some debate as to who is a "stranger". It obviously includes trespassers, but it has been suggested that it should also include licensees over whom the defendant does not exercise control, in order to keep liability within reasonable bounds. This view received support in *Ribee v Norrie*.[185] Here, Miss Ribee, described as a sprightly 70-year-old lady, suffered property damage and personal injury when her home caught fire.[186] The fire had started in an adjoining property which had been divided into bedsit accommodation. It was suspected that the fire had been caused by one of the occupants leaving a smouldering cigarette on the settee in the common area. The Court of Appeal held the landlord of the hostel liable. On the facts, his plea of act of stranger was rejected. He could have exercised some control over the persons occupying the hostel, for example, by putting up notices prohibiting smoking, and could have foreseen such an accident occurring. It could not be said that the fire was due to the unforeseeable act of a stranger.

Secondly, it is unclear whether the defence applies to the *negligent* act of a third party. It would seem, as a matter of logic, that the defence should not be defeated on proof that the third party did not act intentionally. The real emphasis should be on whether the defendant should have been able to foresee, and therefore react to, the actions of the third party. This takes us to our third problem. The formulation of this defence is sounding more and more like an action for negligence. Defendants will not be liable if they can show that they did not foresee, or should not have foreseen, the actions of the third party. *Street on Torts*[187] has gone so far as to say that despite clear authority for this defence, the cases are erroneously decided and have nothing to do with the rule in *Rylands v Fletcher*, but are cases decided in negligence. This, perhaps, is to take conceptual neatness a step too far. Undoubtedly, negligence principles have influenced the development of the rule as much as they have influenced nuisance, but it is still conceptually distinct.

### (3) Act of God

**10–062**   This defence is, due to the advances in modern technology and science, largely defunct. The defendant will not be liable where the escape is due solely to natural causes, in circumstances where no human foresight or prudence could reasonably recognise the possibility of such an occurrence and provide against it. So far, there has been only one successful English case, which was decided in 1876. In *Nichols v Marsland*,[188] the defendant had some ornamental pools on his land, which contained large quantities of water. These pools had been formed by damming up with artificial banks a natural stream which flowed through his property. Due to extraordinary rainfall, the banks broke down, and the rush of escaping water carried away four bridges. The Court of Appeal held that the defendant should not be held liable for an extraordinary act of nature which could not have been reasonably anticipated.

---

[185] [2001] P.I.Q.R. P8.
[186] She was saved, we are told, by her heroic spaniel, which jumped on her bed and whimpered until she awoke! It should be noted that it remains contentious whether liability for the escape of a fire is covered by the rule in *Rylands v Fletcher* or under a parallel rule of the common law: see *Musgrove v Pandelis* [1919] 2 K.B. 43 and *H&N Emanuel v Greater London Council* [1971] 2 All E.R. 835 at 839 per Lord Denning M.R. See A. Ogus (1969) 28 C.L.J. 104.
[187] J. Murphy (12th edn, Butterworths, 2007) p.482.
[188] (1876) 2 Ex. D. 1.

A stricter view was taken in *Greenock Corp v Caledonian Ry*,[189] in which the court was critical of the approach taken by the court in *Nichols*. In this case, a concrete paddling pool for children had been constructed by the local authority in the bed of a stream, requiring the course of the stream to be altered. Again, there was an extraordinary level of rainfall, which caused the stream to overflow at the pool. Due to the construction of the pool, water which would have otherwise flowed down stream flowed down a public street. The House of Lords held that such an event did not qualify as an act of God.

In view of *Greenock*, it is most unlikely that the defence would succeed today. However, it is possible that a situation may exist where modern precautions against exceptional natural conditions were defeated (for example, an earthquake in a London suburb) and the defence might come into play, but such circumstances would be very rare indeed.

*(4) Statutory authority*

Again, this defence is important, and the approach is the same as that taken in nuisance **10–063** (see above). It will therefore be a question of construction in each case. The courts will examine whether the breach of the rule in *Rylands v Fletcher* was authorised by the statute in question. In *Green v Chelsea Waterworks Co*,[190] the defendants, who were under a statutory duty to maintain a continuous supply of water, were not liable when, in the absence of negligence, the water main burst, damaging the plaintiff's premises, horse and stock. However, the defendants were liable for a burst water main in *Charing Cross Electricity Supply Co v Hydraulic Power Co*.[191] Here, the defendants were operating under a statutory power to supply water for industrial purposes. These powers were subject to a "nuisance clause", which provided that nothing in the Act should exonerate the undertakers from liability for nuisance. On this basis, the defendants remained liable even in the absence of negligence.

The Court of Appeal in *Dunne v North Western Gas Board*[192] sought to clarify the different treatment of statutory duties and powers. In this case, there was a series of 46 explosions of coal gas in Liverpool, which resulted when a water main had leaked and water had washed away the soil supporting a gas main. The plaintiffs sued both the Gas Board and the Corporation which was responsible for the water main. The Gas Board had a statutory duty to supply gas and it had, in the absence of negligence, a good defence of statutory authority. The Corporation, in contrast, only acted under a statutory power. Here, unlike *Charing Cross*, the Act did not contain a nuisance clause, and so the Corporation would not be liable in the absence of negligence.

The House of Lords in *Transco* emphasised the significance of this defence in limiting the application of the rule by excluding claims for high risk activities arising from work conducted under statutory authority.[193]

*(5) Consent*

This may be express or implied. Consent will be implied where the escape results from some- **10–064** thing maintained for the common benefit, for example, in a block of flats, from the guttering, or from common utilities such as water, gas or electricity. The tenant in such circumstances is

---

[189] [1917] A.C. 556.
[190] (1894) 70 L.T. 547.
[191] [1914] 3 K.B. 772.
[192] [1964] 2 Q.B. 806 at 833–837.
[193] See Lord Hoffmann [2003] UKHL 61; [2004] 2 A.C. 1 at para.31.

assumed to forego any rights against the landlord, due to the benefit he or she gains, provided the escape occurs without negligence.[194]

## REMEDIES

**10–065**   There are three main remedies:

- Injunctions;

- Abatement;

- Damages.

The main remedy for nuisance is the injunction. Where liability lies under the rule in *Rylands v Fletcher*, the escape has usually occurred, and the damage has already been caused, so the claimant will be seeking damages. Remedies will be discussed generally in Ch.17, but we examine here their particular application in relation to nuisance and the rule in *Rylands v Fletcher*. We will also consider the possibility of a claimant recovering under the Human Rights Act 1998.

*(1) Injunctions*

**10–066**   As will be discussed further in Ch.17, an injunction is an equitable and therefore a discretionary remedy. As a remedy, it is well suited to nuisance, because it can be adapted to meet the balance of competing interests. The courts are generally willing to grant an injunction, unless there are exceptional circumstances which mean that damages are seen as the most appropriate remedy. In such circumstances, damages are said to be given "in lieu of" (instead of) an injunction. Whilst s.50 of the Senior Courts Act 1981 is the section governing this matter, the leading case is that of *Shelfer v City of London Electric Lighting Co.*[195] In this case, A.L. Smith L.J. laid down the four conditions which would lead a court to grant damages in lieu of an injunction:

- Where the injury to the claimant's legal rights is small;

- Where the injury is capable of being estimated in money;

- Where the injury can be adequately compensated by a small money payment; and

- Where it would be oppressive to the defendant to grant an injunction.

In the case itself, the court granted an injunction against vibrations and noise caused by the defendant's machinery, even though the result would deprive many of its customers of electricity. The courts are unwilling to allow a defendant essentially to buy the right to commit the nuisance by paying damages to the claimant.[196]

---

[194] *Kiddle v City Business Properties Ltd* [1942] 1 K.B. 269 at 274. See also *Carstairs v Taylor* (1871) L.R. 6 Ex. 217. See L. Kadirgamar [1973] Conv 179.
[195] [1895] 1 Ch.287. Its ongoing authority was confirmed recently in *Regan v Paul Properties Ltd* [2006] EWCA Civ 1391; [2007] Ch.135 and *Watson v Croft Promo-Sport Ltd* [2009] EWCA Civ 15; [2009] 3 All E.R. 249.
[196] See Lindley L.J. [1895] 1 Ch.287 at 315–316.

The exercise of this discretion was discussed by the Court of Appeal in *Miller v Jackson*[197] and *Kennaway v Thompson*.[198] In the former case, the majority of the court held that an injunction was inappropriate, on the basis that the public interest in cricket should prevail (Lord Denning M.R.) and that the plaintiffs had knowingly bought the property in the knowledge that a nuisance would be likely to occur (Cumming-Bruce L.J.). Damages were therefore awarded.[199] In *Kennaway*, Lawton L.J. held that the relevant authority remained that of *Shelfer*, which did not support either proposition. Accordingly, the plaintiff would be awarded an injunction against power boat racing on a nearby lake, regardless of any public interest in power boat racing, and regardless of the fact that she had chosen to build a house near the lake in the knowledge that some racing took place.[200] Nevertheless, the injunction was awarded on terms. The court used its discretion to stipulate a strict timetable for international, national and club events, thereby allowing the racing to continue in a limited form. By such means, and also by using their power to suspend the injunction to give the defendant the opportunity to remedy the nuisance, the courts recognise and balance the competing rights of the litigants.[201]

### (2) Abatement

This is a form of self-help, by which claimants intervene themselves to stop the nuisance. **10–067** Generally, the courts are reluctant to encourage such actions. Claimants who wish to take the law into their own hands must do so at their peril, and run the risk of countervailing claims for trespass and conversion. Generally, however, it is an acceptable response towards encroaching roots and branches, where it would make little sense to go to court.[202] For example, in *Delaware Mansions Ltd v Westminster City Council*,[203] discussed under private nuisance, the House of Lords accepted that the claimant company was entitled to recover the costs which had been incurred in remedying a continuing nuisance caused to its property by tree roots when the defendant council had refused its request that the tree be removed. Even in the face of such obvious nuisances, however, claimants proceed at their own risk and their actions must be no more than necessary to abate the nuisance. Lord Cooke also warned against imposing unreasonable burdens on local authorities to pay for remedial works and advised that "as a general proposition, I think that the defendant is entitled to notice and a reasonable opportunity of abatement before liability for remedial expenditure can arise."[204] The claimant should therefore take care not to enter his or her neighbour's land, and give notice if entry is necessary, except in an emergency. Any branches or roots which have been lopped off remain the neighbour's property and if they are kept, the claimant may be held liable for conversion (civil theft). Abatement, therefore, is a remedy of limited utility.

---

[197] [1977] Q.B. 966.

[198] [1981] Q.B. 88. See R.A. Buckley (1981) 44 M.L.R. 212.

[199] See also *Dennis v Ministry of Defence* [2003] EWHC 793 (QB); [2003] Env L.R.34: damages appropriate when contrary to public interest to prevent RAF flying Harrier jets from its base. This was justified as consistent with developing human rights case law.

[200] Although it had increased in volume and noise beyond tolerable levels in subsequent years. See also *Watson v Croft Promo-Sport Ltd* [2009] EWCA Civ 15: public interest relevant only in marginal cases and should not, of itself, negate the requirement of exceptional circumstances or oppression of the defendant which *Shelfer* requires.

[201] See S. Tromans (1982) 41 C.L.J. 87 at 93–95, who argues for greater use of damages awards.

[202] See *Lemmon v Webb* [1895] A.C. 1.

[203] [2001] UKHL 55; [2002] 1 A.C. 321.

[204] [2001] UKHL 55; [2002] 1 A.C. 321 at para.34. But see *Kirk v Brent LBC* [2005] EWCA Civ 1701; [2006] Env. L.R. D7 where the Court of Appeal questioned whether this was an absolute rule and refused to strike out a claim where no notice had been given for substantial works until four years after the event and it could be argued that the local authority were put on notice by the fact that similar damage had been caused to other nearby property.

*(3) Damages*

**10–068**   All of the three heads of liability we have discussed in this chapter become actionable only on proof of damage.[205] Special damage must of course be proved for the individual to claim a remedy for public nuisance.

*Personal injury*

**10–069**   Public nuisance, as discussed above, protects the individual who, as a member of the public, has suffered particular damage due to the defendant's actions. Any damages award will therefore cover personal injury, damage to property, loss of custom, and perhaps even particular inconvenience caused to the individual. Private nuisance and the rule in *Rylands v Fletcher*, in contrast, are aimed specifically at protecting the interests of claimants with rights to land. They therefore award damages for the diminution in the value of the land, or lesser enjoyment of the use of land or its fixtures. On this basis, this would seem to exclude damages for personal injury. Professor Newark, in an article cited by Lord Goff in *Cambridge Water* and *Hunter*, explained that the land merely provided the setting for the injury, and therefore there was no special reason for distinguishing personal injury caused by a nuisance from other cases of personal injury to which the ordinary rules of negligence apply.[206]

This view seems to be followed in the leading authorities at the moment, namely *Hunter v Canary Wharf Ltd*[207] and *Transco Plc v Stockport MBC*,[208] although the issue was not strictly in point in either case. The majority in *Hunter* held that only those with an interest in land or exclusive possession could sue in private nuisance, and Lords Lloyd and Hoffmann expressly stated that compensation should not be awarded for personal injury, as it represents harm to the person, not the land. This view was also taken by the House of Lords in *Transco*, despite mixed authority in the past where damages for personal injury had been awarded under the rule in *Rylands v Fletcher*,[209] although not without challenge.[210] Lord Bingham affirmed that "the claim cannot include a claim for death or personal injury, since such a claim does not relate to any right in or enjoyment of land."[211] This position was confirmed recently by Dyson L.J. in *Corby Group Litigation Claimants v Corby BC*[212] who distinguished public from private nuisance. Only public nuisance—a tort seeking to protect against unlawful acts or omissions which endanger the life, safety, health, property or comfort of the public (and which says nothing about enjoyment of land)—will permit damages for personal injury to be recovered. The torts are distinct and the rights created by them different.[213]

As a result of *Hunter v Canary Wharf* and *Transco*, damages for private nuisance are awarded for the injury to the land, not the person, and the sum awarded should not differ however many people reside on the land. Lord Hoffmann in *Hunter* expressly stated that:

---

[205] Although the courts are sometimes generous in finding damage for certain types of private nuisance, e.g. interference with certain easements.

[206] (1949) 65 L.Q.R. 480 at 489.

[207] [1997] A.C. 655. Followed by *Vukelic v Hammersmith and Fulham LBC* [2003] EWHC 188 (QB (TCC)).

[208] [2003] UKHL 61; [2004] 2 A.C. 1.

[209] *Hale v Jennings* [1938] 1 All E.R. 579; *Shiffman v Order of the Hospital of St John of Jerusalem* [1936] 1 All E.R. 557 (although decided on negligence) and *Perry v Kendricks Transport Ltd* [1956] 1 W.L.R. 85 at 92.

[210] See *Read v Lyons* [1947] A.C. 156.

[211] [2004] 2 A.C. 1 at para.9. See also Lord Hoffmann at para.35.

[212] [2008] EWCA Civ 463; [2009] Q.B. 335. Comment: M. Lee (2009) 20 K.L.J. 129.

[213] [2008] EWCA Civ 463 at paras 27–30. There is, however, no reason why claimants cannot raise both torts in litigation; they are not mutually exclusive.

"damages cannot be increased by the fact that the interests in the land are divided; still less according to the number of persons residing on the premises".[214]

Personal injury is therefore protected by the torts of negligence and public nuisance, and should not be confused with the private nuisance concept of "personal discomfort", which is related to the diminished utility of the land. *Bone v Seale*[215] has been cited as an illustration of this distinction. Here, damages were awarded to compensate for the personal discomfort caused by smells from an adjacent pig farm. The award represented the diminished utility value of the land "suffering" from the smells. Such an award could be made even in the absence of evidence that the value of land had diminished, and irrespective of the number of people affected and any injury the smell may have caused them.

   This is not, however, entirely convincing. It is hard to persuade non-lawyers that damages are awarded not for their twitching nostrils, but for the "suffering" of the land on which they are standing. Equally, if such "suffering" cannot always be converted into market loss (i.e. diminution of value of the land), it is difficult to say on what basis such damages are awarded, if not on a personal basis. Lords Lloyd and Hoffmann suggest that the loss is one of "loss of amenity". This was recognised by the House of Lords in the contract law case of *Ruxley Electronics and Construction Ltd v Forsyth*.[216] In this case, Mr Forsyth had required a swimming pool of a certain depth, and this had not been provided, although this did not diminish the actual value of the pool. The House of Lords in *Ruxley* approved the trial judge's award of damages for loss of amenity, although Lord Mustill clearly awarded such damages on the basis that the consumer's subjective preference, expressed in the contract, had not been satisfied. It is questionable whether this case establishes a principle under which damages can be assessed independently of the personality of the occupants of land and indeed, its exact status in contract law remains uncertain. Further doubt was thrown on this issue by the Court of Appeal in *Dobson v Thames Water Utilities Ltd*,[217] where the Court ruled that in the case of a transitory nuisance caused by odours and mosquitoes from a sewage treatment works which did not affect the market value of the land, damages would be assessed by taking account of the actual experiences of the people in occupation of the property. On this basis, an unoccupied house awaiting renovation would receive only nominal damages, whilst damages for a family home would be assessed on the experiences of the family members. This, the Court insisted, was entirely consistent with awarding damages for injury to land; it simply represented a means of placing a value on this loss. It is questionable whether such an approach is in reality consistent with the statement of Lord Hoffmann above. Logically, does it not suggest that a family of four will recover more damages than the old widowed lady next door, suffering exactly the same interference with land? Why should actual occupation be necessary to assess amenity loss when the courts use hypotheticals to assess loss on a regular basis? *Dobson* illustrates the difficulties of conceiving "personal discomfort" as an injury to land and, in so doing, questions how the "personal" element can be removed from the equation.

---

[214] [1997] A.C. 655 at 707.
[215] [1975] 1 All E.R. 787.
[216] [1996] A.C. 344.
[217] [2009] EWCA Civ 28; [2009] 3 All E.R. 319. Comment: S. Tofaris [2009] C.L.J. 273.

*Economic loss*

**10–070**   In *Hunter*, Lord Hoffmann recognised that loss of profits was recoverable as consequential loss when it resulted from the claimant's inability to use the land for the purposes of his or her business.[218] Recovery of such losses has been accepted in a number of cases. For example, in *Andreae v Selfridge & Company Ltd*[219] the owner of a hotel was allowed to recover damages for the loss of custom suffered by her business due to noise and dust caused by the defendants' construction work. More recently, in *Jan de Nul (UK) Ltd v AXA Royale Belge S.A. (Formerly N.V. Royale Belge)*,[220] the Court of Appeal permitted the Hampshire Wildlife Trust to recover over £100,000 for an investigation into silting of feeding grounds at the head of an estuary. Although the report had indicated no long-term damage would occur, the court found that it had acted reasonably in commissioning such a report and the cost of the survey was consequential on physical interference with its property rights.

*Damage to chattels*

**10–071**   By chattels, we mean personal property which happens to be on the land. One would expect that if the courts are reluctant to award damages for personal injuries, they would be equally reluctant to award damages for loss of chattels. If you cannot recover for your own broken leg, it would seem incongruous if you could recover for the broken leg of your poodle. Certainly this is the view of Professor Newark in his much-cited article.[221] Unfortunately, this point is not dealt with in *Hunter*, except by Lord Hoffmann, who supports a continuing right to sue for damage to chattels and livestock in nuisance as consequential loss. There is clear authority in support of this position. In *Halsey v Esso Petroleum Co Ltd*,[222] damage to laundry hanging in the garden was deemed actionable in private nuisance and under the rule in *Rylands v Fletcher*. Equally, damage to the paintwork of the plaintiff's car on the highway was held to be actionable in public nuisance and under the rule in *Rylands v Fletcher*.

Whilst the position seems difficult to justify, it may, perhaps, be explained if we consider the practical impact of not allowing recovery for damage to chattels. For example, a farmer complains that the defendant emits noxious fumes over his land. These fumes have ruined his crops and trees, and harmed the health of his livestock. If only damage to land is recoverable, the farmer will only be awarded damages for his crops and the trees.[223] Yet, these are simply alternative means of farming one's land, and why should the law draw an arbitrary distinction between the different modes of farming? It remains to be seen how this problem might be resolved in the future.

*Remoteness*

**10–072**   Damages under private nuisance, public nuisance and the rule in *Rylands v Fletcher* are all subject to the test set out in *The Wagon Mound (No.1)*,[224] namely that the defendant is only liable for damages of a type which can be reasonably foreseen. Reference should be made here to Ch.6. Lord Reid, in *The Wagon Mound (No.2)*, held foreseeability to be an essential element

---

[218] [1997] A.C. 655 at 706.
[219] [1938] Ch.1. See, also, Lawton J. in *British Celanese v Hunt* [1969] 1 W.L.R. 959.
[220] [2002] EWCA Civ 209; [2002] 1 Lloyd's Rep. 583.
[221] (1949) 65 L.Q.R. 480 at 490.
[222] [1961] 2 All E.R. 145.
[223] Crops and trees are, of course, treated as part of the land in question.
[224] *Overseas Tankship (UK) Ltd v Morts Dock and Engineering Co Ltd* [1961] A.C. 388 at 427.

in determining liability in both public and private nuisance: "It would not be right to discriminate between different cases of nuisance".[225] In *Cambridge Water*, Lord Goff clarified that the *Wagon Mound* test would apply to the rule in *Rylands v Fletcher*. The reader should therefore ignore Blackburn J.'s statement, in the case itself, that the defendant will be liable for all the natural consequences of the escape.

## The Human Rights Act 1998

The case of *Marcic v Thames Water Utilities Ltd*[226] provides a useful illustration of the potential for the Act to supplement and change the law of nuisance, but also of the reluctance of the courts to overwhelm public bodies with excessive liability. Peter Marcic brought a claim against his statutory water and sewage undertaker, Thames Water Utilities Ltd (TWUL). He complained of TWUL's failure since 1992 to prevent persistent external flooding and back flow of foul water from its sewer system into his home at times of heavy rain. Although it was reasonably practicable for TWUL to prevent the flooding, it had refused to do so. Under its then scheme of priorities, there was no prospect of such works being undertaken in the foreseeable future. After nine years, Marcic turned to law and brought this action for damage to his property in nuisance and under the 1998 Act.

**10–073**

Although his claim in private nuisance was rejected at first instance as contrary to existing authority, Judge Havery Q.C. approved the claim under the Human Rights Act 1998 founded on infringement of the claimant's rights to private and family life (under art.8) and peaceful enjoyment of his possessions (art.1 of Protocol 1).[227] TWUL was a public authority under s.6 of the Act, and the case law of the European Court of Human Rights supported use of art.8 and art.1 of Protocol 1 in this context.[228] Although both art.8 and art.1 of Protocol 1 are qualified rights—the court must consider "the protection of the rights and freedoms of others"[229] and "the public interest"[230]—in view of the frequent flooding of Marcic's property and TWUL's unsatisfactory system of prioritisation, the judge supported Marcic's claim under the Act.

The Court of Appeal in supporting Marcic's claim in private nuisance rendered any claim under the Act unnecessary. Section 8(3) of the Act provides that:

> "No award of damages is to be made unless, taking account of all the circumstances of the case, including–(a) any other relief or remedy granted, or order made, in relation to the act in question (by that or any other court) . . . the court is satisfied that the award is necessary to afford just satisfaction to the person in whose favour it is made."

---

[225] *The Wagon Mound (No.2) (Overseas Tankship (UK) Ltd v Miller Steamship Co Pty)* [1967] 1 A.C. 617 at 640.

[226] [2003] UKHL 66; [2004] 2 A.C. 42, HL, [2002] Q.B. 929, CA.

[227] Where there is a demonstrable and significant fall in the value of the property, without proper compensation, this amounted to a partial expropriation: see *S v France* (1990) 65 D. & R. 250 at 261. See D. Anderson [1999] E.H.R.L.R. 543.

[228] The court relying on *Baggs v UK* (1987) 9 E.H.R.R. 235, (a case of nuisance by noise from Heathrow airport affecting the applicant's enjoyment of his home); *S v France* (1990) 65 D. & R. 250 (effect of nuclear power station near home); *Guerra v Italy* (1998) 26 E.H.R.R. 357 (toxic emissions from factory); *Lopez Ostra v Spain* (1994) 20 E.H.R.R. 277 (fumes and smells from waste treatment plant).

[229] Art.8, para.2: "except such as is in accordance with the law and is necessary in a democratic society in the interests of national security, public safety or the economic well-being of the country, for the prevention of disorder or crime, for the protection of health or morals, or for the protection of the rights and freedoms of others."

[230] Art.1, Protocol 1.

Nevertheless, the Court of Appeal supported the reasoning of the first instance judge. The court suggested that even if the court had decided that a fair balance had been struck between the competing interests of Marcic and TWUL's other customers, the defendant might, in any event, be required to pay compensation to ensure that one person did not bear an unreasonable burden.[231]

The Court of Appeal ruling in *Marcic* was applied by Buckley J. in *Dennis v Ministry of Defence*.[232] This involved a claim for compensation by Mr and Mrs Dennis whose property was adjacent to an RAF base and who had suffered deafening noise due to the flying of Harrier jets over their land. Although the court again found a nuisance at common law, it held that the noise and the resultant reduction in the value of the estate did amount to a breach of the Dennis's rights under art.8 and art.1 of Protocol 1, although any breach would be balanced by the state's interest in national security and the cost and inconvenience of uprooting a military base. Nevertheless, the court saw no reason why the Dennis's should bear the cost of this disturbance alone and that damages of £950,000 would have been payable under the Act to cover the period until 2012 when Harrier training was expected to be phased out. This sum was thus awarded for common law nuisance.

When *Marcic* reached the House of Lords, the award in *Dennis* of £950,000 and the potential liability of Thames Water for £1 billion if it compensated every customer in Marcic's position[233] did not go unnoticed. Their Lordships rejected liability either at common law or under the Act. Where Parliament had established an elaborate scheme of regulation in which an independent regulator sought to balance the competing interests of the parties involved, liability would not be imposed. It would be inconsistent with the statutory scheme and, given the need to balance competing interests and the availability of judicial review, this scheme was compatible with art.8 and art.1 of Protocol 1 of the Convention. Following the European Court of Human Rights decision in *Hatton v United Kingdom*,[234] which confirmed the margin of appreciation given to States in matters of general policy, the House found that the scheme did strike a reasonable balance: "Parliament acted well within its bounds as policy maker."[235] The reluctance of the House to intervene on the basis of the Human Rights Act 1998 is particularly notable in view of its criticism of the treatment of Mr Marcic. Such concerns, however, did not persuade the House of Lords to support his claim.[236]

---

[231] See *S v France* (1990) 65 D. & R. 250 at 263 and *James v United Kingdom* (1986) 8 E.H.R.R. 123, para.54: "under the legal systems of the contracting states, the taking of property in the public interest without payment of compensation is treated as justifiable only in exceptional circumstances."

[232] [2003] EWHC 793 (QB); [2003] Env L.R.34. Followed by *Andrews v Reading BC (No.2)* [2005] EWHC 256 (QBD); [2006] R.V.R. 56 (£2,000 for noise arising from new traffic scheme). See also *Moreno Gomez v Spain (4143/02)* (2005) 41 E.H.R.R. 40.

[233] In the financial year 1999–2000, the profits of the whole group (of which TWUL formed only a part) amounted to only £344 million after tax.

[234] Application No. 36022/97, (2003) 37 E.H.R.R. 28.

[235] [2003] UKHL 66; [2004] 2 A.C. 42, HL at para.43. See also *Arscott v Coal Authority* [2004] EWCA Civ 892; [2005] Env. L.R. 6 (common enemy defence to flooding reached a fair balance between interests of person affected and general public and was Convention-compliant. This defence permits the occupier of land to use or develop it so as to prevent floodwaters coming on to the land without being liable if flood water which would have entered the land consequently damages that of another. Contrast *Giacomelli v Italy* (59909/00) (2007) 45 E.H.R.R. 38; *Fadeyeva v Russia* (55723/00) (2007) 45 E.H.R.R. 10.

[236] Although Lord Hoffmann noted that Thames Water had agreed with the Regulator in 2002 to free 250 properties (including that of *Marcic*) from the risk of external flooding. See also *Dobson v Thames Water Utilities Ltd* [2009] EWCA Civ 28 (reluctance to award damages under s.8, Human Rights Act 1998 for child without rights over land who was living with parents who were able to recover damages in private nuisance).

## Conclusion

The House of Lords' decisions in *Hunter v Canary Wharf Ltd*,[237] *Cambridge Water Co v*   **10–074**
*Eastern Counties Leather Plc*[238] and *Transco Plc v Stockport MBC*[239] cast new light on the
nature of the torts of private nuisance and *Rylands v Fletcher* liability. In so doing, their
Lordships clearly distinguish these torts from the tort of negligence, examined earlier in this
book, although in practice the line is not so clear. Nevertheless, these decisions are highly
significant in indicating the future development of these torts, and their importance should not
be underestimated. In contrast, public nuisance has received limited attention, and should be
noted primarily in connection with obstruction of the highway.

In the next chapter, we examine the tort of trespass in its many forms: trespass to the person,
goods and land. In considering trespass to land, readers should note our earlier discussion of
its relationship with private nuisance.

---

[237] [1997] A.C. 655.
[238] [1994] 2 A.C. 264.
[239] [2003] UKHL 61; [2004] 2 A.C. 1.

# Chapter 11

# TRESPASS

## Introduction

The tort of trespass is one of the oldest torts in English law. In modern law, it takes three forms–trespass to the person, to land and to goods. All three torts have the same characteristics: they must be committed intentionally, cause direct and immediate harm and are actionable per se, i.e. without proof of damage. Although these three criteria have not always been followed—for example in the past, the courts have been willing to impose liability for trespass to the person where the tort has been committed negligently[1]—they are generally followed today. They serve to distinguish trespass from other actions, such as negligence and nuisance, which were traditionally called "actions on the case" and deal with indirect harm.

It is important to recognise that the tort of trespass operates in a different manner from torts such as nuisance and negligence. These torts, which we have already looked at, compensate the claimant for damage incurred unintentionally or indirectly, and act as a form of loss-spreading. The aim of trespass, however, is to vindicate the claimant's right to be free from interference either to his or her person, property or goods. On this basis, the torts are actionable per se. Damage is not the trigger for compensation. The wrongful actions of the defendant in interfering with a recognised legal interest possessed by the claimant trigger compensation. Of course, in awarding damages the courts will examine whether any loss or damage has been suffered. They will generally only award nominal damages in trespass to land or goods if no damage exists, but the existence of aggravated and exemplary damages[2] in these fields highlights the willingness of the courts to acknowledge the importance of protecting these interests in modern society.

The tort of trespass does, however, have a close connection with other areas of law. Trespass to the person, in dealing with interference with the person in terms of personal integrity and freedom of movement, bears a close relationship with criminal law and the offences found in the Offences against the Person Act 1861. Trespass to land, in contrast, deals with interference with the claimant's possession of land and therefore bears a close relationship with the tort of private nuisance, discussed in the previous chapter. Trespass to goods is also very closely connected to the tort of conversion. The significance of this will be discussed below.

---

[1] See *Weaver v Ward* (1617) Hob. 134; 80 E.R. 284 and *Scott v Shepherd* (1773) 2 Wm. Bl. 892; 96 E.R. 525.
[2] See Ch.17.

This chapter will concentrate on trespass to the person and trespass to land. Trespass to goods will be dealt with briefly at the end of the chapter.

## TRESPASS TO THE PERSON

**11–002**  As stated above, trespass to the person protects the claimant against interference with his or her person. This may be attempted by means of assault, battery or false imprisonment. These torts possess the classic "trespass" characteristics in that they must be committed intentionally, by direct and immediate actions and are actionable without proof of damage.[3] To the reader, these torts are perhaps better recognised as criminal offences and indeed, the defendant will normally face criminal, rather than civil, charges for such actions. There are a number of reasons for this. First of all, the police will usually be called in, which makes criminal proceedings more likely. Secondly, the claimant may not wish the pressure of further civil proceedings brought at his or her own instigation when the defendant may not have the means to satisfy judgment. Thirdly, the criminal courts now possess at least some means of awarding compensation to a victim of crime,[4] and victims may also recover under the Criminal Injuries Compensation Scheme[5] which is a national fund, granting compensation for personal injury caused by crimes of violence. The Scheme will award compensation to any person who has sustained personal injury directly attributable to a crime of violence or to the apprehension of an offender or the prevention of an offence. Such compensation is unlikely to be as high as that awarded in a successful tort action, but is undoubtedly an easier option for the victim.

A tort action will generally be motivated by more than just a desire for compensation. It may be pursued to highlight a refusal of the Director of Public Prosecutions to bring a criminal prosecution[6] or in the face of an unsuccessful prosecution. As the burden of proof is lower in the civil courts, the claimant may succeed in proving his or her case on the balance of probabilities where the prosecutor has failed to prove the allegations in a criminal court beyond reasonable doubt. In the American case concerning O.J. Simpson, for example, the defendant, an ex-football star and celebrity, was found not guilty of the murder of his ex-wife and her lover, but was nevertheless subsequently found liable to pay damages by a civil court.[7] A tort action may also be brought to highlight abuse of power by public bodies such as the police, and a successful claimant may have his or her point reinforced by an award of exemplary damages.[8] In seeking to gain compensation where criminal proceedings have failed, litigants should note the limitations in ss.44 and 45 of the Offences against the Person Act 1861.[9] These sections relate to assault and battery charges heard in the magistrates' courts.[10] Section 45

[3] See F.A. Trindade (1982) 2 O.J.L.S. 211.
[4] See Powers of the Criminal Courts (Sentencing) Act 2000, ss.130–134 (as amended).
[5] See generally the Criminal Injuries Compensation Act 1995 (see *http//www.justice.gov.uk/guidance/compensation-schemes/cica* [accessed April 21, 2011]).
[6] See, e.g. *Halford v Brookes* [1991] 1 W.L.R. 428.
[7] The controversy continues, as demonstrated by the recent publication of O.J. Simpson and R. Goldman, *If I did it: Confession of the killer* (Gibson Square Books, 2007). See also the more recent example of *Ashley v Chief Constable of Sussex Police* [2008] UKHL 25; 2 W.L.R. 975 (civil claim following death of unarmed man, shot by police, when officer responsible had been acquitted of murder).
[8] See, e.g. the guidelines given by Lord Woolf in *Thompson v Commissioner of Police of Metropolis* [1998] Q.B. 498.
[9] The Law Commission Report No. 218, *Criminal law: Legislating the criminal code: Offences against the person and general principles* (1993) recommended the repeal of these sections.
[10] Note that common assault and battery are summary offences by virtue of the Criminal Justice Act 1988 s.39.

provides that where a summary hearing brought by or on behalf of the party aggrieved has been held and has ended, after a hearing on the merits, either with a certificate of dismissal,[11] or with the accused being convicted and fined or imprisoned, civil proceedings for the same cause will be barred.[12] As most criminal offences, save the most serious, are tried in the magistrates' court, this in practice limits the situations in which the victim can sue for compensation in tort.

Most cases are therefore decided by the criminal courts and for this reason, the civil courts will often reason by analogy to criminal cases. We shall also use criminal cases, where appropriate, to illustrate the likely treatment of a tort claim. Criminal law authorities, however, should be treated with caution. They are not authority in the law of tort and can therefore only be treated as guidance. Proper regard must be had to the differing concerns of criminal law (which are largely punitive) and trespass to the person (which protects the personal integrity and right to self-determination of the claimant). We shall examine battery, assault and false imprisonment in turn.

## Battery

This has a number of components. Force must be applied intentionally by immediate and direct means to another individual. This can vary from the most minor contact with the claimant, such as an unwanted peck on the cheek, to a violent blow in the chest. Because the tort is actionable without proof of damage, both types of battery render the defendant liable to pay damages. The requirements of battery are examined below.   **11–003**

### (1) It must be intentional

This means that the act of force must be voluntary. For example, Y has not committed a battery if X grasps his arm and pulls it to strike Z. Intention relates only to the action of the defendant. It is not necessary that the defendant intends the consequences of his or her actions. On this basis, the defendant will be liable for all the consequences flowing from the tort, whether or not they are foreseeable.[13] Equally, if I intend to hit A and instead hit B, I commit a battery against B.[14] This rule, which is essentially one of convenience, has been explained as the concept of "transferred intent".   **11–004**

The tort may be committed even if the original action was unintentional, if the defendant at some point intends to apply force. For example, in *Fagan v Metropolitan Police Commissioner*,[15] the defendant unintentionally stopped his car on a policeman's foot. At this stage, no tort had been committed. However, by deliberately failing to move until the police officer had shouted

---

[11] This cannot be given when the defendant has pleaded guilty: *Ellis v Burton* [1975] 1 W.L.R. 386.

[12] See *Wong v Parkside Health NHS Trust* [2003] 3 All E.R. 932 at 937, CA. The question focuses on the conduct in question, for example an assault. The courts will not allow the claimant to circumvent s.45 by framing the claim under a different cause of action e.g. under the rule in *Wilkinson v Downton*. See also *Masper v Brown* (1876) 1 C.P.D. 97.

[13] See *Williams v Humphrey, The Times*, February 20, 1975 where the defendant was liable for deliberately pushing a guest in his swimming pool, although he clearly did not intend to cripple the plaintiff, who broke his ankle and foot.

[14] *James v Campbell* (1832) 5 C. & P. 372; 172 E.R. 1015, and *Bici v Ministry of Defence* [2004] EWHC 786 (QB); *The Times*, June 11, 2004. For criticism, see A. Beever (2009) 29 L.S. 400.

[15] [1969] 1 Q.B. 439.

"Get off my foot" several times, he committed a battery. It seems likely that, as in criminal law, recklessness in the use of force is sufficient to establish intent in battery.[16]

*(2)  It must be direct*

**11–005**  It is a basic requirement of any trespass that the injury must be direct. If the injury is indirect, the claimant must find another basis for recovery. However, this requirement has been interpreted flexibly. In the eighteenth century case of *Scott v Shepherd*,[17] for example, the defendant was found liable for battery when he had thrown a lighted squib into a market place. This was despite the fact that the squib had been thrown on by two stallholders, to protect themselves and their wares, before it had exploded in the face of Scott. The majority of the court found the battery to be sufficiently direct. Equally, in *DPP v K*,[18] the force was considered sufficiently immediate and direct where a schoolboy had poured some concentrated sulphuric acid, stolen from a chemistry lesson, into a hand-dryer which was later used by another pupil with horrific results. The court held that the boy had known full well that he had created a dangerous situation, but had nevertheless taken the risk of injury to another. It was no excuse that he had panicked and had intended to remove the acid as soon as he was able.

*(3)  Immediate force*

**11–006**  The tort of battery applies to any form of bodily contact. This causes a potential problem. If applied literally, it would cover all forms of contact. For example, A would commit a battery by tapping B on the shoulder to get his attention. It would clearly be a nonsense if an actionable battery was committed in such circumstances, and the law would, in effect, provide a charter for vexatious litigants to sue. Whilst this is common sense, the courts have experienced difficulties in finding a theoretical basis on which to draw a line between actionable batteries and ordinary social contact. Lord Holt C.J.'s comments in *Cole v Turner*[19] have been cited, where his Lordship held that "the least touching of another in anger is a battery". On this basis, the Court of Appeal in *Wilson v Pringle*[20] held that battery must be committed with "hostile" intent. On the facts of the case, a boy had suffered serious injury due to the antics of a fellow pupil. The defence alleged that the defendant had merely pulled the schoolbag off the schoolboy's shoulder, which had led him to fall on the ground and injure himself. The court held that liability depended on whether the pupil's actions had been "hostile" and not simply a schoolboy prank. It can be questioned whether this is helpful. What is hostile to one person may seem quite the opposite to another. For example, should an over-enthusiastic slap on the back or a surgeon's mistaken amputation of a leg be regarded as non-hostile and therefore not a battery? Even if an objective interpretation is adopted, it simply seems to mean that the reasonable person would view the action as contrary to the ordinary rules of social conduct. If this is so, then the view of Robert Goff L.J. in *Collins v Wilcock*[21] is preferable. His Lordship took the entirely sensible view that instead of adopting complicated legal rules based on implied consent to the battery, or hostile intent, the law should just exclude liability for

---

[16] *R. v Venna* [1976] Q.B. 421. Subjective recklessness will suffice: see *R. v Savage* [1992] 1 A.C. 699, HL and *Bici v MOD* [2004] EWHC 786 (QB) at para.67: "it must be a subjective recklessness that they appreciated the potential harm to the claimants and were indifferent to it."

[17] (1773) 2 W. Bl. 892, 96 E.R. 525.

[18] [1990] 1 W.L.R. 1067. See also *Haystead v Chief Constable of Derbyshire* [2000] 3 All E.R. 890, QBD.

[19] (1704) 6 Mod. Rep. 149; 90 E.R. 958.

[20] [1987] Q.B. 237.

[21] [1984] 1 W.L.R. 1172. See also Lord Goff in *Re F* [1990] 2 A.C. 1.

conduct generally acceptable in the ordinary conduct of daily life—a view which he reiterated in *Re F*:[22]

> "... a broader exception has been created to allow for the exigencies of everyday life: jostling in a street or some other crowded place, social contact at parties and such like. This exception has been said to be founded on implied consent, since those who go about in public places, or go to parties, may be taken to have impliedly consented to bodily contact of this kind. Today this rationalization can be regarded as artificial: and, in particular, it is difficult to impute consent to those who, by reason of their youth or mental disorder, are unable to give their consent. For this reason I consider it more appropriate to regard such cases as falling within a general exception embracing all physical contact which is generally acceptable in the ordinary conduct of everyday life."

## Assault

This tort protects the claimant in fear of battery. Where the defendant's actions cause the claimant reasonably to apprehend the direct and immediate infliction of force on him or her, the tort is committed. It is important to stress first of all that this is distinct from the popular meaning of "assault", which in tort equates with the tort of battery. So, if I point a gun at you, I have only committed an assault. It is irrelevant that the gun is unloaded—you do not know that, and have every reason to apprehend battery.[23] Only when I shoot the gun and hit you have I committed a battery. If my aim is poor and I miss, only an assault has been committed.     **11–007**

The requirements of assault are as follows:

### (1) Reasonable apprehension of harm

The key to assault is the reasonable apprehension of harm. If I creep up and strike you from behind without your knowledge, I have only committed a battery. It is only assault if you are aware of my approach. Equally, if you are lucky enough to be saved from physical harm by the intervention of a third party, or if I change my mind, I have only committed an assault. In *Stephens v Myers*,[24] for example, the plaintiff was threatened with violence whilst attempting to expel the defendant from a parish meeting. The defendant had approached the plaintiff threatening violence, but, due to the intervention of the churchwarden, was liable only for assault. Passive obstruction, however, such as that seen in *Innes v Wylie*,[25] where a policeman stopped the plaintiff from entering a room, will not amount to assault. If the human obstruction is passive, like a door or a wall preventing entry, the claimant has no reason to anticipate the direct and immediate infliction of force, so the defendant cannot be liable. The test of reasonable apprehension is an objective one. It is irrelevant whether the particular claimant was actually in fear, or could have defended himself or herself successfully.     **11–008**

---

[22] [1990] 2 A.C. 1 at 72–73.
[23] *R. v St George* (1840) 9 C. & P. 483 at 493; 173 E.R. 921 at 926. See also *Logdon v DPP* [1976] Crim. L.R. 121.
[24] (1840) 4 C. & P. 349; 172 E.R. 735.
[25] (1844) 1 C. & K. 257 at 263; 174 E.R. 800. Contrast *Chief Constable of Thames Valley Police v Hepburn* [2002] EWCA Civ 1841; *The Times*, December 19, 2002, CA.

*(2)  It must be intentional*

**11–009**   This is a basic requirement of the tort and here signifies that the defendant intended the claimant to apprehend reasonable force would be used or was reckless as to the consequences of his or her actions.[26]

*(3)  It must be immediate and direct*

**11–010**   This is really part of the test of reasonable apprehension. If the claimant can see that the defendant is not in a position to inflict immediate and direct harm on the claimant, then the claimant has nothing to fear and so the defendant is not liable for assault. Therefore, if I threaten you with violence as I am passing you in a train, I have not committed assault. More controversially, in *Thomas v National Union of Miners (South Wales Area)*,[27] striking miners, who hurled insults at working miners who had been transported into work in vehicles, were not held liable for assault, because the vehicles had been protected by a police cordon.

**11–011**   **Can words amount to an assault?:**   There is old authority that words by themselves cannot amount to an assault.[28] This may now be challenged in the light of the House of Lords case of *R. v Ireland*.[29] Here, three women had been harassed by Ireland. He was alleged to have made repeated telephone calls to them, generally at night, during which he remained silent. The women suffered psychiatric illness as a result. The House of Lords rejected the proposition that an assault could never be committed by words as unrealistic and indefensible. Liability would in fact depend on whether the claimant, in the circumstances before the court, reasonably believed that the oral threat could be carried out in the sufficiently near future to qualify as an immediate threat of personal violence. On the facts, the court was prepared to accept that silence would be capable of giving rise to such fears. This seems sensible and it is to be hoped that although the decision was made in criminal law, it will be applied by analogy to tort law. Whilst the old saying goes that "sticks and stones may break my bones, but words will never hurt me", this seems to require an unduly high level of courage by the reasonable person. Few amongst us would not experience fear if telephoned by a stalker. As recognised by the court in *R. v Ireland*, whilst the recipient of the call may have no knowledge of the stalker's whereabouts, the fear lies with the knowledge that the stalker, in contrast, knows exactly where the recipient is at the time of the call.

Conversely, it has long been accepted that words may negative an assault. In the classic case of *Tuberville v Savage*,[30] the defendant placed his hand on his sword and stated that "If it were not assize time, I would not take such language from you". It was assize time and so, in reality, the defendant was stating that he did not intend to strike the plaintiff. This must be distinguished from a conditional threat, where the claimant is merely given an option to avoid violence. It was no excuse for the highwayman to claim that his victims had a viable alternative option when he stated "stand and deliver, your money or your life!" On this basis, in

---

[26] *R. v Venna* [1976] Q.B. 421; *Bici v MOD* [2004] EWHC 786 (QB) (subjective recklessness).

[27] [1986] Ch.20 at 65. More recently, the Court of Appeal rejected a claim by the President of Equatorial Guinea that the advance group participating in an attempted coup (which failed) had the means to carry out the threat alleged: *Mbasogo v Logo Ltd (No.1)* [2006] EWCA Civ 1370; [2007] Q.B. 846.

[28] See *Meade's & Belt's Case* (1823) 1 Lew. C.C. 184, 168 E.R. 1006: "no words or singing are equivalent to an assault".

[29] [1998] A.C. 147.

[30] (1669) 1 Mod. Rep. 3; 86 E.R. 684.

*Read v Coker*,[31] the defendant was liable for assault when he and his servants threatened to break the plaintiff's neck unless he left the defendant's workshop.

## False imprisonment

This tort is concerned with the claimant's right to freedom of movement. A complete restriction of this freedom, unless it is expressly or impliedly authorised by the law, will render the defendant liable. It is necessary to exclude conduct expressly or impliedly authorised by the law from this tort in view of the custodial powers of the state and the powers of the police force, provided, of course, these bodies act within the powers given them by law. It is no excuse that the defendant had wrongfully assumed in good faith that he had a legal right to detain the claimant.[32] In this sense, false imprisonment is a strict liability tort. It is not the conduct of the defendant which is judged, but the injury to the claimant. "False" simply means wrongful. Equally, "imprisonment" does not require the defendant to put the claimant in prison, but will extend to any actions which deprive the claimant of his or her freedom of movement. It should be noted that it need not be shown that force has been used. **11–012**

One question which has arisen is this: where A has given orders to B to restrain C, is A or B liable for false imprisonment? Generally, the actor (here B) will be liable, unless B exercises no discretion in the matter and is forced to obey the instructions of A. An example of this may be found in *Austin v Dowling*.[33] Here, a police inspector had refused to take the responsibility for arresting the plaintiff on a charge made by the defendant's wife, but finally did arrest the plaintiff when the defendant signed the charge sheet. It was held that the defendant was liable for false imprisonment. In modern times, however, the courts have taken the view that the police, as professionals, are expected to exercise their own judgment and not simply follow the instructions of others. This view formed part of the reasoning of the Court of Appeal in *Davidson v Chief Constable of North Wales and Another*,[34] where a store detective had given evidence to the police which led to the arrest of Davidson for shoplifting. Davidson and a friend were detained by the police for two hours before it became clear that the store detective's suspicions were unfounded. Davidson sued the store detective for false imprisonment. The Court of Appeal held that no action lay against the store detective where she had merely given information to the police, who could act as they saw fit. Only if the detective had been the instigator, promoter and active inciter of the action would the detective be liable.

The requirements of false imprisonment are examined below:

*(1) A complete restriction of the claimant's freedom of movement*

This requirement refers to any actions which restrict the claimant's freedom of movement in every direction. It is not satisfied, however, if the claimant is able to move in one direction. For example, in *Bird v Jones*,[35] the plaintiff had insisted on passing along the public footway **11–013**

---

[31] (1853) 13 C.B. 850; 138 E.R. 1437.

[32] See *R v Governor of Brockhill Prison, Ex p. Evans (No.2)* [2001] A.C. 19 (prison governor liable for unauthorised detention of prisoner when his sentence (calculated by him on the law as then understood) was subsequently found to be incorrect). See P. Cane (2001) 117 L.Q.R. 5. Contrast *Quinland v Governor of Swaleside Prison* [2003] Q.B. 306, CA (sentence miscalculated by judge, but detention by prison governor under warrant of commitment was legally justified until warrant set aside).

[33] (1870) L.R. 5 C.P. 534.

[34] [1994] 2 All E.R. 597, CA.

[35] (1845) 7 Q.B. 742.

on Hammersmith Bridge in London, which the defendants had partially enclosed without due permission. The plaintiff had climbed over a fence erected by the defendants to close off the footway on one side of the bridge, but was prevented from moving along the footway by the defendants. He was told that he might go back and use the public footway on the other side of the bridge, but the plaintiff would not do so. The court held that the defendants were not liable for false imprisonment. They had not imposed a complete restriction on the plaintiff's freedom of movement.

Such a restriction will generally involve a positive act. Trespass is concerned with intentional, immediate and direct actions, not omissions. On this basis, an omission or refusal to release the claimant from confinement will not amount to false imprisonment, unless the claimant has a legal right to be released and the defendant is under a positive obligation to release the claimant. The majority of the Court of Appeal in *Iqbal v Prison Officers Association*[36] thus held that the claimant, who was confined to his cell as a result of a prison officers' strike, could not sue for false imprisonment. Their omission to act—in refusing to let him out of his cell—did not entail liability. The claimant was legally detained and the officers were under no duty to the prisoner to release him (their duty was to their employer).[37] Lord Neuberger MR did suggest, however, that a deliberate and dishonest refusal to unlock the cells might give rise to a claim for misfeasance in public office.[38]

The issue of confinement remains a question of fact. If the claimant is able to return in the same direction in which he or she came, or is given reasonable means of escape, the defendant will not be liable. The means of escape must be reasonable—a rope left by the window of a seven storey building will clearly not suffice. This question did, however, divide the House of Lords in *R. v Bournewood Community and Mental Health NHS Trust, Ex p. L.*[39] The majority found that a mentally disordered patient who had been placed voluntarily in an unlocked ward and showed no desire to leave had not been detained, despite the fact that the hospital gave evidence that he had been sedated and would have been detained compulsorily had he sought to leave. Lord Steyn, however, dissented, remarking that, "The suggestion that L was free to go is a fairy tale."[40] The European Court of Human Rights in 2005[41] found unanimously that the applicant had been deprived of his liberty, contrary to art.5.1 of the Convention. The Strasbourg Court noted, however, that the House of Lords had considered the question solely on the basis of false imprisonment,[42] rather than in terms of art.5.1, and the criteria for assessing domestic and Convention issues were different.[43]

**11–014**     It is a matter of contention whether a reasonable means of escape exists when the defendant imposes conditions on the manner in which visitors leave his or her premises. There is authority that, provided the conditions are reasonable, the defendant is not liable if he or she refuses to allow the claimant to leave until these conditions are satisfied. In *Robinson v*

---

[36] [2009] EWCA Civ 1312; [2010] Q.B. 732 (Sullivan L.J. dissenting on the issue of liability).

[37] The court also found that the direct and immediate cause of the prisoner's confinement was the order of the Governor that, because of the strike, prisoners should remain in their cells throughout the day.

[38] [2009] EWCA Civ 1312 at paras. 40–42, discussed at 11–033.

[39] [1999] 1 A.C. 458.

[40] [1999] 1 A.C. at 495. Lord Nolan also dissented on this point.

[41] *HL v United Kingdom (45508/99)* (2005) 40 E.H.R.R. 32. Subsequently applied in *JE v DE* [2006] EWHC 3459 (Fam); [2007] M.H.L.R. 39 (Fam Div).

[42] The decision of the House of Lords pre-dated the coming into force of the Human Rights Act 1998.

[43] *HL v United Kingdom (45508/99)* (2005) 40 E.H.R.R. 32 at para.90.

*Balmain Ferry Co Ltd*,[44] for example, the plaintiff had contracted to enter the defendants' wharf to catch a ferry boat to cross the river. For reasons of efficiency, the fee of one penny was paid on one side of the river, on entering and exiting the wharf. Having a 20 minute wait for the next boat, the plaintiff changed his mind and tried to exit the wharf. He refused to pay the stipulated charge of one penny to leave the wharf, as required by a notice above the turnstile. The defendants refused to let him leave until the charge was paid. In an action for false imprisonment, the Privy Council held that a penny charge was a reasonable condition for leaving by a route different from the one stipulated in the contract:

> "There is no law requiring the defendants to make the exit from their premises gratuitous to people who come there upon a definite contract which involves their leaving the wharf by another way".[45]

This approach was taken a step further by the House of Lords' decision five years later in *Herd v Weardale Steel, Coal and Coke Co Ltd*.[46] Here, a miner had refused to do certain work, on the basis that it was dangerous, and had demanded to be taken to the surface before the end of his shift. His employer refused. Their Lordships held that the employer was not liable for false imprisonment. The miner had voluntarily entered the mine under a contract of employment, and was deemed to have impliedly consented that he would not be brought to the surface until the end of the shift.

These cases involve a worrying invasion of the civil liberties of those involved.[47] However, there is clearly a line to be drawn. As Viscount Haldane points out in *Herd*, a claimant cannot expect to be able to stop an express train because he or she now wishes to get off the train. The traveller consents to a restriction on his or her freedom of movement for the duration of the journey. If this consent is withdrawn, logically he or she should be permitted to alight at the first reasonable opportunity, which will usually be the next designated stop. It does not entail a right to stop the train immediately. On this basis, the miner in *Herd* quite rightly limited his claim for false imprisonment to the period during which the lift was available to take him out of the mine. It is when the defendant refuses to allow the claimant to leave in such circumstances that a claim for false imprisonment should lie.

*Robinson* may, however, be defended on the basis that the plaintiff's restraint was not complete, as he could have crossed the river (subject to a query as to whether this is reasonable). *Herd* is more difficult to defend. It is difficult to see the decision as anything but a harsh ruling in favour of an employer's rights over his employees. It is scarcely legitimate to suggest imprisonment as a reasonable response to the employee's breach of contract. A better explanation of *Herd* (and certainly one more palatable to modern industrial relations) is to view it as an omission case; an interpretation supported by the Court of Appeal in *Iqbal* (above).

*It is unnecessary to show the claimant knew of the imprisonment*

Here the point is simply that the tort protects the claimant's freedom of movement, because it is a recognised interest the legal system wishes to protect. Proof of damage is not required, and so it is not necessary that the claimant has suffered from the knowledge of his or her false    **11–015**

---

[44] [1910] A.C. 295, PC.
[45] [1910] A.C. 295, PC at 299.
[46] [1915] A.C. 67.
[47] See generally K.F. Tan (1981) 44 M.L.R. 166.

imprisonment. *Grainger v Hill*[48] established that the tort exists even if the claimant is too ill to move, and in *Meering's* case,[49] the Court of Appeal held that the tort can be committed even where the claimant does not know that he or she is being detained. In this case, the plaintiff had been suspected of stealing from his employer, the defendants, and so he had been asked to accompany two of his employer's private police force to the company's office. He had agreed and waited as instructed in the waiting room. Unknown to the plaintiff, the two policemen remained nearby and had been instructed not to let him leave the waiting room until the Metropolitan Police arrived. He later sued for false imprisonment. The court held that the tort had been committed as soon as the defendant was under the control of the defendants' police. Atkin L.J. stated the legal position:

> "It appears to me that a person could be imprisoned without his knowing it. I think a person can be imprisoned while he is asleep, while he is in a state of drunkenness, while he is unconscious, and while he is a lunatic . . . Of course the damages might be diminished and would be affected by the question whether he was conscious of it or not."[50]

This is a strong statement, indicating the courts' disapproval of any unjustified and complete restriction on the claimant's freedom of movement.[51] As Lord Griffiths commented in *Murray v Ministry of Defence*[52]:

> ". . . the law attaches supreme importance to the liberty of the individual and if he suffers a wrongful interference with that liberty it should remain actionable even without proof of special damage".

### (2) Without legal authorisation

**11–016**     The burden of proof lies on the defendant to justify the lawfulness of the arrest and the claimant is only required to show that he or she has been denied freedom of movement. On this basis, this requirement should be treated as a defence to be established by the defendant and will be so treated in a later section, below. Again, we can see that the rule seeks to protect the civil liberties of the claimant.

## THE RULE IN *WILKINSON V DOWNTON*

**11–017**     In all three torts above, the three characteristics of a trespass action are apparent: intentional acts which directly harm the claimant, which are actionable without proof of harm. They do not include intentional harm which has been indirectly caused. This gap is filled by the so-called rule in *Wilkinson v Downton*. Like the rule in *Rylands v Fletcher* seen in the

---

[48] (1838) 4 Bing. N.C. 212; 132 E.R. 769.

[49] *Meering v Grahame-White Aviation Co Ltd* (1920) 122 L.T. 44.

[50] (1920) 122 L.T. 44 at 53.

[51] There is authority to the contrary in *Herring v Boyle* (1834) 1 Cr. M. & R. 377; 149 E.R. 1126 which was not cited in *Meering*. This was criticised, however, by Lord Griffiths in *Murray v Ministry of Defence* [1988] 1 W.L.R. 692 at 701.

[52] [1988] 1 W.L.R. 692 at 703 (although the comment was obiter). See also Sedley L.J. in *Chief Constable of Thames Valley Police v Hepburn* [2002] EWCA Civ 1841; *The Times*, December 19, 2002, CA at para.14.

previous chapter, the rule is named after its leading case, where the relevant legal principles were set out. In *Wilkinson v Downton*[53] the defendant falsely told the plaintiff that her husband had been involved in an accident in which he had been seriously injured. The defendant later claimed that it had been a practical joke, but the shock suffered by the plaintiff as a result led her to suffer weeks of illness. She sued the defendant for damages. His actions had been intentional, but the harm had been indirect. Nevertheless, Wright J. held that where the defendant had wilfully undertaken an act calculated to cause physical harm to the plaintiff, there was a good cause of action. It is clear, however, that, unlike trespass, harm must be proved.

The case was applied by the Court of Appeal in *Janvier v Sweeney*.[54] In this case, a private detective had pretended to be a police officer, and, in order to obtain access to her employer's correspondence, had threatened the plaintiff that she was in danger of arrest for association with a German spy (her fiancé was German). The plaintiff suffered psychiatric illness as a result, and was allowed to recover damages under the rule in *Wilkinson v Downton*.

However, despite such a rapid start, and the potential breadth of the rule, it has not been much relied upon by the courts, due to the increasing role of the tort of negligence in recent times. Yet, it was resurrected by the Court of Appeal in the 1993 case of *Khorasandjian v Bush*[55] to deal with the problem of harassment. In the absence of a tort of harassment,[56] the court resorted to existing tortious actions (private nuisance and the rule in *Wilkinson v Downton*) to protect a young woman who had been suffering from a campaign of harassment undertaken by a former boyfriend. The rule was relied upon by the court to support the grant of an injunction against the defendant for wilful actions calculated to cause physical harm to the plaintiff. But one problem existed. In both *Wilkinson* and *Janvier*, the plaintiffs had suffered physical or psychiatric injury. In contrast, in *Khorasandjian*, the plaintiff had merely suffered from stress. Nevertheless, Dillon L.J. took a broad approach. His Lordship held that there was "an obvious risk that the cumulative effect of continued and unrestrained further harassment such as she has undergone would cause [psychiatric] illness",[57] which would suffice for a quia timet injunction (an injunction given to prevent an apprehended tort).

The courts have subsequently disapproved of such a broad approach. Harassment is now dealt with specifically by means of the Protection from Harassment Act 1997 (see below). In *Hunter v Canary Wharf*,[58] the House of Lords found that, in view of the Act, the decision in *Khorasandjian* granting the plaintiff a remedy in private nuisance should be overruled. Whilst their Lordships did not overturn the alternative ground for the decision based on the rule in *Wilkinson v Downton*, Lord Hoffmann in the recent decision in *Wainwright v Home Office*[59] favoured a narrower interpretation of the law. Whilst expressly questioning the continued need for this tort, he was reluctant to see it extended beyond claims for indirectly inflicted physical and recognised psychiatric injury. Both he and Lord Scott expressed concern that to do so would encourage unwarranted litigation:

---

[53] [1897] 2 Q.B. 57.
[54] [1919] 2 K.B. 316.
[55] [1993] Q.B. 727.
[56] *Patel v Patel* [1988] 2 F.L.R. 179.
[57] [1993] Q.B. 727 at 736.
[58] [1997] A.C. 655.
[59] [2003] UKHL 53, [2004] 2 A.C. 406, HL. See also *Wong v Parkside Health NHS Trust* [2001] EWCA Civ 1721; [2003] 3 All E.R. 932, CA.

"In institutions and workplaces all over the country, people constantly do and say things with the intention of causing distress and humiliation to others. This shows lack of consideration and appalling manners but I am not sure that the right way to deal with it is always by litigation."[60]

The view of the court was clearly that, in view of the expansion of the tort of negligence to cover claims for psychiatric illness since 1901,[61] this tort was effectively defunct.[62]

The 1997 Act will be examined later in this chapter.

## TRESPASS TO THE PERSON: DEFENCES

**11–018**   Defences generally are dealt with in Ch.16. Here, we highlight the defences which are of particular importance in actions for trespass to the person.

## (1) Consent

**11–019**   This is an obvious defence. If I expressly consent to contact or implicitly lead the defendant to believe that I am consenting, I cannot later sue the defendant. It would be highly inconvenient if no such rule existed. On this basis, hospitals can ensure that they commit no torts against patients whilst operating by asking them to sign consent forms. Equally, a patient who presents his or her arm for an injection is clearly consenting to the infliction of immediate and direct force on their person. Team sports similarly rely on the ability of the individual to consent to the rough and tumble which may ensue (but not, of course, to a violent blow by an opposing team member contrary to the rules of the game). In this way, the self-determination of the individual is protected.

The consent must, of course, be real and not induced by fraud, misrepresentation or duress. So, in *R. v Williams*,[63] the defendant, a singing tutor, was liable in battery for sexually assaulting a naive plaintiff who had been falsely informed that this would improve her voice. The traditional rule is that the fraud must go to the very nature and quality of the act or to the identity of the assailant, and that fraud as to the effect and consequences of the act is not deemed sufficient to nullify consent.[64] It is submitted that this may lead to unduly harsh results in practice. The criminal court in *R. v Dica*[65] held that this distinction would not apply to the offence of unlawful infliction of grievous bodily harm under s.20 of the Offences against the Person Act 1861. Here, Dica had had unprotected sexual intercourse with the complainants without informing them that he knew himself to be HIV positive. They were later found to be infected with the HIV virus. The Court of Appeal held that although there was consent to

---

[60] [2003] UKHL 53, [2004] 2 A.C. 406, HL at para.46.

[61] *Dulieu v White & Sons* [1901] 2 K.B. 669.

[62] Field J in *C v D* [2006] EWHC 166 (QBD) approved Lord Hoffmann's view, although he found that the sexually abused claimant had succeeded in part in his claim under the principle.

[63] [1923] 1 K.B. 340.

[64] *Hegarty v Shine* (1878) 14 Cox C.C. 124; *R. v Clarence* (1888) 22 Q.B.D. 23; *R. v Linekar* [1995] Q.B. 250, CA. Query its application in *R. v Tabassum (Naveed)* [2000] 2 Cr. App. R. 328.

[65] [2004] EWCA Crim 1103; [2004] Q.B. 1257.

the act of intercourse, his conduct amounted to an offence under s.20.[66] It remains unclear whether what is essentially a claim for fraud as to the risk of infection would give rise to civil liability.

It is not necessary in English law for the claimant to be aware of all the relevant facts in giving his or her consent. As may be recalled from Ch.5, the House of Lords in *Sidaway v Bethlem Royal Hospital*[67] held that a medical practitioner was not obliged to inform the patient of all the risks of a medical procedure, but simply to provide a reasonable level of information, judged according to the practices of a respectable body of opinion in that sector of the medical profession. The patient will therefore usually be given a broad understanding of the procedure, but no more. But if the patient specifically asks a question, the doctor is expected to answer both truthfully and as fully as the questioner requires.[68] Provided the patient is informed in broad terms of the nature of the procedure to be undertaken and of any significant risks which would affect the judgment of a reasonable patient,[69] real consent is given. If the claimant believes the information given is deficient, the remedy lies in the tort of negligence, not trespass to the person.[70] It has been suggested, however, that in the light of the Royal Bristol Infirmary Report, which emphasised the central role of consent in the provision of medical care, and the Human Rights Act 1998, more detailed information may be required.[71] A recent decision suggested that, at the very least, the duty to inform a patient of significant risks extended to making the patient aware that fewer or no risks were associated with another available and alternative treatment.[72] This does not, however, signify that doctors have to disclose every possible alternative treatment, regardless of its feasibility.[73]

One peculiar aspect of consent is that for trespass to the person, but not, it should be noted, for trespass to land, the burden is on the claimant to prove absence of consent. Generally, the burden is on the defendant to establish any defences. This suggests that in trespass to the person, consent is not a defence at all. Rather, absence of consent is part of the cause of action to be proved on the balance of probabilities by the claimant. At first instance, in

---

[66] s.20 does not require proof of assault or battery. cf. *R. v B* [2006] EWCA Crim 2945; [2007] 1 W.L.R. 1567 (failing to disclose HIV status would not vitiate consent (see Sexual Offences Act 2003 s.76 (Conclusive presumptions about consent)) but could amount to s.20 offence).

[67] [1985] A.C. 871. Approved in *Creutzfeldt-Jakob Disease Litigation (No.1)* (2000) 54 B.M.L.R. 1 (QBD).

[68] See *Chester v Afshar* [2004] UKHL 41, [2005] 1 A.C. 134 where the claimant was formerly a journalist who actively sought information as to the risks involved. See Lord Bingham at para.5: "Mr Afshar was however subject to a further, important, duty: to warn Miss Chester of a small (1 per cent–2 per cent) but unavoidable risk that the proposed operation, however expertly performed, might lead to a seriously adverse result . . . The existence of such a duty is not in doubt. Nor is its rationale: to enable adult patients of sound mind to make for themselves decisions intimately affecting their own lives and bodies."

[69] *Pearce v United Bristol Healthcare* [1999] P.I.Q.R. P53, CA. Although it is impossible to state how significant this risk may be, Lord Bridge in *Sidaway* above indicated that it would be something in the region of 10 per cent.

[70] See *Chatterton v Gerson* [1981] Q.B. 432 at 443 per Bristow J. Note that if the patient has consented to one procedure, it does not mean that the patient has consented to any further invasion unless the doctor has ensured that the terms of consent authorise such further treatment as the doctor considers necessary or desirable.

[71] See A. Hockton, *The Law of Consent to Medical Treatment* (2nd edn, Sweet and Maxwell, 2011) at 1–006. Indeed, the guidance given to doctors by the General Medical Council goes beyond that stated in *Sidaway: Consent guidance: Patients and doctors making decisions together* (GMC, 2008) (*http://www.gmc-uk.org/guidance/ethical_guidance/ consent_guidance_index.asp* [Accessed April 21, 2011]). For empirical research into informed consent from a professional and patient perspective, see R. Heywood, A. Macaskill and K. Williams (2010) 18 Med L Rev 152 and (2008) 24 P.N. 104.

[72] *Birch v University College London Hospital NHS Foundation Trust* [2008] EWHC 2237 (QB); (2008) 104 B.M.L.R. 168.

[73] R. Heywood [2009] C.L.J. 30 at 31.

*Freeman v Home Office (No.2)*,[74] McCowan J. held that the burden of proof was on the claimant, because the tort consists of a trespass against the will of the party. In practice, however, the issue of consent will usually be raised by the defendant and is therefore generally treated as a defence.

### Refusal of consent

**11–020**  It seems logical that if I have a right to consent to a trespass to my person, I have a corresponding right to refuse consent to such actions. But whilst it is clearly desirable that I have the right to refuse consent to your violent actions, it is more contentious when I wish to refuse to consent to life-saving medical treatment. The idea of self-determination implies that the doctor should not be allowed to overrule my express wishes, even with my best interests at heart. Therefore, if a Jehovah's Witness clearly states that, because of her religious beliefs, she is not prepared to authorise a blood transfusion, the doctor will commit a battery if he administers blood against her will.[75]

It has been held that an adult of sound mind and full understanding should be able to decide to refuse treatment, even if the treatment is necessary to save his or her life or even, controversially, that of her unborn child.[76] Capacity will be presumed unless shown otherwise.[77] Only where there is doubt as to the patient's free will and capacity will no trespass take place. For example, in *Re T (Adult: Refusal of Treatment)*,[78] a patient had refused a blood transfusion, following a road traffic accident and subsequent Caesarian section to deliver her premature baby. She was not a Jehovah's Witness, but had been brought up by her mother, who was a devout Witness, to believe that blood transfusions were wrong. Her refusal followed time alone with her mother. It was held that in the light of her illness, the incomplete information she had been given, and the perceived influence of her mother, the doctors had acted lawfully in the circumstances in giving her a transfusion. This case shows how narrow the line between autonomy and lack of capacity may sometimes be.

This does not mean that a patient suffering from some mental disability cannot refuse consent. The question remains one of capacity. In *Re J.T. (Adult: refusal of medical treatment)*,[79] the patient had a learning disability which in the past had been associated with extremely severe behavioural disturbance. She was being detained under the Mental Health Act 1983. Wall J. held that, nevertheless, she was capable of comprehending and retaining the information given, believing it, and making a choice in the light of it.[80] She was therefore competent

---

[74] [1984] 1 Q.B. 524, affirmed [1984] 1 Q.B. 548. Contrast majority view of the Supreme Court of Canada in *Non-Marine Underwriters v Scalera* (2000) 185 D.L.R. (4th) 1.

[75] *Malette v Shulman* (1990) 67 D.L.R. (4th) 321.

[76] *St George's Healthcare NHS Trust v S* [1999] Fam 26. Scott (2000) 20 O.J.L.S. 407 highlights the difficulties in determining the nature of moral and legal duties in such situations. See also *Re AK (Adult patient) (Medical Treatment: Consent)* [2001] 1 F.L.R. 129 (victim suffering from motor neurone disease but, although severely disabled, intellect unimpaired). Note also the guidance set out in *Re B v NHS Hospital Trust* [2002] EWHC 429 (Fam); [2002] 2 All E.R. 449, 473–474 by Dame Elizabeth Butler-Sloss.

[77] *Re MB* [1997] 2 F.C.R. 541 at 553 per Butler-Sloss L.J. See also *Trust A v H (an adult patient)* [2006] EWHC 1230 (Fam); [2006] 2 F.L.R. 958.

[78] [1993] Fam. 95.

[79] [1998] 1 F.L.R. 48.

[80] Applying the test stated in *Re C (Refusal of medical treatment)* [1994] 1 F.L.R. 31. See also *Re MB* [1997] 2 F.C.R. 541 (fear of needles rendered patient temporarily incompetent) and *Re W* [2002] EWHC 901 (Fam); *Independent*, June 17, 2002 (psychopathic disorder, but sufficient mental capacity to weigh the information required to reach a decision as to treatment).

to refuse the renal dialysis necessary to keep her alive. These cases will never be easy to decide, but the courts are reluctant to deny the right of the individual to retain self-determination over his or her body.

Difficult problems arise in determining the extent to which a child may be able to refuse to give consent to medical treatment. In relation to consent, s.8(1) of the Family Law Reform Act 1969 permits children of 16 and over to consent to surgical, medical or dental treatment without the consent of a parent or guardian. In relation to children below 16, the House of Lords in *Gillick v West Norfolk Area Health Authority*[81] held by a majority that a child below 16 is capable of giving valid consent, provided that the child is of sufficient intelligence and understanding to appreciate what is proposed. This is regardless of the feelings of his or her parents. However, this is not the same as giving the child a right to refuse consent. In *Re W*,[82] W was a girl of 16 who was suffering from anorexia nervosa. She opposed the local authority's decision to move her to a unit specialising in the treatment of eating disorders. The Court of Appeal held that even if the child is 16 or over, or *"Gillick* competent", a parent or guardian may nevertheless consent on the minor's behalf. The court warned doctors to listen to the objections of minors, whose views would increase in importance according to the age and maturity of the minor, but held that such objections would not be an absolute bar to treatment. In any event, the court has an inherent jurisdiction to intervene to protect minors irrespective of their wishes. This allows the court to intervene and overrule a minor's objection to treatment.

In the case of younger children, parental consent will suffice for general medical treatment. Even where the parents refuse consent, the court's inherent power may be invoked to ensure the child receives the appropriate treatment.[83] In the case of *Re C*,[84] Wilson J. overruled parental objections to HIV testing of their baby girl. The mother was HIV positive and the child had a 20 to 25 per cent chance of infection. Whilst the court was prepared to accord great importance to the wishes of her parents, the arguments in favour of testing the baby were overwhelming. This view was approved by the Court of Appeal,[85] in which Butler-Sloss L.J. emphasised that the welfare of the child was the paramount concern of the court.

*Limits to consent*

Criminal law has refused to accept the defence of consent where the defendant has inflicted **11–021** bodily harm on the claimant: ". . . it is not in the public interest that people should try to cause, or should cause, each other actual bodily harm for no good reason".[86] The House of Lords

---

[81] [1986] A.C. 112.

[82] [1993] Fam. 64. See also *Re M (A child) (Medical treatment)* [1999] 2 F.L.R. 1097. See C. Bridge and M.R. Brazier (1996) 16 L.S. 84, although Morris in 2005 argued that the increasingly rights-based approach in this area may lead to greater autonomy for adolescents: (2005) 21 P.N. 158.

[83] The judgment of the European Court of Human Rights in *Glass v United Kingdom (61827/00)* [2004] 1 F.C.R. 553 stressed the role of the court in protecting the personal integrity of the child under art.8, even where emergency procedures are involved if sufficient time exists.

[84] [2000] Fam. 48, Fam. Div. See also *Re B (A child) (Immunisation: Parental rights)* [2003] Fam Law 731, CA (immunisation ordered despite mothers' objections) and the more drastic *Re A (Children) (Conjoined Twins)* [2001] Fam 147, CA (parents' objections to separation of conjoined twins overruled, although the inevitable result was that one of the girls would die).

[85] [1999] 2 F.L.R. 1004; [2000] Fam. Law 16, CA. See also *Re C (a child) (Immunisation: Parental rights)* [2003] EWCA Civ 1148; [2003] 2 F.L.R. 1095 (mother's opposition to child's immunisation overruled by court in the best interests of the child).

[86] *Att-Gen's Reference (No.6 of 1980)* [1981] Q.B. 715 at 719 per Lord Lane C.J. Infliction of harm is permissible, however, in the course of properly conducted games and sports or the lawful chastisement or correction of children.

decision in *R. v Brown*,[87] which found a group of sado-masochists liable for acts of violence in which they had willingly and enthusiastically participated, was challenged in the European Court of Human Rights. The Strasbourg court held that the decision was not contrary to art.8 of the European Convention on Human Rights, which grants everyone a right to respect for their private and family life.[88] The United Kingdom government was permitted under art.8.2 to take measures necessary to protect its citizens from personal injury and its response had not been disproportionate to the need in question. The same approach has been adopted towards terminally ill patients who, unable to act due to their disability, wish to seek the assistance of another to commit suicide. In *Pretty v United Kingdom*,[89] Diane Pretty had sought an undertaking from the Director of Public Prosecutions that her husband would not be prosecuted under the Suicide Act 1961 for helping her to commit suicide. She was suffering from motor neurone disease and wished to avoid the extremely distressing and undignified final stages of the disease. The DPP refused her request. The European Court of Human Rights found that this refusal did not conflict with Mrs Pretty's human rights. Limiting her right to self-determination might interfere with her rights under art.8, but this could be justified as "necessary in a democratic society"[90] due to the need to safeguard life and protect the weak and vulnerable in society, who might be exploited by permitting assisted suicide. Whilst there was no evidence to suggest that Mrs Pretty fell into this category, this broader social goal was found to justify the DPP's position.[91]

It remains an open question whether such policy arguments will extend to tort. Much no doubt will depend on the nature of the injury inflicted: is the claimant consenting to a tattoo, ear-piercing, or serious physical injury? Lord Denning M.R., in *Murphy v Culhane*,[92] suggested that a defence of voluntary assumption of risk (or volenti non fit injuria, see Ch.16) might still apply, for example where a burglar had taken upon himself the risk that the householder might defend his or her property, but there is little real authority on this point, and a court is unlikely to wish to be seen to condone disproportionate physical injury.

## (2) Necessity

**11–022**    This is a limited defence. It allows the defendant to intervene to prevent greater harm to the public,[93] a third party, the defendant or the claimant. The courts are careful to keep this defence within strict bounds and generally the defendant must act reasonably in all the circumstances.

---

[87] [1994] 1 A.C. 212. See also *R. v Emmett, The Times*, October 15, 1999, but contrast *R. v Wilson* [1997] Q.B. 47, CA (wife able to consent to branding buttocks with hot knife on the basis that it was analogous to tattooing!)

[88] *Laskey, Jaggard and Brown v UK* (1997) 24 E.H.R.R. 39.

[89] (2002) 35 E.H.R.R.1.

[90] Art. 8.2.

[91] The Strasbourg court also found no violation of art.2 (right to life) and art.3 (right not to be subjected to degrading treatment). See now *R (on the application of Purdy) v DPP* [2009] UKHL 45; [2010] 1 A.C. 345 (DPP required to promulgate an offence-specific policy identifying the facts and circumstances to be taken into account in deciding whether to prosecute for assisted suicide).

[92] [1977] Q.B. 94. See also Lord Mustill in *Airedale NHS v Bland* [1993] 1 All E.R. 821.

[93] See, for example, *Austin v Commissioner of Police for the Metropolis* [2007] EWCA Civ 989; [2008] 1 All E.R. 564 (police preventing crowd from leaving public place where unauthorised demonstration was taking place amounted to false imprisonment, but was justified by necessity due to threat of imminent breach of the peace). The appeal to the House of Lords on the basis of breach of art.5(1), ECHR was rejected: crowd control measures resorted to for public order and public safety reasons did not amount to a deprivation of liberty provided that they were not arbitrary, were proportionate and were enforced for no longer than was reasonably necessary [2009] UKHL 5; [2009] 1 A.C. 564. For criticism, see D. Feldman [2009] C.L.J. 243 and D. Mead (2009) E.H.R.L.R. 376.

This defence solves a particular practical problem experienced by the emergency services. If a patient is brought into the accident and emergency section of a hospital unconscious, or is mentally ill and incapable of consenting, when can the medical practitioners involved be certain that their intervention is legal? It would be absurd and discriminatory if they were permitted to refuse to treat such patients in the absence of express evidence of consent.[94] This problem was addressed by the House of Lords in *Re F; F v West Berkshire Health Authority*.[95] Lord Goff held that the doctors may intervene in the best interests of the patient where: (a) it is necessary to act in circumstances where it is not practicable to communicate with the patient; and (b) the action taken is such as a reasonable person would in all the circumstances take. On this basis, where a patient is unconscious but otherwise competent and not known to object to the treatment, treatment may be legally justified. Where the incapacity is temporary, the doctor should do no more than is reasonably required in the best interests of the patient before he or she recovers consciousness.

The situation where the incapacity is permanent, for example where the patient is in a permanent coma or permanently mentally ill, is more difficult. In *Re F* itself, an application was made to the court to authorise a sterilisation operation on a woman of 36, with a mental age between five and six years old, who was clearly incapable of consenting to the operation. The House of Lords held that treatment would be justified if it would be in the patient's best interests and would be endorsed by a reasonable body of medical opinion. Where a number of reasonably suitable treatments were available, treatment should, however, be determined according to the best interests of the patient, taking into account broader ethical, social, moral and welfare considerations.[96] On this basis, hospitals will be permitted to undertake treatment necessary to preserve the life, health and wellbeing of the patient. This may extend beyond surgical operations or substantial treatment to include routine medical and dental treatment, provided it is in the best interests of the patient. Their Lordships held in *Re F* (Lord Griffiths dissenting) that the law should not require judicial approval to be sought on each occasion treatment was given, although they felt it would be "highly desirable" to seek judicial approval for operations such as sterilisations. The sterilisation of a minor or a mentally handicapped adult will in virtually all cases require the prior sanction of a High Court judge.[97]

Although provision already existed for the psychiatric treatment of persons formally detained in a mental hospital,[98] in 2007 the Mental Capacity Act 2005 was brought into force. This is intended to clarify the decision-making process for people of 16 or over who are

---

[94] The situation is exacerbated by the absence of any wardship jurisdiction for adults or the mentally ill in this context.

[95] [1990] 2 A.C. 1. See also *R. v Bournewood Community and Mental Health NHS Trust, ex p. L* [1999] 1 A.C. 458, HL. This application of the defence of necessity in this instance was subsequently found to violate art.5, E.C.H.R. by the European Court of Human Rights in *HL v United Kingdom (45508/99)* (2005) 40 E.H.R.R. 32 (breach of art.5.1 due to absence of procedural safeguards to protect against arbitrary deprivations of liberty). Note the Strasbourg court did not criticise the existence of the defence of necessity. The government has recently introduced new safeguards to close the so-called "*Bournewood* gap": see Sch.7 to the Mental Health Act 2007 which inserts a new Sch.A1 into the Mental Capacity Act 2005: see Hewitt (2007) 157 N.L.J. 1600. This sets out the detailed procedures and requirements relating to standard and urgent authorisations of deprivation of liberty in hospitals or care homes. These have been criticised, however, as overly complex: M.A. Jones (2007) 23 P.N. 238.

[96] *Re S (Adult Patient: Sterilisation: Patient's Best Interests)* [2001] Fam 15, CA. See also *Re A (Mental Patient: Sterilisation)* [2000] 1 F.L.R. 549, CA, *Simms v Simms* [2002] EWHC 2734 (Fam); [2003] Fam 83 and *Portsmouth NHS Trust v Wyatt* [2005] EWCA Civ 1181; [2005] 1 W.L.R. 3995.

[97] See now Mental Capacity Act 2005.

[98] See the limited provision made under the Mental Health Act 1983 for psychiatric treatment of persons formally detained in a mental hospital (now subject to amendment by the Mental Health Act 2007).

unable to make decisions for themselves. For the first time, there is a statutory definition of capacity (ss.1–3). Section 1(2) provides for a presumption of capacity: a person is assumed to have capacity unless it is established otherwise. Sections 4 to 6 provide for care or treatment (within limits) of a person without capacity provided, before doing the act, reasonable steps are taken to establish the patient lacks capacity in relation to the matter in question and it is reasonably believed that the patient lacks capacity and the act is in the patient's best interests. These sections are said to codify existing common law rules. One leading commentator has commented that:

> "it is likely that in substance the outcomes of decisions about medical treatment made in the 'best interests' of incompetent adults will differ little from the common law approach that the courts have developed over the last 20 years or so."[99]

A good example of the dilemmas involved in such decisions is found in the well-known case of *Airedale NHS v Bland*.[100] This involved another victim of the tragic Hillsborough disaster discussed in Ch.4. Tony Bland had been in a persistent vegetative state (PVS) for three and a half years following injuries suffered by him at the match, which had caused him to suffer irreversible brain damage. He continued to breathe unaided and his digestion continued to function, but he could not see, hear, taste, smell or communicate in any way. He was given no prospect of recovery. The doctors, with the support of his parents, applied to the court to withhold all life-sustaining treatment. Lord Goff, in the House of Lords, applied the principles stated in *Re F*. His Lordship held that there was no absolute rule that a patient's life had to be prolonged by treatment or care regardless of all the circumstances and the quality of the patient's life. Treatment could be withdrawn if the patient had no hope of recovery and a reasonable medical practitioner would hold that it was not in the patient's best interests to prolong the patient's life. If an adult of full understanding has the right to withhold consent to medical treatment due to his right to self-determination, his Lordship held that it would be inconsistent if there was no corresponding rule to deal with the refusal of consent where the patient is incapable of indicating his wishes.

This is, with due respect, a questionable analogy. It is difficult to consider a right to self-determination in terms of an individual who lacks capacity. The justification for intervention must surely be a paternalistic concern for the best interests of the individual concerned. One can further criticise the court's distinction between a doctor actively taking life (i.e. euthanasia, which is prohibited) and one in which the doctor discontinues life-saving treatment (which is allowed provided that the court's approval is sought). In the latter case, the patient is allowed to die of his or her pre-existing condition, which the court classifies as an omission for which the doctors will not be judged responsible. Yet, in both cases the doctor may be acting in the best interests of the patient to relieve the patient's condition, and indeed, the latter option will generally result in the patient starving to death or dying from infection, which is a far from dignified end.

---

[99] M.A. Jones (2007) 23 P.N. 238 at 248. For a more detailed discussion of the statutory provisions, see P. Bartlett and R. Sandland, *Mental Health Law: Policy and Practice* (3rd edn, OUP, 2007) and E. Jackson, *Medical Law: Text, Cases and Materials* (2nd edn, OUP, 2009).

[100] [1993] 1 All E.R. 821. The Court of Appeal recently approved the General Medical Council's advice on the withholding and withdrawal of life prolonging treatments, notably artificial nutrition and hydration (ANH): *R. (on the application of Burke) v General Medical Council* [2005] EWCA Civ 1003; [2006] Q.B. 273. Comment: C. McIvor (2006) 22 P.N. 59.

In *NHS Trust A v M*,[101] the court was asked to consider whether discontinuance of treatment did, in fact, violate art.2 (right to life) and art.3 (right not to suffer degrading treatment) of the European Convention on Human Rights. The court held that, generally, art.2 would require a deliberate act, not an omission, by someone acting on behalf of the state, which results in death. Where treatment has been discontinued in the best interests of a patient, in accordance with the views of a respectable body of medical opinion, the state's positive obligations under art.2 were discharged. Equally, there was no violation of art.3. It could not in any event be invoked where the patient was unable to experience pain and was unaware of the nature of the treatment. The court thus approved Lord Goff's distinction in *Re F* as convention-compatible. Such rulings amount to a compromise whereby the judiciary avoids ruling on the controversial question of euthanasia, but provides patients and their families with a limited remedy in extremely distressing circumstances. The court's approval should be sought in virtually all such cases.

## (3) Self-defence

As a defence, the burden of proof lies on the defendant.[102] There is a clear analogy with criminal law where s.3 of the Criminal Law Act 1967 provides that a person has the right to use "such force as is reasonable in the circumstances in the prevention of crime". There are two limbs to the test. The defendant's force must be reasonable and not out of proportion to force exerted against him or her. It must also be based on an honest and, in contrast to criminal law, reasonable belief that the claimant will be attacked by the defendant.[103] In judging what is reasonable, the court will consider all the circumstances of the case, including the fact that the action may have had to be taken in the heat of the moment.[104]     **11–023**

This will be a question of fact. In *Lane v Holloway*,[105] where an elderly plaintiff had struck the young defendant on the shoulder during an argument, and the defendant had responded with an extremely severe blow to the plaintiff's eye, the defendant was held liable. The blow in the circumstances was out of proportion to the plaintiff's actions. This may be contrasted with the more recent case of *Cross v Kirkby*.[106] Here a farmer, who had been struck by a hunt saboteur with a baseball bat, wrestled the bat from him and struck a single blow to the head which, unfortunately, caused him serious injuries. In finding self-defence, the Court of Appeal took into account the anguish of the moment in assessing whether this was an excessive and disproportionate response to the threat posed, and held that the law did not require the defendant to measure the violence to be deployed with mathematical precision. It should be

---

[101] [2001] Fam. 348 (Fam Div). Followed by *Re G (Adult incompetent: Withdrawal of treatment)* (2002) B.M.L.R. 6 and *A Hospital v W* [2007] EWHC 425 (Fam); [2007] LS Law Medical 273.

[102] *Ashley v Chief Constable of Sussex* [2008] UKHL 25; [2008] 1 A.C. 962 (was policeman who fatally shot unarmed and naked suspect in the dark acting in self-defence?) Comment: N.J. McBride [2008] C.L.J. 461.

[103] See *Ashley v Chief Constable of Sussex* [2008] UKHL 25; [2008] 1 A.C. 962, and *Bici v MOD* [2004] EWHC 786 (QB) where both courts distinguished the position in criminal law where an honest belief of attack will suffice. Lord Scott in *Ashley* [2008] UKHL 25 at paras 17 and 18 justified this distinction on the basis of the different functions of criminal and civil law. In *Bici*, the soldiers, who had shot and injured a group of men travelling together in a car in Kosovo, failed to satisfy the court that there were reasonable grounds for them to believe that they were being threatened with being shot by the men.

[104] See *Ashley v Chief Constable of Sussex* [2006] EWCA Civ 1085; [2007] 1 W.L.R. 398 at para.82 per Sir Anthony Clarke M.R.

[105] [1968] 1 Q.B. 379.

[106] *The Times*, April 5, 2000.

noted that the right to defend oneself in self-defence extends to defence of one's spouse, and, if the analogy with s.3 of the Criminal Law Act 1967 is correct, to defence of others.

## (4) Provocation

**11–024**   The general view, stated in *Lane v Holloway*,[107] is that provocation is not a valid defence. It may reduce or extinguish the claimant's entitlement to exemplary damages, but will not reduce ordinary compensatory damages. This was followed by May L.J. in *Barnes v Nayer*[108] where the court held that prolonged abuse and threats from a neighbouring family were insufficient provocation to justify the defendant attacking the mother with a machete. Lord Denning, in *Murphy v Culhane*,[109] modified his view in *Lane*, holding that it could reduce the compensatory measure where the victim is at least partly responsible for the damage suffered. This seems questionable and is really an argument for reducing the damages for contributory negligence (see below). It is submitted that the view in *Lane* is to be preferred.

## (5) Contributory negligence?

**11–025**   There is some authority that the principles of contributory negligence apply to battery, although this has recently been discredited. In *Murphy v Culhane*,[110] Murphy was alleged to have been part of a gang which had set out to attack Culhane. Murphy had been killed when Culhane struck him on the head with a plank. Lord Denning saw no reason why the deceased's fault should not result in a reduction in his widow's damages under ss.1(1) and 4 of the Law Reform (Contributory) Negligence Act 1945. Lord Rodger in *Standard Chartered Bank v Pakistan National Shipping Corp (No.2)*[111] raised doubts, however, whether this line of authority, in fact reflects the common law position. The Court of Appeal in *Co-operative Group (CSW) Ltd v Pritchard*[112] agreed. "Fault", as defined by s.4 of the 1945 Act, signifies:

> "negligence, breach of statutory duty or other act or omission which gives rise to a liability in tort or would, apart from this Act, give rise to the defence of contributory negligence."

The first part of this definition applies to the defendant, i.e. it must be a claim giving rise to liability in tort, and the second half to the claimant—that is, conduct which, before the Act, would have given rise to a complete defence of contributory negligence. The question thus becomes: at common law was there a defence of "contributory negligence" to a claim against a defendant in these circumstances? Just as there is no evidence of such a defence existing in

---

[107] [1968] 1 Q.B. 379.
[108] *The Times*, December 19, 1986.
[109] [1977] Q.B. 94.
[110] [1977] Q.B. 94.
[111] [2002] UKHL 43; [2003] 1 A.C. 959 at para.45, although his Lordship reserved his opinion on this point.
[112] [2011] EWCA Civ 329. Smith LJ, however, expressed the view that although this was correct at law, justice required that apportionment should be available in cases of battery where the claimant had been at fault and this had been one of the causes of his injury.

relation to claims of fraud or deceit,[113] there is no case before 1945 which holds that there is such a defence in the case of an "intentional tort" such as battery. On this basis, Lord Denning in *Murphy v Culhane* was incorrect[114] and contributory negligence is not a defence.

## (6) Lawful authority

This defence is generally applied in relation to false imprisonment where the defendants have **11–026** specific statutory authority to deprive the claimant of his or her complete freedom of movement. It should be noted that even art.5 of the European Convention on Human Rights, which gives a right to liberty and security and which, under the Human Rights 1998, can now be enforced against public authorities such as the police, recognises that this will be limited in accordance with procedures prescribed by law.[115] This is obviously an important defence—without it our criminal justice system would fall apart. Section 12(1) of the Prison Act 1952 authorises the imprisonment of persons sentenced to imprisonment or committed to prison on remand pending trial.

Equally, a lawful arrest will not render a police officer or citizen liable for false imprisonment.[116] Reference should be made here to the provisions of the Police and Criminal Evidence Act 1984, particularly ss.24, 24A and 28. Readers are advised to consult specialist texts for detailed study of the requirements of a lawful arrest.[117] Basically, a police officer may legally arrest a person under a warrant. Section 24 (as amended by the Serious Organised Crime and Police Act 2005)[118] makes provision for a police officer to arrest an individual without a warrant if the individual is about to commit an offence, in the act of committing an offence, or if he or she has reasonable grounds for suspecting the individual to be about to commit an offence or in the act of committing such an offence. These powers of summary arrest are, however, subject to s.24(5): the constable must have reasonable grounds for believing that for one of the listed specific reasons, e.g. to prevent physical injury or damage to property, it is necessary to arrest the person in question.

A different regime applies to private individuals undertaking a "citizen's arrest". The new s.24A[119] states that a person, other than a constable, may arrest without a warrant a person in

---

[113] On this basis, contributory negligence is not a defence to deceit: *Alliance and Leicester BS v Edgestop Ltd* [1994] 2 All E.R. 38 and *Standard Chartered Bank v Pakistan National Shipping Corpn (Nos 2 and 4)* [2002] UKHL 43; [2003] 1 A.C. 959.

[114] See Aikens L.J. at para. 49.

[115] Art.5.1 lists six cases where an individual may legitimately be deprived of his liberty and these include detention after conviction by a competent court and lawful arrest for the purpose of bringing a person before a competent legal authority on reasonable suspicion of having committed an offence.

[116] Note also s.329, Criminal Justice Act 2003: civil proceedings by convicted offender for trespass to the person in circumstances where the act is alleged to be committed on the same occasion as the imprisonable offence for which the claimant has been convicted. An action may only be brought with permission of the court (see ss.329(2) and (3)) and it is a defence if the defendant can prove both that the condition in subs.(5) is met, and that, in all the circumstances, his act was not grossly disproportionate. Subsection (5) provides that the defendant only did the act because (a) he believed that the claimant was about to commit an offence, was in the course of committing an offence or had committed an offence immediately beforehand *and* (b) believed the act necessary to defend himself or another person, protect or recover property, prevent the commission or continuation of an offence or apprehend, or secure the conviction, of the claimant after he had committed an offence or was necessary to assist in achieving any of those things.

[117] e.g. see P. Ozin et al, *PACE: A practical guide to the Police and Criminal Evidence Act 1984* (2nd edn, OUP, 2010).

[118] s.110(1).

[119] As inserted by the Serious Organised Crime and Police Act 2005 s.110(1) and (4).

the act of, or whom he has reasonable grounds for suspecting to be in the act of, committing an indictable offence (that is, an offence which may be put before a judge and jury, not before a magistrate).[120] If the indictable offence has already been committed, s.24A(2) extends the power of arrest to anyone guilty of the offence or whom he or she has reasonable grounds for suspecting guilty of it. However, an offence must actually be committed. As was the case prior to the amendments, private individuals will not be protected from civil liability if they arrest someone under the mistaken belief that an offence has been committed.[121] There are also two further conditions to avoid a claim in tort for false imprisonment or battery.[122] First, the person making the arrest must have reasonable grounds for believing that one of the four conditions listed in s.24A(4) render it necessary to arrest the person in question. Secondly, it must appear to the person making the arrest that it is not reasonably practicable for a constable to make the arrest instead. The four conditions are as follows:

- To prevent the person causing physical injury to himself or others;
- To prevent the person suffering physical injury;
- To prevent the person causing loss or damage to property; or
- To prevent the person making off before a constable can assume responsibility for him.

As one commentator has stated,[123] this is likely to deter all but the foolhardy from exercising their citizen's right of arrest. Few citizens will be aware which offences are indictable and s.24A limits the situations generally when such a right may be exercised. These provisions are much narrower than those applicable to police constables and there is a clear risk that the unwary will find themselves liable in tort.

Finally, reference should also be made to s.3 of the Criminal Law Act 1967, which allows a person to use such force as is reasonable in the circumstances to prevent crime or in effecting or assisting in the lawful arrest of offenders, suspected offenders or persons unlawfully at large. There are also common law powers to intervene and take reasonable steps to prevent breaches of the peace.[124]

## CAN TRESPASS TO THE PERSON BE COMMITTED NEGLIGENTLY?

**11–027**    As stated in the introduction, early authority does seem to indicate the existence of a tort of negligent trespass to the person. It is doubtful, however, whether this tort has survived the growth and dominance of the tort of negligence outlined in earlier chapters of this book. Nevertheless, Diplock J. in *Fowler v Lanning*[125] did not rule out the existence of such a tort.

---

[120] s.24A(1). In force, January 1, 2006.
[121] See *R. v Self* [1992] 3 All E.R. 476 at 480.
[122] s.24A(3).
[123] See R.C. Austin [2007] Crim L.R. 459.
[124] See *Albert v Lavin* [1982] A.C. 546 at 565 and *R. (on the application of Laporte) v Chief Constable of Gloucestershire* [2006] UKHL 55; [2007] 2 A.C. 105. See also police powers to enforce public order, primarily under the Public Order Act 1986 and the Criminal Justice and Public Order Act 1994.
[125] [1959] 1 Q.B. 426 at 433.

In this case, his Lordship held that a pleading which simply stated that "the defendant shot the plaintiff" disclosed no cause of action. The plaintiff should have pleaded either intention or negligence on the part of the defendant and if negligence was alleged, the burden of proof generally lay on the plaintiff. Diplock J. therefore left open the question whether the plaintiff could have brought an action for negligent trespass to the person.

Lord Denning, in *Letang v Cooper*,[126] was perhaps predictably more forthright. Here, the plaintiff had suffered injuries when the defendant had driven over her legs whilst she was sunbathing outside a hotel on a piece of grass which was used as a car park. Her obvious course of action would have been to sue in negligence, but due to the three year limitation period for personal injuries (see Ch.16), she was out of time. She therefore tried to claim within the six year limitation period allocated for trespass, by framing her case as one of unintentional trespass to the person. The Court of Appeal rejected her claim, drawing a distinction between intentional and unintentional trespass to the person. Although Diplock L.J. was more cautious, suggesting that it was irrelevant whether the tort was described as unintentional trespass or negligence, Denning L.J. refused to accept the existence of a tort of unintentional trespass:

> ". . . when the injury is not inflicted intentionally but negligently, I would say the only cause of action is negligence and not trespass."[127]

If this is correct, then any claims for injury to the person which are not intentional must be brought in negligence. This does not seem to involve a dramatic step. It is difficult to see, in any event, why negligent conduct should be actionable without proof of damage. Lord Denning's view consolidates the position of trespass in the law of torts as a tort seeking to compensate for intentional conduct which unduly interferes with the personal integrity and autonomy of the individual.

Before moving on to consider trespass to land, there are two further related torts which should be considered. Harassment has been discussed above, and here we outline the provisions of the Protection from Harassment Act 1997, which are likely to be relevant to litigants considering an action for intentional injury by another. Equally, malicious prosecution, although not a form of trespass and only actionable on proof of damage, is frequently pleaded in common with false imprisonment and it is therefore convenient to consider its operation in this chapter.

## PROTECTION FROM HARASSMENT ACT 1997

Until recently, harassment was not a recognised tort[128] and litigants were forced to frame their **11–028** claims in trespass or nuisance.[129] However, s.3 of the Protection from Harassment Act 1997

---

[126] [1965] 1 Q.B. 232.
[127] [1965] 1 Q.B. 232 at 240. Approved in *Wilson v Pringle* [1987] Q.B. 237. See also *Bici v Ministry of Defence* [2004] EWHC 786 (QB). In *A v Hoare* [2008] UKHL 6; [2008] 1 A.C. 844, the House of Lords ruled that this did not prevent s.11of the Limitation Act 1980 including both claims in negligence and in trespass to the person due to its broad wording and legislative history.
[128] *Patel v Patel* [1988] 2 F.L.R. 179, CA.
[129] See *Khorasandjian v Bush* [1993] Q.B. 727.

creates a statutory tort of harassment. Yet, despite the importance of this provision, it has been the criminal provisions of the Act which have so far received the most attention.[130]

## What is "harassment"?

**11–029**    "Harassment" is described in s.1(1) as a course of conduct which amounts to harassment of another, and which the defendant knows or ought to know amounts to harassment of the other; in other words, the conduct is intentional and harasses another. Section 1(1A), added under the Serious Organised Crime and Police Act 2005 to counteract animal rights extremists, now also provides that

> "A person must not pursue a course of conduct—
>   (a)  which involves harassment of two or more persons, and
>   (b)  which he knows or ought to know involves harassment of those persons, and
>   (c)  by which he intends to persuade any person (whether or not one of those mentioned above)–
>       (i)   not to do something that he is entitled or required to do, or
>       (ii)  to do something that he is not under any obligation to do."

This seeks to prohibit intimidating conduct which prevents people going about their lawful business.

Section 1(2) further provides that the defendant ought to know that his or her conduct amounts to harassment if a reasonable person in possession of the same information would think the course of conduct amounted to harassment of the other. This is an objective test. The court will not take account of any mental disorder from which the defendant is suffering, or any other characteristics, as this would substantially lessen the protection given to victims by the Act.[131]

The description of "harassment" in s.1(1) is somewhat circular. It has been deliberately defined broadly and clearly goes beyond mere stalking which was the principal target of the Act. The general feeling stated in *Thomas v News Group Newspapers Ltd* is that "'Harassment' is . . . a word which has a meaning that is generally understood."[132] Section 7 provides some assistance. "Harassment" is defined as conduct which includes "alarming the person or causing the person distress."[133] "Course of conduct" is stated to involve conduct on

---

[130]  ss.2 and 4. In 1998, for example, there were nearly 6,000 prosecutions under the Act: J. Harris, *An evaluation of the use of the effectiveness of the Protection from Harassment Act 1997*, Home Office Research Study 203 (Home Office, 2000). The police recorded crime statistics for 2009–10 report 53,029 recorded offences of harassment: see *http://rds.homeoffice.gov.uk/rds/crimeew0910.html* [Accessed April 21, 2011].

[131]  *R. v C (Sean Peter)* [2001] 2 F.L.R. 757, CA (Crim).

[132]  *Thomas v News Group Newspapers Ltd* [2002] E.M.L.R. 4, para.30 per Lord Phillips M.R.

[133]  s.7(2).

at least two occasions,[134] and may include speech.[135] Although the cases now give some guidance,[136] Baroness Hale noted in *Majrowski v Guy's and St Thomas's NHS Trust* that:

"A great deal is left to the wisdom of the courts to draw sensible lines between the ordinary banter and badinage of life and genuinely offensive and unacceptable behaviour."[137]

As Lord Nicholls explained in that case, there is a boundary between conduct which is unattractive, even unreasonable, and conduct which is oppressive and unacceptable;[138] the court keeping in mind whether the conduct is of such gravity as to justify the sanctions of criminal law.[139] A recent example of oppressive and unacceptable conduct may be found in *Ferguson v British Gas Trading Ltd*[140] where the persistent sending of unjustified bills and threatening letters to a former customer of British Gas was found to be of sufficient gravity to constitute harassment. The Court of Appeal was unimpressed by British Gas' argument that it could not be held responsible for its own computerised debt recovery system or that the threats were diminished by the fact that Mrs Ferguson knew them to be unjustified. In the words of Jacob L.J.:

"a victim of harassment will almost always know that it is unjustified. The Act is there to protect people against unjustified harassment."[141]

Claims will be restricted in a number of ways. First, a "course of conduct" must be proved. Secondly, s.1(3) provides that a valid defence exists when the conduct was pursued for the purpose of detecting crime, under any legal requirement, or was reasonable in the circumstances.[142] Thirdly, it has been held that remedies will not be granted in favour of limited companies as opposed to individuals.[143] Despite the fact that the Act has been used

[134] s.7(3) (a) in relation to a single person. In the case of conduct in relation to two or more persons (see s.1(1A)), conduct is required on at least one occasion in relation to each of those persons.: s.7(3) (b). See also s.7(3A). See *Lau v DPP* [2000] 1 F.L.R. 799 (the fewer the number of incidents and the wider the time lapse, the less likely a finding of "course of conduct").

[135] s.7(4). It may even on rare occasions extend to press articles which provoke reader hostility to a particular individual, although the courts are very conscious of the risk of violating art.10 of the Convention (freedom of expression): *Thomas v News Group Newspapers Ltd* [2001] EWCA Civ 1233; [2002] E.M.L.R. 4. More recently, see *Howlett v Holding* [2006] EWHC 41 (QB); *The Times*, February 8, 2006 (flying banners from aircraft referring to Mrs Howlett in abusive and derogatory terms).

[136] See *Banks v Ablex Ltd* [2005] EWCA Civ 173; [2005] I.C.R. 819 (failure to show misconduct amounting to harassment on two occasions), *Conn v Sunderland City Council* [2007] EWCA Civ 1492; [2008] I.R.L.R. 324 (foreman shouting at employee and threatening to smash a window did not amount to oppressive conduct).

[137] [2006] UKHL 34; [2007] 1 A.C. 224 at para.66.

[138] [2006] UKHL 34; [2007] 1 A.C. 224 at para.30.

[139] *Veakins v Kier Islington Ltd* [2009] EWCA Civ 1288; [2010] I.R.L.R. 132.

[140] [2009] EWCA Civ 46; [2010] 1 W.L.R. 785.

[141] [2009] EWCA Civ 46; [2010] 1 W.L.R. 785 at para.20.

[142] *KD v Chief Constable of Hampshire* [2005] EWHC 2550 (QB); [2005] Po. L.R. 253 stated that s.1(3)(a) (course of conduct pursued for the purpose of preventing or detecting crime) should be interpreted subject to the defences of necessity and proportionality in the light of art.8.1 of the European Convention on Human Rights.

[143] *DPP v Dziurzynski* [2002] EWHC 1380; (2002) 166 J.P. 545 and *Daiichi Pharmaceuticals UK Ltd v Stop Huntingdon Animal Cruelty* [2003] EWHC 2337; [2004] 1 W.L.R. 1503, although this does not prevent the managing director of the company in question bringing a claim on his own behalf and on behalf of the employees of the company in a representative capacity (see *Bayer Plc v Shook* [2004] EWHC 332 (QB): companies involved in the development of genetically modified crops obtaining interim injunction against protesters in order to prevent harassment of their employees). See J. Seymour [2005] C.L.J. 57.

to curb the activities of activists, for example animal rights protesters, the courts have indicated that the Act should not be used to restrict the citizen's right to protest in the public
interest.[144]

## Remedies

**11–030**   If harassment is shown, s.3 allows the claimant to sue for damages and/or an injunction.[145]
Damages here may include a sum for anxiety and any financial loss resulting from the
harassment.[146] In *Majrowski v Guy's and St Thomas's NHS Trust*[147] the House of Lords recognised that the doctrine of vicarious liability would apply to harassment by employees in the
course of their employment, rendering employee potentially liable under the Act. An injunction may be granted for actual or apprehended acts of harassment. If the defendant breaches
the injunction, s.3(3) controversially permits a civil court to issue a warrant for the arrest of
the defendant.[148] Section 3A[149] provides for injunctions (but not damages) to protect persons
from harassment within s.1(1A).

## MALICIOUS PROSECUTION

**11–031**   This tort has much in common with the tort of false imprisonment. Both torts focus on loss of
liberty. Whilst, in false imprisonment, the defendant exercises direct restraint over the move-
ments of the claimant, malicious prosecution may be seen as indirect restraint by means of
setting the prosecution in motion. This tort is not, however, actionable per se and damage must
be proved. The classic definition of damage was given by Holt C.J. in *Savile v Roberts*,[150]
namely damage to a man's fame (or reputation), person or property. It is clear that an unwarranted prosecution may damage a person's reputation. Harm to the person has been interpreted
broadly to include both the threat of imprisonment and actual imprisonment. Harm to property
signifies the costs incurred by the claimant in defending the charges.

The tort has four requirements:

- the defendant has prosecuted the claimant;

- maliciously (i.e. with some wrongful or improper motive);

- without reasonable and probable cause;

---

[144] See *Huntingdon Life Sciences Ltd v Curtin, The Times*, December 11, 1997, but also *DPP v Moseley, The Times*,
June 23, 1999.
[145] The civil standard of proof is applied to proceedings under s.3: *Hipgrave v Jones* [2004] EWHC 2901 (QB);
[2005] 2 F.L.R. 174.
[146] s.3(2).
[147] [2006] UKHL 34; [2007] 1 A.C. 224.
[148] The court in *Silverton v Gravett* (unreported, October 19, 2001, QBD) held that this did not breach art.10 (freedom
of expression) nor art.11 (freedom of association) of the European Convention on Human Rights as such restrictions
could be justified as being "for the prevention of disorder or crime" or "for the protection of the reputation or rights
of others": see arts 10.2 and 11.2.
[149] Added by the Serious Organised Crime and Police Act 2005 s.125(5).
[150] (1698) 1 Ld. Raym. 374; 91 E.R. 1147. See, more recently, Roch L.J. in *Clark v Chief Constable of Cleveland*
[2000] C.P. Rep. 22.

- the prosecution ended in the claimant's favour. (This may be by acquittal, discontinuance by the prosecution, conviction quashed on appeal or on technical grounds.)

Actions will generally be against the police. Actions may be brought against private individuals, however, if they can be shown to have falsely and maliciously given information to the police, in circumstances where the police had no effective discretion whether to prosecute. This will not be established simply on the basis that the defendant has given information to the police, or prepared a report for the police. A recent example is that of *Martin v Watson*,[151] where the defendant maliciously made a groundless accusation of indecent exposure against the plaintiff, who was subsequently prosecuted. Lord Keith, in his leading judgment, held that:

> "Where an individual falsely and maliciously gives a police officer information indicating that some person is guilty of a criminal offence and states that he is willing to give evidence in court of the matters in question, it is properly to be inferred that he desires and intends that the person he names should be prosecuted. Where the circumstances are such that the facts relating to the alleged offence can be within the knowledge only of the complainant, as was the position here, then it becomes virtually impossible for the police officer to exercise any independent discretion or judgement, and if a prosecution is instituted by the police officer the proper view of the matter is that the prosecution has been procured by the complainant."[152]

This is not an easy tort to establish and the courts are careful not to allow the tort to be used **11–032** to discourage the prosecution of suspected criminals.[153] The most difficult obstacle for a claimant is to prove that the defendant had no reasonable and probable cause for the prosecution. This involves proving a negative, which is always problematic. The claimant must establish on the balance of probabilities that the defendant did not have an honest belief in the guilt of the accused founded on objective facts which gave reasonable grounds for the existence of this belief.[154] Malice alone will not suffice. This is particularly difficult to establish if, for example, the defendant has taken legal advice (provided of course the legal adviser was given all the relevant facts). It will be for the jury to decide whether the defendant honestly believed the guilt of the accused.[155] Malicious prosecution is usually heard by a judge and jury[156] and while it is for the judge to determine whether the prosecutor had reasonable and probable cause, it remains nevertheless for the jury to determine any disputed

---

[151] [1996] 1 A.C. 74 at 86–87. Note further guidance given by Brooke L.J. in *Mahon v Rahn (No.2)* [2000] 1 W.L.R. 2150 at 2205–2206. *Martin* was applied in *Sallows v Griffiths* [2001] F.S.R. 15, CA.

[152] But contrast *H v B* [2009] EWCA Civ 1092 (complainant in prosecution for rape not prosecutor when no more than key witness and had done nothing improper to influence CPS's decision to prosecute).

[153] In Canada, malicious prosecution is now being supplanted by the more straightforward tort of negligent investigation: *Hill v Hamilton-Wentworth Regional Police Services Board* 2007 S.C.C. 41; (2007) 285 D.L.R. (4th) 620 (comment: E. Chamberlain (2008) 124 L.Q.R. 205). However such an approach has been rejected by the English courts for policy reasons: see Ch.2 and *Van Colle v Chief Constable of Hertfordshire* [2008] UKHL 50; [2009] 1 A.C. 225.

[154] See *Herniman v Smith* [1938] A.C. 305 and, more recently, *Isaac v Chief Constable of the West Midlands Police* [2001] EWCA Civ 1405, *Quaquah v Group 4 Falck Global Solutions Ltd (Malicious Prosecution)* [2003] EWHC 1504 (QB); [2004] Prison L.R. 1 and *Moulton v Chief Constable of West Midlands* [2010] EWCA Civ 524.

[155] *Glinski v McIver* [1962] A.C. 726.

[156] In common with false imprisonment.

facts relevant to that question. The jury will also determine whether the defendant was malicious.[157]

Malicious prosecution only relates to prosecution, i.e. criminal charges. It remains questionable whether there is an equivalent tort of malicious institution of civil proceedings. This was doubted in *Metall und Rohstoff v Donaldson, Lufkin & Jenrette Inc*[158] and in the more recent House of Lords case of *Gregory v Portsmouth CC*.[159] Even if it does exist, it will rarely succeed, due to difficulties in proving damage.[160] Equally, it has been held that such proceedings do not affect the claimant's reputation, because his or her fair name is protected by the trial and judgment of the court.[161] Lord Steyn in *Gregory v Portsmouth CC* saw no reason to change the current legal position:

> "I am tolerably confident that any manifest injustices arising from groundless and damaging civil proceedings are either already adequately protected under other torts or are capable of being addressed by any necessary and desirable extensions of other torts. Instead of embarking on a radical extension of the tort of malicious prosecution I would rely on the capacity of our tort law for pragmatic growth in response to true necessities demonstrated by experience."[162]

**11–033**    There does, however, seem to be a tort of malicious abuse of process, although it is of limited importance and should be confined to the heads of damage supporting a claim for malicious prosecution.[163] Examples include malicious procurement of a search-warrant[164] and malicious presentation of a winding up order or petition for bankruptcy[165] without reasonable or probable cause. This is really a variant of the tort of misfeasance in a public office, the test

---

[157] On guidance for juries in awarding damages for malicious prosecution, see *Manley v Commissioner of Police of the Metropolis* [2006] EWCA Civ 879; [2006] Po. L.R. 117. Note that in addition to the civil action, a defendant who maliciously induces the authorities to bring unwarranted charges may face prosecution for wasting police time, for perverting or attempting to pervert the course of justice, or (if he or she gives evidence) for perjury.

[158] [1990] 1 Q.B. 391.

[159] [2000] 1 A.C. 419, which held that the tort does not apply to internal disciplinary proceedings. Lord Steyn held that the law, by providing adequate alternative remedies in defamation, malicious falsehood, conspiracy and misfeasance in public office, made it unnecessary and undesirable to extend this tort. For comment, see P. Cane (2000) 116 L.Q.R. 346. Note also *Strickland v Hertfordshire CC* [2003] EWHC 287 (QB); [2003] Po. L.R. 252.

[160] It is assumed that if the claimant succeeds in the initial action, the order for costs in the claimant's favour will cover any financial loss (this, unfortunately, is untrue unless the court awards indemnity costs, which is exceptional).

[161] Generally, see *Quartz Hill Gold Mining Co v Eyre* (1883) 11 Q.B.D. 674 at 689–690. Note the comments of Lord Steyn in *Gregory v Portsmouth CC* [2000] 1 A.C. 419 at 428: "However realistic this view may have been in its own time, it is no longer plausible".

[162] [2000] 1 A.C. 419 at 432–433.

[163] *Land Securities Plc v Fladgate Fielder (A Firm)* [2009] EWCA Civ 1402; [2010] 2 W.L.R. 1265, where the Court of Appeal refused to extend this tort to applications for judicial review for which the court had given permission and where only general economic losses had been suffered.

[164] *Reynolds v Commissioner of Police of the Metropolis* [1985] Q.B. 881; *Gibbs v Rea* [1998] A.C. 786, PC; *Kennedy v Chief Constable of Merseyside* [2004] Po. L.R. 226. See also *Keegan v Chief Constable of Merseyside* [2003] EWCA Civ 936; [2003] 1 W.L.R. 2187 where the Court of Appeal found, on the facts, no improper motive, but noted that had the Human Rights Act 1998 been in force, art.8 might have made a difference.

[165] *Johnson v Emerson* (1870–71) L.R. 6 Ex 329; *Quartz Hill Gold Mining Co v Eyre* (1883) 11 Q.B.D. 674. See, more recently, *Tibbs v Islington LBC* [2002] EWCA Civ 1682; [2003] B.P.I.R. 743.

for which has recently been restated in *Three Rivers DC v Bank of England (No.3)*.[166] The rationale of this tort is that executive or administrative power should only be exercised for the public good and not for ulterior and improper purposes.[167] In *Three Rivers*, the House of Lords found that liability in the tort of misfeasance in public office arose where the actions of a public officer[168] were carried out in the knowledge of, or with reckless indifference to the probability of,[169] injury being caused to a claimant, or a class[170] of persons of which the claimant was a member. Two forms of liability for misfeasance in public office exist at common law:

(i)   exercise of public power for improper or ulterior motives ("targeted malice");

(ii)  public officer knowingly acting beyond his or her powers and in the knowledge that such actions would probably result in injury to the claimant ("untargeted malice"). Reckless indifference is sufficient to establish liability, but not mere negligence.[171]

Both forms impose liability for an abuse of power by a public official activated by subjective bad faith.[172] The claimant must show special damage.[173] Although this will generally be economic loss, it will include personal injury.[174]

## TRESPASS TO LAND

Trespass to land is clearly a different type of tort from those examined above. Its rationale is not to protect the integrity or reputation of the claimant, but to protect the claimant against direct and unjustifiable interference with his or her possession of land. There is an obvious similarity here with the tort of nuisance which equally deals with an unjustifiable interference with the claimant's use and enjoyment of land. However, there is a notable distinction. Trespass to land, in common with all forms of trespass, must be direct and immediate and is actionable without proof of damage. In contrast, nuisance, as discussed in Ch.10, involves an indirect act which is only actionable on proof of damage. The distinction, which derives

**11–034**

---

[166]   [2003] 2 A.C. 1. The tort itself can be traced back to the 17th century (see *Turner v Sterling* (1671) 2 Vent 25) and was described as "well established" by the Privy Council in *Dunlop v Woollahra Municipal Council* [1982] A.C. 158 at 172 per Lord Diplock.

[167]   See Nourse L.J. in *Jones v Swansea City Council* [1990] 1 W.L.R. 54 at 85.

[168]   This is a broad concept: *Calveley v Chief Constable of the Merseyside Police* [1989] A.C. 1228. In the case, the Bank of England was held to satisfy this requirement.

[169]   *Akenzua v Secretary of State for the Home Department* [2002] EWCA Civ 1470; [2003] 1 W.L.R. 741. Comment: J.R. Spencer [2003] C.L.J. 543.

[170]   This is defined loosely: see *Akenzua v Secretary of State for the Home Department* [2002] EWCA Civ 1470 (victim did not need to be known prior to the expected harm occurring).

[171]   *Muuse v Secretary of State for the Home Department* [2010] EWCA Civ 453.

[172]   *Southwark LBC v Dennett* [2007] EWCA Civ 1091; [2008] H.L.R. 23 at paras 21–22.

[173]   *Watkins v Secretary of State for the Home Department* [2006] UKHL 17; [2006] 2 A.C. 395 (special damage required even where a public officer has infringed a constitutional right—here, that of a prisoner to receive unopened correspondence from his legal advisers or the court). Loss of liberty will, however, by analogy with false imprisonment be regarded as special damage: *Karagozlu v Commissioner of Police of the Metropolis* [2006] EWCA Civ 1691; [2007] 1 W.L.R. 1881.

[174]   *Akenzua v Secretary of State for the Home Department* [2002] EWCA Civ 1470. Mere distress or normal emotion will not suffice: *Hussain v Chief Constable of West Mercia* [2008] EWCA Civ 1205.

from the old rigid forms of action, survives despite the abolition of the forms of actions over 100 years ago. On this basis, if I throw a brick and destroy your prize flowers, I have committed an actionable trespass. If, however, I build a fire in my garden and noxious fumes blow over and harm your prize flowers, I have only committed a nuisance.

Unlike trespass to the person, trespass to land does not generally lead to criminal liability, although there are a number of statutory exceptions.[175] It is actionable per se, which may seem surprising. Tort law in the twenty-first century is generally more concerned with protecting personal interests, such as those discussed above, than with protecting interests in land, but historical concerns that trespass would lead to a breach of the peace led the courts to find liability without proof of harm.[176] Nevertheless, a claimant is likely to receive only nominal damages without proof of loss. Trespass also serves a useful function in determining boundaries to land (although claimants may alternatively seek a declaratory judgment) and in dealing with persistent trespassers by means of injunctive relief.

In common with trespass to the person, it is an intentional tort, but it is the act of entry which must be intentional and not the act of trespass. On this basis, provided your actions are voluntary, you are a trespasser whether you know you are trespassing or not.[177] It is therefore no excuse that you are utterly lost, although the courts will not impose liability where you were forcibly thrown or pushed onto the land.[178] Where animals stray onto another's land, Park J. in *League against Cruel Sports v Scott*[179] indicated that the owner will be responsible for the damage they cause if he or she intended them to enter the claimant's land or, knowing that there was a real risk that they would enter, failed to take reasonable care to prevent their entry. On this basis, the master of a hunt was liable when his hounds entered land belonging to the League against Cruel Sports, who were, unsurprisingly, not prepared to tolerate such a trespass. This case raises the question whether, in spite of *Letang v Cooper*,[180] a defendant may commit a trespass to land negligently. It is submitted that a consistent approach should be adopted to trespass, which should be confined to intentional voluntary acts. It is contrary to the general development of the law for a tort actionable per se to be committed negligently.

Trespass is therefore established where the claimant can show a direct and unjustifiable interference with the claimant's possession of land. The nature of these two requirements will be examined below.

## (1) Direct and unjustifiable interference

11–035   This can occur in a number of ways. The obvious examples are walking on my lawn or entering my house without my permission, but it will also include such diverse examples as throwing a CS gas canister on my land[181] or allowing sheep to stray onto my land.[182] Trespass may be

---

[175] e.g. "aggravated trespass" under the Criminal Justice and Public Order Act 1994 s.68 (as amended), where persons have trespassed on the land to disrupt a lawful activity taking place on the land (e.g. hunt saboteurs).

[176] See *Clerk & Lindsell on Torts* (20th edn, Sweet and Maxwell, 2010), para.19–09.

[177] *Conway v George Wimpey & Co Ltd* [1951] 2 K.B. 266 at 273–274.

[178] *Smith v Stone* (1647) Style 65; 82 E.R. 533.

[179] [1986] Q.B. 240.

[180] [1965] 1 Q.B. 232 (which of course only deals with trespass to the person).

[181] *Rigby v Chief Constable of Northamptonshire* [1985] 1 W.L.R. 1242.

[182] This has been found to extend to the discharge of water into a canal without permission: *British Waterways Board v Severn Trent Water Ltd* [2002] Ch.25, CA.

committed by interference with the subsoil[183] and even airspace if it is within the height necessary for the ordinary use and enjoyment of the land and structures on it.[184] On this basis, the
defendants in *Bernstein v Skyviews & General Ltd*[185] were not liable for taking aerial photographs of the landowner's home at a height of many hundreds of metres above the ground. This
is re-affirmed by the Civil Aviation Act 1982 s.76(1), which provides that civil aircraft flying at
a reasonable height do not commit a trespass. A reasonable height will be determined by the
court with regard to the wind, weather and all the circumstances of the case. A claimant may
recover damages, however, from the owner of the aircraft for property damage or personal
injury caused by something falling from an aircraft while in flight, taking off or landing. The
claimant need not prove negligence or intention, or establish any other cause of action, provided
that the loss or damage was not caused or contributed to by the negligence of the claimant.[186]

It should also be noted that the public have a right to use the public highway for any reasonable purpose, which will extend to peaceful assembly, provided their acts do not amount to a
public or private nuisance and do not obstruct the highway by unreasonably impeding the
public's primary right to pass and repass.[187]

## (2) Possession of land

This is the interest protected by the tort of trespass. Only those with possession of the land can          **11–036**
sue for trespass. It is not enough to be physically on the land or to have control over the land.
A mere licensee, such as a lodger or guest in a hotel, cannot sue for trespass. The claimant
must have an interest in land in possession or at least exclusive possession to maintain an
action for trespass.[188] An interest in land without possession will not suffice. For example,
when a landlord has leased his property, the tenant is the party in possession. The landlord
will only be able to sue if the trespasser injures the interest he or she has in possession,
namely the reversionary interest in land, i.e. the landlord's right to possession at the end
of the term of the lease.[189] Ordinarily, it will be the tenant who sues for trespass. The
similarities with the right to sue in nuisance, discussed in Ch.10, should be noted. The claimant
will be able to sue regardless of the fact that he or she was out of the premises at the time
the trespass took place or had only just acquired the right to possession. The concept
of "trespass by relation" allows the claimant to sue for trespass even if the trespass took place

---

[183] See *Bocardo SA v Star Energy UK Onshore Ltd* [2010] UKSC 35; (2011) 1 A.C. 380 (owner of surface land was
also owner of strata beneath it, including minerals found there unless alienated by conveyance, the common law or
statute to someone else). Lord Hope acknowledged, however, at para.27 that there must be some stopping point where
the concept of strata belonging to anybody would be so absurd to be not worth arguing.
[184] See *Kelsen v Imperial Tobacco Co Ltd* [1957] 2 Q.B. 334 and, more recently, *Anchor Brewhouse Developments
Ltd v Berkley House (Docklands Developments) Ltd* (1987) 38 B.L.R. 82 (injunction awarded to stop a developer's
cranes oversailing the plaintiff's land, even though they were high enough not to affect the normal use of that land).
See also *Laiqat v Majid* [2005] EWHC 1305; [2005] 26 E.G. 130 (C.S.) (an overhanging that occurred four metres
above ground level would be regarded as an interference with airspace and would amount to trespass).
[185] [1978] Q.B. 479.
[186] s.76(2).
[187] *DPP v Jones* [1999] 2 A.C. 240, HL (peaceful assembly on highway did not amount to trespass necessary to
invoke police powers against trespassory assembly under the Public Order Act 1986).
[188] *Nicholls v Ely Beet Sugar Factory* [1931] 2 Ch.84.
[189] See *Jones v Llanrwst Urban DC* [1911] 1 Ch.393 at 404.

between the time when the right to possession was obtained and actual entry into possession.[190]

## TRESPASS TO LAND: DEFENCES

**11–037**    The defences bear a clear resemblance to the defences discussed above for trespass to the person, namely consent, necessity and lawful authority. Similarly to nuisance, there is generally no defence of *jus tertii* to trespass. *Jus tertii* alleges that the claimant cannot succeed because a third party has a better title to the land than the claimant and should therefore be bringing the action instead of the claimant. It has been rejected in a number of cases.[191]

### (1) Licence

**11–038**    The defendant will not be liable for trespass where he or she has permission to act, be it express or implied, from the party in possession. A licence should be distinguished from interests in property, such as easements or profits à prendre which give the grantee a proprietary right to enter the land. These are dealt with in the standard works on land law.[192] Although a licence to act is a good defence, it has two notable limitations. It may be restricted by express or implied terms and if they are exceeded, the defendant has committed a trespass. As noted in Ch.8, "When you invite a person into your house to use the staircase, you do not invite him to slide down the banisters".[193] Equally, permission can be withdrawn, thereby rendering the defendant a trespasser if he or she fails to leave within a reasonable period of time.

Express or implied limits on permission to enter have been discussed above and in Ch.8. However, the ability to withdraw or revoke the licence is more complicated. The licence cannot be revoked where the claimant has also been granted a property interest such as a profit à prendre,[194] or has a licence coupled with an equity.[195] In other circumstances, it will depend on whether the claimant has been given permission to enter under a bare licence (i.e. in the absence of consideration), or under a contractual licence (i.e. in return for consideration, for example by purchasing a ticket to watch a football match). A bare licence may be revoked at any time,[196] although public law may impose some limits on the power of a public body to

---

[190]   See *Clerk & Lindsell on Torts* (20th edn, Sweet and Maxwell, 2010), para.19–026.

[191]   *Nicholls v Ely Beet Sugar Factory* [1931] 2 Ch.84; *Chambers v Donaldson* (1809) 11 East. 65; 103 E.R. 929. It may, however, be used in relation to actions for the recovery of land: see below.

[192]   Note also that such rights may be acquired by prescription (see Ch.10.)

[193]   See Scrutton L.J. in *The Carlgarth* [1927] P. 93 at 110.

[194]   A right to take goods from the land—see *Thomas v Sorrell* (1673) Vaugh. 330; 124 E.R. 1098.

[195]   See *National Provincial Bank Ltd v Hastings Car Mart Ltd* [1964] Ch.665 and Gray and Gray, *Elements of Land Law* (5th edn, OUP, 2008) para.10.4.2.

[196]   See *CIN Properties Ltd v Rawlins* [1995] 2 E.G.L.R. 130 which applied this rule even to quasi-public places such as a shopping centre and survived a challenge to the European Commission on Human Rights (*Anderson v United Kingdom* [1998] E.H.R.L.R. 218). This was applied in *Porter v Commissioner of Police for the Metropolis* (unreported, 20 October 1999), despite the highly critical academic response of Gray and Gray [1999] E.H.R.L.R. 46.

revoke its licence.[197] A contractual licence may be revoked (although this may result in a claim for breach of contract) unless (a) there is an express or implied term in the contract limiting the power to revoke the licence for a defined or reasonable time, and (b) the court would be prepared to grant an injunction to prevent breach of contract.[198] The existence of any implied term will be a question of construction on the facts of the case. For example, if I buy a ticket for the cinema, it is implied that (provided I behave myself) I can stay in the cinema until the end of the film.[199] If the licence is revocable, the defendant must be given reasonable time to leave and remove his or her goods.

## (2) Necessity

Necessity is also a valid defence to trespass to land. The necessity may be public or private, but in both cases, there must be an actual or reasonably perceived danger in relation to which reasonable steps are taken. For example, if there is a fire and the defendant enters another's land or destroys another's property to stop the spread of the fire, the defence will be one of public necessity if the actions are in the public interest. If the defendant has intervened to save his or her own person or property from imminent danger, the defence will be one of private necessity.[200] In *Rigby v Chief Constable of Northamptonshire*,[201] a young psychopath broke into a gun shop and armed himself. To end the siege, the police fired a canister of CS gas into the shop to smoke out the intruder. Unfortunately, it set the shop alight. The shopkeeper sued the police for damages. Taylor J. held that the police could rely on the defence of necessity provided they could show that they had not been negligent in creating or contributing to the necessity. On the facts, the intruder had been a clear threat to the public and the police had clearly not caused or contributed to the problem at hand. They were therefore not liable in trespass.[202]

   In recent years, the Court of Appeal has expressed concern as to the operation of this defence and advocated that it should be confined to very limited circumstances. Lord Denning M.R. in *Southwark LBC v Williams*[203] highlighted the concern that it could be used to justify public unrest. Here, a group of individuals in dire need of accommodation had relied on necessity to justify taking over a number of empty houses belonging to the local authority which were due for development. Lord Denning M.R. held that such behaviour was not acceptable in society and that the defence should only apply to urgent situations of immediate peril:

**11–039**

---

[197] See *Wandsworth v A* [2000] 1 W.L.R. 1246, CA (attempt to deny parent access to a primary school). Applied in *R. (on the application of Montgomery) v Hertfordshire CC* [2005] EWHC 2026; [2006] I.R.L.R. 787.

[198] *Winter Garden Theatre (London) Ltd v Millennium Productions Ltd* [1948] A.C. 173.

[199] Compare *Hurst v Picture Theatres Ltd* [1915] 1 K.B. 1. There is also authority that if the court is prepared to award an order for specific performance, the licence cannot be revoked even where the licensee has yet to enter into possession of the premises: *Verrall v Great Yarmouth BC* [1981] Q.B. 202.

[200] Although it has been held that it is no excuse to an action in trespass that you entered due to threats to your life: *Gilbert v Stone* (1647) Style 72; 82 E.R. 539.

[201] [1985] 1 W.L.R. 1242.

[202] They were, however, liable for negligence, as discussed in Ch.2.

[203] [1971] 1 Ch.734.

"If homelessness were once admitted as a defence to trespass, no-one's house could be safe. Necessity would open a door which no man could shut. It would not only be those in extreme need who would enter. There would be others who would imagine that they were in need or would invent a need, so as to gain entry . . . So, the courts must for the sake of law and order take a firm stand. They must refuse to admit the plea of necessity to the hungry and the homeless, and trust that their distress will be relieved by the charitable and the good."[204]

This approach was approved by the Court of Appeal in *Monsanto Plc v Tilly*.[205] Here, campaigners against genetically modified (G.M.) crops had entered onto land and destroyed some of the G.M. crops growing there. Monsanto, a company licensed by the Department of the Environment to carry out trials on G.M. crops, sought injunctions against the defendants prohibiting them from trespassing on the land. The defendants claimed that they had a valid defence of necessity, but this was dismissed by the Court of Appeal. The court held that the real purpose of the campaign was to attract publicity for their cause, and their actions did not fit within the very narrow defence of necessity. The defence would only apply where the defendants faced an emergency where it was necessary for the defendants to act in the face of immediate and serious danger to life or property, and where their actions were reasonable. In any event, there was a public authority responsible for the public interest in relation to G.M. crops, namely the Department of Environment. Again, the Court of Appeal stressed that the defence of necessity should not be used to justify "all sorts of wrongdoing".

## (3) Justification by law

**11–040**   It is a valid defence that the defendant was legally authorised to enter onto the claimant's land. The most obvious example is that of a police officer entering premises under warrant. Reference should be made again to the Police and Criminal Evidence Act 1984 (ss.16 to 18, as amended) and the Criminal Justice and Public Order Act 1994.[206] One particular problem, which has now been resolved by statute, is the difficulty experienced by householders who needed access to neighbouring land to undertake repairs to their property. Their neighbours at common law were quite entitled to refuse, or charge a premium. The Access to Neighbouring Land Act 1992 now provides that the court may make an order allowing access to land for the purpose of carrying out works which are reasonably necessary for the preservation of adjoining or adjacent land and which cannot be carried out, or would be substantially more difficult to carry out, without entry upon the land. The scope of the Act is limited, however, by the fact that the court cannot make such an order if it would cause unreasonable interference with the neighbour's enjoyment of the land or unreasonable hardship. Equally, it is confined to work to "preserve" the land, although it will extend to improvement work incidental to such works: s.1(5).[207]

Abuse of such legal authority is treated severely. Where the defendant has entered the property with legal authority, but subsequently abuses that authority, the trespass is deemed to have

---

[204] [1971] 1 Ch.734 at 744.
[205] [2000] Env. L.R. 313; *The Times*, November 30, 1999.
[206] See also Countryside and Rights of Way Act 2000 s.2.
[207] See also Party Wall etc. Act 1996.

taken place from the moment of entry (the so-called doctrine of trespass ab initio).[208] This only applies, however, to positive acts of abuse and does not apply to omissions. It also does not seem to apply to cases of partial abuse. In *Elias v Pasmore*,[209] the police had lawfully entered the plaintiff's premises to arrest a man, and had seized a number of documents, some of them unlawfully. Horridge J. held that the original entry was not a trespass to land. The only action was for trespass to the goods unlawfully seized. It is submitted that, despite criticism of trespass ab initio,[210] the doctrine is sound and should be preserved. It is important in a democratic society that any abuse of legal authority which interferes with the claimant's right to possession should not be tolerated.

## TRESPASS TO LAND: REMEDIES

The ordinary remedies of damages and/or an injunction may be obtained for trespass. The trespass may consist of a single act or be continuous. If the trespass is continuous, the claimant will have a right to sue for as long as it lasts. On this basis, the claimant may bring a second action for damages if the trespass persists.[211] The assessment of damages will be discussed in more detail in Ch.17. Here, therefore, we confine our study to remedies which are particularly relevant to the tort of trespass. Further details may be found in texts on land law. **11–041**

### (1) Self-help

This is mentioned to stress its limits.[212] A party in possession may use reasonable force to resist wrongful entry or attempted entry by a trespasser. Such people are therefore perfectly within their rights to erect fences or put up barbed wire fences. The force must be reasonable and any force in excess of what is reasonably necessary will render the person liable for trespass to the person. **11–042**

A guard dog is equally permissible, provided that it is reasonable to keep the dog on the premises for that purpose: s.5(3) of the Animals Act 1971. Section 1 of the Guard Dogs Act 1975 further provides, however, that a guard dog should not be used unless the dog is secured, or his handler is on the premises and the dog is under the control of the handler at all times. In any event, a notice containing a warning that a guard dog is present should be clearly exhibited at each entrance to the premises.[213]

---

[208] See the *Six Carpenters' Case* (1610) 8 Co Rep. 146a; 77 E.R. 695.

[209] [1934] 2 K.B. 164.

[210] The doctrine has been criticised as antiquated and for failing to recognise that a lawful act should not be rendered unlawful by subsequent events: see the Court of Appeal obiter in *Chic Fashions (West Wales) Ltd v Jones* [1968] 2 Q.B. 299 at 313, 317, 320. Lord Denning is critical of the doctrine in *Chic Fashions* when it is used against the police, but nevertheless uses it against taxi-drivers in *Cinnamond v British Airports Authority* [1980] 1 W.L.R. 582 at 588 who had abused their right to set down passengers at London airport by touting for business.

[211] *Holmes v Wilson* (1839) 10 Ad. & E. 503; 113 E.R. 190.

[212] Stressed again by the Court of Appeal recently in *Macnab v Richardson* [2008] EWCA Civ 1631; [2009] 35 E.G. 108, notably where it is not a clear and simple case of trespass, nor an emergency.

[213] See *Hobson v Gledhill* [1978] 1 W.L.R. 215.

Although anyone in possession of land has a right to re-enter at all times,[214] this is limited by the Criminal Law Act 1977.[215] Section 6 renders it an offence for anyone without lawful authority (other than a displaced residential occupier[216]) to use or threaten violence for the purposes of securing entry to any premises occupied by another. Readers should also note the restrictions on entry contained in the Protection from Eviction Act 1977, which renders it an offence to unlawfully evict or harass any person with a right to remain in occupation of the premises.

## (2) Order for possession of land

**11–043**    This is an action for the recovery of land (formerly called "Ejectment"), by which the person entitled to possess the land seeks a court order to recover the land. This is usually achieved by the claimant proving his or her own title to land.[217] There is now a special summary procedure the claimant can use against persons entering or remaining on their premises without the claimant's licence or consent, whether or not the claimant is able to identify them.[218] This permits the claimant to take action against squatters within a short period of time. This is essentially a proprietary action, but is mentioned because it has evolved from the tort of trespass.

## (3) Mesne[219] profits

**11–044**    These will usually be claimed in addition to the action for recovery of possession of land. They are a form of consequential damages, given to the claimant for the time he or she has been kept out of possession of his or her land and allow the owner to make a fair and reasonable charge for the use of the land. By this means, the claimant can seek a reasonable rent for the defendant's possession of the property. The remedy is usually used against a tenant who has refused to leave at the end of the lease. It is irrelevant that the claimant cannot show that the property could have been let during this period or that the defendant did not profit from the property. The damages are for the lost use of the property. Therefore, in *Inverugie Investments Ltd v Hackett*,[220] the Privy Council held that the plaintiff could recover a reasonable rent for every apartment in a hotel block, in spite of the defendants' objections that they had never been fully booked and indeed had an average occupancy of 35 to 40 per cent. Lord Lloyd held that it was not a question of the actual loss suffered, or whether the defendants had derived any

---

[214] Note *Ropaigealach v Barclays Bank Plc* [2000] Q.B. 263, CA (mortgagee permitted to exercise right to take possession without court order).

[215] As amended by the Criminal Justice and Public Order Act 1994 and Serious Organised Crime and Police Act 2005.

[216] This is defined by s.12(3) as any person who was occupying the premises as a residence immediately before being excluded from occupation by a trespasser.

[217] On this basis, there is authority that the defence of *jus tertii* applies to an action for recovery of land. But note the extension of recovery to contractual licensees in *Manchester Airport Plc v Dutton* [2000] Q.B. 133, CA (licensee with right to occupy land entitled to bring action for possession against trespasser even when not in actual occupation), although applied restrictively in *Countryside Residential (North Thames) Ltd v T (A Child)* (2001) 81 P. & C.R. 2, CA.

[218] See the Civil Procedure Rules, Pt 55.

[219] Pronounced "mean".

[220] [1995] 1 W.L.R. 713.

actual benefit from the use of the premises, but of assessing a reasonable rate for the 15½ years the plaintiff had been out of possession:

> "If a man hires a concrete mixer, he must pay the daily hire, even though he may not in the event have been able to use the mixer because of rain. So also must a trespasser who takes the mixer without the owner's consent. He must pay the going rate, even though in the event he had derived no benefit from the use of the mixer."[221]

On this basis, it was acceptable to calculate the sum due on the wholesale rate paid by tour operators, which took into account seasonal variations in the booking fee.

## Trespass to Goods

Finally, we shall briefly examine the tort of trespass to goods. This tort is now largely covered by the Torts (Interference with Goods) Act 1977, which brings together torts dealing with wrongful interference with goods, such as trespass and conversion (essentially theft in civil law[222]).[223] Reference should be made to other texts for a full understanding of wrongful interference with goods.[224] Here, we confine ourselves to a general discussion of trespass to goods.    **11–045**

This form of trespass deals with intentional and direct interference with the possession of goods. This includes removing or damaging goods—in fact, any act interfering with the claimant's possession of the goods. It is unnecessary to show the defendant has removed the goods to establish this tort. Scraping your keys on the side of a vehicle would amount to trespass to goods.[225] In contrast to the other forms of trespass discussed above, the requirements of this tort are not particularly clear. They will be examined below.

### The requirements of trespass to goods

*(1) It must be intentional*

Generally, it would seem that the act of interference with the goods must be intentional. It is, however, irrelevant whether the defendant realised that he or she was committing a trespass. For example, in *Wilson v Lombank Ltd*,[226] a car had been sent to a garage for repair. The defendant, believing wrongly that the car was his, removed it from the garage. It was held    **11–046**

---

[221] [1995] 1 W.L.R. 713 at 718. See also *Horsford v Bird* [2006] UKPC 3; [2006] 1 EGLR 75 (mesne profits awarded up to date that judge awarded damages in lieu of an injunction for trespassory encroachment of boundary wall on Horsford's land).

[222] Conversion is defined as wilfully dealing with the claimant's property in a way which amounts to a denial of the claimant's rights over it, whereby the claimant is deprived of the use and possession of the property. The Act also abolishes the old tort of detinue: s.2(1).

[223] See, generally, S. Green [2010] Conv 15.

[224] See, e.g. M.G. Bridge, *Personal Property Law* (3rd edn, OUP, 2002) and S. Worthington, *Personal property law: Text, cases and materials* (Hart, 2000).

[225] See the example given by Alderson B. obiter in *Fouldes v Willoughby* (1841) 8 M. & W. 540 at 549; 151 E.R. 1153 at 1157: "Scratching the panels of a carriage would be a trespass".

[226] [1963] 1 W.L.R. 1294.

that the defendant was liable in trespass. He had intentionally removed the vehicle and it was irrelevant that it was due to a mistake.

However, a number of cases have suggested negligence to be a sufficient condition of liability. In *National Coal Board v JE Evans & Co (Cardiff) Ltd*,[227] for example, the court excused the conduct of the defendants who, in digging a trench, had damaged an underground cable belonging to the plaintiffs. The court found that the defendants had not been negligent—there was no way they could have known of the presence of the cable, which had been laid by the plaintiffs or by the plaintiffs' predecessors in title without informing the landowner. The cable was not visible and had not been marked on the plan given to the defendants by the landowners. On this basis, where the claimant cannot reasonably know of the existence of the goods, but nevertheless harms them, a court will not find liability for trespass. There are also a number of road accident cases where the courts again look for negligence even when the action is brought in trespass.[228] This raises the "*Fowler v Lanning*[229] question" of whether there is a parallel claim for unintentional trespass to goods. It must be doubted whether such a claim is necessary and it may be preferable simply to treat such claims as negligence. Nevertheless, there is still some support for a tort of unintentional trespass to goods. For example, s.11(1) of the Torts (Interference with Goods) Act 1977 refers to "intentional trespass to goods", which suggests that it should be distinguished from "unintentional" trespass to goods.

*(2)  It must be direct*

11–047    The interference must be direct and immediate.[230] This raises all the questions we have seen considered above in relation to the other forms of trespass. For example, if I put out poison for my neighbour's dog, is this direct enough to amount to trespass to goods? It may be argued that it is no more indirect than the acid put in the hand-dryer in *DPP v K*,[231] discussed above. Nevertheless, the general view is that it is probably not direct enough.[232]

*(3)  Actionable per se?*

11–048    This tort is generally regarded as actionable without proof of damage. Thus, it covers activities such as the unauthorised touching of museum exhibits, which would not otherwise be protected in tort. There is some authority in favour of proof of damage, but these cases can generally be explained as highway cases based on negligence.[233]

*(4)  Possession*

11–049    The key to this tort is interference with the possession, not the ownership, of goods. In *Wilson v Lombank Ltd*,[234] for example, the plaintiff was found not to be the true owner of the car, having purchased the vehicle from a person who had no right to sell the car. Nevertheless, he was found to be in possession at the time of the trespass, and was therefore able to bring an

---

[227] [1951] 2 K.B. 861.
[228] *Holmes v Mather* (1875) 133 L.T. 361 where Bramwell B. at 363 attributes it to "the convenience of mankind in carrying on the affairs of life".
[229] [1959] 1 Q.B. 426.
[230] For a recent example, see *White v Withers LLP* [2009] EWCA Civ 1122; [2010] 1 F.L.R. 859 (estranged wife intercepting husband's post).
[231] [1990] 1 W.L.R. 1067.
[232] See *Clerk & Lindsell on Torts* (20th edn, Sweet and Maxwell, 2010), para. 15–09.
[233] *Everitt v Martin* [1953] N.Z.L.R. 298 and *Slater v Swann* (1730) 2 Str. 872; 93 E.R. 906.
[234] [1963] 1 W.L.R. 1294.

action for trespass to goods. The question is therefore whether the claimant was in possession at the time the interference took place. Bailees,[235] trustees, executors, administrators of estates and owners of franchises will all satisfy this requirement.

## Defences

The defences are similar to those mentioned for other forms of trespass. It is a valid defence **11–050** that the claimant has consented to the interference. Equally, if the trespass in question was necessary for the preservation and protection of the goods and reasonable steps were taken,[236] the defendant has a good defence. Readers should note that under the Police and Criminal Evidence Act 1984,[237] the police are given specific powers to search for and seize property without liability. Section 11(1) of the 1977 Act states that contributory negligence is no defence to proceedings based on "intentional" trespass to goods. Again, this begs the question whether contributory negligence could be a defence should unintentional trespass to goods be recognised, but as this is essentially a claim for negligence, the answer is obviously yes. Section 8 of the 1977 Act also provides a further defence:

> "The defendant in an action for wrongful interference shall be entitled to show, in accordance with rules of court, that a third party has a better right than the plaintiff in respect of all or any part of the interest claimed by the plaintiff, or in right of which he sues."

Under this provision, the defendant may protect himself or herself against double liability by identifying who had the interest protected by the tort at the relevant time. Rules of court now provide that the claimant should give particulars of title and identify any other person who, to his or her knowledge, has or claims to possess an interest in the goods.[238] Readers should also note that the 1977 Act gives the claimant a wider range of remedies than the common law remedies of damages and/or injunction, which include a final order for special delivery, or for delivery or damages, if the defendant is in possession or control of the goods.[239]

Trespass to goods is therefore a means by which the claimant's possession of goods can be protected from unwarranted interference by others. It is limited in scope, but presents an example of one of the many varied interests protected by the law of torts.

---

[235] See *Owen and Smith (trading as Nuagin Car Service) v Reo Motors (Britain) Ltd* (1934) 151 L.T. 274, CA.
[236] See *Kirk v Gregory* (1876) 1 Ex. D. 55 where the defence failed because, although the defendant had acted bona fide, it was not proved that the interference was reasonably necessary.
[237] See ss.8–22.
[238] CPR r.19.5A.
[239] See Torts (Interference with Goods) Act 1977 s.3.

# Chapter 12

# THE ECONOMIC TORTS

## Introduction

In this chapter we look at a number of different torts which protect a claimant (usually a business[1]) from infliction of economic loss by intentional acts. These are the so-called "economic torts". It is important to distinguish these torts from the tort of negligence, in which economic loss may caused by careless, rather than intentional conduct. Until quite recently, there was much confusion about the nature and scope of the economic torts. This is because they were often invoked in rather complex commercial circumstances, and, as the courts wrestled with the appropriate principles to apply in such circumstances, a number of different, overlapping causes of action emerged.

Until recently, it was usual to think in terms of there being at least four different economic torts. These included torts called "conspiracy", "intimidation", "inducing a breach of contract" and "interference with contractual relations". However, some of the case law dealing with the last two of these torts had blurred the distinction between them. In some cases, it had been suggested that both these torts might be dealt with according to a single set of rules (the so-called "unified theory"). To make matters worse, in other cases, it had been suggested that some of the economic torts were in fact just ways of committing a wider "generic" tort called "causing loss by unlawful means".

Thankfully, however, the recent decision of the House of Lords in *OBG v Allan*[2] has provided much-needed clarity. In the light of this decision, we can say that there are nowadays three "economic torts", as follows:

- Inducing a breach of contract

- Causing loss by unlawful means

- Conspiracy

---

[1] Claims are occasionally made outside of a commercial context. See, e.g. *Falconer v ASLEF* [1986] I.R.L.R. 331 (a claim for hotel expenses by a traveller who could not use his train ticket because of unlawful industrial action).
[2] [2007] UKHL 21, [2008] 1 A.C. 1. See also H. Carty (2008) 124 L.Q.R 641; J. O'Sullivan (2008) 24(3) P.N. 164.

The important thing to note is that, in *OBG v Allan*, their Lordships confirmed that the second of these torts is indeed a generic tort. As such, it encompasses a number of torts that formerly went by different names. Although, no doubt, these old names will continue to be used to describe different factual scenarios in which the generic tort is committed, the rules governing these scenarios are now the same.

In earlier times, the economic torts were often invoked to provide a remedy where trade unions caused loss to commercial parties by organising industrial disputes. Nowadays, however, the right to take or incite industrial action without being exposed to tortious liability is enshrined in legislation. Thus, although the economic torts continue to play a small role in regulating trade union activity (claims may be brought where economic loss is caused by "unofficial" action taken in breach of the statutory rules) their main purpose in modern times is to regulate competition between commercial parties. Essentially, they do this by making some forms of unreasonable business practice unlawful.[3] Bearing in mind this purpose, it will be useful, before exploring the rules of each tort, if we consider in general terms the extent to which the courts have felt able to interfere with commercial competition. An understanding of the problem the courts face will help us to understand why the specific rules of the torts are framed as they are.

## Regulating competition: the scope of the economic torts

12–002 In developing the economic torts, the courts have had to strike a delicate balance between the need to protect traders from unreasonable behaviour and the desirability of allowing vigorous competition, which is necessary for a thriving economy. The general approach of the courts was established in *Mogul Steamship Co Ltd v McGregor, Gow & Co*,[4] an important decision of the House of Lords taken at the end of the nineteenth century.

The defendants were various shipowners involved in the highly lucrative trade of importing tea from China. They sought to obtain a monopoly in this trade by driving the plaintiff, a rival shipping company, out of business. To achieve this, the defendants formed an association and began to ship tea at heavily discounted prices, so that the plaintiff company could not compete and lost all its business. The plaintiff company brought an action against the defendants to recover its financial loss, arguing that the defendants' actions should be declared unlawful.

The House of Lords held that the plaintiff company had no cause of action. The defendants had engaged in vigorous, cut-throat competition, but what they had done could not be called unlawful. The effect of this decision was to establish the ground rules for the subsequent development of the economic torts: the courts would be wary of interfering with market competition, even where this had the effect of driving a trader out of business.

What this means, in a modern context, is that where, for example, a new "superstore" opens, selling goods at bargain prices, small local traders whose businesses suffer have no remedy in law—the law does not prohibit simple competition, even though it might be regarded by some as unfair (or, perhaps, as contrary to the wider social interest in preserving

[3] Note that this is also the function of a related tort called "passing off", consideration of which is beyond the scope of this book. Interested readers should consult specialist texts on intellectual property, e.g. Bainbridge, *Intellectual Property* (7th edn, Longman, 2008); Cornish, *Cases and Materials on Intellectual Property* (5th edn, Sweet & Maxwell, 2006).
[4] [1892] A.C. 25.

the traditional identities of communities). For fear of stifling the free market, tort law will only provide a remedy for unfair trading practices in certain very limited circumstances. It is to these that we now turn.

## INDUCING A BREACH OF CONTRACT

This tort is committed where A, knowing of a contract between B and C, and intending that it should be breached, persuades B to breach that contract, and as a result B does breach the contract, causing loss to C. **12–003**

Liability for inducing a breach of contract was established in the famous case of *Lumley v Gye*.[5] The defendant, Mr Gye, was the proprietor of a theatre. He wished to secure the services of a certain opera singer by the name of Miss Wagner, who was, at the time, under a contract to sing for the plaintiff, Mr Lumley. Mr Gye offered Miss Wagner a large sum of money to break this contract. When she did so and performed in Mr Gye's theatre, the plaintiff brought an action claiming that Mr Gye had unlawfully induced Miss Wagner to breach her contract, thereby causing him financial loss. The court upheld this claim, holding that a person who procures another to commit an actionable wrong[6] (in this case a breach of contract) is liable *as an accessory*.

Note that the essence of the *Lumley v Gye* tort is that the defendant, by approaching and persuading, *joins with the contract-breaker* in committing a wrong against the claimant— the breach thereby has the flavour of a joint enterprise. This is what justifies the imposition of accessory liability. Liability cannot be established simply on the basis that the defendant has factually caused non-performance of the contract (say, by making available to the contract-breaker, without persuasion, a more attractive deal). It will also help with our understanding at this stage if we remember that there is no tort of inducing lawful termination of a contract—thus, for example, where a representative of an energy company knocks at your door and persuades you to "switch" service providers, the tort is not committed, because their intention is that you should *lawfully* terminate your contract with your existing provider.

For the *Lumley v Gye* tort to be established, the defendant must:

- know of the existence of the contract; and

- know that his or her behaviour will (if acted on) induce a *breach*; and

- intend to induce that breach.

It is worth considering each point in turn:

---

[5] [1853] 2 El. & Bl. 216.

[6] For the sake of simplicity, it is convenient to refer to the tort as "inducing a breach of contract". Strictly speaking, however, the principles of the tort apply equally to a (limited) number of other situations where the defendant procures a third party to commit an actionable wrong against the claimant. Such situations include procuring a breach of a company director's fiduciary duty, or a breach of an agent's duty to account to a principal. For some modern examples, see *Kallang Shipping SA Panama v AXA Assurances Senegal* [2008] EWHC 2761; *Sotrade Denizcilik Sanayi Ve Ticaret AS v Amadou LO* [2008] EWHC 2762; *Colliers CRE Plc v Pandya* [2009] EWHC 211.

## The defendant must know of the existence of the contract

**12–004**    This requirement is fairly straightforward. The simple point is that there can be no liability where A does something which causes the breach of a contract between B and C unless A knows that there *is* such a contract. The point is illustrated by the decision in *Smith v Morrison*.[7] Here, the first defendant (a farmer) accepted a deposit from the plaintiff in respect of the sale of his farm. In the particular circumstances of the case, he did not believe that this constituted a binding contract to sell the farm. He subsequently sold the farm to the second defendant (a company) which shared his belief that the previous dealings did not amount to a contract. In the action, the plaintiff claimed, amongst other things, that the second defendant had induced a breach of contract by dealing with the first defendant. However, Plowman J. accepted the company's evidence that it had honest and genuine doubts about the existence of any valid previous contract to sell the farm. In these circumstances, there could be no liability for inducing a breach of contract.

The requirement of knowledge of the existence of a contract is, of course, necessary to fulfil the requirement that interference with the contract must be *intentional*. As Lord Nicholls put it in *OBG v Allan*:[8] "Intentional interference presupposes knowledge of the contract." In many situations, however, A may know that B and C have a contractual relationship, but may not fully appreciate its terms. A may therefore not realise (and so not intend) that persuading B to act in a certain way will result in a *breach*. (A may think, for example, that B's conduct will result in terminating the contract lawfully.) In these circumstances, A cannot normally be liable.

## The defendant must know that the induced conduct will amount to a breach

**12–005**    As has been said, the defendant must normally know that his or her inducement will (if acted on) result in a breach of contract. In order for this to be so, two things are necessary:

- the defendant (A) must have knowledge of any relevant contractual terms that might be broken if B acts in response to the inducement;

- the defendant (A) must *realise* that the *legal effect* of B taking the induced course of conduct vis-à-vis C will be to put B in breach of those terms.

*Knowledge of the contractual terms*

**12–006**    The defendant (A) must normally have knowledge of the contractual term(s) between B and C that might be broken as a result of dealing with B. Such knowledge can sometimes be inferred from the fact that the defendant is familiar with the usual terms incorporated into contracts of the relevant kind.[9] But where this is not the case, the law will not fix A with constructive knowledge of the contractual term(s) just because A has dealings with B but carelessly fails to make appropriate inquiries about the extent of B's contractual obligations

---

[7] [1974] 1 W.L.R. 659.
[8] *OBG v Allan* [2007] UKHL 21 per Lord Nicholls at para.192.
[9] *Middlebrook Mushrooms Ltd v Transport and General Workers' Union* [1993] I.C.R. 612 per Neil L.J. at 621.

to C.[10] The position is different, however, where A's failure to acquire the relevant knowledge results from deliberately "turning a blind eye" (i.e. where A deliberately refrains from making inquiries because of a suspicion that they would reveal something to A's disadvantage.)

Thus, in *Emerald Construction Co Ltd v Lowthian*,[11] union officers (A) took unlawful industrial action against a building contractor (B) with the purpose of inducing it to terminate its arrangements with the plaintiff (C) for the supply of labour. One of the issues in the case was whether the union officers *knew* that, if B terminated these arrangements with C, it would amount to a breach of contract. The union officers had had sight of the contract between B and C, but had not investigated its terms. Lord Denning M.R. said:

> "Even if they did not know of the actual terms of the contract, but had the means of knowledge—which they deliberately disregarded—that would be enough. Like the man who turns a blind eye. So here, if the officers deliberately sought to get this contract terminated, heedless of its terms, regardless of whether it was terminated by breach or not, they would do wrong."[12]

### *Knowledge of the legal effect of the induced conduct*

In some situations, the defendant (A) may know about the relevant contractual terms between B and C, but not realise that, as a matter of law, B will be in breach these terms by responding to the inducement. Addressing this sort of situation, Lord Hoffmann, in *OBG v Allan*, said:

**12–007**

> "To be liable for inducing a breach of contract, you must know that you are inducing a breach of contract. It is not enough that you know that you are procuring an act which, as a matter of law or construction of the contract, is a breach. You much actually realize that it will have this effect."[13]

There can therefore be no liability in a case where the defendant (A) is honestly mistaken about the legal effect of B's actions on B's contract with C. Such was the case in *British Industrial Plastics Ltd v Ferguson*.[14] Here, a former employee (B) of the plaintiff company (C) offered the defendant (A) information about one of the company's secret processes which he (B) had invented while working for the company. The defendant knew that the employee had a continuing contractual obligation to the company not to reveal trade secrets. However, he dealt with the employee in the honest (but mistaken) belief that this obligation did not, in law, extend to patentable processes, so that dealing with the employee would not give rise to a breach of contract.

---

[10] See *British Industrial Plastics Ltd v Ferguson* [1940] 1 All E.R. 479. Per Lord Hoffmann in *OBG v Allan* [2007] UKHL 21, at para.41: "Mr Ferguson did not deliberately abstain from inquiry . . . He negligently made the wrong inquiry, but that is an altogether different state of mind." See also *Swiss Bank Corp v Lloyds Bank Ltd* [1979] Ch.548. (Constructive knowledge of the contractual terms will not suffice, per Browne-Wilkinson J. at 572).

[11] [1966] 1 W.L.R. 691 at 700.

[12] *Emerald Construction Co Ltd v Lowthian* [1966] 1 W.L.R. 691 per Lord Denning M.R. at 700. Note that his Lordship's subsequent reference to the liability of one who acts "recklessly" must now be treated with caution, in the light of Lord Hoffmann's assertion in *OBG v Allan* [2007] UKHL 21 (at para.41) that there can be no constructive knowledge even in a case involving "gross negligence". Deliberately refraining from inquiry is not the same as recklessly failing to inquire.

[13] *OBG v Allan* [2007] UKHL 21 per Lord Hoffmann at para.39

[14] [1940] 1 All E.R. 479

In the Court of Appeal, McKinnon L.J. observed that, in accepting this evidence, the trial judge had "vindicated [the defendant's] honesty . . . at the expense of his intelligence".[15] The House of Lords agreed, however, that the defendant's lack of intelligence about the law was nothing to the point—he could not be liable unless he had actually known that the legal effect of the employee's conduct would be a breach of contract.

## The defendant must "intend" to induce the breach

**12–008**   The *Lumley v Gye* tort is a tort of intention. It is not sufficient for liability that a defendant's dealings cause a breach of contract if that is not what was intended. As Lord Nicholls put it in *OBG v Allan*:

> "Causative participation is not enough. A stranger to the contract may know nothing of the contract. Quite unknowingly and unintentionally he may procure a breach of the contract by offering an inconsistent deal to a contracting party which persuades the latter to default on his contractual obligations. The stranger is not liable in such a case. Nor is he liable if he acts carelessly. He owes no duty of care to the victim of the breach. Negligent interference is not actionable."[16]

*What counts as "intending"?*

**12–009**   The difficult question, of course, is to what extent a defendant can be said to "intend" a breach of contract where that is not what he or she necessarily *desires*, but is nevertheless the foreseeable, probable or inevitable consequence of taking a particular course of action. Before the decision in *OBG v Allan*, the law on this point was extremely confused. The leading case, *Millar v Bassey*,[17] was a Court of Appeal decision concerning the well-known singer, Shirley Bassey. She breached a recording contract, knowing that this would result in her record company having to breach its contracts with the plaintiffs—a record producer and a group of musicians who had already been engaged to make the record. A majority of the Court of Appeal declined to strike out the plaintiffs' action. Beldam L.J. thought that Miss Bassey might be said to have "intended" those breaches, even though she had not "desired" them.[18]

This approach, however, was disapproved of by the House of Lords in *OBG v Allan*. Explaining the correct approach to be taken, Lord Hoffmann said that it was necessary to distinguish between "ends, means and consequences". In the first two cases, there would be liability, but not in the third. Thus, in the first case, it is conceivable (though it would be unusual) that a defendant might desire the breach purely as an end in itself, to serve some spiteful purpose. Here, there would be the required degree of intention. Equally, in the second (usual type of) case, the necessary intention will be present. Here, the defendant does not desire the breach as an end in itself, but only as the *means* of achieving a different end (usually his or her own enrichment or advantage). As Lord Hoffmann put it:

---

[15] *British Industrial Plastics Ltd v Ferguson* [1938] 4 All E.R. 504, CA per McKinnon L.J. at 513. (Noted by Lord Hoffmann in *OBG v Allan* [2007] UKHL 21 at para.39.)

[16] *OBG v Allan* [2007] UKHL 21 per Lord Nicholls at para.191.

[17] [1994] E.M.L.R. 44.

[18] Peter Gibson L.J. dissented, expressing a diametrically opposed view, whilst Ralph Gibson L.J.'s judgment was, as *Street on Torts* aptly puts it (J. Murphy, 12th edn., 2007, p.372), "unfathomably equivocal".

"If someone knowingly causes a breach of contract, it does not normally matter that it is the means by which he intends to achieve some further end or even that he would rather have been able to achieve that end without causing a breach. Mr Gye would very likely have preferred to be able to obtain Miss Wagner's services without her having to break her contract. But that did not matter."[19]

In the third type of case, however, the defendant neither desires the breach as an end in itself nor as a means of achieving a further end. This was the situation in *Millar v Bassey*. The breaches of the contracts with the producer and musicians were not a means by which Miss Bassey sought to achieve her desired end (freedom from her own recording obligations), nor, of course, were they a desired end in themselves. Their Lordships in *OBG v Allan* thought that, this being so, Miss Bassey could not be said to have "intended" those breaches in the necessary sense. The Court of Appeal had therefore been wrong to allow the action to proceed.

*Must the defendant intend to cause loss?*

It will suffice if the defendant intends to cause a breach of contract. There is no further require- **12–010** ment that the defendant must intend to cause loss to the claimant.[20] Thus, for example, in *South Wales Miners' Federation v Glamorgan Coal Co Ltd*,[21] the defendant, a miners' union, was held liable for inducing breaches of contracts between miners and their employers when it instructed the miners to stop work for a time. The union's purpose was to restrict the supply of coal, in order to keep the price of coal high (thereby maintaining the level of miners' wages, which were paid by reference to that price). Maintaining the price of coal, of course, would also be of benefit to the employers. It was clear, therefore, that the union did not intend to cause the employers any loss as a result of their members' actions. However, when, in the event, some loss was suffered, the union was liable—it was sufficient that it had intended to cause breaches of contract, and its conduct could not be excused on the basis that it had not intended to cause any loss. (Note, however, that the tort of "causing loss by unlawful means"— discussed below—does require an intention to cause the claimant loss.)

## What counts as "inducing"?

To be liable for the *Lumley v Gye* tort of "inducing"[22] a breach of contract, there must be a **12–011** sufficient causal connection between the behaviour of the defendant (A) and the actions of the third party (B) in breaching his or her contract with C. Since liability under the tort is "accessory" liability, the applicable principles are to be found in other cases dealing with the question of when a defendant can be liable as an accessory to a civil wrong committed by another.[23] In essence, these cases hold that the defendant must "join with" the other person to commit the wrong, in furtherance of some shared purpose. We can see that this was true in

---

[19] *OBG v Allan* [2007] UKHL 21 per Lord Hoffmann at para.42.
[20] Although the claimant must suffer some loss. The tort is not actionable per se. See *Sefton v Tophams Ltd* [1965] Ch.1140, CA. (Overruled by HL on different grounds at [1967] 1 A.C. 50.)
[21] [1905] A.C. 239. (Cited by Lord Hoffmann in *OBG v Allan* [2007] UKHL 21 at para.62.)
[22] Some cases and textbooks refer to the *Lumley v Gye* tort as "procuring" a breach of contract, but nothing turns on this difference in terminology.
[23] *OBG v Allan* [2007] UKHL 21 per Lord Hoffmann at para.36.

*Lumley v Gye*, since both Mr Gye and Miss Wagner sought to achieve the same purpose–namely that she would sing for Mr Gye instead of the plaintiff.

By contrast, no such common purpose existed in *CBS Songs v Amstrad Consumer Electronics Plc*.[24] This case concerned (amongst other things) an allegation of procuring (or "inducing") copyright infringement. The defendants manufactured and marketed a hi-fi music centre featuring an integrated record-player, radio, and twin cassette-deck with high-speed dubbing. This equipment could be used by members of the public to copy commercial broadcasts, records and tapes. Lord Templeman, giving the leading speech in the House of Lords, held that the defendants' conduct could not be regarded as analogous to the situation in *Lumley v Gye*—merely making available the means of committing a wrong was not the same as jointly committing that wrong. It could not be said that the defendants' *purpose* in selling such equipment was to infringe copyrights (though this might, of course, be the purpose of people who bought the machines).

## Defences to inducing a breach of contract

**12–012** The Trade Union and Labour Relations (Consolidation) Act 1992[25] sets out a number of defences to the economic torts, including the *Lumley v Gye* tort. Detailed consideration of the circumstances in which these defences operate is beyond the scope of this book. For present purposes it will suffice to note that, because most forms of industrial action involve breach of a contract of employment, in the absence of such statutory protection it would be impossible for a trade union to encourage its members to take industrial action without exposing itself to a claim by the employer for inducing a breach of contract.

In addition to the statutory defences, there is the common law defence of "justification". This can operate in a number of different circumstances, as follows:

*Where the defendant has an equal or superior right to the third party's performance*

**12–013** This form of justification will arise where the third party (the contract-breaker) has, under a previous contract, assumed obligations towards the defendant which are inconsistent with performing the contract with the claimant. In such a case, it can be said that the defendant has an equal or superior legal right to the third party's services which justifies inducing the third party to breach.[26]

*Where the defendant has statutory authority to interfere with the contract*

**12–014** In *Stott v Gamble*,[27] for example, a licensing authority, constituted under the Cinematograph Act 1909, had a statutory power to prevent films they considered "objectionable or indecent" from being shown in theatres. The plaintiffs, distributors of a film called "Five Nights", had a contract with a theatre-owner under which a fee was to be paid when the film was shown. As a result of the licensing authority's decision to ban the film, the theatre-owner did not show the film or pay the fee. The plaintiffs' action against the licensing authority failed. Horridge J. held

---

[24] [1988] A.C. 1013. See also *Unilever v Chefaro* [1994] F.S.R. 135.
[25] s.219. See also B. Simpson (2007) 36(4) I.L.J. 468.
[26] *Smithies v National Association of Operative Plasterers* [1909] 1 K.B. 310; *Edwin Hill & Partners v First National Finance Corp Plc* [1989] 1 W.L.R. 225.
[27] [1916] 2 K.B. 504.

that the licensing authority had not sought to cause the breach "for their own ends" (as required by *Lumley v Gye*) but had done so to serve a statutory purpose.

*Where the defendant has a moral or social duty to interfere with the contract*

In *Brimelow v Casson*[28] the defence of justification succeeded when the defendant (a trade union official) induced a number of women employed as actresses to breach their contracts of employment. The defendant argued that he was morally justified in taking this action because the women's wages were so low that they were compelled to supplement their income by prostitution.  **12–015**

This form of the defence, however, is of quite limited scope. It will not cover a situation where trade union officials merely seek to improve workers' wages or conditions,[29] and is probably confined to extreme circumstances such as those in *Brimelow v Casson* where (as Goff L.J. subsequently put it) "the conduct of the party whose contracts were interfered with was utterly disgraceful and the circumstances produced were in the nature of a public scandal."[30]

## CAUSING LOSS BY UNLAWFUL MEANS

The key elements of this tort were examined by Lord Hoffmann in *OBG v Allan*. His Lordship said:  **12–016**

> "The essence of the tort . . . appears to be (a) a wrongful interference with the actions of a third party in which the claimant has an economic interest and (b) an intention thereby to cause loss to the claimant."[31]

This general formulation can be taken to encompass the types of wrongdoing that were formerly regarded as the commission of the separate economic torts known as "interference with contractual relations" and "intimidation".

The "unlawful means tort" differs from the "*Lumley v Gye* tort" in that the defendant does not "join with" the third party in committing a wrong against the claimant. Rather, the defendant acts independently to bring about the claimant's loss by doing something unlawful vis-à-vis the third party, which affects the third party's ability to deal with the claimant. Liability for commission of the unlawful means tort is therefore primary or "stand alone" liability, rather than accessory liability.

In summary, to establish the unlawful means tort, the following three things must be shown:

- the defendant must take some action in relation to the third party which is "unlawful" in the relevant sense;

- the action in question must affect the third party's freedom to deal with the claimant;

- the defendant must intend to cause the claimant loss.

We consider each proposition in turn:

---

[28] [1924] 1 Ch.302.
[29] See *South Wales Miners' Federation v Glamorgan Coal Co Ltd* [1905] A.C. 239
[30] *Pritchard v Briggs* [1980] Ch.338 per Goff L.J. at 416.
[31] *OBG v Allan* [2007] UKHL 21 per Lord Hoffmann at para.47.

## The defendant's actions must be "unlawful" in the relevant sense

**12–017**  A memorable example of "unlawful" conduct towards third parties giving rise to liability is to be found in the early case of *Tarleton v McGawley*.[32] Here, the plaintiff, wishing to trade with the native inhabitants of Cameroon, had anchored his ship near the shore, loaded with trading goods. As the inhabitants approached the ship in their canoes, the defendant, the master of a rival trading ship, thought to secure their trade exclusively for himself. He therefore fired a cannon at them, intending to frighten them off and deter them from trading with the plaintiff. This unlawful act produced the desired effect, and the plaintiff suffered economic loss when the inhabitants refused to trade with him. The court held that the plaintiff could recover this loss from the defendant.

Under the modern law (somewhat confusingly perhaps), not every form of conduct that is against the law will count as "unlawful" for the purpose of establishing the tort of "causing loss by unlawful means".[33] As Lord Walker observed in *OBG v Allan*, in deciding what sort of actions should count as "unlawful" for this purpose, it is necessary for the law to identify a suitable control mechanism "to stop the notion of unlawful means getting out of hand". Otherwise (to use his Lordship's example) there might be liability in tort where, say, a pizza delivery business obtains more custom, to the detriment of its competitors, because its drivers regularly exceed the speed limit or jump red lights.[34]

The majority[35] in *OBG v Allan* agreed that a suitable way of confining the scope of the unlawful means tort was to insist that actions by the defendant will only count as "unlawful" if they are *actionable at the suit of the third party* (or, in an "intimidation" scenario—see below—are threats of doing something that would be so actionable).

Taking this approach rules out liability in Lord Walker's pizza delivery example, because the conduct in question, though it involves the commission of criminal offences, is not actionable at the suit of the third parties affected by it (the customers who buy pizzas with a faster delivery time, to the detriment of the claimant). Moreover, there can be no liability in such a case because the conduct in question does not affect the freedom of the third parties to deal with the claimant (see below)—the customers can still order a slower, lawfully-delivered pizza if they want to.

By contrast, such an approach would allow for liability in a case where (to extend Lord Walker's example) a pizza business prevented customers from contracting to buy pizzas from a rival by, say, unlawfully detaining the rival's customers or threatening them with violence.[36] This sort of unlawful conduct gives rise to a cause of action at the suit of the third parties (trespass to the person), and affects their freedom to deal with the claimant.

---

[32] (1794) 1 Peake 270.

[33] What makes matters more confusing is that what counts as "unlawful" for the purpose of this tort is different from what counts as "unlawful" for the purpose of establishing the tort of "unlawful means conspiracy" (discussed in later section).

[34] *OBG v Allan* [2007] UKHL 21 per Lord Walker at para.266.

[35] Lords Hoffmann, Brown and Baroness Hale. Lord Nicholls took an alternative line, based on the idea that the defendant must be said to cause the claimant's loss through the "instrumentality" of the third party. Lord Walker declined to prefer either approach.

[36] What would be the position if a pizza business unlawfully interfered with customers' phone calls, so as to prevent them ordering pizzas from a rival? This would (probably) not give rise to a cause of action at the suit of the customer, but it would prevent the customer from dealing with the claimant. Such an example shows us how, in some circumstances, the wider "instrumentality" test suggested by Lord Nicholls might be useful.

## The defendant's actions must affect the third party's freedom to deal with the claimant

This requirement explains why the courts have refused to impose liability in the so-called **12–018** "bootlegging" cases. In *RCA Corporation v Pollard*,[37] for example, the plaintiff company had the exclusive right to exploit records made by Elvis Presley. The defendant sold bootleg records that had been made without consent at Elvis concerts before his death. The plaintiff company claimed that this activity amounted to an unlawful interference with the contractual relationship between it and the Presley estate, and had the potential to cause the company loss, in the form of lost sales of authorised Elvis records. The Court of Appeal declined to hold the bootlegger liable for causing loss by unlawful means. Although bootleg recording was a criminal offence, it did not interfere with the Presley estate's freedom to deal with the company—it made no difference to the estate's ability to honour its contractual obligation to the company, because that obligation was merely an undertaking not to *consent* to the exploitation of Elvis recordings by persons other than the plaintiff. In other words, there could be no liability because, in spite of the bootlegger's activity, the third party (the estate) was still free to deal with the plaintiff on the same terms as it always had done.

## The defendant must intend to cause the claimant loss

Without an intention to cause the claimant loss, there can be no liability, even if the loss is the **12–019** inevitable result of the defendant's actions. Mere causative participation in the circumstances producing the loss will not suffice. Thus, for example, if you always drive to the supermarket on Saturday afternoons, but one Saturday I crash into your car—inevitably resulting in loss of custom for the supermarket—I will not, without more, be liable to the supermarket. This is because the essence of the unlawful means tort is that I must intend to "strike at" the supermarket through you—it will not be sufficient if I simply could not care less whether you get to the supermarket or not.

As with the *Lumley v Gye* tort, it is necessary here to distinguish between "ends, means and consequences". Intention will be established in the first two cases, but not in the third. In some cases, therefore, it will be sufficient if the defendant's principal desire (the "end") is personal enrichment, and injuring the claimant through the third party is only a means of achieving this end. Thus, as Lord Hoffmann explains in *OBG v Allan*, the ship's master who fired the cannon in *Tarleton v McGawley*:

> ". . . may have had nothing against the other trader. If he had gone off to make his fortune in other waters, he would have wished him well. He simply wanted a monopoly of the local trade for himself. But he nevertheless intended to cause him loss."[38]

By contrast, there will be no "intention" in cases where the loss is only a foreseeable consequence. For example, in *Barretts & Baird (Wholesale) Ltd v Institution of Professional Civil*

---

[37] [1983] Ch.135. See also *Ex p. Island Records* [1978] Ch.122; *Issac Oren v Red Box Toy Factory Ltd* [1999] F.S.R. 785.
[38] *OBG v Allan* [2007] UKHL 21 at para.63.

*Servants*[39] the defendant trade union called a strike by civil servants in the Ministry of Agriculture in support of a pay claim. As a result, the plaintiffs, an abattoir, were unable to obtain certificates necessary for exporting meat and claiming subsidies. The defendants could not be liable, however, because causing economic loss to the abattoir was neither the purpose of the strike nor was it desired as a means of achieving that purpose.

## Ways of committing the unlawful means tort

**12–020**   It will be instructive here to consider a number of scenarios in which, under the old law before *OBG v Allan*, the courts used to say that defendants were liable for committing the economic torts of "interference with contractual relations" and "intimidation". Considering these scenarios will show us how these old economic torts were really just different ways of committing the modern tort of causing loss by unlawful means.

*The "interference with contractual relations" scenarios*

**12–021**   Before *OBG v Allan*, it used to be said that there could be two, additional, "indirect" ways of committing the *Lumley v Gye* tort.[40] Thus, under the old law, the *Lumley v Gye* tort could actually be committed in three ways:

(1) The "classic" or "direct" form of the tort (the only form that now survives) was committed where the defendant made a direct approach to the third party and persuaded or procured ("induced") the third party to breach a contract with the claimant (as in *Lumley v Gye* itself).

(2) One of the (old) "indirect" forms was committed where the defendant brought about the breach by doing something else (other than "inducing") in relation to one of the contracting parties (e.g. taking away a party's tools so they could not perform the contract).[41]

(3) Another of the (old) "indirect" forms was committed where the defendant (a trade union) induced a breach of "Contract A" (e.g. between workers and employer), so as to prevent performance of "Contract B" (e.g. between employer and customer), intending to cause loss to the customer as a means of putting pressure on the employer.[42]

The courts had held that the "indirect" forms of the *Lumley v Gye* tort (scenarios 2 and 3) amounted to the commission of a tort called "interference with contractual relations". They had also held that it was a requirement in such cases that the defendant must have used "unlawful

---

[39] [1987] I.R.L.R. 3. Approved by Lord Hoffmann in *OBG v Allan* [2007] UKHL 21 at para.64.
[40] See, e.g., *DC Thomson & Co Ltd v Deakin* [1952] Ch.646, where the CA adopted the "unified theory" of liability under *Lumley v Gye*.
[41] This example is given by Jenkins L.J. in *Thomson & Co Ltd v Deakin* [1952] Ch.646 at 696. See also *GWK Ltd v Dunlop Rubber Co Ltd* (1926) 42 T.L.R. 376.
[42] See, e.g., *J.T. Stratford & Son Ltd v Lindley* [1965] A.C. 269. Note that an intention to injure the customer was here inferred from the fact that this was an inevitable result of the defendant's conduct. In the new language of *OBG v Allan*, it would have to be said that injuring the customer was a "means" of achieving the union's "end" (putting pressure on the employer) as opposed to a mere by-product of achieving that end. There is an obvious difficulty in distinguishing such a case from *Barretts & Baird (Wholesale) Ltd v Institution of Professional Civil Servants* [1987] I.R.L.R. 3 (considered above). Despite this, it appears that both decisions survive *OBG* (see Lord Hoffmann at paras 47 and 64).

means" to interfere with the contract—e.g. trespass to goods in scenario 2, or the "direct" form of the *Lumley v Gye* tort (which would suffice as "unlawful means") in scenario 3.

However, in *OBG v Allan*, Lord Hoffmann (with whom the majority agreed) stated:

> ". . . the distinction between direct and indirect interference is unsatisfactory and it is time for the unnatural union between the *Lumley* v *Gye* tort and the tort of causing loss by unlawful means to be dissolved."[43]

Nowadays, therefore, we can say, much more simply, that scenarios 2 and 3 are just examples of the tort of "causing loss by unlawful means". The wrongs in question are actionable because they meet the requirements of this tort, as set out in *OBG v Allan*, not because they represent "extensions" of the *Lumley v Gye* principle.

*The "intimidation" scenario*

The classic example of the old tort of "intimidation" is *Rookes v Barnard*.[44] The plaintiff was employed by BOAC. The three defendants were union officials. There was an informal agreement between the union and BOAC that all employees would belong to the union. When the plaintiff resigned from the union, the defendants threatened BOAC with an unlawful strike unless they dismissed him. BOAC gave in to this threat, and lawfully brought the plaintiff's contract to an end. Because he had been dismissed lawfully, the plaintiff, of course, had no remedy against BOAC for breach of contract. He therefore brought an action against the defendants. The House of Lords held that the defendants had committed the tort of intimidation against the plaintiff. This tort would be established where a defendant threatened to use unlawful means against a third party to compel that third party to act in such a way as to cause economic loss to the claimant.

**12–022**

If we re-examine *Rookes v Barnard*, using the language of *OBG v Allan*, we can see that its facts will fit within the rules for establishing the modern unlawful means tort. First, the threat of a strike would count as "unlawful" because, if it had been carried out, it would have been actionable as a breach of contract by the third party (BOAC). Secondly, the threat clearly affected BOAC's ability to deal with the plaintiff (they could no longer employ him). Lastly, the defendants clearly intended to cause loss to the plaintiff (have him dismissed), albeit that causing this loss was only a means of securing their primary objective of maintaining a union-only workforce.

## The modern torts applied: the *OBG v Allan* appeals

In *OBG v Allan* the House of Lords decided three appeals. It will be convenient here to note how the modern torts were applied in the factual context of each case.

**12–023**

*Mainstream Properties Ltd v Young*

Here, two employees of the claimant property company, in breach of their contracts of employment, diverted a development opportunity to another company which they ran. The defendant, who provided financial assistance for this transaction, knew that the employees worked under

**12–024**

---

[43] *OBG v Allan* [2007] UKHL 21 per Lord Hoffmann at para.38.
[44] [1964] A.C. 1129.

contracts with the claimant company, but accepted the employees' assurances that their involvement in the transaction would not put them in breach of those contracts. Their Lordships dismissed the claimant company's contention that the defendant's actions should amount to inducing a breach of contract. On the facts, whilst the defendant had known about the existence of the contracts, he had not known (or turned a blind eye to) their terms. Therefore, it could not be said that he had intended to cause the breaches.

*OBG v Allan*

**12–025**   In this case, the defendants were official receivers, who, it turned out, had been wrongly appointed. Acting in good faith, however, the receivers took control of the claimants' company and so caused them loss that would not have resulted if the company had continued to trade normally. The claimants argued that the receivers' actions amounted not only to trespass to their land and conversion of their goods,[45] but to the commission of an economic tort involving interference with contractual relations. Their Lordships held that, under the rules of the modern unlawful means tort, such a claim could not succeed. The receivers had not done anything unlawful (in the relevant sense) when dealing with the company's assets. Moreover, since they had acted in good faith, the receivers had not intended to cause loss to the claimants.

*Douglas v Hello!*

**12–026**   This appeal concerned the publication of wedding photographs of the film-stars Michael Douglas and Catherine Zeta-Jones. The magazine "OK!" had contracted with the Douglases for the exclusive right to publish photos of the wedding. The defendants—a rival magazine called "Hello!"—published photographs that it knew had been taken secretly at the wedding by an unauthorised photographer pretending to be a waiter. This, of course, deprived "OK!" of their "scoop" and caused them loss, in the form of lost magazine sales. "OK!" claimed that "Hello!" were liable for misuse of confidential information,[46] and also for the tort of causing loss by unlawful means. Their Lordships held that the unlawful means claim could not succeed. The defendants' actions in publishing the secret pictures had not interfered with the third parties' ability to deal with the claimant (the Douglases were not actually prevented from honouring their agreement to supply "OK!" with wedding pictures). This meant that one of the essential ingredients for establishing the modern tort was missing.

## CONSPIRACY

**12–027**   The tort of conspiracy[47] has two forms:

- unlawful means conspiracy

- lawful means conspiracy (also known as "conspiracy to injure" or "simple conspiracy").

[45] The claimants also sought to extend the tort of conversion to cover choses in action (i.e. their outstanding contractual claims at the time the receivers were appointed). However, the majority (Lord Nicholls and Baroness Hale dissenting) declined to extend the scope of this tort.
[46] The majority (Lords Nicholls and Walker dissenting) held that the breach of confidence claim should succeed. This aspect of the case is discussed in Ch.15.
[47] Conspiracy as a tort is not to be confused with criminal conspiracy, which has different rules. See *Meretz Investments v ACP Ltd* [2007] EWCA Civ 1303 at para.174 per Toulson L.J.

Both forms share the requirement that two or more defendants must "combine" with a common purpose so as to cause the claimant loss. Usually, this means that the defendants will *agree* to pursue a common course of action, but there is no need for an express agreement between them.[48]

## Unlawful means conspiracy

This tort is committed where two or more defendants act together with a shared intention of using "unlawful means" to cause loss to the claimant.[49] Until quite recently, the rules of this tort were rather uncertain. Much ink had been spilt by judges and academics alike in discussing two things:                                                                              **12–028**

- What degree of "intention" should be required?
- What should count as "unlawful means"?

It will be helpful to examine these two issues in the light of a number of recent decisions that have clarified the law.

*What must the conspirators intend?*

A distinction must first be drawn between the different degrees of intention required for the two different forms of conspiracy. To establish "lawful means conspiracy" (discussed below) the conspirators must intend to injure the claimant in the sense that this is their *predominant purpose*. (This effectively limits the application of "lawful means conspiracy" to very rare situations where the defendants act purely out of malice.) However, to establish "unlawful means conspiracy" it is sufficient if the conspirators "intend" to injure the claimant in the wider *OBG v Allan* sense that they intend to do so only as a *means* of achieving an *end* (usually their own enrichment).[50] It is clear from the decision of the Court of Appeal in *Meretz Investments v ACP Ltd*[51] that what is said in *OBG v Allan* about intention in the context of the "causing loss by unlawful means" tort applies equally in the context of "unlawful means conspiracy". Thus, the conspirators must intend not simply that unlawful means will be used—they must also *intend to cause the claimant loss*.                                       **12–029**

Although the conspirators must share the relevant degree of intention,[52] they do not all have to share the same degree of participation in the use of the unlawful means. Indeed, the whole purpose of invoking the tort of conspiracy is to attribute to all conspirators responsibility for actions committed by other members of the conspiracy. Thus, for example, where A and B conspire to ruin C's business by shooting all his customers, but B acts alone in firing the gun, A may be liable to C in conspiracy, even though A has not committed the unlawful act.[53] In

---

[48] *Belmont Finance Corp v Williams Furniture Ltd (No.2)* [1980] 1 All E.R. 393.

[49] See, e.g., *Tullett Prebon Plc v BGC Brokers LP* [2011] EWCA Civ 131; *Bank of Tokyo-Mitsubishi UFJ Ltd v Baskan Gida Sanayi Ve Pazarlama AS* [2009] EWHC 1276; *Digicel (St Lucia) Ltd v Cable & Wireless Plc* [2010] EWHC 774.

[50] *Lonrho Plc v Fayed* [1992] 1 A.C. 448.

[51] [2007] EWCA Civ 1303.

[52] Arguably, a conspirator who has played some part in the proceedings but lacks the required degree of intention might be liable on the basis that other conspirators have that intention. This is doubtful, however, because it would involve the proposition that persons can be liable for being in a combination without a true meeting of their minds.

[53] Responsibility may be attributed on the basis of the "common enterprise" principle. See *Brook v Bool* [1928] 2 K.B. 578.

this example, of course, one of the conspirators (B) has also committed the tort of "causing loss by unlawful means". Invoking the tort of conspiracy here simply has the effect of creating secondary liability for that tort, and so widening the class of potential defendants.

In the recent past, it was sometimes said that "unlawful means conspiracy" was a tort of rather limited usefulness, because its only function seemed to be to impose secondary liability for committing the tort of "causing loss by unlawful means". In other words, whenever the tort was invoked, it was merely an "added extra", because one or more of the conspirators would turn out to be liable anyway for "causing loss by unlawful means".[54] However, the recent House of Lords decision in *Total Network SL v Revenue and Customs Commissioners*[55] shows us that the tort is, in fact, much more useful than this. First, it can be used in situations where it is extremely unlikely that a single defendant acting alone would have been able to cause the loss in question. Secondly, because of the extended meaning given to the phrase "unlawful means", it can be used in situations where none of the conspirators has actually committed the unlawful means tort.

*What counts as "unlawful means" for the purpose of establishing this tort?*

**12–030**     In *Total Network SL v Revenue and Customs Commissioners* the defendants had perpetrated a complex VAT fraud—known as a "carousel fraud"—with the intention of obtaining tax rebates from the Revenue to which they were not entitled. For technical reasons, the Revenue were unable to use statutory procedures to reclaim the money they had wrongly paid out. They therefore sought to recover the money in an action for "unlawful means conspiracy". The Court of Appeal thought that, in principle, such an action ought to succeed. The problem, however, was that what the defendants had done, although a criminal offence, was not actionable in civil law as a tort. This meant that, according to existing authority,[56] it could not qualify as "unlawful means" for the purpose of establishing the tort. The relevant cases had held (as in *OBG v Allan*) that not every illegal act would count as "unlawful means"—an act would only count as "unlawful" if it was unlawful in the special sense of being actionable in civil law. The Court of Appeal therefore felt constrained to decide the issue in the defendants' favour, but gave leave to the Revenue to appeal to the House of Lords.

In the House of Lords, Lord Walker observed that the development of the economic torts had been "a long and difficult process" that had resulted in some confusion. A particular difficulty, he said, was that:

> ". . . it has been generally assumed, throughout the 20th-century cases, that "unlawful means" should have the same meaning in the intentional harm tort and in the tort of conspiracy".[57]

His Lordship went on to explain, however, that this assumption was unnecessary—there was no reason why "unlawful means" could not mean different things for the purposes of the two different torts.

---

[54] See, e.g. per Lord Devlin in *Rookes v Barnard* [1964] A.C. 1129, at 1204: ". . . the element of conspiracy is usually only of secondary importance since the unlawful means are actionable by themselves."

[55] [2008] UKHL 19.

[56] *Powell v Boladz* [1998] Lloyd's Med. Rep. 116.

[57] *Total Network SL v Revenue and Customs Commissioners* [2008] UKHL 19 per Lord Walker at para.89. His Lordship uses the phrase "intentional harm tort" to mean what we (and their Lordships in *OBG v Allan*) refer to as the tort of "causing loss by unlawful means".

Following this reasoning, the House of Lords concluded that, in the context of the tort of "unlawful means conspiracy", the phrase "unlawful means" can have a wider meaning than it does in the context of the tort of "causing loss by unlawful means". For the latter tort, following *OBG v Allan*, the defendant's actions must be "unlawful" in the special sense that they are actionable in civil law by the party against whom they are directed, and affect that party's ability to deal with the claimant. However, this restrictive meaning of "unlawful" does not apply in the context of "unlawful means conspiracy"—it will be sufficient to establish this tort if the conspirators have merely done something unlawful in the wider sense, like committing a crime. On this basis, the defendants in the case could be held liable.

The problem with their Lordships' approach in *Total Network SL*, of course, is that it raises the prospect of widespread liability for unlawful means conspiracy. It will be recalled that, in *OBG v Allan*, Lord Walker noted that a restricted definition of "unlawful means" was needed in order to stop liability for "causing loss by unlawful means" from getting out of hand. Thus, where a pizza delivery business employs motorcyclists who exceed the speed limit and jump red lights (criminal offences), intending to take custom away from a rival, no action will lie, because the "unlawful means" in question are not actionable in civil law. But what if (as seems not unlikely) the owners, managers, chefs and motorcycle-riders involved in the defendant pizza business are all acting in combination, with a common intention to enrich themselves at the claimant's expense by breaking the law? Surely then we have an "unlawful means conspiracy" in the terms allowed by *Total Network SL*?

There are potentially two ways in which this problem of expansive liability might be avoided. The first is to confine the application of the new, wider, meaning of "unlawful means" to situations where the criminal offences committed are breaches of criminal laws *designed specifically for the protection of the claimant's interests*. On this basis, it would, as in *Total Network SL*, be a conspiracy where defendants combine to defraud the Revenue by committing the offence of common law "cheat" (specifically preserved in revenue cases by Theft Act 1968 s.32(1)(a)) because the very reason that offence exists is to protect the Revenue from loss of money. On the other hand, it would not be a conspiracy to combine to exceed the speed limit or jump red lights with an intention to injure the claimant's business, because the criminal offences in question are not designed to protect the claimant from economic loss, but to serve very different purposes.

The second possibility is that the application of the tort in its wider form could be limited to "two-party" situations—as in *Total Network SL* itself—where the conspirators use the "unlawful means" in question directly against the claimants, rather than—as in the pizza example—against third parties (customers, or other road users) with the purpose of "striking at" the claimant's business through the third parties. The reasoning of their Lordships in *Total Network SL* suggests that either or both of these approaches might serve as a suitable control mechanism to confine the scope of liability in future cases.

## Lawful means conspiracy

The anomalous tort of "lawful means conspiracy" is committed where two or more persons in combination cause loss to the claimant by acts that would be perfectly lawful if done by one person alone. Essentially, the tort makes defendants liable for "ganging up" on the claimant for no good reason and exercising their (lawful) rights in such a way as to cause the claimant loss. The tort's distinguishing feature is that, to establish liability, it must be shown that **12–031** causing the claimant loss is the defendants' *predominant purpose*—if it can be shown that their predominant purpose was to achieve some other objective (e.g. their own enrichment) there will be no liability.[58] (In the language of *OBG v Allan*, it will not be sufficient if the defendants intend to injure the claimant only as a means of achieving an end—they must intend to injure the claimant as an end in itself.) Thus, the tort could not apply in a case like *Mogul Steamship Co Ltd v McGregor, Gow & Co*—which we considered at the beginning of this chapter—because the predominant purpose of the defendants in that case was to further their own interests by gaining a monopoly in the tea trade—intentionally driving the plaintiff out of business was just the means of achieving that goal.

Of course, this restrictive "predominant purpose" requirement makes the tort very difficult to establish. It was, however, said to have been established by the House of Lords in the turn-of-the-century case of *Quinn v Leathem*,[59] where a number of butchers (at the behest of their trade union) agreed to inflict economic loss on the plaintiff (who was employing non-union workers) by exercising their lawful entitlement not to handle the plaintiff's meat. Subsequent attempts to establish the tort have not been so successful. For example, in *Crofter Hand Woven Harris Tweed Co Ltd v Veitch*,[60] dock workers lawfully refused to handle the plaintiffs' machine-spun imported yarn. Their hope was that preventing mill-owners from obtaining such yarn would advance the pay claims of workers in traditional mills (using hand-spun, home-produced yarn) who were members of the dock workers' union. It was held that the plaintiffs had no cause of action against the dock workers, whose "predominant purpose" had not been to injure the plaintiffs but to further the interests of their fellow union members.[61]

It may seem strange that liability should ever attach to lawful acts simply because they are done in concert with others. The traditional rationale for such liability, as expressed by Bowen L.J. in *Mogul Steamship Co Ltd v McGregor, Gow & Co* (when that case was before the Court of Appeal) is that:

> ". . . a combination may make oppressive or dangerous that which if it proceeded only from a single person would be otherwise."[62]

In *Lonrho v Shell*,[63] however, Lord Diplock pointed out that such a proposition is really quite absurd when seen in the context of the modern business world. His Lordship said:

> ". . . to suggest today that acts done by one street-corner grocer in concert with a second are more oppressive and dangerous to a competitor than the same acts done by a string of supermarkets under a single ownership or that a multinational conglomerate such as Lonrho or oil company such as Shell or B.P. does not exercise greater economic power than any combination of small businesses, is to shut one's eyes to what has been happening in the business and industrial world since the turn of the century."

---

[58] See *Lonrho Plc v Fayed* [1992] A.C. 448.

[59] [1901] A.C. 495.

[60] [1942] A.C. 435.

[61] Compare *Huntley v Thornton* [1957] 1 W.L.R. 321. Union officials were liable when they sought to prevent the plaintiff from getting a job, after losing their argument with the union that he should be expelled. Harman J. (at 340) found that the officials had not acted to further the union's interest, but to uphold "their own ruffled dignity", and this did not qualify as a legitimate ulterior purpose.

[62] *Mogul Steamship Co Ltd v McGregor, Gow & Co* (1889) 23 Q.B.D. 598, CA per Bowen L.J. at 616.

[63] [1982] A.C. 173.

His Lordship concluded, however, by saying:

> "The civil tort of conspiracy to injure . . . must I think be accepted by this House as too well-established to be discarded however anomalous it may seem today."

The application of the tort is not extensively considered in either *OBG v Allan* or *Total Network SL*. On the other hand, its continued existence is not doubted by their Lordships. Conceivably, therefore, it remains applicable in very special circumstances.

## The economic torts: conclusion

We have seen that the economic torts, though complex, have gained a good deal of coherence from recent House of Lords decisions. Thanks to modern industrial-relations legislation, these torts no longer serve so directly one of the main purposes for which they were developed—the regulation of trade union activity. However, it is clear that they still have an important function in setting the boundaries of acceptable commercial conduct.     **12–032**

# Chapter 13

# DEFAMATION

## Introduction

Defamation is a different type of tort from those examined in earlier chapters. It does not **13–001** protect the personal safety of the individual or even the personal integrity and right to self-determination of the claimant. It protects something far more indistinct: the reputation of the claimant. On this basis, while abuse of the claimant in private can only give rise to liability for harassment or possibly assault, unjustified criticism of the claimant to another, which makes society think less of the claimant, gives rise to the tort of defamation. It is the claimant's reputation, not injured feelings, which the tort aims to protect.

The tort raises a number of difficult problems. For example, a basic democratic right stated in art.10 of the European Convention on Human Rights is the right to freedom of expression, which includes the right to "hold opinions and to receive and impart information and ideas without interference by public authority". Article 10 is now incorporated into English law by the Human Rights Act 1998 and s.6 of the Act provides that it is unlawful for a public authority (which includes courts) to act in a way which is incompatible with a Convention right.[1] Freedom of expression includes the right to criticise, and is particularly important in relation to politicians and officials who occupy positions of power. This is further supported by s.12 of the 1998 Act which provides that when a court is considering whether to grant any relief which, if granted, might affect the exercise of freedom of expression, it must have particular regard to the importance of this right and, inter alia, the public interest in the publishing of such material by the press.[2]

On the other hand, the reader will be fully aware of the frequent complaints of press intrusion and irresponsible reporting where journalists, anxious for a "scoop" in a very competitive media market, publish without fully checking their facts. Unfortunately the old adage that "there is no smoke without fire" still applies, and a person mistakenly named as a serial rapist is unlikely to fight the corner of freedom of expression. Article 10.2 of the Convention recognises that the right to freedom of expression cannot go unchallenged. Such a right:

---

[1] The Act came into force on October 2, 2000.
[2] See s.12(1) and (4).

"carries with it duties and responsibilities [and so] may be subject to such formalities, conditions, restrictions or penalties as are prescribed by law and are necessary in a democratic society . . . for the protection of the reputation or rights of others".

The law of defamation must therefore attempt to balance the competing rights of freedom of expression and protection of one's reputation. This is a far from easy task and, unfortunately for the reader, has led to a complex and frequently confusing area of law. This will be examined below.

We will approach defamation in four logical stages. This aids clarity and helps to minimise the difficulties outlined above. Four main questions must be addressed:

(a)  Is the statement defamatory?

(b)  Does it refer to the claimant?

(c)  Has it been published?

(d)  Do any of the defences apply?

These will be considered in this and the following chapter. This chapter will focus on the first three stages, establishing when a claimant can bring an action for defamation and who can sue and be sued. Chapter 14 will set out the defences available to defendants, particularly in the light of the Defamation Act 1996 and the important House of Lords judgment in *Reynolds v Times Newspapers Ltd*.[3] It will also consider alternatives to defamation law (for example the tort of malicious falsehood[4]) and the ability of regulatory bodies such as the Press Complaints Commission to deal with complaints of media excess.

The first step must, however, be to examine the long-standing division of defamation into two parts: libel and slander. Both are examples of defamation, but for historical reasons are treated separately. It would make life easier for all if this distinction were abolished (unless the reader has a particular desire to maintain a distinction logical in Tudor times, but sadly not our own), but this does not appear to be imminent. Abolition has been suggested from 1843 without success[5] and it is therefore unlikely to occur in the near future. The distinction will therefore be examined below.

## LIBEL AND SLANDER

13–002     These torts are generally distinguished on the basis that libel takes permanent form, for example, an article or a photograph published in a daily newspaper,[6] while slander is temporary, for example words shouted across a classroom or gestures made to a crowd.[7] The permanency of libel is deemed to make it more serious—more people will possibly see it and it will

---

[3] [2001] 2 A.C. 127.

[4] A claimant may also wish to consider an action in negligence or breach of confidence. See Chs 2 and 15.

[5] See, in particular, Ch.2 of the report of the Faulks Committee in 1975 (Report of the Committee on Defamation, Cmnd 5909).

[6] Or even a waxwork: *Monson v Tussauds Ltd* [1894] 1 Q.B. 671, CA.

[7] It is generally suggested that sign language would be treated as slander.

not be forgotten. Damage is presumed,[8] and libel is therefore actionable *per se* (i.e. without proof of damage). Slander, in contrast, requires proof of special damage, which can be proved by evidence of financial loss or any other material loss capable of estimation in financial terms. Being shunned by friends is not sufficient. However, being shunned by clients will suffice, due to the financial impact on your business.[9] The damage must, as always, not be too remote. In defamation cases, the test for remoteness, as stated by *Lynch v Knight*,[10] is that the loss is such as might fairly and reasonably on the facts of the case have been anticipated and feared to result. Libel, unlike slander, is also a crime, although few prosecutions are brought.

Unfortunately, the distinction between libel and slander is far from watertight. A spoken insult in the presence of your peers may do more harm to your reputation than insults in a disreputable newspaper. The distinction may also be quite complicated. For example, I dictate a letter to my secretary who then posts it. It contains defamatory material. On the current case law, the letter once sent amounts to libel for which I am responsible, but my dictation to the secretary is merely slander.[11] Further problems arise if you consider what happens if the spoken words are recorded on tape: do they now amount to libel? What about insulting words in a long-running play—can they really be considered slander when repeated every night? In the latter case, Parliament has helpfully intervened and stated that performances of a play (except when given on a domestic occasion in a private dwelling) shall be treated as publication in permanent form and therefore libel.[12] Equally, broadcasts on television or on radio are treated as libel.[13] *Youssoupoff v MGM Pictures Ltd*[14] deals somewhat confusingly with our first problem. Here, a Russian Princess complained about words used in the film soundtrack to "Rasputin, the Mad Monk", which she claimed had falsely suggested that she had been raped or seduced by Rasputin. The court took the view that speech which was synchronised with the film took a permanent form and should be treated as libel. Logically, therefore, if the film broke down but the words continued it would be slander. Yet, this ignores the fact that although the words are merely heard, they are permanently recorded which, it is submitted, suggests that they should be considered to be libel. Further examples of unresolved problems include whether writing in chalk on a wall[15] or sky-writing by aeroplanes[16] amounts to libel or slander. Such uncertainty, it is submitted, is as good a reason as any for abolishing the distinction between libel and slander.

---

[8] See *Jameel v Dow Jones & Co Inc* [2005] EWCA Civ 75; [2005] Q.B. 946 in which the Court of Appeal held that the presumption of damage is compatible with art.10: "It would not be right to abandon this principle in the absence of a convincing case that it is in conflict with article 10 of the Convention" per Lord Phillips of Worth Matravers MR at para.37.

[9] See *Storey v Challands* (1837) 8 Car. & P. 234; 173 E.R. 475 and *McManus v Beckham* [2002] EWCA Civ 939; [2002] 1 W.L.R. 2982.

[10] (1861) 9 H.L.Cas. 577 at 600; 11 E.R. 854 (Lord Wensleydale).

[11] *Osborn v Thomas Boulter & Son* [1930] 2 K.B. 226.

[12] Theatres Act 1968 s.4(1).

[13] Broadcasting Act 1990 s.166.

[14] (1934) 50 T.L.R. 581.

[15] See *Monson v Tussauds Ltd* (1894) 1 Q.B. 671 at 692 which suggests it should be treated as libel.

[16] The Faulks Committee at para.76 suggested that it would be libel due to the fact that the vapour takes some time to disperse.

## Types of slander actionable per se

**13–003**   Further remnants of the past are the four occasions where slander is actionable without proof of damage. These represent occasions where the court feels safe in presuming damage, because of the nature of the allegations made.

*(1)  Imputation of a criminal offence punishable by imprisonment*

**13–004**   There must be an imputation that a criminal offence has been committed. For example, in *Webb v Beavan*,[17] it was stated that "I will look you up in Gloucester gaol next week. I know enough to put you there". This was held to imply that a criminal offence had been committed and so was actionable per se. An allegation that an individual is suspected of a criminal offence will not suffice.[18]

*(2)  Imputation of a contagious disease*

**13–005**   This, with the rise of AIDS, could have some contemporary relevance. An accusation that a physician has AIDS or is HIV positive would clearly harm the reputation of the physician. However, the last reported case brought under this head was in 1844,[19] which removes its topicality somewhat. The rule has been used in relation to diseases such as venereal disease, leprosy and plague, but it must be questioned whether, with advances in medicine, this exception ought to survive when it can no longer be assumed that people with contagious diseases will be shunned.

*(3)  Imputation of unchastity or adultery by a female*

**13–006**   This is stated to be actionable per se under s.1 of the Slander of Women Act 1891. In modern times, it seems very outdated and potentially discriminatory.

The Government in 2011[20] expressed its intention to repeal this provision and category (2) above (imputation of a contagious disease) in its proposed Repeals Bill.[21]

*(4)  Imputation of professional unfitness or incompetence*

**13–007**   This is the only exception with any contemporary relevance (and on which there are reported cases in the last 100 years). A statement criticising a person's professional competence or fitness for office may affect his or her reputation and will be difficult to brush off. The only question which has arisen here relates to the scope of the exception. At common law, it was held that the accusation had to relate directly to the person's professional competence. The exception therefore did not apply where the accusation was unrelated to the post, for example where a headmaster was accused of committing adultery with one of the school's cleaners.[22] The exception was broadened by s.2 of the Defamation Act 1952 to include all words likely to disparage the claimant's official, professional or business reputation, whether or not the words relate to the claimant's office, profession, calling, trade or business.

---

[17]  (1883) 11 Q.B.D. 609.
[18]  *Simmons v Mitchell* (1880) 6 App. Cas. 156, PC.
[19]  *Bloodworth v Gray* (1844) 7 Man. & Gr. 334; 135 E.R. 140 (venereal disease).
[20]  See *Draft Defamation Bill Consultation* (Consultation Paper CP3/11) at 9.
[21]  See Ministry of Justice, 'Business Plan 2011–2015' (November 2010).
[22]  *Jones v Jones* [1916] 2 A.C. 481. Applied in *Hopwood v Muirson* [1945] K.B. 313 (solicitor criticised whilst acting as referee for friend).

As may be seen, the distinction between libel and slander still has a basis at law, although its rationale is questionable. It has been suggested that it excludes minor claims for slander where the claimant has suffered little harm, but in reality the cost of bringing a defamation claim, and procedural rules against vexatious litigants, are likely to deter such claimants in any event.

## THE GENERAL REQUIREMENTS OF DEFAMATION

As stated above, the best way of approaching defamation is by logically answering the following four questions:                                                           **13–008**

- Is the statement defamatory?
- Does it refer to the claimant?
- Has it been published to a third party?
- Can the defendant rely on any of the defences?

## The role of the judge and jury

An action for defamation, unlike one for negligence, will usually be heard by a judge and jury, unless the court is of the opinion that the trial requires any prolonged examination of documents or accounts, or any scientific or local investigation which cannot conveniently be made with a jury.[23] The judge will determine, as a matter of law, whether the words are capable of being defamatory, that is, could a reasonable jury come to the conclusion that the statement was capable of bearing a defamatory meaning?[24] The jury will determine whether, as a matter of fact, the words in the case are defamatory. The jury will also determine the level of damages and may, if appropriate, award aggravated or punitive damages.                      **13–009**

The first three questions will be examined in this chapter. Defences will be examined in Ch.14.

## (1) Is the statement defamatory?

The statement is defamatory if it harms a person's reputation. It is more difficult, however, to state exactly when a person's reputation will be harmed. The classic definition is found in *Sim v Stretch*,[25] where statements were held to be defamatory and therefore to harm a person's reputation when they "tend to lower the plaintiff in the estimation of right-thinking members of society generally".[26] This has been extended by *Youssoupoff v MGM Pictures Ltd*[27] to    **13–010**

---

[23] Senior Courts Act 1981 s.69. See *Beta Construction Ltd v Channel Four Television Co Ltd* [1990] 1 W.L.R. 1042, CA and *Armstrong v Times Newspapers Ltd (No.2)* [2006] EWCA Civ 519; [2006] 1 W.L.R. 2462.
[24] *Capital and Counties Bank Ltd v Henty* (1882) 7 App. Cas. 741, although the application of the test in this case is less than satisfactory. See also *Mark v Associated Newspapers Ltd* [2002] EWCA Civ 772; [2002] E.M.L.R. 38, CA.
[25] [1936] 2 All E.R. 1237.
[26] [1936] 2 All E.R. 1237 at 1240, HL per Lord Atkin. This presumes that the claimant's reputation can be lowered: see *Williams v MGN Ltd* [2009] EWHC 3150 (QB) claimant in a libel action with a background of serious criminal convictions had no reputation capable of protection.
[27] (1934) 50 T.L.R. 581. See L. Treiger-Bar-Am (2000) 20 L.S. 291.

circumstances where the claimant is "shunned or avoided" as a result of the statements. The question is therefore whether your reputation has been harmed in the eyes of "right-thinking members of society". Essentially, this is the standard of the "reasonable person", who is, of course, a fiction, but this sets at least an objective standard to be applied by the courts. The reasonable person, we are told, is fair-minded, neither unduly suspicious nor unduly naive, nor avid for scandal, nor bound to select one defamatory meaning when non-defamatory meanings are available.[28] In practice, it will be determined partly by the judge, who decides whether the statement in question is capable of being defamatory before it can be put before a jury. This can raise questions as to the ability of the courts to relate to the standards of society in general. For example, in *Byrne v Deane*,[29] a verse had been placed on the notice-board of a golf club which stated: "But he who gave the game away, may he byrnne [*sic*] in hell and rue the day". Mr Byrne, who was a member of the club, alleged that it implied that he had informed the police of certain illegal gambling machines which had been on the premises and which had been removed as a result. The Court of Appeal held that the verse was not defamatory. An allegation that he had reported a crime to the police could not be regarded as lowering the reputation of Mr Byrne, certainly not in the eyes of a "good and worthy subject of the King". The resulting distress and perhaps isolation suffered by Mr Byrne as a result of the verse were regarded as irrelevant. There is therefore a distinct danger that the standard of "right-thinking people" may rise far above the general standards of society, and fail to protect the claimant's reputation adequately by assuming that right-thinking people could not possibly conclude that a particular statement is defamatory.

Further difficulties may be seen when this test is applied to allegations of adultery and homosexuality. Whilst clearly defamatory in the past, it might be suggested that in more liberal times, they would no longer affect a person's reputation. The court must choose between a liberal approach and an appreciation that such a view may not be shared by every member of society. Who, then, is the right-thinking member of society? In *R. v Bishop*,[30] the court recognised that the legalisation of homosexuality in the Sexual Offences Act 1967 did not necessarily change the views of society, and that, in 1975, many still regarded homosexuality as immoral. It is an open question whether this is still the case today. Arguably, the situation is different for adultery. In a society where one in three marriages fail, one might expect a more tolerant view of adultery and sex outside marriage. On this basis, a statement that X is an adulterer should not be regarded as defamatory, unless it suggests that X is a hypocrite, for example, he is a clergyman or the Minister for the Family. It should be remembered, however, that provided the judge rules that the statement is capable of being defamatory, it is the jury who finally resolves whether the statement is, in fact, defamatory. It is to be hoped that the jury will reflect current trends in society when reaching its decision.

**13–011**    It should also be noted that it is no excuse that the defendant did not intend the words to be defamatory.[31] The law protects reputation and it cannot be said that the statement does not

---

[28] See *Lewis v Daily Telegraph* [1964] A.C. 234 at 259–260 per Lord Reid. Society would appear to signify society as a whole and not simply a section of the community: *Tolley v Fry* [1930] 1 K.B. 467 at 479. It has been suggested that, in view of the more diverse nature of society today and the fact that the reputation of a person within his or her own racial or religious community may be damaged by a statement which would not be regarded as damaging by society at large, this may need to be re-addressed in future: *Arab News Network v Al-Khazen* [2001] EWCA Civ 118.

[29] [1937] 1 K.B. 818 at 833.

[30] [1975] Q.B. 274 at 281. The case itself concerned the admissibility of character evidence.

[31] The intention of the defendant may, however, be relevant in relation to possible defences (see Ch.14) or at least diminish the award of damages.

affect the claimant's reputation just because the insult was unintentional. The test is objective, and it is irrelevant that the defendant did not intend to defame the claimant, or even whether the people to whom the statement was communicated actually believed the statement to be true.[32] The defendant may, however, be able to claim that the words should not be treated as defamatory because the statement was mere abuse uttered in rage ("You idiot!") and was not intended to be taken seriously. This is a very fine line. While the courts may be prepared to disregard words spoken in the heat of the moment, which the hearer must have understood to be mere abuse, they are unlikely to dismiss written words on this basis. The general view is that the writer will have had the opportunity to cool down and repent, so that if the words are published nevertheless, they cannot be dismissed as mere abuse. In *Berkoff v Burchill*,[33] the majority of the Court of Appeal held that a published description of the actor, director and writer Steven Berkoff as "hideously ugly" was capable of being defamatory and could not be dismissed as mere abuse. He was a person in the public eye and it was held that such a description would expose him to ridicule as it suggested that he had a repulsive appearance.

Defamation is not confined to direct attacks on the claimant's reputation. If this were so, a defendant could easily resort to indirect attacks, safe in the knowledge that the audience would be well aware of what was actually being alleged, and yet the claimant could do nothing. To protect the claimant's reputation, defamation must also include implied or veiled attacks, which are generally known as "innuendo".

*Innuendo*

An innuendo consists of an implied attack on a person's reputation. The test is objective: **13–012** what view would a reasonable person take of the statement? There are two types of innuendo: true (or legal) and false (or popular). A true innuendo is one where the attack is truly hidden in the absence of special facts and circumstances, which the claimant must show are known by some of the people to whom the statement is published. The court will obviously have to be informed in the Statement of Case what special meanings are alleged and what facts support this meaning.[34] A false or popular innuendo is one which a reasonable person guided by general knowledge would infer from the natural and ordinary meaning of the words.[35] The court does not have to be informed of any specific facts to draw this inference. This is a complicated distinction, and an example will help the reader to understand the distinction between true and false innuendo. Suppose that A publishes a statement that B works for "the family business". By itself, this is not defamatory unless:

(i) B's father has been arrested for involvement with the Mafia. With this extra knowledge, we now know that A is implying that B works for the Mafia and is involved in organised crime. This is defamatory as a true innuendo

---

[32] See *Morgan v Odhams Press* [1971] 1 W.L.R. 1239 at 1246 and 1252.

[33] [1996] 4 All E.R. 1008. But contrast *Norman v Future Publishing Ltd* [1999] E.M.L.R. 325, CA.

[34] Practice Direction–Defamation Claims Pt 53, r.2.3 of the Civil Procedure Rules (CPR): "(1) The claimant must specify in the particulars of claim the defamatory meaning which he alleges that the words or matters complained of conveyed, both (a) as to their natural and ordinary meaning; and (b) as to any innuendo meaning (that is a meaning alleged to be conveyed to some person by reason of knowing facts extraneous to the words complained of) and (2) In the case of an innuendo meaning, the claimant must also identify the relevant extraneous facts."

[35] See, generally, *Lewis v Daily Telegraph Ltd* [1964] A.C. 234 at 271–272 per Lord Hodson.

(ii) B can show that the term "family business" is known to be a slang term for the Mafia. This is unlikely here, but if B were successful, he would be relying on a false or popular innuendo.

A true innuendo was relied upon in *Tolley v J.S. Fry & Sons Ltd*,[36] where a famous amateur golfer alleged that a caricature of him had appeared without his knowledge or consent in an advertisement for Frys Chocolate. This, in itself, was not defamatory. However, Tolley claimed that for people who knew of his amateur status it would imply that, contrary to acceptable amateur conduct, he had accepted money. The House of Lords held the advertisement to be capable of bearing the meaning alleged in the innuendo. People knowing of Tolley's amateur status might think less of him and therefore his reputation would be diminished.[37] Equally, in *Cassidy v Daily Mirror Newspapers Ltd*,[38] there was nothing defamatory in publishing a photograph depicting Cassidy and a young woman announcing that they were engaged. However the fact that Mr Cassidy was still married led the majority of the Court of Appeal to recognise that the words were defamatory of the existing Mrs Cassidy, on the basis that a reasonable person knowing of their relationship might assume that she had cohabited with Cassidy outside marriage. This, in 1928, would be regarded in a negative light. It was no excuse that the newspaper did not know that Cassidy was already married, and had in fact been told by Cassidy that he was engaged to the woman with whom he had been photographed.

*Lewis v Daily Telegraph Ltd*[39] is a good illustration of how courts deal with a false innuendo. Here, the defendants had published a paragraph in their newspaper which indicated that the Fraud Squad was investigating the affairs of a company and its chairman, Mr Lewis. This was in fact true, and so the claim for defamation on the literal meaning of the words failed. However, it was also claimed that the paragraph contained an innuendo—it indicated that the company was being operated in a fraudulent and dishonest way. The majority of the House of Lords held that the words were not capable of bearing that meaning. The test was an objective one: what would an ordinary and reasonable person infer as the natural and ordinary meaning of these words? The court held that a reasonable person might infer from the paragraph that the company and Lewis were *suspected* of fraud, but held that a reasonable person would not assume that a police investigation indicated that Lewis and the company were *guilty* of such conduct. This has to be correct, otherwise newspapers would be unable to report investigations prior to their final result. The court also recommended that, for clarity, claimants should set out the meaning of the false innuendo on which they wish to rely if it does not speak for itself.[40] This will enable the defendant to be fully aware of the case against him or her and will clarify issues prior to trial.

---

[36] [1931] A.C. 333.

[37] Evidence was given that he would have been called on to resign the membership of any reputable golf club.

[38] [1929] 2 K.B. 331.

[39] [1964] A.C. 234 at 258. See also *Mapp v News Group Newspapers Ltd* [1998] Q.B. 520. Contrast *Hayward v Thompson* [1982] Q.B. 47, where the words "connected with" a murder plot were held to be plainly capable of conveying to ordinary persons the imputation of Hayward's guilt.

[40] [1964] A.C. 234 at 281 and 273. Note Lord Denning M.R. in *Allsop v Church of England Newspaper Ltd* [1972] 2 Q.B. 161 at 167 who stated that, in most cases, it is not only desirable but necessary for the claimant to set out in the Case Statement the meaning which he or she says the words bear unless there is only one ordinary meaning which is clear and explicit. See now CPR, Pt 53.

The general test is therefore: would the reasonable person view the statement as defamatory      **13–013**
on the particular facts of the case? The courts do look at the statements in context. It is not
enough to point to a particular sentence or isolated paragraph. The court will look at the article
as a whole. This is illustrated by the approach of the House of Lords in *Charleston v News
Group Newspapers Ltd*.[41] The *News of the World* had run a story about a computer game,
which featured near-naked bodies of models in pornographic poses, on which the heads of two
characters from the Australian soap "Neighbours" (Madge and Harold Bishop) had been
superimposed. The headline read "Strewth! What's Harold up to with our Madge?" and was
accompanied by photographs of the characters as depicted in the game. The actors complained
that the photographs suggested that they had participated in some way in the making of the
game. Although the accompanying article made it clear that the actors had not participated in
any way, it was argued that a significant proportion of readers skimming through the newspaper would only read the headlines and look at the photographs, and would come to the
wrong conclusions. The court refused to approach the case in this way. "Defamatory" was
judged by the standard of the ordinary reasonable person, who would have taken the trouble
to discover what the article was about. It was therefore irrelevant that the *News of the World*
may have some readers who only read the headlines.[42] Lord Nicholls did warn newspapers,
however, that they were "playing with fire", and that if the explanatory text were tucked
away further down the article or on a continuation page, the court would be likely to take a
different view.[43]

Once the claimant has shown that the words used were defamatory, he or she must move on
to the second requirement and show that the words in fact referred to him or her.

## (2) Does the statement refer to the claimant?

This is obviously not a problem if the claimant is mentioned by name, but otherwise the ques-      **13–014**
tion is again the view of the reasonable person: would the reasonable person, having knowledge of the special circumstances, understand the words to refer to the claimant?[44] This was
considered by the House of Lords in *Morgan v Odhams Press Ltd*.[45] A newspaper article in
*The Sun* had reported that a girl had been kidnapped by a dog-doping gang. This was incorrect
and the girl had been staying at Mr Morgan's flat at the relevant time. Morgan produced a
small number of witnesses who had seen the two together and who claimed that, having read
the article, they assumed it to suggest that Morgan was part of the dog-doping gang. The
majority of the House held that on the facts there was sufficient material for a jury to find that
the statement referred to him. It was not necessary to find a specific "pointer" in the article, or
a "peg" on which to hang such a reference. Although a careful study of the article would have
suggested that it could not refer to Morgan, it was held that the ordinary, reasonable reader did
not have the forensic skills of a lawyer. The majority of the House held that, taking account of
the sensationalist nature of the article, and the fact that the average reader was likely to read
the story casually, gaining a general impression of it, the ordinary reasonable person would,

---

[41] [1995] 2 A.C. 65.
[42] [1995] 2 A.C. 65 at 73 per Lord Bridge.
[43] [1995] 2 A.C. 65 at 74.
[44] *Morgan v Odhams Press Ltd* [1971] 1 W.L.R. 1239.
[45] [1971] 1 W.L.R. 1239 at 1245 and 1269–1270.

on the facts, have drawn the inference that the article referred to Morgan[46] A new trial was ordered nevertheless, due to the judge's misdirection to the jury on the assessment of damages.

It is generally the rule that the meaning of any statement must be judged at the time of publication. Liability will not arise where an innocent statement is later rendered defamatory by subsequent events.[47] However, the courts will not allow this rule to be used to "cover up" defamatory statements where the defendant has made a defamatory statement, but only identified the claimant in a later article. Therefore, in *Hayward v Thompson*,[48] the Court of Appeal admitted in evidence a later article identifying the plaintiff where the first article had merely referred to "a wealthy benefactor of the Liberal party". On this basis, both articles were found to be defamatory of the defendant.[49]

**13–015**     As stated above, it is irrelevant whether the defendant intended the words to be defamatory. It is equally irrelevant whether the defendant intended to refer to the claimant. Provided reasonable persons would find the statement defamatory, and to refer to the claimant, the defendant who publishes the statement will be liable. *Hulton & Co v Jones*[50] is the classic example. The defendant newspaper had published a humorous account of a motor festival in Dieppe, featuring the antics of a fictional churchwarden from Peckham called Artemus Jones. Unfortunately for the newspaper, this was also the name of a barrister, who sued for libel. The real Mr Jones was not a churchwarden, had not gone to the Dieppe festival and did not live in Peckham, but friends of his swore that they believed the article to refer to him. The House of Lords held that there was evidence upon which the jury could conclude that reasonable people would believe Mr Jones was referred to and it was irrelevant that the defendants had no intention to defame him.[51]

It is of no assistance to the defendant that the words were true of another individual. In *Newstead v London Express Newspaper Ltd*,[52] a report of the conviction for bigamy of a Harold Newstead, aged 30, of Camberwell, London provoked an action for defamation from another Harold Newstead who also lived in Camberwell and who was about the same age. The Court of Appeal upheld his claim against the newspaper. *Newstead* is perhaps a more meritorious case than *Hulton*. Such a coincidence was obviously prejudicial to the reputation of the innocent Mr Newstead, and the newspaper should therefore have made greater efforts to identify the real culprit. The decision does impose a considerable burden on newspapers, however, which cannot possibly check every story to ascertain whether there is any chance of confusion as to the identity of the person involved. This was recognised by the court, but it was held that it was not unreasonable to place a burden on the party who puts the statements into circulation to identify the person so closely that little or no risk of confusion arises.[53]

The question arises, however, whether it is reasonable to expect newspapers to bear the risk of a person being mistaken for another individual in a photograph in the paper. This problem

---

[46] Note the contrast with the approach taken by the House of Lords in the more recent case of *Charleston v News Group Newspapers Ltd* [1995] 2 A.C. 65, discussed above.

[47] *Grappelli v Derek Block (Holdings) Ltd* [1981] 1 W.L.R. 822.

[48] [1982] Q.B. 47.

[49] In any event, there was evidence that a number of people had identified Mr Hayward from the context of the first article, including his family, other members of the Liberal party and innumerable journalists.

[50] [1910] A.C. 20. The Faulks Committee recommended no change in the rule of *Hulton v Jones* (para.123).

[51] W.V.H. Rogers, *Winfield & Jolowicz on Torts* (18th edn, Sweet and Maxwell, 2010), 12–19, notes that Jones had once worked for the newspaper. This might have influenced the jury, even though his counsel accepted that the author of the article and the newspaper editor did not know of the existence of the respondent.

[52] [1940] 1 K.B. 377.

[53] [1940] 1 K.B. 377 at 388 per Greene M.R.

arose in *O'Shea v MGN Ltd*,[54] where the *Sunday Mirror* had published an advertisement for an adult internet service featuring a "glamour" model, who resembled the claimant. Ms O'Shea complained that ordinary sensible readers, who were aware of her resemblance to the model, would have concluded that she had consented to appear on a highly pornographic website. Whilst concluding that, as a matter of law, the image was defamatory,[55] Morland J. held that liability would be contrary to art.10 of the European Convention on Human Rights. Protection of Ms O'Shea's reputation could not be said to meet a "pressing social need"[56] and to be necessary in a democratic society for the protection of the reputation of others.[57] The judge distinguished *Hulton* and *Newstead* on the basis that the existence of the claimants could have been discovered in those cases, whereas it would have been impossible in *O'Shea*. Liability would impose an "impossible burden" on the publisher, which could not be justified.[58]

It may be questioned whether such a distinction is valid. Ms O'Shea had been accidentally defamed, as had Mr Jones, and it may be challenged whether the form the statement takes should be of such crucial importance. If the true objection is to liability for unintentional defamation, can the art.10 right to freedom of expression be confined to photographs? At present, *O'Shea* appears to be treated as an isolated exception and the general rule remains. It remains to be seen whether the case can in future found a basis to challenge this form of liability.

If confusion does arise, the defendant has only two options:

(i) To argue that there is not enough evidence for a reasonable person to find confusion as to identity.

(ii) To adopt a defence of unintentional defamation. This will be discussed in the next chapter, but generally involves an apology and offer to pay some compensation.

## Group defamation

If the statement in question relates to a group of individuals, it will be difficult for the claimant to establish that the words refer to him or her directly. Unless the group in question has legal identity, for example is a company, and can therefore sue for loss of the group's reputation, no action will stand unless: **13–016**

(i) the class is so small that the claimant can establish that the statement must apply to every member of the class; or

(ii) the claimant can show that the statement refers to him or her directly.

The leading case on group defamation is the House of Lords case of *Knuppfer v London Express Newspaper Ltd*.[59] In this case, an article had been published which criticised the Young Russian political party, Mlado Russ. The party consisted of several thousand members,

[54] [2001] E.M.L.R. 40 (QBD).
[55] See *Dwek v Macmillan Publishers Ltd* [2000] E.M.L.R. 284, CA (photograph described as Dodi Fayed with a prostitute was, in fact, of the claimant).
[56] See Lord Keith in *Derbyshire CC v Times Newspapers* [1993] A.C. 534 at 550.
[57] See art.10.2.
[58] para.43. Morland J. was additionally concerned that liability would inhibit investigative journalism into drug dealing, corruption, child abuse and prostitution.
[59] [1944] A.C. 116.

but they were mainly overseas and the British branch consisted of only 24 members. Knuppfer was one of these members. To establish that the libel referred directly to him, he alleged that because he was the head of the British branch, British readers would assume the remarks referred to him. This argument was rejected by the House of Lords. It was held that the article was not capable of referring to Knuppfer. There had been no mention of the activities of the party in the United Kingdom and their Lordships found no evidence to infer that the article referred to Knuppfer. Lord Porter advised that in deciding whether the article was capable of referring to the claimant, the court should examine the size of the class, the generality of the charge and the extravagance of the accusation.[60] The true test was whether a reasonable jury could find that the article was capable of referring to the claimant.

As a general rule, therefore, a statement aimed at a group will not be considered to refer to its individual members. On this basis, a politician could not sue a newspaper which printed "All politicians are liars" unless he or she could show something which referred specifically to him or her.[61] It will depend on the facts of the case. Obviously, the smaller the group and more specific the charge, the easier it will be to show that the article refers to the claimant. For example, a statement that the local five-a-side team are utterly incompetent obviously refers to five particular individuals.[62]

## (3) Has the statement been published to a third party?

**13–017**   This third requirement is vital. It is not enough, for example, that the defendant sends a letter to the claimant making lurid accusations against him or her. This will not harm his or her reputation, although he or she may be distressed by it. It is only when the letter is seen by a third party (or "published") that the claimant's reputation will be harmed.[63] It can be seen that "publication" has nothing to do with printing presses, but signifies that the libel or slander has come to the knowledge of a third party. The claimant's reputation will only suffer harm when the offending words are communicated to someone other than the claimant and the defendant. Insulting words spoken to the claimant in private by the defendant are not defamatory, although they may of course give rise to claims for harassment or assault. Although readers may see the term "malicious publication" used, this should not be taken literally. Malice is not required. We therefore use the simple term "publication".

The requirement of publication is obviously met by printing an article in a newspaper or book, or by shouting a remark in a lecture theatre, and will not generally be a problem. It is really a matter of common sense. For example, if I make defamatory statements in my lecture and the students (a) cannot understand me because I am speaking in old Norse,[64] or (b) cannot hear me because my microphone is not working, I have not published my statements. Publication requires that the words must be intelligible and reach the third party. Problems have arisen when the defendant alleges that he or she did not intend to publish the words. For example, A sends a letter defamatory of B to B. B alleges in court that it was opened by his

---

[60] [1944] A.C. 116 at 124.

[61] It would seem that although political parties cannot sue for defamation, politicians can sue in their own right. This is discussed below under "Who can sue?"

[62] See also *Aspro Travel v Owners Abroad Group Plc* [1996] 1 W.L.R. 132, where directors of a limited family company were allowed to sue for defamation in their own right.

[63] This is not the case, however, for criminal libel, where publication to the prosecutor alone will suffice.

[64] Unless I am very unlucky and one of my audience understands old Norse!

wife, Mrs B, and it has therefore been published to a third party enabling him to sue for defamation. A states that he did not intend the letter to be published and therefore he should not be liable. The courts deal with this by having a test of reasonable foresight: if it is reasonably foreseeable that a third party would see the statement, then the defendant will be liable. On that basis, in *Theaker v Richardson*,[65] the defendant was liable for sending a defamatory letter to a married woman, which had been opened by her husband. The letter, which had been addressed to the wife, had been sealed in a brown envelope which looked like an election circular. The court upheld the view of the jury that it was foreseeable that the husband would open the letter. In contrast, in *Huth v Huth*,[66] it was found that it was not foreseeable that a butler would open his employer's mail. Defendants wishing to avoid publication should ensure that the document is in a sealed envelope marked "private and confidential". Making defamatory remarks on a postcard or telegram is obviously unwise and the court will presume, in the absence of evidence to the contrary, that someone will have read the remarks along the way.[67] Similarly, a careless defendant who leaves documents open on his or her desk runs the risk of publication to visitors or perhaps cleaners, but not, it would seem, to a burglar who steals the document from a locked drawer.[68]

A few odd rules remain. It is still the rule (despite the fact that the law no longer regards husband and wife as one person) that a husband does not publish words by telling his wife (or vice versa).[69] A modern explanation for this rule may be a concern for "marital harmony" whereby the courts are reluctant, save in exceptional circumstances, to see spouses give evidence against one another. It also seems to be the rule that while an author who dictates a document to a typist is liable for publication,[70] a typist or printer who hands back to the author a document containing defamatory statements made by the author is deemed not to be liable for publication. This is easier to explain. The typist can hardly publish the document to the author of the document itself.[71] The typist and printer are effectively acting as the author's agents, and an agent repeating back the statements of the principal cannot be treated as publication to a third party. However, if the documents are shown to anyone else, the typist or printer (as well as the author) may be liable for publication of the statements.

In this regard, it should be noted that it is no defence that the defendant is merely repeating the defamatory statements of another.[72] Repetition will increase the harm to the claimant's reputation, for which the defendant will be obliged to pay compensation. The fact that the person repeating the libel or slander expresses a doubt or disbelief as to the truth of the statement is irrelevant—repetition is sufficient to incur liability.[73]

There are a limited number of situations, however, where the original defamer will remain liable, namely:

---

[65] [1962] 1 W.L.R. 151.

[66] [1915] 3 K.B. 323.

[67] See, e.g. *Sim v Stretch* [1936] 2 All E.R. 1237.

[68] *Pullman v Hill* [1891] 1 Q.B. 524 at 527 per Lord Esher M.R.

[69] *Wennhak v Morgan* (1888) 20 Q.B.D. 635.

[70] *Osborn v Thomas Boulter & Son* [1930] 2 K.B. 226.

[71] See *Eglantine Inn Ltd v Smith* [1948] N.I. 29 at 33 and *Osborn v Thomas Boulter & Son* [1930] 2 K.B. 226 at 237 per Slesser L.J.

[72] *Weld-Blundell v Stephens* [1920] A.C. 956. See also *Stern v Piper* [1997] Q.B. 123 and *Shah v Standard Chartered Bank* [1999] Q.B. 241. This rule was strongly affirmed in *Mark v Associated Newspapers Ltd* [2002] E W C A Civ 772; [2002] E.M.L.R. 38, CA, where it was held to be consistent with art.10 of the European Convention on Human Rights.

[73] *Slipper v BBC* [1991] 1 Q.B. 283.

(a) Where the original defamer has authorised or requested publication;[74]

(b) Where he or she intended that the statement should be repeated or republished;

(c) Where he or she has informed a person who is under a moral duty to repeat or republish the statement,[75] or, generally,

(d) Where the re-publication is, on the facts, the natural and probable result of the original publication.

**13–018**    This last point was argued in *Slipper v BBC*.[76] Slipper, a former detective superintendent, had complained about a film made and broadcast by the BBC which dealt with his abortive efforts to bring back one of the Great Train Robbers, Ronnie Biggs, from Brazil. Slipper claimed that a press review of the film portrayed him in a defamatory light, and that the BBC were responsible for the repetition of the libel in the newspaper reviews of the film. The Court of Appeal treated the matter as one of causation and remoteness, rather than turning on any particular rule relating to defamation: did the reviews amount to a *novus actus interveniens* breaking the chain of causation? Therefore, if repetition of the libel was the natural and probable consequence of the original publication, the original publisher would remain liable. On the facts, the court held that this was a question for the jury and refused to strike out this part of Slipper's case.

The application of this test was discussed more recently in *McManus v Beckham*.[77] Here, McManus had complained that Victoria Beckham, wife of footballer David Beckham, had entered his memorabilia shop and had advised customers that a signed photograph of her husband for sale in the shop was a forgery. The incident received extensive press coverage, and McManus brought a claim based on subsequent damage to his business. The question remained whether it was a natural and probable consequence of her outburst that it would receive media attention. The Court of Appeal rejected a simple test of reasonable foresight, which had been suggested in *Slipper*. This would impose an unfair burden on the defendant. A just and reasonable result would be achieved by imposing liability:

(a) Where the defendant is actually aware that what she says or does is likely to be reported, and, that if she slanders someone that slander is likely to be repeated in whole or in part; or

(b) Where she should have appreciated that there was a significant risk that what she said would be repeated in whole or in part in the press and that that would increase the damage caused by the slander.[78]

In other words, she will be liable where it was foreseeable to a reasonable person in the position of the defendant that there was a significant risk of repetition, either in whole or in part,

---

[74] e.g. by requesting journalists present to note allegations made during a parish meeting: see *Parkes v Prescott* (1869) L.R. 4 Ex. 169 at 179.

[75] *Slipper v BBC* [1991] 1 Q.B. 283 at 301 per Slade L.J.

[76] [1991] 1 Q.B. 283.

[77] [2002] EWCA Civ 939; [2002] 1 W.L.R. 2982.

[78] [2002] 1 W.L.R. 2982 at 2998 per Waller L.J.

and that, in consequence, increased harm to the claimant would ensue.[79] On the facts of the case, it could not be said that it was impossible for the claimants to satisfy this test.[80]

One last question is whether it is possible to publish by omission. For example, in *Byrne v Deane*,[81] discussed earlier, the question arose whether the club could be liable for failing to remove the notice in question. The court held that those responsible for the club would be liable if they failed to remove defamatory matter attached to the club notice-board within a reasonable time. However, if the defamatory matter was not readily removable (for example, carved deep into stonework) and could only be removed at great inconvenience and expense, its non-removal would not amount to publication. Equally, the host of a phone-in show might find himself or herself liable for failing to take reasonable care to prevent controversial guests making defamatory statements. It is therefore a question of control. In this last case, however, the host may now have a defence of innocent dissemination under s.1 of the Defamation Act 1996 (see Ch.14).

## Who can sue?

### (1) Any living human being

We have seen numerous examples of this already, such as Princess Youssoupoff and Artemus Jones. It should be noted, however, that the action does not survive death,[82] so the estate of a person who has been defamed has no cause of action.     **13–019**

### (2) Companies

This is more controversial. A company is a corporate entity, not a real person, and is incapable of having its "personal feelings" injured by the defendant's statements. Yet, as we stated at the start of this chapter, the tort of defamation is concerned with reputation, not personal feelings. A company does have a business reputation to protect. Despite arguments that this interest is not sufficient to merit the benefit of a tort actionable per se, and is sufficiently protected by other torts, such as malicious falsehood and deceit, it is clear that companies can sue for defamation. The classic authority is *South Hetton Coal Co v North-Eastern News Association Ltd*,[83] where the Court of Appeal held that the company was entitled to sue a newspaper which had alleged that properties in which the company housed its employees were highly insanitary. A libel calculated to injure the company's trading reputation was held to be actionable. Readers may remember the more modern example in the long-running "McLibel" trial[84] in which the fast-food chain McDonalds brought a case against two environmental campaigners for allegedly defamatory statements about the company. The Faulks Committee in 1975 recommended     **13–020**

---

[79] [2002] 1 W.L.R. 2982 at 3001 per Laws L.J.

[80] The case was ultimately settled, Mrs Beckham paying the claimants £55,000 for the hurt and damage suffered together with a set of official merchandise signed by her husband: Statement in Open Court, March 11, 2003 (QBD, Gray J.).

[81] [1937] 1 K.B. 818.

[82] Law Reform (Miscellaneous Provisions) Act 1934 s.1(1).

[83] [1894] 1 Q.B. 133.

[84] *McDonald's Corp v Steel (No.4)* [1995] 3 All E.R. 615. The trial itself lasted 313 days (the longest trial in English history). See J. Vidal, *McLibel–Burger culture on trial* (Pan, 1997).

that companies should not be able to sue unless they had suffered financial loss or the words were likely to cause the company financial damage.[85] This has not been implemented.

The reasoning of the Court of Appeal in *South Hetton* was approved by the House of Lords in *Jameel v Wall Street Journal Europe SPRL (No.3).*[86] In this case, a trading company, incorporated in Saudi Arabia, had brought an action for libel in response to a newspaper article which suggested that its bank accounts were being monitored to prevent their use for channelling funds to terrorist organisations. The company was found to have a trading reputation in the UK, despite the fact that it conducted no business in the jurisdiction. It was argued that to allow such a company to bring a claim in libel without proof of damage amounted to an undue restriction of freedom of speech, contrary to art.10. The majority of the Lords disagreed.[87] In the words of Lord Bingham:

> "the good name of a company, as that of an individual, is a thing of value. A damaging libel may lower its standing in the eyes of the public and even its own staff, make people less ready to deal with it, less willing or less proud to work for it . . . I find nothing repugnant in the notion that this is a value which the law should protect."[88]

In view of the margin of appreciation given to national courts in their interpretation of art.10,[89] his Lordship was not prepared to alter the well-established rule in *South Hetton* and require a company to show special damage. He added, however, that where the trading corporation had suffered no financial loss, damages should be kept strictly within modest bounds.[90]

## Who cannot sue?

### (1) Governmental bodies

**13–021** The House of Lords in *Derbyshire CC v Times Newspapers Ltd*[91] held that institutions of central or local government, such as local authorities, could not sue for defamation. This is an important decision. The plaintiff, a local authority, had brought an action for damages for libel against *The Times* in respect of two newspaper articles which had questioned the propriety of its financial dealings. On a preliminary issue as to whether the plaintiff had a cause of action against the defendants, the House of Lords upheld the view of the Court of Appeal that a local authority could not bring an action for libel. Lord Keith, giving the leading judgment, commented that:

---

[85] para.342.

[86] [2006] UKHL 44; [2007] 1 A.C. 359.

[87] Lord Hoffmann and Baroness Hale dissenting. Lord Hoffmann at para.91 distinguished an individual's reputation (part of his or her personality) from that of a company (really no more than a commercial asset) and questioned why defamation should differ from other torts, such as malicious falsehood, where a company is required to show proof of damage to bring an action to protect its commercial assets from tortious harm.

[88] [2006] UKHL 44; [2007] 1 A.C. 359 at para.26. Concern was also raised that if special damage was required, a company would not be able to avert irreparable damage to its reputation by a prompt issue of proceedings: see Lord Bingham at para.26 and Lord Hope at para.102.

[89] See *Steel and Morris v United Kingdom (68416/01)* (2005) 41 E.H.R.R. 403.

[90] [2006] UKHL 44; [2007] 1 A.C. 359 at para.27. See also his remark at para.19.

[91] [1993] A.C. 534. See B. Bix and A. Tomkins (1993) 56 M.L.R. 738; S. Palmer [1993] C.L.J. 363, and E. Grant and J.G. Small (1994) 14 O.J.L.S. 287.

"It is of the highest public importance that a democratically elected governmental body, or indeed any governmental body, should be open to uninhibited public criticism. The threat of a civil action for defamation must inevitably have an inhibiting effect on freedom of speech."[92]

The decision is therefore significant in recognising that it is in the public interest that individuals are free to question and criticise central and local government. It would be contrary to the democratic process and freedom of expression for such bodies to have a right to sue in defamation, and would "place an undesirable fetter on freedom of speech".[93] In reaching this conclusion, the House of Lords, unlike the Court of Appeal,[94] did not rely on the European Convention on Human Rights, but relied on English and United States case law.[95] In future, however, with the incorporation of the Convention into English law by the Human Rights Act 1998, art.10 will form the main focus of any discussion of freedom of expression. The decision marks welcome recognition that open government is a valuable part of modern democratic society and that any restrictions of freedom of expression in this context should be examined very carefully.

*(2)  Political parties*

The logic of (1), namely the requirement that the public should be able to question the executive, applies equally to political parties. Buckley J. in *Goldsmith v Bhoyrul*[96] applied *Derbyshire* to exclude a claim for defamation by the Referendum Party.[97] Despite the fact that the party had yet to be elected, Buckley J. held that defamation actions, or the threat of such actions, would restrict free speech, which would be contrary to the public interest. The public should be free to discuss and criticise political parties putting themselves forward for election.        **13–022**

It is important, however, to note the limited effect of these two decisions. These decisions do not prevent individual politicians from suing, and indeed a number of politicians have sued in recent years (for example, former Conservative MPs Rupert Allason and Neil Hamilton) with mixed success.[98] There is an obvious argument that politicians, involved in the democratic process, should also be prevented from suing for defamation for the reasons stated in *Derbyshire*, at least when the statements relate to their performance as Members of Parliament.[99] This is not the legal position at present. There is no English equivalent to the United States restrictions on the ability of public figures to sue for defamation, stated by the United States

---

[92] [1993] A.C. 534 at 547.

[93] [1993] A.C. 534 at 549 per Lord Keith.

[94] [1992] Q.B. 770.

[95] Lord Keith commented ([1993] A.C. 534 at 541): "My Lords, I have reached my conclusion upon the common law of England without finding any need to rely upon the European Convention . . . I can only add that I find it satisfactory to be able to conclude that the common law of England is consistent with the obligations assumed by the Crown under the Treaty in this particular field."

[96] [1998] Q.B. 459 at 463.

[97] The Referendum party had been founded by the late Sir James Goldsmith. It sought to secure a referendum on Britain's future in Europe and put up 547 candidates in the 1997 election.

[98] Re-iterated recently by Tugendhat J. in *McLaughlin v Lambeth LBC* [2010] EWHC 2726 (QB); [2011] E.M.L.R. 8: the right to sue of any individual who carried on the day to day management of the affairs of a governmental body was subject to no limitation other than the requirement that the words complained of should refer to, and be defamatory of, that individual.

[99] See E. Barendt [1993] P.L. 449.

Supreme Court in *New York Times v Sullivan*.[100] In that case, the Supreme Court held that in the light of the protection of free speech in the First Amendment, public figures may only sue if they can present clear and convincing evidence of actual malice by the publisher. Actual malice is shown by proving that the defendant published the piece with knowledge that the defamatory statement was false or at least with reckless disregard as to its falsity. The rule in *Derbyshire* is further undermined by the fact that governmental bodies still have the right to sue for malicious falsehood (see Ch.14) and to prosecute for criminal libel. The impact of the decision must therefore be questionable when the restriction can so easily be circumvented in this way.[101] In *Derbyshire* itself, the council leader, Bookbinder, was able to sue in his own right for damages. Mr Bookbinder's earlier action against Norman Tebbit, former Chairman of the Conservative party, will be discussed in the next chapter.

## Conclusion

**13–023**    In this chapter, we have examined the necessary elements which the claimant must establish to bring an action for defamation. The next chapter will concentrate on the defences available to the defendant. As we shall see, it is with the defences that the real tensions between the right of freedom of speech and the need to protect the claimant's reputation show themselves. Whilst recognising that a claimant should have a right to defend his or her reputation against publication of defamatory words, the courts nevertheless consider whether publication can be defended, either on the basis that the words are true, or that publication is in the public interest. The defences available in defamation are somewhat complicated and therefore warrant a chapter of their own.

---

[100]  376 U.S. 254 (1964). See also *Lingens v Austria* (1986) 8 E.H.R.R. 407 in which the European Court of Human Rights adopted an approach towards public figures similar to that adopted in the U.S. For a comparison, see D. Elder (1986) 35 I.C.L.Q. 891.

[101]  See B. Bix and A. Tomkins (1993) 56 M.L.R. 738.

# Chapter 14

## DEFENCES TO DEFAMATION

### Introduction

In the last chapter we examined the basic requirements of a defamation action. The burden is **14–001** on the claimant to establish (a) that the statement is defamatory, (b) that it refers to the claimant and (c) that it has been published to a third party. In this chapter, we examine the defences open to the defendant once the claimant has established these three requirements. The main defences are justification (or truth), fair (now renamed honest) comment and privilege. These defences protect the defendant in two ways: first, where he or she has told the truth, and, secondly, where the words have been published in circumstances where it is in the public interest that the defendant should be free to publish. These defences must now also be considered in the light of the Human Rights Act 1998. The Act places particular importance on freedom of expression (Art.10) and requires the courts to balance the protection of a party's reputation against the public interest in allowing individuals to "hold opinions and to receive and impart information and ideas without interference" by the courts. Section 12(4) of the Act further provides that the courts "must have particular regard to the importance of the Convention right to freedom of expression." Although the law of defamation has always recognised these two conflicting interests, it cannot be denied that the 1998 Act has brought this debate to the fore.

It should also be noted that although justification, honest comment and privilege are the most important defences, other defences exist. It is a defence if the claimant has expressly or impliedly consented to the publication of the defamatory matter,[1] and under the Defamation Act 1996[2] a number of further options arise: unintentional defamation and innocent dissemination. Consent will be discussed generally in Ch.16, but the other five defences will be examined below. If all the defences fail, the defendant has one final option. This is to mitigate the level of damages (to be assessed by the jury) by raising arguments in his or her favour, for example that an apology was made or that the defamatory material was not shown to a large number of people. Such arguments will not amount to a defence, but may at least lead the jury to award a lesser amount of damages against the defendant.

We shall discuss each defence in turn.

---

[1] *Cookson v Harewood* [1932] 2 K.B. 478n; *Chapman v Lord Ellesmere* [1932] 2 K.B. 431 at 463–465 per Slesser L.J.
[2] See K. Williams (1997) 5 Tort L. Rev. 206.

## (1) JUSTIFICATION (OR TRUTH)[3]

**14–002**     It is a valid defence to show that the defamatory statements were in fact true. Two points
should be noted here. First, defamatory statements are presumed to be untrue.[4] The claimant
does not have to show that the statements were false. The burden therefore will be on the
defendant to show that the statements were true and so justified. Secondly, the claimant has no
right to complain about true statements which lower his or her reputation. Logically, such
statements merely bring the individual's reputation down to its appropriate level.[5] It is also
irrelevant whether the statements are published out of malice or to let others know the truth.
The only exception to this is contained in s.8 of the Rehabilitation of Offenders Act 1974.
Section 8(5) provides that where the claimant complains that the defendant has published
information concerning his or her spent convictions, the defendant cannot rely on the defence
of justification if the publication is proved to have been made with malice. The burden will be
on the claimant to show the presence of malice.[6]

The difficulties in proving that a particular allegation is true should not be underestimated.
The defendant will have to justify, on the balance of probabilities, not only the express
meaning of the words, but any innuendoes deriving from the statement. In *Wakley v Cooke*,[7]
for example, the defendant had called the plaintiff a "libellous journalist". He was able to
show that a judgment had once been obtained against the plaintiff for libel. However, because
the words, by innuendo, were capable of meaning that the plaintiff was in the habit of libelling
people, the comment could not be justified by referring to only one previous incident of libel.
The defendant's claim of justification therefore failed.

The burden on the defendant is reduced, however, by the fact that the defendant is only
required to show that the words used were substantially true. In *Alexander v North Eastern
Railway Co*,[8] the defendants had stated that the plaintiff had been convicted of an offence of
dishonesty and sentenced to three weeks' imprisonment in default of payment of a fine. In fact,
they could only prove the conviction and a sentence of two weeks' imprisonment. Nevertheless,
the court found the statement to be substantially true and the defendants therefore succeeded
in their defence of justification.

Section 5 of the Defamation Act 1952 also assists the defendant when several allegations
have been made against the claimant. Section 5 provides that:

---

[3] The term favoured by the Faulks Committee (Report of the Committee on Defamation, 1975, Cmnd 5090) para.129,
who believed that it would save confusion.

[4] This was challenged in the Court of Appeal in *Jameel v Wall Street Journal Europe SPRL (No.3)* [2005] EWCA
Civ 74; [2005] Q.B. 904 at paras 55–57 for infringing arts 6 and 10 of the ECHR (not raised on appeal to HL).
Although the point was dismissed as having been raised too late in proceedings, the court gave it little support,
stressing that it would require a major change of the law of defamation. The point does, however, remain open and
there is some indication in *Steel and Morris v United Kingdom (68416/01)* (2005) 41 E.H.R.R. 22 that it may, in
exceptional circumstances, give rise to a breach of art.10.

[5] *M'Pherson v Daniels* (1829) 10 B. & C. 263 at 272; 109 E.R. 448 at 451. It is irrelevant that the defendant did not
know the statements to be true at the time they were made, provided they are of course in fact true.

[6] Eady J. in *Silkman v Heard* (February 28, 2001, QBD) raised the question whether this is compatible with the right
to freedom of expression in art.10 of the European Convention on Human Rights in that the information is in the
public domain and this section has been relied on so rarely in defamation actions.

[7] (1849) 4 Exch. 511; 154 E.R. 1316.

[8] (1865) 6 B. & S. 340; 122 E.R. 1221. Note also the comments of Eady J. in *Turcu v News Group Newspapers Ltd*
[2005] EWHC 799 (QB) at para.109: "English law is generally able to accommodate the policy factors underlying
the Article 10 jurisprudence by means of established common law principles; for example that a defamatory allegation need only be proved, on a balance of probabilities, to be *substantially* true."

"... in an action for libel or slander in respect of words containing two or more distinct charges against the plaintiff a defence of justification shall not fail by reason only that the truth of every charge is not proved if the words not proved to be true do not materially injure the plaintiff's reputation having regard to the truth of the remaining charges."

On this basis, if the defendant has made a number of distinct charges against the claimant and the defendant cannot prove the truth of all the charges, this does not necessarily mean that the defendant cannot establish the defence. It will be sufficient that the defendant has proved the truth of the most serious charges such that the other statements do not injure the claimant's reputation materially. An example will help: X has published an article which alleges that Y (i) had stolen all the Christmas presents from a children's home, (ii) had written on the wall "Santa Claus does not exist", and (iii) had spelt "Santa Claus" incorrectly. If X could justify allegation (i) and (ii), his defence would not fail because he could not also prove allegation (iii).     **14–003**

The burden is therefore on the defendant to justify the substantial truth or "sting" of the allegations. To achieve this, the defendant may also wish to raise matters with a "common sting" in support of his or her claim of justification. For example, in *Williams v Reason*,[9] a Welsh amateur rugby player sued in respect of an article which accused him of writing a book for profit, contrary to his amateur status. The defendants claimed justification and were permitted to allege in support of the article that the player had previously taken money for wearing a particular brand of boots. The sting of the defamatory words was that Williams had compromised his amateur status (so-called "shamateurism") and the evidence of the boots money went to justify that charge. However, if the allegation against the claimant is specific, then the claimant can simply sue on the basis of this individual allegation and the defendant will not be permitted to raise matters with a "common sting".[10] On this basis, the Court of Appeal in *Bookbinder v Tebbit*[11] struck out part of the defence put forward by Norman Tebbit, the former chairman of the Conservative party, which referred to general examples of irresponsible spending by Derbyshire City Council. The court found that Tebbit had made a specific allegation against Bookbinder that the council, under his leadership, had squandered public money by overprinting stationery with a political message. He would therefore have to justify that particular allegation.

The defendant can also, when appropriate, rely on s.13 of the Civil Evidence Act 1968 (as amended by s.12(1) of the Defamation Act 1996). This provides that if the defendant has alleged that the claimant has committed an offence, this can be proved to be true simply by giving evidence of the conviction. It is not necessary to prove that the claimant was rightly convicted.

If the defendant cannot show that the statements were substantially true, the defence fails. Partial justification will not constitute a defence, although it may serve to reduce the jury's assessment of damages. Should the defendant fail completely in the defence of justification, it

---

[9] [1988] 1 W.L.R. 96 at 103 per Stephenson L.J.

[10] *Polly Peck (Holdings) Plc v Trelford* [1986] Q.B. 1000. See also *Cruise v Express Newspapers Plc* [1999] Q.B. 931, CA (where the article in question contains two separate and distinct allegations, the defendant will not be permitted to rely on the other allegation to support a defence of justification or fair comment) and *McKeith v News Group Newspapers Ltd* [2005] EWHC 1162 (QB); [2005] E.M.L.R. 32 (rejecting common sting argument: real issue was the validity of the claimant's qualifications).

[11] [1989] 1 W.L.R. 640.

is likely that a jury will award the claimant a higher level of damages. An unsuccessful attempt to justify the defamatory statement aggravates the injury to the claimant by giving the statement extra publicity at trial, and so merits a higher award.[12] It is therefore a calculated risk whether to raise this defence. Where the defendant raises a defence of justification or honest comment, the defendant must make it clear which of the words complained of are statements of fact, and must set out the facts and matters relied upon to support the allegation that the words are true.[13] The defendant must also state the meaning he or she seeks to justify.[14]

## (2) HONEST COMMENT

**14–004**  This defence, known until 2010 as fair comment,[15] is a very different defence to justification. Here, the defendant does not have to show that his or her words are true, but that he or she has exercised the right to criticise the claimant. Inevitably, however, the defendant's right to freedom of expression will be kept within bounds. The difficult question for the court is where the law should draw the line between the defendant's democratic right to comment and the claimant's right to protect his or her reputation. In applying the defence, the courts have imposed three main limitations on the extent to which a defendant can escape liability for criticism: (a) it must be in the public interest, (b) it must be "comment", and (c) it must be honest. These limitations are discussed below.

### In the public interest

**14–005**  This is the first limitation on the defence: it is only acceptable if the defendant comments in the "public interest" or in relation to a matter submitted for public criticism (for example, a book).[16] This raises the obvious question of what is meant by the "public interest". A mere glance at the tabloid press indicates that the public are interested in all sorts of things! "Public interest" is therefore not interpreted as what interests the public, but rather what a judge considers it is in the public's interest to know. In other words, matters which affect people generally, in which they are legitimately interested or concerned.[17] Such matters range from the conduct of politicians,[18] to the insanitary conditions in which employees are housed,[19] to the sudden closure of a West End play.[20]

---

[12]  See Lord Diplock in *Broome v Cassell & Co Ltd* [1972] A.C. 1027 at 1125.

[13]  See Practice Direction to Pt 53, para.2.5 to the Civil Procedures Rules.

[14]  *Lucas-Box v News Group Newspapers Ltd* [1986] 1 W.L.R. 147.

[15]  The change of name was introduced by Lord Phillips in *Spiller v Joseph* [2010] UKSC 53 at para. 117.

[16]  Lord Phillips enquired, however, in the 2010 case of *Spiller v Joseph* whether there was a case for widening the scope of the defence by removing the requirement that it must be in the public interest: [2010] UKSC 53 at para. 113. He further commented that the defence generally merits consideration by the Law Commission or an expert committee. See 14–042 below.

[17]  See Lord Denning M.R. in *London Artists v Littler* [1969] 2 Q.B. 375 at 391.

[18]  *Seymour v Butterworth* (1862) 3 F. & F. 372; 176 E.R. 166.

[19]  *South Hetton Coal Co v North-Eastern News Association Ltd* [1894] 1 Q.B. 133.

[20]  *London Artists v Littler* [1969] 2 Q.B. 375.

## It must be comment

The defendant must be able to show that the words in question consist of a comment on a **14–006** given set of facts.[21] Whereas for justification, the defendant must prove that the words used are true, the defendant is not required to show that the comment is true, merely that it is his or her honest view. It is important, however, that the comment should be based on a true set of facts.[22] (The defendant will obviously not be able to invent facts and then "comment" on them). The only exception to this rule is where the facts commented upon have been published by a person on a privileged occasion, for example where a witness has made a statement in court.[23] Otherwise, the facts on which the comment is made must be shown to be true.

It is sometimes a difficult question whether the defendant has sufficiently stated or indicated the facts on which the comment is made. In *Kemsley v Foot*,[24] for example, Lord Kemsley (a well-known newspaper proprietor at the time) complained about an article entitled "Lower than Kemsley", which criticised the quality of a newspaper unconnected with him. The article contained no other reference to Kemsley, but the inference was obviously that Kemsley produced low quality newspapers. The defendants claimed honest (then fair) comment, but it was questioned whether the defendants could rely on this defence when there were no facts in the article to "comment" upon. The House of Lords took a very broad view of the headline and held that where a "substratum of fact" could be inferred from the words used, the defence of honest comment could be put to the jury. Here, the defendants had clearly referred to Lord Kemsley, who was well-known to the public generally.[25] A stricter line was taken, however, by the House of Lords in the later case of *Telnikoff v Matusevitch*.[26] In this case, a letter was published in the *Daily Telegraph* which criticised an article by the plaintiff, published in the same newspaper, concerning recruitment to the BBC Russian service. The letter suggested that the plaintiff was racist. The plaintiff brought an action against the letter writer for libel. The question arose whether, in considering the letter writer's defence of honest comment, the letter should be considered in the context of the article it criticised. The majority of the House of Lords held that in considering whether the letter amounted to "comment", the court should not look at the article, since many readers of the letter would not have read the article or, if they had read it, would not have had its terms fully in mind. If, in isolation, remarks in the letter were adjudged to be statements of fact rather than comment, then the defence of honest comment would not lie, and the defendant would have to resort to the

---

[21] A recent case demonstrated the difficulties of distinguishing statements of fact from expressions of opinion: *British Chiropractic Association v Singh* [2010] EWCA Civ 350 (criticism of lack of scientific evidence to support treatment amounted to an opinion).

[22] These must be known to the commentator at the time of publication, at least in general terms, although they need not be at the forefront of his or her mind: see Eady J. in *Lowe v Associated Newspapers Ltd* [2006] EWHC 320 (QB); [2007] Q.B. 580 at para.74.

[23] *Mangena v Wright* [1909] 2 K.B. 958; *Brent Walker Group Plc v Time Out Ltd* [1991] 2 Q.B. 33, CA (provided the report is fair and accurate).

[24] [1952] A.C. 345. Described by Lord Phillips in *Spiller v Joseph* [2010] UKSC 53 (at para.91) as "an absurd libel action. It was not about vindicating the reputation of Viscount Kemsley but about amour propre".

[25] Eady J. in *Lowe v Associated Newspapers Ltd* [2006] EWHC 320 (QB); [2007] Q.B. 580 approved the view that comment may be made if the matter is already before the public without the need to set out the facts on which the comment is made, provided that the subject-matter of the comment is plainly stated. *Telnikoff v Matusevitch* (see below) was not cited by the judge.

[26] [1992] 2 A.C. 343.

alternative defence of justification. Lord Keith denied that this would require future letter writers to include the entire text of the article in the letter. The onus would simply be on the letter writer to make it clear that he or she was writing comment and not making statements of fact. His Lordship thought that newspaper editors would not have any difficulty in observing whether this had in fact been achieved.[27]

The Supreme Court in the now leading case of *Spiller v Joseph*[28] reviewed these cases and determined that the comment must explicitly or implicitly indicate, at least in general terms, the facts on which it is based. It was not, however, necessary to identify the facts with such particularity that the reader could judge for himself whether it was well founded. In the words of Lord Phillips, the key issue is that:

> "the reader can understand what the comment is about and the commentator can, if challenged, explain by giving particulars of the subject matter of his comment why he expressed the views that he did. A fair balance must be struck between allowing a critic the freedom to express himself as he will and requiring him to identify to his readers why it is that he is making the criticism."[29]

There is, therefore, a fine line between a statement of fact (to which the defence of honest comment does not apply) and comment based on ascertainable facts. Whilst *Spiller* offers some assistance, one might still question what is meant by the phrase "indicate at least in general terms". The case-law suggests that where the statement in question refers generally to a given set of facts, including those which are common knowledge, then it is comment. So, if I state that "X has just been convicted of murder. His conduct has been disgraceful", I will be able to rely on the defence, provided I can prove that X has been convicted of murder. Equally, it would seem, if X is well-known to the public as a murderer, on the basis of *Kemsley*, I could still rely on the defence if I simply stated "X's conduct is disgraceful". In contrast, if I stated "Y is untrustworthy", I am not referring, even in general terms, to any facts upon which I can claim to be commenting.

It will fall to the judge to decide whether the words are capable of amounting to comment (the jury will decide ultimately whether the words do amount to comment). The defendant may be assisted, however, by s.6 of the Defamation Act 1952. This states:

> ". . . in an action for libel or slander in respect of words consisting partly of allegations of fact and partly of expressions of opinion, a defence of fair comment shall not fail by reason only that the truth of every allegation of fact is not proved if the expression of opinion is fair comment having regard to such of the facts alleged or referred to in the words complained of as are proved."

This means that the truth of every statement of fact need not be proved. For example, A publishes an article which states that schoolteacher B failed his examinations at university, is always late and is therefore incompetent to teach at the local school. B sues for libel. A is able to prove that B failed his examinations, but finds that B is noted for his punctuality. Here, A

---

[27] Note, however, Lord Ackner's vigorous dissenting judgment in favour of freedom of speech.
[28] [2010] UKSC 53.
[29] [2010] UKSC 53 at para. 104.

can rely on s.6 to show that his comment is honest, and it will not matter that he cannot show the truth of all the allegations of fact.

## Honest

This final limitation is difficult to define. The courts apply the following test: was the opinion, **14–007** however exaggerated, obstinate or prejudiced, honestly held by the person expressing it?[30] The judge will decide whether a hypothetical person could honestly express the commentator's views on the assumption that he knew the facts accurately stated in the article (the objective test). The jury will decide whether the defendant in fact acted honestly and not maliciously. It should be noted that the jury need not agree with the comment, but must decide whether the statement is within the bounds of honest comment. The fact that the comment is expressed strongly, provided it does not descend into mere abuse, will make no difference.[31]

The defence of honest comment, unlike the defence of justification, will be defeated by malice. (As we will see later, malice also defeats the defence of qualified privilege). It is for the claimant to allege malice, and the judge will only put the allegation to the jury where he or she is satisfied that the claimant can adduce evidence to support a finding that the defendant was malicious. It has been assumed in the past that "malice" possesses the same meaning for the defences of honest comment and qualified privilege, namely that the courts are required to consider whether the defendant was acting under some indirect or improper motive. However, Lord Nicholls in the Court of Final Appeal in Hong Kong took a different view. In *Cheng v Tse Wai Chun*,[32] his Lordship focused on the key question of honesty, which he found to be the touchstone of this defence. Regardless of motive, if the defendant honestly believed the truth of his comment, then a court would not find malice. Spite, animosity, intention to injure or other motivation would only be relevant as evidence that the defendant did not genuinely believe the view expressed. Although only persuasive in English law, Eady J. has supported this development in a number of judgments.[33] In *Branson v Bower (No.2)*, he emphasised the rationale for this change:

> "It is necessary to acknowledge that if a defendant does indeed have to pass any more restrictive test, going beyond that of honesty, then the consequence would be a significant inhibiting effect on freedom of expression on matters of public interest . . . As Lord Nicholls makes clear, the whole point about a defence of fair comment is that it is to allow citizens to express hard-hitting opinions on matters of public interest honestly without fear of being brought before the courts."[34]

---

[30] See *Reynolds v Times Newspapers Ltd* [2001] 2 A.C. 127 at 193 per Lord Nicholls; *Slim v Daily Telegraph* [1968] 2 Q.B. 157 at 170; *Merivale v Carson* (1887) 20 Q.B.D. 275 at 281; *Turner v Metro-Goldwyn-Mayer Pictures* Ltd [1950] 1 All E.R. 449 at 461; *Silkin v Beaverbrook Newspapers Ltd* [1958] 1 W.L.R. 743 at 747.

[31] *Merivale v Carson* (1887) 20 Q.B.D. 275.

[32] Also known as *Tse Wai Chun Paul v Albert* [2001] E.M.L.R. 777 at 797; 10 B.H.R.C. 525 (CFA (HK)). Comment F.A. Trindade (2001) 117 L.Q.R. 169. See also *Associated Newspapers Ltd v Burstein* [2007] EWCA Civ 600; [2007] 4 All E.R. 319.

[33] See, for example, *Branson v Bower (No.2)* [2002] Q.B. 737 and *Hughes v Risbridger* [2010] EWHC 491 (QB). See also *Spiller v Joseph* [2010] UKSC 53.

[34] [2002] Q.B. 737 at 746. Lord Nicholls had held that the right to express comments honestly held lay at the heart of the defence and so would allow politicians, social reformers, busybodies, those with or without political or other ambitions to "grind their axes": above at 789.

## (3) PRIVILEGE

**14–008**   This is the third main defence. Here, we are concerned with a list of occasions when the public interest in freedom of expression is such that it overrides any concerns as to the effect of this freedom on the claimant's reputation. A defendant who makes a defamatory statement on such an occasion may raise the defence of privilege. The defence is somewhat technical: the defendant must show the court that the occasion on which the statement was made falls within an established head of privilege.

There are two types of privilege in English law. Absolute privilege is the stronger form of privilege and applies on occasions where the need to protect freedom of speech is so important as to create an absolute defence to any action for defamation, irrespective of the motives or words of the author. Qualified privilege is the weaker form of privilege. It applies on occasions where it is desirable that freedom of speech should be protected, but only where the author is acting honestly and without malice. If the claimant can show that the defendant has acted maliciously, the qualified privilege is lost. The judge decides whether the occasion is a privileged one, and whether a reasonable jury could find that the author's dominant motive was malice. The jury will decide whether any allegation of malice has been proved.

Decisions determining the occasions which merit absolute or qualified privilege have been taken over the last 500 years and represent the policy choices of Parliament and the judiciary at particular moments in history. The most recent consideration of privilege by the legislature has resulted in the Defamation Act 1996. The House of Lords also reconsidered privilege in the important case of *Reynolds v Times Newspapers*.[35] Both are discussed below.

### Absolute privilege

**14–009**   Absolute privilege applies to statements made in Parliament, in court and by certain officers of state. There are five main occasions when the defence will apply.

*(1) Statements in Parliament*

**14–010**   Article 9 of the Bill of Rights 1689 provides that:

> "the freedom of speech and debates or proceedings in Parliament ought not to be impeached or questioned in any court or place out of Parliament".

This preserves parliamentary autonomy, and allows Members of Parliament freely to criticise individuals as they feel appropriate. It also prevents the courts from inquiring into the conduct of parliamentary business.[36] The defence is confined, however, to statements made in Parliament.[37] As the Privy Council recently commented:

---

[35] [2001] 2 A.C. 127.

[36] The defence has been found to be consistent with the European Convention on Human Rights in that it does not impose a disproportionate restriction on the individual's right of access to the court: *A v United Kingdom (35373/97)* (2003) 36 E.H.R.R. 51.

[37] *Buchanan v Jennings* [2004] UKPC 36; [2005] 1 A.C. 115 (absolute privilege does not extend to repetition of statements outside Parliament even where the MP merely adopts and confirms a previous statement made in Parliament).

"A degree of circumspection is accordingly called for when a Member of Parliament is moved or pressed to repeat out of Parliament a potentially defamatory statement previously made in Parliament."[38]

In *Church of Scientology of California v Johnson-Smith*,[39] the plaintiff was not permitted to rely upon statements made by an MP in Parliament as evidence of malice, even though the action was based on comments made by the MP outside Parliament. The rule can be a mixed blessing for MPs. When the former Conservative MP, Neil Hamilton, sued *The Guardian* for libel, the action was stayed by May J., on the basis that the defendants would be unable to mount an effective defence because of parliamentary privilege.[40] This left Hamilton unable to clear his own name and pressure mounted for a change in the law. In an attempt to avoid any unfairness, Parliament passed s.13 of the Defamation Act 1996, which provides that an MP may waive privilege for the purpose of defamation proceedings.[41] However, even with the benefit of this section, Mr Hamilton later chose to withdraw his action against *The Guardian*. This section has been criticised for unduly favouring MPs over their opponents. The section gives no corresponding right to the opponent to ask for parliamentary privilege to be removed.

*(2) Reports, papers, votes and proceedings ordered to be published by either House of Parliament*

Statements in these documents are absolutely privileged by virtue of s.1 of the Parliamentary Papers Act 1840. Absolute privilege does not extend, however, to extracts from, or abstracts of, parliamentary papers, or to reports of parliamentary proceedings, but all of these are covered by qualified privilege, which will be discussed below.    **14–011**

*(3) Judicial proceedings*

It is important that the court should hear all relevant and admissible evidence, and it would be contrary to public policy if witnesses were reluctant to give evidence for fear that they may subsequently be sued for defamation. To ensure a fair trial, absolute privilege is therefore given to all oral and written statements made in the course of judicial proceedings. "Judicial proceedings" are defined broadly, and cover all tribunals exercising functions equivalent to a court of justice.[42] The privilege extends to statements made by the judge, jury, advocates, the parties and    **14–012**

---

[38] Lord Bingham [2004] UKPC 36; [2005] 1 A.C. 115 at para.20.

[39] [1972] Q.B. 522.

[40] *Hamilton v Guardian Newspapers, The Times*, July 22, 1995, following the Privy Council decision in *Prebble v Television New Zealand* [1995] 1 A.C. 321 (see A. Sharland and I. Loveland [1997] P.L. 113). For a recent example of parliamentary privilege, see *Office of Government Commerce v Information Commissioner* [2008] EWHC 774 (Admin); [2010] Q.B. 98.

[41] s.13 came into force on September 4, 1996. s.13(1) provides "(1) Where the conduct of a person in or in relation to proceedings in Parliament is in issue in defamation proceedings, he may waive for the purposes of those proceedings, so far as concerns him, the protection of any enactment or rule of law which prevents proceedings in Parliament being impeached or questioned in any court or place out of Parliament." See *Hamilton v Al Fayed (No.1)* [2001] 1 A.C. 395, where the House of Lords applied s.13 in Hamilton's favour—a short lived victory for Mr Hamilton whose claim ultimately failed. Comment: A.W. Bradley [2000] P.L. 556.

[42] See *O'Connor v Waldron* [1935] A.C. 76 and *Trapp v Mackie* [1979] 1 W.L.R. 377, HL. This has recently been found to include the Authorisation Tribunal of the self—regulatory Securities Association (*Mahon v Rahn (No.2)* [2000] 1 W.L.R. 2150) and the police disciplinary board (*Heath v Commissioner of Police of the Metropolis* [2004] EWCA Civ 943; [2005] I.C.R. 329).

witnesses.[43] This freedom to comment may be abused, but it is for the judge to regulate the conduct of the case in court. The defence also applies to statements made on occasions that can be regarded as a step in judicial proceedings, for example witness statements.[44] Whilst the defence applies to the solicitor/client relationship in connection with litigation, it is not clear whether it applies to communications between a solicitor and client which are not related to judicial proceedings. Logically, perhaps, it should not. In *More v Weaver*,[45] however, the Court of Appeal held that all relevant communications between solicitor and client were absolutely privileged. The question was left open by the House of Lords in *Minter v Priest*,[46] and it is more likely that such communications are covered by qualified privilege (discussed below).

*(4) Reports of United Kingdom court proceedings*

**14–013**    Section 14 of the Defamation Act 1996[47] provides that absolute privilege is accorded to all fair and accurate contemporaneous reports of public proceedings in a court in the United Kingdom, in the European Court of Justice (or any court attached to that court) and in the European Court of Human Rights.[48] Thus, a newspaper can give an account of court proceedings without fearing actions for defamation. "Contemporaneous" is the main limiting factor. This seems to mean as soon as practicable.[49] It is for the jury to decide whether the report is a fair and accurate one.

*(5) Communications between certain officers of state*

**14–014**    The argument here is that officers of state will perform their duties better if they are not acting under fear of litigation. This is essentially the familiar public policy argument that is used in the tort of negligence to justify not imposing liability on the police and other public bodies (see Ch.2). The leading case on this category of absolute privilege is *Chatterton v Secretary of State for India*.[50] Here, the Court of Appeal held that an action for libel based on a letter written by the Secretary of State for India to his parliamentary under-secretary, to enable the latter to answer questions in Parliament concerning the plaintiff, was rightly dismissed by the trial judge. To allow any judicial inquiry into such matters would tend to deprive officers of state of their freedom of action. The scope of this immunity is a matter of some debate, and it has been narrowly construed in more recent times. The immunity does not, for example,

---

[43] *Royal Aquarium and Summer and Winter Garden Society v Parkinson* [1892] 1 Q.B. 431 at 451 per Lopes L.J. , but see now *Jones v Kaney* [2011] UKSC 13 (no justification for holding expert witnesses immune from suit in relation to evidence given in court).

[44] *Watson v McEwan* [1905] A.C. 480 at 487; *Buckley v Dalziel* [2007] EWHC 1025 (QB); [2007] 1 W.L.R. 2933. This avoids the potential difficulty of individuals being reluctant to make witness statements due to their fear of being sued for defamation. However, the rule has boundaries and it does not extend to cover the fabrication of documentary evidence: *Darker v Chief Constable of the West Midlands* [2001] 1 A.C. 435.

[45] [1928] 2 K.B. 520, CA.

[46] [1930] A.C. 558 (see Lord Buckmaster at 570, Viscount Dunedin at 575 and Lord Atkin at 586). Note also the judgments of Brooke L.J. (with whom Nourse L.J. and Sir Brian Neill agreed) in *Waple v Surrey County Council* [1998] 1 W.L.R. 860 and Gray J. in *Clarke v Davey* [2002] EWHC 2342, 8 November 2002, who found a realistic prospect that Ms Clarke would be able to establish at trial that *More v Weaver* could no longer stand in the light of subsequent authority.

[47] This replaces the very similar Law of Libel Amendment Act 1888 s.3 (as amended) which was confined to television, newspapers and the radio.

[48] It also extends to certain international criminal tribunals: s.14(3).

[49] s.14(2). The privilege extends to the reporting of previous court hearings, insofar as it was reasonably necessary to give context to a contemporaneous report of a court hearing: *Crossley v Newsquest (Midlands South) Ltd* [2008] EWHC 3054 (QB).

[50] [1895] 2 Q.B. 189.

extend to communications between civil servants. Henn-Collins J. in *Szalatnay-Stacho v Fink*[51] suggested that it does not extend to officials below the rank of Minister, and in *Merricks v Nott-Bower*[52] the Court of Appeal refused to strike out a claim simply because the report was written by high-ranking police officers.

## Qualified privilege

This is the more limited form of privilege, and again largely consists of a list of occasions when the defendant has a valid defence to an action for defamation. The defendant must establish that the statement was made on such an occasion, or that he or she can satisfy the general test at common law. The privilege will be lost, however, if the claimant[53] can show either that the statement was made maliciously (for example, the defendant abused the privilege by using it for some purpose other than that for which the privilege was given) or that the defendant has exceeded the privilege (for example by publishing the statements more widely than necessary). In *Horrocks v Lowe*,[54] Lord Diplock considered the meaning of "malice", and held that the defendant is entitled to be protected by the privilege unless a "dominant and improper" motive is proved. His Lordship emphasised, however, that judges and juries should be slow to find a defendant malicious on the sole ground that the publication of the defamatory words (even though he believed them to be true) was prompted by the dominant motive of injuring the claimant. Generally an extra element was required. The defence of qualified privilege would be lost only if it could be shown that the defendant did not honestly believe that what he or she said was true, or was reckless as to its truth or falsity.[55]

The occasions when qualified privilege exists are listed below. The Defamation Act 1996 put on a statutory basis a number of miscellaneous occasions on which qualified privilege had previously arisen at common law. We will start, however, with the common law doctrine of qualified privilege which, as we will see, has undergone considerable development in recent years.

*Qualified privilege at common law*

Here, we are concerned with qualified privilege which arises in situations where there is a "reciprocal duty and interest" between the defamer and the person to whom the statement is published. Unfortunately, as we shall see, it has proved difficult to define precisely when such situations will arise. The defence has a number of forms, but in its basic form has two requirements:

- X has a duty or interest in communicating with Y (this duty may be legal, moral or social); and

- Y has a corresponding interest or duty in receiving the information in question.[56]

**14–015**

**14–016**

---

[51] [1946] 1 All E.R. 303 at 305; not considered by Court of Appeal [1947] K.B. 1.

[52] [1965] 1 Q.B. 57.

[53] Although the burden of proving malice is usually on the claimant, the burden will be on the defendant in cases of qualified privilege under the Parliamentary Papers Act 1840 s.3 (see below) to prove that the extract was published bona fide and without malice.

[54] [1975] A.C. 135 at 149–150.

[55] Except where the person is under a duty to pass on, without endorsing, defamatory reports made by some other person.

[56] See *Adam v Ward* [1917] A.C. 309 at 334 per Lord Atkinson.

The element of reciprocity is essential. On this basis, if X writes a letter to Y which contains false defamatory statements about Z, but (a) X has a duty to inform Y, and (b) Y has an interest in receiving this information, X has a good defence of qualified privilege.

Qualified privilege will also extend to situations where X publishes a statement to Y who shares a "common interest" with X, for example in the business in which they both work.[57] Further, it will include the situation where X has published the statement to defend his or her own interests and it is in the interest of Y to receive and consider the statement. For example, in *Osborn v Boulter*[58] the plaintiff had claimed that he had been supplied with poor quality beer. The defendant's response—that the plaintiff watered down his beer—was sent to meet this accusation and was therefore privileged. The courts have found that the law will generally attach privilege more readily to communications within an existing relationship than to communications between strangers.[59] The privilege will not be lost by dictating a letter to a secretary or delivering a circular to a printer.[60] These are reasonable and ordinary means of communication in business and are therefore privileged. It is not clear, however, whether they are covered by an ancillary form of privilege, which is dependent on the defendant establishing qualified privilege between the defendant and the intended recipient of the letter, or whether they form their own head of qualified privilege because of the common interest between the author and the typist in getting the letter written. Divergent views were expressed in *Bryanston Finance Ltd v de Vries*,[61] and the point therefore remains open.

The rationale for this head of qualified privilege is said to be the "common convenience and welfare of society".[62] In other words, it is necessary at times for people to be free to communicate without fear of litigation, in order to protect their own interests or because they are under a duty to communicate. The law will respect this freedom as being in the public interest provided it is not abused (i.e. exercised with malice).[63] A few examples will assist. On applying for a job, your new employer will generally require a reference from your former employer. Your former employer is under no legal duty to provide the reference, but is under a social duty to do so. It is very much in the interest of your new employer to see your reference. Therefore the reference will be protected by qualified privilege: *Spring v Guardian Assurance*.[64] The same reasoning will apply in respect of complaints made or information given to the police or appropriate authorities regarding suspected crimes.

A more graphic example may be seen in the case of *Watt v Longsdon*.[65] In this case, the plaintiff was managing director of a company overseas. The defendant was also a director of the

---

[57] See, e.g. *Bryanston Finance Ltd v de Vries* [1975] Q.B. 703.

[58] [1930] 2 K.B. 226 at 233–234.

[59] See *Kearns v General Council of the Bar* [2003] EWCA Civ 331; [2003] 1 W.L.R. 1357.

[60] *Osborn v Boulter* [1930] 2 K.B. 226 at 234.

[61] [1975] Q.B. 703—Lord Denning M.R. arguing for original privilege at 719 and Lawton L.J arguing for ancillary privilege at 736–738.

[62] *Toogood v Spyring* (1834) 1 Cr.M. & R. 181 at 193 per Parke B.; 149 E.R. 1044 at 1049–1050; *Davies v Snead* (1870) LR 5 QB 608 at 611 per Blackburn J.

[63] See Lord Nicholls in *Reynolds v Times Newspapers* [2001] 2 A.C. 127 at 194.

[64] [1995] 2 A.C. 296. In this case, the plaintiff relied on negligence and breach of contract following a finding that none of the persons involved in the giving of the reference had acted maliciously.

[65] [1930] 1 K.B. 130. See also *W v Westminster City Council* [2005] EWHC 102 (QB); [2005] 4 All E.R. 96 (Note) (social workers in child protection case conference protected by qualified privilege, although in breach of art.8) and *Clift v Slough BC* [2010] EWCA Civ 1171 (defence of qualified privilege when local authority placed C on Violent Persons register would be confined to communications to employees likely to deal with C. The defence would not extend to communication to other supernumerary departments e.g. trade union officials, which was disproportionate and a breach of art.8. ECHR).

company. The defendant had been informed by a manager (B) of various allegations of misconduct relating to the plaintiff. The defendant wrote back to B, adding his own suspicions, and asking B to obtain sworn statements to support the allegations. Without waiting to verify the complaints, the defendant wrote to the chairman of the board of directors, and to the plaintiff's wife (who was an old friend of his), informing them of the allegations. The allegations proved to be false and the plaintiff sued the defendant for libel. The question arose whether publication of the allegations to the chairman of the board and to the plaintiff's wife were covered by qualified privilege. The Court of Appeal held that the defendant's letter to the chairman of the board of directors was covered by qualified privilege. Employees of a company would have a common interest in the affairs of the company, which entitled them to discuss the behaviour and conduct of another employee. Additionally, there was a possibility that the chairman might be asked to provide a reference for the plaintiff at a future date. The qualified privilege did not extend, however, to the defendant's letter to the plaintiff's wife. Here, the defendant was held to have no duty to pass this information to the wife, particularly when it had not been verified. Yet, this is not clear-cut. Arguably, a wife has an interest in hearing about the misconduct of her husband, and there may sometimes be a "moral" or "social" duty to inform her of his misconduct. The court held that it would depend on the circumstances of each case. If the defendant had known the information to be genuine, it may have been found that the defendant had a moral duty to pass the information to the wife.[66] This case illustrates the problems of dealing with vague concepts of "duty" and "interest". The law's attempt to define these concepts will be examined below.

**What is a legal, moral or social duty?**    The observations of Lindley L.J., in *Stuart v Bell*,[67]    **14–017**
make it clear that the law simply leaves this question to be answered at the discretion of the judge:

> "The question of moral or social duty being for the judge, each judge must decide it as best as he can for himself. I take moral or social duty to mean a duty recognised by English people of ordinary intelligence and moral principle, but at the same time not a duty enforceable by legal proceedings, whether civil or criminal."

This provides little assistance. At best, we can say that the law applies an objective test, having regard to the moral and social duties prevalent in society. This inevitably raises a question as to the ability of the courts to ascertain the views of modern society. In practice, it will be a matter of looking at past case law and ascertaining what situations in recent times have given rise to such duties.

**What is an interest?**    Generally, this is easier to define. The courts will interpret "interest"    **14–018**
broadly to include, for example, financial and business interests such as an interest in the financial stability of an individual or company. Again, an objective test will be applied, and the question will be decided by the judge, who will ascertain whether the interest is legitimate and should be protected for the common convenience and welfare of society.

**The duty/interest test and the media:**    The leading case on common law qualified privi-    **14–019**
lege is now the House of Lords decision in *Reynolds v Times Newpapers Ltd*,[68] in which the

---

[66] See Scrutton L.J. [1930] 1 K.B. 130 at 149–150.
[67] [1891] 2 Q.B. 341 at 350.
[68] [2001] 2 A.C. 127, HL; [1998] 3 W.L.R. 862, CA. Comment F.A. Trindade (2000) 116 L.Q.R. 185; I. Loveland [2000] P.L. 351; K. Williams (2000) 63 M.L.R. 748; I. Loveland [2000] E.H.L.R.L. 476.

relationship between qualified privilege and the press was called into question. The House of Lords recognised that in a democracy the press play a vital role in ensuring that the public are informed and aware of the laws and regulations which affect their daily lives. This fact is recognised expressly in the Human Rights Act 1998. Section 12(4) of the Act provides that the courts should have a particular regard to the importance of freedom of expression in deciding cases which concern journalistic, literary or artistic material, and should examine (i) the extent to which the material has, or is about to, become available to the public; (ii) the extent to which it is, or would be, in the public interest for the material to be published; and (iii) any relevant privacy code.[69] This section was introduced by the Government in response to concern that the Act might undermine press freedom and result in the introduction of a privacy law "through the back door". The Act was therefore amended by the Government to include s.12, which was "designed solely to ensure that free speech, free expression, is abundantly safeguarded after the Bill becomes law".[70]

In view of such advocacy of press freedom, there is a clear argument that the defence of qualified privilege should be extended to all statements published in the public interest. Society has a clear interest in such stories, and the press may regard itself as under a duty to publish such material. Such an extension would ensure that the press, provided it acted without malice, would have the freedom to discuss important issues without the "chill" of a potential libel claim. This argument is particularly strong in relation to political discussion. Political matters are of direct concern to the electorate. Therefore it can be argued that the electorate has a "right to know". The courts have nevertheless traditionally opposed qualified privilege in this context, except in extreme circumstances such as a national emergency.[71] In *Reynolds v Times Newspapers*, the House of Lords reiterated that the media did not possess its own head of qualified privilege, even when dealing with matters of political information. However, a more liberal stance was suggested. This decision, and its implications, will be examined below.

**14–020**     In *Reynolds*, the former Prime Minister of the Republic of Ireland, Albert Reynolds, brought an action against *The Times* over an article which he claimed implied that he had deliberately misled the Irish Parliament and his cabinet colleagues during a political crisis in Ireland in 1994. He succeeded at first instance, but the jury awarded him one penny in damages. He appealed. *The Times* also appealed, claiming that it was protected by qualified privilege. The Court of Appeal set aside the jury's verdict and ordered a retrial, but held that the article was not covered by qualified privilege. *The Times* appealed to the House of Lords, but the majority of the House rejected its appeal. It was held that there was no special head of qualified privilege for the media based on the public interest in political information and discussion. On this basis, the ordinary "duty/interest" test outlined above would apply. However, their Lordships were of the view that this test was flexible enough to include consideration of diverse factors such as the nature, status and source of the material published and the circumstances of publication.[72] The court disagreed that such factors formed a third test of their own (the

---

[69] s.12(1) provides that "This section applies if a court is considering whether to grant any relief which, if granted, might affect the exercise of the Convention right to freedom of expression". Section 12(5) adds that "relief" includes any remedy or order (other than in criminal proceedings).

[70] Lord Williams of Mostyn, Hansard, H.L. col. 2113, October 29, 1998.

[71] See *Blackshaw v Lord* [1984] Q.B. 1 at 27 per Stephenson L.J.: "There may be extreme cases where the urgency of communicating a warning is so great, or the source of the information so reliable, that publication of suspicion or speculation is justified; e.g. where there is danger to the public from a suspected terrorist or the distribution of contaminated food or drugs; but there is nothing of that sort here".

[72] See *Blackshaw v Lord* [1984] Q.B. 1 at 27.

"circumstantial test" which had been adopted by the Court of Appeal). Lord Nicholls, who gave the leading opinion, held that:

> "With all due respect to the Court of Appeal, this formulation . . . gives rise to conceptual and practical difficulties and is better avoided . . . These factors are to be taken into account in determining whether the duty-interest is satisfied, or, as I would prefer to say in a simpler and more direct way, whether the public are entitled to know the particular information."[73]

Applying this test, the majority agreed with the Court of Appeal that the article did not contain **14–021** information which the public had a right to know.[74] Their Lordships particularly focused on the fact that the article had failed to mention Mr Reynolds' own explanation of his conduct to the Irish Parliament. The case nevertheless marked a clear recognition by the House of Lords of the importance of art.10 of the European Convention on Human Rights, and of the need to balance the countervailing interests of reputation and freedom of speech. It also gave the press some hope, in recognising that, in the right circumstances, the press could rely on qualified privilege when discussing political matters. Lord Nicholls advised future courts to consider a number of factors (which are not exhaustive) in deciding whether a duty to publish political discussion could be established, namely:

(i) The seriousness of the allegation—the more serious the charge, the more the public is misinformed and the individual harmed if the allegation is not true;

(ii) The nature of the information—whether it is a matter of public concern;

(iii) Its source;

(iv) What steps had been taken to verify the information;

(v) The status of the information, i.e. the reliability of the report;

(vi) The urgency of the matter (news being a perishable commodity);

(vii) Whether comment is sought from the claimant;

(viii) Whether the gist of the claimant's side of the story has been told;

(ix) The tone of the article; and

(x) The general circumstances and timing of the publication.

Such a flexible approach leaves the courts free to weigh up the competing interests of freedom of expression and reputation on the facts of each case. Yet such flexibility brings also uncertainty. While Lord Nicholls asserted that courts should be slow to find that publication is not in the public interest, particularly in relation to political discussion,[75] it remained for the courts to determine how his Lordship's ten guidelines would be applied. As Lord Lester of Herne Hill Q.C. commented following judgment in *Reynolds*:

---

[73] [2001] 2 A.C. 127 at 197.
[74] The minority felt that the issue of qualified privilege should be re-considered at the re-trial in the light of their Lordships' judgments.
[75] Lord Nicholls [2001] 2 A.C. 127 at 205.

"What matters now is for the media to develop and monitor their own codes of responsible journalism so that they are able to take advantage of the new opportunities created by *Reynolds*. The temptation is for the media to follow the easy line of least resistance and to censor themselves rather than to meet the challenge of *Reynolds*: namely, to maintain the high professional and ethical standards that they expect of those who govern on our behalf. To avoid that professional challenge would not be in the best interests of free expression and an informed public."[76]

**14–022**    **The application of *Reynolds*:**    Post-*Reynolds*, the courts in a number of decisions sought to clarify the operation of the test for qualified privilege, notably in the *Loutchansky* litigation[77] and in *Bonnick v Morris*.[78] In the former, a Russian businessman, Mr Loutchansky, had brought a libel claim in relation to two articles which appeared in *The Times* newspaper in 1999. It was alleged, amongst other matters, that the claimant was a Russian mafia boss, and that he was involved in money laundering and the smuggling of nuclear weapons. In the consolidated hearing of *Loutchansky v Times Newspapers Ltd (Nos 2–5)*,[79] the Court of Appeal ruled on a number of issues (including internet defamation and s.8 of the Defamation Act 1996 which will be considered later in this chapter) and stressed that the *Reynolds* test was one of responsible journalism. If the newspaper could satisfy the *Reynolds* criteria and demonstrate that it had acted responsibly, the defence of qualified privilege would apply. In determining the public interest, the Court of Appeal noted three matters of individual and public concern which would be predominant in the mind of the court:

(i) If qualified privilege was allowed, then, to all intents and purposes, the publisher would have a complete defence and the claimant would be denied a remedy;

(ii) Setting the standard of journalistic responsibility too low would inevitably encourage too great a readiness to publish defamatory matter; and

(iii) Setting the standard too high would deter newspapers from their proper function of keeping the public informed.

The court additionally recognised that where privilege is found, little room is left for a finding of malice: a responsible journalist will not act maliciously.[80] The ten factors thus incorporate both the test for privilege and the question of malice and limit the role of the jury in this context. In stipulating the test to be one of responsible journalism, the court rejected the test applied by Gray J. below—whether a publisher would be open to legitimate criticism if he failed to publish the information in question—as too stringent.[81]

---

[76] *The Times*, December 7, 1999. Lord Lester Q.C. represented *The Times* in *Reynolds*.

[77] See below.

[78] [2002] UKPC 31; [2003] 1 A.C. 300.

[79] [2001] EWCA Civ 1805; [2002] Q.B. 783. See also *Loutchansky v Times Newspapers Ltd (No.1)* [2001] EWCA Civ 536; [2002] Q.B. 321 (the factors identified by the court for consideration in *Reynolds* to be determined on the basis of the defendant's state of knowledge at the time of publication). Note that the same rule applies to fair/honest comment, but that further facts may be pleaded for justification: see *Cohen v Daily Telegraph* [1968] 1 W.L.R. 916.

[80] See also *GKR Karate (UK) Ltd v Yorkshire Post Newspapers Ltd* [2000] 1 W.L.R. 2571 at 2580 per May L.J.

[81] The case was remitted to Gray J., who, applying the above principles, found against *The Times*: *Loutchansky v Times Newspapers Ltd and others* [2002] EWHC 2490 (QB); [2002] All E.R. (D) 371 (Nov), (Approved judgment).

In *Bonnick v Morris*,[82] Lord Nicholls indicated that a flexible approach should be adopted where the words used were ambiguous and could have conveyed either a defamatory and non-defamatory meaning to the ordinary reasonable reader. Here, the article had referred to the dismissal of Mr Bonnick in the context of contractual litigation in which irregularities had been alleged. Mr Bonnick alleged that the article suggested that there was a connection between his dismissal and the irregularities stated. In the view of the court, the defamatory meaning was not obvious. Here, the article related to a matter of considerable public concern and was generally well-balanced and, in such circumstances, it was prepared to overlook the failure of the journalist to inquire into the truth of the statement or refer to the claimant's own explanation in the article. Lord Nicholls emphasised, however, that the court would not have been so generous if an expressly defamatory statement had been made.

Further signs of flexibility may be found in the so-called "reportage"[83] cases. This is a special form of qualified privilege where the media neutrally reports the allegations made by one named party against another without adopting, embellishing or endorsing the allegations.[84] Whilst the newspaper here is still subject to the *Reynolds* test, there is a difference— the journalist is not required to verify the truth of the allegation because he or she is simply reporting in a neutral fashion the *fact* that the statement has been made. This will not always be easy to show and to date there have only been two successful cases.[85] In *Galloway v Telegraph Group Ltd*,[86] the court rejected the defence of reportage in circumstances where the *Daily Telegraph* was found to have gone a long way to adopt and embellish the allegations contained in documents found by its reporter and had done so with relish.

Despite such guidance, the House of Lords in *Jameel v Wall Street Journal Europe SPRL (No.3)*[87] found that the lower courts were interpreting the *Reynolds* defence in an unduly restrictive manner and that it was necessary to restate its principles.[88] The Court of Appeal in this case had rejected the defence of qualified privilege due to the failure of the newspaper to delay publication to allow the claimant to comment. Whilst this is one of Lord Nicholls' relevant factors, the House of Lords stressed that the ten factors are not hurdles, but merely pointers towards the correct approach to adopt.[89] Their Lordships identified two questions to be addressed in cases of media qualified privilege: **14–023**

- That the subject-matter of the article, taken in context and as a whole, was in the public interest; *and*

- That the publication met the objective standard of responsible journalism.[90]

---

[82] [2002] UKPC 31; [2003] 1 A.C. 300.

[83] Described by Ward L.J. as a "fancy word": *Roberts v Gable* [2007] EWCA Civ 721; [2007] E.M.L.R. 16 at para.34.

[84] See *Al-Fagih v HH Saudi Research & Marketing (UK) Ltd* [2001] EWCA Civ 1634; [2002] E.M.L.R. 13 (Mantell L.J. dissenting) and *Roberts v Gable* [2007] EWCA Civ 721; [2007] E.M.L.R. 16.

[85] Namely *Al-Fagih v HH Saudi Research & Marketing (UK) Ltd* [2001] EWCA Civ 1634 and *Roberts v Gable* [2007] EWCA Civ 721. Sedley L.J. also suggested in *Roberts v Gable* that there may be cases where the responsible journalism tests requires verification, although it will usually be beside the point.

[86] [2006] EWCA Civ 17; [2006] E.M.L.R. 11. The defence also failed in *Charman v Orion Publishing Group Ltd* [2007] EWCA Civ 972; [2008] 1 All E.R. 750.

[87] [2006] UKHL 44; [2007] 1 A.C. 359 (also discussed in Ch.13 in the context of a company's right to sue in defamation).

[88] [2006] UKHL 44; [2007] 1 A.C. 359 at para.38 per Lord Hoffmann.

[89] [2006] UKHL 44; [2007] 1 A.C. 359 at para.33 per Lord Bingham and at para.56 per Lord Hoffmann.

[90] Explained in *Flood v Times Newspapers* [2010] EWCA Civ 804; [2011] 1 W.L.R. 153 as existing when the inclusion of the allegations was part of the story and made a real contribution to it, and the steps taken to gather and publish the information were responsible and fair: at para. 55 per Lord Neuberger M.R.

Guidance should be gained from decided cases and reference could be made to media Codes of Practice. On the facts of the case, their Lordships were in no doubt that, despite the failure to contact Mr Jameel,[91] the article as a whole, dealing with the thorny issue of the funding of international terrorism in the wake of the 9/11 attacks, raised a matter of public interest and that the Wall Street Journal (described as a respected, influential and unsensational newspaper)[92] had acted responsibly in taking reasonable steps to verify the facts relied upon. In the words of Baroness Hale:

> "We need more such serious journalism in this country and our defamation law should encourage rather than discourage it . . . if the public interest defence[93] does not succeed on the known facts of this case, it is hard to see it ever succeeding."[94]

The strong views of their Lordships can be contrasted with those of the Court of Appeal[95] and lower court judge, Eady J.,[96] that the defence of qualified privilege should not stand. The House of Lords stressed the need to apply the *Reynolds* test more generously and with greater flexibility. Lord Hoffmann commented that allowance should be made for editorial judgement:

> "The fact that the judge, with the advantage of leisure and hindsight, might have made a different editorial decision should not destroy the defence."[97]

This amounts to a clear indication that it should be easier for the media to establish this defence in future.

The recent Court of Appeal decision in *Flood v Times Newspapers*[98] does suggest, however, that this should not render newspapers complacent, and that the courts will draw a line when a newspaper's attempt at investigative journalism is based on unfounded (and unchecked) allegations from an unknown source. In rejecting the defence where the newspaper had linked a senior police officer with the acceptance of bribes in exchange for confidential police information, the Court distinguished *Jameel*. These were serious allegations, largely unchecked and unsupported, and a distinction had to be made between publication of the fact that a complaint had been made and the details of the allegations underlying the complaint. Here, the article ran the risk of "trial by media" and, in particular, the failure of the newspaper to amend its online journal when Flood had been cleared by an internal police investigation received particular condemnation.[99]

---

[91]  Scepticism was expressed whether any useful response could in any event have been obtained.

[92]  Lord Bingham [2006] UKHL 44; [2007] 1 A.C. 359 at para.2. Query to what extent the "quality" of the newspaper should be relevant.

[93]  The House was divided whether the *Reynolds* defence should be seen as a development of the common law duty/ interest test (Lords Bingham, Scott and Hope) or whether it is, in reality, a distinct public interest defence (Lord Hoffmann and Baroness Hale). This does not appear, however, to have any impact on the actual content of the defence and their Lordships were in agreement as to its application to the facts of the case.

[94]  [2006] UKHL 44; [2007] 1 A.C. 359 at paras 150–151.

[95]  *Jameel v Wall Street Journal Europe SPRL (No.3)* [2005] EWCA Civ 74; [2005] Q.B. 904.

[96]  *Jameel v Wall Street Journal Europe SPRL (No.3)* [2004] EWHC 37 (QB); [2004] E.M.L.R. 11.

[97]  [2006] UKHL 44; [2007] 1 A.C. 359 at para.51.

[98]  [2010] EWCA Civ 804.

[99]  Note that the newspaper has been given leave to appeal to the Supreme Court: UKSC 2010/0166.

The general view remains, however, that the *Reynolds* test, as interpreted in *Jameel*, repre- **14–024** sents a liberalisation of traditional rules and that it will be generally easier to satisfy than the traditional duty/interest test for qualified privilege. The Privy Council in *Seaga v Harper*[100] rejected the view of the Court of Appeal in *Kearns v General Council of the Bar*[101] that *Reynolds* privilege was confined to media publications. In that case, the *Reynolds* test was held to be inapplicable to a letter circulated to the 10,000 members of the Bar. It has already been established that the defence is not confined to political matters, but extends to any question of interest to the public.[102] The Privy Council went further and found:

> "no valid reason why it should not extend to publications made by any person who publishes material of public interest in any medium, so long as the conditions framed by Lord Nicholls as being applicable to 'responsible journalism' are satisfied".[103]

On this basis, *Reynolds* privilege might extend to quasi-media defendants, such as bloggers, and other bodies acting in the public interest such as NGOs. If followed by the domestic courts, it has the potential to encourage far greater resort to this defence.

The English position may be compared with that of New Zealand, where the New Zealand **14–025** Court of Appeal has rejected *Reynolds* as too uncertain and restrictive and favoured a press-specific head of privilege rejected so firmly by the House of Lords.[104] In so doing, the court commented that this could be justified on the basis that New Zealand newspapers were more responsible than their English counterparts.[105] English law also remains distinct from the position in the United States where, following *New York Times v Sullivan*,[106] public figures may only recover damages for defamation if they are able to show by clear and convincing evidence that the defendant published with malice. It may also be questioned whether *Reynolds* succeeds in striking an adequate balance between freedom of speech and protection of reputation. The European Court of Human Rights in *Lingens v Austria*,[107] in finding that the conviction of a journalist for defamation was in breach of art.10, strongly advocated the right of the press to impart information and ideas on political issues in the public interest. Following the liberalisation of *Jameel*, one must assume that its objective two-stage test does provide an adequate response and that the test of:

---

[100] [2008] UKPC 9; [2008] 1 All E.R. 965.

[101] [2003] EWCA Civ 331; [2003] 1 W.L.R. 1357.

[102] Although most cases have some political element. See *GKR Karate (UK) Ltd v Yorkshire Post Newspapers Ltd* [2000] 1 W.L.R. 2571, which concerned allegedly sub-standard karate courses!

[103] [2008] UKPC 9 at para.11. See also Lord Hoffmann in *Jameel* at para.54.

[104] See *Lange v Atkinson* [2000] 3 N.Z.L.R. 385 (where a genuine political discussion is involved). This decision affirmed and elaborated its original decision in *Lange v Atkinson* [1998] 3 N.Z.L.R. 424 after the Privy Council ([2000] 1 N.Z.L.R. 257) had remitted the case for rehearing in the light of *Reynolds* (comment N.W. Barber and A.L. Young (2001) 117 L.Q.R. 175). Consider also the different Australian test set out in *Lange v Australian Broadcasting Co* (1997) 189 C.L.R. 520 based on a test of reasonableness. On December 22, 2009, the Supreme Court of Canada issued its judgment in *Grant v Torstar Corp.* (2009 SCC 61) establishing a new "responsible communication" defence, hailed as a victory for public interest journalism and freedom of the press: see R. Mullender (2010) 126 L.Q.R. 368.

[105] [2000] 3 N.Z.L.R. 385 at 398.

[106] 66 376 U.S. 254 (1964).

[107] (1986) 8 E.H.R.R. 407. See also *De Haes and Gijsels v Belgium* (1997) 25 E.H.R.R. 1 and *Castells v Spain* (1992) 14 E.H.R.R. 445.

"Responsible journalism is the point at which a fair balance is held between freedom of expression on matters of public concern and the reputations of individuals."[108]

*Qualified privilege under statute*

**14–026**   The Defamation Act 1996 provides for numerous occasions on which qualified privilege will arise. Section 15(1) provides that:

"The publication of any report[109] or other statement mentioned in Sch.1 to this Act is privileged unless the publication is shown to be made with malice."[110]

Some of the most important examples in Sch.1 are considered below.

**14–027**   **(i) Reports of parliamentary proceedings:**   Absolute privilege only extends to reports, papers, votes and proceedings ordered to be published by either House of Parliament. It does not include fair and accurate reports of parliamentary proceedings, which were covered by common law qualified privilege[111] and are now covered by the Defamation Act 1996. Schedule 1, para.1 provides that there is privilege for a fair and accurate report of proceedings in public of a legislature anywhere in the world.[112] Schedule 1, para.7 also provides that a fair and accurate copy of, or extract from, matter published by or on the authority of a government or legislature anywhere in the world is privileged. This expands the previous privilege granted under s.3 of the Parliamentary Papers Act 1840.[113] In both cases, publication is covered by qualified privilege "without explanation or contradiction" (the meaning of this phrase is discussed later).

**14–028**   **(ii) Reports of judicial proceedings:**   As stated above, absolute privilege is accorded to fair and accurate contemporaneous reports of court proceedings in public. Fair and accurate non-contemporaneous reports of public judicial proceedings are covered by qualified privilege.[114] The common law is now replaced by the Defamation Act 1996 (Sch.1, para.2) which provides that a fair and accurate report of proceedings in public before a court anywhere in the world is privileged without explanation or contradiction.

**14–029**   **(iii) Registers:**   Likewise, publications of a fair and accurate copy of or extract from a register required by law to be open to public inspection, for example the register of county court judgments, was privileged under the common law[115] and is now privileged without explanation or contradiction under the Defamation Act 1996 (Sch.1, para.5).

---

[108] *Bonnick v Morris* [2002] UKPC 31; [2003] 1 A.C. 300 at para.23 per Lord Nicholls. Note also the comments of the Court of Appeal in *Galloway v Telegraph Group Ltd* [2006] EWCA Civ 17; [2006] E.M.L.R. 11 at para.80: "it also seems to us that Lord Nicholls was himself according particular importance to freedom of expression and thus freedom of the press in just the same way as the European Court [of Human Rights] has done. We detect no difference in principle between the approach of the House of Lords in *Reynolds* and that of the European Court."

[109] *Henry v BBC (Qualified Privilege)* [2005] EWHC 2787 (QB): broadcast was so heavily laden with editorial comment that it did not qualify as a report protected by Defamation Act 1996 s.15.

[110] Sch.1 and s.15 only came into force on April 1, 1999: Defamation Act 1996 (Commencement No.1) Order (SI 1999/817).

[111] *Wason v Walter* (1868) L.R. 4 Q.B. 73.

[112] For a recent application, see *Curistan v Times Newspapers Ltd* [2008] EWCA Civ 432; [2009] Q.B. 231.

[113] As amended by Defamation Act 1952 s.9(1).

[114] This did not extend to fair and accurate reports of judicial proceedings in foreign courts: *Webb v Times Publishing Co* [1960] 2 Q.B. 535.

[115] *Sealers v Scarlett* [1892] 2 Q.B. 56.

**(iv) Other matters covered by s.15 and Sch.1 to the Defamation Act 1996:** We have   **14–030**
already seen the operation of Sch.1 in the examples above. Schedule 1 replaces previous
statutory provisions for privilege in the Law of Libel Amendment Act 1888 and the Defamation Act 1952. It also covers some of the common law examples of qualified privilege. It is
divided into two sections. Part I deals with reports which are privileged "without explanation
or contradiction". Part II deals with reports which are privileged "subject to explanation or
contradiction". This distinction is important. Qualified privilege may be lost (for Pt II reports
only) if it is proved that the defendant has been requested, by the claimant, to publish in a suitable manner[116] a reasonable letter or statement by way of explanation or contradiction, and
has refused or neglected to do so: s.15(2). In other words, the claimant must be given the right
of reply with respect to Pt II reports. However, the courts will not permit Sch.1 to be abused.
Section 15(3) provides that the privilege will not extend to matters which are not of public
concern and the publication of which is not for the public benefit. It will equally not protect
the publication of matters prohibited by law.[117]

We shall refrain from repeating the long list of reports and statements given in Sch.1. Readers
are advised to look at the Defamation Act 1996. Generally, Pt I covers fair and accurate reports
of legislative, court or government body proceedings anywhere in the world, as may be seen
from the examples given above. The Pt II list consists of a number of different types of reports,
including fair and accurate copies of or extracts from documents made available by a court in
any Member State, or by the European Court of Justice[118] (para.10); fair and accurate reports
of proceedings at any public meeting held in a Member State (para.12); and fair and accurate
reports of proceedings at a general meeting of a UK public company (para.13).[119]

**Schedule 1 and freedom of expression:** It is inevitable that, following *Reynolds*, the courts   **14–031**
would be asked to consider the relationship between freedom of expression and statutory
qualified privilege. In *McCartan Turkington Breen v Times Newspapers Ltd*[120] (a case heard
the day after the Human Rights Act 1998 came into force), the court considered the meaning of the term "public meeting" in the Northern Irish equivalent to para.12 (see above).[121]
Did it include a press conference? It was alleged that defamatory statements had been made
against the plaintiffs in a report of a press conference organised by an informal committee,
which sought to secure the release from prison of a British serviceman, Private Lee Clegg.
At first instance, Girvan J. had found that the issue of invitations to members of the press, but
not to the general public, indicated that the press conference was not a "public meeting" and
accordingly no privilege attached to the report. The Northern Ireland Court of Appeal affirmed
this view. The House of Lords rejected such a narrow definition. "Public meeting" was to be
interpreted in the context of contemporary conditions, and a meeting would be public if its
organisers opened it to the public or, by issuing a general invitation to the press, manifested

---

[116] That is, in the same manner as the publication complained of or in a manner that is adequate and reasonable in the
circumstances: s.15(2).

[117] s.15(4)(a).

[118] Or by a judge or officer of any such court.

[119] The recent case of *Flood v Times Newspaper* [2010] EWCA Civ 804 deals with a further type of report: Sch.1,
para.9(1)(b): a fair and accurate copy of or extract from a notice or other matter issued for the information of the
public by any authority performing governmental functions (here the police).

[120] [2001] 2 A.C. 277. Comment I. Loveland [2001] P.L. 233.

[121] s.7 and para.9 of the Schedule to the Defamation Act (Northern Ireland) 1955 granted qualified privilege to "a fair
and accurate report of the proceedings at any public meeting." These provisions have now been repealed and replaced
by the Defamation Act 1996.

an intention to communicate the proceedings to a wider public. A meeting did not lose its public character because admission was subject to some restriction. The organisers' object had been to stimulate public pressure to rectify a perceived injustice, and a press conference was an important vehicle to promote discussion and furtherance of matters of public concern. There was nothing in its nature to exclude it from the ordinary meaning of a "public meeting".[122]

Lord Bingham emphasised the importance of the media in keeping the public informed:[123]

> "It is very largely through the media, including of course the press, that [the public] will be so alerted and informed. The proper functioning of a modern participatory democracy requires that the media be free, active, professional and enquiring. For this reason the courts, here and elsewhere, have recognised the cardinal importance of press freedom and the need for any restriction on that freedom to be proportionate and no more than is necessary to promote the legitimate object of the restriction."

Such statements must give hope to journalists that the courts will adopt a more generous interpretation of qualified privilege in future. Nevertheless, the courts will, as seen in *Loutchansky* and *Jameel*, still seek to ensure that the standard of responsible journalism is maintained, and will continue to be alert to any suggestion that they have given a green light to a general media head of qualified privilege. The *Reynolds* criteria will be monitored, and it should be recalled that whilst the newspapers were successful in *McCartan Turkington Breen* and *Jameel*, *The Times* failed to satisfy the Court of Appeal that it should be accorded qualified privilege in *Loutchansky*.

## (4)  Offer of Amends Under the Defamation Act 1996

**14–032**    This defence applies to unintentional defamation. It may be recalled that the publication of a statement may amount to defamation even though the defendant did not intend to harm the claimant's reputation. For present purposes, there are two senses in which the publication of a defamatory statement might be said to be "unintentional". First, there is the situation where, for example, a newspaper publishes a defamatory statement, knowing that it refers to the claimant, but honestly and reasonably believing that the statement is true (as in *Cassidy v Daily Mirror*, discussed in Ch.13). Secondly, there is the "mistaken identity" situation, where a newspaper publishes a statement which is false and defamatory in relation to the claimant, but intends the statement to refer to someone else, about whom it is true (as in *Newstead v London Express*, also discussed in Ch.13).

Section 4 of the Defamation Act 1952 did provide some mechanism whereby a defendant could, in such circumstances, make an "offer of amends" which, if accepted, would end proceedings, and if not accepted would amount to a defence. But this provision was little used, mainly because of the difficulties defendants had in proving that the statement was published "innocently", as required by s.4(5). A revised version appears in the Defamation Act 1996.[124]

---

[122]   The House of Lords also ruled that a press release issued at the press conference, but not read aloud, could be part of the relevant proceedings.

[123]   [2001] 2 A.C. 277 at 290–291.

[124]   As recommended by the *Neill Committee on Practice and Procedure in Defamation*, 1991, Ch. VII.

Sections 2 to 4 set out the new procedure for making an offer of amends. As May L.J. stated in *Milne v Express Newspapers*:[125]

"The main purpose of the statutory provisions is plain. It is to encourage the sensible compromise of defamation proceedings without the need for an expensive jury trial."

Under s.2, the defendant must be prepared:

  (i) To admit that he or she was wrong (or partly wrong);

  (ii) To offer in writing to make a suitable correction and apology;

  (iii) To publish the correction and apology in a manner that is reasonable and practicable in the circumstances; and

  (iv) To pay the claimant such compensation (if any) and such costs as may be agreed or determined to be payable.

The offer may relate to the statement generally, or only to a specific defamatory meaning (known as a "qualified offer"). Timing is important. The offer must be made before service of a defence.[126] This forces the defendant to decide whether to fight the action or admit that he or she is wrong. If the offer is accepted, the claimant must discontinue the action against the defendant.[127] If the parties cannot agree the amount of compensation to be paid, s.3(5) provides that it will be settled by the court, sitting without a jury, "on the same principles as damages in defamation proceedings".[128] This will involve questions such as mitigation, aggravation and causation of loss. Recent case law has clarified that if an early unqualified offer to make amends is accepted and an agreed apology published, the court is likely to find substantial mitigation, reducing the level of damages awarded.[129]

    If the offer is not accepted, the action may continue, but the defendant may use the making of the offer as a defence unless the claimant is able to show that the defendant knew or had reason to believe that the statement referred to the claimant (or was likely to be understood as referring to him) and was both false and defamatory of him. The test is one of bad faith, not negligence.[130] In other words, the burden is on the claimant to show that the defamation was intentional or reckless. Section 4(4) provides that the defendant cannot rely on an offer of amends by way of defence in combination with any other defence. The defence is therefore of limited use, and a defendant would be wise to consider his or her tactical position before

---

[125] [2004] EWCA Civ 664; [2005] 1 W.L.R. 772 at para.14.

[126] s.2(5).

[127] Subject to a residual court discretion to allow a party to resile from an accepted offer in exceptional circumstances: *Warren v Random House Group Ltd* [2008] EWCA Civ 834; [2009] Q.B. 600.

[128] See *Abu v MGN Ltd* [2002] EWHC 2345 (QB); [2003] 1 W.L.R. 2201.

[129] See *Nail v News Group Newspapers Ltd* [2004] EWCA Civ 1708; [2005] 1 All E.R. 1040 (reduced by 50 per cent but no standard percentage discount and each case would require individual consideration). See also *Campbell-James v Guardian Media Group Plc* [2005] EWHC 893 (QB); [2005] E.M.L.R. 24. This is because, due to the early capitulation of the defendant, the claimant's reputation has been vindicated whilst he or she has been spared the anxiety and costs risk of contested proceedings. Where only one defendant (out of several) makes an unqualified offer of amends with published apology, the court will cap his liability when considering joint and several liability with the other defendants: *Veliu v Mazrekaj* [2006] EWHC 1710 (QB); [2007] 1 W.L.R. 495.

[130] s.4(3). "Reason to believe" imports the concept of recklessness, discussed by Lord Diplock in *Horrocks v Lowe* [1975] A.C. 135: see *Milne v Express Newspapers* [2004] EWCA Civ 664; [2005] 1 W.L.R. 772.

relying on an offer or qualified offer of amends as a defence. It should be noted that even if the offer is not accepted, it may be relied upon in mitigation of damages.[131]

On a historical note, the defendant still has a defence under s.2 of the Libel Act 1843 (as amended by the Libel Act 1845). This provides that it is a defence, when a libel is published in a newspaper without actual malice or gross negligence, for the defendant to publish a full apology in the newspaper and pay money into court by way of amends. This has not been repealed by the Defamation Act 1996, but has been little used due to substantial procedural disadvantages to the defendant. The Faulks Committee in 1975 recommended its repeal "with a view to simplifying this aspect of the law of defamation",[132] but this sensible suggestion has not been taken up. After the 1996 Act, however, it is likely to be of only historical interest.

## (5) INNOCENT DISSEMINATION

14-033    This defence applies to parties involved in the distribution process, who inadvertently become involved in the publication of defamatory material. It therefore has no application to the actual author of the defamatory material, or to the publisher who actively produces the defamatory material. An example will help us understand the problem. I write a defamatory article for the Daily Rag. I have published the libel and will be liable, but so have the editor, publisher and the distributors of the Daily Rag, including Mr X, the newsagent. Each repetition of the libel is actionable by the claimant. It seems harsh to allow the claimant to sue all of the above parties. Therefore the defence of innocent dissemination seeks to draw a distinction between those who produce the libel (here myself, my editor and publisher) and those who "disseminate" or distribute it (here the distributors and Mr X). Until recently, the defence was part of the common law, as stated in *Vizetelly v Mudie's Select Library Ltd*.[133] The court in this case held that the mechanical distribution of defamatory material by agencies such as newsagents or libraries would be protected against claims for defamation provided they could show that:

(i) They did not know that the work contained a libel of the claimant;

(ii) It was not by negligence that they did not know of the libel; and

(iii) The defendants did not know, nor ought to have known, that the works were of such a character that they were likely to contain defamatory material.

In the case itself, the defendants were held liable for defamation because they had overlooked a publisher's circular which had requested the return of copies of the book in question, and in fact had no procedure for checking whether the books they lent contained defamatory material.

The common law has now been replaced and updated by s.1 of the Defamation Act 1996. It is now a defence to show that:

---

[131] s.4(5): "The offer may be relied on in mitigation of damage whether or not it was relied on as a defence".

[132] At para.373.

[133] [1900] 2 Q.B. 170, applying *Emmens v Pottle* (1885) 16 Q.B.D. 354.

(i)   The defendant is not the author,[134] editor or commercial publisher (in the sense of issuing material to the public in the course of business)[135] of the statement;

(ii)  The defendant took reasonable care in relation to the publication; and

(iii) The defendant did not know, and had no reason to believe, that what he or she did caused or contributed to the publication of a defamatory statement.

In assessing the above criteria, the court will have regard to the extent of the defendant's responsibilities for the content of, or decision to publish, the statement; the nature or circumstances of the publication; and the previous conduct or character of the author, editor or publisher (s.1(5)). For example, if the defendant distributes work by an author renowned for controversy, the defendant will be expected to vet the work carefully for defamatory material. Sections 1(3)(a) to (e) list a number of individuals who do not qualify as "authors", "editors" or "publishers". These provisions are not comprehensive, and do not prevent the courts reasoning by analogy. Section 1(3)(a) provides that distributors and printers[136] can rely on a s.1 defence. Interestingly, broadcasters of live programmes may also rely on the defence if, in the circumstances, they have no effective control over the maker of the statement, for example in live phone-in programmes.[137] Again, however, if controversial guests are invited, editors would be wise to employ some kind of screening process, and consider devices such as a delay mechanism on the transmission of material, if they wish to show that they have taken reasonable care.

Even the internet is provided for, in s.1(3)(c) and (e). Section 1(3)(e) covers the "operator    **14–034** or provider of access to a communications system by means of which the statement is transmitted, or made available, by a person over whom he had no effective control"—essentially an internet service provider or "ISP". This particular provision was considered in the case of *Godfrey v Demon Internet Ltd.*[138] The defendants were an ISP which provided a particular newsgroup, which stored postings for about a fortnight. In January 1997, an unknown person made a posting to the newsgroup which was defamatory of Dr Godfrey. Godfrey contacted the defendants four days later, requesting that the posting be removed from their news server. The defendants failed to do so, and the posting remained on the server for the full two week period. It was accepted that the defendants could have removed the posting had they chosen to do so. Godfrey sued the defendants for libel. Morland J. struck out the defendants' s.1 defence. The defendants had known of the posting's defamatory contents and, by failing to remove the statements, lost the protection of s.1 of the Act. While the defendants were not the author, editor or commercial publisher of the statement, they could not show that they had taken reasonable care in relation to the publication, or that they did not know that what they did caused or contributed to the publication of a defamatory statement. Morland J. also refused to

---

[134] s.1(2) defines "author" as originator of the statement, but does not include a person who did not intend that his or her statement be published at all.
[135] s.1(2).
[136] Ch.11 of the report of the Faulks Committee in 1975 (Report of the Committee on Defamation, Cmnd 5909) recommended that the defence of innocent dissemination should be extended to printers.
[137] s.1(3)(d).
[138] [2001] Q.B. 201.

accept that an ISP could not "publish" information.[139] An ISP which transmitted a defamatory posting on a news server would, by analogy to a bookseller, be deemed to publish the information contained in the posting.[140]

Fears have been expressed that Godfrey has led to a restriction of freedom of speech on the internet. Faced with an allegation that a posting is defamatory, most ISPs will simply withdraw the posting to avoid potential litigation and will not bother to check whether the allegation is well-founded. Arguably, this will give individuals the opportunity to "veto" any posting which contains information they do not wish to be published and consequently limit free speech. It is notable that the United States Supreme Court, when faced with a similar case in Lunney v Prodigy,[141] chose to find in favour of the ISP. The Electronic Commerce (EC Directive) Regulations 2002[142] offer little comfort to ISPs. These Regulations, implementing EC Directive 2000/31/EC, limit the potential liability of ISPs in relation to a number of legal claims, including defamation, obscenity and copyright. Regulation 19 grants immunity to the ISP which hosts the relevant site, but only if two conditions are met:

(i) The ISP does not have actual knowledge of the unlawful activity or information and is not aware of facts or circumstances from which it would have been apparent to the ISP that the activity or information was unlawful; and

(ii) It acts expeditiously to remove such information on obtaining any such knowledge.

The Law Commission in the report discussed below concluded that this would act in the same manner as s.1, again leaving the ISP potentially liable where it has been notified of an allegedly defamatory posting.[143]

Loutchansky v Times Newspapers Ltd (No.2)[144] mentioned above under "qualified privilege", highlights a further risk of liability. Here, the article in question had been posted as part of The Times' publicly accessible online archive. The Court of Appeal held that every hit of the article on this site would amount to publication. This is consistent with Godfrey, but must be considered in the light of the rule of English law established in Duke of Brunswick v Harmer that every publication will give rise to a cause of action.[145] On this basis, the claimant would be able to sue every time someone accessed the article. It was argued that such ongoing liability would be contrary to free speech, place an unfair burden on the ISP and totally undermine the one-year limitation period for defamation claims (see below under "Limitation").

[139] In effect, rejecting the "mere conduit" argument that has gained acceptance in the US. Contrast the position where the information is "cached", that is stored temporarily on the computer system for the purpose of enabling the efficient availability of internet material. Here, Bunt v Tilley [2006] EWHC 407 (QB); [2007] 1 W.L.R. 1243 held that the role of the ISP is passive and it would not be liable unless it had been knowingly involved in the process of publication (see also reg.18, Electronic Commerce (EC Directive) Regulations 2002). See also Metropolitan International Schools Ltd (t/a SkillsTrain and t/a Train2game) v Designtechnica Corp (t/a Digital Trends) [2009] EWHC 1765 (QB); [2010] 3 All E.R. 548 (Google not publisher of allegedly defamatory material appearing on a search return).

[140] Dr Godfrey's claim against Demon was finally settled, with much publicity, with an agreement to pay Godfrey £15,000 in damages plus costs which amounted to almost £250,000: The Times, March 31, 2000. As a result, a number of servers were closed down to avoid potential defamation claims.

[141] See 529 US 1098 (2000), The Times, May 3, 2000, where the US Supreme Court let stand a decision of the New York Court of Appeals (94 N.Y. 2d 242; 701 N.Y.S. 2d 684; 723 N.E. 2d 539) that Prodigy was a "common carrier" who would not be responsible for what appeared on its site.

[142] SI 2002/2013, in force from August 21, 2002.

[143] Defamation and the Internet: A preliminary investigation: para.2.23.

[144] [2001] EWCA Civ 1805; [2002] Q.B. 783.

[145] (1849) 14 Q.B. 185; 117 E.R. 75. Upheld in Berezovsky v Michaels [2000] 1 W.L.R. 1004, HL.

The court rejected these arguments. As "stale news", such information had limited public interest value and, in any event, the court concluded that the attachment of an appropriate notice, warning that any suspected article should not be treated as the truth, would remove the sting from the material. In any event, any claims for damages would be modest. The court thus refused to change the law in favour of the US "single publication" rule,[146] whereby an article is published only once when it is first posted on the archive.[147]

The Court of Appeal in *Jameel v Dow Jones & Co Inc*[148] suggested that defendants would find more success in claiming abuse of process. Here, an article listed a number of alleged donors, including the claimant, to an organisation that was claimed to be a front for Al Qaeda. It had been posted on the internet in the United States for the Wall Street Journal On-Line, a subscriber service. Evidence suggested that only five[149] subscribers had accessed the article in the UK. It was held that, in such circumstances, the court could strike out the libel action as an abuse of process. Where publication within the jurisdiction was minimal and did not amount to a real and substantial tort harming the claimant's reputation, the claim could be struck out on the basis that the costs of proceeding to trial would be out of all proportion to what would be achieved. The burden is therefore on the claimant to establish that there has been more than minimal access to the material and the courts are not prepared to presume at law that there has been substantial publication, even where the site is open to general access.[150]

## Reform

Doubts have been expressed whether the current state of the law is satisfactory. The Law Commission in its preliminary report, "Defamation and the Internet: A preliminary investigation",[151] found a "strong case" for changing the law. It had been given evidence that ISPs were receiving over a 100 complaints each year, and concluded that, under the present law, the safest course for any ISP in such circumstances would be to remove the material, whether or not the alleged defamatory material was in the public interest or true. This caused a potential conflict with art.10. Equally, although it agreed with the view expressed above that damages arising from online archives would generally be modest, it noted concerns as to the costs and difficulties facing publishers in defending such cases if brought many years after the original publication.

**14–035**

---

[146] *Gregoire v GP Putnam's Sons* (1948) 81 NE 2d 45 (applied to a website publication in *Firth v State of New York* (2002) NY Int 88).

[147] The Times' appeal to the European Court of Human Rights was dismissed in that it was not a disproportionate interference with the right of freedom of expression to require that the newspaper publish an appropriate qualification to the internet version of the article: *Times Newspapers Ltd v United Kingdom (3002/03 and 23676/03)* [2009] E.M.L.R. 14. The Court did, however, express concern that, on different facts, libel proceedings against a newspaper after a significant lapse of time might, in the absence of exceptional circumstances, give rise to a disproportionate interference with press freedom under Art. 10, ECHR.

[148] [2005] EWCA Civ 75; [2005] Q.B. 946.

[149] Three of whom were said to be agents or associates of the claimant.

[150] *Al Amoudi v Brisard* [2006] EWHC 1062; [2007] 1 W.L.R. 113. See also *Carrie v Tolkien* [2009] EWHC 29 (QB) and *Kaschke v Gray* [2010] EWHC 1907 (QB).

[151] Scoping study No.2, December 2002. See *The Guardian*, December 18, 2002. Note also Scoping Study No.1, "Aspects of Defamation Procedure" (May, 2002) which also highlights the need to reform s.1 of the Defamation Act 1996 to ensure that the right balance is struck between claimants and defendants in defamation cases.

The Ministry of Justice in 2009 opened consultation on the merits of the multiple publication rule and, in particular, the impact of the rule that each publication of defamatory material can form the basis of a new defamation claim on online archives.[152] In the light of the responses to consultation and the views of the Culture Media and Sport Select Committee and Ministry of Justice's Libel Group, the Labour government in March 2010 announced that it had decided in principle to introduce a single publication rule (with the court having a discretion to extend the one year limitation period where appropriate), but that further consideration was needed to resolve how this rule would operate in practice.[153] In March 2011, following the May 2010 general election, the new Coalition Government announced that it intends to implement the single publication rule as part of its proposed Defamation Bill,[154] and will also engage in further consultation in relation to internet publications. In particular, it will seek views on whether the law should be changed to give greater protection to secondary publishers such as internet service providers, discussion forums and (in an offline context) booksellers, or alternatively how the existing law should be updated and clarified.

## (6) LIMITATION

14–036    This is not really a defence, but an assertion that the claimant has run out of time to bring his or her claim for defamation. As will be discussed in Ch.16, the claimant has a limited time in law to bring a claim. In defamation the time limit is very short. Sections 5 and 6 of the Defamation Act 1996 amend the Limitation Act 1980 to reduce the time limit from three years to one year. Section 4A of the Limitation Act 1980 now provides that the ordinary six year time limit for claims in tort does not apply. After one year has expired, the claimant cannot normally sue, however bad the injury to his or her reputation. The assumption is that if your reputation has been injured, you should have realised this and be sufficiently incensed to bring the claim within a short period of time.[155] The court does, however, have a largely unfettered discretion to hold that the time limit should not apply under s.32A of the Limitation Act 1980.[156] In so doing, it must balance the interests of the parties with regard to all the circumstances of the case. Section 32A(1) provides that:

> "If it appears to the court that it would be equitable to allow an action to proceed having regard to the degree to which–(a) the operation of s.4A of this Act prejudices the plaintiff . . . and (b) any decision of the court under this subsection would prejudice the defendant . . . the court may direct that that section shall not apply to the action."

The court will consider the length of the delay, why it occurred and, if it is due to lack of knowledge of certain facts, how soon the claimant acted once these facts were known.[157] The

---

[152] "Defamation and the internet: The multiple publication rule" Consultation Paper CP 20/09.

[153] "Response to Defamation and the internet: The multiple publication rule" Consultation Paper CP(R) 20/09, March 23, 2010.

[154] *Draft Defamation Bill Consultation* (Consultation Paper CP3/11): *http://www.justice.gov.uk/docs/draft-defamation-bill-consltation,pdf* [Accessad April 22, 2011].

[155] Although it should be noted that in the case of slander not actionable per se, the one year time limit will only start to run from the date on which the special damage occurs. These points are dealt with in more detail in Ch.16.

[156] See *Steedman v BBC* [2001] EWCA Civ 1534; [2002] E.M.L.R. 17.

[157] See s.32A(2)(a) and (b).

court will also examine the extent to which the delay has weakened the evidential basis for the claim.[158]

It should be noted that the one year time limit also applies to claims for malicious falsehood, which will be examined below.

## THE NEED FOR REFORM

In this section, we examine some of the problems which have arisen in the tort of defamation, and the continuing need for reform in this area of law. Criticism of the operation of the law of defamation is nothing new. We have already mentioned some of the criticisms contained in the Faulks Committee report of 1975.[159] The Neill Report on Practice and Procedure in Defamation of July 1991 made a number of further recommendations, many of which formed the basis for the 1996 Act. Nevertheless, problems remain.[160] Readers will have noted how complicated many of the rules of the tort are, but there remain fundamental difficulties in its application and procedure. There have been a number of high profile cases, for example the case brought by Jeffrey Archer against the *Daily Star*,[161] where the media publicised the extravagant awards given by juries in libel trials. Such awards are particularly questionable when compared with the level of personal injury awards, which are strictly controlled by the courts and considerably less in value.

**14–037**

Readers may also note that the claimants are usually people of means. Legal Aid has never been available for defamation.[162] Conditional fees[163] now provide a possible source of funding for litigants, provided that they can find a firm prepared to take their case on such a basis, and deal with any expenses not covered by the conditional fee arrangement. The House of Lords in *Campbell v Mirror Group Newspapers Ltd (Costs)*[164] denied that a conditional fee arrangement entered into by supermodel Naomi Campbell in her privacy action against the *Mirror*,[165] which provided for an additional "success fee" for solicitors and counsel of 95 per cent and 100 per cent respectively, was contrary to art.10.[166] The *Mirror* had argued that, bearing in mind Ms Campbell was able to fund the litigation without the assistance of a conditional fee agreement (CFA), the threat of having to pay a huge award of costs (ordinary costs plus success fee) if it lost, was a disproportionate restriction on the defendant's freedom of expression. The

---

[158] See s.32A(2)(c).

[159] Report of the Committee on Defamation, Cmnd 5909.

[160] See I. Loveland (1997) 46 I.C.L.Q. 561.

[161] This decision is perhaps now better known for providing the basis for Mr Archer's later conviction for perjury. The sum awarded was later repaid by Mr Archer: see *The Guardian*, October 2, 2002.

[162] Although the European Court of Human Rights in *Steel v United Kingdom (68416/01)* [2005] E.M.L.R. 15; (2005) 41 E.H.R.R.22 (ECHR) found that financial aid may in lengthy and complex defamation actions be necessary for a fair hearing (denial of Legal Aid to Steel and Morris in "McLibel" litigation (see Ch.13) amounted to violation of art.6.1). See also *McVicar v United Kingdom (46311/99)* (2002) 35 E.H.R.R. 22.

[163] This is an arrangement by which legal advisers risk not recovering their fee unless their client is successful (commonly referred to as a "no win, no fee" arrangement). See Courts and Legal Services Act 1990 s.58 (as substituted and amended).

[164] [2005] UKHL 61; [2005] 1 W.L.R. 3394, Comment: Caddell [2006] C.L.J. 45.

[165] This is discussed in Ch.15.

[166] As the losing party, the Mirror Group was liable for its own costs and those of the claimant. It had complained when faced with the claimant's bill of costs which amounted to over £1 million in a case where Ms Campbell had been awarded £3,500 in damages.

House of Lords disagreed, although with some reservations as to the wisdom or justice of the CFA system as it is presently constituted.

Such reservations received support from the European Court of Human Rights in January 2011.[167] Noting that the Ministry of Justice had since 2003 been engaged in public consultation as to the recoverable success fee scheme and that the Labour government, prior to losing the May 2010 election had proposed measures to reduce the level of success fees recoverable, the Court found unanimously that in *Campbell* the success fees had been disproportionate and violated the art.10 right to freedom of expression. This decision has been welcomed by campaigners, who feared the chilling effect of large success fees, and the new Government is now proposing extensive reforms to civil litigation funding and costs.[168]

In general, though, it remains the case that defamation is a tort which protects the reputation of those with the means to invoke it. As such, it is a far from efficient means of ensuring the right balance between protection of reputation and freedom of speech in modern society.

## Procedural reforms

14-038    Much of the cost of defamation cases comes from the complicated trial process. The Defamation Act 1996 therefore contemplates that some cases should be dealt with by a summary non-jury procedure.[169] Under s.8(2), where the claimant has no realistic prospect of success, and there is no reason why it should be tried, a judge without a jury may dismiss the claim. Alternatively, where there is no defence which has a realistic prospect of success, and there is no other reason why the claim should be tried,[170] a judge may give judgment for the claimant and grant the claimant summary relief.[171] The remedies open to the claimant are limited, however. Under s.9(1), the court has a range of options which consist of: (i) a declaration that the statement was false and defamatory; (ii) an order that the defendant publish a suitable correction and apology; (iii) an award of damages not exceeding £10,000; and (iv) an injunction restraining publication. It is for the parties to arrange the correction and apology. If they cannot agree on its content, s.9(2) provides that the claimant must be satisfied by a summary of the court's judgment. The advantages to the parties are obvious: a speeded-up procedure which avoids a long-winded and costly trial. The claimant can ensure that the statement is corrected and may obtain a certain amount of damages. The judge is given a discretion

---

[167] *MGN Ltd v United Kingdom* (39401/04) Times, January 20, 2011.

[168] See 'Reforming civil litigation funding and costs in England and Wales—Implementation of Lord Justice Jackson's Recommendations: The Government Response' (Cm 8041, March 2011) which proposes to abolish the general recoverability of CFA success fees and ATE ("after the event") insurance premiums from the losing side: *http://www.justice.gov.uk/docs/jackson-report-government-response.pdf* [Accessed April 22, 2011].

[169] The new procedure was brought into force (together with all the other provisions of the Defamation Act 1996 which apply in England and Wales and which had not so far been brought into force) by the Defamation Act 1996 (Commencement No.2) Order 2000 (SI 2000/222), on February 28, 2000.

[170] In deciding whether the claim should be tried, the judge will consider, amongst other things, how serious the defamation is and whether it is justifiable in the circumstances to proceed to a full trial: s.8(4).

[171] s.8(3). See *James Gilbert Ltd v MGN Ltd* [2000] E.M.L.R. 680 and, generally, CPR r. 53.2. The test is the same as that under CPR Part 24, which allows for summary disposal of cases generally. In *Loutchansky v Times Newspapers Ltd (Nos 2–5)* [2001] EWCA Civ 1805; [2002] Q.B. 783, the Court of Appeal held that there was no reason why the summary procedure should not also be used for disposing of questions of quantum alone once liability had been determined or admitted.

under s.8(3) to force the claimant to follow the summary route if it "will adequately compensate him for the wrong he has suffered".

Use of this provision will inevitably be confined to straightforward cases where the claimant is prepared to accept an award not exceeding £10,000. Additionally, in the light of the European Convention on Human Rights, which (under art.6) grants the defendant a right to a fair trial, it must be questioned to what extent courts should restrict the defendant's ability to assert his or her right to freedom of expression in a full trial. It is a first step, however, in trying to simplify the complicated and costly procedure involved in defamation cases.

## Control of damages

This has been one of the main complaints about the law of defamation in recent years. Damages are assessed by the jury, not the judge, and in the past the Court of Appeal has been reluctant to interfere with jury awards. However, after a series of notoriously high awards, this attitude has had to change.[172] Section 8 of the Courts and Legal Services Act 1990 empowered the Court of Appeal to substitute its own figure of damages for that of the jury without the need for a retrial.[173] More fundamentally, the Court of Appeal has recognised that the judge must exercise some degree of control over jury awards, by ensuring that they receive appropriate guidance in the summing-up.

14–039

This can be seen in the 1994 case of *Rantzen v Mirror Group Newspapers (1986) Ltd*,[174] where the newspaper had accused the television presenter Esther Rantzen, who had founded the children's charity ChildLine, of knowingly protecting a person guilty of sexual abuse. The jury had awarded £250,000. The Court of Appeal set this aside under s.8 of the Courts and Legal Services Act 1990 and substituted the figure of £110,000. Neill L.J. held that:

> "We consider therefore that the common law if properly understood requires the courts to subject large awards of damages to a more searching inquiry than has been customary in the past. It follows that what has been regarded as the barrier against intervention should be lowered. The question becomes: 'Could a reasonable jury have thought that their award was necessary to compensate the plaintiff and to re-establish his reputation?' "[175]

The court held that the judge should refer to previous Court of Appeal decisions under s.8 for guidance, but was not prepared to say that the judge should refer the jury to other awards in libel actions or personal injury cases. It acknowledged that it would take some time for case law to develop under s.8 and, in the meantime, the jury should be invited to consider the purchasing power of their award (for example, could it buy a house, a car or a holiday?) and whether the award was proportionate to the damage suffered. A sum should be awarded which

---

[172] In *Tolstoy Miloslavsky v United Kingdom* (1995) 20 E.H.R.R. 442, the European Court of Human Rights found the law prior to the Courts and Legal Services Act 1990 and *Rantzen v Mirror Group Newspapers (1986) Ltd* [1994] Q.B. 670 to be contrary to art.10 of the European Convention on Human Rights. The jury's award of £1.5 million in damages (which was three times the size of the highest libel award previously made in England) was therefore a violation of art.10.

[173] Note also that in *Grobbelaar v News Group Newspapers Ltd* [2002] 1 W.L.R. 3024, the House of Lords exercised its inherent power to alter the award.

[174] [1994] Q.B. 670.

[175] [1994] Q.B. 670 at 692.

ensured that the claimant was provided with adequate compensation.[176] The court's judgment, which the court held to be consistent with art.10 of the European Convention on Human Rights, provided some guidance for juries, but was taken a step further in the now leading case of *John v Mirror Group Newspapers Ltd*.[177]

In this case, which was brought by the entertainer Elton John against the *Daily Mirror*, the Court of Appeal provided juries with further guidance. Despite the ruling in *Rantzen*, the court found that there was still evidence of disproportionate libel awards, and thought further action was necessary. On this basis, the court finally accepted that juries should be informed, by way of guidance, of the level of damages awarded in personal injury cases. While it was clearly impossible to compare severe brain damage with an attack on a person's reputation, it did give the jury some guidance as to the level of damages necessary in the circumstances. The judge, and advocates for both sides, would now be permitted to address the jury on what they considered to be the correct level of damages. Such changes, it was hoped, would make the assessment of damages "more rational and so more acceptable to public opinion".[178] The courts would continue to refer to decisions under the 1990 Act (as suggested in *Rantzen*) and would continue to refuse to allow references to defamation awards which had been made on different sets of facts. The Court of Appeal reduced the jury's award of compensatory damages from £75,000 to £25,000.

**14–040**     Two further points should be made here. First, any compensatory sum awarded may be supplemented by aggravated or exemplary damages, which will be discussed generally in Ch.17. Aggravated and exemplary damages play a significant role in defamation, which remains one of the few occasions when exemplary or punitive damages may be awarded. Aggravated damages will be awarded for additional injury to the claimant's feelings. The court will award exemplary damages where the defendant, either knowing a statement to be false or careless whether it be true or false, has deliberately published the statement because the profit gained from publication will outweigh any financial penalties.[179] This obviously is particularly apposite to newspapers publishing sensational stories such as the one concerning Elton John in *John*. Nevertheless, such sums are controlled, and the Court of Appeal reduced the exemplary damages in *John* from £275,000 to £50,000. Sir Thomas Bingham M.R. warned that:

> "principle requires that an award of exemplary damages should never exceed the minimum sum necessary to meet the public purpose underlying such damages, that of punishing the defendant, showing that tort does not pay and deterring others".[180]

---

[176] [1994] Q.B. 670 at 696.

[177] [1997] Q.B. 586. Applied in *Kiam v MGN Ltd* [2002] EWCA Civ 43; [2003] Q.B. 281.

[178] [1997] Q.B. 586 at 616 per Sir Thomas Bingham M.R. It might also be helpful to take account of previous awards made by judges sitting alone which would be reasoned: *Gur v Avrupa Newspaper Ltd* [2008] EWCA Civ 594. But note the doubts expressed by Lord Hoffmann in *Gleaner Co Ltd v Abrahams* [2003] UKPC 55; [2004] 1 A.C. 628 as to the comparability of personal injury and defamation awards due to their different purpose and differing impact on society. His Lordship underlined, in particular, the deterrent role played by defamation damages in preventing the media riding roughshod over the rights of citizens: see paras 53–56. May L.J. in *Nail v News Group Newspapers Ltd* [2004] EWCA Civ 1708; [2005] 1 All E.R. 1040 at para.39 commented, however, that the possibility of deterrence is more often associated with conduct which might result in aggravated or exemplary damages and with malice.

[179] See *Broome v Cassell* [1972] A.C. 1027.

[180] [1997] Q.B. 586 at 619.

Secondly, the main problem here is still the jury. In *Kiam v MGN Ltd*,[181] Sedley L.J. dissenting complained that the *John* case had failed in its purpose of limiting damages: "the train has left the station again and is now accelerating".[182] The Court of Appeal noted that whatever guidance is given to juries, the sums awarded remain large. This has been exacerbated recently by changes in personal injury law which have increased awards for non-pecuniary loss[183]—to which libel juries are asked in *John* to refer—although it now seems to be accepted that there is a ceiling for compensatory damages, reserved for the most serious cases following trial, of about £200,000.[184] Yet, however one refines the guidance given to juries, ultimately the question must arise whether it would be simpler just to abolish the jury in defamation cases.[185] or, less drastically, place assessment of damages in the hands of the judge. It is the judge, after all, who assesses damages in personal injury cases. This ensures a roughly coherent framework which at least allows parties some means of predicting the level of damages to be awarded. Uncertainty makes it difficult to settle defamation cases, which the general rules of civil litigation seek to encourage. The Faulks Committee in 1975 recommended removing the right to trial by jury and permitting only a judicial discretion to allow trial by jury if necessary.[186] However, the Law Commission, in its report on damages for non-pecuniary loss, decided that it was not appropriate at the present time to take assessment of damages away from the jury.[187] In the light of the changes likely to result from full implementation of the Defamation Act 1996 and the incorporation of the European Convention on Human Rights into English law, the Commission decided to wait, believing that such a change would require, in any event, a full examination of how defamation cases are tried. It nevertheless thought that it should never be left to a jury to decide whether exemplary damages should be awarded, or their amount.[188]

A graphic illustration of the difficulties invoked by the use of juries in libel trials may be seen in *Grobbelaar v News Group Newspapers Ltd*.[189] Grobbelaar—a well-known goalkeeper—had complained about articles which appeared in *The Sun*, based on covert audio and video recordings in which he was recorded agreeing to a proposed match fixing conspiracy, accepting £2,000 in cash, and claiming that he had previously accepted bribes for fixing particular games. The trial jury had found in his favour and awarded him damages of £85,000. The Court of Appeal, however, overturned the verdict as perverse in view of the evidence presented in court. In so doing, it demonstrated a clear lack of faith in the reasoning of the jury and re-affirmed the doubts of many as to the ability of the jury to act objectively in the course of such trials. The House of Lords (Lord Steyn dissenting) reinstated the jury's verdict and held that only exceptionally should the verdict of a jury be overturned as perverse. Lord Bingham found it:

**14–041**

---

[181] [2003] Q.B. 281.

[182] [2003] Q.B. 281 at 302.

[183] See Ch.17; *Heil v Rankin* [2001] Q.B. 272.

[184] This does not include exemplary damages or any special damages and is as at 2004. See *Lillie & Reed v Newcastle City Council* [2002] EWHC 1600 (QB), as acknowledged by Lord Hoffmann in *Gleaner Co Ltd v Abrahams* [2003] UKPC 55; [2004] 1 A.C. 628 at para.49.

[185] Lord Phillips recently asked in *Spiller v Joseph* [2010] UKSC 53 at para. 116: "has not the time come to recognise that defamation is no longer a field in which trial by jury is desirable?"

[186] At para.516.

[187] Law Commission Report No. 257, *Damages for personal injury: Non-pecuniary loss* (1999), para.4.23.

[188] At para.4.32.

[189] [2002] UKHL 40; [2002] 1 W.L.R. 3024.

"a very serious thing to stigmatise as perverse the unanimous finding of jurors . . . that is not a conclusion to be reached lightly or if any alternative explanation not involving perversity presents itself."[190]

The majority found such an alternative explanation: the article contained two stings—first, that Grobbelaar had taken bribes and, secondly, that he had actually fixed matches. Whilst the first had been proved, the evidence at trial had not supported the latter. On this basis, the jury's finding of liability could be explained on the basis that it found insufficient justification for this latter allegation. However, the majority was unable to accept that this justified an award of £85,000. It again refused to declare this perverse, but reduced the award to £1. By accepting bribes, Grobbelaar had acted in a way in which no decent or honest footballer would act and had undermined the integrity of the game. Lord Millett found it an "affront to justice"[191] to award more than derisory damages to a sportsman whose reputation had been so destroyed.
    The current problem therefore remains unsolved.

## Government intervention?

**14–042**    In November 2010, the newly elected Coalition Government set out a timetable for a new Defamation Act which would reform the law of defamation to protect freedom of speech.[192] In accordance with this timetable, a draft Defamation Bill was published in March 2011[193] and opened up for consultation with the goal of introducing the final bill in May 2012, aiming to reach the statute books in 2013. Justice Secretary, Kenneth Clarke expressed the goals of the Government in unveiling the draft Bill:

> "The right to speak freely and debate issues without fear of censure is a vital cornerstone of a democratic society. In recent years though, the increased threat of costly libel actions has begun to have a chilling effect on scientific and academic debate, and investigative journalism . . . The Government's draft Defamation Bill will ensure that anyone who makes a statement of fact or expresses an honest opinion can do so with confidence."[194]

With this in mind, the Defamation Bill proposes:

- A new requirement that a statement must have caused, or is likely to cause, substantial harm in order for it to be defamatory (clause 1).

- A new statutory defence of responsible publication on matters of public interest (clause 2).

- A statutory defence of truth (replacing the current common law defence of justification) (clause 3).

---

[190] [2002] 1 W.L.R. 3024 at 3034–3035.
[191] [2002] 1 W.L.R. 3024 at 3050.
[192] Ministry of Justice Business Plan 2011–2015: *http://www.justice.gov.uk/moj-business-plan2011–15-nov10.pdf* [Accessed April 22, 2011].
[193] *Draft Defamation Bill Consultation* (Consultation Paper CP3/11): *http://www.justice.gov.uk/docs/draft-defamation-bill-consutation.pdf* [Accessed April 22, 2011]..
[194] *http://www.justice.gov.uk/news/press-release-150311a.htm* [Accessed April 22, 2011].

- A statutory defence of honest opinion (replacing the current common law defence of fair/honest comment) (clause 4).

- Provisions updating and extending the circumstances in which the defences of absolute and qualified privilege are available (clause 5).

- Introduction of a single publication rule to prevent an action being brought in relation to publication of the same material by the same publisher after a one year limitation period has passed (clause 6).

- Action to address libel tourism by ensuring a court will not accept jurisdiction unless satisfied that England and Wales is clearly the most appropriate place to bring an action against someone who is not domiciled in the UK or an EU Member State (clause 7).

- Removal of the presumption in favour of jury trial, so that the judge would have a discretion to order jury trial where it is in the interests of justice (clause 8).

In addition, the Government will consult on the following:

- Responsibility for publication on the internet. The paper seeks views on whether the law should be changed to give greater protection to secondary publishers such as internet service providers, discussion forums and (in an offline context) booksellers, or alternatively how the existing law should be updated and clarified.

- A new court procedure to resolve key preliminary issues at as early a stage as possible, so that the length and cost of defamation proceedings can be substantially reduced.

- Whether the summary disposal procedure under s.8 and 9, Defamation Act 1996, should be retained and, if so, whether improvements are needed.

- Whether further action is needed beyond the proposals in the draft Bill and the introduction of a new court procedure to address issues relating to an inequality of arms in defamation proceedings, including whether any specific restrictions should be placed on the ability of corporations to bring a defamation action.

- Whether the current provisions in case law restricting the ability of public authorities and bodies exercising public functions to bring defamation actions should be placed in statute and whether these restrictions should be extended to other bodies exercising public functions.

The provisions seek to simplify and clarify law and to speed up defamation cases, notably by removing the right to trial by jury under Senior Courts Act 1981 s.69 and introducing a "threshold of seriousness" in clause 1 to allow trivial cases to be struck out. Further, by placing on a statutory footing defences such as *Reynolds* privilege, justification and honest/fair comment, the Government hopes to clarify the law and thereby encourage their use. It remains to be seen which provisions will survive the consultation process (the removal, for example, of the right to jury trial is likely to prove controversial) and whether the opportunity will be taken to address in more depth the issue of publication on the internet beyond the welcome introduction of the single publication rule.

## INTERIM INJUNCTIONS

**14–043**    It is worth noting briefly that although the claimant may wish to obtain an injunction to prevent publication of the statement in question, the courts will only rarely grant an injunction prior to a full hearing at the trial. Therefore, even if the claimant is given prior notice of publication of statements which may diminish his or her reputation, it will be difficult to prevent publication. The court's discretion to grant interim relief will not ordinarily be exercised to restrain a libel where the defendant alleges a defence or claims justification, unless the claimant can prove that the libel is plainly untrue.[195] In *Holley v Smyth*,[196] the majority of the Court of Appeal upheld this rule as supporting the right to free speech, even where the defendant's motives were questionable.[197] More recently, the Court of Appeal in *Greene v Associated Newspapers Ltd*[198] confirmed that such a rule was consistent with the European Convention on Human Rights and that a lesser test would seriously weaken the effect of art.10.[199]

In view of the problems associated with a defamation action, litigants may wish to consider two alternative options. Where the defamatory material has been published by the media, the individual may wish to send a complaint to the Press Complaints Commission or Ofcom and take advantage of the remedies they provide. This is cost effective, but it should be considered whether the remedies are sufficient. Alternatively, the claimant may wish to sue for malicious falsehood. The advantages and disadvantages of these two options will be examined below.

## COMPLAINTS TO REGULATORY BODIES

**14–044**    A person aggrieved by inaccurate statements in the media may complain to the Press Complaints Commission (the self-regulating body of the press) or Ofcom, the regulator for the UK communications industries. These bodies do not award compensation, but may require the offending newspaper or broadcaster to publish a summary of any adjudication. The Press Complaints Commission (PCC) follows a Code of Practice which protects "the rights of the individual and the public's right to know".[200] The Code deals specifically with issues such as accuracy, the right to reply, privacy, harassment and intimidation, intrusion into grief and shock, and the treatment of children and other vulnerable parties. In 2009, the PCC investigated 1,134 complaints. Where the complainant is successful, the PCC will generally try to negotiate the publication of an agreed correction and/or apology, a letter from the journal to the complainant, or a follow-up article. If this fails, it can require the publication of a critical adjudication in full, with a headline reference to the PCC. A copy of the adjudication will be published on the PCC website. Generally the Commission will not accept complaints made

---

[195] See *Bonnard v Perryman* [1891] 2 Ch.269, CA. See also *William Coulson & Sons v James Coulson and Co* (1887) 3 T.L.R. 846: an interim injunction should only be used in the clearest of cases.

[196] [1998] Q.B. 726. (Staughton L.J. dissenting.)

[197] The defendant had used the threat of publication as a means of putting pressure on the claimant to compensate him for an alleged wrong.

[198] [2004] EWCA Civ 1462; [2005] Q.B. 972.

[199] For example, that it was more likely than not that the defendant could not show that what it wished to say about the claimant was true. The Court of Appeal accepted that a different rule would apply for breach of confidence: see Ch.15 and *LNS v Persons Unknown* [2010] EWHC 119 (QB).

[200] Preamble to the Code of Practice: *http://www.pcc.org.uk/cop/practice.html* [Accessed April 22, 2011].

more than two months after publication of the article unless there are special circumstances, and the procedure cannot be used if legal action has commenced.

Ofcom has more extensive powers.[201] It is the independent regulator and competition authority for the UK's communications industries and covers television, radio, telecommunications and wireless communications services. Operating under the Communications Act 2003 and the Broadcasting Acts 1990 and 1996 (as amended), it is concerned with broadcasting standards (matters of taste and decency) and fairness (unfair or unjust treatment and the infringement of privacy). If it deems it necessary, Ofcom may issue a Direction not to repeat a programme, to broadcast a correction or a summary of the adjudication, or even fine the broadcaster. Again, short time limits apply. Because of restrictions on the period for which broadcasters have to retain recordings, complaints concerning fairness and/or privacy should be brought within 20 working days after broadcast of the relevant programme. Ordinarily, Ofcom will not accept a complaint which is submitted after this deadline, although it may at its discretion decide to consider the complaint despite the delay in its submission.[202] Complaints concerning broadcasting standards should also be submitted within 20 working days of broadcast. Where a complaint is submitted later than 20 working days of the broadcast, complainants should explain why the complaint was not submitted earlier. In deciding whether to investigate late complaints, Ofcom will take into account all relevant factors, including the reason for the delay in submitting the complaint and the fact that broadcasters are only required to keep recordings for a limited time after the date of the broadcast. [203]

These are therefore very limited provisions, both in terms of the remedies available and the time limits, but they provide some means of redress for complainants who feel that they have been misrepresented by the media. A further option which the claimant should consider, however, is whether he or she would be able to bring a claim for malicious falsehood.

## MALICIOUS OR INJURIOUS FALSEHOOD

This is a different tort from defamation and can be classified as an economic tort, i.e. a tort which specifically protects the economic interests of the claimant.[204] Here, the claimant is complaining that the defendant has made a false statement to a third party which has damaged his or her business interests. This is distinct from defamation. Defamation protects the business reputation of the claimant. Malicious falsehood protects the financial interests of the claimant. This distinction is illustrated in the following example. The defendant has told X that the claimant's shop does not sell paper. This is untrue. X, as a result, buys his paper from the defendant's shop. Such a statement does not affect the claimant's trading reputation but will obviously reduce the income of the shop, and affect the claimant's financial position. On this basis, the Court of Appeal in *Ratcliffe v Evans*[205] held that the plaintiff had a valid action when a newspaper published a statement that the plaintiff's firm had gone out of business. It

**14-045**

---

[201] Website *http:// www.ofcom.org.uk* [Accessed April 22, 2011]: Ofcom replaced the Broadcasting Standards Commission in December 2003, and, in addition to regulating standards of taste and decency on all TV and radio channels, licences commercial TV and radio and oversees the telecommunications industry.

[202] Ofcom procedures for the handling of Fairness and Privacy complaints (2009) para. 9.

[203] Ofcom procedures for the handling of broadcasting standards investigations (2009) para. 15.

[204] For economic torts generally, see Ch.12.

[205] [1892] 2 Q.B. 524.

was held that the statement did not reflect on the plaintiff's character, but nevertheless the plaintiff could sue for the general loss of business which resulted from publication.

To bring a case for malicious falsehood, there are four main requirements:

(i) The defendant made a false statement concerning the claimant or his or her property;

(ii) Maliciously;

(iii) To some person other than the claimant; and

(iv) As a result the claimant suffered economic loss.

The tort is therefore not actionable per se. Special damage must be proved, such as loss of business.[206] However, the claimant may be assisted by s.3(1) of the Defamation Act 1952. This provides that it is no longer necessary to allege or prove special damage if the words complained of:

". . . are calculated to cause pecuniary damage to the plaintiff and are published in writing or other permanent form or if the said words are calculated to cause pecuniary damage to the plaintiff in respect of any office, profession, calling, trade or business held or carried on by him at the time of the publication."

This provision covers many of the occasions giving rise to the action and makes the tort largely actionable without proof of damage, provided the words are calculated to cause the claimant financial loss. The other requirements must, however, be met. The statement must be proved to be false.[207] This, unlike in defamation, will not be presumed. The claimant must also show that the statement was made maliciously, i.e. that the defendant knew that the statement was false, or was reckless as to whether it was true or not,[208] or was actuated by some indirect, dishonest or improper motive.[209] It is always a defence that the statement was made in good faith.[210]

**14–046**     Damages may extend to distress and injury to feelings consequential on financial loss. In *Khodaparast v Shad*,[211] an Iranian woman had lost her part-time job as a teacher in a religious school and found it difficult to gain employment when a former lover had distributed mock-up advertisements for telephone sex services using her photograph. At trial, he had persisted in claiming that these were genuine advertisements and such behaviour was typical of her loose morals. The trial judge had found in favour of the claimant and awarded additional aggravated damages[212] to reflect the injury to the claimant's feelings from the defendant's conduct prior to and during the trial. The Court of Appeal approved this award. As stated by Stuart-Smith L.J.:

---

[206] *Royal Baking Powder Co v Wright Crossley & Co* (1900) 18 R.P.C. 95 at 99: "The damage is the gist of the action and therefore . . . it must be especially alleged and proved."

[207] It does not include mere advertising "puffs": *White v Mellin* [1895] A.C. 154.

[208] *Shapiro v La Morta* (1923) 40 T.L.R. 201.

[209] *Balden v Shorter* [1933] Ch.427.

[210] *Spring v Guardian Assurance* [1995] 2 A.C. 296.

[211] [2000] 1 W.L.R. 618. Applied in *Smith v Stemler* [2001] C.L.Y. 2309 (Central London County Court).

[212] See Ch.17: Damages.

"once the plaintiff is entitled to sue for malicious falsehood, whether on proof of special damage or by reasons of s.3 of the 1952 Act I can see no reason why, in an appropriate case, he or she should not recover aggravated damages for injury to feelings . . . justice requires that it should be so."[213]

It should be noted that this is an additional claim. It does not permit a claimant to obtain damages solely for emotional distress or injury to his or her reputation. Any claim for the latter must be brought under the tort of defamation.

Generally, therefore, defamation will be easier (depending of course on the facts) for the claimant to prove, so few actions are brought for malicious falsehood. The claimant will also have the benefit of a jury in defamation, which he or she will not have for malicious falsehood, which will be heard by a judge alone. There may nevertheless be advantages to suing for malicious falsehood. First, the claimant does not have to show an attack on his or her business reputation, but simply that the false statement has resulted in the business losing money. Secondly, the tort may prove useful where other causes of action fail. For example, in *Kaye v Robertson*,[214] the court, horrified by the behaviour of the newspaper in question, relied on malicious falsehood to support Kaye's claim. Gorden Kaye, a popular actor, had been seriously injured when a piece of wood smashed through his car windscreen during a bad storm in 1990. He was in a critical condition for many days, and a special notice was placed on his door to keep out visitors. A journalist and photographer from the *Sunday Sport* newspaper nevertheless entered the room, obtained a picture of Mr Kaye using a flash camera, and claimed that Kaye had consented to an "interview". The paper alleged that it had obtained "a great old-fashioned scoop". In fact, Kaye was in intensive care and could not remember the incident 15 minutes after the event. The Court of Appeal took a dim view of such conduct, but struggled to find a basis for liability in tort. Trespass to the person (see Ch.11) did not work. The use of a flash by itself did not amount to battery.[215] The judges were tempted by libel, on the basis that it was defamatory to state falsely that Kaye had consented to give an exclusive interview to the *Sunday Sport*. However, the court adhered to the rule that interim injunctions (i.e. injunctions before the final hearing) should be used sparingly in libel.[216] The court therefore resorted to malicious falsehood: the paper's allegation that the story and photograph had been taken with Kaye's consent was clearly false, and Kaye had lost the right to sell his first interview after the accident for profit.[217] Bingham L.J. commented that:

---

[213] [2000] 1 W.L.R. 618 at 630–631, relying heavily on dicta from Nicholls V.C. and Sir Michael Kerr in *Joyce v Sengupta* [1993] 1 W.L.R. 337 and distinguishing previous negative dicta in *Fielding v Variety Inc* [1967] 2 Q.B. 841.

[214] [1991] F.S.R. 62.

[215] Although Glidewell L.J. suggested at 68 that a bright light deliberately shone into another's eyes which injured his sight or damaged him in some other way might at law be a battery.

[216] See above.

[217] The Court of Appeal also considered the economic tort of passing off, in which the claimant sues for a misrepresentation made to the claimant's prospective or existing customers which is calculated to injure the business or goodwill of the claimant and which has caused or threatened actual damage to the business or goodwill of the claimant. The claimant must be a "trader". The court held that the possibility of Kaye selling the story of his accident did not make him a "trader".

"this case nonetheless highlights, yet again, the failure of both the common law of England and statute to protect in an effective way the personal privacy of individual citizens".[218]

## Defamation: conclusion

**14–047**     As may be seen, defamation is a difficult and complex area of law, but one which is of considerable interest to anyone who is concerned how the law of tort deals with the difficult issues of freedom of expression and the rights of individuals to protect their reputation from attack. The best way to approach this area of law is in stages, following the method indicated above. In this way, the reader can understand the reasoning adopted by the courts and appreciate the problems inherent in this area of law. Although the Defamation Act 1996 has attempted to deal with these problems, there is clearly a long way to go. It remains to be seen whether the current government proposals for reform will be implemented and to what extent they will simplify this area of law. One thing is clear. The incorporation of art.10 (freedom of expression) of the European Convention on Human Rights into English law by the Human Rights Act 1998 will ensure an ongoing debate as to the scope of this tort.

---

[218] [1991] F.S.R. 62 at 70. Arguably, this deficiency has now been met by the courts' development of breach of confidence to protect an individual's right to privacy (see Ch.15).

# Chapter 15

# PRIVACY (OR MISUSE OF PRIVATE INFORMATION)

As stated in Ch.13, defamation protects the reputation of the claimant against untrue state-  **15–001** ments of fact. The common law has found more difficulty in deciding whether the claimant should be able to obtain a remedy in tort for the publication of *true* facts which the claimant does not wish others to know. Until recently, litigants were forced to resort to torts such as trespass and private nuisance to find some protection. With the advent of the Human Rights Act 1998, the question has arisen whether English law should now accept a new tort based on invasion of privacy.

Such a tort would be contentious. Whilst it would protect the claimant from invasion of his or her private life, it would be at the expense of the public's right to know and the defendant's freedom of expression, protected by art.10 of the European Convention on Human Rights (ECHR). At worst, it would give claimants a means of suppressing true, but damaging, infor- mation which it is in the public interest to disclose. Yet, it cannot be denied that publication of details of an individual's private life, even when they are accurate, can be distressing. In particular, advances in modern technology have led to an increasing number of intrusions into the private lives of individuals, be they public or private figures. Many other countries have accepted the need for laws protecting privacy.[1] The 1998 Act, which incorporates art.8, ECHR (right to respect for private and family life), brings to the fore the question of whether, and to what extent, English law should recognise a right to privacy.

## Protection of privacy by existing torts

Prior to the Human Rights Act 1998, it seemed clear that there was no right to privacy in  **15–002** English law. Tort law did, however, offer some protection on an ad hoc basis. Whilst the claimant would have to satisfy the basic requirements for each tort, some protection could

---

[1] For example, the United States Restatement (Second) of Torts recognises four types of invasion of privacy: intrusion, appropriation of name or likeness, unreasonable publicity and placing a person in a false light (paras 652A–652I) (1977). New Zealand finally confirmed the existence of a tort protecting informational privacy in *Hosking v Runting* [2005] 1 N.Z.L.R. 1. In contrast, France introduced a new provision into its Civil Code: art.9 (by virtue of the Law 70–643 of 17 July 1970), whilst German courts recognised privacy as a right (*Persönlichkeitsrecht*) protected by para.823(1) of its Civil Code in the 1950s: see W. van Gerven, J. Lever and P. Larouche, *Tort Law* (Hart, 2000).

thereby be obtained, even if it was merely indirect and the remedy often ill-suited to the protection of privacy. Trespass to land, private nuisance, malicious falsehood and even defamation were therefore relied upon by claimants.

Trespass, notably, provided a means of preventing direct interference with the claimant's possession of land and has long been used to protect the claimant against invasion of privacy.[2] Yet, with the advent of long-range lenses, photographers are no longer required to intrude onto the claimant's land, thereby limiting the effectiveness of this action. For example, in *Bernstein v Skyviews Ltd*,[3] Lord Bernstein failed in his action for trespass against the defendants. The defendants had taken aerial photographs of his country house without his consent, but the court held that the rights of a landowner did not extend to airspace exceeding that necessary for the ordinary use and enjoyment of land.[4] Equally, private nuisance may assist in preventing indirect interference with one's enjoyment of land, although its use is limited by the House of Lords decision in *Hunter v Canary Wharf Ltd*,[5] which confined the right to sue for private nuisance to those with an interest in land or exclusive possession.[6] Defamation can offer only limited protection against the invasion of privacy, although innuendo may assist a claimant in bringing an action. In *Tolley v Fry*,[7] for example, Tolley successfully sued the defendants for an advertisement in which his caricature was pictured promoting the defendants' chocolate bars. However, this case rested on the innuendo that Tolley (an amateur golfer) had violated his amateur status. He would have been unable to sue simply on the basis that he had been caricatured in an advertisement. More fundamentally, the protection provided by defamation is subject to the defence of justification, which permits the defendant to publish any statement provided he or she can show that it is substantially true.[8] Malicious falsehood also came to the assistance of Gorden Kaye in *Kaye v Robertson*[9] where the court, horrified by the behaviour of the newspaper in question, sought to find some way of supporting his claim. Following an accident, Kaye was in intensive care in hospital, and a special notice was placed on his door to keep out visitors. A journalist and photographer from the *Sunday Sport* newspaper nevertheless entered the room, obtained a picture of Mr Kaye using a flash camera, and claimed that Kaye had consented to an "interview", although he was unable to recollect the incident 15 minutes after the event.[10] The Court of Appeal took a dim view of such conduct, but struggled to find a basis of liability in tort,[11] resorting finally to malicious falsehood: the paper's allegation that the story and photograph had been taken with Kaye's consent was clearly false, and Kaye had lost the right to sell his first interview after the accident for profit. Bingham L.J. commented that:

[2] See *Entick v Carrington* (1765) 2 Wils. K.B. 275; 95 E.R. 807.

[3] [1978] 1 Q.B. 479.

[4] See Ch.11.

[5] [1997] A.C. 655, discussed in Ch.10.

[6] Thereby overturning the Court of Appeal's decision in *Khorasandjian v Bush* [1993] Q.B. 727 that the daughter of the house (who was a licensee) could obtain an injunction for private nuisance to stop harassment by a former boyfriend.

[7] [1931] A.C. 333. See also *Charleston v News Group Newspapers* [1995] 2 A.C. 65.

[8] Note, however, that under s.8 (as amended) of the Rehabilitation of Offenders Act 1974 justification is not a defence where the defendant has maliciously published details of a person's distant criminal past. The defences of fair (now honest) comment and privilege may also limit the claimant's ability to complain.

[9] [1991] F.S.R. 62.

[10] The paper alleged that it had obtained "a great old-fashioned scoop".

[11] Trespass to the person failed as the use of a flash by itself did not amount to battery. Nor did Kaye have sufficient possessory rights to bring an action for trespass to land. Defamation (that is, the newspaper had falsely stated that Kaye had consented to give an exclusive interview to the *Sunday Sport*) equally failed as the court was not prepared to impose an interim injunction except in the clearest of cases.

"this case nonetheless highlights, yet again, the failure of both the common law of England and statute to protect in an effective way the personal privacy of individual citizens."[12]

Such provisions are thus limited and, at best, provide only indirect protection of an individual's private life. However, the Human Rights Act 1998 raised the prospect of change. The Act expressly refers to the art.8 right to respect for one's private and family life. The remainder of this chapter will examine the impact of this development. Has the Act, despite Government denials, introduced a right to privacy into English law?

## The impact of the Human Rights Act 1998

In October 2000, the Human Rights Act 1998 came into force in England and Wales. This Act **15–003** gives domestic legal effect to the vast majority of the rights contained in the European Convention on Human Rights. Under s.6, the courts (as a public authority) must act in a way which is compatible with the Convention.

Article 8 of the Convention states that:

"(1) Everyone has the right to respect for his private and family life, his home and his correspondence.
(2) There shall be no interference by a public authority with the exercise of this right except such as is in accordance with the law and is necessary in a democratic society in the interests of national security, public safety or the economic well-being of the country, for the prevention of disorder or crime, for the protection of health or morals, or for the protection of the rights and freedoms of others."

This imposes a positive obligation on States to see that such rights are respected.[13] Nevertheless, it is qualified. It must also be considered in the light of art.10, which protects freedom of expression:

"(1) Everyone has the right to freedom of expression. This right shall include freedom to hold opinions and to receive and impart information and ideas without interference by public authority and regardless of frontiers. This Article shall not prevent States from requiring the licensing of broadcasting, television or cinema enterprises.
(2) The exercise of these freedoms, since it carries with it duties and responsibilities, may be subject to such formalities, conditions, restrictions or penalties as are prescribed by law and are necessary in a democratic society, in the interests of national security, territorial integrity or public safety, for the prevention of disorder or crime, for the protection of health or morals, for the protection of the reputation or the rights of others, *for preventing the disclosure of information received in confidence*, or for maintaining the authority and impartiality of the judiciary."[14]

---

[12] [1991] F.S.R. 62 at p.70. Further protection is provided by copyright law where the claimant owns the copyright of the work or photograph disclosed: see *Williams v Settle* [1960] 1 W.L.R. 1072; s.85 of the Copyright, Designs and Patents Act 1988. Specific statutes also offer protection: Protection from Harassment Act 1997, Data Protection Act 1998 (which extends the rights of individuals to control the use of personal data stored on computers or manually). Note also the Codes of Practice applicable to the media, discussed in Ch.14.

[13] *Von Hannover v Germany (59320/00)* (2005) 40 E.H.R.R. 1.

[14] Emphasis added.

The question arises whether such provisions are sufficient to give claimants a "right" to privacy, or require or empower the courts to develop a tort protecting claimants from invasion of their privacy. The Government's response was in the negative. The Lord Chancellor, during the reading of the Human Rights Bill, stated:

> "This Bill does not impose any statutory controls on the press by a back-door privacy law . . . I would not agree with any proposition that the courts as public authorities will be obliged to fashion a law on privacy because of the terms of the Bill."[15]

Further, s.12(4) of the 1998 Act provides that:

> "The court must have particular regard to the importance of the Convention right to freedom of expression and, where the proceedings relate to material which the respondent claims, or which appears to the court, to be journalistic, literary or artistic material (or to conduct connected with such material), to—
>
> (a)  the extent to which–
>    (i)  the material has, or is about to, become available to the public; or
>    (ii) it is, or would be, in the public interest for the material to be published;
>
> (b)  any relevant privacy code."

This does not prevent, however, the courts choosing to develop the common law in a way which provides greater protection of privacy rights.[16] The subsequent development of the law illustrates two propositions:

- there is still no general tort of invasion of privacy,

- claimants may nevertheless seek a remedy against the publication of private information relating to their personal lives under the action for breach of confidence.

These two propositions will be discussed below.

## THE CURRENT LEGAL POSITION

### (1)  Rejection of a new tort of invasion of privacy

**15–004**    The leading case is that of *Wainwright v Home Office*.[17] Here, a mother and son visiting a relative in prison were strip-searched for drugs under humiliating conditions. No drugs were found. The search was conducted in breach of prison rules (and therefore not protected by statutory authority) and both claimants suffered distress as a result; the son, who suffered from

---

[15]  Lord Irvine of Lairg, *Hansard*, 24 November 1997, cols. 784–5.
[16]  The so-called "indirect" horizontal effect: see Hunt [1998] P.L. 423 and Buxton (2000) 116 L.Q.R. 48.
[17]  [2003] UKHL 53, [2004] 2 A.C. 406. See Morgan (2004) 120 L.Q.R. 393 and Johnston [2004] C.L.J. 15.

physical and learning difficulties, developing post-traumatic stress disorder. It was claimed that such conduct invaded their rights to privacy.[18]

In the House of Lords, Lord Hoffmann rejected the existence of a common law tort of invasion of privacy. Whilst existing torts might provide some protection, this did not indicate that the common law should regard privacy as a principle of law worthy of protection in itself. Any such development could only be undertaken by Parliament, which could provide specific detailed rules to deal with privacy issues.[19] In any event with the coming into force of the Human Rights Act 1998, in future claims could be brought under s.6 of the Act. The creation of a general tort was not, in his Lordship's opinion, necessary to comply with art.8.

The 1998 Act was not applicable on the facts of *Wainwright* which occurred before the Act was in force. Their Lordships accepted that a challenge might subsequently be made to the European Court of Human Rights in Strasbourg. This, indeed, occurred and the Strasbourg Court held unanimously that the prison officers' conduct was a breach of art.8. The requirement to submit to a strip-search would generally amount to an interference with the right to respect for private life under art.8, and it could not be said that the searches were a proportionate response to the legitimate aim of combating the drugs problem within the prison.[20] Each applicant was awarded €3,000 in compensation.

Nevertheless, the basic proposition in *Wainwright* stands: a general tort of privacy has not been accepted by the courts.

## (2) The "extended" breach of confidence action

Lord Hoffmann in *Wainwright* noted that the law of breach of confidence had in recent years undergone "judicious development" to provide a remedy for some invasions of privacy.[21] This is somewhat of an understatement. Despite the courts' doubts in relation to a new tort protecting privacy, they have been far less reticent in re-moulding the equitable doctrine of breach of confidence[22] as a means of protecting the private lives of claimants. This has long provided a remedy in equity where there has been unauthorised disclosure or use of information in

**15–005**

---

[18] It was also argued that the parties could claim under the rule in *Wilkinson v Downton*. This claim, which was rejected, is discussed in Ch.11.

[19] [2004] 2 A.C. 406 at para.33.

[20] *Wainwright v United Kingdom (12350/04)* (2007) 44 E.H.R.R. 40. See also *Peck v United Kingdom (44647/98)* (2003) 36 E.H.R.R. 41 (footage broadcast of Mr Peck's suicide attempt captured on CCTV cameras breached his art.8 rights and no effective remedy existed at the time). Both cases indicate that the law prior to the Human Rights Act 1998 was not fully compatible with art.8, as interpreted by the European Court of Human Rights (contrast the Commission ruling in *Earl Spencer v United Kingdom (28851/95)* (1998) 25 E.H.R.R. CD 105: applicants did not demonstrate that the remedy of breach of confidence was insufficient or ineffective in the circumstances of their case).

[21] [2004] 2 A.C. 406 at para.18. The first step was taken by Lord Goff in *Att-Gen v Guardian Newspapers Ltd (No.2)* [1990] A.C. 109 at 281–282.

[22] This is not really a tort at all but an independent equitable principle: see *Att-Gen v Guardian Newspapers Ltd (No.2)* [1990] A.C. 109 at 280–3 per Lord Goff. It is a matter of dispute whether the "extended" breach of confidence action is to be treated as a tort. As we will see, Lord Nicholls appears content to consider it to be a tort, but the Court of Appeal in *Douglas v Hello! Ltd (No.3)* [2005] EWCA Civ 595, [2006] Q.B. 125 at para.96 dispute this, and the willingness of the courts to award an account of profits supports a basis in equity.

circumstances where a duty of confidentiality exists. For example, in *Argyll v Argyll*,[23] an ex-wife was able to obtain an injunction preventing her former husband revealing confidences of their married life.

Yet, whilst the old doctrine focused on circumstances where there was a genuine relationship of confidence between the parties and was confined to information said to possess the necessary quality of confidence,[24] modern law has adopted a far more generous interpretation.[25] As Lord Nicholls has stated in a leading case:

> "The time has come to recognise that the values enshrined in articles 8 and 10 are now part of the cause of action for breach of confidence . . . The values embodied in articles 8 and 10 are as much applicable in disputes between individuals or between an individual and a non-governmental body such as a newspaper as they are in disputes between individuals and a public authority."[26]

The key modern cases are *Campbell v Mirror Group Newspapers Ltd*[27] and *McKennitt v Ash*.[28] These cases provide a framework for the modern action.

*Campbell v Mirror Group Newspapers Ltd*

**15–006**    Naomi Campbell is a well-known "supermodel". The *Daily Mirror* published a number of articles which revealed that, contrary to her previous statements, she was a drug addict and attending Narcotics Anonymous meetings to deal with her addiction. Photographs were taken without her knowledge, showing her in a public street leaving a group meeting, and details were given of her treatment. In response to her action for breach of confidence,[29] the *Daily Mirror* alleged that it had acted in the public interest in correcting her previous denials and that the photographs and other details were merely peripheral to this information.

The House of Lords accepted that the *Mirror* was entitled to set the record straight and correct Ms Campbell's previous untrue statements, but their Lordships were divided whether the additional details were peripheral or not. The majority argued in favour of Ms Campbell[30]: details relating to her treatment were akin to the private and confidential information contained in medical records and their publication might deter Ms Campbell from seeking help for her addiction and thereby harm her health. On balance, her art.8 rights therefore

---

[23] [1967] Ch 302. See also *Stephens v Avery* [1988] Ch 449 and the early case of *Prince Albert v Strange* (1849) 1 De G & Sm 652; 1 Mac. & G. 25 (publisher obtaining copies of private etchings made by the Prince Consort of members of the royal family at home from an employee of a printer to whom the Prince had entrusted the plates).

[24] See *Coco v AN Clark (Engineers) Ltd* [1969] R.P.C. 41, 47–48 per Megarry J.

[25] Note the influential article, G. Phillipson, "Transforming breach of confidence? Towards a common law right of privacy under the Human Rights Act" (2003) 66 M.L.R. 726.

[26] *Campbell v Mirror Group Newspapers Ltd* [2004] UKHL 22, [2004] 2 A.C. 457 at para.17. See also Lord Woolf C.J. in *A v B Plc* [2003] Q.B. 195 at para.4.

[27] [2004] UKHL 22; [2004] 2 A.C. 457. Comment: Morgan (2004) 120 L.Q.R. 563 and Moreham [2004] C.L.J. 555. Appeal to the European Court of Human Rights for violation of art.10 was rejected by a majority of 6:1: *MGN Ltd v United Kingdom* (39401/04) (2011) 29 B.H.R.C. 686.

[28] [2006] EWCA Civ 1714; [2008] Q.B. 73. Comment: Moreham (2007) 123 L.Q.R. 373.

[29] A claim was also brought under the Data Protection Act 1998, but all parties agreed that this claim would succeed or fail depending on the success of the breach of confidence action.

[30] Lords Nicholls and Hoffmann dissenting.

outweighed the newspaper's right to freedom of expression, entitling Ms Campbell to an award of damages.

A number of points arise from the *Campbell* decision. First, it is clear that although the action is in breach of confidence, their Lordships are focussing on issues of privacy. Lord Nicholls is perhaps most overt in his approach:

> "The common law or, more precisely, courts of equity have long afforded protection to the wrongful use of private information by means of the cause of action which became known as breach of confidence . . . This cause of action has now firmly shaken off the limiting constraint of the need for an initial confidential relationship. In doing so it has changed its nature . . . Now the law imposes a 'duty of confidence' whenever a person receives information he knows or ought to know is fairly and reasonably to be regarded as confidential. Even this formulation is awkward. The continuing use of the phrase 'duty of confidence' and the description of the information as 'confidential' is not altogether comfortable. Information about an individual's private life would not, in ordinary usage, be called 'confidential'. The more natural description today is that such information is private. The essence of the tort is better encapsulated now as misuse of private information."[31]

Secondly, this action does not protect all privacy rights, but is confined to private information. For example, the strip-searches in *Wainwright* would not fit under this action. Future Wainwrights would have to seek a remedy not in tort, but under ss.7 and 8 of the Human Rights Act 1998. Thirdly, liability will only arise if the defendant discloses private, not public, information. This is therefore a key issue. When will information be private? Clearly if a public figure discusses her private life in the press, she will run the risk, as with Ms Campbell, that this will be viewed as a matter of public debate. Finally, art.8 rights are not, as stated above, absolute. The courts will in each case balance the claimant's rights to private and family life against the defendant's freedom of expression. It is clear in *Campbell* that, despite s.12 of the Human Rights Act 1998, neither right has pre-eminence.[32] The test is whether publication pursues a legitimate aim and whether the benefit of publication is proportionate to the harm done by interference with privacy.[33]

### *McKennitt v Ash*

Unlike Naomi Campbell, Loreena McKennitt, despite being a well-known Canadian folk musician, had carefully guarded her personal life and was distressed when a former close friend wrote a book which contained personal and private details of her life. She sought an injunction on the basis of breach of privacy or confidence to prevent further publication of certain private material. Her friend, Niema Ash, alleged that this prevented her telling her own story which includes her friendship with Ms McKennitt.

**15–007**

The Court of Appeal was, perhaps understandably, unconvinced by Ms Ash's argument. In reality, her book (entitled *Travels with Loreena McKennitt*) was only of interest due to

---

[31] [2004] 2 A.C. 457 at paras 13–14. See also Lord Hoffmann at para.50: "What human rights law has done is to identify private information as something worth protecting as an aspect of human autonomy and dignity."
[32] *Douglas v Hello! Ltd (No.1)* [2001] Q.B. 967 at 1004–5 per Sedley L.J.
[33] [2004] 2 A.C. 457 at para.113 per Lord Hope.

revelations arising from her close and confidential relationship with Ms McKennitt. As Buxton L.J. commented:

> "the matters related in the book were specifically experiences of . . . Ms McKennitt. Ms Ash cannot undermine their confidential nature by the paradox of calling in aid the confidential relationship that gave her access to the information in the first place."[34]

Yet, *McKennitt* is important not due to its application of the law, which can be argued to satisfy even the traditional conception of the breach of confidence action, but in its guidance as to the nature of the "extended" action. Buxton L.J. confirmed that the English law of breach of confidence lies in the case law of arts 8 and 10 and that, as a result, there are two key questions for the court to resolve:[35]

(i) Is the information private in the sense that it is in principle protected by art.8? If no, that is the end of the case. If yes, then

(ii) In all the circumstances, must the interest of the owner of the private information yield to the right of freedom of expression conferred on the publisher by art.10? (the "balancing exercise")

Much then will depend on the facts of the case, although undoubtedly some guidance may be gained from examining previous decisions. Caution must, however, be taken with early cases such as *Douglas v Hello! Ltd (No.1)*[36] and *A v B Plc*,[37] in that more recent decisions indicate that the courts would now be far more willing to protect the privacy rights of the claimants in question.[38]

## Application of the two-stage test:

### (i) Is the information private?

**15–008** Whether a particular piece of information qualifies as private will depend on all the circumstances of the case, and the courts proceed case by case. At times this may be obvious. For example, the journals of the Prince of Wales recording his impressions of the handing over of

---

[34] [2008] Q.B. 73 at para.32.
[35] [2008] Q.B. 73 at para.11.
[36] [2001] Q.B. 967. The later Court of Appeal decision in *Douglas v Hello! Ltd (No.3)* [2005] EWCA Civ 595, [2006] Q.B. 125 stated, obiter, that in the light of the subsequent development of the law, the decision to lift the interlocutory injunction had been wrong (Decision in favour of Douglases' claim not appealed to HL: *OBG Ltd v Allan* [2007] UKHL 21; [2008] A.C. 1).
[37] [2003] Q.B. 195. The Court in *McKennitt v Ash* [2008] Q.B. 73 commented at para.62: "The width of the rights given to the media by *A v B* cannot be reconciled with *Von Hannover*."
[38] Note, in particular, the influence of the subsequent decision of the European Court of Human Rights in *Von Hannover v Germany (59320/00)* (2005) 40 E.H.R.R. 1 (photographs taken of Princess Caroline of Monaco in her daily life without her consent were not in the public interest. The publication of the photos and articles, the sole purpose of which was to satisfy the curiosity of a particular readership regarding the applicant's private life, did not contribute to any debate of general interest—breach of art.8). See also *Murray v Express Newspapers Plc* [2008] EWCA Civ 446; [2009] Ch 481 (arguable that photograph of J.K. Rowling's infant son in a public street infringed the child's reasonable expectation of privacy—case ultimately settled prior to trial).

Hong Kong in 1993 were considered to be paradigm examples of confidential documents.[39] If not, then the courts have used a variety of formulations. The Court of Appeal in *Douglas v Hello! Ltd (No. 3)*[40] asked:

> "What is the nature of 'private information'? It seems to us that it must include information that is personal to the person who possesses it and that he does not intend shall be imparted to the general public. The nature of the information, or the form in which it is kept, may suffice to make it plain that the information satisfies these criteria."[41]

In *Campbell*, their Lordships expressed themselves in a number of different ways. Perhaps the most useful statement is by Lord Nicholls: "Essentially the touchstone of private life is whether in respect of the disclosed facts the person in question had a reasonable expectation of privacy."[42] This is clearly an objective test.

When the question is not obvious, the courts will look to the nature of the activity in which the claimant was engaged, the place at which it was happening, the nature and purpose of the intrusion, absence of consent (known or inferred), the effect on the claimant, and the circumstances in which, and purposes for which, the information came into the hands of the publisher.[43] The attributes of the claimant will also be relevant (although not decisive), for example, is the claimant a publicity-seeking celebrity or a mere child?[44] The cases show that details which are of a sexual nature[45] or concern health or personal matters will be regarded as private. Information may also be private even if the individual in question wishes to exploit it commercially, although this is likely to reduce the level of damages awarded.[46]

*(ii) Balancing Article 8 and Article 10*

Here, the key is to identify whether it is proportionate to prevent disclosure of private information, having regard to the competing Convention right of freedom of expression. Neither Article has precedence over the other. The cases indicate that a number of factors may affect the balancing exercise. A court is far more likely to permit discussion of matters of legitimate public interest, for example information relating to politicians in the exercise of their functions, than tittle-tattle related to parties with no real public function,[47] as exemplified by the European Court of Human Rights judgment in favour of Princess Caroline of Monaco who, despite having no official functions, had been photographed dining, with her children,

**15–009**

---

[39] *HRH Prince of Wales v Associated Newspapers Ltd* [2006] EWCA Civ 1776; [2008] Ch.57 at para.35 per Lord Phillips C.J. Prince Charles brought proceedings for breach of confidence and infringement of copyright when *The Mail on Sunday* published extracts from his journal headed "The Handover of Hong Kong—or 'The Great Chinese Takeaway'".

[40] [2006] Q.B. 125.

[41] [2006] Q.B. 125 at para.83.

[42] [2004] 2 A.C. 457 at para.21. See also Lord Hope: "a duty of confidence will arise whenever the party subject to the duty is in a situation where he knows or ought to know that the other person can reasonably expect his privacy to be protected" [2004] 2 A.C. 457 at para.85.

[43] *Murray v Express Newspapers Plc* [2008] EWCA Civ 446 per Sir Anthony Clarke MR at para. 36.

[44] As in *Murray v Express Newspapers Plc* [2008] EWCA Civ 446 (photograph of 19 month child in public place taken covertly without parents' consent).

[45] See *Mosley v News Group Newspapers Ltd* [2008] EWHC 1777 (QB).

[46] *Douglas v Hello! Ltd (No. 3)* [2005] EWCA Civ 595; [2006] Q.B. 125.

[47] See Baroness Hale in *Campbell* at paras 148–149.

shopping, playing tennis and bicycling.[48] The court found that "the publication of the photos and articles in question, of which the sole purpose was to satisfy the curiosity of a particular readership regarding the details of the applicant's private life, cannot be deemed to contribute to any debate of general interest to society despite the applicant being known to the public."[49] Certain matters may help tip the balance. Special considerations apply to photographs, which are, by their very nature, more intrusive than words.[50] In the *Prince of Wales* case, the fact that the information was disclosed to the newspaper by an employee in Prince Charles' private office, who was under a contractual obligation to keep the contents of the journal confidential, was said to support Prince Charles's claim.[51] The breach of confidence defence of "public domain" will also fall to be considered at this stage—information will not be protected against publication if it is already known to the public. This raises difficult questions of degree. For example, in *McKennitt*, despite Ms KcKennitt's insistence of her avoidance of publicity, evidence was given that she had discussed the death of her fiancé in a drowning accident and its impact on her in a number of articles. The Court of Appeal refused to accept that limited disclosure of personal details permitted subsequent scrutiny of every detail of her personal life. On the facts, the articles had been part of a campaign by McKennitt to promote water safety and it was regarded as "cruelly insensitive"[52] to suggest that this opened up her entire life to scrutiny as a result.

## Remedies

**15–010**    Claimants, if aware of or suspecting disclosure, will frequently seek an injunction to prevent publication. As noted in Ch.14, English courts are particularly aware of the dangers that the award of interlocutory injunctions may pose to the right of freedom of expression. This does not, of course, prevent a claim for damages, but the damages awarded have until recently not been large. Michael Douglas and Catherine Zeta-Jones in the *Douglas v Hello! Ltd* litigation were awarded £3,750 each for the distress arising from infringement of their privacy rights when an unauthorised photographer sold photographs of their wedding reception (although this was no doubt reduced by their willingness to grant exclusive rights to their wedding pictures to Hello!'s rival, OK! Ltd).[53] A claim for an account of profits was accepted to be possible, but unavailable on the facts.[54] Ms McKennitt received a mere £5,000. In *Mosley v*

---

[48]   *Von Hannover v Germany (59320/00)* (2005) 40 E.H.R.R. 1. For criticism, see Sanderson [2004] EHRLR 631. See also *Sciacca v Italy* (50774/99), (2006) 43 E.H.R.R. 20 (ECHR).

[49]   At para.65.

[50]   See *Von Hannover* at para.59; *Campbell* at paras 123 and 155 (Lord Hope and Baroness Hale respectively) and *Douglas v Hello! Ltd (No.3)* [2005] EWCA Civ 595; [2006] Q.B. 125 at paras 84–91. In *Theakston v MGN Ltd* [2002] EWHC 137 (QB); [2002] E.M.L.R. 22, for example, Ouseley, J. was prepared to restrain photographs of the celebrity, but not the information that he had visited a brothel.

[51]   [2008] Ch.57 at para.71: "There is an important public interest in employees in the position of Ms Goodall respecting the obligations of confidence that they have assumed. Both the nature of the information and of the relationship of confidence under which it was received weigh heavily in the balance in favour of Prince Charles."

[52]   [2008] Q.B. 73 at para.54.

[53]   They were also awarded £7,000 for the cost and inconvenience of making a hurried selection of photographs for *OK! Magazine*, which represented their commercial interest in exploiting private information about their wedding: see Bagshaw (2005) 121 L.Q.R. 550. The House of Lords, on appeal by *OK!* Magazine only, made it clear that the ordinary principles of breach of confidence would apply to claims to protect commercial confidential information, which did not concern privacy rights: see Lord Hoffmann, who adopts a pragmatic commercial approach to such claims: *OBG Ltd v Allan* [2007] UKHL 21; [2008] A.C. 1 at para.118.

[54]   At para.249. See the classic article of Jones (1970) 80 L.Q.R. 463.

*News Group Newspapers Ltd*,[55] however, Eady J. was prepared to award the claimant £60,
000 in view of the scale of distress and indignity suffered by Mr Mosley. The newspaper had
published salacious details of the claimant's involvement in sado-masochistic activities,
which, it alleged, had a Nazi theme and mocked the way that Holocaust victims had been
treated in concentration camps. In addition to being (at the time) President of the FIA (the
organization running Formula 1 motor-racing), Mr Mosley is the son of Sir Oswald Mosley,
a noted Fascist leader during the Second World War, rendering such allegations doubly embar-
rassing. Sexual activity of this nature was, predictably, deemed to give rise to a reasonable
expectation of privacy and, in the absence of proof of the Nazi or concentration camp
allegations, publication could not be said to be in the public interest. In awarding damages,
Eady J. highlighted that the court should award an adequate financial remedy, capable
of acknowledging the infringement of privacy and compensating for injury to feelings, embarrassment and distress. Exemplary damages would not, however, be awarded. Whilst accepting
the sums previously awarded had been modest, in view of the infringement in question, which
included video footage of the claimant which was freely accessible on the News of the World's
website and persistent reference to the unproven Nazi allegations, Eady J. was prepared to be
more generous.[56]

For many, however, it is the question of obtaining an interlocutory injunction to prevent the
information being revealed in the first place which is the most important issue. In *Cream
Holdings Ltd v Banerjee*,[57] the House of Lords indicated when a court should make an interim
order in a breach of confidence claim. The question is complicated by s.12(3) of the Human
Rights Act 1998, which states:

> "No such relief is to be granted so as to restrain publication before trial unless the
> court is satisfied that the applicant is likely to establish that publication should not be
> allowed."

This form of wording differs from the traditional test stated in *American Cyanamid Co v
Ethicon Ltd*,[58] namely that the court must be satisfied that there is a real prospect of success.
Lord Nicholls, with the full agreement of the House, considered the meaning of the word
"likely" in s.12(3) and how it differed from the traditional test. Did it, in other words, make it
easier or harder for the claimant to obtain an interlocutory injunction for breach of confidence,
or did it simply maintain the status quo? In his Lordship's view, the principal purpose of this
section was to buttress the protection given to freedom of expression. It thus set a higher
threshold for the grant of an interlocutory injunction than existed previously. Although bearing
in mind that confidentiality, once breached, is lost forever, his Lordship concluded:

---

[55] [2008] EWHC 1777 (QB). Mr Mosley subsequently brought a case to the European Court of Human Rights,
arguing for a prior notification rule by which newspapers, intending to publish details of an individual's private life,
must notify the individual in advance and thereby give him or her the opportunity to apply for an interlocutory injunction to block publication. As acknowledged by Eady J. in *Mosley*, unlike defamation, no amount of damages can fully
compensate the claimant for the damage done once the public are made aware of private information relating to the
claimant: para.236. The Court ruled unanimously, however, that Art. 8 ECHR does not require a legally binding
pre-notification requirement: *Mosley v United Kingdom (48009/08)* Times, May 11, 2011.
[56] Eady J. remarked at para.236 that: "[Mr Mosley] is hardly exaggerating when he says that his life was ruined." For
a review of the law to date, see D. Eady (2010) 29 C.J.Q. 411.
[57] [2004] UKHL 44; [2005] 1 A.C. 253.
[58] [1975] A.C. 396, 407–408 per Lord Diplock.

"There can be no single, rigid standard governing all applications for interim restraint orders. Rather, on its proper construction the effect of section 12(3) is that the court is not to make an interim restraint order unless satisfied the applicant's prospects of success at the trial are sufficiently favourable to justify such an order being made in the particular circumstances of the case. As to what degree of likelihood makes the prospects of success "sufficiently favourable", *the general approach should be that courts will be exceedingly slow to make interim restraint orders where the applicant has not satisfied the court he will probably ("more likely than not") succeed at the trial*. In general, that should be the threshold an applicant must cross before the court embarks on exercising its discretion, duly taking into account the relevant jurisprudence on article 10 and any countervailing Convention rights."[59]

His Lordship accepted that there will be cases where the courts will be required to depart from this general approach and require a lesser degree of likelihood, for example, where the potential adverse consequences of disclosure are particularly grave or where a short-lived injunction is needed to enable the court to hear and give proper consideration to an application for interim relief pending the trial or any relevant appeal. Generally, however, the test enunciated by Lord Nicholls places the burden on the claimant to persuade the judge that his prospects of success at trial are sufficiently favourable.[60] The court will, in most cases, be slow to grant an interim restraint order where the claimant has *not* satisfied the court that, once the relevant balancing exercise between art.8 and art.10 rights has been carried out, he or she would be more likely than not to succeed at the trial.

## Conclusion

15–011  This is an area of law which is still developing. The judiciary has openly expressed its misgivings that the recognition of privacy rights has been "shoehorned" into the existing action for breach of confidence.[61] The law thus becomes particularly unclear when the courts face "real" breach of confidence actions such as *McKennitt*[62] and the *Prince of Wales* case, where no legal expansion is required. All such cases must now be reviewed in the light of the Human Rights Act 1998 whether they involve "confidential" information due to an express or implied duty of confidence or merely private information for which the claimant has a reasonable expectation of privacy. More recently, Lord Nicholls has openly distinguished between an action to

[59] [2005] 1 A.C. 253 at para.22 (emphasis added). For recent examples, see *CDE v MGN Ltd* [2010] EWHC 3308 (QB) and *CTB v News Group Newspapers Ltd*, [2011] EWHC 1232 (QB). Contrast with the treatment of interlocutory injunctions in defamation: see *LNS v Persons Unknown* [2010] EWHC 119 (QB); [2010] 2 F.L.R. 1306 (nub of applicant's true complaint was protection of reputation rather than private life and defamation rule in *Bonnard v Perryman* would thus be applied: see 14–043).
[60] See *Browne v Associated Newspapers Ltd* [2007] EWCA Civ 295; [2008] Q.B. 103. But compare *CC v AB* [2006] EWHC 3083 (QB); [2007] E.M.L.R. 11 (QBD): "in order to protect [the claimant's relationship with his wife] it is necessary to prevent the defendant going directly or indirectly to the media for no better reason than spite, money-making or 'tittle tattle'." (Eady J.)
[61] See Lord Phillips M.R. in *Douglas v Hello! Ltd (No.3)* [2006] Q.B. 125 at para.53: "We cannot pretend that we find it satisfactory to be required to shoehorn within the cause of action of breach of confidence claims for publication of unauthorised photographs of a private occasion." Academics have also been critical of reliance on breach of confidence: see, for example, Morgan [2003] C.L.J. 444 and Mulheron (2006) 69 M.L.R. 679, who proposes a potential framework for a tort of privacy.
[62] Ms Ash was a long-term confidant of Ms McKennitt and had at one stage signed a contract with her containing express obligations of confidence.

protect privacy and an action to protect secret (or "confidential") information. Both at present are still encompassed by the action for breach of confidence.[63] It is to be hoped that formal recognition of a tort of misuse of private information will bring clarity to this area of law and permit the law to develop its own rules and remedies out of the shadow of the action for breach of confidence.

---

[63] See Lord Nicholls in *OBG Ltd v Allan* [2008] A.C. 1 at para.255.

# Chapter 16

# GENERAL DEFENCES AND EXTINCTION OF LIABILITY

## Introduction

In this chapter, we examine defences generally and the ways in which the defendant's liability **16–001** can be extinguished. We have already considered a number of defences in this book, for example defences to defamation claims in Ch.14, defences such as act of God or statutory authority in our nuisance chapter, and necessity in our trespass chapter. These will therefore not be considered here. This chapter will examine the remaining general defences in tort and should therefore be used in conjunction with earlier chapters outlining the requirements of the tort in question. We examine each defence in turn. It should be noted that, in general, the burden of proof in establishing a defence will rest on the defendant on the balance of probabilities. There is no limit on the number of defences a defendant may allege.

The second half of this chapter deals with ways in which the defendant's liability can be extinguished. The primary method is limitation. The Limitation Act 1980 imposes strict time limits within which the claimant must start his or her action. If these time limits are missed, then, subject to certain statutory discretions, the court will refuse to hear the claimant's action, however strong the claim. This ensures that claimants do not bring stale claims which it would be difficult for the defendant to defend. We shall also consider the effect of death of either party to the action, and the more technical grounds of waiver, and accord and satisfaction. We begin by examining the main general defences in the law of torts.

## DEFENCES

### (1) Consent

We saw the defence of "consent" in our chapter on trespass to the person where the surgeon, **16–002** for example, operates on a patient. The surgeon is not committing a trespass if he or she has obtained the patient's consent to the procedure in question. In negligence, the terminology is different, and the courts prefer the term volenti non fit injuria or "voluntary assumption of risk". In relation to property, it is usually termed "leave" or "licence". Although the courts may use the terms interchangeably,[1] the defence is applied differently and we shall therefore divide consent into three categories:

    (i)   consent;

    (ii)  voluntary assumption of risk; and

    (iii) leave or licence.

We shall examine each category in context. Therefore, consent will be examined in the context of trespass to the person, voluntary assumption of risk in relation to negligence and leave or licence in relation to property torts.[2]

*(i) Consent*

**16–003**    The defendant will not be liable for trespass to the person where the claimant has consented to such actions. Consent may be express or implied. For example, by presenting your arm for an injection, you are impliedly showing that you consent to the physical contact involved. Following *Freeman v Home Office (No.2)*,[3] the burden is on the claimant to show the absence of consent. Although ordinarily the burden is on the defendant to establish a defence, the nature of trespass to the person is such that the claimant must show that the physical contact was incurred without his or her consent. In reality, however, the defendant is more likely to produce evidence showing consent than rely on the hope that the claimant will be unable to establish absence of consent. Practically, therefore, it works as a defence. This topic is discussed fully in Ch.11 and therefore readers are advised to refer further to the section on "Consent" in that chapter.

*(ii) Voluntary assumption of risk*

**16–004**    In the tort of negligence, consent takes the form of an agreement to run the risk of the defendant's negligence. It may be express or implied and forms an absolute defence. There are traditionally said to be three main requirements for the defence:

    (a)  agreement to the risk;

    (b)  full knowledge of the nature and extent of the risk; and

    (c)  voluntary choice by the claimant.

The three requirements will be examined below.

**16–005**    **(a) Agreement:**   There is mixed authority as to what is meant by "agreement". Lord Denning in *Nettleship v Weston*[4] took a very formalistic view, holding that "nothing will suffice short of an agreement to waive any claim for negligence".[5] This clearly did not exist on the facts of the case. It may be recalled from earlier chapters that a friend, who had been teaching the defendant to drive, had been injured by the defendant's negligent driving. The court held that the friend had not agreed to take the risk of this happening as he had specifically asked, prior

---

[1]  See, e.g. *Arthur v Anker* [1997] Q.B. 564 at 572.
[2]  By "property torts", we mean torts protecting land such as private nuisance and trespass to land.
[3]  [1984] 2 W.L.R. 130; affirmed [1984] 1 Q.B. 524.
[4]  [1971] 2 Q.B. 691.
[5]  [1971] 2 Q.B. 691 at 701.

to the lesson, whether he would be protected by the car-owner's insurance policy. It is unclear, however, whether such a stringent test for agreement applies generally. Such a test would rarely be satisfied, and his Lordship's view would severely limit the application of this defence. A more flexible approach was clearly evident in the House of Lords' decision in *ICI v Shatwell*.[6]

In this case, the plaintiff and his brother worked together at the defendant's quarry. With complete disregard to their employer's safety instructions (and certain statutory duties imposed on them) which required them to test detonators from a proper shelter, they decided to test the detonators in the open to save time. There was an explosion in which the plaintiff was seriously injured. He sued his employer as vicariously liable for his brother's negligence. The House of Lords was not prepared to allow him to recover damages. It was held that the plaintiff had voluntarily assumed the risk, having fully appreciated the potential danger which led to the injury. Although it is possible to explain this decision in terms of an implied agreement between the two brothers, little attention was paid by their Lordships to the requirement of agreement.[7] A clearer example of the artificiality of a formal requirement of express or implied agreement may be found in the House of Lords case of *Titchener v British Railways Board*.[8] In this case, a 15-year-old girl had been struck by a train while crossing a railway line. She was seriously injured. She was a trespasser, having passed through a gap in the boundary fence, and it was held that she clearly knew of the risk of being hit by trains when crossing the line. She had nevertheless taken that risk and, had the train driver been negligent, a defence of voluntary assumption of risk would have applied. In this case, it is difficult to see how any agreement (express or otherwise) could be found between the plaintiff and the train driver. The defence seemed to be based simply on her free acceptance of the risks involved.

"Agreement" should thus be interpreted loosely to mean that the claimant has clearly consented to the risk.[9] Obviously this will be easier to establish where the claimant has openly agreed with the defendant to undertake the risk, but this is not a necessary requirement. On this basis, "agreement" cannot be considered as a separate requirement. It is simply part of the question whether the defendant has fully consented to the risk, which also involves an examination of the claimant's knowledge and understanding of the risks involved. It is submitted therefore that (a) and (b) should be merged to form a single requirement that the claimant has full knowledge of and has accepted the nature and extent of the risks involved.

**(b) Full knowledge and acceptance of the nature and extent of the risk:** This is the key **16–006** issue. To lose the right to sue for negligence, it is not sufficient that the claimant simply consented to the defendant's activities. Such consent will only provide a defence if it is of a particular quality: it is given with a full understanding and acceptance of the nature and extent of the risks involved. For example, if I agree to attend your barbecue, I accept the risk of smoke and perhaps even the risk of undercooked food. However, unless you tell me, I do not accept the risk that you will try to set the barbecue alight with petrol, causing a massive explosion. My agreement to attend the barbecue was not with the full knowledge of the risks involved. This can lead to difficult questions of fact and has given rise to a number of controversial decisions, none more so than the Court of Appeal decision in *Dann v Hamilton*.[10]

---

[6] [1965] A.C. 656, see, in particular, Lord Reid.
[7] Although Lord Pearce referred to a genuine full agreement at 687.
[8] [1983] 1 W.L.R. 1427.
[9] Note, however, A.J.E. Jaffey (1985) 44 C.L.J. 87.
[10] [1939] 1 K.B. 509. See D.M. Gordon (1966) 82 L.Q.R. 62 for criticism.

In this case, the plaintiff and her mother had accepted a lift from Hamilton to see the coronation decorations. During the evening, Hamilton had consumed a certain amount of alcohol, but the plaintiff nevertheless accepted a lift home. This was despite the warning from a fellow passenger, who refused to travel any further in the car, that she should find an alternative means of transport. Due to Hamilton's negligent driving, the vehicle was involved in an accident in which Hamilton was killed and the plaintiff injured. The question arose whether the plaintiff had voluntarily assumed the risk of negligent driving. When warned by her friend, she had merely responded: "You should be like me. If anything is going to happen, it will happen". Was this statement sufficient to establish the defence?

Perhaps surprisingly, Asquith J. held that it was not. He distinguished between knowledge of a risk and consent to the risk. The plaintiff clearly knew that the driver was intoxicated, but Asquith J. held that this did not mean that she had accepted the risk of him driving negligently. However, the judge did concede that if the drunkenness of a driver was so extreme and glaring that to travel with him would be to engage in an intrinsically and obviously dangerous occupation, such as meddling with an unexploded bomb, or walking on the edge of an unfenced cliff, the defence would be established.

This decision draws the defence very narrowly indeed.[11] One explanation is the fact that it is a driving case where, of course, the driver is required to be insured.[12] The insurance cover ensures that the victim is fully compensated whilst the cost is spread throughout the driving community. This explanation is nowadays further supported by s.149 of the Road Traffic Act 1988, which excludes the defence of voluntary assumption of risk in all road traffic cases. It provides that when a person uses a motor vehicle which is required by law to be insured:

> "any antecedent agreement or understanding between them (whether intended to be legally binding or not) shall be of no effect so far as it purports or might be held:
>
> (a) to negative or restrict any such liability of the user in respect of persons carried in or upon the vehicle as is required . . . to be covered by a policy of insurance, or
>
> (b) to impose such conditions with respect to the enforcement of any such liability of the user."

The defence will therefore never work against car passengers, who should be regarded as in a category of their own. This provision does not, however, prevent other defences applying, such as contributory negligence. In *Owens v Brimmell*,[13] for example, the plaintiff had accompanied the defendant to a number of public houses and finally to a club. Both men had drunk about eight to nine pints of beer. Driving home, the defendant lost control of the car, which collided with a lamp-post. The plaintiff suffered severe injuries and brain damage. Watkins J. held that where a passenger rides in a car with a driver whom he knows has consumed enough alcohol to impair to a dangerous degree his ability to drive properly and safely, the passenger will be found to be contributorily negligent. This will obviously apply where a passenger,

---

[11] The decision was questioned by the Court of Appeal in *Pitts v Hunt* [1991] 1 Q.B. 24 who suggested that riding pillion on a motorbike after the plaintiff and the driver had been drinking for hours would, but for s.149 of the Road Traffic Act 1988, have amounted to voluntary assumption of risk. In any event, the court found a good defence of illegality and the case will be considered fully in that section.

[12] The Road Traffic Act 1930 first introduced compulsory third party insurance.

[13] [1977] Q.B. 859.

knowing that he is relying on the driver for a lift home, accompanies him on a bout of drinking which diminishes the driver's ability to drive properly and safely. On this basis, although the defence of voluntary assumption of risk was not available, damages were reduced by 20 per cent.

In addition, s.149 does not mean that the defence of voluntary assumption of risk will not work in relation to other types of vehicle. The leading modern case on the nature and extent of the risk is now *Morris v Murray*.[14] In this case, the plaintiff chose to fly in a light aircraft piloted by his friend, with whom he had consumed a considerable amount of alcohol prior to the flight.[15] The aircraft crashed shortly after take-off, killing the pilot and badly injuring the plaintiff. The Court of Appeal found in such circumstances that the defence had been established. The plaintiff was well aware of the extreme risk involved in flying with his friend. It was so dangerous that it amounted to an intrinsically dangerous activity, such as that outlined by Asquith J. in *Dann v Hamilton*. Such an adventure was wildly irresponsible.[16]

**(c) Voluntary choice by the claimant:**   Even if the claimant has clearly consented, with full     **16–007**
knowledge of the risks involved, the defence will not be established if the consent cannot be said to be voluntary. Whilst this may seem obvious, the question of "voluntary choice" has at times been contentious. For example, in the nineteenth century the courts held that the defence applied to employees working under dangerous conditions, and refused to acknowledge that an employee's desire to keep his or her job might force him or her to agree to work under appalling conditions. In such circumstances, the employee, in the absence of statutory rights, was in no position to threaten the employer that unless working conditions improved, he or she would leave. The employer would simply accept the employee's resignation. The House of Lords' decision in *Smith v Charles Baker & Sons*[17] marked welcome recognition of the injustice of this approach. Here, the plaintiff was an employee, who worked on the construction of a railway where a crane would swing heavy stones above his head without warning. The employee was fully aware of the danger of stones falling, but carried on working. He was seriously injured when a stone fell from the crane. The House of Lords (Lord Bramwell dissenting) held the employer liable. Their Lordships refused to accept the argument that by continuing to work, the employee had voluntarily accepted the risk of the stones falling. Nevertheless, it was recognised that a balance had to be struck. If the work was intrinsically dangerous, despite reasonable steps by the employer to minimise risks, the employee would be deemed to accept those risks.[18] Here, this was not the case, and so the employer would be found liable.

No such risk of pressure was found in *ICI v Shatwell*[19] where the brothers, testing the detonators in the quarry, had been clearly instructed to take precautions, but nevertheless chose to accept the risk. The court held that, in the light of *Smith v Baker*, it would apply the rule very carefully to employees and be alert to pressure from employers. However, on the facts of this case, no such pressure had been exerted.

Consent is equally not voluntary if the claimant is so drunk that he or she is incapable of     **16–008**
understanding the nature and extent of the risk. Again this is a fine line. In *Morris v Murray*, despite his consumption of alcohol, it seems that the plaintiff was capable of realising the risks

---

[14]  [1991] 2 Q.B. 6. Comment K. Williams (1991) 54 M.L.R. 745.
[15]  The pilot was found to have consumed 17 whiskies.
[16]  See Fox L.J. at 17.
[17]  [1891] A.C. 325, HL.
[18]  See Lord Herschell [1891] A.C. 325, HL at 360.
[19]  [1965] A.C. 656.

of flying with an intoxicated pilot,[20] but if he had drunk even more, the defence might not have been established. It has equally been questioned whether a defendant should be liable where, due to the defendant's negligence, the claimant has been given the opportunity to commit suicide. There is a clear argument that where the claimant has deliberately decided to end his or her life, the defence of voluntary assumption of risk should stand. This issue has been raised in two cases where the suicide took place when the deceased was under the care of the police or custodial authorities. In *Kirkham v Chief Constable of Greater Manchester*,[21] the plaintiff's husband had committed suicide while in a remand centre. The plaintiff had warned the police at time of his arrest of her husband's suicidal tendencies, but the police had negligently failed to pass on this information to the remand authorities. The Court of Appeal held that in the light of her husband's clinical depression, he could not be held to have voluntarily accepted the risk. This must be correct. If you are found to be of unsound mind, then an argument that you weighed up and decided to assume the risks of injury can hardly stand.

However, Lloyd L.J. indicated (obiter) that the defence would apply if the deceased had been of sound mind at the time of the suicide.[22] This was not followed by the House of Lords in the later case of *Reeves v Metropolitan Police Commissioner*.[23] In this case, Martin Lynch had committed suicide in police custody by hanging himself from a cell door. Although a doctor had found Lynch to be of sound mind, the police had known that he was a suicide risk and had kept him under frequent observation. Nevertheless, they had failed to take all adequate precautions to prevent the suicide. In an action for negligence under the Fatal Accidents Act 1976, the majority of the House of Lords (Lord Hobhouse dissenting) found the police liable. They had undertaken a specific duty to protect Lynch from the risk of suicide and this they had failed to do. Any defence of voluntary assumption of risk would be inconsistent with such a duty:

> "If the defence were available in circumstances such as the present where a deceased was known to have suicidal tendencies it would effectively negative the effect of any duty of care in respect of such suicide."[24]

It made no difference whether the victim was of sound or unsound mind at the time of the suicide. The limitations of this decision should be noted:

- The police admitted to owing a specific duty to protect Lynch from the risk of suicide. If it was simply a duty to take reasonable care of him, voluntary assumption of risk could still be argued. This duty will only arise where the police knew or ought to have known that the individual was a suicide risk.[25]

- The House of Lords stressed that such a specific duty of care would be rare.

- Their Lordships were far from happy in treating Lynch as being of sound mind (the main reason for departing from the view of Lloyd L.J. in *Kirkham*). Lord Hoffmann

---

[20] He had in fact driven from the public house to the airfield and had helped start the aircraft and fuel it.
[21] [1990] 2 Q.B. 283.
[22] [1990] 2 Q.B. 283 at 290.
[23] [2000] 1 A.C. 360, HL.
[24] Lord Jauncey [2000] 1 A.C. 360, HL at 375–376.
[25] See *Orange v Chief Constable of West Yorkshire Police* [2001] EWCA Civ 611; [2002] Q.B. 347, CA. cf. *Keenan v United Kingdom* (2001) 33 E.H.R.R. 38 concerning art.2 of the European Convention on Human Rights.

remarked that "I confess to my unease about this finding, based on a seven minute interview with a doctor of unstated qualifications".[26] This highlights the practical difficulties which would arise if liability were held to depend on whether the deceased was of sound or unsound mind.

- The damages were reduced in any event by 50 per cent for contributory negligence (see below).

A final example of where the courts have considered the "voluntariness" of the assumption of risk is in relation to rescuers. We have considered liability towards rescuers in Ch.4, but one argument against liability would be that, in relation to non-professional rescuers at least, they have chosen to act. They are under no obligation to intervene, but have chosen to do so freely and so (arguably) have voluntarily accepted the risk of injury involved. If I choose to go into a burning building to save a baby, I must have appreciated the risk of injury and so (arguably) I have voluntarily accepted the risk and cannot sue. The courts have rejected this argument. It is obviously contrary to public policy, but the courts have chosen to analyse it as a situation where the rescuer is not acting voluntarily. The legal, social or moral duty which forces the rescuer to intervene is such that he or she does not act voluntarily in the circumstances. On this basis, the defence of voluntary assumption of risk will not work against rescuers.

A good example is the well-known case of *Haynes v Harwood*.[27] Here, a police officer had been injured whilst stopping runaway horses attached to a van in a crowded street. The defendant had negligently left the horses unattended on the highway and they had bolted when a boy had thrown a stone at them. The Court of Appeal held that the police officer's reaction had been reasonably foreseeable in the circumstances and refused to accept a defence of voluntary assumption of risk.[28] It was also held that the reaction need not be instinctive to be reasonable. This seems sensible. It is surely better to intervene having considered the dangers than to jump in immediately.

*Other uses of "consent" in negligence*

The courts have not always approached consent in negligence on a consistent basis. In addition to the defence of voluntary assumption of risk, the claimant's consent has been used by the courts in two further ways. First, the claimant's consent may limit the standard of care owed to the claimant by the defendant. Secondly, the claimant's consent may amount to an exclusion clause. These will be examined below. In both situations, the courts deny that they are applying the defence of voluntary assumption of risk, but the dividing line, as will be seen, is far from clear.

**16–009**

(a) **Setting the standard of care in negligence:** Here, the claimant's acceptance of risk does not go to establish a defence but lowers the standard of care owed by the defendant to the claimant. This is particularly relevant to injuries suffered in the course of sporting activities. Here, in establishing the standard of care, the court will look at all the circumstances of the case, including the fact that a competitive sport, with associated risks to participants, is taking place. This is illustrated by the case of *Wooldridge v Sumner*.[29] In this case, a professional photographer at a horse show had been knocked down by a galloping horse whose rider had

**16–010**

---

[26] [2000] 1 A.C. 360 at 372. See also Lord Hope at 385.
[27] [1935] 1 K.B. 146.
[28] Greer L.J. [1935] 1 K.B. 146 at 156–157. See also *Baker v T.E. Hopkins* [1959] 1 W.L.R. 966.
[29] [1963] 2 Q.B. 43. See also *Condon v Basi* [1985] 1 W.L.R. 866, C.A, *Caldwell v Maguire* [2001] EWCA Civ 1054; [2002] P.I.Q.R. P6 and C. Gearty [1985] C.L.J. 371.

taken the corner too fast.[30] The Court of Appeal held that the question in issue was the standard of care expected of a jockey in a race. In setting the standard, regard would be had to the fact that any reasonable spectator would: (a) expect the jockey to concentrate his attention on winning the race, and (b) accept the existence of certain risks, provided the jockey stayed within the rules of the race and was not reckless. On this basis, the jockey was not in breach of his duty of care to the spectator. The Court of Appeal in *Blake v Galloway*[31] extended this approach to informal games which could be said to be played subject to a tacitly agreed understanding or convention—in this case, a group of 15-year-old friends, throwing twigs and pieces of bark chipping at each other. In examining such "horseplay", Dyson L.J. found that a breach of duty would only occur where the defendant's conduct amounted to recklessness[32] or a very high degree of carelessness, which was not the case here.

The dividing line between "no breach of duty" and the defence of voluntary assumption of risk is unclear. The principle on which they rest is the same: the defendant is not liable where the claimant knows and assents to a particular risk. The courts utilise both approaches, and Fox L.J. in *Morris v Murray*[33] held that the gap between the two approaches is not a wide one.

**16–011** **(b) Exclusion clauses:** There is an obvious similarity between an express agreement to assume the risk of negligence and an exclusion clause, in which the claimant agrees to exclude or limit the defendant's liability. However, they are treated as distinct. *White v Blackmore*[34] is a good example of this distinction in operation. The plaintiff's husband had been killed in an accident at a race meeting for old cars. He had been thrown in the air when the rope behind which he was standing had been pulled away by an accident some distance away. Buckley L.J. held that the defendants (who organised the meeting) had successfully excluded liability by notices which absolved them from all liability for accidents howsoever caused. The circumstances did not, however, support the defence of voluntary assumption of risk. By simply standing behind a rope to observe a race, the spectator did not accept the risk of such injury due to the defendants' negligence. Buckley L.J. nevertheless admitted the close relationship between the defence and the operation of exclusion clauses.

The distinction between voluntary assumption of risk and exclusion clauses is nevertheless important, particularly in the light of the strict legal requirements applied to exclusion clauses. For example, to be valid an exclusion clause must be incorporated either by writing, custom or reasonable notice. Equally, exclusion clauses are now regulated by statute. The Unfair Contract Terms Act 1977[35] limits the ability of the defendant to rely on exclusion clauses to exclude or limit liability for negligence as follows[36]:

- The Act regulates exclusion clauses dealing with business liability, i.e. where liability arises:

[30] Who went on to win!
[31] [2004] EWCA Civ 814; [2004] 1 W.L.R. 2844.
[32] There is some debate as to whether "reckless disregard" sets too low a standard—compare *Wooldridge v Sumner* with *Caldwell v Maguire* [2001] EWCA Civ 1054. See 5–019.
[33] [1991] 2 Q.B. 6 at 15.
[34] [1972] 2 Q.B. 651.
[35] See also Unfair Terms in Consumer Contracts Regulations 1999 (SI 1999/2083). However, these regulations apply to standard form terms in consumer contracts and are unlikely to be relevant here.
[36] We list here only the main provisions of the Act relevant to this topic. Further reference should be made to works on the law of contract.

(a)  from things done or to be done by a person in the course of a business (whether his own business or another's); or

(b)  from the occupation of premises used for business purposes of the occupier.[37]

Clauses not dealing with business liability are not affected by the 1977 Act.[38]

- Negligence is dealt with in s.2. This provides that a person cannot by reference to any contract term or notice exclude or restrict liability for death or personal injury resulting from negligence.[39] If the claim is for property or other damage, s.2(2) provides that a person cannot exclude or restrict liability for negligence except in so far as the term or notice satisfies the requirement of reasonableness.

- The reasonableness test is set out in s.11 and Sch.2. These provide that the term must be reasonable having regard to all the circumstances at the time liability arose, including the relative bargaining positions of the parties, any inducement to agree to the clause and, where liability is limited, the resources available to the defendant to meet such liability and the ability of the defendant to obtain insurance cover.

- Section 2(3) deals specifically with the defence of voluntary assumption of risk and distinguishes the defence from exclusion clauses generally. It states: "Where a contract term or notice purports to exclude or restrict liability for negligence, a person's agreement to or awareness of it is not of itself to be taken as indicating his voluntary acceptance of any risk". Therefore, the defendant cannot necessarily ensure that the defence will apply by means of a notice excluding liability. It will remain a question of fact, although it may be questioned what extra element is required to establish the defence of voluntary assumption of risk where the claimant has by notice or contract agreed to exclude liability.

### *(iii)  Leave or licence*

Consent in relation to claims for property torts such as trespass to land or private nuisance has been mentioned in earlier chapters. As stated earlier, the courts prefer to use the terms "leave" or "licence" in this context. Reference should be made to the relevant chapter.     **16–012**

## (2)  Public policy and illegality[40]

This defence is also known by its Latin name, ex turpi causa non oritur actio, which means that an action cannot be founded on a base cause.[41] It is essentially founded on public policy, which prevents a person from obtaining compensation for the consequences of his own     **16–013**

---

[37]  Unfair Contract Terms Act 1977 s.1(3).
[38]  Except where the contrary is stated in s.6(4) (sale and hire purchase contracts under s.6) or where ss.2–7 do not apply (see misrepresentation under s.8).
[39]  Unfair Contract Terms Act 1977 s.2(1).
[40]  Note that this defence does not operate to bar a claim based on the European Convention on Human Rights and so is inapplicable to claims under the Human Rights Act 1998: *Al Hassan-Daniel v Revenue and Customs Commissioners* [2010] EWCA Civ 1443, "Human rights are not just for the virtuous" per Sedley L.J., at para. 12.
[41]  The classic statement is by Lord Mansfield in *Holman v Johnson* (1775) 1 Cowp. 341 at 343; 98 E.R. 1120: "No Court will lend its aid to a man who founds his cause of action upon an illegal or an immoral act".

criminal act.[42] It is obviously a matter of degree. If you are attacked when your car is parked on a double yellow line, then a court is not going to dismiss your claim because you were parked illegally. However, if you were involved in a burglary and seriously injured by your fellow burglar negligently handling explosives while trying to blow open the safe, the court would not tolerate your claim.[43] It is clearly a question whether the criminal or immoral act is the basis for the claim or simply background information. This can be a matter of degree. In *Ashton v Turner*,[44] the plaintiff and two other men had been in a car crash which was due to the negligent driving of the defendant. All three men were involved in a burglary, and the crash occurred while driving away from the scene of the crime. The court held that any negligence during the course of the burglary and the subsequent flight in the getaway car would be met by the defence of illegality. The plaintiff's claim was therefore rejected.

A good illustration of the defence may be found in *Pitts v Hunt*.[45] In this case, the plaintiff and Hunt had been drinking together and then set off home together on a motorbike. The plaintiff knew that Hunt was under age, drunk, uninsured, and did not even possess a licence to drive the motorbike. Nevertheless, the plaintiff rode pillion and encouraged Hunt to drive recklessly and deliberately frighten other road-users. There was an accident in which Hunt was killed and the plaintiff seriously injured. The Court of Appeal refused the plaintiff's claim against Hunt's personal representatives on the basis of illegality. On the facts of the case, both the plaintiff and Hunt were involved in the criminal activity of reckless driving.

**16–014**       Attempts to establish a single test for illegality have nevertheless proved inconclusive. Beldam L.J. in *Pitts v Hunt* favoured a test based on public policy and whether it would be an affront to the public conscience to compensate the claimant.[46] In *Tinsley v Milligan*,[47] however, the House of Lords was openly critical of the uncertainty inherent in the public conscience test. Yet, despite such comments, a few isolated decisions have still continued to adopt this broad approach, for example, the Court of Appeal decision in *Reeves v Metropolitan Police Commissioner*.[48] (Illegality was not raised in the House of Lords.) It may be recalled that the police were sued for negligence following a death in police custody. It was held that the police had a duty of care to prevent Lynch from committing suicide, which they had breached. The Court of Appeal considered whether such liability should be denied due to illegality. Although suicide has not been a crime since the Suicide Act 1961, the court considered whether there was sufficient evidence to conclude that ordinary citizens would be shocked or affronted by an award of damages in respect of the death of a man (known to be a suicide risk) while involuntarily in police custody. The court concluded that there was not and, according to the majority, such a defence would be invalid as contradicting the police's duty of care to prevent the risk of suicide in the first place.

---

[42] See Lord Hoffmann in *Gray v Thames Trains Ltd* [2009] UKHL 33 at para. 24.

[43] See *National Coal Board v England* [1954] A.C. 403 at 429. Contrast, however, the approach of criminal law which is prepared to find manslaughter due to gross negligence where the victim has participated in the unlawful activity: see *R v Wacker* [2002] EWCA Crim 1944; [2003] Q.B. 1207, where a lorry driver was convicted for the manslaughter of 58 illegal immigrants who suffocated when he closed the air vent in the back of his lorry.

[44] [1981] Q.B. 137.

[45] [1991] 1 Q.B. 24.

[46] Using the test set out by Hutchison J. in *Thackwell v Barclays Bank Plc* [1986] 1 All E.R. 676. Contrast Balcombe L.J. who argued that due to the nature of the joint illegal activity undertaken by the plaintiff and Hunt, it was impossible for the court to determine the standard of care which is appropriate to this situation (see also *Jackson v Harrison* (1978) 138 C.L.R. 438). Unfortunately the Balcombe test is by its nature limited in application to the tort of negligence.

[47] [1994] 1 A.C. 340. See also disapproval of the "public conscience" test in *Stone & Rolls Ltd (in liquidation) v Moore Stephens (a firm)* [2009] UKHL 39 at para.97.

[48] [1999] Q.B. 169, CA.

This decision may be contrasted with the later Court of Appeal decision in *Vellino v Chief Constable of the Greater Manchester Police*,[49] where the court drew a distinction between claims from prisoners in custody and on arrest. Here, the police had attempted to arrest Vellino at his second floor flat. He had previously evaded arrest by climbing out of a window and lowering himself onto the ground. On this occasion, however, his escape had tragic consequences when he fell badly and was left with severe brain damage and tetraplegia. The majority of the Court gave his claim short shrift. His injuries were inextricably linked to his criminal conduct in escaping lawful custody. Further,

> "to suggest that the police owe a criminal the duty to prevent the criminal from escaping, and that the criminal who hurts himself while escaping can sue the police for the breach of that duty, seems to me self-evidently absurd."[50]

Only Sedley L.J. was prepared to contemplate a duty on the police not to afford both the temptation to escape and an opportunity to do so where there is a known risk that the prisoner will do himself real harm, and even so, damages under this limited duty would have been substantially reduced for contributory negligence.

The nature of the test for illegality was considered more recently by the House of Lords in 2009 in *Gray v Thames Trains Ltd*.[51] Here, Gray, whilst suffering from post-traumatic stress disorder (PTSD), had stabbed to death a drunken pedestrian, who had stepped in front of his car. He was found guilty of manslaughter on the grounds of diminished responsibility and detained in a hospital indefinitely as a result. The PTSD, however, had been caused by the negligence of the defendants (Mr Gray had been involved in the Ladbroke Grove rail crash in which 31 people had been killed) and Gray argued that, despite his conviction for manslaughter, he should be able to recover for ongoing loss of earnings caused by the accident. The defendants argued that any claim for loss of earnings must terminate once he had been imprisoned and that the defence of illegality would bar any financial losses resulting from his conviction for manslaughter.

Their Lordships found in favour of the defendants. It would be inconsistent with the sentence of the criminal court, which held Gray responsible for his crime albeit whilst suffering from diminished responsibility, for a civil court to compensate him for an injury or disadvantage resulting from the punishment for the crime.[52] Equally, it rejected Gray's claim for an indemnity against any claims brought against him by the victim's family and damages for feelings of guilt and remorse consequent on the killing. These, held Lord Hoffmann, were caused by Gray's own crime, not the defendants' negligence.[53] In so doing, their Lordships approved the earlier Court of Appeal decision of *Clunis v Camden & Islington Health*

---

[49] [2001] EWCA Civ 1249; [2002] 1 W.L.R. 218. Comment C.A. Hopkins [2002] C.L.J. 257. See also *Sacco v Chief Constable of the South Wales Constabulary* (Unreported, May 15, 1998), CA.

[50] See Schiemann L.J. [2002] 1 W.L.R. 218 at 224.

[51] [2009] UKHL 33; [2009] 1 A.C. 1339. There was also some discussion of illegality in *Stone & Rolls Ltd (in liquidation) v Moore Stephens (a firm)* [2009] UKHL 39; [2009] 1 A.C. 1391, but in view of the disparate reasoning of their Lordships, it is difficult to ascertain any clear guidance from this case: for criticism, see Davies [2009] C.L.J. 505.

[52] Their Lordships rejected the argument that the conviction for manslaughter should be disregarded in assessing damages for loss of earnings. The court would examine the facts as they happened, not a counter-factual scenario. His loss of earnings was thus caused by his conviction for manslaughter.

[53] [2009] UKHL 33; [2009] 1 A.C. 1339 at para.51.

*Authority*.[54] In this case, Clunis had been convicted of manslaughter on the grounds of diminished responsibility when he had, for no reason, attacked and killed a man at an underground station. He had a long history of mental illness and seriously violent behaviour, but had been discharged from hospital, with after-care services in the community to be provided by the defendant health authority. The plaintiff claimed that, due to the negligence of the health authority, his condition had not been properly assessed and he was therefore not prevented from committing the attack. The Court of Appeal rejected this claim. The criminal court had found Clunis to be of diminished responsibility, rather than insane, which indicated that he had appreciated what he was doing and that it was wrong. It would be contrary to public policy to support such a claim arising out of commission of a crime.[55]

In his leading opinion, Lord Hoffmann addressed the question of *when* the illegality defence would apply. He rejected the tests, mentioned in earlier case-law, of "an inextricable link"[56] between the claim and the illegality, or the claim arising "directly ex turpi causa"[57] as unhelpful.[58] Much would depend on context. There are a number of different justifications for the illegality defence, which will vary according to the situation. In each case the policy reasons must be considered against the facts of the case to reach a fair outcome.[59] His Lordship identified narrow and broad forms of the illegality defence:

**Narrow policy ground**: you cannot recover for damage which flows from loss of liberty, a fine or other punishment lawfully imposed upon you in consequence of your own unlawful act. The policy here is to avoid inconsistency between criminal and civil law and is used in both *Gray* and *Clunis*.

**Wide policy ground**: you cannot recover compensation for loss which you have suffered in consequence of your own criminal act. It would be offensive to public notions of the fair distribution of resources to permit compensation in such circumstances. An example of such reasoning may be seen in *Vellino* above.

Other factors may also be relevant. Would, for example, the result in *Gray* have been different if the claimant had been convicted of a trivial offence, but, due to the severity of his mental disorder, had been detained under a hospital order? In such extreme cases, Lords Phillips, Rodger and Brown suggested that the hospital order was a consequence of the mental condition, not the criminal act, and in such circumstances the defence of illegality would not apply.[60]

**16–015**     Finally, it should be noted that illegal activities will not always obstruct the claimant's action in tort. In *Revill v Newbery*,[61] for example, the plaintiff was a burglar who had been shot whilst attempting to enter the defendant's shed to steal his property. The owner of the shed, who was 76, had been concerned about the spate of burglaries in the area and had resolved to wait in his

---

[54] [1998] Q.B. 978.
[55] The court refused to follow *Meah v McCreamer* [1985] 1 All E.R. 367 where a convicted rapist had been allowed to recover damages when a head injury in a road accident had led to a dramatic personality change (see also *Gray v Thames Trains Ltd* [2009] UKHL 33 per Lord Rodger at para.65). *Clunis* was applied in *Wilson v Coulson* [2002] P.I.Q.R. P22 where the court refused to allow recovery of a head of damages based on an illegal act, i.e. injuries resulting from a heroin overdose. In any event, the health authority was not found to owe Clunis a duty of care, relying on *X v Bedfordshire CC* [1995] 2 A.C. 633, discussed in Ch.2.
[56] The "inextricable link" test was suggested by Judge L.J. in *Cross v Kirkby*, *The Times*, April 5, 2000 and adopted by Sir Murray Stuart-Smith in *Vellino v Chief Constable of the Greater Manchester Police* [2001] EWCA Civ 1249.
[57] *Saunders v Edwards* [1987] 1 W.L.R. 1116 at 1134.
[58] See para.54. See also Lord Rodger at para.74.
[59] See paras 30–31.
[60] See comments by Lord Phillips, Rodger and Brown in *Gray* at paras 15, 83 and 103 respectively.
[61] [1996] Q.B. 567.

shed with a shotgun to defend his property. The burglar sued the defendant for negligence and the court rejected the defence of illegality. Parliament, in enacting the Occupiers' Liability Act 1984,[62] had clearly indicated that in future trespassers, including burglars, should not be treated as outlaws by the occupiers of land. The illegal activities of the burglar therefore did not affect his claim. It should be noted that the court did reduce the damages awarded to the burglar by two-thirds, under the principle of contributory negligence.

*Reform*

Despite some clear-cut cases, the defence of illegality remains shrouded in uncertainty. The **16–016** best that can be said is that the defence will operate when the claim is clearly founded on an illegal act, which is sufficiently serious (e.g. a crime leading to imprisonment), and the illegality in question cannot be dismissed as incidental. The Court of Appeal in *Vellino* saw no need to distinguish cases which dealt with illegality: (a) to deny a duty of care on the basis that it would not be fair, just and reasonable, and (b) as an absolute defence. In the case itself the majority adopted different approaches, but such a distinction was dismissed as irrelevant. On a basic level this is true—either way, the claimant's action will not succeed—although this is to ignore the different burdens of proof applicable to the duty of care (burden on claimant) and defence (burden on defendant). The Law Commission in its 2001 Consultation Paper, *The Illegality Defence in Tort*,[63] was critical of the current state of the law which it found to be sometimes confusing, lacking a clear rationale. It therefore proposed a structured statutory discretion directing the court to ask itself whether the claim should be allowed in the light of the rationale behind the illegality defence—in general, it stated, to maintain the internal consistency of the law in the interest of promoting the integrity of justice[64]—and taking certain factors into account. These factors would be:[65]

(i)   the seriousness of the illegality;

(ii)  the knowledge and intention of the claimant;

(iii) whether denying relief would act as a deterrent;

(iv)  whether denying relief would further the purpose of the rule which renders the claimant's conduct illegal;

(v)   whether denying relief would be proportionate to the illegality involved; and

(vi)  the degree of connection between the illegal act and the facts giving rise to the claim.

This Consultation Paper received, however, a mixed reception. There was a fear, in our view justifiable, that a statutory discretion would introduce greater uncertainty to the law. The Law Commission, in its final report of March 2010,[66] concluded that, in the light of recent case law such as *Gray v Thames Trains* which expressly took into account the policy factors which

---

[62] See Ch.8.
[63] Law Commission Consultation Paper No.160 (2001).
[64] Relying on the test stated by McLachlin J. in *Hall v Herbert* (1993) 2 S.C.R. 159 at 178, Supreme Court of Canada.
[65] See paras 6.23–6.45.
[66] Law Commission, *The Illegality Defence,* Law Com. No. 320, HC Paper No. 412. (2010): These final recommendations followed the provisional recommendations made in *The Illegality Defence: A Consultative Report* (Consultation Paper No 189), published in January 2009.

underlie the illegality defence, no proposals for reform would be made. The law will thus be left to develop through case law. The Law Commission suggested in its 2009 Consultative Report that policy factors should include (a) furthering the purpose of the rule which the illegal conduct has infringed; (b) consistency; (c) that the claimant should not profit from his or her own wrong; (d) deterrence; and (e) maintaining the integrity of the legal system.[67] The Law Commission concluded that whenever the illegality defence is successful, the court should make clear the justification for its application.

## (3) Contributory negligence[68]

**16–017**    It is convenient to refer to the principle of contributory negligence as a "defence", although, as will be seen, it can no longer operate as a complete defence to a claimant's action. Contributory negligence is generally raised in cases involving the tort of negligence, although it has a wider application, for example in breach of statutory duty.[69] It permits a defendant to argue that the damages awarded in favour of the claimant should be reduced because some of the damage was caused by the fault of the claimant. It has obvious links with causation, examined in earlier chapters. Indeed, it is impossible to have 100 per cent contributory negligence for the very reason that this in fact amounts to a statement that the claimant is the cause of the accident (or the novus causa interveniens) and has no right to sue the defendant.[70]

The principle of contributory negligence is now found in s.1(1) of the Law Reform (Contributory Negligence) Act 1945. The common law position prior to 1945 was complicated. The rule at common law was that the claimant could recover nothing if he or she was contributorily negligent.[71] The obvious injustice of this rule led the courts to modify this rule to:

- First, the rule of last opportunity. This was where the court found that although both parties were negligent, the defendant had the last chance to avoid the accident.[72] If so, the claimant would recover in full.

- Secondly, the rule of constructive last opportunity. This is where the defendant would have had the last opportunity to avoid the accident, but for his or her own negligence.[73] If proved, the claimant again would recover in full.

Such solutions served only to complicate the law, and of course did not remove the injustice of the former rule. Instead of the claimant's action failing, the claimant recovered full damages. This ignored his or her fault entirely. Neither the old rule nor the courts' modifications were

---

[67] *The Illegality Defence,* Law Com. No. 320 at para. 7.69.
[68] See N. Gravells (1977) 93 L.Q.R. 581.
[69] Although it cannot be used in deceit (*Alliance and Leicester BS v Edgestop Ltd* [1994] 2 All E.R. 38 and *Standard Chartered Bank v Pakistan National Shipping Corpn (Nos 2 and 4)* [2002] UKHL 43; [2003] 1 A.C. 959) nor for intentional torts such as trespass to the person: *Co-operative Group (CSW) Ltd v Pritchard* [2011] EWCA Civ 329. The Torts (Interference with Goods) Act 1977 s.11(1) also provides that it is not a defence to proceedings founded on conversion or intentional trespass to goods.
[70] See *Pitts v Hunt* [1991] 1 Q.B. 24 and *Anderson v Newham College of Further Education* [2002] EWCA Civ 505; [2003] I.C.R. 212.
[71] See *Butterfield v Forrester* (1809) 11 East 60; 103 E.R. 926.
[72] *Davies v Mann* (1842) 10 M. & W. 546; 152 E.R. 588.
[73] *British Columbia Electric Ry v Loach* [1916] 1 A.C. 719.

fair to both parties. The law is now stated in the Law Reform (Contributory Negligence) Act 1945 (the Act).

*The statutory position*

Section 1(1) of the Act provides:                                                    **16–018**

> "Where any person suffers damage as the result partly of his own fault and partly of the fault of any other person or persons, a claim in respect of that damage shall not be defeated by reason of the fault of the person suffering the damage, but the damages recoverable in respect thereof shall be reduced to such extent as the court thinks just and equitable having regard to the claimant's share in the responsibility for the damage."

This section finally allowed the courts to apportion damages as they felt "just and equitable" and marked a welcome move away from the technicalities of the common law. Damages will be reduced according to the claimant's responsibility for the damage (not the accident). On this basis, damages may be reduced in a car crash when the claimant has failed to wear a seat-belt.[74] This may not have led to the accident, but may have added to the injury suffered.

"Damage" is defined in s.4 to include loss of life and personal injury, and it continues to include property damage. It would also appear to cover claims for pure economic loss.[75] Section 4 also defines "fault" as:

> "... negligence,[76] breach of statutory duty or other act or omission that gives rise to liability in tort or would, apart from the Act, give rise to the defence of contributory negligence."

This is not particularly clear. The accepted view is that s.1 refers to "fault" both in relation to the claimant and the defendant. On this basis, the first part of the definition refers to the nature of the claim against the defendant, which can be for negligence, breach of statutory duty or any other act or omission giving rise to liability in tort. The second part of the definition refers to negligence, breach of statutory duty or the acts or omissions of the claimant which would at common law have given the defendant an absolute defence. On this basis, negligence by the claimant which would not at common law have given rise to a defence of contributory negligence—the classic example being deceit/fraud—would not affect the claim.[77]

---

[74] See *Froom v Butcher* [1976] Q.B. 286.

[75] See *Platform Home Loans v Oyston Shipways Ltd* [2000] 2 A.C. 190, HL.

[76] This has raised problems whether contributory negligence can be a defence when the claimant alleges that the defendant's negligence amounts to breach of contract. The leading case of *Forsikringsaktieselskapet Vesta v Butcher* [1988] 3 W.L.R. 565 limits the defence to where the defendant's liability in contract is the same as his liability in the tort of negligence independently of the existence of any contract. See also *Barclays Bank Plc v Fairclough Building Ltd* [1995] Q.B. 214 and *Raflatac Ltd v Eade* [1999] 1 Lloyd's Rep 506, Colman J.

[77] This was confirmed by the House of Lords in *Standard Chartered Bank v Pakistan Shipping Corp (Nos 2 and 4)* [2002] UKHL 43; [2003] 1 A.C. 959 noted by R. Grantham [2003] C.L.J. 15, approving earlier authority in *Alliance and Leicester BS v Edgestop Ltd* [1993] 1 W.L.R. 1462, *Corporacion Nacional del Cobre de Chile v Sogemin Metals Ltd* [1997] 1 W.L.R. 1396 and *Nationwide BS v Thimbleby & Co* [1999] Lloyd's Rep P.N. 359. In deceit, it is irrelevant that the claimant may have allowed himself or herself to be influenced by other factors or has failed to verify the statement in question: *Edgington v Fitzmaurice* (1885) L.R. 29 Ch. D. 459 and *Redgrave v Hurd* (1881–82) L.R. 20 Ch.D. 1.

A very broad interpretation of s.4 was adopted by the majority of the House of Lords in *Reeves v Metropolitan Police Commissioner*,[78] where their Lordships held that it included intentional acts by the claimant. On this basis, the deliberate act of the deceased in committing suicide in police custody amounted to contributory negligence within the Act. This is a very generous interpretation of "fault"—it can hardly be termed "negligent" to deliberately commit suicide—and it is somewhat artificial to claim that a person's act of suicide "contributed" to the damage, i.e. his death. However, the section is broadly phrased, and in view of the defendant's duty to prevent this very act occurring, the majority held that a "common sense" approach should prevail. Both the deceased's intentional act and the negligence of the police had contributed to his death and so a 50:50 division of responsibility was appropriate.[79]

It should be noted that the aim of this section is not to show that the claimant owes the defendant a duty of care to protect him or her against liability, but to show that the claimant failed to exercise reasonable care and this added to his or her injuries.[80] In applying the test the court will have regard both to the relative blameworthiness of the parties and the causal "potency" of the claimant's acts, that is, the relative importance of his acts in causing the damage apart from his blameworthiness.[81] It will be a question of fact in each case. There are three main questions the court should address:

(i) Was the claimant acting negligently?

(ii) Did his or her actions contribute to the damage suffered?

(iii) To what extent should his or her damages be reduced?

These questions will be examined below.

*(i) Was the claimant acting negligently?*

**16–019**    As we have seen above, the question is whether the claimant has exercised reasonable care. As Lord Denning stated in *Jones v Livox Quarries*:

"A person is guilty of contributory negligence if he ought reasonably to have foreseen that, if he did not act as a reasonable, prudent man, he might hurt himself; and in his reckonings, he must take into account the possibility of others being careless".[82]

[78] [2000] 1 A.C. 360, HL. Contrast *Barings Plc (in liquidation) v Coopers & Lybrand (No.7)* [2003] P.N.L.R. 34 where the intentionally false statements by Nick Leeson to hide his unauthorised trading were not held to amount to contributory negligence for which his employers would be vicariously liable in relation to their claim of negligence against the accountants for failing to detect and report fraud. Nevertheless, the claimants' damages were reduced for contributory negligence due to their failure to supervise their own employees properly.
[79] But note the divergence in the House of Lords in *Corr v IBC Vehicles Ltd* [2008] UKHL 13; [2008] 1 A.C. 884 as to the correct approach to use when a victim, driven by severe depression caused by the defendant's negligence, takes his own life. Lords Scott, Mance and Neuberger were all prepared to contemplate a reduction for contributory negligence, but argued in favour of a more nuanced approach which would take into account to what extent the deceased's personal autonomy had been overborne by the impairment to his mind attributable to the defendant.
[80] *Nance v British Columbia Electric Ry Co Ltd* [1951] 2 All E.R. 448.
[81] See Lord Reid in *Stapley v Gypsum Mines Ltd* [1953] A.C. 663 at 682.
[82] [1952] 2 Q.B. 608 at 615. Reference will be made to changes in the public perception of risk. On this basis, the reasonable man, warned that there was a substantial risk that smoking would seriously damage his health, would stop smoking: *Badger v Ministry of Defence* [2005] EWHC 2941 (QB); [2006] 3 All E.R. 173 (contributory negligence to fail to give up smoking when risk to health known).

It is clearly an objective test, but the courts will make allowances for children[83] and the aged and infirm. The courts will equally recognise that in an emergency (which is due to the fault of the defendant), some allowance must be made for decisions taken in the heat of the moment. In *Jones v Boyce*,[84] for example, the plaintiff was a passenger on top of the defendant's coach. In realising correctly that the coach was in danger of being overturned due to a defective coupling rein, he decided to jump off and broke his leg. The coach, in fact, did not overturn. The court nevertheless held that it was a question of whether the plaintiff had acted reasonably, and allowances should be made for the actions of parties placed in such a dangerous predicament. However, the reaction must be reasonable and respond to some danger. In *Adams v Lancashire and Yorkshire Ry Co*,[85] for example, it was not deemed reasonable to deal with the inconvenience of a draft from an open train door by leaning out of the moving train to close it. The court held that the plaintiff should simply have moved seats or waited until the next station.[86] He therefore had no right to sue the defendant for negligence when he fell out of the train.

The same restrictions apply to rescuers. Whilst allowances will be made for the heat of the moment, the rescuer cannot claim for injuries which are due to his or her unreasonable response to the danger. For example, in *Harrison v British Railways Board*,[87] a misguided train guard attempted to assist a passenger who was trying to join a moving train by signalling the driver to stop. Unfortunately, he gave the wrong signal and the driver continued to accelerate. He then tried to pull the passenger into the rapidly accelerating train, but both of them fell out. The guard sued the passenger for negligence. The court held that the passenger did owe the guard a duty of care when, through lack of care for his own safety, he had put himself in a situation of danger in which it was reasonably foreseeable that someone would intervene to help, but that a reasonable guard would have applied the emergency brake. On this basis, the guard's damages were reduced by 20 per cent. Boreham J. warned, however, that rescuers should be treated leniently: "One has a feeling of distaste about finding a rescuer guilty of contributory negligence. It can rarely be appropriate to do so".[88]

*(ii) Did the claimant's actions contribute to the damage suffered?*

The classic case is that of *Stapley v Gypsum Mines Ltd*.[89] Stapley had been killed in a mining **16–020** accident when a large piece of the roof where he was working fell upon him. He, and another miner, Dale, had been instructed earlier to make that part of the mine safe by bringing down a section of the roof. The men tried unsuccessfully to bring down the roof and then carried on working. In an action by Stapley's widow, it was argued that Stapley's own negligence had been the substantial cause of his death. The majority of the House of Lords held that Dale had also been responsible for the accident, for whom the employers were vicariously liable, but that damages should be reduced by 80 per cent for contributory negligence. Lord Reid found the question of who had contributed to the damage to be one of common sense, depending on the facts of each particular case. Where a number of people had been at fault, it would be a

---

[83] See *Yachuk v Oliver Blais Co Ltd* [1949] A.C. 386 and *Gough v Thorne* [1966] 3 All E.R. 398, depending on the age of the child.
[84] (1816) 1 Stark 493; 171 E.R. 540.
[85] (1869) L.R. 4 C.P. 739.
[86] The next station was three minutes away.
[87] [1981] 3 All E.R. 679.
[88] [1981] 3 All E.R. 679 at 686.
[89] [1953] A.C. 663. Note, however, PS Atiyah (1965) 43 Can. Bar. Rev. 609, who criticises the court's analysis of causation, and our discussion of this point in Ch.6.

matter of isolating those parties whose fault had led to the accident and was not too remote. Here, the question was whether the fault of Dale was so mixed up with the accident that, as a matter of common sense, his actions must be regarded as having contributed to his accident.[90] On the facts, there was insufficient separation of time, place or circumstance to find that Dale had not contributed to the accident.

It is also important that the claimant's negligence exposed him or her to the particular type of damage suffered. For example, if I drive without a seatbelt and suffer injuries whilst stationary when a lorry negligently drops its load on my car, it cannot be said that my failure to wear a seatbelt exposed me to that particular risk of damage. Conversely, the damages were reduced in *Jones v Livox Quarries*,[91] where the plaintiff had been injured when, whilst riding on the back of a vehicle to the works canteen, he was struck from behind by the driver of a dumper truck. Riding on the back of the vehicle was contrary to his employers' express instructions and what materialised was precisely the type of danger to be expected from such conduct. However, if a passing sportsman had negligently shot him in the eye, he could hardly be said to be contributorily negligent since this was not a risk to which his negligent actions exposed him.[92]

*(iii)  To what extent should the claimant's damages be reduced? What is "just and equitable" in these circumstances?*

16–021    This is generally a matter of the court's discretion and therefore will depend on the facts of the case. The wording of the Act gives the courts considerable flexibility, which they utilise to the full.[93] Indeed, it is difficult critically to evaluate the court's assessment of contributory negligence, because the courts generally give a bald figure, with little guidance as to the reasoning underlying the sum. The courts have given some indications that they will be influenced by the relative blameworthiness of each party in addition to considering the degree to which their fault contributed towards the damage suffered,[94] but this will not always be the case. However, in certain circumstances, guideline figures have been given to provide some certainty and consistency, and these are generally followed.

16–022    (a)  **Failure to wear a seatbelt:**    Guidelines were given by the Court of Appeal in *Froom v Butcher*.[95] In this case, despite driving carefully, Mr Froom had been struck head-on by a speeding

---

[90]  See *Casey v Morane* [2001] I.C.R. 316, CA, which equally adopts a "common sense" approach to causation.
[91]  [1952] 2 Q.B. 608.
[92]  Lord Denning's somewhat graphic example [1952] 2 Q.B. 608 at 616. This is, however, cited in *St George v Home Office* [2008] EWCA Civ 1068; [2009] 1 W.L.R. 1670 (drug addict, who suffered brain damage due to the negligence of the prison service when suffering withdrawal symptoms whilst in custody, at fault in becoming addicted to drugs from the age of 16, but such fault was too remote in time, place and circumstances to be sufficiently connected with the negligence of the prison staff and to be regarded as a cause of the injury).
[93]  An appeal court will only overturn a finding of contributory negligence where it finds that the judge had gone wrong in principle, misunderstood the facts or was clearly wrong: see *Kerry v Carter* [1969] 1 W.L.R. 1372 at 1376. Note, however, the ruling of the European Court of Justice in *Candolin v Pohjola (C537/03)* [2005] E.C.R. I-5745 that European law, as stated in the EU's Motor Insurance Directives, rendered any national law excluding or disproportionately limiting compensation to passengers in motor vehicle accidents due to contributory negligence ineffective. Merkin finds that "Happily, English law complies with these rules" ((2005) 17 I.L.M. 12), although clearly any "disproportionate" reduction would lead to difficulties.
[94]  See *Davies v Swan Motor Co (Swansea) Ltd* [1949] 2 K.B. 291 at 326 per Lord Denning. Hale L.J. more recently recognised that the role of the court is to compare the claimant's share in responsibility for the damage with that of the defendant: 'to do what is "just and equitable" . . . includes being fair to the claimant as well as to the defendant. Realistically, therefore, the court has to compare the one with the other": *Eagle v Chambers* [2004] R.T.R. 9, at para.14.
[95]  [1976] Q.B. 286.

car overtaking in the opposite direction. He suffered head and chest injuries, which were found to have been caused by his failure to wear a seatbelt. At the time, it was not compulsory to wear a seatbelt, and Froom had argued that he had made a conscious decision not to wear one, having seen a number of accidents where drivers wearing seatbelts had been trapped in the vehicle following an accident. The Court of Appeal held that his failure to wear a seatbelt did amount to contributory negligence. It had added to the injury suffered and it was irrelevant that Froom believed that it would be safer not to wear a seatbelt—the test was of the reasonable person who would, according to the court, wear a seatbelt. Damages were therefore reduced by 20 per cent.

The court gave general guidance as to the appropriate reduction for not wearing a seatbelt:

- 25 per cent if the injury would have been prevented altogether;

- 15 per cent if the injury would have been less severe; and

- 0 per cent if wearing the seatbelt would not have prevented injury.

This will tend to be followed save in exceptional cases; the courts acknowledging the value of having clear guidelines which will encourage parties to reach sensible settlements.[96] The binding nature of these guidelines was recently reaffirmed in *Stanton v Collinson*,[97] where the Court of Appeal acknowledged the powerful public interest in there being no intensive inquiry into fine degrees of contributory negligence so that the vast majority of cases could be settled according to a well-understood formula and that exceptional cases did not get out of control.

It should be noted that seatbelt wearing is now compulsory for front and back seats (where available).[98] Although Lord Denning also suggested in *Froom* that exceptions may be made for pregnant women or "unduly fat" passengers,[99] pregnant women are not exempt, unless their doctor certifies that they should be for medical reasons.[100] A doctor may exempt any party if he or she decides that it is warranted and issue a formal "Certificate of Exemption from Compulsory Seat Belt wearing".[101] This must be produced on request by the police.[102]

**(b) Failure to wear a crash helmet:** *Capps v Miller*[103] applied the *Froom* guidelines to    **16–023**
crash helmets,[104] although the majority held that a reduction of only 10 per cent would be

---

[96] See Keene L.J. in *J (a minor) v Wilkins* [2001] P.I.Q.R. P12.

[97] [2010] EWCA Civ 81; [2010] R.T.R. 26.

[98] For adults, see s.14, Road Traffic Act 1988 (Seat belts: adults), as amended. Regulation 5 of the Motor Vehicles (Wearing of Seat Belts) Regulations SI 1993/176 requires adults and children aged 14 and over to wear seat belts where available in the rear of all classes of motor vehicle (as amended by Motor Vehicles (Wearing of Seat Belts) (Amendment) Regulations SI 2006/1892). This new requirement does not apply where a large or small bus is being used to provide a local service in a built-up area, or where the bus is constructed or adapted for the carriage of standing passengers and standing is permitted. For children under 14, see Road Traffic Act 1988 s.15 (as amended). (Restriction on carrying children not wearing seat belts in motor vehicles) and Motor Vehicles (Wearing of seat belts) (Amendment) Regulations 2006 (SI 1006/1892).

[99] [1976] Q.B. 286 at 295.

[100] See s.14(2)(b)(iii), Road Traffic Act 1988 and reg.6 and Sch.1 (exemptions), Motor Vehicles (Wearing of Seat Belts) Regulations 1993 (SI 1993/176).

[101] See Sch.1 of 1993 Regulations.

[102] Road Traffic Act 1988 s.14(4).

[103] [1989] 1 W.L.R. 839. See also *O'Connell v Jackson* [1972] 1 Q.B. 270.

[104] This is now authority that failure to wear a bicycle helmet, which is recommended by the Highway Code but not legally required, may be treated as contributory negligence: *Smith v Finch* [2009] EWHC 53 (QB) (but not causative of injury on the facts). Griffith Williams J. held that "there can be no doubt that the failure to wear a helmet may expose the cyclist to the risk of greater injury" (para.44). Fulbrook commented in 2004 that, in practice, a 25 per cent deduction was becoming the standard response in settlements of traffic accidents in any event: [2004] J.P.I. 171.

appropriate where a crash helmet had been worn but not fastened. Section 16 of the Road Traffic Act 1988 provides that it is compulsory to wear protective head gear when riding a motor bike. It should be noted that exceptions are made for Sikhs wearing turbans.[105]

Apart from this guidance, the court is free to assess what is just and equitable. It should be remembered that the reduction cannot be 100 per cent, as this is essentially a denial of causation.[106] Croom-Johnson L.J. in *Capps v Miller*[107] also advised the courts against making fine distinctions in percentages, although he disapproved of dicta indicating that an award of less than 10 per cent should not be given.[108]

**16–024**    **(c) Negligent valuation cases:**    The House of Lords in *Platform Home Loans Ltd v Oyston Shipways Ltd*[109] dealt with the application of the defence of contributory negligence in the wake of the House of Lords' decision in *South Australia Asset Management Corp v York Montague Ltd* (commonly known as *SAAMCO*).[110] This decided that damages for a negligent valuation would not extend to losses due to a fall in market price,[111] but would be capped at the amount of the overvaluation at the time the valuation takes place. Here, the lender was found to be contributorily negligent in making the loan without having obtained from the borrower information required by its own form, and in advancing as much as 70 per cent of the valuation of the property. Due to the negligent valuation of the property and fall in the market, it had lost £611,748 ("the basic loss"). However, under *SAAMCO*, this would be capped at the overvaluation: the property was valued at £1.5 million but actually worth at that time £1 million, therefore £500,000. Controversially, the majority of the House deducted 20 per cent contributory negligence from the whole losses suffered by the claimant (£611,748). In the view of the majority, the damage referred to in s.1(1) was the damage suffered by the claimant as a result of the transaction (the basic loss). Although the claimant's damages would be capped under *SAAMCO*, the majority held that it was not just and equitable to reduce the capped amount by 20 per cent. This left the claimants with damages of £489,398.

*Multiple defendants*

**16–025**    One final problem we must address before moving on to the next defence is how to approach a situation where the claimant is suing more than one defendant. For example, the claimant (C) is suing two defendants (D and T) for negligence. C's contributory negligence is assessed at 20 per cent. How will this sum be deducted from the defendants' liability for damages?

The first point is that the two defendants are treated as jointly and severally liable at law.[112] This means that the claimant is entitled to sue one or both of the defendants for the full sum due. Under s.1 of the Civil Liability (Contribution) Act 1978, if only one defendant is sued, he

---

[105] s.16(2).
[106] See *Pitts v Hunt* [1991] 1 Q.B. 24 at 48 per Beldam L.J. and *Anderson v Newham College of Further Education* [2002] EWCA Civ 505; [2003] I.C.R. 212 (breach of statutory duty).
[107] [1989] 1 W.L.R. 839 at 849.
[108] As suggested by the Court of Appeal in *Johnson v Tennant Bros Ltd*, November 19, 1954 (unreported).
[109] [2000] 2 A.C. 190 (Lord Cooke dissenting). For criticism, see J. Stapleton (1999) 115 L.Q.R. 527.
[110] [1997] A.C. 191, HL.
[111] Such losses are not within the scope of the duty owed to the lender by the valuer.
[112] This is discussed more fully in Ch.17. A more complicated situation is where not all defendants can plead contributory negligence against the claimant (for example, where one defendant is liable for deceit for which contributory negligence is not a defence): see *Nationwide Building Society v Dunlop Haywards (DHL) Ltd (t/a Dunlop Heywood Lorenz)* [2009] EWHC 254 (Comm); [2010] 1 W.L.R. 258 (comment: J. O'Sullivan (2009) 25 P.N. 32) where Christopher Clarke J. applied the contributory negligence deduction to the "relevant damage" before apportioning liability.

or she is fully liable, but is entitled to claim a contribution from any other person liable in respect of the same damage. The contribution, under s.2, will be assessed by the court as the sum which is "just and equitable having regard to the extent of that person's responsibility for the damage in question". This is therefore a matter for the defendants to sort out and not for the claimant to worry about. Secondly, the contributory negligence of the claimant will be compared with the total responsibility of the defendants. In our example, the 20 per cent contributory negligence of C would be compared with the 80 per cent liability of D and T, and C would be awarded 80 per cent of the damages due. This is irrespective of whether C is suing D, T, or D and T together. It is irrelevant at this stage to what extent D and T are individually responsible. Thirdly, it is for D and T to argue their individual degree of responsibility.

By this means, the claimant is fully compensated and it is for the defendants to sort out the division of responsibility between them. This is seen in practice in *Fitzgerald v Lane*,[113] a case mentioned in Ch.6. Here, the plaintiff had stepped out into traffic on a busy road when the lights at the pedestrian crossing had been against him. He had been struck by a vehicle driven by the first defendant, which pushed him into the path of the second defendant's car. Both the defendants were negligent, but the plaintiff had also been contributorily negligent in not looking properly before crossing the road. The House of Lords adopted the reasoning outlined above. First of all, to what extent was the plaintiff contributorily negligent in comparison with the fault of both defendants? Here, it was found to be 50 per cent. Secondly, how should the remaining 50 per cent be divided between the two defendants?

Contributory negligence is a popular defence. Under the statute, the courts now have flexibility to allocate damages according to the fault of the parties involved. Unlike the defences of voluntary assumption of risk and illegality, this defence gives the courts the power to reduce damages without removing the claim altogether, and therefore is more readily used than the former, more drastic, defences.

## (4) Inevitable accident

This is a little used defence, although readers may find reference to the defence in earlier case law. It is essentially a defence that, despite using all reasonable care, the accident nevertheless happened: "People must guard against reasonable probabilities, but they are not bound to guard against fantastic possibilities".[114]    **16–026**

In negligence, a claim that all reasonable care has been used will not tend to be treated as an independent defence, but as a matter relevant to the claimant's allegation that reasonable care has not been used. The allegation therefore goes to the question of breach of duty. It equally can have no application to torts where the defendant is liable despite the exercise of reasonable care, for example the tort of defamation. It is difficult therefore to see a modern role for this defence, except perhaps where the claimant is relying on the doctrine of res ipsa loquitur to establish breach of duty.[115] Here, the claimant relies on the circumstances of the

---

[113] [1989] A.C. 328. See also *J (a minor) v Wilkins* [2001] P.I.Q.R. P12, where the Court of Appeal, in assessing apportionment under the 1978 Act, drew an analogy with the *Froom v Butcher* guidelines under the 1945 Act. However, Sedley L.J. in the later case of *Pride Valley Foods Ltd v Hall & Partners* [2001] EWCA Civ 1001; (2001) 76 Con L.R. 1 stressed that this was just one of the three questions to be addressed in contributory negligence and therefore 1978 Act case law was unlikely to prove helpful in dealing with questions under the 1945 Act.
[114] *Fardon v Harcourt-Rivington* (1932) 146 L.T. 391 at 392 per Lord Dunedin.
[115] See earlier chapters and Lord Denning in *Southport Corp v Esso Petroleum Co Ltd* [1954] 2 Q.B. 182 at 200, CA, (reversed HL [1956] A.C. 218).

accident to place the burden on the defendant to establish that reasonable care was taken. Yet, even this use has been criticised as an over-simplification of the doctrine,[116] and we must conclude that the role of this defence in the twenty-first century is highly questionable.

## (5) Mistake

**16–027**   The fact the defendant made a genuine mistake is not generally a defence. It is no defence that the surgeon mistakenly believed that the patient had consented to open heart surgery, or that the defendant mistakenly believed that it was perfectly safe to drive at 100 mph in a residential area at night.

## General defences: conclusion

**16–028**   We can therefore conclude that out of the defences referred to in this chapter, contributory negligence is the most flexible, permitting the courts to limit the claimant's damages, but to not disallow the claim altogether. This is preferred by the courts to more drastic defences which provide a full defence to the claimant's action for damages. As stated earlier, these are not the only defences, and reference should be made to defences which apply to particular torts, discussed in the relevant chapters.

We now move on to consider the means by which the claimant's right of action can be lost. If a claim is extinguished, there is no further scope for the claim, however strong the claim may be. The main grounds for extinction will be set out below. The primary example is that of limitation, essentially where the claimant has run out of time to bring his or her claim. It should be noted that this is a significant source of negligence claims against solicitors, who are frequently sued by their clients for failing to commence proceedings within the time limits set by law.

## EXTINCTION OF LIABILITY

## (1) Limitation of Actions

**16–029**   Limitation is the main reason why claims in tort are extinguished.[117] It would cause obvious problems if there were no time limit within which the claimant should bring an action in tort. For example, if the victim of a car accident were able to claim damages in tort 20 years after the accident, a number of problems would arise:

- Witnesses would be unlikely to remember the event;

- Witnesses may have disappeared or have died;

- Documentation would be lost; and

---

[116]   W.V.H Rogers, *Winfield & Jolowicz on Torts* (18th edn, Sweet & Maxwell, 2010), para.25–27.
[117]   We use the term "extinguished" for convenience, but generally, limitation only amounts to a statutory bar to the claim.

- The defendant, for an indeterminate time, would have to live with the possibility of being sued.

In view of such objections, the law sets a time limit on such claims.[118] The Limitation Act 1980 contains the main provisions.[119] Section 2 of the Act provides that actions founded on a tort[120] should be brought within six years of the date when the cause of action accrued, i.e. when the cause of action arises against a potential defendant. Where the tort is actionable on proof of damage, for example negligence, then the cause of action will only arise when the damage has taken place. Where the tort is actionable per se (i.e. without proof of damage), the cause of action will arise on the date of the defendant's act or omission.

However, not all tort claims are within s.2. There are special provisions for personal injury claims (s.11), defamation (s.4A) and defective products (s.11A). We shall examine each in turn.

*Personal injury claims—ss.11, 12, 14 and 33 of the Limitation Act 1980*

**Section 11:**   This provides that where, due to negligence, nuisance or breach of duty,[121] the claimant's action for damages consists of or includes damages for personal injury, the claim must be brought within three years from the date on which:   **16–030**

(a) the action accrued; or

(b) the date of knowledge (if later) of the injured person.[122]

"Personal injury" is defined in s.38 as including any disease or impairment of a person's physical or mental condition and will thus extend to psychiatric injuries, including dyslexia.[123] If the injured person dies before the expiration of either of these periods, then the action will run for the benefit of the estate for three years from: (a) the date of death; or (b) the date of the personal representative's knowledge; whichever is later.[124] It should be noted that s.11 covers claims which *include* damages for personal injury. The time limit will therefore apply to any additional claims, for example for property damage.

---

[118] It should be noted that limitation periods are purely statutory and have been part of English law since the first Limitation Act of 1623. There were no time limits imposed at common law.

[119] The Act is subject to amendments, in particular by the Latent Damage Act 1986 and the Consumer Protection Act 1987. Note also the limitation period under the Human Rights Act 1998, s.7(5): "Proceedings under subsection (1)(a) must be brought before the end of—(a) the period of one year beginning with the date on which the act complained of took place; or (b) such longer period as the court or tribunal considers equitable having regard to all the circumstances, but that is subject to any rule imposing a stricter time limit in relation to the procedure in question." See, recently, *M (A Child) v Ministry of Justice* [2009] EWCA Civ 419; (2009) 159 N.L.J. 860.

[120] "Tort" is defined widely by Toulmin Q.C. in *R. v Secretary of State for Transport, Ex p. Factortame* [2001] 1 W.L.R. 942, QBD (T & CC) at para.171 to cover: "breach of non-contractual duty which gives a private law right to the party injured to recover compensatory damages at common law from the party causing the injury". This broad definition includes the so-called Eurotorts, discussed in Ch.7.

[121] This can be breach of statutory duty or contractual duty or any other breach of duty. It covers breach of contract, whether the duty is strict or to take reasonable care: *Foster v Zott GmbH & Co* (Unreported, 24 May 2000), CA.

[122] s.11(4). This does not apply to damages under s.3 of the Protection from Harassment Act 1997—s.11(1A) inserted by Protection from Harassment Act 1997 s.6—which will be governed by s.9. Section 9 deals with sums recoverable by statute and sets a six year limitation period.

[123] See *Phelps v Hillingdon LBC* [2001] 2 A.C. 619, *Robinson v St Helens MBC* [2002] EWCA Civ 1099; [2003] P.I.Q.R. P9 and *Adams v Bracknell Forest BC* [2004] UKHL 29; [2005] 1 A.C. 76.

[124] s.11(5).

**16–031**　　**Section 14:**　Section 14 defines "the date of knowledge".[125] This is deemed to be the date on which the claimant first had knowledge:

(a) that the injury in question was significant; and

(b) that the injury was attributable in whole or in part to the act or omission which is alleged to constitute negligence, nuisance or breach of duty; and

(c) of the identity of the defendant; and

(d) if it is alleged that the act or omission was that of a person other than the defendant, of the identity of that person and the additional facts supporting the bringing of an action against the defendant.

It is irrelevant that the claimant is unaware that, as a matter of law, the acts or omissions in question gave him or her a legal right to sue.[126] Section 14(2) provides that the injury is "significant" if the claimant would reasonably have considered it sufficiently serious to justify instituting proceedings for damages against a defendant who did not dispute liability and was able to satisfy judgment. After some debate,[127] this has been found to set an impersonal standard[128]—in the words of Lord Hoffmann in *A v Hoare*:

> "you ask what the claimant knew about the injury he had suffered, you add any knowledge about the injury which may be imputed to him under section 14(3) and you then ask whether a reasonable person with that knowledge would have considered the injury sufficiently serious to justify his instituting proceedings for damages against a defendant who did not dispute liability and was able to satisfy a judgment."[129]

Section 14(3) provides for constructive knowledge, which includes knowledge which the claimant might reasonably be expected to acquire from facts observable or ascertainable by the claimant, or from facts ascertainable with the help of medical or other professional advice it is reasonable to expect the claimant to seek.[130] The majority of the House of Lords in *Adams v Bracknell Forest BC* held that this would be a mainly objective test: what would a reasonable person, placed in the situation in which the claimant was placed, have said or done?[131] This

---

[125] For guidance, see *Spargo v North Essex District Health Authority* [1997] P.I.Q.R. P235, CA.

[126] s.14(1).

[127] See *McCafferty v Receiver for the Metropolitan Police District* [1977] 1 W.L.R. 1073, which is no longer good authority.

[128] For a recent application, see *Albonetti v Wirral MBC* [2008] EWCA Civ 783: A person who had been raped must know that he or she had suffered not only a grave wrong but also a significant injury for the purposes of the Limitation Act 1980 s.14.

[129] [2008] UKHL 6; [2008] 1 A.C. 844 at para.34. See also *McCoubrey v Ministry of Defence* [2007] EWCA Civ 17; [2007] 1 W.L.R. 1544 in which Neuberger L.J. noted at para.44 that this means that s.14(2) has a comparatively limited application, having been enacted to extend the limitation period for personal injury victims who were effectively unaware that they had been injured at all or who had suffered an injury originally thought (reasonably) to be minor but which subsequently turned out to be very serious.

[130] The claimant will not be fixed with expert knowledge which he or she has failed to obtain despite taking all reasonable steps to consult (and, where appropriate, to act on) expert advice.

[131] [2004] UKHL 29; [2005] 1 A.C. 76. Baroness Hale, in contrast to the majority, favoured a more subjective approach. Applied in *Smith v Hampshire CC* [2007] EWCA Civ 246; [2007] E.L.R. 321 and *Whiston v London SHA* [2010] EWCA Civ 195; [2010] 1 W.L.R. 1582. Constructive knowledge may arise when claimant given reasonable opportunity to acquire information but declines to do so: *Pierce v Doncaster MBC* [2008] EWCA Civ 1416; [2009] 1 F.L.R. 1189.

may, however, take account of the effect of the injury on the claimant, for example, if it renders the claimant blind, the court will not assume that the claimant should have acquired knowledge by seeing something, or if it causes celebral palsy, the level of disability of the claimant.[132]

As Lord Hoffmann made clear in *A v Hoare*,[133] more subjective matters, such as the victim's character or intelligence, should not be considered under s.14. They will still be relevant, however, under the s.33 discretion, discussed below.[134]

**Section 12:**     Section 12 makes special provision for dependants claiming under the Fatal Accidents Act 1976 (which will be discussed in Ch.17).[135] Section 12(1) requires the dependant to show that the deceased had a valid cause of action on death. If the action had been lost, for example due to a time limit or any other reason, the claim under the Fatal Accidents Act is lost. If the deceased did have a valid cause of action on death, then the dependant has three years to bring the action starting from:

    **16–032**

(a)  the date of death; or

(b)  the date of knowledge of the person for whose benefit the action is brought; whichever is the later. ("Knowledge" is as defined in s.14, discussed above.)

**Section 33:**     It can be seen that, generally, claims for personal injury, or under the Fatal Accidents Act 1976, are subject to the short time limit of three years. This, however, must be considered in the light of the discretion provided under s.33 of the Act.[136] Section 33 permits the court to override the statutory time limits if it appears equitable to the court to allow the case to proceed, having regard to the prejudice of denying the claim to the claimant[137] and the prejudice of allowing the claim to the defendant.[138] Section 33(3) directs the court, in considering whether to exercise its discretion, to have regard to all the circumstances of the case and in particular to:

    **16–033**

(a)  the length of, and the reasons for, the delay on the part of the claimant;

(b)  the extent to which, having regard to the delay, the evidence in the case is likely to be less cogent;

(c)  the conduct of the defendant after the cause of action arose, including (when relevant) the response made to any reasonable request by the claimant for information or inspection for the purpose of ascertaining facts which were or might be relevant to the claimant's cause of action against the defendant;

---

[132] *Whiston v London SHA* [2010] EWCA Civ 195. The court also noted that account should also be taken of the fact that a claimant born with a disability was likely to be less curious about the reasons for his disability than one who had become disabled in adulthood following an adverse incident: at paras 60–63.

[133] [2008] UKHL 6; [2008] 1 A.C. 844 at para.45.

[134] Notably s.33(3)(a): "In acting under this section the court shall have regard to all the circumstances of the case and in particular to the length of, and the reasons for, the delay on the part of the plaintiff."

[135] See also s.13.

[136] In narrowing its interpretation of s.14, the courts have assumed that there will be a more generous exercise of the s.33 discretion in future: see Lord Hoffmann in *Adams v Bracknell Forest BC* [2004] UKHL 29; [2005] 1 A.C. 76 at para.45.

[137] Or any person he or she represents.

[138] Or any person he or she represents.

(d) the duration of any disability[139] of the claimant arising after the date of the accrual of the cause of action;

(e) the extent to which the claimant acted promptly and reasonably once he or she knew that there was a possible action for damages; and

(f) the steps, if any, taken by the claimant to obtain medical, legal or other expert advice and the nature of any such advice he or she may have received.

The House of Lords, in *Thompson v Brown*[140] and *Donovan v Gwentoys*[141] indicated at an early stage that s.33 was not confined to exceptional cases and that the courts could adopt a broad approach to its provisions. The judge is therefore given an unfettered discretion to assess the matter generally with reference to the factors highlighted in s.33(3).[142] The burden, however, of showing that it would be equitable to disapply the limitation period lies on the claimant and the courts have re-iterated that it is a heavy burden.

A recent issue arose as to the courts' treatment of so-called "windfall defence" claims where the claimant (having otherwise a good case) issues proceedings out of time due to the negligence of his solicitor. The Court of Appeal in the conjoined road traffic cases of *Cain v Francis; McKay v Hamlani*[143] took the opportunity to lay down guidelines. In both cases there was no dispute over liability, but in *Cain* proceedings had been issued one day late and in *McKay* just under a year late. The Court of Appeal ruled that in such a case, where the defendant had had early notice of the claim, the accrual of a limitation defence would be regarded as a complete windfall to the defendant and he could not argue that losing this defence would itself amount to prejudice to be considered under s.33.[144] The relevant prejudice was harm to the defendant's ability to defend his claim. Equally, the existence of an alternative claim against the claimant's solicitor for negligence would not necessarily signify that the time limit should not be disapplied. As Smith L.J. observed in *Cain*:

"It seems to me that, in the exercise of the discretion, the basic question to be asked is whether it is fair and just in all the circumstances to expect the defendant to meet this claim on the merits, notwithstanding the delay in commencement. The length of the delay will be important, not so much for itself as to the *effect* it has had".[145]

---

[139] s.38(2) provides that "For the purposes of this Act a person shall be treated as under a disability while he is an infant, or lacks capacity (within the meaning of the Mental Capacity Act 2005) to conduct legal proceedings" (as amended by the Mental Capacity Act 2005).

[140] [1981] 1 W.L.R. 744.

[141] [1990] 1 W.L.R. 472. See also the Court of Appeal in *Nash v Eli Lilly & Co* [1993] 1 W.L.R. 782 and *Firman v Ellis* [1978] Q.B. 886.

[142] Confirmed more recently by the House of Lords in *Horton v Sadler* [2006] UKHL 27; [2007] 1 A.C. 307. For example, in *Robinson v St Helens MBC* [2002] EWCA Civ 1099; [2003] P.I.Q.R. P9, the Court of Appeal refused to exercise its discretion to support a claim by a 33-year-old claimant that the local authority had negligently failed to treat his dyslexia during his primary and secondary schooling where there was no cogent medical evidence showing serious injury and the long delay would place the defendant in great difficulty in contesting the claim. See also *Rowe v Kingston upon Hull City Council* [2003] EWCA Civ 1281; [2004] P.I.Q.R. P16 and *B v Ministry of Defence* [2010] EWCA Civ 1317.

[143] [2008] EWCA Civ 1451; [2009] Q.B. 754, notably at paras 69–74. Contrast *McDonnell v Walker* [2009] EWCA Civ 1257; [2010] P.I.Q.R. P5 (inexcusable delay causing prejudice to defendant and little if any prejudice to claimant in suing solicitors).

[144] At most it was slight prejudice as in the case of *Donovan v Gwentoys Ltd* [1990] 1 W.L.R. 472.

[145] [2008] EWCA Civ 1451 at para.73 (emphasis added).

On the facts, the slight delay was deemed to have no prejudicial effect—the defendants had had early notification of a claim and every possible opportunity to investigate and to collect evidence. Section 33 would therefore be exercised in the claimants' favour.

It should be noted that s.33 only applies to claims for personal injury or under the Fatal Accidents Act 1976 under s.11. It has no application to torts outside these sections. Until recently, the House of Lords had found that it did not apply to actions for trespass to the person which were solely governed by s.2.[146] This led to difficulties in relation to claims by adults for child abuse. Even with the provision under s.28 (see below) that time will only run from the age of majority, the trauma of childhood sexual abuse may take many years to manifest itself or to be appreciated by the victim. However, the courts only have the discretion to extend the time limit under s.33 if it is classified as a personal injury claim under s.11. It does not apply to s.2 claims. The House of Lords in *A v Hoare* finally overruled its previous decision in *Stubbings v Webb* and accepted that all personal injury claims, caused by negligence or trespass to the person, should fall within s.11.[147] In *A v Hoare* itself, the defendant had been convicted in 1989 of the attempted rape of the claimant and sentenced to life imprisonment. Only when he won £7 million on the lottery, whilst on day release in 2004, did the victim consider it worthwhile pursing a claim for compensation, only to face the argument that she was out of time. Their Lordships confirmed that, having suffered personal injury from the assault, she was entitled to rely on s.11 and ask the court to exercise its discretion in her favour under s.33.[148] This is an important ruling. As Case has commented:

"[t]he strict construction of section 14 required by *A v Hoare* . . . will mean that most claimants seeking compensation for historic abuse will be reliant on a generous application of the court's discretion under section 33 if they are to defeat the limitation defence."[149]

Subsequent case law has indicated a willingness by the courts to apply s.33 in cases involving allegations of vicarious liability for acts of sexual abuse by employees in the course of their employment.[150]

*Defamation—ss.4A and 32A of the Limitation Act 1980*

We looked at s.4A in Ch.14. This section was introduced by s.5 of the Defamation Act 1996. Section 4A provides a one-year time limit for claims for defamation. Under s.32A of the Act, however, the court retains a discretion to allow a claim out of time if it would be equitable, having regard to the prejudice to the claimant and defendant respectively.[151] This operates in the same manner as s.33 above, except that the courts will take account of the policy behind the much shorter limitation period for defamation, that is, that the defamatory impact of libel or slander is likely to be transient and that Parliament evidently intended that a claimant should assert and

**16–034**

---

[146] See *Stubbings v Webb* [1993] A.C. 498 which held that the ordinary s.2 six-year limit would apply. *Stubbings* was upheld by the European Court of Human Rights in *Stubbings v United Kingdom (22083/93)* (1997) 23 E.H.R.R. 213.
[147] [2008] UKHL 6.
[148] Discretion was ultimately exercised in the claimant's favour on the basis of its exceptional circumstances: [2008] EWHC 1573 (QB); (2008) 152(29) S.J.L.B. 29, Coulson J.
[149] See P. Case, "Limitation and sexual abuse" (2009) 25 P.N. 22 at 25.
[150] P. Case "Limitation and sexual abuse" (2009) 25 P.N. 22, although she finds that this is less so for straightforward negligence claims. The Court of Appeal delivered guidance as to the correct approach to the application of section 33 to historic sexual abuse claims in *B v Nugent Care Society* [2009] EWCA Civ 827; [2010] 1 W.L.R. 516.
[151] See, for example, *Steedman v BBC* [2001] EWCA Civ 1534; [2002] E.M.L.R. 17 (extension rejected where good claim against solicitor and absence of any contemporary complaint).

pursue his need for vindication speedily. On this basis, ss.33 and 32A represent "differing manifestations of the application of the same principles to be derived from the different circumstances to which [they] are applicable".[152] The provisions also apply to malicious falsehood.[153]

*Defective products—s.11A of the Limitation Act 1980*

**16–035** Section 11A makes special provision for defective products and was set out in Ch.9. Generally, it provides a three year period of limitation when the claim consists of or includes damages for personal injury or loss of or damage to any property, starting from:

    (a)  the date on which the cause of action accrued; or

    (b)  if later, the date of knowledge of the injured person or, in the case of loss of or damage to property, the date of knowledge of the claimant.[154]

This is similar to s.11 above, but it should be noted that the date of knowledge is specifically dealt with under s.14(1A), which applies the s.14(1) criteria to defective products. Section 11A(3) provides for a 10-year long-stop, preventing any claim 10 years after the date on which the product was supplied to another or when the product was last supplied by a person.[155] The courts have a discretion under s.33 to override the statutory limitation period for death and personal injury claims, but the 10 year-long-stop will continue to apply.[156]

As discussed in Ch.9, in 2009 the Grand Chamber of the European Court of Justice in *O'Byrne v Aventis Pasteur SA*[157] held that where national legislation allowed for substitution of parties, it should not be applied in a way which permitted the producer to be sued after the expiry of the 10 year period (even though the action had been begun within time, albeit against the wrong defendant). It did accept, however, that where the proceedings had been issued within time against a wholly-owned subsidiary of the producer, a national court would be permitted to substitute the producer for that subsidiary if it found that the putting into circulation of the product had been determined by the producer. This narrow exception was not found to apply by the Supreme Court in *O'Byrne v Aventis Pasteur MSD Ltd*[158] in 2010, despite the fact that the producer in question wholly-owned the English subsidiary which had been mistakenly sued within the time limit. The Supreme Court ruled that the exception for wholly-owned subsidiaries should be interpreted narrowly to indicate a situation where, as a matter of fact, a distribution subsidiary was so closely involved with the parent producer that they could, in effect, also be regarded as a producer.

*Limitation problems*

**16–036** **(i) Deliberate concealment:** One obvious problem with limitation periods is where the defendant has concealed the damage. Section 32 deals directly with this problem. If the action is based on fraud or mistake, or where the defendant has deliberately concealed any fact relevant to the cause of action from the claimant, the limitation period will only start when the

---

[152] Sir Anthony May, President QBD in *Brady v Norman* [2011] EWCA Civ 107 at para.21.
[153] See *Cornwall Gardens Pty Ltd v RO Garrard & Co Ltd* [2001] EWCA Civ 699; *The Times*, June 19, 2001.
[154] Or (if earlier) of any person in whom the claimant's cause of action was previously vested.
[155] See Consumer Protection Act 1987 s.4.
[156] s.33(1A) provides that "The court shall not under this section disapply—(a) subs.3 of s11A". Section 11A(3) also applies regardless of the provisions for extension of time due to fraud, concealment or mistake (see s.32(4A)) or disability (see s.28(7)(a)).
[157] (C-358/08) [2010] 1 W.L.R. 1375.
[158] [2010] UKSC 23; [2010] 1 W.L.R. 1412, reversing Court of Appeal in [2007] EWCA Civ 966.

claimant has discovered the fraud, mistake or concealment or could, with reasonable diligence, have discovered it. An example of concealment may be found in the case of *Kitchen v RAF Association*[159] where a claim was made against a firm of solicitors for negligence. It was held that the solicitors' failure to inform Mrs Kitchen of her possible claim against the local electricity board, when her husband had been electrocuted by a defectively installed cooker, did not amount to concealment. It was certainly negligent, but there was no evidence to show deliberate concealment of this fact. However, their failure to inform her of an offer by the electricity board to pay £100 was within the relevant section, as it amounted to deliberate concealment (basically to cover up for their mistake).

This interpretation of s.32 was confirmed by the House of Lords in *Cave v Robinson Jarvis & Rolf*,[160] which overturned the Court of Appeal ruling in *Brocklesby v Armitage & Guest*.[161] In *Brocklesby*, the Court had interpreted s.32 very broadly, notably relying on s.32(2) which defines deliberate concealment as the "deliberate commission of a breach of duty in circumstances in which it is unlikely to be discovered for some time". The Court of Appeal held that, in view of s.32(2), deliberate concealment could be proved by showing simply that the defendant's negligence consisted of an intentional act or omission in circumstances where the negligence would not be immediately apparent. It was not necessary to show that the defendant was aware of the breach of duty in question.[162] The House of Lords in *Cave* rightly pointed out that this would disapply the limitation period in every case where a professional had acted on behalf of a client and was subsequently found to be negligent. This would extend dramatically professional liability,[163] and force such defendants to defend every action, however stale. Lord Millett considered such a result to be "neither just, nor consistent with the policy of the Limitation Acts".[164] "Deliberate concealment" should therefore be interpreted as requiring the defendant to be aware of the breach of duty, and to conceal or fail to disclose the wrongdoing in circumstances where it is unlikely to be discovered for some time.[165]

The section does also seek to protect innocent third parties. Section 32(3) states that nothing in the section shall extend the limitation period for actions (a) to recover property or recover its value or (b) to enforce a charge against any property or set aside a transaction affecting property, when the action is brought against an innocent third party who purchased the property for valuable consideration after the fraud, mistake or concealment had taken

---

[159] [1958] 1 W.L.R. 563 (although the case concerned s.26 of the Limitation Act 1939, the statutory predecessor of s.32).

[160] [2002] UKHL 18; [2003] 1 A.C. 384, HL. See T. Dugdale (2002) 18 P.N. 156.

[161] [2002] 1 W.L.R. 598.

[162] In *Brocklesby*, for example, the solicitors' negligence in failing to secure the claimant's release from his mortgage obligations had not become apparent until much later. The solicitors had not been aware that they had been negligent, but were nevertheless found to have acted "deliberately" in that they had intended to act for the claimant.

[163] Particularly in view of s.32(5) (discussed below) which denies the defendant the benefit of the 15-year long-stop provision of s.14B.

[164] [2002] UKHL 18; [2003] 1 A.C. 384, HL at para.15. The Law Commission in its report, *Limitation of Actions* (2001), was also critical at 3.136: "*Brocklesby* . . . ignores the rationale of s.32, which is that the defendant should not be able to profit from his own behaviour in concealing facts relevant to the claimant's claim."

[165] See *Williams v Fanshaw Porter & Hazelhurst* [2004] EWCA Civ 157; [2004] 1 W.L.R. 3185 (if the defendant appreciated that he or she had committed a serious mistake or had been negligent and made a conscious decision not to disclose that fact, this amounted to deliberate concealment even though the defendant had acted to avoid embarrassment or for some other innocent reason). See also *AIC Ltd v ITS Testing Services (UK) Ltd (The Kriti Palm)* [2006] EWCA Civ 1601; [2007] 1 All E.R. (Comm) 667. The breach of duty in question does not include *any* legal wrongdoing whatsoever, but legal wrongdoing of a kind that could properly be raised in an action to which s.32 applied and would not include legal wrongs which were not justiciable: *Giles v Rhind* [2008] EWCA Civ 118; [2009] Ch. 191, para.38.

place. Section 32(5) also provides that the s.14B time limit for latent damage (discussed below) does not apply to cases of deliberate concealment.

**16–037**    **(ii) Disability:**    A further problem arises where the claimant cannot sue due to a disability. This is dealt with in s.28 which provides that if the person is under a disability on the date on which the action accrues, the six year limitation period will only start when he or she has ceased to be under a disability or has died (whichever occurs first). By "disability", we mean that a person is under 18 or lacks capacity (within the meaning of the Mental Capacity Act 2005) to conduct legal proceedings.[166] The main problem arises when the disability affects the claimant after the cause of action has arisen. In such cases, there is nothing in s.28 to stop the ordinary limitation period applying.[167]

**16–038**    **(iii) Latent damage: property damage or financial loss:**[168]    "Latent damage" signifies damage which cannot be detected immediately. Prior to *Murphy v Brentwood*,[169] such claims raised considerable limitation problems. *Anns v Merton LBC*[170] had established that damages for structural damage to a building—for example defective foundations—would be recoverable. On this basis, the limitation period for latent damage would start from the time the defect came into existence, even though the defect might not be detectable until many years later.[171] This served to exclude a large number of claims. The Latent Damage Act 1986 therefore added ss.14A and 14B into the Act to deal specifically with this problem.

Subsections 14A(4) and (5) provide that the action for negligence[172] must be brought within:

(a)  six years of the cause of action; or

(b)  if later, three years from the earliest date on which the claimant[173] first had both the knowledge required for bringing the action for damages for the relevant damage and a right to bring such an action.

The test for knowledge mirrors that set out in s.14 above, namely knowledge of the material facts about the damage in respect of which damages are claimed, and any other facts relevant to the current action.[174] Section 14A is subject to an overriding time limit, stated in s.14B to be 15 years from the date of the last negligent act or omission which caused the damage in question. Section 3 of the Latent Damage Act 1986 also provides that where the property with the latent defect has changed ownership before the material facts about the damage are known, the new owner will have a fresh cause of action, to which ss.14A and B will apply.

---

[166]  s.38(2).

[167]  See s.28(1) and (2) and *Purnell v Roche* [1927] 2 Ch.142. However, disability is expressly mentioned as a ground for extending the time limit for personal injury under s.33 above.

[168]  See N. Mullany (1991) 54 M.L.R. 349. For personal injury and death, see s.11 above.

[169]  [1991] 1 A.C. 398. See also Ch.3.

[170]  [1978] A.C. 728.

[171]  See, e.g. *Pirelli General Cable Works Ltd v Oscar Faber & Partners* [1983] 2 A.C. 1. Approved in *Abbott v Will Gannon & Smith Ltd* [2005] EWCA Civ 198; [2005] P.N.L.R. 30.

[172]  This is interpreted strictly. The sections will not apply to other torts such as nuisance or even claims in contract where the breach is founded on negligent conduct: see *Iron Trades Mutual Insurance Co Ltd and Others v J.K. Buckenham Ltd* [1990] 1 All E.R. 808, approved by the Court of Appeal in *Société Commerciale de Réassurance v Eras International Ltd (formerly Eras (UK))* [1992] 2 All E.R. 82 (Note).

[173]  Or any person in whom the cause of action was vested before him or her.

[174]  See s.14A(6)–(10) and *Haward v Fawcetts (A Firm)* [2006] UKHL 9; [2006] 1 W.L.R. 682 (the first House of Lords decision on the interpretation of s.14A, commented by J O'Sullivan (2006) 22 P.N. 127).

Post-*Murphy*, where claims for defective premises are regarded as non-recoverable pure economic loss, these sections may seem somewhat defunct. There is no longer a cause of action to put a time limit on. However, they are still worth noting because they apply generally to negligence claims for latent damage (although not for personal injury and death, which is covered by s.11). They would therefore still apply to claims for property damage, for example, under the complex structure argument outlined in Ch.3, or for financial losses resulting from negligent advice.[175]

### The burden of proof

The issue of limitation will generally be raised by the defendant. However (although the law is not clear on this point), it seems that it is the claimant who bears the burden of proof, and who has to establish that the cause of action arose during the limitation period.[176] Claimants should note that it is not always enough to start the action within the limitation period. The court retains the power to dismiss a claim for want of prosecution where there has been prolonged or "inordinate and inexcusable" delay in the prosecution of the action. It should be noted that this is now governed by r.3.4(2) of the Civil Procedure Rules and the courts have discouraged judges from seeking guidance from case law prior to the implementation of the Rules.[177] In practice, it would seem that, in keeping with the strict timetables established by the Rules, the courts will be less tolerant of delays in pursuing a claim. Further, a court may find that a failure to proceed promptly amounts to an abuse of process, for example, where the claimant has commenced and continued litigation which he or she has no intention of bringing to a conclusion.[178]

**16–039**

### Reform

There has been much criticism of the limitation regime. It is complicated, leads to uncertainty and, on a number of occasions, unjust results. In its 1998 Consultation Paper, the Law Commission came to the conclusion that:

**16–040**

> "the present law on limitation suffers from a number of defects: it is incoherent, needlessly complex, outdated, uncertain, unfair and wastes costs."[179]

In its 2001 Report (No.270), *Limitation of Actions*, the Commission put forward a simplified regime based on a primary limitation period of three years for the majority of claims, subject to a long-stop of 10 years. Its main recommendations are outlined below:

---

[175] See, e.g. *Henderson v Merrett Syndicates* [1995] 2 A.C. 145, discussed in Ch.3. For recent examples, see *Babicki v Rowlands* [2001] EWCA Civ 1720; [2002] Lloyd's Rep PN 121 where the defendant firm of solicitors had been negligent whilst acting for the Babickis in the purchase of business premises and *Haward v Fawcetts (A Firm)* [2006] UKHL 9; [2006] 1 W.L.R. 682, where economic loss was alleged to be due to negligent investment advice from the defendants.

[176] See *Crocker v British Coal Corp* (1996) 29 B.M.L.R. 159 and the Law Commission Report No.270 (2001), *Limitation of Actions*, para.5.29, although it is for the defendant in his or her defence to raise the question of limitation: Practice Direction to Civil Procedure Rules Pt 16, para. 13.1.

[177] In, for example, *Biguzzi v Rank Leisure Inc* [1999] 1 W.L.R. 1926 (Lord Woolf M.R. himself), *Axa Insurance Co Ltd v Swire Fraser Ltd* [2001] C.P. Rep. 17 and *Securum Finance Ltd v Ashton* [2001] Ch.291, the Court of Appeal has warned against restricting the wide discretion to strike out granted by rule 3.4(2) by reference to earlier authorities such as *Allen v Alfred McAlpine & Sons Ltd* [1968] 2 Q.B. 229 and *Birkett v James* [1978] A.C. 297.

[178] *Grovit v Doctor* [1997] 1 W.L.R. 640 per Lord Woolf. See also *Arbuthnot Latham Bank Ltd v Trafalgar Holdings Ltd* [1998] 1 W.L.R. 1426, but contrast *Aktas v Adepta* [2010] EWCA Civ 1170 (something more than a single negligent oversight in timely service of claim form was required).

[179] Law Commission Consultation Paper No. 151 (1998), *Limitation of Actions*, para.11.1.

- The primary or "core" limitation period of three years should run from the date on which the claimant knows, or ought reasonably to know: (a) the facts which give rise to the cause of action, (b) the identity of the defendant, and (c) that the injury suffered is significant. This will cover claims in most torts (including defamation), contract, restitution and trust law.

- The long-stop period of 10 years should normally run from the date on which the cause of action arises.[180]

- Personal injury should continue to be treated differently. The Commission backed down on its more radical proposals in the Consultation Paper that personal injury claims should be included within the core regime, subject only to an extended long-stop of 30 years.[181] It now proposes that the courts should continue to have a discretion to disapply the three-year limitation period and that no long-stop should apply.[182]

- For minors, the core limitation period should not run until the minor is 18. However, the long-stop period should apply, although it will not bar an action before the claimant reaches 21. Adult disability will similarly suspend the core limitation period, but not the long-stop period.

- The long-stop should not apply to deliberate concealment, but only where the concealment is dishonest.

Some caution is, nevertheless, advisable. Consultation has led to a watering down of a number of the proposals of the Consultation Paper and the suggested scheme would continue to raise uncertainty as to the "date of knowledge", the personal injury discretion and the meaning of "dishonesty". The judiciary has also been critical of the decision to reverse the one year limitation period for defamation and malicious falsehood. This was only introduced under the Defamation Act 1996 and the Commission has been accused of failing to appreciate:

"that a major, if not the major, objective of a defamation action is the vindication of the claimant's reputation, an objective which in most cases can only be attained by swift remedial action."[183]

One must now be doubtful whether these recommendations will ever be implemented. The recommendations were accepted in principle by the Labour Government in 2002,[184] subject to further consideration of several issues, but the government did state that it would legislate

---

[180] Where (as in negligence) loss or damage must be proved, time would run from the date of the act or omission that gives rise to the cause of action. This would also apply to claims for breach of statutory duty.

[181] This was largely due to evidence which indicated that the long-term effects of sexual abuse and mesothelioma, caused by exposure to asbestos, could manifest themselves over a period greater than 30 years: paras 3.102–3.104.

[182] This is subject to a number of exceptions, for example, where an adult claimant is suffering from a disability (paras 3.127–3.133) and under the Consumer Protection Act 1987 (para.4.37). Claims under the Fatal Accidents Act 1976 and under the Law Reform (Miscellaneous Provisions) Act 1934 will equally be subject to the statutory discretion to disapply the primary limitation period and will not be subject to a long-stop.

[183] See Hale L.J. at para.32 in *Steedman v BBC* [2001] EWCA Civ 1534; [2002] E.M.L.R. 17. Note also Brooke L.J. at para.46: "While I can understand the Commission's desire to remove the anomalies to which they draw their attention in their report, it appears to me that the experience of judges in this highly specialist field of practice needs to be taken carefully into account before there is any question of re-introducing a more relaxed limitation regime for defamation cases in this jurisdiction."

[184] See Lord Chancellor's Department Press Release of 16 July 2002: *www.gnn.gov.uk*.

when a suitable opportunity arose. In January 2007, it announced that it would consult on the detailed contents of a draft Bill. Meanwhile, signs of judicial impatience were clearly apparent in the House of Lords' decision in *A v Hoare*.[185] The Law Commission had recommended that personal injuries claims in negligence and trespass to the person should be treated in the same way. In *KR v Bryn Alyn Community (Holdings) Ltd (In Liquidation)*,[186] Auld L.J. had warmly commended this proposal which would, in the words of the judge, "obviate much arid and highly wasteful litigation turning on a distinction of no apparent principle or other merit."[187] In the absence of legislative intervention, the House of Lords in *Hoare* used its 1966 Practice Statement to ensure that "justice may henceforth be done".[188] Somewhat ironically such legislative intervention was used in November 2009 by the Labour government to justify its decision not to proceed with any reform of limitation law.[189]

## (2) Waiver

Waiver provides a further means by which a claimant may lose the right to bring his or her **16–041** action. The term itself may lead to some confusion, as it has a number of legal meanings. First of all, waiver can be used to signify a choice between two inconsistent rights. The claimant cannot take advantage of both rights, and if the claimant, expressly or by unequivocal conduct, with full knowledge, indicates his or her intention to adopt one of these inconsistent rights, the other right will be lost. For example, A (an agent) commits a tort against his principal (P), for whom he works. P has not authorised such conduct. P then has a choice: ratify A's conduct or sue A in tort. If P ratifies the defendant's actions, P no longer has a claim against A in tort, but may have an action under the agency contract.[190]

The second meaning forms the basis for the doctrine of "waiver of tort". This term is misleading[191] because it does not mean that the remedy in tort is extinguished, but that for certain proprietary torts such as trespass to land,[192] the claimant may sue and receive either tortious damages (for reliance loss) or restitutionary damages (to recover the gain obtained by the defendant at his or her expense). Following the House of Lords decision in *Attorney General v Blake*,[193] which accepted that the restitutionary remedy of account of profits might be available for breach of contract albeit in exceptional circumstances, it has been suggested by a number of commentators that the choice of tortious or restitutionary damages should be available more generally in tort law. The recent Court of Appeal decision of *Devenish Nutrition Ltd*

---

[185] [2008] UKHL 6.
[186] [2003] EWCA Civ 85; [2003] Q.B. 1441.
[187] [2003] EWCA Civ 85; [2003] Q.B. 1441 at para.100.
[188] [2008] UKHL 6 at para.82 per Lord Brown.
[189] The government held that consultation with key stakeholders had demonstrated that there were insufficient benefits and potentially large-scale costs associated with the reform. In addition, the courts had, in the government's view, remedied some of the most significant difficulties with the law that the Law Commission identified, for example, in relation to the limitation aspects of child abuse cases. On this basis, the limitation reforms would not be taken forward: Bridget Prentice (Parliamentary Under-Secretary, Ministry of Justice) HC Deb (November 19, 2009).
[190] See *United Australia Ltd v Barclays Bank Ltd* [1941] A.C. 1 at 28 per Lord Atkin.
[191] And thankfully little used in recent case law.
[192] The key is misappropriation of the claimant's property rights and so this will not include torts which merely interfere with such rights as demonstrated by the nuisance case of *Stoke-on-Trent v W. and J. Wass Ltd* [1988] 1 W.L.R. 1406.
[193] [2001] 1 A.C. 268.

*v Sanofi-Aventis SA*[194] does not, however, support this view.[195] The Court of Appeal held that account of profits would not be available in an action for breach of statutory duty[196] and that purely compensatory damages were sufficient for the purpose of safeguarding the rights of private persons under art.81 (now art.101, TFEU).

It should be noted that where such damages are available, the claimant cannot obtain both forms of damages, as they overlap. The claimant's action in tort will only be extinguished once final judgment has been given for restitutionary damages.[197]

## (3) Accord and satisfaction

**16–042**  This is where the parties have agreed, for valuable consideration or by deed, to extinguish liability. "Accord" means agreement and "satisfaction" is the consideration and performance of that agreement. The agreement may be conditional, for example: I will accept £30,000 as compensation for my claim, subject to the right to return to court if my condition worsens; or may simply be in full satisfaction of the claim. If the defendant fails to pay the sum stipulated, the claimant may return to court, but it is a moot point whether the claimant goes to court to enforce the accord or to restart his or her claim. The answer depends on the nature of the agreement reached. If the agreement is to discharge the previous liability, the claimant must sue on the new agreement. If, however, the agreement can be construed as an agreement to discharge liability provided the sum is paid, then the claimant has a choice: pursue the original claim or the new agreement.

## (4) Judgment

**16–043**  A final judgment in a case will extinguish the right of future action. The action effectively merges into the judgment. This is primarily on public policy grounds, and prevents the parties to litigation disputing the validity of the decision. The rule only applies where the decision is final, and it does not of course prevent either party appealing that the decision is wrong, in terms of law or fact, up until final judgment.

## (5) Death

**16–044**  At common law, the general rule was that the death of either party extinguished any existing cause of action in tort (*actio personalis moritur cum persona*). It was not until 1934 that the problems arising from this rule forced the legislature to act. The growth of road traffic, and its accompanying accidents, led to complaints that it was unjust that where the defendant's negligent

---

[194] [2008] EWCA Civ 1086; [2009] Ch 390, but note the minority view of Longmore L.J. See also *Forsyth-Grant v Allen* [2008] EWCA Civ 505; [2008] Env L.R. 41 (remedy of account of profits not available for tort of nuisance post- *AG v Blake*).
[195] For criticism, see C. Rotherham, 'Gain-based relief in tort after *AG v Blake*' (2010) 126 L.Q.R. 102 and O. Odudu and G. Virgo [2009] C.L.J. 32, who argue that the conclusions reached in *Devenish Nutrition* and *Forsyth-Grant* are unnecessarily restrictive.
[196] Unlawful operation of cartel contrary to art.81, TEC (now art.101, TFEU).
[197] See *United Australia Ltd v Barclays Bank Ltd* [1941] A.C. 1 at 30 per Lord Atkin. Further reference should be made to A. Burrows, *The Law of Restitution* (3rd edn, OUP, 2010), Ch.23. Note also the cases of *Island Records Ltd v Tring International Plc* [1995] 3 All E.R. 444, *Tang Man Sit v Capacious Investments Ltd* [1996] A.C. 514, PC and *Westminster CC v Porter (No.2)* [2003] Ch.436, Hart J.

driving had led to an accident in which the defendant had been killed, the claimant would receive nothing from the defendant's estate or insurers. Section 1(1) of the Law Reform (Miscellaneous Provisions) Act 1934 now provides for the general survival of actions in tort. It states that:

"... all causes of action subsisting against or vested in [any person on death] shall survive against, or, as the case may be, for the benefit of [the] estate."

This does not provide a cause of action for death itself. It is simply a question of the survival of actions existing at the time of death. This leaves one remaining problem. The claimant is penalised if the defendant dies before the claimant suffers damage due to the defendant's wrongful actions. For example, I negligently bake a cake which is contaminated, but die before you eat it. An action for negligence is dependent on proof of damage and so your action would only arise after my death. Section 1(4) deals with this problem. It provides that where damage has been suffered as a result of a wrongful act which would have allowed the claimant to sue the defendant if the wrongdoer had not died before or at the same time as the damage was suffered, an action will nevertheless subsist against him as if he had died after the damage had been suffered.

Section 1(1) does not apply to defamation claims. It was deemed too controversial to allow an action for defamation once the person defamed had died. However, there is no real reason why an action should not continue just because the defendant making the defamatory remarks is deceased. The harm to the reputation may still continue. The Faulks Committee[198] made some proposals for the survival of claims against the estate of the deceased defamer, and for limited recovery when the defendant has defamed a person now dead, but such recommendations have not been implemented.[199]

## Extinction of liability: conclusion

In this chapter, we have examined a number of defences and considered ways in which the **16–045** claimant can lose his or her claim due to extinction of liability. The courts, as we have seen, have a number of alternatives open to them when considering defences, and will tend to favour those defences which allow them to take a flexible approach to the claim. The Limitation Act 1980 forms a considerable barrier to claims where the claimant has delayed and, as we have shown, provides rules of considerable complexity. It is to be regretted that the proposals forwarded by the Law Commission are now unlikely to be implemented.

In our final chapter, we consider the matter most important to claimants: what remedies will the law award them for the torts committed against them?

---

[198] Cmnd 5909 (1975), Ch.15.
[199] The Neill Committee on defamation found the recommendations problematic and resolved that the law should not be changed.

# Chapter 17

# REMEDIES

## Introduction

In this chapter, we examine the remedies available to claimants in actions in tort. We concentrate on three main remedies: damages, injunctions and self-help. Readers will note that other remedies specific to particular torts have been discussed in earlier chapters. The main subject of this chapter will be damages. The courts have developed a complex framework of rules which govern the assessment of damages, which will be set out below. Readers should not forget, however, that for certain torts, such as nuisance, the equitable remedy of an injunction may prove more effective than damages, for example where the claimant wishes to prevent further interference with his or her enjoyment of land.

**17–001**

## DAMAGES

Damages are the most commonly sought remedy in the law of tort. They provide a means by which the courts can vindicate the rights of the claimant against the defendant by means of a financial award. They can therefore be awarded for torts which are actionable without proof of damage, such as trespass and libel, where they vindicate the claimant's right to be free from interference with his or her person, land and goods, or vindicate the claimant's reputation. They are equally significant, however, where the claimant has suffered actual damage or loss. Here, the claimant seeks not only to vindicate his or her rights, but a financial award which compensates the claimant for his or her losses (provided they are not too remote). The claimant may also seek a sum which further compensates for any additional distress, or which punishes the defendant for his or her appalling misconduct. The rules as to the assessment of such awards are complex and will be set out below, but first we shall outline the different types of damages available to the claimant. Although the claimant will generally seek compensatory damages, these are not the only form of damages available. We will also examine the relationship between tortious damages and damages awarded under the Human Rights Act 1998.

**17–002**

## Types of damages

17–003    The court may award six different kinds of damages:

- Compensatory;

- Contemptuous;

- Nominal;

- Aggravated;

- Exemplary or punitive; and

- Restitutionary.

We shall examine all six types of damages in turn.

*(1)  Compensatory*

17–004    Tort law seeks to fully compensate the victim. The underlying principle is expressed by the
term restitutio in integrum. This is explained by Lord Blackburn in *Livingstone v Rawyards
Coal Co*[1] as:

> "the sum of money which will put the party who has been injured, or who has suffered,
> in the same position as he would have been in if he had not sustained the wrong for which
> he is now getting his compensation or reparation."

The aim is therefore to award a sum in compensation to the claimant which puts the claimant
in his or her pre-tort position. Obviously this is not always possible. If the claimant has
suffered personal injury, a court cannot literally return the claimant to his or her pre-tort position. The court therefore seeks to find a financial sum which, as far as possible, will compensate the claimant. This is an inexact science. It is impossible to state the precise sum necessary
to achieve this aim, and therefore the court seeks an approximate figure. While financial losses
before trial can be estimated with some exactitude, the claimant may seek damages for future
financial loss due to the tort, and again the court is forced to produce an approximate figure
which it believes will cover this head of loss.

17–005        Assessing compensation is, therefore, often a far from easy task. The main problems arise
in relation to personal injury claims and those consequent on a victim's death. This chapter
will therefore concentrate on these particular claims. It should not be forgotten, however, that
damages may also be available in tort for other types of loss, and reference should be made to
the discussion in earlier chapters. There is also generally a duty to mitigate loss in tort. The
courts will not allow a claimant to recover losses which he or she could have reasonably
avoided. Although the main authorities on mitigation are in contract law (where the same rule
applies), it seems clear that a court in tort will not require strenuous attempts by the claimant

---

[1]  (1880) 5 App. Cas. 25 at 39 per Lord Blackburn.

to reduce the loss suffered.[2] The old rule that losses incurred due to lack of funds were irrecoverable, e.g. expensive hire charges where it would have been more economical to purchase a new vehicle[3] has been overturned.[4]

The courts will generally award damages in one lump sum. This gives a claimant one chance to go to court to obtain damages, and the court will not allow a claimant to go back to court to recover a further award of damages, even if his or her loss has significantly increased, unless:

(i) the claimant is suing for breach of a separate and distinct legal right;[5]

(ii) the injury continues, such as under a continuing nuisance where a fresh cause of action occurs (see Ch.10);

(iii) a provisional award of damages has been made under s.32A of the Senior Courts Act 1981 (see below); or

(iv) the first award was an interim award prior to trial (see below).

Compensatory damages are often divided in personal injury claims into special and general damages. These are terms used by the parties in their case statements. General damages are damages which cannot be precisely quantified, for example loss of future earnings or pain and suffering. Special damages are claimed for particular forms of pre-trial loss resulting from the tort, which the claimant can quantify, for example medical expenses and loss of earnings prior to trial. These should be set out clearly in the case statements.

*(2) Contemptuous*

This is a derisory award of the lowest coin in the land—now one penny—by which the court **17–006** indicates that although the claimant has a good cause of action, it is a bare technical victory. Such awards are often found in libel actions.[6] The court, more drastically, can deny the claimant his or her costs, and this imposes a greater penalty on the claimant. In English law, costs usually follow the event, so the losing defendant will have to pay not only his or her own costs but also those of the claimant. However, under s.51 of the Senior Courts Act 1981, the award of costs is at the discretion of the court, and contemptuous damages may lead a court to exercise its discretion to order the claimant to pay his or her own costs. In such circumstances, any victory is wholly illusory.

---

[2] See *British Westinghouse Electric & Manufacturing Co Ltd v Underground Electric Railways Co of London Ltd (No.2)* [1912] A.C. 673, HL; *Andros Springs v World Beauty (The World Beauty)* [1970] P. 144 and *Morris v Richards* [2003] EWCA Civ 232; [2004] P.I.Q.R. Q3. The burden of proof rests on the defendant to show that the claimant has unreasonably neglected to mitigate the damages.

[3] See *The Liesbosch* [1933] A.C. 449.

[4] *Lagden v O'Connor* [2003] UKHL 64; [2004] 1 A.C. 1067. Comment: B. Coote (2004) 120 L.Q.R. 382.

[5] See *Brunsden v Humphrey* (1884–85) L.R. 14 Q.B.D. 141 where the plaintiff was able to claim for damage to his vehicle and later for personal injury. However, note the rule in *Henderson v Henderson* (1843) 3 Hare 100; 67 E.R. 313 that it would be an abuse of process if the claimant did not bring forward their whole case in the first action. The court in *Talbot v Berkshire CC* [1994] Q.B. 290 cast doubt on *Brunsden* for not considering *Henderson* in its decision. For a more recent application of the *Henderson* rule, see *Johnson v Gore Wood & Co* [2002] 2 A.C. 1, notably Lord Bingham at 30, *Stuart v Goldberg* [2008] EWCA Civ 2; [2008] 1 W.L.R. 823 and *Henley v Bloom* [2010] EWCA Civ 202; [2010] 1 W.L.R. 1770 (not abuse of process to complain of disrepair of flat following earlier possession proceedings as issues involved were conceptually distinct).

[6] See the jury award in *Reynolds v Times Newspapers Ltd* discussed in Ch.14.

### (3) Nominal

**17–007**     Nominal damages are a token amount which recognises that the claimant's legal right has been infringed, but that no actual damage has been caused.[7] They therefore generally will apply to torts actionable per se (i.e. without proof of damage) such as trespass to the person or land and libel. An award of nominal damages should not affect the ordinary rule as to costs, as it does not indicate any negative finding.

### (4) Aggravated

**17–008**     These form a further level of compensatory damages granted by the courts to compensate for additional mental distress inflicted on the claimant due to the malicious, high-handed, insulting or oppressive conduct of the defendant.[8] The manner in which the tort is committed or the motives of the defendant may therefore justify an award of aggravated damages.[9] For example, in libel, if the defendant has published the statement out of malice, or has persisted at trial with an insupportable plea of justification, an additional sum on top of compensatory damages may be awarded to the claimant. Such damages are not available for all torts. The courts will award aggravated damages for torts where the injury to the claimant's feelings and self-esteem are closely connected to the type of damage for which compensation is awarded.[10] On this basis, they are not awarded for negligence[11] but are commonly awarded for intentional torts such as trespass[12] and for libel.[13] This raises a potential problem of double recovery. The Court of Appeal in *Richardson v Howie*[14] suggested that, in view of their compensatory nature, this should be dealt with by including the award of damages for injury to feelings within the general damages award and only in exceptional cases making a separate award of aggravated damages.[15] Nevertheless, the Court of Appeal in *Rowlands v Chief Constable of Merseyside Police*[16] remained willing to impose an award of aggravated damages where

---

[7] See, e.g. *Constantine v Imperial Hotels Ltd* [1944] K.B. 693, and, more controversially, *Lumba v Secretary of State for the Home Department* [2011] UKSC 12 (false imprisonment where suffered no loss or damage as a result of the unlawful exercise of the power to detain.).

[8] See Law Commission Report No.247, *Aggravated, exemplary and restitutionary damages* (1997) which recommended at para.6.1 that for clarity, these damages should in future be termed "damages for mental distress". See, however, Murphy, 'The nature and domain of aggravated damages" [2010] C.L.J. 353, who argues that aggravated damages provide compensation for violation of dignitary interests and on that basis may extend to high-handed and malicious breaches of contract and negligence.

[9] See Lord Devlin in *Rookes v Barnard* [1964] A.C. 1129 at 1221 and Lord Diplock in *Cassell v Broome* [1972] A.C. 1027 at 1124.

[10] See Judge Toulmin Q.C. in *R. v Secretary of State for Transport, ex p. Factortame (No.7)* [2001] 1 W.L.R. 942 where he rejected a claim for aggravated damages for the Government's breach of EC legislation providing for freedom of establishment of nationals in Member States, although he expressly left open the question whether the revisions of the Treaty would affect his decision.

[11] *Kralj v McGrath* [1986] 1 All E.R. 54.

[12] e.g. *Appleton v Garrett* [1996] P.I.Q.R. P1 where a dentist had deliberately undertaken unnecessary dental work on unsuspecting young patients and *Owers v Bailey* [2007] 1 P. & C.R. DG17 (interference with right of way).

[13] See *John v MGN Ltd* [1997] Q.B. 586 at 607. Pearson L.J. gives an excellent summary of the law in *McCarey v Associated Newspapers* Ltd [1965] 2 Q.B. 86 at 104–105. Gray J suggested in *Collins Stewart Ltd v Financial Times Ltd (No.2)* [2005] EWHC 262 (QB); [2006] E.M.L.R. 5, however, that corporations, which have no feelings, cannot claim aggravated damages (distinguishing *Messenger Newspaper Group v National Graphical Association (NGA)* [1984] I.R.L.R. 397, but see below).

[14] [2004] EWCA Civ 1127; [2005] P.I.Q.R. Q3.

[15] Query whether a separate award should be made for psychiatric injury arising from the tort: *Martins v Choudhary* [2007] EWCA Civ 1379; [2008] 1 W.L.R. 617 (question of fact how distinct from injury to feelings).

[16] [2006] EWCA Civ 1773; [2007] 1 W.L.R. 1065.

police misconduct in the arrest and prosecution of Mrs Rowlands had induced feelings of humiliation and resentment, which had been exacerbated by the willingness of the police to give false evidence in support of an unjustified prosecution. The Court warned, however, that attention should be paid to the dangers of compensating the claimant twice in respect of the same harm.

The sum awarded is at the discretion of the court, but is usually moderate. Some guidelines exist. For example, the Court of Appeal in *Thompson v Metropolitan Police Commissioner*[17] indicated the level of awards suitable for damages against the police for false imprisonment and malicious prosecution. Indeed, claims against the police form a major reason for the award of aggravated damages.

## (5) Exemplary or punitive

The leading case here is that of *Rookes v Barnard*.[18] In this case, Lord Devlin distinguished punitive damages[19] from aggravated damages and set out when punitive damages would be granted in English law. The concept of punitive damages may seem odd in tort. They are a form of damages which punish the defendant for his or her conduct, and attempt to deter the defendant and others from undertaking such conduct in future. Punitive damages are concerned with the conduct of the defendant rather than the damage suffered by the claimant. Although they are sometimes confused with aggravated damages, there is a clear division. Aggravated damages seek to compensate the claimant for any additional injury due to the manner in which the tort was committed. In contrast, punitive damages aim to punish the defendant.

**17–009**

In *Rookes v Barnard*, Lord Devlin restricted punitive damages to three kinds of case. His Lordship doubted the legitimacy of such damages, which, in his view, confused the civil and criminal functions of the law, and brought punishment into civil law without the procedural safeguards of criminal law. However, his Lordship admitted that punitive damages were firmly established in English law and therefore decided not to abolish this head of damages, but held that a restrictive approach should be taken in future. Further, juries (if present) should be directed that they should only award punitive damages when ordinary compensatory damages are inadequate to punish the defendant for his or her outrageous conduct, to show that tort does not pay, and to deter others.[20] The means of the parties would be taken into consideration in determining any award. This approach was approved by the House of Lords in the later case of *Cassell v Broome*.[21]

*The three kinds of punitive damages*

Lord Devlin recommended that punitive damages should only be awarded in the three following situations:

**17–010**

---

[17] [1998] Q.B. 498.

[18] [1964] A.C. 1129. See P.R. Ghandhi (1990) 10 L.S. 182 and H. Koziol and V. Wilcox (eds), *Punitive damages: Common law and civil law perspectives (Tort and Insurance Law)* (Springer, 2009).

[19] The Law Commission recommended that the term "punitive" should be used in future rather than "exemplary" in their 1997 Report No.247. It will therefore be used in this section.

[20] [1964] A.C. 1129 at 1228. Punitive damages cannot be awarded where there is no material damage to be compensated: *Watkins v Secretary of State for the Home Department* [2006] UKHL 17; [2006] 2 A.C. 395.

[21] [1972] A.C. 1027.

- oppressive, arbitrary or unconstitutional actions by government servants;

- conduct calculated by the defendant to make a profit, which may well exceed any compensation payable to the claimant; and

- when expressly authorised by statute.

These will be examined below.

**17–011**    **(i) Oppressive, arbitrary or unconstitutional actions by government servants:**    Here, the defendant is penalised for the abuse of executive power. It is therefore no excuse, as in *Huckle v Money*,[22] that the claimant was only wrongfully detained for no more than six hours, had been treated well, and provided with beefsteaks and beer. The court held that "to enter a man's house by virtue of a nameless warrant, in order to procure evidence, is worse than the Spanish Inquisition".[23] However, punitive damages will not be awarded on this basis against private individuals or corporations, however powerful they may be. They will also not be awarded against public bodies such as a nationalised water authority which is not exercising an executive function.[24] However, they may be awarded against the police or local government officials.[25] The court in *Holden v Chief Constable of Lancashire*[26] held that not all false arrests will merit punitive damages and that this will be a matter for the jury.[27] The court did find, however, that the claimant was not required to show oppressive, arbitrary *and* unconstitutional conduct by the official. Punitive damages could therefore be awarded where there was no oppressive behaviour by the arresting officer. Nor, it would seem, is it necessary to prove that the official's conduct was malicious, fraudulent, insolent, cruel, or other similar conduct. It must simply be outrageous and thus require punitive damages to mark disapproval, to deter and to vindicate the strength of the law.[28]

There is no clear reason why punitive damages under this head should be confined to misconduct by the executive. In modern times, where much power lies with private individuals or corporations, the distinction between public and private bodies seems increasingly arbitrary. This, however, is the inevitable result of the approach taken by Lord Devlin in *Rookes v Barnard*, which sought to limit punitive damages to the bare minimum required by existing case law. It would be too much to expect analytical consistency from such an approach.

**17–012**    **(ii) Conduct calculated by the defendant to make a profit which may well exceed any compensation payable to the claimant:**    The aim here is to teach the defendant that tort does not pay and to deprive the defendant of the fruits of his or her tort. However, it is approached in a rough and ready way, and the court will not require the claimant to set out the profit obtained by the defendant from the tort. The real question is whether the conduct of the defendant was "calculated" to make a profit. To prove this, the claimant must show something calculated and deliberate in the defendant's actions, although it is not necessary that the defendant engaged in any precise balancing of the chances of profit and loss.[29] The most

---

[22] (1763) 2 Wils. K.B. 206; 95 E.R. 768.
[23] (1763) 2 Wils. K.B. 206 at 207.
[24] *AB v South West Water Services* [1993] Q.B. 507.
[25] See *Cassell v Broome* [1972] A.C. 1027.
[26] [1987] Q.B. 380.
[27] False imprisonment being one of the few torts usually heard by a judge and jury.
[28] *Muuse v Secretary of State for the Home Department* [2010] EWCA Civ 453 at paras 67–71 per Thomas L.J.
[29] See *Cassell v Broome* [1972] A.C. 1027 at 1094 per Lord Morris.

frequent example is found in libel.[30] In *Cassell v Broome*,[31] the House of Lords held that the court should investigate whether the defendant was aware of the fact that what he was planning to do was against the law (or had shown reckless disregard as to whether the proposed conduct was legal or illegal) and had nevertheless decided to carry on because the prospects of material advantage outweighed the prospects of material loss.

**(iii) Expressly authorised by statute:** This is very rare. It has been argued that s.97(2) of the Copyright, Designs and Patents Act 1988[32] authorises punitive damages by virtue of its reference to "additional damages",[33] although its statutory predecessor did not.[34] The House of Lords in *Redrow Homes Ltd v Bett Brothers Plc*[35] left this question expressly open, although Lord Clyde suggested obiter that they should be regarded as aggravated only.[36] More recently, Pumfrey J. in *Nottinghamshire Healthcare National Health Service Trust v News Group Newspapers Ltd*[37] has found that the section permits only aggravated damages, but on a basis far wider than that admitted at common law, and contains an element of restitutionary damages. It may be questioned whether "a wider form of aggravated damages" which expressly addresses the flagrancy of the breach can be viewed as distinct from exemplary damages or, more likely, the statute in reality gives a discretion to award damages which include a punitive element.[38]

**17–013**

*The "cause of action" test*

The Court of Appeal decision in *AB v South West Water Services*[39] imposed one further restriction on punitive damages: they should only be awarded for torts which had received punitive awards

**17–014**

---

[30] Although such awards are frequently made against landlords evicting tenants to obtain a higher level of rent from a new tenant: see *Drane v Evangelou* [1978] 1 W.L.R. 455, *Asghar v Ahmed* (1985) 17 H.L.R. 25 and *Design Progression Ltd v Thurloe Properties Ltd* [2004] EWHC 324; [2005] 1 W.L.R. 1 (breach of statutory duty under Landlord and Tenant Act 1988 s.1).

[31] [1972] A.C. 1027. See also *John v MGN Ltd* [1997] Q.B. 586 at 618 per Bingham M.R.

[32] "(2) The court may in an action for infringement of copyright having regard to all the circumstances, and in particular to—(a) the flagrancy of the infringement, and (b) any benefit accruing to the defendant by reason of the infringement, award such additional damages as the justice of the case may require."

[33] See also Reserve and Auxiliary Forces (Protection of Civil Interests) Act 1951 s.13(2). The High Court in *R. v Secretary of State for Transport, Ex p. Factortame (No.5)* [1998] C.M.L.R. 1353 held that liability for breach of European legislation did not entitle the claimants to punitive damages. Lewison J. in *Devenish Nutrition Ltd v Sanofi-Aventis SA* [2007] EWHC 2394 (Ch); [2008] E.C.C. 4 rejected this analysis as based on the discredited cause of action test. Under the principle of equivalence (litigants in EU law should be subject to rules equivalent to those in domestic actions), punitive damages could be available for breach of EU law. In *Devenish*, however, they were precluded because the defendants had already been fined by the Commission for their breach of competition law and any award would have led to double punishment for the same wrong (point not appealed: [2009] Ch.390).

[34] s.17(3) of the Copyright Act 1956. This is the accepted view. However, cases such as *Williams v Settle* [1960] 1 W.L.R. 1072 do little to clarify this question.

[35] [1999] 1 A.C. 197.

[36] [1999] 1 A.C. 197 at 207. For a contrary view, see C. Michalos (2000) 22 E.I.P.R. 470.

[37] [2002] EWHC 409 (Ch); [2002] E.M.L.R. 33. See also Pumfrey J. in *Phonographic Performance Ltd v Reader* [2005] EWHC 416; [2005] E.M.L.R. 26.

[38] Gray J. in *Collins Stewart Ltd v Financial Times Ltd (No.2)* [2005] EWHC 262 (QB); [2006] E.M.L.R. 5 at para.33 described them as having more in common with punitive damages than aggravated damages. Note, however, that the Labour Government Consultation Paper, *The Law on Damages* (CP 09/07, May 2007) recommended that the term "additional damages" in the 1988 Act should be replaced by "aggravated and restitutionary" damages and that, overturning *Collins* on this point, such damages would be available to corporate claimants. It also recommended that the term "exemplary damages" should also be replaced by "aggravated damages" in the 1951 Act above, thereby leaving rendering the question of punitive damages entirely for the common law: see at para.216. This recommendation has not been taken forward by the new Coalition government: see Ministry of Justice, "Civil Law Reform Bill: Response to Consultation" (January 2011).

[39] [1993] Q.B. 507. In any event, the defendants had been convicted for contamination of the water supply and fined (see *Archer v Brown* [1985] Q.B. 401, below). See generally A.S. Burrows (1993) 109 L.Q.R. 358.

at the time of *Rookes v Barnard* (the "cause of action" test). If no such case had been reported, then no award would be given. This excluded punitive damages awards for torts such as negligence, public nuisance, deceit and for sex and race discrimination. This rule had no basis in principle and was simply a crude method of limiting claims. It predictably received well-deserved criticism in the Law Commission report on *Aggravated, Exemplary and Restitutionary Damages*.[40] The House of Lords in *Kuddus v Chief Constable of Leicestershire Constabulary*[41] finally overturned this "arbitrary and irrational restriction".[42] In future, the court would examine the facts of the case and would not be deflected by the claimant's cause of action.[43] In the case itself, the fact that no-one had received punitive damages for the tort of misfeasance in public office prior to *Rookes v Barnard* did not preclude the claimant from recovering such damages.

The House in *Kuddus* expressed concern, however, that counsel had not raised the fundamental question of the role of punitive damages in English tort law. Views varied from the critical approach of Lord Scott[44] to the more positive view of Lord Nicholls who considered that punitive damages perform an important function in buttressing civil liberties, for example in relation to claims of false imprisonment and wrongful arrest by the police.[45] It is an ongoing question whether punitive damages should continue to be part of English law. The Law Commission felt that they still played a valuable role and that they should be available for all torts or equitable wrongs (but not for breach of contract) where the defendant, in committing the tort, or by his or her subsequent conduct, has deliberately and outrageously disregarded the claimant's rights.[46] The Law Commission recommended, nevertheless, that punitive damages should remain a last resort remedy, and should not be awarded when other remedies adequately punish the defendant for his or her conduct. The Commission also noted the problem of high jury awards in libel and false imprisonment. Despite cases such as *John v MGM*[47] and *Thompson v Metropolitan Police Commissioner*,[48] where the Court of Appeal set down guidelines for awards, the Commission sensibly advocated that punitive awards should in future be dealt with by the judge.

Such suggestions are helpful, although the Government has stated that it does not intend to implement the reforms.[49] Although the primary aim of the law of tort is compensation, this does not mean that tort law cannot have other objectives, including deterrence of particularly reprehensible behaviour. Indeed, other Commonwealth countries, such as Canada,[50] Australia[51]

[40] Law Commission Report No.247 (1997).
[41] [2001] UKHL 29; [2002] 2 A.C. 122.
[42] See Lord Nicholls [2001] UKHL 29; [2002] 2 A.C. 122 at para.55.
[43] Eady J. ruled out, however, the award of exemplary damages for invasion of privacy in *Mosley v News Group Newspapers Ltd* [2008] EWHC 1777 (QB) on the basis that any such award would, in the context of the balancing of rights under arts 8 and 10 of the ECHR, fail the tests of necessity and proportionality.
[44] [2001] UKHL 29; [2002] 2 A.C. 122 at paras 119–121. Note also the view of A. Beever (2003) 23 O.J.L.S. 87, who argues that punitive damages are an anomaly which should be expunged from the law.
[45] [2001] UKHL 29; [2002] 2 A.C. 122 at para.63.
[46] Law Commission Report No.247 (1997) at para.6.3.
[47] [1997] Q.B. 586.
[48] [1998] Q.B. 498.
[49] *Hansard* (HC Debates), November 9, 1999, col.502. The Government suggested that further judicial development of the law in this area might help clarify the issues.
[50] *Hill v Church of Scientology of Toronto* (1995) 126 D.L.R. (4th) 129 and *Whiten v Pilot Insurance Company* (2002) 209 DLR (4th) 257. See M. Graham [2002] L.M.C.L.Q. 453.
[51] *Uren v John Fairfax & Sons Pty Ltd* (1966) 117 C.L.R. 118, High Court of Australia.

and New Zealand[52] have adopted a more generous treatment of punitive damages. A problem arises, however, in relation to vicarious liability. Lord Scott in *Kuddus* maintained that no defendant should pay punitive damages unless he or she had committed punishable behaviour and that, on this basis, an employer should not be vicariously liable for the punitive damages awarded against an errant employee.[53] To allow such damages would be to punish the wrong person and to allow the guilty party to escape punishment. However, the Law Commission has argued that punitive damages may play a positive role in encouraging employers to exercise greater control over their workforce and will assist claimants who are unable to identify which member of the employer's workforce had committed the tort. In *Rowlands v Chief Constable of Merseyside Police*,[54] the Court of Appeal confirmed that an employer could be vicariously liable for punitive damages. Despite arguments to the contrary, it was felt desirable to make such an award which would ensure that the victim received damages of an adequate amount which would be paid by those who bore ultimate responsibility for the tortfeasor's conduct. It is submitted that such an award is contentious. It subverts the punitive element of the damages and places an extra burden on the employer, who is *not* at fault. The Supreme Court of Canada in *Blackwater v Plint*[55] recently rejected punitive damages in this context, although there is no Commonwealth consensus on this controversial issue.[56]

Further concerns may be raised. Punitive damages are paid, not to the State as is the case with criminal fines, but to the claimant. The victim thus receives a windfall irrespective of his or her actual loss. In addition, there is the potential for double or excessive punishment if the defendant's conduct amounts to a crime for which he or she has been prosecuted. This problem was addressed by the court in *Archer v Brown*,[57] which held that if the defendant had already been prosecuted and sentenced in a criminal court for precisely the conduct which forms the basis of the suit, no punitive award should be made. Peter Pain J. stated that a man should not be punished twice for the same offence.[58] The Law Commission, in their 1997 report, proposed that the courts should have a discretion in such circumstances to refuse to consider or make an award of punitive damages where a defendant had already been convicted by a criminal court.[59]

---

[52] Note the recent Supreme Court decision of *Couch v Attorney-General (No 2)* [2010] NZSC 27 (Sup Ct (NZ)) which overturned the earlier Privy Council decision in *A v Bottrill* [2002] UKPC 44; [2003] 1 A.C. 449 and now requires at least conscious awareness of the risk, or subjective recklessness, to be shown when suing for exemplary damages in negligence claims (Elias C.J. dissenting). This issue is particularly contentious in New Zealand in the light of the no-fault compensation scheme, discussed in Ch.1, which serves to exclude any common law claim for personal injury but permits a claim for exemplary damages. See H. Wilberg [2010] P.L. 809.

[53] [2001] UKHL 29; [2002] 2 A.C. 122 at paras 123–137. Such comments were, however, obiter.

[54] [2006] EWCA Civ 1773, [2007] 1 W.L.R. 1065. Comment H. Gow (2007) 157 N.L.J. 164.

[55] (2005) 258 D.L.R. (4th) 275. The Court dealt with the point in only one paragraph, commenting that "The trial judge . . . correctly stated that punitive damages cannot be awarded in the absence of reprehensible conduct specifically referable to the employer": at para.91.

[56] See the High Court of Australia in *State of New South Wales v Ibbett* [2006] HCA 57, (2007) 231 A.L.R. 485 (punitive damages may be awarded against the police).

[57] [1985] Q.B. 401, but contrast *Messenger Newspaper Group Ltd v National Graphical Association* [1984] I.R.L.R. 397 where Caulfield J. refused to take into account a £675,000 fine imposed for contempt of court and ordered the defendant to pay an additional £25,000 as punitive damages.

[58] [1985] Q.B. 401 at 423. Contrast *Borders (UK) Ltd v Commissioner of Police of the Metropolis* [2005] EWCA Civ 197; [2005] Po. L.R. 1 (award of punitive damages did not duplicate criminal penalties).

[59] Law Commission Report No.247, paras 5.112–5.115.

*(6) Restitutionary*

**17–015**  We looked at the doctrine of "waiver of tort" briefly in Ch.16, where the claimant has the option to choose between compensatory and restitutionary damages. Here, damages are assessed not on the loss caused to the claimant, but on the gain obtained by the defendant at the claimant's expense. It should be noted that not all torts allow for restitutionary damages,[60] and further reference should be made to works on the law of restitution.[61] The Law Commission, in their 1997 report, decided that no attempt should be made at present to state comprehensively in legislation the situations in which torts should trigger restitutionary damages, and this should be left to common law development.[62] They nevertheless proposed legislation which would allow the courts to award restitutionary damages as an alternative to punitive damages.[63]

## The relationship between tort damages and damages under the Human Rights Act 1998[64]

**17–016**  Section 8(1) of the Act sets out the judicial remedies which arise when a public authority has acted in a way which is incompatible with a Convention right (see s.6 and Ch.2).[65] It states that, in such a case, the court "may grant such relief or remedy, or make such order, within its powers as it considers just and appropriate." This broad discretion, which includes the award of damages, has three main limitations:

> (i) damages can only be awarded where the court has the power to award damages in civil proceedings;[66]
>
> (ii) no award of damages can be made unless, taking account of all the circumstances of the case,[67] the court is satisfied that the award is necessary to afford just satisfaction to the claimant; and

---

[60] See *Devenish Nutrition Ltd v Sanofi-Aventis SA* [2008] EWCA Civ 1086; [2009] Ch.390 holding that non-proprietary torts (that is, torts not involving the misappropriation of the claimant's property rights) are still bound by Court of Appeal authority in *Stoke on Trent City Council v W&J Wass Ltd (No 1)* [1988] 1 W.L.R. 1406 that only compensatory damages could be awarded for such torts). It is not always clear even for proprietary torts such as trespass whether the basis for damages is compensatory or restitutionary. See, for example, the damages awarded for trespass to land in *Horsford v Bird* [2006] UKPC 3; [2006] 1 E.G.L.R. 75 which some authors have described as restitutionary (Edelman (2006) 122 L.Q.R. 391) and *Severn Trent Water Ltd v Barnes* [2004] EWCA Civ 570; [2004] 2 E.G.L.R. 95 (described as compensatory). See also Lord Scott, "Damages" [2007] L.M.C.L.Q. 465 at 467.

[61] See, e.g. G. Virgo, *Principles of the Law of Restitution* (2nd edn, OUP, 2006) Ch.16.

[62] At para.6.2.

[63] At paras 3.48–3.57. See para.3.51: "We therefore recommend that: legislation should provide that restitutionary damages may be awarded where: (a) the defendant has committed: (i) a tort or an equitable wrong, or (ii) a civil wrong (including a tort or an equitable wrong) which arises under an Act, and an award of restitutionary damages would be consistent with the policy of that Act, and (b) his conduct showed a deliberate and outrageous disregard of the plaintiff's rights. (Draft Bill, cl.2(1), 12(3))".

[64] See, generally, the Law Commission Report No.266, *Damages under the Human Rights Act 1998* (2000), J. Steele, 'Damages in tort and under the Human Rights Act: remedial or functional separation?' [2008] C.L.J. 606 and J. Wright, *Tort Law and Human Rights* (2nd ed, Hart, 2012).

[65] See also s.7.

[66] s.8(2).

[67] These include: (a) any other relief or remedy granted, or order made, in relation to the act in question (by that or any other court), and (b) the consequences of any decision (of that or any other court) in respect of that act: s.8(3).

(iii) in determining whether to award damages or the amount of the award, the court
must take into account the principles applied by the European Court of Human
Rights.[68]

There is thus no right to damages. The courts will examine all the circumstances of the case
and consider whether "just satisfaction" has been achieved, even in the absence of an award
of damages under the Act. Damages are thus a residual remedy and, as recognised by the DCA
review of the implementation of the Human Rights Act, awarded rarely.[69]

There is some dispute as to how such damages should be assessed. It has been argued that
these damages should differ from the ordinary compensatory damages discussed above and be
lower than those awarded for any comparable tort.[70] This question was resolved by Lord
Bingham in *R. (on the application of Greenfield) v Secretary of State for the Home Department*[71]
where his Lordship stated that damages would indeed be distinct from those awarded in
ordinary tort law:

"the 1998 Act is not a tort statute. Its objects are different and broader. Even in a case
where a finding of violation is not judged to afford the applicant just satisfaction, such a
finding will be an important part of his remedy and an important vindication of the right
he has asserted . . . Secondly, the purpose of incorporating the Convention in domestic
law through the 1998 Act was not to give victims better remedies at home than they could
recover in Strasbourg but to give them the same remedies without the delay and expense
of resort to Strasbourg."[72]

This is consistent with s.8(4), which instructs the court to take account of the principles
applied by the European Court of Human Rights. In practice, however, this court rarely gives

---

[68] s.8(4). These are set out under art.41 of the Convention.

[69] See Department of Constitutional Affairs, *Review of the implementation of the Human Rights Act* (2006) p.18
(*http://www.justice.gov.uk/docs/full_review.pdf* [Accessed April 25, 2011]). At the time of the report, there were only
three reported cases in which damages had been awarded: *R. (Bernard) v Enfield London Borough Council* [2003]
H.R.L.R. 4—£8,000 was awarded to a disabled claimant who was required to live in unsuitable accommodation for
20 months; *R. (KB) v Mental Health Review Tribunal* [2003] EWHC 193 (Admin); [2004] Q.B. 936—£750 to £4,000
for delays to Mental Health Review Tribunal hearings and *Van Colle v Chief Constable of Hertfordshire* [2006]
EWHC 360 (QB)—£50,000 to parents of a witness murdered because of inadequate police protection (reduced on
appeal to £10,000 to estate and £15,000 to parents for grief and suffering: [2007] EWCA Civ 325; [2007] 1 W.L.R.
1821, although liability was ultimately rejected by the House of Lords: [2008] UKHL 50, see Ch.2).

[70] See Lord Woolf C.J.,"The Human Rights Act 1998 and Remedies" in M. Andenas and D. Fairgrieve (eds), *Judicial
Review in International Perspective: II* (Kluwer Law International, 2000), pp.429–436, but contrast *R. (KB) v Mental
Health Review Tribunal (Damages)* [2003] EWHC 193 (Admin); [2004] Q.B. 936 and *Anufrijeva v London Borough
of Southwark* [2003] EWCA Civ 1406; [2004] Q.B. 1124 at para.73.

[71] [2005] UKHL 14; [2005] 1 W.L.R. 673 at para.19.

[72] *Greenfield* was applied in *Savage v South Essex Partnership NHS Foundation Trust* [2010] EWHC 865 (QB);
[2010] P.I.Q.R. P14 (£10,000 for breach of art.2 in permitting compulsorily detained mental patient to escape and
commit suicide) and *R. (on the application of Pennington) v Parole Board* [2010] EWHC 78 (Admin) (£1,750 for
breach of art.5(4) due to 3 month delay in informing prisoner that he was to be released on licence, rejecting the argument raised by Varuhas (2009) 72 M.L.R. 750 for a tort-based approach to damages under the Human Rights Act).
The existence of a tortious remedy may, however, impact on the remedy awarded under the Human Rights Act: see
*Dobson v Thames Water Utilities Ltd* [2009] EWCA Civ 28; [2009] All E.R. 319 (award of damages in private
nuisance to property owner was relevant in deciding whether to award damages to person living in the same household whose art.8 rights had been infringed, discussed in Ch.10).

guidance as to the principles adopted or even a breakdown of the award in question.[73] Nevertheless, a number of observations may be made. The primary principle (in common with English law) is that the victim should, as far as possible, be placed in the same position as if the violation of his or her rights had not occurred. Further, the court is clearly more willing to award damages for distress and disappointment than the English courts, although it has been suggested that such injury must be significant and of sufficient intensity before it could sound in damages.[74] The court is equally willing to consider the character and conduct of the parties and the scale and manner of the violation of rights in deciding on the most appropriate response. The court does not, however, award exemplary damages.[75] It should also be noted that proceedings for damages must be brought quickly under the Act, normally within one year of the act complained of.[76]

## ACTIONS FOR PERSONAL INJURY

17–017    Having discussed the different kinds of damages available to claimants, we now focus on a specific type of action: a claim for compensation for personal injury. As highlighted above, the courts experience particular problems in assessing such awards. It is impossible to put a financial price on the loss of a limb, or the pain and suffering endured during an accident. Further, even financial losses cause difficulties when future financial loss is claimed. The courts are required to predict the future financial position of the claimant if the tort had not taken place. For example, if the claimant wishes to recover future loss of earnings, a court should take account of the fact that he or she may have been dismissed or made redundant, or taken a career break, or even promoted to run the company. Such prospects should be brought into any compensatory sum, but achieving this with any degree of accuracy is obviously difficult. As Lord Scarman commented in *Lim v Camden Area Health Authority*[77]: "There is really only one certainty: the future will prove the award to be either too high or too low".

The courts have adopted a number of principles which seek to achieve the goal of full compensation, which will be considered below, but a number of matters should be noted. First, the courts assess the claimant's loss on an individual basis. They therefore have no problem with the fact that claimant X, who is a company director living in a large house in Surrey, will receive far more damages than claimant Y, a worker in a fast food outlet living in rented accommodation, even though they have received exactly the same injuries due to

---

[73] See Law Commission Report No.266; para.3.4: "Perhaps the most striking feature of the Strasbourg case-law, to lawyers from the UK, is the lack of clear principles as to when damages should be awarded and how they should be measured."

[74] *R. (KB) v Mental Health Review Tribunal* [2003] EWHC 193 (Admin); [2004] Q.B. 936, relying on *Silver v United Kingdom* (1983) 6 E.H.R.R. 62. The Court is equally more willing to award damages for negligently-incurred pure economic loss than in English law: see Ch.3.

[75] See Law Commission Report No.266 para.3.47 which examines the case law of the European Court of Human Rights. Note also s.9(3): "In proceedings under this Act in respect of a judicial act done in good faith, damages may not be awarded otherwise than to compensate a person."

[76] See s.7(5): "Proceedings under subs.7(1)(a) must be brought before the end of—(a) the period of one year beginning with the date on which the act complained of took place; or (b) such longer period as the court or tribunal considers equitable having regard to all the circumstances, but that is subject to any rule imposing a stricter time limit in relation to the procedure in question."

[77] [1980] A.C. 174 at 183.

the tort.[78] X will have suffered greater financial losses than Y and will therefore deserve a larger award. The courts have also traditionally been wary of the use of actuarial evidence in the calculation of awards. Actuarial evidence is used by insurance companies to calculate premiums, and it has been suggested that it may form a more accurate basis for assessing future financial losses in tort. The courts have been reluctant to embrace such evidence, a judge commenting in 1985 that "the predictions of an actuary can be only a little more likely to be accurate (and will almost certainly be less interesting) than those of an astrologer".[79] Nevertheless, in the House of Lords in *Wells v Wells*[80] (which will be discussed in more detail below), Lord Lloyd adopted a far more positive view of actuarial evidence, holding that whilst such evidence should not govern personal injury claims, it should certainly be referred to, and used as a starting-point rather than a check. It would seem that, in future, actuarial tables will have an active role in setting the level of awards for pecuniary loss.[81]

We shall look first at how the courts assess past and future financial losses (or pecuniary loss). This will be followed by an examination of the most difficult category to assess: non-pecuniary loss.

## Pecuniary loss

If the claimant has suffered severe injuries, the largest part of the claim is likely to be for **17–018** financial loss, including loss of earnings, cost of care and expenses. As stated above, while financial losses before trial can be assessed with some degree of accuracy, future losses are very difficult to calculate. This is not assisted by the general rule that the courts will award a once-and-for-all lump sum. The court must find a sum which, if properly invested, will cover the claimant for all future losses incurred due to the tort. The best the courts can do is to make a "guesstimate" of future losses. The difficulties in assessing the different types of financial loss suffered by the claimant will be examined below.

*(1) Loss of earnings*

While loss of earnings before trial can be assessed with a degree of accuracy, calculation of **17–019** loss of future earnings is obviously more problematic. The method used by the courts is known as the "multiplier/multiplicand method". Essentially, a figure is reached by the court multiplying the multiplier by the multiplicand.

$$\text{MULTIPLIER} \times \text{MULTIPLICAND} = \text{future loss of earnings}$$

The multiplicand is the claimant's net annual loss.[82] This is his or her gross annual salary, less income tax and National Insurance.

The multiplier is the number of years for which this loss will continue. However, this is not a question of the difference between the claimant's age at the time of the accident and the age he or she resumes work or retires. The courts will take account of the possibilities of unemployment, redundancy and other factors reducing salary (although they will also take account of promotion prospects, etc. to increase the figure). They will also note the fact that the

---

[78] See *H West & Son Ltd v Shephard* [1964] A.C. 326.

[79] *Auty v National Coal Board* [1985] 1 All E.R. 930 at 939 per Oliver L.J.

[80] [1999] 1 A.C. 345.

[81] See, e.g. *Worrall v Powergen Plc* [1999] Lloyd's Rep. Med. 177 which followed Lord Lloyd's dictum.

[82] See *British Transport Commission v Gourley* [1956] A.C. 185, HL.

claimant is being paid "up front". On this basis, the multiplier will be discounted to take account of these contingencies. The multiplier will therefore usually be set at a rate far lower than the actual number of years during which the injury will be suffered.

This formula is stated to give a lump sum sufficient, if invested, to produce an income equal to the loss of income suffered by the claimant.[83] Whether in fact this is achieved is highly questionable and in fact most unlikely. However, this myth persists in tort law.

Pressure has mounted, however, for the courts to adopt a more scientific approach. The Ogden Tables, which first appeared in 1984,[84] have made a considerable impact in persuading the courts of the merits of actuarial evidence. These are a set of actuarial tables, prepared by a working party of lawyers, insurers, accountants and actuaries for use in personal injury and fatal accident cases, which are published by the Government Actuary's Department. They assist in identifying the most appropriate multiplier, using the projected future mortality rates from the 2004-based national population projections for the United Kingdom. The Ogden Tables are now regularly cited in court, and s.10 of the Civil Evidence Act 1995 provides that they are admissible as evidence in court. Yet, reference to the Ogden Tables has only added to the criticism of the courts' refusal to take account of inflation when establishing the multiplier.[85] In setting up the multiplier, the courts assume that the interest on the lump sum will cover inflation, and so this can be ignored.[86]

**17–020**     The courts had in the past presumed a return on investments of 4 to 5 per cent.[87] It was questioned whether this was a realistic figure, since it assumed that the successful claimant would invest in equities which, in an unstable stock market, could prove a risky investment. With the advent of index-linked government securities (I.L.G.S.) a safer alternative existed. These are bonds under which the return on capital is fully protected against inflation. On this basis, if inflation increases and so the lump sum is worth less, the claimant will be protected by the bond. However, greater security comes at a price, and the interest on such bonds is less than the general commercial rate. The Law Commission, in its 1994 report *Structured Settlements and Interim and Provisional Damages*,[88] recommended that the courts, in assessing the multiplier, should use the rate for index-linked government securities unless there are special reasons affecting the individual case. Section 1 of the Damages Act 1996 would seem to resolve this problem. Section 1 provides that the court is to "take into account such rate of return as may from time to time be prescribed by an order made by the Lord Chancellor". Until recently, however, the Lord Chancellor had failed to act on this provision.

In the absence of legislative intervention, the House of Lords intervened in July 1998 in the important case of *Wells v Wells*.[89] Their Lordships overruled the Court of Appeal, which had adhered to the recognised practice of assuming a 4 to 5 per cent return on investments. It was

---

[83] Assuming the claimant will draw on the income and part of the capital from the sum invested so that the lump sum is exhausted at the end of the relevant period.

[84] Now in their 6th edition (2007). As well as providing tables of multipliers, the publication provides explanatory notes as to how the tables should be used: see *http://www.gad.gov.uk/services/other%20services/compensation_for_injury_and_death.html* [Accessed April 25, 2011].

[85] In *Lim Poh Choo v Camden and Islington Area Health Authority* [1980] A.C. 174 at 193 Lord Scarman held that only in exceptional circumstances would any allowance be made for inflation.

[86] This process was affirmed by the Court of Appeal in *Cooke v United Bristol Health Care* [2003] EWCA Civ 1370; [2004] 1 W.L.R. 251.

[87] Since *Mallett v McMonagle* [1970] A.C. 166, HL.

[88] Law Commission Report No.224 paras 2.25–2.28.

[89] [1999] 1 A.C. 345, HL. See D Kemp (1998) 114 L.Q.R. 570 who, at p.571, describes it as "one of the most important decisions in personal injury litigation since the Second World War".

held that it was no longer appropriate to act on the assumption that the claimant will invest his or her damages in equities and to apply a discount rate of 4 to 5 per cent. Rather, the courts should recognise the suitability of index-linked government securities for a prudent investment of a large lump sum of damages, and, in the light of this, their Lordships applied a discount rate of 3 per cent.

This led to a dramatic increase in multipliers, previously capped at 18. In the case of *Thomas v Brighton Health Authority* (which was joined in *Wells*), serious injuries had been suffered by a child at birth, and the court raised the multiplier from 17 to 26.58. The Court of Appeal held in *Warren v Northern General Hospital Trust*[90] that the discount rate should remain at 3 per cent until the Lord Chancellor set a rate under s.1 of the Damages Act 1996. This was regardless of the fact that the net yield of index-linked government securities was found to have dropped to 2.5 per cent.

The court was influenced by the imminent intention of the Lord Chancellor to prescribe a rate under s.1,[91] and, in 2001, this rate was indeed set at 2.5 per cent.[92]

Yet, this has not prevented a number of challenges to this rate. Section 1(2) of the Damages Act 1996 provides that the setting of the rate of return:

"shall not however prevent the court taking a different rate of return into account if any party to the proceedings shows that it is more appropriate in the case in question"

and, as might be expected, litigants have relied on this provision to question the rate used. Guidance was finally given by the Court of Appeal in *Warriner v Warriner*.[93] A departure would only be justifiable if the case:

(i) fell into a category which the Lord Chancellor had not taken into account when setting the rate; and/or

(ii) had special features which were material to the choice of rate of return and were shown not to have been taken into account when the rate was set.

In the court's view, it would be appropriate to alter the rate in comparatively few cases. Here, the mere fact that Ms Warriner, who had suffered serious brain damage in a road accident, had

---

[90] [2000] 1 W.L.R. 1404. See also *J v Grocott* [2000] P.I.Q.R. Q17 (Hale J.) and *Barry v Ablerex Construction (Midlands) Ltd* [2001] EWCA Civ 433, (2001) 98(22) L.S.G. 35 (CA) in which both courts affirm that the House of Lords in *Wells* clearly contemplated that the rate would remain at 3 per cent until the Lord Chancellor set a rate under the Act in the absence of significant economic changes. The lowering of the I.L.G.S. rate did not constitute such a change.

[91] See Consultation Paper, *The discount rate and alternatives to lump sum payments* (March 2000) (*http://www.dca. gov.uk/consult/general/damagesfr.htm* [Accessed April 25, 2011]). Publication is noted by Stuart-Smith L.J. in his leading judgment in *Warren v Northern General Hospital Trust* [2000] 1 W.L.R. 1404.

[92] Damages (Personal Injury) Order 2001(SI 2001/2301), art.2. Note the subsequent consultation paper, *Setting the discount rate: Lord Chancellor's Reasons* (July 2001) (*http://www.dca.gov.uk/civil/discount.htm* [Accessed April 25, 2011]) and the 2002 report, *Analysis of the Impact of the Prescribed Discount Rate of 2.5%* (*http://www.dca.gov.uk/ risk/pdrria.htm*).

[93] [2002] EWCA Civ 81; [2002] 1 W.L.R. 1703. Note also *Cooke v United Bristol Health Care* [2003] EWCA Civ 1370; [2004] 1 W.L.R. 251, where the Court of Appeal rejected an indirect challenge to the discount rate by means of increasing the multiplicand and *Eagle v Chambers (No.2)* [2004] EWCA Civ 1033; [2004] 1 W.L.R. 3081 where the Court of Appeal rejected an additional claim for investment management fees, stating that any desire to increase the sum awarded by investing more broadly was to be set off by any gains made and was not recoverable from the defendant.

a long life expectancy would not justify any alteration of the rate and, indeed, such claims were included in the category which the Lord Chancellor had in mind in setting the 2.5 per cent rate. Generally, then, the court will stick to 2.5 per cent in the interests of certainty to facilitate settlements and save the expense of expert evidence at trial. Whilst this is admittedly a "rough and ready" approach, such policy reasons would be undermined if every shift in market conditions required the courts to revise the rate. Nevertheless this has not prevented criticism, notably from the former Government Actuary, that this rate is far too high in the light of current economic conditions and that a fundamental review is needed if victims are not to go undercompensated.[94]

Nevertheless, the impact of *Wells* and the Lord Chancellor's intervention has been dramatic. Damages for future pecuniary loss have risen considerably. It should not be forgotten that this carries with it a consequential rise in liability insurance premiums.[95] It should also be noted that the courts do not check what the claimant actually does with the sum awarded, and it is generally accepted that, in reality, it is unlikely that a claimant would place the entire award of damages in index-linked government securities. Nevertheless, if the claimant chooses to invest all the lump sum in the stock market or in his or her bank account, this is disregarded and will not affect the court's calculation of damages.[96]

### (2) Lost years

**17–021**     This is a claim for loss of earnings during the period the claimant would have been able to work, but for the fact that his or her life has been shortened by the defendant's tort. In other words, suppose that claimant A was expected to live to 80. Following the tort, A will only live to 40. The claim will be for the loss of earnings from the age of 40. In the past, A could have claimed damages for loss of expectation of life for which the courts awarded a small sum, even though the claimant might be unaware of the loss or had been killed instantaneously.[97] In view of this award, the court in *Oliver v Ashman*[98] held that no additional award for loss of earnings during the "lost years" would be allowed. However, damages for loss of expectation of life were abolished by s.1(1)(a) of the Administration of Justice Act 1982. In 1980, the majority of the House of Lords in *Pickett v British Rail Engineering Ltd*[99] finally overturned *Oliver v Ashman* and accepted that a claim for loss of earnings during the "lost years" should stand. Their Lordships were influenced by the predicament of dependants, for whom the victim would have provided financial support during this period. If the victim cannot claim, and they are unable to bring a claim in their own right under the Fatal Accidents Act 1976 (see below),[100] then this head of damage would go uncompensated.

[94] C Daykin, "Fair compensation needs actuaries" [2009] J.P.I.L 48. Note that on 9 November 2010, the Lord Chancellor agreed, after pressure from the Association of Personal Injury Lawyers (APIL), to review the discount rate used by the courts to calculate personal injury awards: see *Solicitors Journal* November 9, 2010.

[95] The Lord Chancellor's Department March 2000 Consultation Paper para.14, reports that insurance industry sources estimate that reducing the guideline rate of return from 4.5 per cent to 3 per cent increased by £115 million the sum needed to be paid out in damages.

[96] See Lord Lloyd [1999] 1 A.C. 345 at 365. The Court of Appeal in *Warren* [2000] 1 W.L.R. 1404, for example, noted that the Court of Protection generally invested 70 per cent of the fund in equities, which was likely to give a higher rate of return than index-linked government securities. This was not treated as a relevant concern, although it may have influenced the court's adherence to the then 3 per cent rule when it seemed clear that the claimant would not be under-compensated.

[97] e.g. £200 in *Benham v Gambling* [1941] A.C. 157.

[98] [1962] 2 Q.B. 210.

[99] [1980] A.C. 136.

[100] A claim by dependants under the Fatal Accidents Act 1976 can only stand when the deceased's claim has not proceeded to judgment or settled.

This was held to be contrary to logic and justice.[101] In assessing the award, the court will look at the claimant's life expectancy before the accident and deduct the sum the claimant would have spent on supporting him or herself, including a proportion of the household bills.[102] The sum awarded will vary, but for a very young child any such loss is highly speculative and the court is likely to award nil damages.[103]

### (3) Loss of earning capacity

This is a claim for losses due to the fact that, although the claimant can carry on working, his or her ability to obtain employment is hindered by the continuing effects of the accident. For example, claimants disabled due to the accident may find it more difficult to obtain a new job if their employment ends for some reason, particularly if they were employed in a physically demanding job. This is often difficult to assess[104] and, particularly in relation to children,[105] highly speculative.

**17–022**

### (4) Deductions

In assessing the claimant's compensation, the court seeks to compensate the victim fully, but is also careful to avoid over-compensation, which may unnecessarily penalise the defendant for his or her tort and be a wasteful use of resources. This problem of over-compensation arises when it is shown that, following the accident, the claimant has received sums of money which also compensate him or her for the loss suffered. The obvious example is where the defendant's tort stops the claimant working. Prior to trial, unless the claimant can obtain an interim award or has savings, the claimant may be dependent on income support. Alternatively, the claimant might have an insurance policy providing critical illness cover, or be entitled to statutory sick pay. If the claimant is awarded damages covering losses suffered prior to trial regardless of such sums, he or she will be compensated twice for some of these pre-trial losses. There are a number of options open to the courts to avoid over-compensation:

**17–023**

- Make the defendant liable only for the actual losses suffered by the claimant, deducting income support, etc., received. This option means that the state, employer or insurance company which has provided financial support is effectively subsidising the defendant who is at fault.

- Ignore other benefits and make the defendant fully liable. Here, it is accepted that the claimant is over-compensated.

- Make the defendant liable only for the actual losses suffered by the claimant, but render the defendant liable to repay all those who supported the claimant prior to trial.

---

[101] This action does not, however, survive for the benefit of the claimant's estate. Section 1(2)(a) of the Law Reform (Miscellaneous Provisions) Act 1934 (as amended by the Administration of Justice Act 1982 s.4) provides that the estate cannot recover any damages for loss of income in respect of any period after the victim's death. This prevents any possibility of double recovery by the claimant as the executor of the estate and dependant.

[102] See *Harris v Empress Motors Ltd* [1984] 1 W.L.R. 212. This is far stricter than the approach under the Fatal Accidents Act 1976 which will be discussed below.

[103] *Croke v Wiseman* [1982] 1 W.L.R. 71. See P.J. Davies (1982) 45 M.L.R. 333. Followed unenthusiastically by *Iqbal v Whipps Cross University Hospital NHS Trust* [2007] EWCA Civ 1190; [2008] P.I.Q.R. P9.

[104] See *Smith v Manchester Corpn* (1974) 17 K.I.R. 1, CA.

[105] See, e.g. *Croke v Wiseman* [1982] 1 W.L.R. 71 where the plaintiff was 21 months old at the time of the accident.

The courts confusingly adopt all three approaches. Lord Reid in *Parry v Cleaver* explains the rules as depending on justice, reasonableness and public policy,[106] but this takes us little further. We therefore set out in this section how these rules work. Essentially, it depends on the nature of the benefit received by the claimant. The principles involved are not particularly clear. The general approach seems to be that when the claimant has received a benefit which reduces the actual loss suffered, it should be deducted, but that the claimant should keep all "collateral payments". This distinction is not, however, always apparent. The simplest way is to examine each individual benefit in turn.

*(i) Charity*

17–024    The law is reluctant to reduce the damages payable to the claimant due to receipt of charitable payments. There is a no doubt realistic fear that individuals would be reluctant to donate money to charity if the net result was to reduce the defendant's liability for damages at trial. Policy therefore dictates that such sums should not be deducted.[107]

*(ii) Voluntary payments by the defendant*

17–025    If the defendant has given any money to the claimant, or provided facilities such as a wheelchair, this will be deducted from the award. This will not include a company pension, as this is distinguishable from compensation for lost wages.[108] In *Williams v BOC Gases Ltd,*[109] an *ex gratia* payment from the defendant employers, given as an advance against any damages awarded, was deducted. The Court of Appeal held that, as a matter of public policy, employers ought to be encouraged to make payments of this kind. This would not be treated as a charitable payment, even if given for benevolent reasons, unless the employer explicitly spelt out that it should be ignored if damages were awarded in future litigation.[110]

*(iii) Insurance*

17–026    Again, if the claimant has had the foresight to purchase an insurance policy to cover some of his or her losses, the courts are reluctant to penalise the claimant.[111] It would seem wrong that a claimant who has paid no premiums should obtain a higher damages award. Arguably this could be met by giving the claimant a credit for the premiums paid, but the courts have not chosen this path. In any event, if the insurance policy is one of indemnity (for example property insurance is usually indemnity insurance), the insurer is likely to seek to recover the monies paid by exercising its right of subrogation. The action will then be brought by the insurance company in the claimant's name. However, personal injury insurance is not generally indemnity insurance, and the claimant will be able to recover both the proceeds of the policy and the damages awarded by the court.[112]

---

[106] [1970] A.C. 1 at 13.
[107] See *Parry v Cleaver* [1970] A.C. 1: *Hussain v New Taplow Paper Mills Ltd* [1988] A.C. 514: and *Gaca v Pirelli General Plc* [2004] EWCA Civ 373; [2004] 1 W.L.R. 2683.
[108] See *Parry v Cleaver* [1970] A.C. 1.
[109] [2000] I.C.R. 1181.
[110] See *Gaca v Pirelli General Plc* [2004] EWCA Civ 373; [2004] 1 W.L.R. 2683, overruling *McCamley v Cammell Laird Shipbuilders Ltd* [1990] 1 W.L.R. 963.
[111] See *Bradburn v Great Western Rail Co* (1874) L.R. 10 Ex 1.
[112] See, generally, P. Cane, *Atiyah's Accidents, Compensation and the Law* (7th edn, Cambridge University Press, 2006), at 15.4.3.

*(iv) Sick pay*

This is deductible from damages for loss of earnings, whether or not it is paid by the defendant. It is not treated as insurance against loss of earnings, but as a substitute for wages. This extends to long-term sickness benefit paid by the employer.[113]  **17–027**

*(v) Pension*

If, as a result of the injury, the claimant retires from his or her job and receives a pension, this is not deductible from the claim for loss of earnings, because the pension is not deemed to be of the same nature as lost wages, but a form of insurance. In *Parry v Cleaver*, a 35-year-old policeman had been severely injured in a road accident and was discharged from the police force. However, whilst in employment, he had made compulsory contributions to a police pension fund, and he became entitled to a pension for life on being discharged. The question was whether this pension should be taken into account when assessing the policeman's loss of earnings following the accident. The majority of the House of Lords held that it should be ignored. A contributory pension scheme was treated as a form of insurance, rather than sick pay, and should not be taken into account when assessing future loss of earnings. It would, however, be taken into account in assessing the loss suffered on reaching police retirement age, when there would be a diminution in pension entitlement. Lord Reid stressed that it was simply a case of comparing "like with like".[114] The minority favoured deduction. Lord Morris (dissenting) held that where there is no discretionary element, and the arrangements leading to the pension are an essential part of the contract, then the pension payments should be taken as a form of deferred pay, and deducted.[115] The majority view, however, was approved by the House of Lords in *Smoker v London Fire and Civil Defence Authority*.[116] Lord Templeman approved Lord Reid's statement in *Parry* that:  **17–028**

> "a pension is the fruit, through insurance, of all the money which was set aside in the past in respect of [an employee's] past work".[117]

The House of Lords, in *Hussain v New Taplow Paper Mills Ltd*,[118] however, distinguished payments under a permanent health insurance scheme set up by the employer, to which employees were not required to contribute. Lord Bridge, delivering the unanimous opinion of the House, viewed such payments as the very opposite of a pension, and indistinguishable from long-term sick pay. On this basis, such payments were deductible. His Lordship commented:

> "It positively offends my sense of justice that a plaintiff, who has certainly paid no insurance premiums as such, should receive full wages during a period of incapacity to work from two different sources, his employer and the tortfeasor".[119]

---

[113] *Hussain v New Taplow Paper Mills Ltd* [1988] A.C. 514.

[114] [1970] A.C. 1 at 21.

[115] [1970] A.C. 1 at 32.

[116] [1991] 2 A.C. 502. See also *Longden v British Coal Corpn* [1998] A.C. 653, HL: contributory incapacity and disability pensions are non-deductible.

[117] [1991] 2 A.C. 502 at 543.

[118] [1988] A.C. 514.

[119] [1988] A.C. 514 at 532.

It would therefore seem that, in his Lordship's view at least, the claimant must have contributed to the pension to avoid any deduction of this benefit.

*(vi)  Social security benefits*

**17–029**  For political reasons, deduction of social security benefits is largely governed by statute. At the commencement of the National Health Service, this matter was governed by the Law Reform (Personal Injuries) Act 1948.[120] Section 2 provided for a deduction from damages for loss of earnings of one-half the value of certain benefits, such as sickness benefit and invalidity benefit, receivable by the claimant in the five years following the accident. This did not include all benefits, however, and the common law developed complementary rules deducting these other benefits in full for the period of the disability.[121]

The current legal position modifies the rules to resemble the third option mentioned above.[122] It represents a political decision to ensure that the overstretched welfare state is not subsidising defendants, and that social security payments made to claimants should be recovered whenever possible. Section 6 of the Social Security (Recovery of Benefits) Act 1997 now provides for the defendant to pay to the Department for Work and Pensions an amount equal to the total amount of specified social security benefits[123] payable to the victim in respect of his or her injury during the five years immediately following the accident (or until the making of the compensation payment whichever is earlier[124]). The claimant will get the difference (if any) between the damages awarded and recoverable benefits.[125] Section 4 provides that the defendant should not make any compensation payment in consequence of an accident, injury or disease suffered by the claimant until he or she has applied to the Secretary of State for a certificate of recoverable benefits.[126] These are processed by the Compensation Recovery Unit (CRU) of the Department for Work and Pensions.[127] The provisions apply not only to court judgments, but extend to out-of-court settlements.[128]

---

[120] This still applies to torts which occurred before January 1, 1989 and which are not barred by the Limitation Act 1980.

[121] See *Hodgson v Trapp* [1989] A.C. 807. These rules still apply for benefits not covered by the 1997 Act, e.g. statutory payments under the Pneumoconiosis etc (Workers' Compensation) Act 1979 (*Ballantine v Newalls Insulation Co Ltd* [2001] I.C.R. 25, CA) or housing benefit (*Clenshaw v Tanner* [2002] EWCA Civ 1848).

[122] Namely that the defendant is liable only for the actual losses suffered by the claimant, but the defendant is rendered liable to repay all those who supported the claimant prior to trial.

[123] They are listed in Sch.2, col.2 and cover most benefits. There are exemptions, however, such as payments made under the Criminal Injuries Compensation Scheme and charitable trusts: see Sch.1, Pt I. Claims under the Fatal Accidents Act 1976 are also excluded: Social Security (Recovery of Benefits) Regulations 1997 (SI 1997/2205), reg.2(2)(a).

[124] s.3. This is inserted to encourage early settlements.

[125] s.8(2).

[126] s.4.

[127] See *http://www.dwp.gov.uk/other-specialists/compensation-recovery-unit/* [Accessed April 25, 2011]. Note also the right of the NHS to recover the costs of treatment at a NHS hospital for victims of road traffic accidents: Health and Social Care (Community Health and Standards) Act 2003, which establishes the Injury Costs Recovery Scheme which permits the NHS to recover the cost of hospital treatment and/or ambulance services from a person liable to pay compensation: see Pt 3 and ss.150–169 (in force, 2007: SI 2006/3397) and is also administered by CRU. This does not, however, include disease cases, unless the disease in question is attributable to the injury suffered, nor any compensation payments made under the Fatal Accidents Act 1976 in respect of the deceased person. There is also a limit to the amount of NHS charges that can be recovered. This is known as the "capped" tariff amount and increases every year (in 2010 £42,999 (S.I. 2010/189)). Further, contributory negligence will be taken into account. Contrast the position of the local authority: *Islington LBC v University College Hospital NHS Trust* [2005] EWCA Civ 596; [2006] P.I.Q.R. P3.

[128] See s.1(3) of the 1997 Act.

The 1997 Act is more generous to claimants than the earlier Social Security Act 1989.[129] Benefits are now deducted only from certain heads of damages, namely loss of earnings, cost of care and loss of mobility, which are set out in Sch.2. This Schedule helpfully lists the relevant benefits to be deducted from each individual head. On this basis, income support will be deducted from any award for loss of earnings, and attendance allowance from damages for the costs of nursing and care. The state can no longer deduct any sum from damages awarded for pain and suffering and loss of amenity, because there is no equivalent state benefit. The defendant, who remains liable to the Secretary of State for "an amount equal to the total amount of the recoverable benefits",[130] may therefore be in a difficult position. Consider the following example. The claimant suffers injuries in an accident caused by the defendant's negligence. Damages are assessed at £10,000 (£7,000 loss of earnings and £3,000 non-pecuniary losses). The claimant has received £8,000 in income support. Under the 1997 Act, the defendant is liable to pay £8,000 to the state, although the claimant's award will only be reduced by £7,000 as no deduction can be made against non-pecuniary losses. The claimant will in such circumstances receive £3,000 damages (£10,000 minus £7,000). The defendant will be liable to pay £11,000 in total (£8,000 to the state and £3,000 to the claimant).[131]

The 1989 Act had separate provisions for damages for £2,500 or less, but at present, there is no provision for small payments under the 1997 Act.[132]

The current law on deductions therefore demonstrates no clear overall policy. Whilst trying to prevent over-compensation, the courts are generous in relation to charitable donations, insurance and pensions, but tough in relation to sick pay. The current distinction between a disablement pension and sick pay also demonstrates the confusion existing in this area of law.[133] The strict line taken in relation to recovery of social security benefits may additionally be criticised. The system involves administration costs, and may leave the successful claimant without any damages and the defendant incurring considerable costs in ascertaining his or her liability to the state. In examining the current legal position, the Law Commission concluded that in view of the lack of consensus as to any reform, it could not at present recommend any changes to the law.[134] Nevertheless, the Commission hoped that its report might assist the judiciary, and also the Government, in developing this area of law. The confusion is therefore likely to continue in the immediate future.

[129] Later incorporated in the Social Security Administration Act 1992. The 1997 Act came into force on October 6, 1997.

[130] s.6(1).

[131] The Court of Appeal in *Griffiths v British Coal Corpn* [2001] EWCA Civ 336; [2001] 1 W.L.R. 1493 modified this result slightly by allowing defendants to offset their liability to the State against any award of interest under each head. Further potential difficulties arise due to the failure of the 1997 Act to make allowances for any reduction in the claimant's damages for contributory negligence.

[132] Although it is possible for the Secretary of State to make regulations exempting payments below a certain amount: Sch.1, Pt 2.

[133] See Law Commission Report No.262, *Damages for Personal Injury: Medical, Nursing and Other Expenses; Collateral Benefits* (1999). The Commission rejected (at paras 11.51–11.52) treating pensions and sick pay alike and deducting both. It felt that there would be practical difficulties in distinguishing between some disablement pensions and some insurance policies.

[134] Law Commission Report No.262, *Damages for Personal Injury: Medical, Nursing and Other Expenses; Collateral Benefits* (1999), para.11.53.

*(5) Expenses*

**17–030**  The claimant can also recover reasonably incurred expenses, which will include medical expenses, increased living expenses and the cost of transport to and from hospital.[135] These will include past and future expenses incurred due to the injury. It is not unreasonable to choose private medical treatment instead of treatment under the National Health Service. Section 2(4) of the Law Reform (Personal Injuries) Act 1948 provides that the claimant is not obliged to use the NHS to mitigate loss.[136] Equally, provided that there is no risk of double recovery, claimants are entitled to claim cost of future private health care even where a local authority would have a statutory obligation to care and accommodate them.[137] However, any saving the claimant makes due to being wholly or partly maintained at public expense in a hospital, nursing home or other institution will be set off against any loss of income due to the injury.[138] The courts are careful to avoid overcompensation, and therefore will deduct the cost of food, heating, etc. from the award.[139]

*Cost of a carer*

**17–031**  A further expense following a serious accident may be the cost of a carer.[140] The court again will award compensation for the cost of a carer if such expense is reasonably incurred. However, the carer in question may not be a professional carer, but a close relative or partner who wishes to care for their loved one. Such relatives are unlikely to charge a fee, but of course make considerable sacrifice in both financial and emotional terms. The Court of Appeal in *Donnelly v Joyce*[141] recognised that such carers should not go unrewarded.

In *Donnelly v Joyce*, the victim's mother had given up her part-time job to nurse her six-year-old son. The court awarded a sum for her nursing services, but held that the loss was suffered by the victim, namely the need to receive nursing services due to the tort. It was not the loss of the mother which was being compensated. The court held, however, that it was unnecessary to show a contract between the victim and his mother to obtain the award.[142]

---

[135] *Cunningham v Harrison* [1973] Q.B. 942. The courts will reject "unreasonable" expenses, for example, the costs of surrogacy with a slim chance of success: *Briody v St Helen's & Knowsley HA* [2001] EWCA Civ 1010; [2002] Q.B. 856, CA.

[136] The Government in its Consultation Paper, *The Law on Damages* (CP 09/07, May 2007) queried whether the time had come to repeal this section to prevent litigants claiming the cost of medical care and then using the NHS free of charge, although there seems little empirical evidence to suggest this is widespread in practice: Ch.5.

[137] *Peters v East Midland Strategic Health Authority* [2009] EWCA Civ 145; [2010] Q.B. 48. Where the claimant lacks capacity (as in *Peters*) the Court held that the Court of Protection could provide against the risk of double recovery eg by requiring notification of any future application for public funding of the claimant's care.

[138] Administration of Justice Act 1982 s.5. *Lim Poh Choo v Camden and Islington Area Health Authority* [1980] A.C. 174 applies the same rule to private care. See, by analogy, deduction applied to claims for compensation for loss of earnings by victims of miscarriages of justice: *R. (on the application of O'Brien) v Independent Assessor* [2007] UKHL 10; [2007] 2 A.C 312.

[139] See *Housecroft v Burnett* [1986] 1 All E.R. 332.

[140] A recent decision suggested that this may extend to the cost of palliative care prior to death, despite the fact that hospices do not charge for care but request a voluntary contribution from relatives: *Drake v Foster Wheeler Ltd* [2010] EWHC 2004 (QB); [2011] 1 All E.R. 63 (criticism: Cooksley [2010] J.P.I.L. 203).

[141] [1974] Q.B. 454.

[142] The Court of Appeal in *Hardwick v Hudson* [1999] 3 All E.R. 426 distinguished this situation from where the victim's wife had provided commercial services for the claimant's business. Different considerations apply in a commercial environment where such services are usually paid for and the victim could only recover if there was evidence of an express or implied contract for the work. This approach is approved by the Law Commission in their Report No.262, *Damages for Personal Injury: Medical, Nursing and Other Expenses; Collateral Benefits* (1999).

*Donnelly* was taken a step further by the House of Lords in *Hunt v Severs*.[143] In this case, the victim had been injured when riding as a pillion passenger on a motorbike driven by the defendant, who later became her husband. In claiming damages, she requested a sum for her carer, namely her husband. The House of Lords held that although the sum was awarded to the victim, it would be held on trust for the carer.[144] Here, the carer and the defendant were the same person. On this basis, the court held that there was no ground in public policy or otherwise to justify requiring the defendant to pay a sum to the claimant to be held on trust for himself.

On its face, the decision of the House of Lords seems entirely correct. It would be ridiculous to force the defendant to pay a sum to the claimant to be paid back to the defendant, but this ignores the reality of the situation. The husband was insured, and therefore the person paying the money (the real defendant) was not the husband, but his insurance company.[145] On this analysis, there is nothing wrong with an insurance company paying a sum to the wife to compensate her carer, whoever he or she may be. Following *Hunt v Severs*, if the carer is the tortfeasor, in order to obtain full compensation, the victim is forced to contract for a carer or use a different relative, even though the best person to care for the victim may be the tortfeasor. Certain disabilities render the victim very wary of strangers, and it seems a worrying development for the law to penalise a victim financially for choosing to be cared for by a loved one who happened to have caused the accident in question. The Law Commission, in their 1999 report, recommended that there should be a legislative provision reversing the result in *Hunt*, and that the carer should have a legal entitlement to the claimant's damages for past (although not future) care.[146] The Labour Government in its 2007 Consultation Paper, *The Law on Damages*[147] proposed that the claimant should be under a personal obligation to account to the carer for damages awarded for past and future care, but that where services were provided by the defendant, damages could only be awarded for future gratuitous services. The current Government, elected in May 2010, has decided, however, not to proceed with these reforms.[148]

The cost of a carer is generally assessed at the commercial rate for such services.[149] If a mother gives up a highly paid employment, the loss will be capped at the commercial rate for the services provided.[150] Equally, if, due to the accident, a person cannot undertake the household tasks undertaken prior to injury, the reasonable cost of substitute services should be awarded.[151]

---

[143] [1994] 2 A.C. 350. See D. Kemp (1994) 110 L.Q.R. 524.

[144] Adopting the view of Lord Denning M.R. in *Cunningham v Harrison* [1973] Q.B. 942 at 951–952. Watson and Barrie highlight the practical difficulties that might arise if this was treated strictly as a trust: see (2003) 19 PN. 320.

[145] Lord Bridge held that at common law the fact that the defendant is insured can have no relevance in assessing damages: [1994] 2 A.C. 350 at 363.

[146] Law Commission Report No.262 (1999) paras 3.76 and 3.62. The High Court of Australia has refused to follow *Hunt* and followed the principle of *Donnelly v Joyce: Kars v Kars* (1996) 141 A.L.R. 37.

[147] Government Consultation Paper, *The Law on Damages* (CP 09/07, May 2007), at paras 114–120.

[148] Ministry of Justice, *Civil Law Reform Bill: Response to Consultation* (January 2011): *http://www.justice.gov.uk/consultations/docs/consult-response-civil-law-reform-bill.pdf* [Accessed April 25, 2011].

[149] This is usually subject to a discount to represent non-payment of tax and national insurance and the belief that care provided out of love and care makes commercial considerations less relevant: *Evans v Pontypridd Roofing Ltd* [2001] EWCA Civ 1657; [2002] P.I.Q.R. Q5, CA.

[150] *Housecroft v Burnett* [1986] 1 All E.R. 332 at 343 per O'Connor L.J.

[151] See *Daly v General Steam Navigation Co Ltd* [1981] 1 W.L.R. 120. In *Lowe v Guise* [2002] EWCA Civ 197; [2002] Q.B. 1369, the Court of Appeal extended recovery to a claimant who, due to the injury, was unable to continue to provide gratuitous care for his disabled brother on which the family depended.

*(6) Other damages*

**17–032**  The examples of expenses listed above are not exhaustive, and damages claims will often consist of a large number of claims, depending on the particular facts of the case. For example, a claimant may wish to sue for the loss of pension rights or the inability to continue a profitable hobby. Subject to the rules of remoteness, the claimant may sue for any losses which are due to the defendant's tort.

## Non-pecuniary loss

*(1) Pain and suffering*

**17–033**  The court will award a sum which represents the pain and suffering experienced by the claimant. The two are generally considered together. The Law Commission in 1995 defined "pain" as "the physical hurt or discomfort attributable to the injury itself or consequent on it", whilst "suffering" was defined as "mental or emotional distress which the plaintiff may feel as a consequence of the injury: anxiety, worry, fear, torment, embarrassment and the like".[152] It is a subjective test, and no sum will be awarded if the claimant is unconscious or unable to experience pain or suffering due to his or her condition.[153] The courts will concentrate on the actual condition of the victim and consider past, present and future suffering.

Section 1(1)(b) of the Administration of Justice Act 1982 also permits an award of damages to victims suffering or likely to suffer on the realisation that their expectation of life has been reduced as a result of the injuries.[154] This will form part of the award for pain and suffering. As the award is subjective, the claimant must be aware of his or her condition. Damages will be refused if the victim is rendered permanently unconscious either immediately or within a short time of the injury. In *Hicks v Chief Constable of South Yorkshire*,[155] for example, where medical evidence indicated that the plaintiffs' daughters, crushed in the Hillsborough disaster, would have lost consciousness within a matter of seconds and would have died within five minutes, the court rejected a claim for the distress suffered by the girls in their last moments.

*(2) Loss of amenity*

**17–034**  This is distinct from pain and suffering and is a claim for the loss of enjoyment of life experienced after the injury. For example, suppose that due to an injury to her leg, the claimant cannot play tennis or go for long country walks as she could prior to the accident. An objective

---

[152] Law Commission Consultation Paper No.140, *Damage for Personal Injury: Non-Pecuniary Loss* (1995), para.2.10. The Law Commission Report No.257, *Damages for Personal Injury: Non-Pecuniary Loss* (April 1999) recommends that the present system of assessment by judges should continue and makes no proposals for reform. In *A v National Blood Authority* [2001] 3 All ER 289 at 382 (discussed in Ch.9), Burton J. was prepared to award the claimants damages under this heading for the social handicap of carrying the Hepatitis C virus.

[153] *H. West & Son Ltd v Shephard* [1964] A.C. 326; *Lim Poh Choo v Camden and Islington Area Health Authority* [1980] A.C. 174 in contrast to loss of amenity which is assessed objectively.

[154] Administration of Justice Act 1982 s.1(1)(a) abolished a claim for loss of expectation of life per se.

[155] [1992] 2 All E.R. 65. See also *Grieves v FT Everard & Sons Ltd* [2007] UKHL 39; [2008] 1 A.C. 281 (no recovery for anxiety caused by fear of future life-threatening disease. Presence of pleural plaques in lungs indicated that the claimant had been exposed to asbestos, but, being symptomless, did not amount to compensatable physical injury).

test is applied, so the fact that the claimant is unable to appreciate this loss is irrelevant. This is clearly seen in *H. West & Son Ltd v Shephard*.[156] Here, the plaintiff had been badly injured in a road traffic accident and had sustained severe head injuries, resulting in cerebral atrophy and paralysis of all four limbs. Due to her injuries, her ability to appreciate her condition was severely limited. She was 41 at the time of accident, but had no prospect of improvement, and required full-time hospital nursing for the rest of her life, which was estimated as five years. The majority of the House of Lords held that she had suffered loss of amenity and approved the trial judge's award of £17,500.[157] The court was not prepared to treat such a victim as dead and reduce the damages on this basis.

This was approved by the House of Lords in *Lim v Camden Area Health Authority*.[158] In this case, a 36-year-old senior psychiatric registrar had suffered extensive and irremediable brain damage following a minor operation. As a result, Dr Lim was barely conscious and totally dependent on others. She was awarded £20,000 for pain and suffering and loss of amenity. This was approved by the House of Lords, which held that *West* could only be reversed by a comprehensive Act of Parliament which dealt with all aspects of damages for personal injury. The court was not prepared to overturn a decision which had formed the basis for settlements and damages awards for almost 20 years. A review of the position was undertaken by the Law Commission which, in its April 1999 Report No.257, *Damages for Personal Injury: Non-Pecuniary Loss*, did not recommend changing the rules for damages for non-pecuniary loss in respect of permanently unconscious or conscious but severely brain-damaged claimants.[159]

The same report stated that damages for non-pecuniary loss in cases of serious personal injury were generally too low, and should be increased generally by a factor of at least 50 per cent for awards over £3,000.[160] It was recommended that this should be achieved by guidelines set down by the Court of Appeal or House of Lords, but if this was not achieved within a reasonable period, then legislation should follow. A five judge Court of Appeal responded in March 2000 in *Heil v Rankin*.[161] In dealing with eight conjoined appeals, Lord Woolf M.R. proposed a more modest increase in awards than that suggested by the Law Commission. His Lordship suggested that in seeking to make compensation awards for non-pecuniary losses which were fair, reasonable and just, the awards should be subject to a tapered increase, from a maximum of one third, to nil when the award was below £10,000. Such increases would take account of the fact that people now live longer, but his Lordship also noted the impact of any increase on the level of insurance premiums.[162] This decision has given rise to a considerable increase in the level of awards. However, the threshold of £10,000, rather than the £3,000 suggested by the Law Commission, has limited the impact of the decision and excluded a large number of claims for minor injuries. In the case itself, Heil lost his appeal because the award was less than £10,000.

---

[156] [1964] A.C. 326 at 368–369 per Lord Pearce. See also *Wise v Kaye* [1962] 1 Q.B. 638.

[157] The minority (Lords Reid and Devlin) favoured a far smaller award.

[158] [1980] A.C. 174.

[159] See paras 2.19 and 2.24.

[160] See para.5.8.

[161] [2001] Q.B. 272. Comment R. Lewis (2001) 64 M.L.R. 100.

[162] *The Times*, March 24, 2000 reported that the Association of British Insurers believed that, following *Heil v Rankin*, the likely rise in premiums would be less than 10 per cent.

*(3) Injury itself*

**17–035**    This is difficult to assess. The courts have developed a system of tariffs which guide judges. Reference is made to previous case law and to the Judicial Studies Board guidelines,[163] with the stated aim of ensuring uniformity whilst keeping the level of such claims within reasonable bounds.

## Interest

**17–036**    Interest will be added to damages depending on the nature of the injury suffered. Unless the claimant is awarded interim damages, he or she will be deprived of the damages award until the case is finally heard in court, which unfortunately may take a considerable amount of time. Section 35A of the Senior Courts Act 1981 provides for interest in actions for personal injuries in which the claimant recovers more than £200, unless the court is satisfied that there are special reasons why interest should not be given.[164] The rates are as follows.

*(1) Pecuniary loss*

**17–037**    No interest will be awarded for future pecuniary loss, because there has been no delay in receipt. For sums due from the date of the accident up to the date of trial, interest will be awarded at half the current short-term rate during that period to reflect the gradual nature of the loss.[165]

*(2) Non-pecuniary loss*

**17–038**    Interest will be awarded at 2 per cent from the date of service of proceedings to the date of trial.[166] The figure is deliberately low, because the only loss suffered is the inability to use the money prior to trial.[167]

## Alternatives to lump sum payments

**17–039**    Damages will usually be awarded, as stated earlier, in the form of a lump sum. This does possess, however, a number of disadvantages. There is a distinct danger that a lump sum may run out due to poor investment, reckless spending, a higher than expected life expectancy, or inflation, leaving the claimant with insufficient funds to meet his or her needs. The lump sum is a "once-and-for-all" payment. This has led to calls for alternative forms of award which

---

[163] Since 1992, the Judicial Studies Board has published *Guidelines for the Assessment of General Damages in Personal Injury Cases* (latest edition: 10th edn, OUP, 2010) and summaries of awards may be found in *Kemp & Kemp: Quantum of Damages* (Sweet and Maxwell, 2011) and in Current Law.

[164] County Courts Act 1984 s.69 makes similar provision for actions in the county court. The interest awarded will be simple interest, although the Law Commission has recommended that the court should have a discretion to award compound interest: Law Commission Consultation Paper No.167, *Compound Interest* (2002) and Report No.287, *Pre-judgment Interest on Debts and Damages* (2004).

[165] See *Jefford v Gee* [1970] 2 Q.B. 130 at 151. *Cookson v Knowles* [1979] A.C. 556 applies the decision to fatal accident cases. Guidelines approved in *A Train & Sons Ltd v Fletcher* [2008] EWCA Civ 413; [2008] 4 All E.R. 699.

[166] See *Birkett v Hayes* [1982] 1 W.L.R. 816 and *Wright v British Railways Board* [1983] 2 A.C. 773. Affirmed in *L (a patient) v Chief Constable of Staffordshire* [2000] P.I.Q.R. Q349, CA, which rejected the argument based on Lord Lloyd's reasoning in *Wells v Wells* [1999] 1 A.C. 345 that the rate should also be set at the I.L.G.S. rate.

[167] Damages for non-pecuniary loss being assessed as at the date of trial.

more closely reflect the actual needs of the claimant. Although there is already provision for provisional damages and interim awards, Parliament has recently shown its support for the use of periodic payments in certain cases. These will be examined below.

*(1) Provisional damages*

Section 32A of the Senior Courts Act 1981[168] provides for provisional damages where it is proved or admitted that there is a chance that, at some definite or indefinite time in the future, the injured person will develop some serious disease, or suffer some serious deterioration in his or her physical or mental condition. Damages will be awarded on the basis that the claimant's condition will not deteriorate, but that the claimant can return to court for further damages if this occurs. The claimant is only entitled, however, to apply once for further damages, and these must be for a disease or type of injury specified in the original action.[169]

**17–040**

In *Willson v Ministry of Defence*,[170] the plaintiff sued his employer following an injury to his ankle at work when he slipped on a polished floor. He applied for an award of provisional damages on the basis that there was a possibility that he would develop arthritis, which might require surgery. Scott Baker J. refused to award provisional damages. The judge asked three questions:

(i) Was there a chance of deterioration?

(ii) Would the deterioration be serious?

(iii) Should the court exercise its discretion in the claimant's favour in the circumstances of the case?

Whilst the plaintiff had shown a chance of deterioration which was measurable, rather than fanciful, the judge held that "serious deterioration" required more than the ordinary progression of a disease. A clear and severable risk was required which would trigger entitlement to further compensation. Arthritis following an ankle injury was not such an event. Epilepsy following a head injury would, however, seem to satisfy this test.[171] In practice, therefore, provisional damages will very rarely be awarded.

*(2) Interim payments*

The court has also, under s.32 of the Senior Courts Act 1981, a discretion to make an interim award prior to trial where the defendant has admitted liability to pay damages, the claimant has obtained judgment against the defendant with damages to be assessed, or where it is

**17–041**

---

[168] Inserted by Administration of Justice Act 1982 s.6. See also CPR r.41.

[169] Damages Act 1996 s.3 provides that a provisional award will not stop the victim's dependants from bringing a claim under the Fatal Accidents Act 1976, but any part of the provisional award which was intended to compensate the victim for pecuniary loss during a period that in the event falls after his or her death shall be taken into account in assessing the amount of any loss of support suffered by the dependants under the Act.

[170] [1991] 1 All E.R. 638.

[171] See *Wan v Fung* [2003] 7 CL 113 (QBD)—1–2 per cent risk sufficient on the facts. See also *Chewings v Williams* [2009] EWHC 2490 (QB); [2010] P.I.Q.R. Q1 (real and not just fanciful chance that claimant would suffer further extremely serious physical damage as a result of chance he would seek surgery with real risk of complications leading to amputation of lower leg).

satisfied that claimant will obtain substantial damages at trial.[172] The court may order an interim payment to be paid in one sum or by instalments.[173]

*(3) Periodic payments[174]*

**17–042**   The option of a structured settlement has been available to claimants from 1988. Here, the idea is to structure the payment of damages such that the traditional lump sum would be replaced by annuities purchased by the tortfeasor and managed by an assurance company.[175] The concept of the structured settlement received a boost in 1987 when the Inland Revenue indicated that the revenue from such annuities would not be taxed. On this basis, the recipient would receive income free from tax, and, if an index-linked annuity was chosen, protected against inflation. If the claimant's disability continued for a long time, there was also the possibility that the annuity might exceed any lump sum. It would also benefit the defendant's insurers, who might be able to negotiate a lower settlement to produce the necessary annual income. Lewis noted in 2006 that since 1988, more than 1500 seriously injured people had received part of their compensation via a structured settlement.[176]

Yet, in recent years, support has increased for a more radical proposal, namely to give the court the power to award periodic payments instead of/in conjunction with a lump sum award.[177] Originally, s.2 of the Damages Act 1996 provided that such awards could only be made with the consent of both parties.[178] As recognised by Lord Steyn, this provision was effectively a dead letter as the consent of both parties was virtually never forthcoming.[179] The majority of the Pearson Commission had recommended that the court should be obliged to award damages for future pecuniary loss caused by death or serious and lasting injury in the form of periodic payments, unless it is satisfied, on the application of the claimant, that a lump sum award would be more appropriate.[180] This proposal was not, however, adopted.

From 2000, however, the Lord Chancellor's Department in two Consultation Papers recommended that the courts should be given the power to order periodic payments for significant future financial loss, which should be reviewable in the light of changing medical or other exceptional circumstances.[181] These proposals now form the basis of ss.100–101 of the Courts Act 2003, which came into force on 1 April 2005, and replace ss.2, 4 and 5 of the Damages

---

[172]   See CPR r.25.6–25.9.

[173]   CPR r.25.6(7).

[174]   See *DCA Guidance on Periodical Payments in Personal Injury cases* (2005) (*http://www.dca.gov.uk/pubs/pps-guidance-final.pdf* [Accessed April 25, 2011]) and R. Lewis "The politics and economics of tort law: Judicially imposed periodical payments of damages" (2006) 69 M.L.R. 418.

[175]   See R. Lewis, *Structured Settlements: the Law and Practice* (Sweet and Maxwell, 1993) and Law Com. No.224 (1994), *Structured Settlements and Interim and Provisional Damages*. Following the Law Commission Report, structured settlements received legislative support in the Finance Act 1995 and Damages Act 1996.

[176]   See R. Lewis (2006) 69 M.L.R. 418 at 420.

[177]   PPOs are distinct from structured settlements in that damages do not have to be calculated as a lump sum which is then "structured" to purchase an annuity. Instead, the courts adopt a "bottom up" approach by which the court assesses the periodical payment the claimant will need for the future, regardless of the capital cost.

[178]   s.2(1): "A court awarding damages in an action for personal injury may, with the consent of the parties, make an order under which the damages are wholly or partly to take the form of periodical payments."

[179]   Lord Steyn in *Wells v Wells* [1999] 1 A.C. 345 at 384.

[180]   *Royal Commission on Civil Liability and Compensation for Personal Injury*, Cmnd 7054 (1978), vol.1, para.576.

[181]   *The discount rate and alternatives to lump sum payments* (March 2000) (*http://www.dca.gov.uk/consult/general/damagesfr.htm* [Accessed April 25, 2011]) and *Damages For Future Loss: Giving the Courts the Power to Order Periodical Payments for Future Loss and Care Costs in Personal Injury Cases* (March 2002) (*http://www.dca.gov.uk/consult/general/periodpay.htm* [Accessed April 25, 2011]). Note also recommendations of the Master of the Rolls' Working Party on Structured Settlements in August 2002.

Act 1996. The revised s.2 of the Damages Act 1996 now states that a court, in awarding damages for future pecuniary loss due to personal injury, "(a) may order that the damages are wholly or partly to take the form of periodical payments, and (b) shall consider whether to make that order."[182] With respect to other forms of damages, the rule remains that the consent of the parties is required.[183] In considering whether periodical payments are appropriate for all or part of an award of damages, the courts will look at all the circumstances of the case and in particular the form of award which best meets the claimant's needs.[184]

One particular concern has been the security of these future payments. What will happen, for example, if the defendant (or his or her insurers) becomes insolvent? Section 2(3) of the Act provides that no order should be made unless the court is satisfied that the continuity of payments is reasonably secure.[185]

Controversy has arisen over one particular provision. Once the court considers that a peri‑ **17–043** odical payment order (PPO) is appropriate, the question of indexation, that is, the rate by which the payment should be increased to cover inflation, should be resolved. Section 2(8) provides that:

> "An order for periodical payments shall be treated as providing for the amount of payments to vary by reference to the retail prices index" (RPI),

but is qualified by s.2(9) which allows for an order to include a provision which disapplies or modifies subs.(8). To what extent does this provision allow claimants to argue for a different index by which their payments should be updated?[186] Despite strong arguments that the RPI should be the ordinary index of choice until Parliament indicated otherwise,[187] the Court of Appeal in *Thompstone v Tameside and Glossop Acute Services NHS Trust*[188] sought to provide general guidance for future courts and accepted that in deciding what order would best meet the claimant's needs, the court should consider the RPI in the light of other alternative indexes.[189] In the cases before the court, the claimants had suffered severe injuries at birth as a result of negligence. In such actions, the main claim is likely to be for future care costs and expert evidence suggested that the wages of carers would increase at a faster rate than the RPI.

---

[182] s.2(1). Note, however, that this power only arises when the matter is before the court, that is, the court is giving judgment on damages or required to approve a settlement made on behalf of a minor or a person lacking capacity. It will not arise when the parties settle out of court.

[183] s.2(2).

[184] CPR r.41.7. This directs the courts to have regard to the factors set out in the Practice Direction 41B (1) which include the scale of the annual payments taking into account any deduction for contributory negligence, and the form of award preferred by the claimant and defendant.

[185] See also s.2(4)–(5) and the provisions of s.101, which substitutes a new s.4 which provides enhanced protection for claimants and replaces the old ss.4 and 5 of the Damages Act 1996.

[186] Such an argument seems to conflict with the approach taken by the Court of Appeal in *Cooke v United Bristol Health Care* [2003] EWCA Civ 1370; [2004] 1 W.L.R. 251 above. The latter issue was resolved in *Thompstone* (see below) by distinguishing *Cooke* on the basis that lump sums raised distinct investment questions to periodical payments.

[187] W. Norris [2005] J.P.I.L. 59.

[188] [2008] EWCA Civ 5; [2008] P.I.Q.R. Q2, approving *Flora v Wakom (Heathrow) Ltd (formerly Abela Airline Catering Ltd)* [2006] EWCA Civ 1103; [2007] 1 W.L.R. 482. Comment: R. Lewis, "The indexation of periodical payments of damages in tort: the future assured?" (2010) 30 L.S. 391.

[189] Suitability should be tested by the following criteria: (i) Accuracy of match of the particular data series to the loss or expenditure being compensated; (ii) Authority of the collector of the data; (iii) Statistical reliability; (iv) Accessibility; (v) Consistency over time; (vi) Reproducibility in the future; and (vii) Simplicity and consistency in application: [2008] EWCA Civ 5 at para.75.

There was thus a danger of the claimant receiving insufficient funds. In such circumstances, the principle of full compensation indicated that use of the ASHE 6115 index (annual earnings survey for care assistants and home carers) would be appropriate, fair and reasonable.

Although the Court of Appeal expressed its wish that the NHS and other defendants would now accept the appropriateness of indexation on the basis of ASHE 6115 in catastrophic injury cases and only seek to reopen the issue on production of significantly different evidence,[190] it remains to be seen whether *Thompstone* will open the door to lengthy discussions of the correct index to be used in relation to PPOs. It will undoubtedly render PPOs more popular with claimants in future.[191]

Section 2B also provides for variation of orders and settlements. If there is a chance that at some time in the future the claimant will, as a result of the tortious act, develop some serious disease or suffer some serious deterioration or enjoy some significant improvement, the court may provide that the order for periodical payments may be varied.[192] These provisions largely reflect those which apply to provisional damages (see above), except significant improvements will also allow for variation and the defendant, as well as the claimant, may apply. It is anticipated that the use of such orders would be very limited.[193]

The aim of these reforms is to promote the widespread use of periodic payments for awards for future pecuniary loss in personal injury cases. It was described at the time as a "revolutionary change".[194] It is important to recognise, however, that such payments are aimed at claimants with long-term or permanent personal injuries where a significant award for future care costs and loss of earnings will be made. They offer few advantages where the level of future loss is low or where the care is only needed for a short time. Most claimants will thus continue to be awarded lump sums.

## ACTIONS ON DEATH

17–044　The death of a victim of a tort gives rise potentially to two different claims: claims from the deceased's estate and from those who were financially dependant on the deceased. Both will be examined below.

### (1) Action by the deceased's estate

17–045　In Ch.16, we looked at the survival of actions for or against the deceased's estate. Such claims are governed by the provisions of the Law Reform (Miscellaneous Provisions) Act 1934. Section 1(1) of the 1934 Act provides for the general survival of actions in tort:

[190] [2008] EWCA Civ 5 at para.100. Indeed, in *Thompstone v Tameside Hospital NHS Trust* [2008] EWHC 2948 (QB); [2009] P.I.Q.R. P9 the High Court set out a model periodical payments order for use in personal injury cases and suggested that departure from it in future cases would have to be justified before being approved by the court.
[191] See N. Bevan (2008) 158 N.L.J. 283: "This decision will propel the periodical payments regime from the backwaters into the mainstream as a means of delivering compensation for future loss in personal injury claims." See also Daykin [2009] J.P.I.L 48.
[192] See Damages (Variation of Periodical Payments) Order 2005 (SI 2005/841), art.2.
[193] See DCA Guidance at para.11.
[194] H. McGregor, *McGregor on Damages* (17th edn, Sweet and Maxwell, 2003).

"... all causes of action subsisting against or vested in [any person on death] shall survive against, or, as the case may be, for the benefit of [the] estate."

It is important to remember that this does not give the estate a cause of action for death itself. It simply means that the estate may pursue actions existing at the time of victim's death.

Damages for pecuniary and non-pecuniary losses up to the date of death may be recovered under the 1934 Act. Any claim for non-pecuniary loss will consist of pain and suffering and loss of amenity during any significant period between injury and death. No sum will be awarded if death is instantaneous or quick.[195] Pecuniary loss may be claimed, but s.1(2)(a) excludes a claim for damages for loss of income in respect of any period after a person's death. Section 1(2)(a) also excludes any award of punitive damages.[196] Any loss or gain to the estate consequent on death will not be taken into account, but a sum in respect of funeral expenses may be claimed.[197] The Law Reform (Contributory Negligence) Act 1945 will also apply to such claims.

## (2) Action by the deceased's dependants

There is a second possible claim arising from the death of the victim. This is a claim not by the deceased's legal representatives, but by those for whom the deceased provided financial support. For example, the death of a victim who is a father is likely to affect his family financially as well as emotionally. At common law, the rule was that the victim's death would not give a cause of action to other persons, even when they were financially dependent on the deceased.[198] However, legislation has intervened, first in the Fatal Accidents Act 1846 (also known as Lord Campbell's Act) and more recently in the form of the Fatal Accidents Act 1976.

17–046

*Fatal Accidents Act 1976*

This consolidates earlier legislation. Sections 1(1) and (2) provide that:

17–047

"(1) If death is caused by any wrongful act, neglect or default which is such as would (if death had not ensued) have entitled the person injured to maintain an action and recover damages in respect thereof, the person who would have been liable if death had not ensued shall be liable to an action for damages, notwithstanding the death of the person injured. (2) ... every such action shall be for the benefit of the dependants of the person ("the deceased") whose death has been so caused."

This is not particularly clear, but s.1 essentially provides an action for damages for the deceased's "dependants", i.e. the group of persons, defined in s.1(3), who were financially dependent on the deceased. The statute creates a hybrid action: it is the action of the dependants, but relies on the fact that the deceased could have sued the tortfeasor. If the deceased's action would have

---

[195] *Hicks v Chief Constable of South Yorkshire* [1992] 2 All E.R. 65.

[196] Law Commission report No.247, *Aggravated, exemplary and restitutionary damages* (1997), para.6.3 proposed that this should be repealed and the Act amended to allow claims to survive for the benefit of the estate of a deceased victim, but that they should not be available against a wrongdoer's estate.

[197] s.1(2)(c).

[198] See *Baker v Bolton* (1808) 1 Camp. 493; 170 E.R. 1033 where the plaintiff failed despite the fact that he "was much attached to his deceased wife and that, being a publican, she had been of great use to him in conducting his business". See also *The Amerika (Admiralty Commissioners v SS Amerika)* [1917] A.C. 38, HL.

failed, for example because the defendant had a good defence or could rely on a valid exclusion clause (unlikely in the event of death),[199] the dependants have no claim. Equally, if the deceased had settled the claim[200] or obtained judgment[201] prior to death,[202] then the dependants have no right of action. Under s.5 of the Act, any damages may be reduced due to the contributory negligence of the deceased. If the dependant has also contributed to the accident, the share of that particular dependant will also be reduced, but this will not affect other dependants.[203]

The dependants will not usually sue in their own right. Section 2 provides for the action to be brought by and in the name of the executor or administrator of the deceased. If there is no such person, or no action has been brought within six months after the demise of the deceased, then an action may be brought by and in the name of all or any of the dependants.[204]

The action, as stated above, is brought on behalf of the deceased's dependants. The court must be satisfied that each dependant:

(1) is a dependant within s.1(3) of the Act; and

(2) was, as a matter of fact, financially dependent on the deceased.

Only if the court is satisfied on (1) and (2) will any sum be awarded. We therefore examine each question in turn.

*(1) Is the claimant a dependant within s.1(3) of the Act?*

**17–048**    Section 1(3) (as amended by the Administration of Justice Act 1982 and Civil Partnership Act 2004) gives a statutory list of those parties classified by law as dependants, namely:

(i) the spouse or former spouse of the deceased;[205]

(ii) the civil partner or former civil partner of the deceased;[206]

(iii) a common law spouse, i.e. a person who was living with the deceased in the same household immediately before the date of the death and had been living with the deceased in the same household for at least two years before that date and was living during the whole of that period as the husband or wife or civil partner of the deceased;

(iv) the deceased's parents, ascendants or anyone treated by the deceased as a parent;

---

[199] Unfair Contract Terms Act 1977 s.2(1) renders invalid terms excluding liability in negligence for personal injury and death if the clause concerns business liability.

[200] *Read v Great Eastern Ry* (1868) L.R. 3 Q.B. 555. Applied in *Thompson v Arnold* [2007] EWHC 1875 (QB); [2008] P.I.Q.R. P1.

[201] *Murray v Shuter* [1976] Q.B. 972.

[202] But not where the deceased's solicitors had negligently discontinued his action *after* his death which does not extinguish the dependants' FAA claim: *Reader v Molesworths Bright Clegg* [2007] EWCA Civ 169; [2007] 1 W.L.R. 1082.

[203] *Dodds v Dodds* [1978] Q.B. 543.

[204] s.2(2), although not more than one action shall lie for and in respect of the same subject matter of complaint (s.2(3), but see now *Cachia v Faluyi* [2001] EWCA Civ 998; [2001] 1 W.L.R. 1966, CA.

[205] Including a person whose marriage to the deceased had been annulled or declared void as well as a person whose marriage to the deceased has been dissolved: s.1(4).

[206] s.1(3)(aa), as inserted by the Civil Partnership Act 2004. This includes a person whose civil partnership with the deceased has been annulled as well as a person whose civil partnership with the deceased has been dissolved: s.1(4A).

(v) the deceased's children (including any person treated as a child of the family in relation to a marriage/civil partnership to which the deceased was at any time a party) and other descendants; and

(vi) any person who is, or is the issue of, a brother, sister, uncle or aunt of the deceased.

Section 1(5) adds that

"for the purposes of subs.(3) above:

(a) any relationship by marriage or civil partnership shall be treated as a relationship of consanguinity (i.e. blood), any relationship of the half blood as a relationship of the whole blood, and the stepchild of any person as his child; and

(b) an illegitimate person shall be treated as the legitimate child of his mother and reputed father."

As can be seen, the above list has been extended to cover stepchildren, adopted and illegitimate children, some cohabitees and, from 2005, civil partners. The provision in relation to cohabitees, brought in under the 1982 amendment, still leaves much to chance,[207] and is further weakened by s.3(4), which states that under s.1(3)(b) [iii above], in assessing damages:

"there shall be taken into account . . . the fact that the dependant had no enforceable right to financial support by the deceased as a result of their living together".[208]

This means that the award for a cohabitee is likely to be lower than for a lawful spouse or civil partner. The Law Commission, in its 1999 report, *Claims for Wrongful Death*, recommended adding a further class of claimant to the s.1(3) list, namely any individual:

"who was being wholly or partly maintained by the deceased immediately before the death or who would, but for the death, have been so maintained at a time beginning after the death".[209]

This is a considerable improvement, which fits neatly with the Commission's stated aim of bringing this area of law into line with the values of modern society. The Government, in its 2007 response, supported only the first part of this test—persons wholly or partly maintained by the deceased immediately before death.[210] The newly elected Coalition Government indicated, however, in January 2011 that it would not proceed with these changes.[211]

[207] See, for example, *Kotke v Saffarini* [2005] EWCA Civ 221; [2005] 2 F.L.R. 517 (claimant unable to obtain compensation for the death of her partner, despite the fact that the relationship had lasted some years and they had a child together due to failure to satisfy s.1(3)(b) test).

[208] The Government in its 2007 Consultation Paper, *The Law on Damages* proposed that s.3(4) should be repealed and replaced by a provision to the effect that the prospect of breakdown in the relationship between the deceased and his or her partner should not be taken into account when assessing damages under the FAA.

[209] para.3.45; Draft Bill, cl.1. A person is treated as being wholly or partly maintained by another if that person "otherwise than for full valuable consideration, was making a substantial contribution in money or money's worth towards his reasonable needs".

[210] *The Law on Damages*, Ch.1 (CP 09/07, May 2007). The second part of the definition was rejected as meeting no significant need, being too open-ended and encouraging loosely framed and speculative claims: at para.8.

[211] Ministry of Justice, "Civil Law Reform Bill: Response to Consultation" (2011): *http://www.justice.gov.uk/ consultations/docs/consult-response-civil-law-reform-bill.pdf* [Accessed April 25, 2011].

*(2) Was the claimant financially dependent on the deceased?*

**17–049**     Even if the individual is within s.1(3), the court will only make an award if it is shown that the individual was financially dependent on the deceased. It is the financial, not emotional, dependency of the claimant on the deceased which is in question.[212] The assessment of damages is dealt with under s.3, which provides that damages should be awarded "as are proportioned to the injury resulting from the death to the dependants respectively". This is far from clear. It seems that the courts will examine whether the individual had a reasonable expectation of pecuniary benefit, as of right or otherwise, from the deceased.[213] This will be assessed at the date of death.[214] Public policy will exclude some forms of benefit, for example if the deceased provided for his family by means of armed robberies.[215] It will be a matter of common sense. For example, if the deceased child helped out in the family business, or the deceased spouse cared for the children and the home, the court will award a sum representing the benefit given to the family. However, if the child was employed by the family business and received a wage, then it would be a different matter, since the family has not suffered any financial loss.[216] The court will have to look at the prospects of the deceased (as we saw in personal injury claims), but also this time the prospects of the dependants. For example, if a husband dies and leaves an elderly wife who was financially dependent on him, then the length of the dependency is unlikely to be long. Equally, children are (hopefully) not financially dependent forever, and account must be made for their increasing independence as they grow older.

One point of controversy has been in estimating the likely period of dependency of a widow. If she remarries, then she has a right to be supported by her new husband and would be overcompensated if she could also claim loss of dependency under the Act. However, the only way to prevent this overcompensation was for the court to estimate the widow's likelihood of remarrying and reduce damages accordingly. It is clearly somewhat objectionable for the court to be seen to assess the widow's possible value on the marriage market, and in view of this, the law was changed by the Law Reform (Miscellaneous Provisions) Act 1971. Section 3(3) of the Fatal Accidents Act 1976 now provides that the court should not take into account the remarriage of the widow or her prospects of remarriage. Arguably, this goes too far in ignoring the fact that the widow may have remarried prior to trial, but if this was not included, the inevitable result would be the postponement of such marriages until after the trial.

Again, this problem was addressed by the Law Commission in their 1999 report, *Claims for Wrongful Death* whose proposals were considered by the Government in its 2007 Consultation Paper, *The Law on Damages*. The Commission recommended that s.3(3) should be repealed, and the fact of a marriage or financially supportive cohabitation taken into account when

---

[212] See Latham L.J. in *Thomas v Kwik Save Stores Ltd, The Times*, June 27, 2000.

[213] See, e.g. *Davies v Taylor* [1974] A.C. 207 where a wife, who had deserted her husband, failed to show some significant prospect, rather than a mere speculative possibility, of a reconciliation with her husband had he lived. Consider also *Welsh Ambulance Service NHS Trust v Williams* [2008] EWCA Civ 81, family members, who worked for family business but received benefits far exceeding the value of their services due to profits created by deceased, deemed dependants.

[214] On this basis, a dependant cannot by his own conduct after death reduce the value of the dependency: *Welsh Ambulance Service NHS Trust v Williams* [2008] EWCA Civ 81, dependency of family members not reduced despite the fact they had successfully taken over the family business.

[215] See *Burns v Edman* [1970] 2 Q.B. 541.

[216] *Sykes v North Eastern Ry* (1875) 44 L.J.C.P. 191.

relevant.[217] This removes the problem of overcompensation, but does not mean a return to pre–1971 law. The Commission proposed that unless a person is engaged to be married at the time of trial, the prospect that he or she will marry, remarry, or enter into financially supportive cohabitation with a new partner, should not be taken into account when assessing the claim.[218] Neither should the prospect of divorce or breakdown in the relationship be taken into account, unless the couple were no longer living together at the time of death, or one of the couple had petitioned for divorce, judicial separation or nullity.[219] The Labour Government agreed in part to these proposals. It endorsed the proposals on divorce or breakdown of the relationship and recommended that the fact of a person's remarriage, entry into a civil partnership and, possibly, financially supportive cohabitation of at least two years following death should be taken into account. This seems a valid compromise and would be a welcome development. Nevertheless, in January 2011, the newly elected Coalition government announced its intention not to proceed with these reforms.[220]

*Assessment*

The courts adopt an approach similar to that used in the assessment of awards for future **17–050** pecuniary loss in a personal injury claim. Again, the claimant will receive a lump sum, which represents the loss of dependency of that particular claimant (although a court in practice will tend to determine the total liability of the defendant and then apportion damages between the various dependants). The court will use the multiplier/multiplicand method. This time the multiplicand will be the net loss of support, namely the deceased's net income less expenditure on his or her own behalf.[221] This will be multiplied by the multiplier. The multiplier will take account of the possible duration of the support, based on the likelihood of continued provision by the deceased and factors such as the life expectancy of the dependant (for example, if the dependant is a widow) or likely period of dependency (for example, if the dependant is a child). It will also be reduced for accelerated receipt.

The multiplier will be set at the date of death, not the date of trial as is the case in personal injury claims.[222] This is because, in contrast to personal injury claims, the court has the added uncertainty of what would have happened to the deceased prior to trial. The multiplier therefore is set at the earlier date to meet this uncertainty. Whilst this is straightforward, it does create a problem of under-compensation for pre-trial losses which, under the multiplier, will also be discounted for early receipt which, of course, does not in fact occur.[223] In any event, the courts will treat the period between death and trial differently and take the deceased's average rate of earnings in the past as the relevant factor on which loss of dependency is assessed.

---

[217] Note also the compromise position taken by the High Court of Australia in *De Sales v Ingrilli* (2002) 193 A.L.R. 130.

[218] para.4.53, Draft Bill, cl.4 and 6(5).

[219] para.4.66, Draft Bill, cl.4.

[220] Civil Law Reform Bill: Response to Consultation (2011).

[221] See *Harris v Empress Motors* [1984] 1 W.L.R. 212 at 216–217 per O'Connor L.J.

[222] See *Cookson v Knowles* [1979] A.C. 556 and *Graham v Dodds* [1983] 1 W.L.R. 808.

[223] See Nelson J. in *White v ESAB Group (UK) Ltd* [2002] P.I.Q.R. Q6 who agreed with the criticisms of the Law Commission that a multiplier which has been discounted for the early receipt of damages should only be used in the calculation of post trial losses, but held that he was bound by House of Lords authority to maintain the current legal position.

*Deductions*

**17–051**   Again, concerns as to overcompensation arise when the deceased's dependants receive money, such as insurance or a widow's pension, from other sources which reduce their financial losses. Here the position is far simpler than for personal injury. Section 4 of the Act provides that:

> "benefits which have accrued or will or may accrue to any person from his estate or otherwise as a result of his death shall be disregarded".[224]

In *Arnup v MW White Ltd*,[225] Smith L.J. clarified that all benefits received as a result of death were to be disregarded. A defendant providing dependants with Ex gratia financial support, could only avoid this result and have the payment taken into account when damages are assessed if the payment was made subject to the stipulation that it was a conditional payment on account. This is very generous (and may be contrasted with the position relating to damages for personal injury described above). Whilst it may be welcomed for its simplicity, it will result in some dependants being overcompensated at the expense of the state or insurance company.

Unfortunately the apparent simplicity of s.4 has been thrown into question by two Court of Appeal decisions which interpret the meaning of "benefit" in that section somewhat differently. In *Stanley v Saddique*,[226] the Court of Appeal was asked whether, in awarding a child damages under the Act following the death of his mother, account should be taken of the fact that his father had remarried soon after his mother's death, and that he received better care from his stepmother. It was argued that this was a benefit which accrued as a result of his mother's death and should be disregarded under s.4. Such a benefit is indirect at best, but the court was prepared to give "benefit" a wide meaning and held that it was not confined to direct payments in money or money's worth. It would include the benefit of absorption into a new family unit of father, stepmother and siblings. On this basis, the child was able to recover damages for the loss of his mother's care, even though he was currently receiving better care from his stepmother. A further implication of *Stanley* is that the benefit of a widow or widower remarrying should be regarded as a "benefit" under s.4 and disregarded. This renders s.3(3) defunct.

*Stanley* can be contrasted with the court's decision in *Hayden v Hayden*.[227] Here, the child's mother had been killed in an accident caused by the negligent driving of the defendant, the child's father. As a result, the defendant gave up work and looked after the child himself, who was four years old at the time of the accident. The majority (McCowan L.J dissenting) held that s.4 did not apply in this case, and therefore the care given by the father would be taken into account when assessing loss of care. The majority judges adopted different reasoning, however. Croom-Johnson L.J. (who had also given judgment in *Stanley*) held that *Stanley* could be distinguished on the facts. In *Stanley*, death had led to an unstable relationship being

---

[224] As amended by Administration of Justice Act 1982, s.3(1). Reg.2(2)(a) of the Social Security (Recovery of Benefits) Regulations 1997 (SI 1997/2205) also provides that the recovery provisions for social security benefits do not apply to fatal accidents claims. See *McIntyre v Harland & Wolff Plc* [2006] EWCA Civ 287; [2006] 1 W.L.R. 2577 for a literal interpretation of the section.

[225] [2008] EWCA Civ 447; [2008] I.C.R. 1064: refusal to deduct sums paid to dependants from death in service benefit scheme and discretionary trust by defendant employer.

[226] [1992] Q.B. 1.

[227] [1992] 1 W.L.R. 986.

replaced by a successful marriage, whereas in *Hayden* the child remained in the family home with her father, who continued to look after her. The continuing care of a father could not be regarded as a benefit accruing as a result of death. Parker L.J., in contrast, chose not to follow *Stanley* in reaching his conclusion,[228] and found that no loss had in fact been suffered when the child enjoyed uninterrupted care.

The law was left far from clear after *Hayden*. The Divisional Court in *R. v Criminal Injuries* **17–052** *Compensation Board, Ex p. K*[229] reviewed the conflict between the two cases and preferred the decision in *Stanley*. *Hayden* was distinguished on its own particular facts, namely that it concerned a situation where the replacement care was provided by the tortfeasor who was an existing carer, who had been looking after the child prior to her mother's death. *Hayden* was further isolated by the Court of Appeal in the later case of *H v S*.[230] Again, the children had been cared for by their father after the death of their mother, but in this case, the parents had been divorced, and the father had lived separately with his new wife. He had, in fact, offered no financial support to the children prior to their mother's death. The court distinguished *Hayden*. It could not be argued that the father was discharging pre-existing parental obligations where he had not supported his children in the past and had shown no real likelihood of doing so in the future. On such a basis, his care was a "benefit" resulting from death which could be disregarded by the court. The situation would have been different, however, if the parents had been living together before the death, or there had been a financial order[231] or actual/potential support in place before the mother died.[232]

*H v S* thus supports the general proposition that the tortfeasor should not be allowed to benefit from the generosity of a third party volunteering to care gratuitously for the victim's dependants by a reduction in the damages awarded. The term "benefit" is thus a disguised claim for the cost of care to be held on trust for the carer by the claimant (see *Hunt v Severs*, above). Yet, in this light, it becomes increasingly difficult to understand why an immediate family member (as in *Hayden*) undertaking greater parental duties should be denied the cost of his care whilst an uncle or estranged father will succeed, unless his claim is to be excluded due to the fact he or she is the tortfeasor.[233] It would seem to penalise parents taking their parental responsibilities seriously. Clarification of the status of cost of care claims for dependants, removed from the artificial wording of s.4, would be a welcome addition to the law.

The operation of s.4 was examined by the Law Commission in *Claims for Wrongful Death*. The Commission's proposal was radical. Section 4 should be repealed and the position in fatal accident claims made consistent with that in personal injury claims. On this basis, charity, insurance, survivors' pensions and inheritance would continue to be non-deductible.[234] The Commission also recommended extending the recoupment of social security benefits to claims under the Fatal

---

[228] Relying on the pre-s.4 case of *Hay v Hughes* [1975] Q.B. 790, CA. This was disapproved by the Divisional Court in *R. v Criminal Injuries Compensation Board, Ex p. K* [1999] Q.B. 1131. Parker L.J. also added as a postscript that difficulties would arise in any event where the carer was in fact the tortfeasor; a reason which the Divisional Court did support (see below).

[229] [1999] Q.B. 1131. It may be noted that the case concerned a claim to the Criminal Injuries Compensation Board. However, the courts use similar criteria to those adopted in ordinary civil claims for damages and so the issue was in point.

[230] [2002] EWCA Civ 792; [2003] Q.B. 965. Comment: M. Lunney [2002] K.C.L.J. 219.

[231] There was a maintenance order in place against the father, but solely for a nominal sum which the court decided to ignore.

[232] See also *L v Barry May Haulage* [2002] P.I.Q.R. Q3.

[233] Assuming, of course, the correctness of *Hunt v Severs* [1994] 2 A.C. 350.

[234] para.5.39, Draft Bill, cl.5.

Accidents Act. Whilst this makes economic sense and would clarify the law, it is unlikely to prove popular with the public, as it would have a significant impact on the level of dependants' claims. It was not adopted by the Government in its 2007 Consultation Paper on damages.

*Damages for bereavement*

**17–053**   It should be noted that under s.1A of the Act (as inserted by s.3 of the Administration of Justice Act 1982 and amended by the Civil Partnership Act 2004), bereavement damages will be awarded to:

- the spouse or civil partner of the deceased; or

- the parents (the mother only if the child is illegitimate) of a minor who was never married or a civil partner.

This is a rare example of a third party succeeding in a claim for mental distress, which is rarely compensated in the law of torts, although it is important to note that the claimant need not prove actual distress.[235] It is in reality a form of consolatory damages. This is shown by the relatively low amount awarded, which is increased periodically: the current figure is £11,800.[236] The sum will be awarded to the spouse/civil partner or between the parents equally[237] and the claim does not survive for the benefit of the recipient's estate on death.[238]

The Law Commission, in its 1999 report, *Claims for Wrongful Death*, proposed a significant reform of bereavement damages. First of all, their availability should be extended to include the child of the deceased (including adoptive children), the parents of the deceased (including adoptive parents), a fiancé(e), a brother or sister of the deceased (including adoptive brothers and sisters) and a cohabitee who lived with the deceased for not less than two years immediately prior to the accident.[239] This latter provision would include same sex relationships. Secondly, the Commission recommended that the sum should increase to £10,000, and should be linked to the Retail Prices Index.[240] The award would be reduced if the deceased had been contributorily negligent.

In its 2007 consultation paper, *The Law on Damages*, the Labour Government announced its intention (at para.60) to increase the award of bereavement damages on a regular basis in line with the Retail Prices Index (rounded to the nearest £100). By increasing the sum every three years in line with inflation, the Goverment seeks to ensure a regular and consistent increase which will assist insurers and the NHS in building the effect of future increases into their reserves and financial plans. Consistent with this intention, the amount was raised from £10,000 to £11,800 on January 1, 2008. From 2005, civil partners have been able obtain bereavement damages and the Government proposed a more limited extension than that put forward by the Law Commission: to children of the deceased under 18 at the time of death

---

[235] For claims for mental distress in tort generally, see P. Giliker (2000) 20 L.S. 19.

[236] See the Damages for Bereavement (Variation of Sum) (England and Wales) Order 2007 (SI 2007/3489). The amount was previously increased from £3,500 to £7,500 by the Damages for Bereavement (Variation of Sum) (England and Wales) Order 1990 (SI 1990/2575) from April 1, 1991, and to £10,000 under the Damages for Bereavement (Variation of Sum) (England and Wales) Order 2002 (SI 2002/644) from April 1, 2002.

[237] s.1A(4).

[238] Law Reform (Miscellaneous Provisions) Act 1934 s.1A.

[239] para.6.31, Draft Bill, cl.2.

[240] such damages would be capped at £30,000 and, if there are more than three claimants, apportioned accordingly: paras 6.41–6.51, Draft Bill, cl.2.

(confined to half the full award i.e. £5,900 each), any person living with the deceased as spouse/civil partner for at least two years immediately prior to the accident,[241] and unmarried fathers with parental responsibility.[242] This, in the Government's view, will:

> "strike an appropriate balance between making this award available to those in what are generally regarded as the closest categories of relationship to the deceased and ensuring that any expansion of compensation is proportionate and reasonable."[243]

Despite general approval for such reforms in the consultation exercise, the current Government in 2011 concluded that the proposed reforms "would not contribute to the delivery of the Government's key priorities".[244]

## ACTIONS FOR LOSS OR DAMAGE TO PROPERTY

This will be dealt with briefly. Loss or damage to property is subject to the same compensatory **17–054** principles outlined above: to put, as far as possible, the claimant in the position as if the tort had not taken place.[245] Where the property has been totally destroyed, the courts will assess the market value of the property at the time and place of its destruction. The market value is the sum of money required to enable the claimant to purchase a replacement in the market at the price prevailing at the date of destruction or as soon thereafter as is reasonable. The claimant will also be able to claim consequential damages, provided they are not too remote. A good example may be found in the case of *Liesbosch Dredger v SS Edison*.[246] Here, the plaintiffs' dredger had been sunk as a result of the defendants' negligence. The court awarded the plaintiffs the market value of a comparable dredger, the cost of adapting the new dredger, insuring it and transporting it to where they were working, and compensation for disturbance and loss in carrying out their contract work from the date of the loss until a substitute dredger could reasonably have been available for use. A claimant will also be able to claim for such things as the reasonable amount of hire of a substitute until a replacement can be bought.[247] The claimant is unlikely to be awarded the cost of restoration of the property, unless there are exceptional circumstances, for example that there is no market for the property destroyed.[248]

If the property is merely damaged, then the court will award a sum for the diminution in value of the property, normally assessed as the cost of repair.[249] The cost of repair will normally be calculated at the time of damage, but there are exceptions to this rule where it would lead to

---

[241] Should the deceased have both a spouse/partner from whom s/he is separated and a cohabiting partner of over two years duration, the sum will be divided between the two: at para.64.

[242] Government Consultation Paper, *The Law on Damages* (CP 09/07, May 2007) Ch.2.

[243] Government Consultation Paper, *The Law on Damages* (CP 09/07, May 2007) at para.65.

[244] Ministry of Justice, "Civil Law Reform Bill: Response to Consultation" (2011) at p.3.

[245] *Livingstone v Rawyards Coal Co* (1880) 5 App. Cas. 25 at 39 per Lord Blackburn.

[246] [1933] A.C. 449. The case is also authority for the rule that losses incurred due to impecuniosity are not recoverable. This rule was overturned by the House of Lords in *Lagden v O'Connor* [2003] UKHL 64; [2004] 1 A.C. 1067 on the basis that the law has moved on and that such a rule would be inconsistent with the general rules of remoteness: see Lord Hope at 1590.

[247] See *Moore v DER Ltd* [1971] 1 W.L.R. 1476.

[248] *Hall v Barclay* [1937] 3 All E.R. 620.

[249] *The London Corporation* [1935] P. 70.

injustice,[250] for example where it is reasonable for the claimant to postpone repairs to a later date.[251] The cost of repair will only be awarded if reasonable in the circumstances. Consistent with the duty to mitigate, the court will not award such damages if they exceed the market value of the goods, although allowance is made if the goods are unique.[252] If the claimant reasonably intends to sell the property in its damaged state, the court will not award the cost of repair, but a sum representing the diminution in capital value of the property. Consequential damages may be awarded, such as cost of substitute hire[253] and loss of use during the period of repairs.

## JOINT AND SEVERAL LIABILITY

**17–055**    So far we have looked at damages generally. This section will examine the legal position where two or more defendants are liable for the same damage,[254] that is, where two or more defendants have committed concurrent torts which lead to a single indivisible injury.[255] This is distinct from the situation where the claimant has suffered different injuries due to the independent actions of two or more people—here it is for the claimant to bring independent claims against each of them. Our situation is where A has suffered one set of injuries resulting from an incident where both D1 and D2 are at fault, for example A was hit when crossing the road because of a car crash between two cars negligently driven by D1 and D2. Here the defendants are said to be jointly and severally liable. This means that the claimant has the choice to sue one or all of the defendants. In either case, the claimant will receive the full amount of damages. Therefore, if A suffered damages assessed at £300,000, A could sue D1 or D2 or both D1 and D2 for this sum. This means that the claimant can sue any of the defendants without worrying whether all the possible defendants are in court, and is able to avoid defendants who have no funds or are uninsured. It is of no concern to the claimant that one defendant is paying for liability for which he or she is only partially at fault.

It will, however, be seen differently from the perspective of the defendant who is the only person sued, but in fact only partially at fault. This situation is now governed by the Civil Liability (Contribution) Act 1978.[256] Section 1(1) provides that:

---

[250] See Lord Wilberforce in *Miliangos v George Frank (Textiles) Ltd* [1976] A.C. 443 at 468.

[251] *Dodd Properties (Kent) Ltd v Canterbury City* Council [1980] 1 W.L.R. 433 where it made commercial good sense to delay repairs until the time when the action had been heard and liability decided. See also *Alcoa Minerals of Jamaica Inc v Broderick* [2002] 1 A.C. 371 (PC), applied by the CA in *Smith v South Gloucestershire DC* [2002] EWCA Civ 1131; [2002] 38 E.G. 206.

[252] See *O'Grady v Westminster Scaffolding* [1962] 2 Lloyd's Rep. 238: 1938 MG car known as Mademoiselle Hortensia!

[253] Although the court will seek proof that the goods were indeed hired and that the price paid was reasonable: HL *Motorworks (Willesden) Ltd v Alwahbi* [1977] R.T.R. 276, CA. On the use of credit hire companies, see the House of Lords in *Dimond v Lovell* [2002] 1 A.C. 384 and *Lagden v O'Connor* [2003] UKHL 64; [2004] 1 A.C. 1067 (cost of credit hire agreement recoverable when claimant could not afford hire of a private car while his car was being repaired, but note the limitations: *Beechwood Birmingham Ltd v Hoyer Group UK Ltd* [2010] EWCA Civ 647; [2010] 3 W.L.R. 1677 (motor dealer with substantial stock of alternative vehicle denied cost of hire)).

[254] "Same damage" is be interpreted according to its natural and ordinary meaning and does not extend to substantially or materially similar damage: *Royal Brompton Hospital NHS Trust v Hammond (No. 3)* [2002] UKHL 14; [2002] 1 W.L.R. 1397, HL. For discussion of the application of the principle of joint and several liability to victims of mesothelioma and asbestosis, see Ch.6.

[255] *Rahman v Arearose Ltd* [2001] Q.B. 351, CA, although the application of the rule in this case is questionable: see T. Weir [2001] C.L.J. 237.

[256] See generally T. Dugdale (1979) 42 M.L.R. 182 and Law Commission, *Report on Contribution* No.79 (1977).

"any person liable in respect of any damage suffered by another person may recover a contribution from any other person liable in respect of the same damage".

Liability includes liability in tort, for breach of contract, breach of trust or otherwise.[257] The defendant (D1) may therefore claim a contribution from any other wrongdoer (D2) responsible for the "same damage" for the amount by which his payment to the claimant exceeds his responsibility for the loss.[258] The contribution must be claimed, however, within the limitation period of two years.[259]

## Assessment

Section 2 deals with assessment of contribution. Section 2(1) provides that:                    **17–056**

"in any proceedings under s.1 above the amount of the contribution recoverable from any person shall be such as may be found by the court to be just and equitable having regard to the extent of that person's responsibility for the damage in question".

This is very similar to the wording of s.1 of the Law Reform (Contributory Negligence) Act 1945 and the same principles seem to apply. The courts will look at causation, and at times, the blameworthiness of the defendants involved.[260] The court has a considerable discretion and may even, if it considers it appropriate, at one extreme, exempt the defendant from any liability to make a contribution or, at the other extreme, direct that the contribution to be recovered from any person shall amount to a complete indemnity.[261] The court will also take into account any defence of contributory negligence, any enforceable exclusion clause[262] and any statutory limits on liability which the other wrongdoer could have used against the original claimant.[263] The Act also does not stop any tortfeasor contracting to indemnify him or herself against liability for contribution.[264]

By this means, the claimant is fully compensated and it is for the defendants to sort out the division of responsibility between them. A good example is *Fitzgerald v Lane*,[265] discussed in Chs

---

[257] s.6(1).

[258] D1 is entitled to recover a contribution ". . . notwithstanding that he has ceased to be liable in respect of the damage in question since the time when the damage occurred, provided that he was liable immediately before he made or was ordered or agreed to make the payment in respect of which the contribution is sought": s.1(2).

[259] Limitation Act 1980 s.10. Time runs from the date on which the right to a contribution accrues, which is the date on which the judgment is given, the date of the arbitration award or the date on which the amount of settlement is agreed between the defendant and the person to whom the payment is to be made: ss.10(3), (4) of the Limitation Act 1980. The relevant date for the running of time against a tortfeasor who sought contribution under the 1978 Act was a judgment or award that ascertained the quantum, and not merely the existence, of the tortfeasor's liability: *Aer Lingus Plc v Gildacroft Ltd* [2006] EWCA Civ 4; [2006] 1 W.L.R. 1173.

[260] See *Madden v Quirk* [1989] 1 W.L.R. 702; *Re-Source America International Ltd v Platt Site Services Ltd* [2004] EWCA Civ 665; [2004] N.P.C. 89 and *Brian Warwicker Partnership Plc v HOK International Ltd* [2005] EWCA Civ 962; [2006] P.N.L.R. 5: causative responsibility is likely to be the most important factor, but the court can consider non-causative fault.

[261] s.2(2). Apportionment by the trial judge will only be interfered with on appeal where it is clearly wrong or where there has been an error in principle or a mistake of fact: *Kerry v Carter* [1969] 1 W.L.R. 1372 at 1376.

[262] Subject to the Unfair Contract Terms Act 1977, discussed in Ch.16.

[263] s.2(3).

[264] s.7(3).

[265] [1989] A.C. 328.

6 and 16, where the plaintiff had negligently stepped out into traffic on busy road and had been struck by a vehicle driven by the first defendant, which pushed him into the path of the second defendant's car. Both the defendants were negligent, but the plaintiff had also been contributorily negligent in not looking properly before crossing the road. The House of Lords held the plaintiff to be 50 per cent contributorily negligent. It then examined the position of the two defendants and found that they were jointly and severally liable, but that each of them was 25 per cent responsible for the injuries. Thus, if only one defendant had been sued, he would have been liable to the claimant for 50 per cent of the damages due, but could have claimed a contribution from the other driver of 25 per cent. In practice, the parties will attempt to get all other relevant parties before the court, and a defendant may take advantage of the "third party" procedure to add a defendant to the case, even when that person has not been mentioned in the claimant's statement of case.[266]

## Settlements

**17–057**  The 1978 Act also makes special provision for settlements. A settlement does not deprive a defendant, who has agreed to make a payment in bona fide settlement or compromise of the claim, from seeking a contribution from any other parties he or she believes liable for the same damage.[267] However, a settlement with one defendant which is "full and final and in satisfaction of all causes of action" may prevent the claimant from pursuing other tortfeasors responsible for the same damage,[268] although much depends on the context and the actual words used.[269]

## OTHER REMEDIES

### Self-help

**17–058**  Reference should be made to earlier chapters where we have discussed other remedies available for specific torts. Readers should specifically note occasions where the claimant can resort to self-help. In Ch.10, we looked at abatement in nuisance, and in Ch.11 we saw that the claimant may use reasonable force to resist trespass. However, such rights should to be exercised with extreme caution. Overstepping the mark can lead to legal action, as the householder found in *Revill v Newbery*[270] when he was found liable to a burglar while seeking to defend his allotment shed with a gun (see Chs 8, 11 and 16). Here, we will concentrate on the equitable remedy of an injunction.

---

[266]  See now Civil Procedure Rules, Pt 19: Parties and group litigation.
[267]  Provided the defendant would have been liable assuming that the factual basis of the claim against him could be established: see s.1(4). For the impact of a settlement on potential claims by the victim's dependants, see *Jameson v CECB (No.1)* [2000] 1 A.C. 455.
[268]  See *Jameson v CECB (No.1)* [2000] 1 A.C. 455, HL, which was applied in *Rawlinson v North Essex HA* [2000] Lloyd's Rep Med 54.
[269]  *Heaton v Axa Equity & Law Life Assurance Society Plc* [2002] UKHL 15; [2002] 2 A.C. 329, HL.
[270]  [1996] Q.B. 567.

# Injunctions

Injunctions are an important tool by which the court can order the defendant to stop a continuing or recurring act, or order the defendant to act in a certain way. The courts will only grant
an injunction if the claimant has a good cause of action; the most obvious examples being
nuisance or trespass.[271] It is an equitable remedy and so lies at the discretion of the court. An
injunction cannot be demanded as of right, and will not be awarded where damages are an
adequate remedy, or where the claimant's conduct is such that it would not be equitable to
make such an award. The court has the option to award damages in addition to or in substitution for an injunction,[272] but a court will only award damages instead of (or "in lieu of") an
injunction in exceptional circumstances. The leading case is that of *Shelfer v City of London
Electric Lighting Co*[273] where A.L. Smith L.J. laid down the four conditions which would lead
a court to grant damages in lieu of an injunction:

**17–059**

    (i) where the injury to the claimant's legal rights is small;

    (ii) where the injury is capable of being estimated in money;

    (iii) where it can be adequately compensated by a small money payment; and

    (iv) where it would be oppressive to the defendant to grant an injunction.

The court in *Shelfer* was keen to resist greater use of damages in lieu of an injunction, as it
would amount to a licence to commit a nuisance. For example, if drilling at night entitled the
claimant to an injunction, but the court chose to award damages of £5,000, this would entitle
the defendant to drill at a cost of £5,000. The court felt that damages should not be used to
legalise a wrongful act by placing a premium on the right to injure the claimant's legal rights.[274]
The authority of *Shelfer* was recently affirmed by the Court of Appeal in *Regan v Paul
Properties Ltd*[275] and *Watson v Croft Promo-Sport Ltd*.[276]

There are a number of different types of injunction, which will be discussed below.

*Prohibitory and mandatory injunctions*

A prohibitory injunction is an injunction which orders the defendant not to act in a certain way.
This is the most common injunction granted, and deals with situations where, unless it is granted,
the defendant is likely to continue acting in a tortious manner. A mandatory injunction, in contrast,
is an injunction ordering the defendant to act in a certain way, and is granted more rarely. The
courts will look at the facts of the case and decide whether damages would be appropriate. For
example, the courts are generally more likely to award damages in lieu of an injunction where the
defendant has obstructed the claimant's right to light, or the defendant has erected a building in

**17–060**

---

[271] Injunctive relief is not generally be granted for negligence, but see J. Murphy (2007) 27 O.J.L.S. 509.
[272] See now Senior Courts Act 1981 s.50.
[273] [1895] 1 Ch.287. See also J.A. Jolowicz [1975] C.L.J. 224 and our discussion in Ch.10.
[274] But see *Jaggard v Sawyer* [1995] 1 W.L.R. 269.
[275] [2006] EWCA Civ 1391; [2007] Ch.135 (comment D. Fox [2007] C.L.J 267): it is for the defendant to demonstrate that the four conditions of *Shelfer* have been satisfied.
[276] [2009] EWCA Civ 15; [2009] 3 All E.R. 249 where Sir Andrew Morritt reiterated that the fact that the wrongdoer
is in some sense a public benefactor is not in itself a sufficient reason for refusing an injunction, although it should be
taken into account in marginal cases where the damage to the claimant is minimal.

breach of a restrictive covenant.[277] The court must also be careful that, in granting an injunction, it ensures that the defendant knows exactly what in fact he or she has to do or not to do.[278]

*Interim injunctions*[279]

**17–061** Prohibitory and mandatory injunctions can be given provisionally prior to the final hearing (interim injunctions), or at the final hearing (perpetual injunctions). The court, faced with an application for an interim injunction, is in a difficult position. The rights of the parties have yet to be determined, and the full facts of the case have yet to be set out. Nevertheless, due to the likely harm of letting the defendant's conduct continue, the court may award an interim injunction but place conditions on its grant. For example, it is common for the court to require the claimant to give an undertaking to pay damages to the defendant for any loss suffered while the injunction is in force, should it prove to be wrongfully issued. This may be expensive. For example, the claimant (C) obtains an interim injunction which prevents the defendant (D) from operating his car plant during the night. At the full hearing of C's claim for nuisance, it is found that the area is classified as an industrial zone and the conduct does not amount to a nuisance. C therefore had no right to an interim injunction, and may find himself liable for the loss of profits experienced by D during the period of the injunction. The principles for the grant of an interim injunction are set out in *American Cyanamid Co v Ethicon Ltd*,[280] and reference should be made to specific practitioners' texts. It should be noted that, as seen in Ch.14, the courts are very reluctant to impose interim injunctions for claims for libel, despite *American Cyanamid*. If the defendant has pleaded justification, fair/honest comment or qualified privilege, the court will only grant such an injunction when convinced that the defence will fail. The Court of Appeal in *Greene v Associated Newspapers Ltd*[281] recently confirmed that such a rule was consistent with the European Convention of Human Rights and that a lesser test would seriously weaken the effect of art.10.[282] It will, however, be marginally easier to obtain an interim injunction for breach of confidence/misuse of private information.[283] In *Cream Holdings Ltd v Banerjee*,[284] the House of Lords found, having regard to s.12(3) of the Human Rights Act 1998,[285] that, in most cases, an interim injunction should only be awarded

---

[277] [1995] 1 W.L.R. 269 at 284. Much, however, will depend on the facts of each case: see *Regan v Paul Properties Ltd* [2006] EWCA Civ 1391; [2007] Ch.135.

[278] per Lord Upjohn in *Redland Bricks Ltd v Morris* [1970] A.C. 652 at 666.

[279] See CPR Pt 25.

[280] [1975] A.C. 396.

[281] [2004] EWCA Civ 1462; [2005] Q.B. 972.

[282] For example, that it was more likely than not that the defendant could not show that what it wished to say about the claimant was true. The Court of Appeal accepted that a different rule would apply for breach of confidence: see below.

[283] The courts accept that there is currently a difference between the treatment of interlocutory injunctions in defamation and privacy law: see *LNS v Persons Unknown* [2010] EWHC 119 (QB); [2010] 2 F.L.R. 1306 (nub of applicant's true complaint was protection of reputation rather than private life and so defamation rule in *Bonnard v Perryman* would be applied).

[284] [2004] UKHL 44; [2005] 1 A.C. 253 (discussed in more detail in Ch.15).

[285] "(3) No such relief is to be granted so as to restrain publication before trial unless the court is satisfied that the applicant is likely to establish that publication should not be allowed."

where it is more likely than not that the applicant will succeed at trial, although there could be no single, rigid standard governing all applications in such cases.[286]

*Quia timet injunctions*

These are injunctions granted to prevent a legal wrong before it occurs. This is obviously an extreme remedy, and the courts will be careful to ensure that the conduct of the defendant is such that substantial damage to the claimant is almost bound to occur, and that damages are not an adequate remedy. As may be expected, the court uses the power to grant such an injunction rarely. The main authority here is Lord Upjohn's judgment in *Redland Bricks Ltd v Morris*,[287] which held that *quia timet* injunctions are granted in two particular types of case:

**17–062**

(1) Where the defendant has, as yet, not harmed the claimant, but is threatening and intending to do so, and if the defendant acts it will cause irreparable harm to the claimant or his or her property; and

(2) Where the claimant has been compensated for past damage, but alleges that the earlier actions of the defendant may lead to future causes of action.

## Remedies: conclusion

The courts therefore employ a number of remedies in dealing with claims in tort. Although the primary remedy is that of compensatory damages, the courts will also use injunctions to meet the needs of claimants, or use damages to punish the misconduct of the defendant or vindicate his or her rights. The claimant may seek to use self-help remedies, but should be careful to stay within the remit of the law. In the field of damages for personal injury and death, the proposals for reform by the Law Commission and Labour government should be noted. It is disappointing that the current government's response has been to abandon the proposed reforms in that they do not "contribute to the delivery of the Government's key priorities",[288] and it is to be hoped that reform of damages for personal injury and death will return to the government's agenda at a future date. Both sets of recommendations may be praised for recognising that tort law must continue to evolve in line with developments in modern society. The Civil Partnership Act 2004 has led to recognition of the rights of civil partners, but cohabitees still remain vulnerable. As non-marital relationships become more common, legal recognition is a necessary step forward. Equally, as medical science improves and life expectancies increase, compensatory principles must adapt to these new conditions. A system of tort law which is responsive to such needs, and sufficiently flexible to change, is one which will hopefully thrive and continue to develop in the twenty-first century and beyond.

**17–063**

---

[286] Lord Nicholls accepted in *Cream Holdings Ltd v Banerjee* [2004] UKHL 44; [2005] 1 A.C. 253 at para.22, that there will be cases where the courts will be required to depart from this general approach and require a lesser degree of likelihood, for example, where the potential adverse consequences of disclosure are particularly grave or where a short-lived injunction is needed to enable the court to hear and give proper consideration to an application for interim relief pending the trial or any relevant appeal.

[287] [1970] A.C. 652 at 665–666.

[288] Ministry of Justice, "Civil Law Reform Bill: Response to Consultation" (2011) at p.3.

# Index

pecuniary loss
  care costs, 17–031
  charities, 17–024
  deductions, 17–023
  expenses, 17–030
  generally, 17–018
  insurance, 17–026
  interest, 17–037
  loss of earning capacity, 17–022
  loss of earnings, 17–019—17–020
  lost years, 17–021
  other damages, 17–032
  pensions, 17–028
  sick pay, 17–027
  social security benefits, 17–029
  voluntary payments by defendants,
    17–025
periodic payments, 17–042—17–043
provisional damages, 17–040

**Police**
  defendants 2–042
**Political parties**
  defamation, 13–022
**Premises**
  meaning, of, 8–013
**Prescription**
  private nuisance, 10–034
**Primary victims**
  psychiatric harm
    actual danger, 4–020
    fear for own safety, 4–021
    generally, 4–018—4–019
**Privacy**
  breach of confidence, 15–005—15–007
  conclusion, 15–011
  human rights, 15–003
  introduction, 15–001
  protection of, 15–002
  rejection of new tort, 15–004
  remedies, 15–010
  two-stage test, 15–008—15–009
**Private nuisance**
  defences
    generally, 10–032
    ineffective defences, 10–037—10–041
    inevitable accident, 10–035
    prescription, 10–034
    statutory authority, 10–033
    third party acts, 10–036
  defendant's land, emanating from,
    10–031
  generally, 10–003
  liability
    generally, 10–020
    landlords, 10–027—10–030
    occupiers, 10–021—10–026

  meaning, 10–004
  negligence, and, 10–043
  reasonable user
    abnormal sensitivity, 10–010—10–011
    duration, 10–008
    factors determining, 10–006
    frequency, 10–008
    locality, 10–007
    malice, 10–012
    meaning, 10–005
    utility of defendant's conduct, 10–009
  title to sue
    actionable nuisance, 10–014—10–015
    generally, 10–013
    human rights, 10–019
    landlords, 10–018
    losses prior to acquisition of land, 10–017
    rights in land, 10–016
  trespass, and, 10–044
**Privilege**
  *see also* **Absolute privilege; Qualified
    privilege**
  defamation, defences to, 14–008—14–031
**Procuring breach of contract**
  defences, 12–012—12–015
  generally, 12–003
  intention, 12–008—12–010
  knowledge of existence of contract,
    12–004
  knowledge that conduct will result in breach,
    12–005—12–007
**Producers**
  consumer protection, 9–016
**Product Liability Directive**
  consumer protection, 9–041
**Products**
  meaning of, 9–020
**Professional opinion**
  standard of care, 5–023
**Professionals**
  occupiers' liability, 8–022
**Prohibitory injunctions**
  generally, 17–060
**Proof**
  causation
    all or nothing, 6–013
    contribution between defendants, 6–016
    generally, 6–012
    material increase in risk, 6–015, 6–017
    vindication of rights, 6–014
  employers' liability, 7–017
  limitations, 16–039
**Property**
  tortuous liability, 1–013
**Proprietary interests**
  economic loss, 3–022